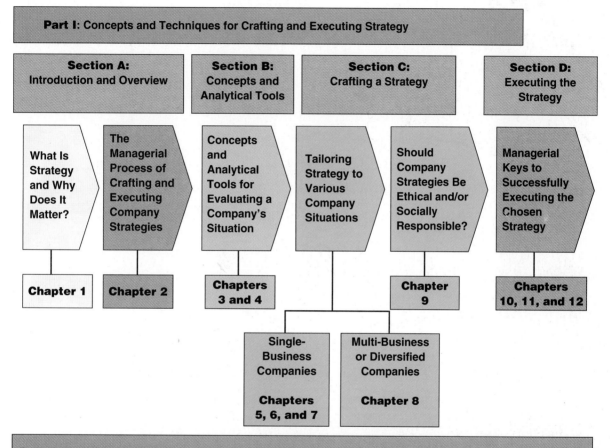

Part I: Concepts and Techniques for Crafting and Executing Strategy

Section A: Introduction and Overview	**Section B:** Concepts and Analytical Tools	**Section C:** Crafting a Strategy	**Section D:** Executing the Strategy

What Is Strategy and Why Does It Matter?

The Managerial Process of Crafting and Executing Company Strategies

Concepts and Analytical Tools for Evaluating a Company's Situation

Tailoring Strategy to Various Company Situations

Should Company Strategies Be Ethical and/or Socially Responsible?

Managerial Keys to Successfully Executing the Chosen Strategy

Chapter 1

Chapter 2

Chapters 3 and 4

Chapter 9

Chapters 10, 11, and 12

Single-Business Companies

Chapters 5, 6, and 7

Multi-Business or Diversified Companies

Chapter 8

Part II: Readings in Crafting and Executing Strategy

Section A: What Is Strategy and How Is the Process of Crafting and Executing Strategy Managed? (2 readings)
Section B: Crafting Strategy in Single-Business Companies (11 readings)
Section C: Crafting Strategy in Diversified Companies (1 reading)
Section D: Strategy, Ethics, and Social Responsibility (2 readings)
Section E: Executing Strategy (4 readings)

Crafting and Executing Strategy

Text and Readings

Arthur A. Thompson, Jr.
The University of Alabama

A. J. Strickland III
The University of Alabama

John E. Gamble
University of South Alabama

Crafting and Executing Strategy

Text and Readings

17TH EDITION

McGraw-Hill
Irwin

Boston   Burr Ridge, IL   Dubuque, IA   New York   San Francisco   St. Louis
Bangkok   Bogotá   Caracas   Kuala Lumpur   Lisbon   London   Madrid   Mexico City
Milan   Montreal   New Delhi   Santiago   Seoul   Singapore   Sydney   Taipei   Toronto

McGraw-Hill
Irwin

CRAFTING AND EXECUTING STRATEGY: TEXT AND READINGS

Published by McGraw-Hill/Irwin, a business unit of The McGraw-Hill Companies, Inc., 1221 Avenue of the Americas, New York, NY, 10020. Copyright © 2010, 2007, 2005, 2003, 2001, 1999, 1998, 1996, 1995, 1993, 1992, 1990, 1987, 1984, 1981, 1978 by The McGraw-Hill Companies, Inc. All rights reserved. No part of this publication may be reproduced or distributed in any form or by any means, or stored in a database or retrieval system, without the prior written consent of The McGraw-Hill Companies, Inc., including, but not limited to, in any network or other electronic storage or transmission, or broadcast for distance learning.

Some ancillaries, including electronic and print components, may not be available to customers outside the United States.

This book is printed on acid-free paper.

1 2 3 4 5 6 7 8 9 0 WCK/WCK 0 9

ISBN 978-0-07-724769-0
MHID 0-07-724769-8

Vice president and editor-in-chief: *Brent Gordon*
Senior sponsoring editor: *Michael Ablassmeir*
Developmental editor II: *Laura Griffin*
Editorial coordinator: *Kelly Pekelder*
Senior marketing manager: *Anke Braun Weekes*
Marketing coordinator: *Michael Gedatus*
Senior project manager: *Harvey Yep*
Lead production supervisor: *Michael R. McCormick*
Design coordinator: *Cara Hawthorne*
Senior photo research coordinator: *Lori Kramer*
Senior media project manager : *Susan Lombardi*
Cover design: *Jillian Lindner*
Cover image: *Punchstock*
Interior design: *Jillian Lindner*
Typeface: *10.5/12 Times New Roman*
Compositor: *Laserwords Private Limited*
Printer: *Quebecor World Versailles Inc.*

Photo Credits: *Chapter 1, p. 4, © Images.com/Corbis, Bek Shakirov; Chapter 2, p. 22, © Images.com/ Corbis, Robert Rogers; Chapter 3, p. 54, © Images.com/Corbis, Lael Henderson; Chapter 4, p. 100, © Images.com/Corbis; Chapter 5, p. 138, © Images.com/Corbis, Bruno Budrovic; Chapter 6, p. 164, © Images.com/Corbis; Chapter 7, p. 206, © Images.com/Corbis; Chapter 8, p. 238, © Images.com/ Corbis, Christopher Zacharow; Chapter 9, p. 288, © Images.com/Corbis, Sheila Golden; Chapter 10, p. 326, © Images.com/Corbis, Rob Colvin; Chapter 11, p. 356, Images.com/Corbis, David C. Chen; Chapter 12, p. 384, © Images.com/Corbis, Paul Anderson.*

Library of Congress Cataloging-in-Publication Data
Thompson, Arthur A., 1940-
    Crafting and executing strategy : text and readings / Arthur A. Thompson, Jr., A. J.
Strickland III, John E. Gamble.—17th ed.
        p. cm.
    Includes index.
    ISBN-13: 978-0-07-724769-0 (alk. paper)
    ISBN-10: 0-07-724769-8 (alk. paper)
    1. Strategic planning. 2. Business planning. I. Stickland, A. J. (Alonzo J.) II. Gamble,
John (John E.) III. Title.
HD30.28.T525 2010
658.4'012–dc22

www.mhhe.com

To our families and especially our wives:
Hasseline, Kitty, and Debra

About the Authors

Arthur A. Thompson, Jr., earned his B.S. and Ph.D. degrees in economics from The University of Tennessee, spent three years on the economics faculty at Virginia Tech, and served on the faculty of The University of Alabama's College of Commerce and Business Administration for 24 years. In 1974 and again in 1982, Dr. Thompson spent semester-long sabbaticals as a visiting scholar at the Harvard Business School.

His areas of specialization are business strategy, competition and market analysis, and the economics of business enterprises. In addition to publishing over 30 articles in some 25 different professional and trade publications, he has authored or co-authored five textbooks and six computer-based simulation exercises that are used in colleges and universities worldwide.

Dr. Thompson spends much of his off-campus time giving presentations, putting on management development programs, working with companies, and helping operate a business simulation enterprise in which he is a major partner.

Dr. Thompson and his wife of 47 years have two daughters, two grandchildren, and a Yorkshire terrier.

Dr. A. J. (Lonnie) Strickland, a native of North Georgia, attended the University of Georgia, where he received a bachelor of science degree in math and physics in 1965. Afterward he entered the Georgia Institute of Technology, where he received a master of science in industrial management. He earned a Ph.D. in business administration from Georgia State University in 1969. He currently holds the title of Professor of Strategic Management in the Graduate School of Business at The University of Alabama.

Dr. Strickland's experience in consulting and executive development is in the strategic management area, with a concentration in industry and competitive analysis. He has developed strategic planning systems for such firms as The Southern Company, BellSouth, South Central Bell, American Telephone and Telegraph, Gulf States Paper, Carraway Methodist Medical Center, Delco Remy, Mark IV Industries, Amoco Oil Company, USA Group, General Motors, and Kimberly Clark Corporation (Medical Products). He is a very popular speaker on the subject of implementing strategic change and serves on several corporate boards.

John E. Gamble is currently Associate Dean and Professor of Management in the Mitchell College of Business at the University of South Alabama. His teaching specialty at USA is strategic management and he also conducts a course in strategic management in Germany, which is sponsored by the University of Applied Sciences in Worms.

Dr. Gamble's research interests center on strategic issues in entrepreneurial, health care, and manufacturing settings. His work has been published in various scholarly journals and he is the author or co-author of more than 30 case studies published in an assortment of strategic management and strategic marketing texts. He has done consulting on industry and market analysis for clients in a diverse mix of industries.

Professor Gamble received his Ph.D. in management from The University of Alabama in 1995. Dr. Gamble also has a Bachelor of Science degree and a Master of Arts degree from The University of Alabama.

Preface

The objective of this text is to effectively and interestingly cover what every senior-level or MBA student needs to know about crafting and executing business strategies. It features a *substantive* presentation of core concepts and analytical techniques and an attractive collection of 20 readings that amplify important topics in managing a company's strategy-making, strategy-executing process. A combination chapters–readings text works quite well for courses where instructors wish to provide students with a foundation in the core concepts and analytical tools of strategic management and a taste of the literature of strategic management before having them tackle a customized set of cases and/or participate in a strategy simulation exercise where the class is divided into teams of 2 to 5 members and each team manages a company that competes head-to-head against companies run by the other teams. Two best-selling state-of-the-art online strategy simulations, *The Business Strategy Game* and *GLO-BUS,* are optional companions for this text—both simulations were created by this text's senior author as a means for instructors to give students *an engaging, learn-by-doing* experience in crafting and executing a strategy and applying the concepts and analytical tools covered in the chapters.

In preparing this 17th edition, our central goals have been to refine the explanations of core concepts and analytical tools, to update and refresh all of the examples, and to incorporate the latest research findings from the literature. As in any substantive revision, coverage was trimmed in some areas, expanded in others. The content of two chapters in the prior edition was condensed into a single chapter in this edition. A new section on strategic leadership has been added to Chapter 2. There is important new coverage of corporate and environmental sustainability. At the end of each chapter, you will now find (1) "Assurance of Learning Exercises" that will help you measure student comprehension of the chapter contents and (2) "Exercises for Simulation Participants" that tightly connect the topics covered in the chapters to the issues and decisions that students have to wrestle with in managing their simulation company. Complementing the 12 chapters and 20 readings is a comprehensive package of support materials that are a breeze to use, highly effective, and flexible enough to fit most any course design.

ON-TARGET CONTENT: THE HALLMARK OF THE 17TH EDITION CHAPTERS

In our view, for a senior/MBA-level strategy text to qualify as having on-target content, it must:

- Explain core concepts in language that students can grasp and provide first-rate examples of their relevance and use by actual companies.
- Thoroughly describe the tools of strategic analysis, how they are used, and where they fit into the managerial process of crafting and executing strategy.

- Incorporate the latest developments in the theory and practice of strategic management in every chapter to keep the content solidly in the mainstream of contemporary strategic thinking.
- Focus squarely on what every student needs to know about crafting, implementing, and executing business strategies in today's market environments.

We believe this 17th edition measures up on all four criteria. The explanations of core concepts and analytical tools are *thorough and carefully crafted to maximize understanding*—the enterprise of sound teaching is never well served by page-saving succinctness that leaves too much unsaid. Chapter content is driven by the imperative of covering well-settled strategic management principles, recent research findings and contributions to the literature of strategic management, the latest thinking of prominent academics and practitioners in the field, and the practices and behavior of real world companies.

There is solid, up-to-date coverage of the continuing march of industries and companies to *wider globalization,* the growing scope and strategic importance of *collaborative alliances,* the spread of *high-velocity change* to more industries and company environments, and how *advancing Internet technology* is driving fundamental changes in both strategy and internal operations in companies across the world. All the chapters are flush with convincing examples that students can relate to. There's a logical flow from one chapter to the next. And we have strived to hammer home the whys and hows of successfully crafting and executing strategy in an engaging and convincing fashion.

The result is a presentation with mainstream chapter content that mirrors contemporary academic thinking and actual management practice. But there are two standout features that strongly differentiate our 12-chapter presentation:

1. *Our coverage of resource-based theory of the firm in the 17th edition is unsurpassed by any other leading strategy text.* RBV principles and concepts are prominently and comprehensively integrated into our coverage of crafting both single-business and multi-business strategies. In Chapters 3 through 8 it is repeatedly emphasized that a company's strategy must be matched *not only* to its external market circumstances *but also* to its internal resources and competitive capabilities. Moreover, an RBV perspective is thoroughly integrated into the presentation on strategy execution (Chapters 10, 11, and 12) to make it unequivocally clear how and why the tasks of assembling intellectual capital and building core competencies and competitive capabilities are absolutely critical to successful strategy execution and operating excellence.

2. *In addition, our coverage of business ethics, core values, social responsibility, and environmental sustainability is unsurpassed by any other leading strategy text.* In this edition, we have embellished the highly important chapter on "Ethical Strategies, Social Responsibility, and Environmental Sustainability" with fresh content so that it can better fulfill the important functions of (1) alerting students to the role and importance of ethical and socially responsible decision-making and (2) addressing the accreditation requirements of the AACSB International that business ethics be visibly and thoroughly embedded in the core curriculum. Moreover, discussions of the roles of values and ethics are integrated into portions of Chapters 1, 2, 10, and 12 to further reinforce why and how considerations relating to ethics, values, social responsibility, and sustainability should figure prominently into the managerial task of crafting and executing company strategies.

ORGANIZATION, CONTENT, AND FEATURES OF THE 17TH EDITION TEXT CHAPTERS

The following rundown summarizes the noteworthy features and topical emphasis in the 12 chapters comprising this edition:

- Chapter 1 is focused directly on "what is strategy and why is it important?" There are substantive discussions of what is meant by the term strategy, the different elements of a company's strategy, and why management efforts to craft a company's strategy tend to be squarely aimed at building sustainable competitive advantage. Considerable emphasis is given to how and why a company's strategy is partly planned and partly reactive and why a company's strategy tends to evolve over time. There's an important section discussing what is meant by the term business model and how it relates to the concept of strategy. The thrust of this first chapter is to convince students that good strategy + good strategy execution = good management. The chapter is a perfect accompaniment for your opening day lecture on what the course is all about and why it matters.

- Chapter 2 concerns the managerial process of actually crafting and executing a strategy—it makes a great assignment for the second day of class and is a perfect follow-on to your first day's lecture. The focal point of the chapter is the five-step managerial process of crafting and executing strategy: (1) forming a strategic vision of where the company is headed and why, (2) the managerial importance of developing a balanced scorecard of objectives and performance targets that measure the company's progress, (3) crafting a strategy to achieve these targets and move the company toward its market destination, (4) implementing and executing the strategy, and (5) monitoring progress and making corrective adjustments as needed. Students are introduced to such core concepts as strategic visions, mission statements, strategic versus financial objectives, and strategic intent. An all-new section underscores that this 5-step process requires strong strategic leadership. There's a robust discussion of why *all managers are on a company's strategy-making, strategy-executing team* and why a company's strategic plan is a collection of strategies devised by different managers at different levels in the organizational hierarchy. The chapter winds up with a concise but meaty section on corporate governance.

- Chapter 3 sets forth the now-familiar analytical tools and concepts of industry and competitive analysis and demonstrates the importance of tailoring strategy to fit the circumstances of a company's industry and competitive environment. The standout feature of this chapter is a presentation of Michael Porter's "five forces model of competition" that we think is the clearest, most straightforward discussion of any text in the field. Globalization and Internet technology are treated as potent driving forces capable of reshaping industry competition—their roles as change agents have become factors that most companies in most industries must reckon with in forging winning strategies.

- Chapter 4 presents the resource-based view of the firm and convincingly argues why a company's strategy must be built around its resources, competencies, and competitive capabilities. The roles of core competencies and organizational resources and capabilities in creating customer value are *center stage* in the discussions of company resource strengths and weaknesses. SWOT analysis is cast as a simple, easy-to-use way to assess a company's resources and overall situation.

There is solid coverage of value chain analysis, benchmarking, and competitive strength assessments—standard tools for appraising a company's relative cost position and market standing vis-à-vis rivals. *An important feature of this chapter is a table showing how key financial and operating ratios are calculated and how to interpret them;* students will find this table handy in doing the number-crunching needed to evaluate whether a company's strategy is delivering good financial performance.

- Chapter 5 deals with a company's quest for competitive advantage and is framed around the five generic competitive strategies—low-cost leadership, differentiation, best-cost provider, focused differentiation, and focused low-cost.

- A much revamped Chapter 6 extends the coverage of the previous chapter and deals with what *other strategic actions* a company can take to complement its choice of a basic competitive strategy and to employ a strategy that is wisely matched to both industry and competitive conditions and to company resources and capabilities. The chapter features sections on what use to make of strategic alliances and collaborative partnerships; merger and acquisition strategies; vertical integration strategies; outsourcing strategies; and the broad strategy options for companies competing in six representative industry and competitive situations: (1) emerging industries, (2) rapid growth industries; (3) mature, slow-growth industries, (4) stagnant or declining industries, (5) turbulent, high velocity industries, and (6) fragmented industries. The concluding section of this chapter covers first-mover advantages and disadvantages, including the first-mover benefits of pursuing a blue ocean strategy.

- Chapter 7 explores the full range of strategy options for competing in foreign markets: export strategies, licensing, franchising, multicountry strategies, global strategies, and collaborative strategies involving heavy reliance on strategic alliances and joint ventures. The spotlight is trained on two strategic issues unique to competing multinationally: (1) whether to customize the company's offerings in each different country market to better match the tastes and preferences of local buyers or whether to offer a mostly standardized product worldwide and (2) whether to employ essentially the same basic competitive strategy in the markets of all countries where it operates or whether to modify the company's competitive approach country-by-country as may be needed to fit the specific market conditions and competitive circumstances it encounters. There's also coverage of the special issues of competing in the markets of emerging countries and the strategies that local companies in emerging countries can use to defend against global giants.

- Our rather meaty treatment of diversification strategies for multibusiness enterprises in Chapter 8 begins by laying out the various paths for becoming diversified, explains how a company can use diversification to create or compound competitive advantage for its business units, and examines the strategic options an already-diversified company has to improve its overall performance. In the middle part of the chapter, the analytical spotlight is on the techniques and procedures for assessing the strategic attractiveness of a diversified company's business portfolio—the relative attractiveness of the various businesses the company has diversified into, a multi-industry company's competitive strength in each of its lines of business, and the *strategic fits* and *resource fits* among a diversified company's different businesses. The chapter concludes with a brief survey of a company's four main post-diversification strategy alternatives: (1) broadening the diversification base, (2) divesting some businesses and retrenching to a narrower diversification base, (3) restructuring the makeup of the company's business lineup, and (4) multinational diversification.

- Chapter 9 provides comprehensive coverage of some increasingly pertinent front-burner strategic issues: (1) whether and why a company has a *duty* to operate according to ethical standards and (2) whether and why a company has a *duty* or *obligation* to contribute to the betterment of society independent of the needs and preferences of the customers it serves. Is there a credible business case for operating ethically and/or operating in a socially responsible manner? Why should a company's strategy measure up to the standards of being environmentally sustainable?

  The opening section of the chapter addresses whether ethical standards are universal (as maintained by the school of ethical universalism) or dependent on local norms and situational circumstances (as maintained by the school of ethical relativism) or a combination of both (as maintained by integrative social contracts theory). Following this are sections on the three categories of managerial morality (moral, immoral, and amoral), the drivers of unethical strategies and shady business behavior, the approaches to managing a company's ethical conduct, the concept of a "social responsibility strategy", the moral and business cases for both ethical strategies and socially responsible behavior, the concept of environmental sustainability, and why every company's strategy should be crafted in an manner that promotes environmental sustainability. The contents of this chapter will definitely give students some things to ponder and, hopefully, will make them far more ethically aware and conscious of why *all companies* should conduct their business in a socially responsible and sustainable manner. Chapter 9 has been written as a "stand-alone" chapter that can be assigned in the early, middle, or late part of the course.

- The three-chapter module on executing strategy (Chapters 10-12) is anchored around a pragmatic, compelling conceptual framework: (1) building the resource strengths and organizational capabilities needed to execute the strategy in competent fashion; (2) allocating ample resources to strategy-critical activities; (3) ensuring that policies and procedures facilitate rather than impede strategy execution; (4) instituting best practices and pushing for continuous improvement in how value chain activities are performed; (5) installing information and operating systems that enable company personnel to better carry out their strategic roles proficiently; (6) tying rewards and incentives directly to the achievement of performance targets and good strategy execution; (7) shaping the work environment and corporate culture to fit the strategy; and (8) exerting the internal leadership needed to drive execution forward.

  The recurring theme throughout these three chapters is that implementing and executing strategy entails figuring out the specific actions, behaviors, and conditions that are needed for a smooth strategy-supportive operation and then following through to get things done and deliver results—the goal here is to ensure that students understand the strategy-implementing/strategy-executing phase is a make-things-happen and make-them-happen-right kind of managerial exercise that leads to operating excellence and good performance.

We have done our best to ensure that the 12 chapters hit the bull's-eye in covering the concepts, analytical tools, and approaches to strategic thinking that should comprise a senior/MBA course in strategy. The ultimate test of the text, of course, is the positive pedagogical impact it has in the classroom. If this edition sets a more effective stage for your lectures and does a better job of helping you persuade students that the discipline of strategy merits their rapt attention, then it will have fulfilled its purpose.

THE COLLECTION OF READINGS

In selecting a set of readings to accompany the chapter presentations, we opted for articles that (1) had been recently published (most appeared in the 2006–2008 period), (2) extended the chapter coverage and expanded on a topic of strategic importance, and (3) were both quite readable and relatively short. At the same time, we endeavored to be highly selective, deciding that a manageable number of on-target readings was a better fit with the teaching/learning objectives of most senior and MBA courses in strategy than a more sweeping collection of readings. The 20 readings we chose came from recent issues of the *Business Strategy Review, Strategy & Leadership, Harvard Business Review, MIT Sloan Management Review, Business Ethics Quarterly, Journal of Business Strategy, European Management Journal, Ivey Business Journal,* and *The TQM Magazine.*

Aside from providing an introductory look at the literature of strategic management literature, the readings offer nice variety. The first reading by Collis and Rukstad on "Can You Say What Your Strategy Is?" discusses the challenges of coming up with an accurate, straight-to-the-point strategy statement. The Ready and Conger article on "Enabling Bold Visions" sets forth a framework for ensuring that strategic visions take root and end up being put into practice, rather than being reduced to empty words or failed hopes. These two articles tie tightly to the material in Chapters 1 and 2.

There are eight readings that complement and expand on topics covered in Chapters 3 through 6. The article by Holger Schiele on "Location, Location: The Geography of Industry Clusters," explores why rival companies and their suppliers sometimes cluster in particular locations and geographic regions and powerful benefits which can flow from clustering; we recommend assigning it in conjunction with Chapter 3. The article by Bowman and Ambrosini on "Identifying Valuable Resources" is a must-assign reading because it adds power to the role and importance of the resource-based view of the firm that dominates the presentation in Chapter 4 (and that is integral to other chapters as well); the article tackles the question of "what is a valuable resource," the ways of valuing a resource, and the means of exploiting a valuable resource. Reading 5 on "The Battle of the Value Chains" also complements the material in Chapter 4 and will give students additional insight into why the value chain concept is such a critically important analytical tool. George stalk's article on "Playing Hardball" is must reading and will open eyes about how companies play competitive hardball in the marketplace. Reading 7 on "Hitting Back: Strategic Responses to Low-Cost Rivals" is a nice complement to the topics covered in Chapter 5 (and also Chapter 6). The article on "Limited Potential Niche or Prospective Market Foothold: Five Tests" also should be assigned in conjunction with Chapter 5. The piece by Kim and Mauborgne on "Value Innovation: A Leap into the Blue Ocean" deepens the coverage of blue ocean strategy in Chapter 6. The Markides and Geroski article on "Racing to Be Second: Conquering the Industries of the Future" provides excellent insight into first-mover disadvantages and fast follower advantages (topics covered in Chapter 6).

We chose three articles to complement and expand on the topics of globalization and global strategy covered in Chapter 7. Pankaj Ghemawat's article on "Globalization Is an Option Not an Imperative or, Why the World Is Not Flat" is definitely a must-assign article; it contains a persuasive presentation on the important differences that often exist between and among country markets and thus why multicountry strategies sometimes must be employed rather than global strategies. The timely reading on "The Challenge for Multinational Corporations in China: Think Local, Act Global" makes a case for why the often sage strategic advice of "think global, act local" needs to be reversed in the case of China. Reading 13 on "How to Win in Emerging Markets" adds breadth and depth to the discussion of the same topic in Chapter 7.

We included one reading to be assigned in conjunction with Chapter 8 on diversification strategies. It is titled "Why Is Synergy So Difficult in Mergers of Related Businesses?" It is a perfect fit with the content of this chapter.

There are two readings that tie very tightly to the Chapter 9 coverage of ethical business strategies, social responsibility, and environmental sustainability. Reading 15 by Bansal and Kandola explores in some detail the very pertinent issue of why good people sometimes behave badly in organizations; this topic is definitely worth exploring at some length in a wide open class discussion. A second reading deals with how differing competitive conditions affect a company's use of commitment to social responsibility; the central thesis (which is somewhat provocative) is that depending on whether competition is weak or fierce, different acts and strategies become morally acceptable as well as economically rational. The authors argue that a firm has to develop its social responsibility strategy in light of its competitive position, as well as ethical considerations.

Four readings were chosen for use with the three chapters on executing strategy (Chapters 10–12). The Neilson, Martin, and Powers article "The Secrets to Successful Strategy Execution" from the *Harvard Business Review* is a splendid treatise on how to avoid breakdowns in strategy execution; it fits in nicely with the framework we use in Chapter 10–12 to introduce students to the managerial tasks of implementing and executing the chosen strategy. Reading 18 on "Some Pros and Cons of Six Sigma" is a good fit with the material in Chapter 11. The Edwin Locke reading on "Linking Goals to Monetary Incentives" reinforces and expands the discussion in the last section of Chapter 11 on how to use incentives to further the cause of good strategy execution. This group of readings concludes with a very provocative article by Sidney Finkelstein on "The Seven Habits of Spectacularly Unsuccessful Executives."

TWO ACCOMPANYING ONLINE, FULLY AUTOMATED SIMULATION EXERCISES— THE BUSINESS STRATEGY GAME AND GLO-BUS

The Business Strategy Game and *GLO-BUS: Developing Winning Competitive Strategies*—two competition-based strategy simulations that are delivered online and that feature automated processing of decisions and grading of performance—are being marketed by the publisher as companion supplements for use with this and other texts in the field. *The Business Strategy Game* is the world's leading strategy simulation, having been played by over 500,000 students at more than 600 universities across the world. *GLO-BUS,* a somewhat simpler online simulation introduced in 2004, has been used at more than 150 universities across the world in courses involving over 50,000 students.

The two simulations are very tightly linked to the material that your class members will be reading about in the text chapters—the senior author of this text is a co-author of both *The Business Strategy Game* and *GLO-BUS*. Moreover, both simulations were painstakingly developed with an eye toward economizing on instructor course preparation time and grading. You'll be pleasantly surprised—and we think quite pleased—at how little time it takes to gear up for and to administer a fully automated online simulation like *The Business Strategy Game* or *GLO-BUS*.

In both *The Business Strategy Game (BSG)* and *GLO-BUS*, class members are divided into management teams of 1 to 5 persons and assigned to run a company in head-to-head competition against companies run by other class members. In *BSG*, the co-managers of each team run an athletic footwear company, producing and marketing both branded and private-label footwear. In *GLO-BUS*, the co-managers of each team operate a digital camera company that designs, assembles, and markets entry-level digital cameras and upscale, multi-featured cameras. In both simulations, companies compete in a global market arena, selling their products in four geographic regions—Europe-Africa, North America, Asia-Pacific, and Latin America. There are decisions relating to plant operations, workforce compensation, pricing and marketing, finance, and corporate social responsibility.

You can schedule 1 or 2 practice rounds and 4 to 10 regular (scored) decision rounds; each decision round represents a year of company operations. When the instructor-specified deadline for a decision round arrives, the algorithms built into the simulation award sales and market shares to the competing companies, region by region. Each company's sales are totally governed by how its prices compare against the prices of rival brands, how its product quality compares against the quality of rival brands, how its product line breadth and selection compares, how its advertising effort compares, and so on for a total of 11 competitive factors that determine unit sales and market shares. The competitiveness of each company's product offering *relative to rivals* is all-decisive—this is what makes them "competition-based" strategy simulations. Once sales and market shares are awarded, the company and industry reports are then generated and all the results made available 15–20 minutes after the decision deadline.

Both simulations feature a Learning Assurance Report that rates your students' performance on facets of learning included in accreditation standards for most business school programs. Also, at the end of each of the 12 chapters in the text is a section containing exercises for simulation participants that require students to utilize what they have read in the chapter in running their simulation company.

The Compelling Case for Incorporating Use of a Strategy Simulation

There are *exceptionally important benefits* associated with using a competition-based simulation in strategy courses taken by seniors and MBA students:

- Assigning students to run a company that competes head-to-head against companies run by other class members *gives students immediate opportunity to experiment with various strategy options and to gain proficiency in applying the core concepts and analytical tools that they have been reading about in the chapters.* The issues and decisions that co-managers face in running their simulation company embrace the very concepts, analytical tools, and strategy options they encounter in the text chapters. Giving class members immediate *"learn-by-doing" opportunity* to apply and experiment with the material covered in their text, while at the same time honing their business and decision-making skills, generates solid learning results.

- *A competition-based strategy simulation arouses positive energy and classroom excitement, engages students in the subject matter of the course, is a fun way for students to learn, and steps up the whole tempo of the course by a notch or two—all of which greatly facilitate the achievement of course learning objectives.* The healthy rivalry that emerges among the management teams of competing companies can be counted upon to stir competitive juices and spur class members to fully exercise their strategic wits, analytical skills, and decision-making prowess. *Nothing energizes a class quicker or better than concerted efforts on the part of class members to gain a high industry ranking and avoid the perilous consequences of falling too far behind the best-performing companies.* Case analysis assignments lack the capacity to generate the interest and excitement that occur when the results of the latest decision round become available and co-managers renew their quest for strategic moves and actions that will strengthen company performance. As soon as your students start to say "Wow! Not only is this fun but I am learning a lot," which they will, you have won the battle of engaging students in the subject matter and moved the value of taking your course to a much higher plateau in the business school curriculum. This translates into a livelier, richer learning experience for students and better instructor-course evaluations.

- Because a simulation involves making decisions relating to production operations, worker compensation and training, sales and marketing, distribution, customer service, finance, and corporate social responsibility and requires analysis of company financial statements and market data, *the simulation helps students synthesize the knowledge gained in a variety of different business courses. The cross-functional, integrative nature of a strategy simulation helps make courses in strategy more of a true capstone experience.*

- *Using both case analysis and a competition-based strategy simulation to drive home the lessons* that class members are expected to learn *is far more pedagogically powerful and lasting than case analysis alone.* Both cases and strategy simulations drill students in thinking strategically and applying what they read in your text, thus helping them connect theory with practice and gradually building better business judgment. What cases do that a simulation cannot is give class members broad exposure to a variety of companies and industry situations and insight into the kinds of strategy-related problems managers face. But what a competition-based strategy simulation does far better than case analysis is thrust class members squarely into an active managerial role where they have to take the analysis of market conditions, the actions of competitors, and their company's situation seriously. Because they are held fully accountable for their decisions and their company's performance, co-managers are strongly motivated to dig deeply into company operations, probe for ways to be more cost-efficient, and ferret out strategic moves and decisions calculated to boost company performance. Such diligent and purposeful actions on the part of company co-managers translate into a productive and beneficial learning experience.

- *Use of a fully automated online simulation can reduce the time instructors spend on course preparation and grading papers.* Simulation adopters often compensate for the added student workload of a simulation by trimming the number of assigned cases from, say, 10 to 12 to perhaps 4 to 6, which significantly reduces the time instructors have to spend on case preparation. Course preparation time can be further cut because you can use several class days to have students meet in the computer lab to work on upcoming decisions or a 3-year strategic plan (in lieu of lecturing on a chapter or covering an additional assigned case). Lab sessions provide a splendid opportunity for you to visit with teams, observe the interplay among co-managers, and view the caliber of the learning experience that is going on. Furthermore, the added student workload associated with participating in a simulation can be compensated for by cutting back on other assignments that entail considerable grading on your part. Grading one less written case or essay exam or other written assignment saves enormous time. With either simulation, grading is effortless, requiring only that you enter percentage weights for each assignment in your online grade book.

In sum, *a three-pronged text-case-simulation course model has significantly more teaching/learning power than the traditional text-case model.* Indeed, a very convincing argument can be made that a competition-based strategy simulation is *the single most effective teaching/learning tool that instructors can employ to teach the discipline of business and competitive strategy, to make learning more enjoyable, and to achieve course learning objectives.*

A Bird's-Eye View of *The Business Strategy Game*

The setting for *The Business Strategy Game* (*BSG*) is the global athletic footwear industry (there can be little doubt in today's world that a globally competitive strategy simulation is *vastly superior* to a simulation with a domestic-only setting). Global market demand for footwear grows at the rate of 7–9% annually for the first five years and 5–7% annually for the second five years. However, market growth rates vary by geographic region—North America, Latin America, Europe-Africa, and Asia-Pacific.

Companies begin the simulation producing branded and private-label footwear in two plants, one in North America and one in Asia. They have the option to establish production facilities in Latin America and Europe-Africa, either by constructing new plants or buying previously constructed plants that have been sold by competing companies. Company co-managers exercise control over production costs based on the styling and quality they opt to manufacture, plant location (wages and incentive compensation vary from region to region), the use of best practices and Six Sigma programs to reduce the production of defective footwear and to boost worker productivity, and compensation practices.

All newly produced footwear is shipped in bulk containers to one of four geographic distribution centers. All sales in a geographic region are made from footwear inventories in that region's distribution center. Costs at the four regional distribution centers are a function of inventory storage costs, packing and shipping fees, import tariffs paid on incoming pairs shipped from foreign plants, and exchange rate impacts. At the start of the simulation, import tariffs average $4 per pair in Europe-Africa, $6 per pair in Latin America, and $8 in the Asia-Pacific region. However, the Free Trade Treaty of the Americas allows tariff-free movement of footwear between North America and Latin America. Instructors have the option to alter tariffs as the game progresses.

Companies market their brand of athletic footwear to footwear retailers worldwide and to individuals buying online at the company's Web site. Each company's sales and market share in the branded footwear segments hinge on its competitiveness on

11 factors: attractive pricing, footwear styling and quality, product line breadth, advertising, the use of mail-in rebates, the appeal of celebrities endorsing a company's brand, success in convincing footwear retailers dealers to carry its brand, the number of weeks it takes to fill retailer orders, the effectiveness of a company's online sales effort at its Web site, and customer loyalty. Sales of private-label footwear hinge solely on being the low-price bidder.

All told, company co-managers make as many as 53 types of decisions each period that cut across production operations (up to 10 decisions each plant, with a maximum of 4 plants), plant capacity additions/sales/upgrades (up to 6 decisions per plant), worker compensation and training (3 decisions per plant), shipping (up to 8 decisions each plant), pricing and marketing (up to 10 decisions in 4 geographic regions), bids to sign celebrities (2 decision entries per bid), financing of company operations (up to 8 decisions), and corporate social responsibility and environmental sustainability (up to six decisions).

Each time company co-managers make a decision entry, an assortment of on-screen calculations instantly shows the projected effects on unit sales, revenues, market shares, unit costs, profit, earnings per share, ROE, and other operating statistics. The on-screen calculations help team members evaluate the relative merits of one decision entry versus another and put together a promising strategy.

Companies can employ any of the five generic competitive strategy options in selling branded footwear—low-cost leadership, differentiation, best-cost provider, focused low-cost, and focused differentiation. They can pursue essentially the same strategy worldwide or craft slightly or very different strategies for the Europe-Africa, Asia-Pacific, Latin America, and North America markets. They can strive for competitive advantage based on more advertising or a wider selection of models or more appealing styling/quality, or bigger rebates, and so on.

Any well-conceived, well-executed competitive approach is capable of succeeding, provided it is not overpowered by the strategies of competitors or defeated by the presence of too many copycat strategies that dilute its effectiveness. The challenge for each company's management team is to craft and execute a competitive strategy that produces good performance on five measures: earnings per share, return on equity investment, stock price appreciation, credit rating, and brand image.

All activity for *The Business Strategy Game* takes place at www.bsg-online.com.

A Bird's-Eye View of *GLO-BUS*

The industry setting for *GLO-BUS* is the digital camera industry. Global market demand grows at the rate of 8–10% annually for the first five years and 4–6% annually for the second five years. Retail sales of digital cameras are seasonal, with about 20 percent of consumer demand coming in each of the first three quarters of each calendar year and 40 percent coming during the big fourth-quarter retailing season.

Companies produce entry-level and upscale, multi-featured cameras of varying designs and quality in a Taiwan assembly facility and ship assembled cameras directly to retailers in North America, Asia-Pacific, Europe-Africa, and Latin America. All cameras are assembled as retail orders come in and shipped immediately upon completion of the assembly process—companies maintain no finished goods inventories and all parts and components are delivered on a just-in-time basis (which eliminates the need to track inventories and simplifies the accounting for plant operations and costs). Company co-managers exercise control over production costs based on the designs and components they specify for their cameras, work force compensation and training, the length of warranties offered (which affects warranty costs), the amount spent for technical support provided to buyers of the company's cameras, and their management of the assembly process.

Competition in each of the two product market segments (entry-level and multi-featured digital cameras) is based on 10 factors: price, camera performance and quality, number of quarterly sales promotions, length of promotions in weeks, the size of the promotional discounts offered, advertising, the number of camera models, size of retail dealer network, warranty period, and the amount/caliber of technical support provided to camera buyers. Low-cost leadership, differentiation strategies, best-cost provider strategies, and focus strategies are all viable competitive options. Rival companies can strive to be the clear market leader in either entry-level cameras or upscale multi-featured cameras or both. They can focus on one or two geographic regions or strive for geographic balance. They can pursue essentially the same strategy worldwide or craft slightly or very different strategies for the Europe-Africa, Asia-Pacific, Latin America, and North America markets. Just as with *The Business Strategy Game,* most any well-conceived, well-executed competitive approach is capable of succeeding, *provided it is not overpowered by the strategies of competitors or defeated by the presence of too many copycat strategies that dilute its effectiveness.*

Company co-managers make 49 types of decisions each period, ranging from R&D, camera components, and camera performance (10 decisions) to production operations and worker compensation (15 decisions) to pricing and marketing (15 decisions) to the financing of company operations (4 decisions) to corporate social responsibility (5 decisions). Each time participants make a decision entry, an assortment of on-screen calculations instantly shows the projected effects on unit sales, revenues, market shares, unit costs, profit, earnings per share, ROE, and other operating statistics. These on-screen calculations help team members evaluate the relative merits of one decision entry versus another and stitch the separate decisions into a cohesive and promising strategy. Company performance is judged on five criteria: earnings per share, return on equity investment, stock price, credit rating, and brand image.

All activity for *GLO-BUS* occurs at www.glo-bus.com.

Administration and Operating Features of the Two Simulations

The Internet delivery and user-friendly designs of both *BSG* and *GLO-BUS* make them incredibly easy to administer, even for first-time users. And the menus and controls are so similar that you can readily switch between the two simulations or use one in your undergraduate class and the other in a graduate class. If you have not yet used either of the two simulations, you may find the following of particular interest:

- Time requirements for instructors are minimal. Setting up the simulation for your course is done online and takes about 10–15 minutes. Once set-up is completed, no other administrative actions are required beyond that of moving participants to a different team (should the need arise) and monitoring the progress of the simulation (to whatever extent desired).

- Participant's Guides are delivered at the Web site—students can read it on their monitors or print out a copy, as they prefer.

- There are extensive built-in "Help" screens explaining (a) each decision entry, (b) the information on each page of the Industry Reports, and (c) the numbers presented in the Company Reports. *The Help screens allow company co-managers to figure things out for themselves, thereby curbing the need for students to always run to the instructor with questions about "how things work."*

- The results of each decision round are processed automatically and are typically available to all participants *15 minutes* after the decision round deadline specified by the instructor/game administrator.

- Participants and instructors are notified via e-mail when the results are ready.

- Schedules for the decision rounds are instructor-determined. Decision rounds can be scheduled once per week, twice per week, or even twice daily, depending on how instructors want to conduct the exercise.

- Following each decision round, participants are provided with a complete set of reports—a 6-page Industry Report, a 1-page Competitive Intelligence report for each geographic region that includes strategic group maps and bulleted lists of competitive strengths and weaknesses, and a set of Company Reports (income statement, balance sheet, cash flow statement, and assorted production, marketing, and cost statistics).

- Two "open-book" multiple choice tests of 20 questions are built into each simulation. The quizzes, which you can require or not as you see fit, are taken online and automatically graded, with scores reported instantly to participants and automatically recorded in the instructor's electronic grade book. Students are automatically provided with three sample questions for each test.

- Both simulations contain a 3-year strategic plan option that you can assign. Scores on the plan are automatically recorded in the instructor's online grade book.

- At the end of the simulation, you can have students complete online peer evaluations (again, the scores are automatically recorded in your online grade book).

- Both simulations have a Company Presentation feature that enables students to easily prepare PowerPoint slides for use in describing their strategy and summarizing their company's performance in a presentation either to the class, the instructor, or an "outside" board of directors.

- *A Learning Assurance Report provides you with convincing empirical data concerning how well your students performed vis-à-vis students playing the simulation worldwide over the past 12 months.* The report is based on 9 measures of student proficiency, business know-how, and decision-making skill and can also be used in evaluating the extent to which your school's academic curriculum produces the desired degree of student learning insofar as accreditation standards are concerned.

For more details on either simulation, please consult Section 2 of the Instructor's Manual accompanying this text or register as an instructor at the simulation Web sites (www.bsg-online.com and www.glo-bus.com) to access even more comprehensive information. Using Internet conferencing technology, the simulation authors conduct seminars several times each month (sometimes each week) to demonstrate how the software works, walk you through the various features and menu options, and answer any questions. To sign up for a demonstration, please visit www.mhhe.com/thompsonsims. By all means, please feel free to call the senior author of this text at (205) 722-9145 to arrange a personal demonstration or talk about how one of the simulations might work in one of your courses. We think you'll be quite impressed with the capabilities that have been programmed into *The Business Strategy Game* and *GLO-BUS,* the simplicity with which both simulations can be administered, and their exceptionally tight connection to the text chapters, core concepts, and standard analytical tools.

RESOURCES AND SUPPORT MATERIALS FOR THE 17TH EDITION

FOR STUDENTS

Key Points Summaries

At the end of each chapter is a synopsis of the core concepts, analytical tools and other key points discussed in the chapter. These chapter-end synopses, along with the margin notes scattered throughout each chapter, help students focus on basic strategy principles, digest the messages of each chapter, and prepare for tests.

Two Sets of Chapter-End Exercises

Each chapter concludes with two sets of exercises. The "Assurance of Learning Exercises" can be used as the basis for class discussion, oral presentation assignments, short written reports, and substitutes for case assignments. The "Exercises for Simulation Participants" are designed expressly for use by adopters who have incorporated use of a simulation and wish to go a step further in tightly and explicitly connecting the chapter content to the simulation company their students are running. The questions in both sets of exercises (along with those Illustration Capsules that qualify as "mini-cases") can be used to round out the rest of a 75-minute class period should your lecture on a chapter last only for 50 minutes.

A Value-Added Web Site

The student version of the Online Learning Center (OLC) or Web site www.mhhe. com/thompson contains a number of helpful aids:

- 20-question self-scoring chapter tests that students can take to measure their grasp of the material presented in each of the 12 chapters.
- A "Guide to Case Analysis" containing sections on what a case is, why cases are a standard part of courses in strategy, preparing a case for class discussion, doing a written case analysis, doing an oral presentation, and using financial ratio analysis to assess a company's financial condition. We suggest having students read this Guide prior to the first class discussion of a case.
- PowerPoint slides for each chapter.

Premium Content Delivered at the Web Site

The publisher's Web site for the text has an assortment of offerings that you may find valuable for your course. Purchasing access to our premium learning resources right on the Web site provides students with the following value-added resources—narrated slides and videos, which along with chapter tests, are also available for iPod download to help students prepare for exams.

FOR INSTRUCTORS

Online Learning Center (OLC)

In addition to the student resources, the instructor section of www.mhhe.com/thompson includes an Instructor's Manual and other support materials. Your McGraw-Hill representative can arrange delivery of instructor support materials in a format-ready Standard Cartridge for Blackboard, WebCT and other Web-based educational platforms.

Instructor's Manual

The accompanying IM contains a section on suggestions for organizing and structuring your course, sample syllabi and course outlines, a set of lecture notes on each chapter, a copy of the test bank, and some of the most comprehensive case teaching notes available with any strategy textbook.

Test Bank and EZ Test Online

There is a test bank containing over 900 multiple choice questions and short-answer/essay questions. It has been tagged with AACSB and Bloom's Taxonomy criteria. All of the test bank questions are also accessible within a computerized test bank powered by McGraw-Hill's flexible electronic testing program EZ Test Online (www.eztestonline.com). Using EZ Test Online allows you to create paper and online tests or quizzes. With EZ Test Online, instructors can select questions from multiple McGraw-Hill test banks or author their own, and then either print the test for paper distribution or give it online.

PowerPoint Slides

To facilitate delivery preparation of your lectures and to serve as chapter outlines, you'll have access to approximately 500 colorful and professional-looking slides displaying core concepts, analytical procedures, key points, and all the figures in the text chapters. The slides are the creation of Professor Jana Kuzmicki of Troy State University.

Instructor's Resource CD-ROM

All of our instructor supplements are available in this one-stop multimedia resource, which includes the complete Instructor's Manual, Computerized Test Bank (EZ Test), accompanying PowerPoint slides, and the Digital Image Library with all the figures from the text. It is a useful aid for compiling a syllabus and daily course schedule, preparing customized lectures, and developing tests on the text chapters.

The *Business Strategy Game* and *GLO-BUS* Online Simulations

Using one of the two companion simulations is a powerful and constructive way of emotionally connecting students to the subject matter of the course. We know of no more effective and interesting way to stimulate the competitive energy of students and prepare them for the rigors of real-world business decision-making than to have them match strategic wits with classmates in running a company in head-to-head competition for global market leadership. Please visit www.mhhe.com/thompsonsims for more information.

ACKNOWLEDGMENTS

A great number of colleagues and students at various universities, business acquaintances, and people at McGraw-Hill provided inspiration, encouragement, and counsel during the course of this project. Like all text authors in the strategy field, we are intellectually indebted to the many academics whose research and writing have blazed new trails and advanced the discipline of strategic management. The following reviewers provided seasoned advice and splendid suggestions for improving the chapters in this 17th edition:

Dennis R. Balch	University of North Alabama
Jeffrey R. Bruehl	Bryan College
Edith C. Busija	Murray State University–Murray, Kentucky
Donald A. Drost	California State University–San Bernardino
Randall Harris	California State University–Stanislaus
Mark Lewis Hoelscher	Illinois State University
Phyllis Holland	Valdosta State University
James W. Kroeger	Cleveland State University
Sal Kukalis	California State University–Long Beach
Brian W. Kulik	Central Washington University
Paul Mallette	Colorado State University
Anthony U. Martinez	San Francisco State University
Lee Pickler	Baldwin-Wallace College
Sabine Reddy	Calilfornia State University–Long Beach
Thomas D. Schramko	The University of Toledo
V. Seshan	Pepperdine University
Charles Strain	University of Houston–Downtown
Sabine Turnley	Kansas State University
S. Stephen Vitucci	Tarleton State University–Central Texas
Andrew Ward	University of Georgia
Sibin Wu	University of Texas–Pan American

We also express our thanks to Lynne Patten, Nancy E. Landrum, Jim Goes, Jon Kalinowski, Rodney M. Walter, Judith D. Powell, Seyda Deligonul, David Flanagan, Esmerlda Garbi, Mohsin Habib, Kim Hester, Jeffrey E. McGee, Diana J, Wong, F. William Brown, Anthony F. Chelte, Gregory G. Dess, Alan B. Eisner, John George, Carle M. Hunt, Theresa Marron-Grodsky, Sarah Marsh, Joshua D. Martin, William L. Moore, Donald Neubaum, George M. Puia, Amit Shah, Lois M. Shelton, Mark Weber, Steve Barndt, J. Michael Geringer, Ming-Fang Li, Richard Stackman, Stephen Tallman, Gerardo R. Ungson, James Boulgarides, Betty Diener, Daniel F. Jennings, David Kuhn, Kathryn Martell, Wilbur Mouton, Bobby Vaught, Tuck Bounds, Lee Burk, Ralph Catalanello, William Crittenden, Vince Luchsinger, Stan Mendenhall, John Moore, Will Mulvaney, Sandra Richard, Ralph Roberts, Thomas Turk, Gordon VonStroh, Fred Zimmerman, S. A. Billion, Charles Byles, Gerald L. Geisler, Rose Knotts, Joseph Rosenstein, James B. Thurman, Ivan Able, W. Harvey Hegarty, Roger Evered, Charles B. Saunders, Rhae M. Swisher, Claude I. Shell, R. Thomas Lenz, Michael C. White, Dennis Callahan, R. Duane Ireland, William E. Burr II, C. W. Millard, Richard Mann, Kurt Christensen, Neil W. Jacobs, Louis W. Fry, D. Robley Wood, George J. Gore, and William R. Soukup. These reviewers provided valuable guidance in steering our efforts to improve earlier editions.

As always, we value your recommendations and thoughts about the book. Your comments regarding coverage and contents will be taken to heart, and we always are grateful for the time you take to call our attention to printing errors, deficiencies, and other shortcomings. Please e-mail us at athompso@cba.ua.edu, astrickl@cba.ua.edu, or jgamble@usouthal.edu; fax us at (205) 348-6695; or write us at P. O. Box 870225, Department of Management and Marketing, The University of Alabama, Tuscaloosa, Alabama 35487-0225.

Arthur A. Thompson

A. J. Strickland

John E. Gamble

Guided Tour

Chapter Structure and Organization

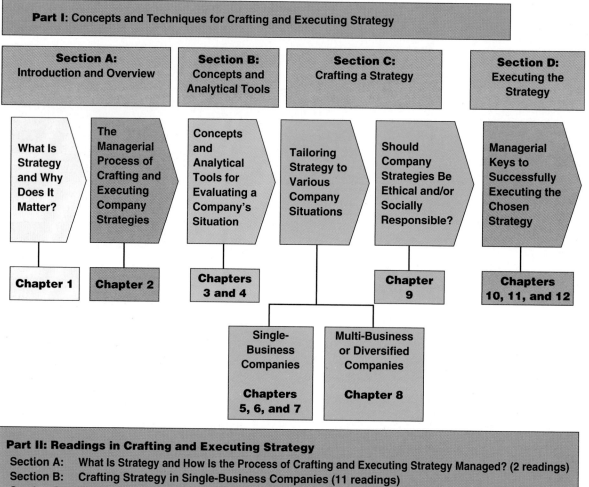

Part I: Concepts and Techniques for Crafting and Executing Strategy

Section A: Introduction and Overview

Section B: Concepts and Analytical Tools

Section C: Crafting a Strategy

Section D: Executing the Strategy

What Is Strategy and Why Does It Matter?

The Managerial Process of Crafting and Executing Company Strategies

Concepts and Analytical Tools for Evaluating a Company's Situation

Tailoring Strategy to Various Company Situations

Should Company Strategies Be Ethical and/or Socially Responsible?

Managerial Keys to Successfully Executing the Chosen Strategy

Chapter 1

Chapter 2

Chapters 3 and 4

Chapter 9

Chapters 10, 11, and 12

Single-Business Companies

Chapters 5, 6, and 7

Multi-Business or Diversified Companies

Chapter 8

Part II: Readings in Crafting and Executing Strategy

Section A: What Is Strategy and How Is the Process of Crafting and Executing Strategy Managed? (2 readings)
Section B: Crafting Strategy in Single-Business Companies (11 readings)
Section C: Crafting Strategy in Diversified Companies (1 reading)
Section D: Strategy, Ethics, and Social Responsibility (2 readings)
Section E: Executing Strategy (4 readings)

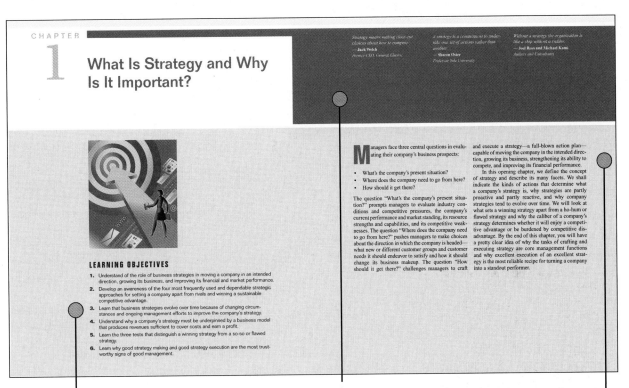

CHAPTER 1
What Is Strategy and Why Is It Important?

Strategy means making clear-cut choices about how to compete.
—**Jack Welch**
Former CEO, General Electric

A strategy is a commitment to undertake one set of actions rather than another.
—**Sharon Oster**
Professor, Yale University

Without a strategy the organization is like a ship without a rudder.
—**Joel Ross and Michael Kami**
Authors and Consultants

LEARNING OBJECTIVES

1. Understand of the role of business strategies in moving a company in an intended direction, growing its business, and improving its financial and market performance.
2. Develop an awareness of the four most frequently used and dependable strategic approaches for setting a company apart from rivals and winning a sustainable competitive advantage.
3. Learn that business strategies evolve over time because of changing circumstances and ongoing management efforts to improve the company's strategy.
4. Understand why a company's strategy must be underpinned by a business model that produces revenues sufficient to cover costs and earn a profit.
5. Learn the three tests that distinguish a winning strategy from a so-so or flawed strategy.
6. Learn why good strategy making and good strategy execution are the most trustworthy signs of good management.

Managers face three central questions in evaluating their company's business prospects:

- What's the company's present situation?
- Where does the company need to go from here?
- How should it get there?

The question "What's the company's present situation?" prompts managers to evaluate industry conditions and competitive pressures, the company's current performance and market standing, its resource strengths and capabilities, and its competitive weaknesses. The question "Where does the company need to go from here?" pushes managers to make choices about the direction in which the company is headed—what new or different customer groups and customer needs it should endeavor to satisfy and how it should change its business makeup. The question "How should it get there?" challenges managers to craft and execute a strategy—a full-blown action plan—capable of moving the company in the intended direction, growing its business, strengthening its ability to compete, and improving its financial performance.

In this opening chapter, we define the concept of strategy and describe its many facets. We shall indicate the kinds of actions that determine what a company's strategy is, why strategies are partly proactive and partly reactive, and why company strategies tend to evolve over time. We will look at what sets a winning strategy apart from a ho-hum or flawed strategy and why the caliber of a company's strategy determines whether it will enjoy a competitive advantage or be burdened by competitive disadvantage. By the end of this chapter, you will have a pretty clear idea of why the tasks of crafting and executing strategy are core management functions and why excellent execution of an excellent strategy is the most reliable recipe for turning a company into a standout performer.

Each chapter begins with a series of chapter **learning objectives,** pertinent **quotes** and an introductory preview of the chapter's contents.

In-depth examples— **Illustration Capsules**— appear in boxes throughout each chapter to expand on important chapter topics, connect the text presentation to real-world companies, and convincingly demonstrate "strategy in action." Some are appropriate for use as mini-cases.

ILLUSTRATION CAPSULE 1.1
Starbucks' Strategy in the Specialty Coffee Industry

In 2008, Starbucks was the world's leading specialty coffee retailer, with more than 11,000 stores in the United States and in approximately 4,500 stores in 43 other countries. Since 2000, the company's sales of ready-to-drink coffee, coffee beans, coffee-flavored products, pastries, and coffee accessories had grown by more than 20 percent annually to reach $9.4 billion in 2007. Its net earnings had increased from $95 million in 2000 to $672 million in 2007.

The company's success and dramatic growth were attributable to its superior execution of an excellent strategy. Starbucks' business strategy was made up of the following elements:

- *Expand the number of Starbucks stores domestically by blanketing metropolitan areas, then adding stores on the city's perimeter.* Starbucks also made its locations readily available to consumers by entering into licensing agreements with food service vendors operating in airports, universities, hospitals, and other places where people congregated.
- *Make Starbucks a global brand by opening stores in an increasing number of foreign locations.* The international expansion effort involved opening company-owned-and-operated stores in some foreign countries, while entering into licensing agreements with reputable and capable local companies in other countries.
- *View each store as a billboard for the company and as a contributor to building the company's brand and image.* Each detail was scrutinized to enhance the mood and ambience of the store, to make sure everything signaled best-of-class and reflected the personality of the community and the neighborhood. The thesis was "Everything matters." The company went to great lengths to make sure the store fixtures, the merchandise displays, the colors, the artwork, the banners, the music, and the aromas all blended to create a consistent, inviting, stimulating environment that evoked the romance of coffee, that signaled the company's passion for coffee, and that rewarded customers with ceremony, stories, and surprise.
- *Broaden in-store product offerings.* Starbucks stores went beyond coffee to include coffee-flavored ice cream, Frappuccino, teas, fresh pastries and other food items, candy, juice drinks, music CDs, coffee mugs, and coffee accessories.
- *Fully exploit the growing power of the Starbucks name and brand image with out-of-store sales.* Examples of such out-of-store sales included the sale of ground coffee and coffee beans in U.S. grocery stores. Starbucks also sold Frappuccino in U.S. grocery and convenience

stores through a partnership with PepsiCo and sold coffee-flavored ice cream in grocery stores through a partnership with Dreyer's Grand Ice Cream.

- *Display corporate responsibility and environmental sustainability.* Key social responsibility and sustainability initiatives included purchasing Fair Trade Certified coffees, donating more than $30 million annually to charitable organizations, purchasing paper cups made from recycled materials, and implementing in-store recycling programs.
- *Control the costs of opening new stores.* The company centralized buying, developed standard contracts and fixed fees for certain items, and consolidated work under those contractors who displayed good cost-control practices. The retail operations group outlined exactly the minimum amount of equipment each core store needed so that standard items could be ordered in volume from vendors at 20 to 30 percent discounts, then delivered just in time to the stores either from company warehouses or the vendor. Most designs for display cases were developed, and the whole store layout was developed on a computer, with software that allowed the costs to be estimated as the design evolved. All this cut store-opening costs significantly and reduced store development time from 24 to 18 weeks.
- *Promote customer-friendly service and enhance store ambience by making Starbucks a great place to work.* Schultz's thesis was that high employee morale would spill over to inject energy, positive vibes, and a feel-good atmosphere into the operations of its stores, thereby making the Starbucks experience more pleasing to patrons.

However, while Starbucks strategy was largely on target, it was far from being set in concrete. In early 2008, co-founder and CEO Howard Schultz announced that Starbucks would slow the pace of store expansion in the U.S. and close 600 of its U.S. stores that were underperforming; over 70 percent of the stores scheduled for closing had been opened since 2006 and were in areas where Starbucks already had a number of other stores nearby. The basic reason why so many new Starbucks stores had failed to reach the expected sales and profit levels had to do with putting stores so close together that they cannibalized each others sales—a number of customers found it more convenient to shop at a newly-opened store rather than go to the nearby store they had previously patronized. Schultz also began launching a series of new initiatives to re-ignite sales at Starbucks stores via new product offerings and actions to wow customers with an even better experience, by offering new products and providing store patrons with an even more intriguing Starbucks' experience.

Sources: Information posted at www.starbucks.com (accessed March 17, 2008 and July 26, 2008); various annual reports and company press releases.

xxix

Margin notes define core concepts and call attention to important ideas and principles.

WHAT DO WE MEAN BY *STRATEGY?*

> **CORE CONCEPT**
>
> A company's *strategy* consists of the competitive moves and business approaches that managers are employing to grow the business, attract and please customers, compete successfully, conduct operations, and achieve the targeted levels of organizational performance.

A company's **strategy** is management's action plan for running the business and conducting operations. The crafting of a strategy represents a managerial *commitment to pursue a particular set of actions* in growing the business, attracting and pleasing customers, competing successfully, conducting operations, and improving the company's financial and market performance. Thus, a company's strategy is all about *how*:

- *How* management intends to grow the business.
- *How* it will build a loyal clientele and outcompete rivals.
- *How* each functional piece of the business (research and development, supply chain activities, production, sales and marketing, distribution, finance, and human resources) will be operated.
- *How* performance will be boosted.

In choosing a strategy, management is in effect saying, "Among all the many different ways of competing we could have chosen, we have decided to employ this combination of competitive and operating approaches to move the company in the intended direction, strengthen its market position and competitiveness, and boost performance." The strategic choices a company makes are seldom easy decisions, and some of them may turn out to be wrong—but that is not an excuse for not deciding on a concrete course of action.[1]

In most industries companies have considerable freedom in choosing the hows of strategy.[2] Thus, some rivals strive to improve their performance and market standing by achieving lower costs than rivals, whereas others pursue product superiority or personalized customer service or the development of competencies and capabilities that rivals cannot match. Some opt for wide product lines, whereas others concentrate their energies on a narrow product lineup. Some competitors position themselves in only one part of the industry's chain of production/distribution activities (preferring

Figures scattered throughout the chapters provide conceptual and analytical frameworks.

Figure 4.5 Translating Company Performance of Value Chain Activities into Competitive Advantage

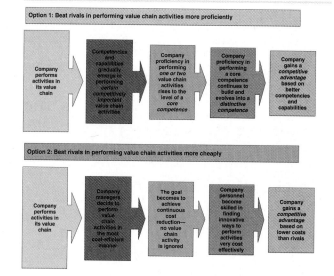

KEY POINTS

The tasks of crafting and executing company strategies are the heart and soul of managing a business enterprise and winning in the marketplace. A company's strategy is the game plan management is using to stake out a market position, conduct its operations, attract and please customers, compete successfully, and achieve organizational objectives. The central thrust of a company's strategy is undertaking moves to build and strengthen the company's long-term competitive position and financial performance and, ideally, gain a competitive advantage over rivals that then becomes a company's ticket to above-average profitability. A company's strategy typically evolves over time, emerging from a blend of (1) proactive and purposeful actions on the part of company managers and (2) as-needed reactions to unanticipated developments and fresh market conditions.

Closely related to the concept of strategy is the concept of a company's business model. A company's business model is management's story line for how and why the company's product offerings and competitive approaches will generate a revenue stream and have an associated cost structure that produces attractive earnings and return on investment—in effect, a company's business model sets forth the economic logic for making money in a particular business, given the company's current strategy.

Key Points sections at the end of each chapter provide a handy summary of essential ideas and things to remember.

---

substitute for doing cutting-edge strategic thinking about a company's external situation—anything less weakens managers' ability to craft strategies that are well matched to industry and competitive conditions.

ASSURANCE OF LEARNING EXERCISES

1. Using your favorite Internet search engine, do some research on competitive forces and driving forces that are at work in the snack food industry. Draw a five-forces diagram for the snack food industry and briefly discuss the nature and strength of each of the five competitive forces. Make a list of the driving forces operating in the snack foods industry and draw some conclusions about whether the likely impact of these driving forces on snack foods companies will be favorable or unfavorable.

2. Refer back to the strategic group map in Illustration Capsule 3.1: Who are Toyota's closest competitors? Between which two strategic groups is competition the strongest? Why do you think no automobile manufacturers are positioned in the upper right corner of the map? Which company/strategic group faces the weakest competition from the members of other strategic groups?

3. Using the information provided in Table 3.2 and your knowledge as a casual dining patron, what are the key success factors for restaurants such as Outback Steakhouse or Carrabba's Italian Grill? Your list should contain no more than six industry key success factors. In deciding on your list, it's important to distinguish between factors critical to success in the industry and factors that enhance a company's overall well-being.

EXERCISES FOR SIMULATION PARTICIPANTS

1. Which of the five competitive forces is creating the strongest competitive pressures for your company?

2. What are the "weapons of competition" that rival companies in your industry can use to gain sales and market share? Refer back to Figure 3.4 to help you identify the various competitive factors.

3. What are the factors affecting the intensity of rivalry in the industry in which your company is competing? Use Figure 3.4 and the accompanying discussion to help you pinpoint the specific factors most affecting competitive intensity. Would you characterize the rivalry and jockeying for better market position, increased sales, and market share among the companies in your industry as fierce, very strong, strong, moderate, or relatively weak? Why?

4. Are there any driving forces in the industry in which your company is competing? What impact will these driving forces have? Will they cause competition to be more or less intense? Will they act to boost or squeeze profit margins? List at least two actions your company should consider taking in order to combat any negative impacts of the driving forces.

Value-added **exercises** at the end of each chapter provide a basis for class discussion, oral presentations, and written assignments. Several chapters have exercises that qualify as "mini-cases."

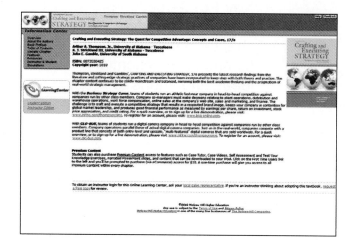

Web site: *www.mhhe.com/thompson*
The student portion of the Web site features 20-question self-scoring chapter tests, a Guide to Case Analysis, and PowerPoint slides for each chapter.

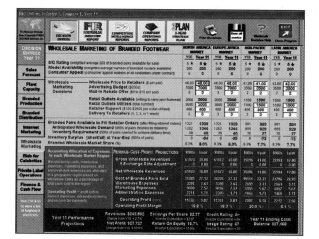

The *Business Strategy Game* or *GLO-BUS* Simulation Exercises Either one of these text supplements involves teams of students managing companies in a head-to-head contest for global market leadership. Company co-managers have to make decisions relating to product quality, production, work force compensation and training, pricing and marketing, and financing of company operations. The challenge is to craft and execute a strategy that is powerful enough to deliver good financial performance despite the competitive efforts of rival companies. Each company competes in North America, Latin America, Europe-Africa, and Asia-Pacific.

Brief Contents

Table of Contents

9. Ethical Business Strategies, Social Responsibility, and Environmental Sustainability   288

Part Two Readings in Crafting and Executing Strategy 415

Crafting and Executing Strategy

Text and
Readings

part one 1

Concepts and Techniques for Crafting and Executing Strategy

What Is Strategy and Why Is It Important?

LEARNING OBJECTIVES

1. Understand the role of business strategies in moving a company in the intended direction, growing its business, and improving its financial and market performance.

2. Develop an awareness of the four most reliable strategic approaches for setting a company apart from rivals and winning a sustainable competitive advantage.

3. Learn that business strategies evolve over time because of changing circumstances and ongoing management efforts to improve the company's strategy.

4. Understand why a company's strategy must be underpinned by a business model that produces revenues sufficient to cover costs and earn a profit.

5. Gain awareness of the three tests that distinguish a winning strategy from a so-so or flawed strategy.

6. Learn why good strategy making and good strategy execution are the most trustworthy signs of good management.

Managers face three central questions in evaluating their company's business prospects:

- What's the company's present situation?
- Where does the company need to go from here?
- How should it get there?

The question "What's the company's present situation?" prompts managers to evaluate industry conditions and competitive pressures, the company's current performance and market standing, its resource strengths and capabilities, and its competitive weaknesses. The question "Where does the company need to go from here?" pushes managers to make choices about the direction in which the company is headed—what new or different customer groups and customer needs it should endeavor to satisfy and how it should change its business makeup. The question "How should it get there?" challenges managers to craft and execute a strategy—a full-blown action plan—capable of moving the company in the intended direction, growing its business, strengthening its ability to compete, and improving its financial performance.

In this opening chapter, we define the concept of strategy and describe its many facets. We shall indicate the kinds of actions that determine what a company's strategy is, why strategies are partly proactive and partly reactive, and why company strategies tend to evolve over time. We will look at what sets a winning strategy apart from a ho-hum or flawed strategy and why the caliber of a company's strategy determines whether it will enjoy a competitive advantage or be burdened by competitive disadvantage. By the end of this chapter, you will have a pretty clear idea of why the tasks of crafting and executing strategy are core management functions and why excellent execution of an excellent strategy is the most reliable recipe for turning a company into a standout performer.

WHAT DO WE MEAN BY *STRATEGY?*

A company's **strategy** is management's action plan for running the business and conducting operations. The crafting of a strategy represents a managerial *commitment to pursue a particular set of actions* in growing the business, attracting and pleasing customers, competing successfully, conducting operations, and improving the company's financial and market performance. Thus, a company's strategy is all about *how*:

- *How* management intends to grow the business.
- *How* it will build a loyal clientele and outcompete rivals.
- *How* each functional piece of the business (research and development, supply chain activities, production, sales and marketing, distribution, finance, and human resources) will be operated.
- *How* performance will be boosted.

In choosing a strategy, management is in effect saying, "Among all the many different ways of competing we could have chosen, we have decided to employ this combination of competitive and operating approaches to move the company in the intended direction, strengthen its market position and competitiveness, and boost performance." The strategic choices a company makes are seldom easy decisions, and some of them may turn out to be wrong—but that is not an excuse for not deciding on a concrete course of action.[1]

In most industries companies have considerable freedom in choosing the hows of strategy.[2] Thus, some rivals strive to improve their performance and market standing by achieving lower costs than rivals, whereas others pursue product superiority or personalized customer service or the development of competencies and capabilities that rivals cannot match. Some opt for wide product lines, whereas others concentrate their energies on a narrow product lineup. Some competitors position themselves in only one part of the industry's chain of production/distribution activities (preferring to be just in manufacturing or wholesale distribution or retailing), while others are partially or fully integrated, with operations ranging from components production to manufacturing and assembly to wholesale distribution or retailing. Some competitors deliberately confine their operations to local or regional markets; others opt to compete nationally, internationally (several countries), or globally (all or most of the major country markets worldwide). Some companies decide to operate in only one industry, while others diversify broadly or narrowly, into related or unrelated industries.

At companies intent on gaining sales and market share at the expense of competitors, managers typically opt for offensive strategies, frequently launching fresh initiatives of one kind or another to make the company's product offering more distinctive and appealing to buyers. Companies already in a strong industry position are more prone to strategies that emphasize gradual gains in the marketplace, fortifying their market position and defending against the latest maneuvering of rivals. Risk-averse companies often prefer "conservative" strategies, preferring to follow the successful moves of pioneering companies whose managers are willing to take the risks of being first to make a bold and, perhaps, pivotal move.

There is no shortage of opportunity to fashion a strategy that both tightly fits a company's own particular situation and is discernibly different from the strategies of rivals. In fact, a company's managers normally attempt to make strategic choices about the key building blocks of its strategy that differ from the choices made by competitors—not 100 percent different but at least different in several important respects. A company's strategy stands a better chance of succeeding when it is predicated on actions, business approaches, and competitive moves aimed at appealing to buyers in ways that set the company apart from rivals and at carving out its own market position. Simply copying successful companies in the industry and trying to mimic their market position rarely works. Rather, there needs to be some distinctive element to the strategy that draws in customers and produces a competitive edge. Carbon-copy strategies among companies in the same industry are the exception rather than the rule.

For a concrete example of the actions and approaches that comprise strategy, see Illustration Capsule 1.1, which describes Starbucks' strategy in the specialty coffee industry.

Strategy and the Quest for Competitive Advantage

The heart and soul of any strategy are the actions and moves in the marketplace that managers are taking to improve the company's financial performance, strengthen its long-term competitive position, and gain a competitive edge over rivals. A creative, distinctive strategy that sets a company apart from rivals and yields a competitive advantage is a company's most reliable ticket for earning above-average profits. Competing in the marketplace with a competitive advantage tends to be more profitable than competing with no advantage. And a company is almost certain to earn significantly higher profits when it enjoys a competitive advantage as opposed to when it is hamstrung by competitive disadvantage. It's nice when a company's strategy produces at least a temporary competitive edge, but a **sustainable competitive advantage** is plainly much better. What make a competitive advantage sustainable as opposed to temporary are actions and elements in the strategy that cause an attractive number of buyers to have a *lasting preference* for a company's products or services. Competitive advantage is the key to above-average profitability and financial performance because strong buyer preferences for the company's product offering translate into higher sales volumes (Wal-Mart) and/or the ability to command a higher price (Mercedes-Benz), thus driving up earnings, return on investment, and other measures of financial performance.

> **CORE CONCEPT**
>
> A company achieves *sustainable competitive advantage* when an attractive number of buyers prefer its products or services over the offerings of competitors and when the basis for this preference is durable.

Four of the most frequently used and dependable strategic approaches to setting a company apart from rivals, building strong customer loyalty, and winning a sustainable competitive advantage are:

1. *Striving to be the industry's low-cost provider.* Wal-Mart and Southwest Airlines have earned strong market positions because of the low-cost advantages they have achieved over their rivals and their consequent ability to underprice competitors. Achieving a cost-based advantage over rivals can produce a durable competitive edge when rivals find it hard to match the low-cost leader's approach to driving costs out of the business. While United Airlines, Delta Airlines, US Airways, and Northwest Airlines have moved in and out of bankruptcy, Southwest Airlines' proficient execution of its low-cost strategy—which includes point-to-point routes, no-frills service, and efficient ground operations—has yielded profits for 35 consecutive years.

In 2008, Starbucks was the world's leading specialty coffee retailer, with more than 11,000 stores in the United States and approximately 4,500 stores in 43 other countries. Since 2000, the company's sales of ready-to-drink coffee, coffee beans, coffee-flavored products, pastries, and coffee accessories had grown by more than 20 percent annually to reach $9.4 billion in 2007. Its net earnings had increased from $95 million in 2000 to $672 million in 2007.

The company's success and dramatic growth were attributable to its superior execution of an excellent strategy. Starbucks' business strategy was made up of the following elements:

- *Expand the number of Starbucks stores domestically by blanketing metropolitan areas, then adding stores on the city's perimeter.* Starbucks also made its locations readily available to consumers by entering into licensing agreements with food service vendors operating in airports, universities, hospitals, and other places where people congregated.

- *Make Starbucks a global brand by opening stores in an increasing number of foreign locations.* The international expansion effort involved opening company-owned-and-operated stores in some foreign countries, while entering into licensing agreements with reputable and capable local companies in other countries.

- *View each store as a billboard for the company and as a contributor to building the company's brand and image.* Each detail was scrutinized to enhance the mood and ambience of the store, to make sure everything signaled best-of-class and reflected the personality of the community and the neighborhood. The thesis was "Everything matters." The company went to great lengths to make sure the store fixtures, the merchandise displays, the colors, the artwork, the banners, the music, and the aromas all blended to create a consistent, inviting, stimulating environment that evoked the romance of coffee, that signaled the company's passion for coffee, and that rewarded customers with ceremony, stories, and surprise.

- *Broaden in-store product offerings.* Starbucks stores went beyond coffee to include coffee-flavored ice cream, Frappuccino, teas, fresh pastries and other food items, candy, juice drinks, music CDs, coffee mugs, and coffee accessories.

- *Fully exploit the growing power of the Starbucks name and brand image with out-of-store sales.* Examples of such out-of-store sales included the sale of ground coffee and coffee beans in U.S. grocery stores. Starbucks also sold Frappuccino in U.S. grocery and convenience stores through a partnership with PepsiCo and sold coffee-flavored ice creams in grocery stores through a partnership with Dreyer's Grand Ice Cream.

- *Display corporate responsibility and environmental sustainability.* Key social responsibility and sustainability initiatives included purchasing Fair Trade Certified coffees, donating more than $30 million annually to charitable organizations, purchasing paper cups made from recycled materials, and implementing in-store recycling programs.

- *Control the costs of opening new stores.* The company centralized buying, developed standard contracts and fixed fees for certain items, and consolidated work under those contractors who displayed good cost-control practices. The retail operations group outlined exactly the minimum amount of equipment each core store needed so that standard items could be ordered in volume from vendors at 20 to 30 percent discounts, then delivered just in time to the store site from either company warehouses or the vendor. Modular designs for display cases were developed, and the whole store layout was developed on a computer, with software that allowed the costs to be estimated as the design evolved. All this cut store-opening costs significantly and reduced store development time from 24 to 18 weeks.

- *Promote customer-friendly service and enhance store ambience by making Starbucks a great place to work.* CEO Howard Schultz's thesis was that high employee morale would spill over to inject energy, positive vibes, and a feel-good atmosphere into the operations of its stores, thereby making the Starbucks experience more pleasing to patrons.

However, while Starbucks' strategy was largely on target, it was far from being set in concrete. In early 2008, co-founder and CEO Schultz announced that Starbucks would slow the pace of store expansion in the U.S. and close 600 of its U.S. stores that were underperforming; over 70 percent of the stores scheduled for closing had been opened since 2006 and were in areas where Starbucks already had a number of other stores nearby. The basic reason why so many new Starbucks stores had failed to reach the expected sales and profit levels had to do with putting stores so close together that they cannibalized each other's sales—a number of customers found it more convenient to shop at a newly opened store rather than go to the nearby store they had previously patronized. Schultz also began launching a series of new initiatives to re-ignite sales at Starbucks stores via new product offerings and actions to wow customers with an even better experience, by offering new products and providing store patrons with an even more intriguing Starbucks experience.

Sources: Information posted at www.starbucks.com (accessed March 17, 2008, and July 26, 2008); various annual reports and company press releases.

2. *Creating a differentiation-based advantage keyed to such features as higher quality, wider product selection, added performance, value-added services, more attractive styling, technological superiority, or unusually good value for the money.* Successful adopters of differentiation strategies include Johnson & Johnson in baby products (product reliability), Harley-Davidson (outlaw image and distinctive sound), Chanel and Rolex (luxury and prestige), Porsche and BMW (engineering design and performance), and Amazon.com (wide selection and convenience). Differentiation strategies can be powerful so long as a company is sufficiently innovative to thwart clever rivals in finding ways to copy or closely imitate the features of a successful differentiator's product offering.

3. *Focusing on serving the special needs and tastes of buyers comprising a narrow market niche.* Prominent companies that enjoy competitive success in a specialized market niche include eBay in online auctions, Best Buy in home electronics, McAfee in virus protection software, Starbucks in premium coffees and coffee drinks, Whole Foods Market in natural and organic foods, and The Weather Channel in cable TV.

4. *Developing expertise and resource strengths that give the company competitively valuable capabilities that rivals can't easily match, copy, or trump with substitute capabilities.* FedEx has developed a resource-based competitive advantage through its superior capabilities in next-day delivery of small packages. Walt Disney has hard-to-beat capabilities in theme park management and family entertainment. Dell's build-to-order manufacturing capabilities in computer hardware have consistently allowed it to earn healthy profit margins while offering businesses and consumers competitive prices. Ritz-Carlton and Four Seasons have uniquely strong capabilities in providing their hotel and resort guests with an array of personalized services. Very often, winning a durable competitive edge over rivals hinges more on building competitively valuable expertise and capabilities than it does on having a distinctive product. Clever rivals can nearly always copy the attributes of a popular or innovative product, but for rivals to match experience, know-how, and specialized competitive capabilities that a company has developed and perfected over a long period is substantially harder to duplicate and takes much longer.

The tight connection between competitive advantage and profitability means that *the quest for sustainable competitive advantage always ranks center stage in crafting a strategy.* The key to successful strategy making is to come up with one or more strategy elements that act as a magnet to draw customers and that produce a lasting competitive edge over rivals. Indeed, what separates a powerful strategy from a run-of-the-mill or ineffective one is management's ability to forge a series of moves, both in the marketplace and internally, that set the company apart from its rivals, tilt the playing field in the company's favor by giving buyers reason to prefer its products or services, and produce a sustainable competitive advantage over rivals. The bigger and more sustainable the competitive advantage, the better are the company's prospects for winning in the marketplace and earning superior long-term profits relative to rivals. Without a strategy that leads to competitive advantage, a company risks being outcompeted by stronger rivals and/or locked into mediocre financial performance. Hence, company managers deserve no gold stars for coming up with a ho-hum strategy that results in ho-hum financial performance and a ho-hum industry standing.

Figure 1.1   Identifying a Company's Strategy—What to Look For

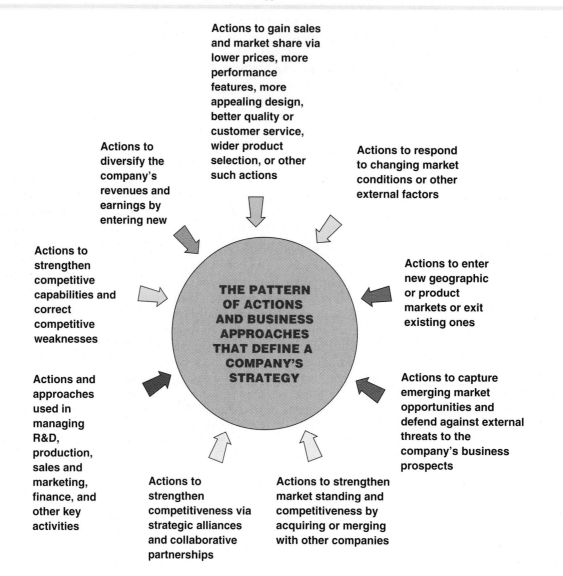

Identifying a Company's Strategy

The best indicators of a company's strategy are its actions in the marketplace and the statements of senior managers about the company's current business approaches, future plans, and efforts to strengthen its competitiveness and performance. Figure 1.1 shows what to look for in pinpointing the key elements of a company's strategy.

Discovering what strategy a company is employing entails researching the company's business approaches and actions in the marketplace. In the case of publicly owned enterprises, the strategy is often openly discussed by senior executives in the company's annual report and 10-K report, in press releases, and in information posted on the company's Web site. To maintain the confidence of investors and Wall Street, most public companies have to be fairly open about their strategies. Company executives typically lay out key elements of their strategies in presentations to securities analysts (the accompanying PowerPoint slides are usually posted in the investor relations section of the company's Web site) and stories in the business media about the company often include aspects of the company's strategy. Hence, except for some about-to-be-launched moves that remain under wraps, there's usually nothing secret or undiscoverable about a company's present strategy.

Why a Company's Strategy Evolves over Time

Regardless of where a company's strategy comes from—be it the product of top executives or the collaborative product of numerous company personnel—it is unlikely that the strategy, as originally conceived, will prove entirely suitable over time. Every company must be willing and ready to modify its strategy in response to changing market conditions, advancing technology, the fresh moves of competitors, shifting buyer needs and preferences, emerging market opportunities, new ideas, and mounting evidence that the strategy is not working well. Thus, *a company's strategy is always a work in progress.*

> **CORE CONCEPT**
> Changing circumstances and ongoing management efforts to improve the strategy cause a company's strategy to evolve over time—a condition that makes crafting a strategy a process, not a one-time event.

Most of the time a company's strategy evolves incrementally from management's ongoing efforts to fine-tune this or that piece of the strategy and to adjust certain strategy elements in response to unfolding events. But, on occasion, major strategy shifts are called for, such as when a strategy is clearly failing and the company faces a financial crisis, when market conditions or buyer preferences change significantly, or when important technological breakthroughs occur. In some industries, conditions change at a fairly slow pace, making it feasible for the major components of a good strategy to remain in place for long periods. But in industries where industry and competitive conditions change frequently and sometimes dramatically, the life cycle of a given strategy is short.[3] For example, companies in industries with rapid-fire advances in technology like medical equipment, electronics, Internet retailing, and wireless devices often find it essential to adjust one or more key elements of their strategies several times a year, sometimes even finding it necessary to reinvent their approach to providing value to their customers.

> A company's strategy is shaped partly by management analysis and choice, and partly by the necessity of adapting and learning by doing.

But regardless of whether a company's strategy changes gradually or swiftly, the important point is that a company's present strategy is always temporary and on trial, pending new ideas from management, changing industry and competitive conditions, and any other new developments that management believes warrant strategy adjustments. Thus, a company's strategy at any given point is fluid, representing the temporary outcome of an ongoing process that, on the one hand, involves reasoned and creative management efforts to craft an effective strategy and, on the other hand, involves ongoing responses to market change and constant experimentation and tinkering. Adapting to new conditions and constantly learning what is working well enough to continue and what needs to be improved are consequently normal parts of the strategy-making process and results in an evolving strategy.

A Company's Strategy Is Partly Proactive and Partly Reactive

The evolving nature of strategy means that the typical company strategy is a blend of (1) proactive decisions to improve the company's financial performance and secure a competitive edge, and (2) as-needed reactions to unanticipated developments and fresh

Figure 1.2   A Company's Strategy Is a Blend of Proactive Initiatives and Reactive
Adjustments

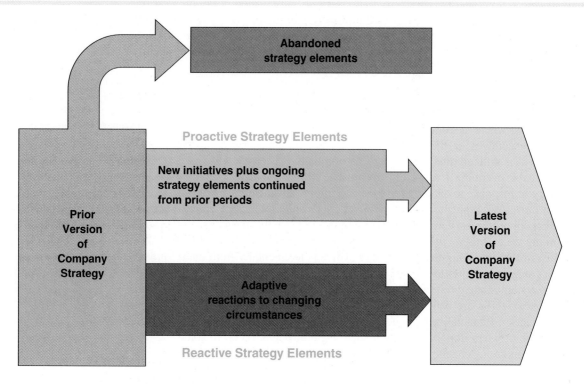

market conditions—see Figure 1.2.[4] The biggest portion of a company's current strategy flows from previously initiated actions and business approaches that are working well enough to merit continuation and newly launched initiatives aimed at boosting financial performance and edging out rivals. This part of management's action plan for running the company consists of its *proactive strategy elements.*

But managers must always be willing to supplement or modify all the proactive strategy elements with as-needed reactions to unanticipated developments. Inevitably, there will be occasions when market and competitive conditions take an unexpected turn that call for some kind of strategic reaction or adjustment. Hence, a portion of a company's strategy is always developed on the fly, coming as a response to fresh strategic maneuvers on the part of rival firms, unexpected shifts in customer requirements and expectations, fast-changing technological developments, newly appearing market opportunities, a changing political or economic climate, or other unanticipated happenings in the surrounding environment. These adaptive strategy adjustments form the *reactive strategy elements.*

As shown in Figure 1.2, a company's strategy evolves from one version to the next as managers abandon obsolete or ineffective strategy elements, settle upon a set of *proactive/intended strategy elements,* and then adapt the strategy as new circumstances unfold—an ongoing process that results in a strategy that is a *combination* of proactive and reactive elements.

STRATEGY AND ETHICS: PASSING THE TEST OF MORAL SCRUTINY

In choosing among strategic alternatives, company managers are well advised to embrace actions that can pass the test of moral scrutiny. Just keeping a company's strategic actions within the bounds of what is legal does not mean the strategy is ethical. Ethical and moral standards are not governed by what is legal; rather, they involve issues of right versus wrong and of duty—what one *should* do. A strategy is ethical only if (1) it does not entail actions and behaviors that cross the line between "should do" and "should not do" (because such actions are unsavory, unconscionable, or injurious to other people or unnecessarily harmful to the environment), and (2) it allows management to fulfill its ethical duties to all stakeholders— owners/shareholders, employees, customers, suppliers, the communities in which it operates, and society at large.

> **CORE CONCEPT**
>
> Ethics go beyond legality; to meet the standard of being ethical, a strategy must entail actions that can pass moral scrutiny in the sense of not being shady, unconscionable, or injurious to others or unnecessarily harmful to the environment.

Admittedly, it is not always easy to categorize a given strategic behavior as definitely ethical or definitely unethical; many strategic actions fall in a gray zone in between. Whether they are deemed ethical or unethical hinges on how high one sets the bar. For example, is it ethical for advertisers of alcoholic products to place ads in media with a largely underage audience? (In 2003, growing concerns about underage drinking prompted some beer and distilled spirits companies to agree to place ads in media with an audience at least 70 percent adult, up from a standard of 50 percent adult.) Is it ethical for an apparel retailer attempting to keep prices attractively low to source clothing from foreign manufacturers who pay substandard wages, use child labor, or subject workers to unsafe working conditions? Many people would say no, but some might argue that a company is not unethical simply because it does not police the business practices of its suppliers. Is it ethical for the makers of athletic uniforms, shoes, and equipment to pay coaches large sums of money as an inducement for the coaches to use the manufacturer's products in their sport? (The compensation contracts of many college coaches include substantial payments from sportswear and sport equipment manufacturers; the teams subsequently end up wearing the uniforms and using the products of these same manufacturers.) Is it ethical for pharmaceutical manufacturers to charge higher prices for life-saving drugs in some countries than they charge in others? (This is a fairly common practice that has recently come under scrutiny.) Is it ethical for a company to turn a blind eye to the damage its operations do to the environment (even though its operations are in compliance with current environmental regulations)—especially if it has the know-how and the means to alleviate some of the environmental impacts by making relatively inexpensive changes in its operating practices?

Senior executives with strong ethical convictions are generally proactive in linking strategic action and ethics; they forbid the pursuit of ethically questionable business opportunities and insist that all aspects of company strategy reflect high ethical standards.[5] They make it clear that all company personnel are expected to act with integrity, and they put organizational checks and balances into place to monitor behavior, enforce ethical codes of conduct, and provide guidance to employees regarding any gray areas. Their commitment to conducting the company's business in an ethical manner is genuine, not hypocritical lip service.

Ethical misconduct, corporate misdeeds, and fraudulent accounting practices all entail substantial downside risk. Aside from just the embarrassment and black marks that accompany headline exposure of a company's misbehavior, the hard fact is that many customers and many suppliers are wary of doing business with a company that engages in sleazy practices or that turns a blind eye to illegal or unethical behavior on the part of employees. They are turned off by unethical strategies and unbecoming conduct—rather than become victims or get burned themselves, wary customers will quickly take their business elsewhere and wary suppliers will tread carefully. Moreover, employees with character and integrity do not want to work for a company whose strategies are shady or whose executives lack character and integrity. The damage that unethical strategies and behavior can do to a company's reputation and overall business is substantial. Besides, immoral or unethical actions are plain wrong.

THE RELATIONSHIP BETWEEN A COMPANY'S STRATEGY AND ITS BUSINESS MODEL

CORE CONCEPT

A company's *business model* explains the rationale for why its business approach and strategy will be a moneymaker. Absent the ability to deliver good profitability, the strategy is not viable and the survival of the business is in doubt.

Closely related to the concept of strategy is the concept of a **business model**. A company's business model is management's story line for how the strategy will be a moneymaker. The story line sets forth the key components of the enterprise's business approach, indicates how revenues will be generated, and makes a case for why the strategy can deliver value to customers and create a profit for the company.[6] A company's business model thus identifies the basis for why its strategy will result in enough revenues to cover costs and realize a profit.

The nitty-gritty issue surrounding a company's business model is whether the chosen strategy makes good business sense from a moneymaking perspective. Why is there convincing reason to believe that the strategy is capable of producing a profit? How will customers be served? How will the business generate its revenues? Will those revenues be sufficient to cover operating costs? The concept of a company's business model is, consequently, more narrowly focused than the concept of a company's strategy. A company's strategy *relates broadly to its competitive initiatives and action plan for running the business* (but it may or may not lead to profitability). However, a company's business model zeros in on *the principle business components by which the business will generate revenues sufficient to cover costs and produce attractive profits and return on investment.* Absent the ability to deliver good profits, the strategy is not viable, the business model is flawed, and the business itself will fail.

Companies that have been in business for a while and are making acceptable profits have a proven business model—because there is hard evidence that their strategies are capable of profitability. Companies that are in a start-up mode or that are losing money have questionable business models; their strategies have yet to produce good bottom-line results, putting in doubt their story line about how they intend to make money and their viability as business enterprises.

Magazines and newspapers employ a business model based on generating sufficient subscription and advertising revenue to cover the costs of delivering their products to readers. Cable TV companies, mobile phone providers, satellite radio companies, and broadband providers also employ a subscription-based business model. The business model of network TV and radio broadcasters entails providing free programming to audiences and then charging advertisers fees based on audience size. Wal-Mart has perfected the business model for big-box discount retailing—a model also used by The Home Depot, Costco, and Target. Gillette's business model in razor blades has involved selling the razor at an attractively low price and then making money on repeat purchases of razor blades. Printer manufacturers like Hewlett-Packard, Lexmark, and Epson have pursued much the same business model as Gillette—selling printers at a low (virtually break-even) price and making large profits on the repeat purchases of printer supplies, especially ink cartridges. Illustration Capsule 1.2 discusses the contrasting business models of Microsoft and Red Hat.

WHAT MAKES A STRATEGY A WINNER?

Three questions can be used to distinguish a winning strategy from a so-so or flawed strategy:

1. *How well does the strategy fit the company's situation?* To qualify as a winner, a strategy has to be well matched to industry and competitive conditions, a company's best market opportunities, and other aspects of the enterprise's external environment. At the same time, it has to be tailored to the company's resource strengths and weaknesses, competencies, and competitive capabilities. Unless a strategy exhibits tight fit with both the external and internal aspects of a company's overall situation, it is likely to produce less than the best possible business results.

> **CORE CONCEPT**
> A winning strategy must fit the enterprise's external and internal situation, build sustainable competitive advantage, and improve company performance.

2. *Is the strategy helping the company achieve a sustainable competitive advantage?* Winning strategies enable a company to achieve a competitive advantage that is durable. The bigger and more durable the competitive edge that a strategy helps build, the more powerful and appealing it is.

3. *Is the strategy resulting in better company performance?* A good strategy boosts company performance. Two kinds of performance improvements tell the most about the caliber of a company's strategy: (*a*) gains in profitability and financial strength and (*b*) gains in the company's competitive strength and market standing.

Strategies that come up short on one or more of the above questions are plainly less appealing than strategies passing all three test questions with flying colors. Additional criteria for judging the merits of a particular strategy include (1) the degree of risk the strategy poses as compared to alternative strategies and (2) the degree to which it is flexible and adaptable to changing circumstances. These criteria are relevant and merit consideration, but they seldom override the importance of the three test questions posed above.

Managers can also use the same questions to pick and choose among alternative strategic actions. A company evaluating which of several strategic options to employ can size up how well each option measures up against each of the three questions. The strategic option with the highest prospective passing scores on all three questions can be regarded as the best or most attractive strategic alternative.

ILLUSTRATION CAPSULE 1.2
Microsoft and Red Hat: Two Contrasting Business Models

The strategies of rival companies are often predicated on strikingly different business models. Consider, for example, the business models for Microsoft and Red Hat in operating system software for personal computers.

Microsoft's business model for making money from its operating system products is based on the following revenue-cost-profit economics:

- Employ a cadre of highly skilled programmers to develop proprietary code; keep the source code hidden so as to keep the inner workings of the software proprietary.

- Sell the resulting operating system and software package to personal computer (PC) makers and to PC users at relatively attractive prices (around $75 to PC makers and about $100 at retail to PC users); strive to maintain a 90 percent or more market share of the 150 million PCs sold annually worldwide.

- Keep costs on the front end (in developing the software) fixed; set the variable costs of producing and packaging the CDs provided to users at only a couple of dollars per copy—once the break-even volume is reached, Microsoft's revenues from additional sales are almost pure profit.

- Provide a modest level of technical support to users at no cost.

- Keep rejuvenating revenues by periodically introducing next-generation software versions with features that will induce PC users to upgrade the operating system on previously purchased PCs to the new version.

Red Hat, a company formed to market its own version of the open-source Linux operating system, employs a business model based on sharply different revenue-cost-profit economics:

- Rely on the collaborative efforts of volunteer programmers from all over the world who contribute bits and pieces of code to improve and polish the Linux operating system. The global community of thousands of programmers who work on Linux in their spare time do what they do because they love it; because they are fervent believers that all software should be free (as in free speech); and, in some cases, because they are anti-Microsoft and want to have a part in undoing what they see as a Microsoft monopoly.

- Collect and test enhancements and new applications submitted by the open-source community of volunteer programmers. Linux's originator, Linus Torvalds, and a team of 300-plus Red Hat engineers and software developers evaluate which incoming submissions merit inclusion in new releases of Red Hat Linux—the evaluation and integration of new submissions are Red Hat's only up-front product development costs.

- Market the upgraded and tested family of Red Hat Linux products to large enterprises and charge them a subscription fee that includes 24/7 support within one hour in seven languages. Provide subscribers with updated versions of Red Hat Linux every 12–18 months to maintain the subscriber base.

- Make the source code open and available to all users, allowing them to create a customized version of Linux.

- Capitalize on the specialized expertise required to use Linux in multiserver, multiprocessor applications by providing fees-based training, consulting, software customization, and client-directed engineering to Red Hat Linux users. Red Hat offers Linux certification training programs at all skill levels at more than 60 global locations—Red Hat certification in the use of Linux is considered the best in the world.

Microsoft's business model—sell proprietary code software and give service away free—is a proven money maker that generates billions in profits annually. On the other hand, the jury is still out on Red Hat's business model of selling subscriptions to open-source software to large corporations and deriving substantial revenues from the sales of technical support, training, consulting, software customization, and engineering to generate revenues sufficient to cover costs and yield a profit. Red Hat's fiscal 2007 revenues of $400 million and net income of $60 million are quite meager in comparison to Microsoft's.

Sources: Information posted at www.microsoft.com and www.redhat.com (accessed May 6, 2008).

WHY ARE CRAFTING AND EXECUTING STRATEGY IMPORTANT?

Crafting and executing strategy are top-priority managerial tasks for two very big reasons. First, there is a compelling need for managers to proactively shape, or craft, how the company's business will be conducted. A clear and reasoned strategy is management's prescription for doing business, its road map to competitive advantage, its game plan for pleasing customers and improving financial performance. High-achieving enterprises are nearly always the product of astute, creative, proactive strategy-making that sets a company apart from its rivals. Companies don't get to the top of the industry rankings or stay there with imitative strategies or with strategies built around timid resolutions to try to do better. And only a handful of companies can boast of strategies that hit home runs in the marketplace due to lucky breaks or the good fortune of having stumbled into the right market at the right time with the right product. So there can be little argument that a company's strategy matters—and matters a lot.

Second, a *strategy-focused enterprise* is more likely to be a strong bottom-line performer than a company whose management team does not take its strategy making responsibilities seriously. There's no escaping the fact that the quality of managers' strategy making and strategy execution has a highly positive impact on revenue growth, earnings, and return on investment. A company that lacks clear-cut direction, has vague or undemanding performance targets, has a muddled or flawed strategy, or can't seem to execute its strategy competently is a company whose financial performance is probably suffering and whose business is at long-term risk. The chief executive officer of one successful company put it well when he said:

> In the main, our competitors are acquainted with the same fundamental concepts and techniques and approaches that we follow, and they are as free to pursue them as we are. More often than not, the difference between their level of success and ours lies in the relative thoroughness and self-discipline with which we and they develop and execute our strategies for the future.

Good Strategy + Good Strategy Execution = Good Management

Crafting and executing strategy are thus core management functions. Among all the things managers do, nothing affects a company's ultimate success or failure more fundamentally than how well its management team charts the company's direction, develops competitively effective strategic moves and business approaches, and pursues what needs to be done internally to produce good day-in, day-out strategy execution and operating excellence. Indeed, *good strategy and good strategy execution are the most trustworthy signs of good management.* Managers don't deserve a gold star for designing a potentially brilliant strategy but failing to put the organizational means in place to carry it out in high-caliber fashion. Competent execution of a mediocre strategy scarcely merits enthusiastic applause for management's efforts either. The rationale for using the twin standards of good strategy making and good strategy execution to determine whether a company is well managed is therefore compelling: *The better conceived a company's strategy and the more competently it is executed, the more likely that the company will be a standout performer in the marketplace.*

Throughout the text chapters to come and the accompanying case collection, the spotlight is trained on the foremost question in running a business enterprise: What must managers do, and do well, to make a company a winner in the marketplace? The answer that emerges, and that becomes the message of this book, is that doing a good job of managing inherently requires good strategic thinking and good management of the strategy-making, strategy-executing process.

The mission of this book is to provide a solid overview of what every business student and aspiring manager needs to know about crafting and executing strategy. This requires exploring what good strategic thinking entails; presenting the core concepts and tools of strategic analysis; describing the ins and outs of crafting and executing strategy; and, through the cases that have been included, helping build skills both in diagnosing how well the strategy-making, strategy-executing task is being performed in actual companies and in prescribing actions for how the companies in question can improve their approaches to crafting and executing their strategies. At the very least, we hope to convince you that capabilities in crafting and executing strategy are basic to managing successfully and merit a prominent place in every manager's toolkit.

As you tackle the following pages, ponder the following observation by the essayist and poet Ralph Waldo Emerson: "Commerce is a game of skill which many people play, but which few play well." If the content of this book helps you become a more savvy player and equips you to succeed in business, then your journey through these pages will indeed be time well spent.

KEY POINTS

The tasks of crafting and executing company strategies are the heart and soul of managing a business enterprise and winning in the marketplace. A company's strategy is the game plan management is using to stake out a market position, conduct its operations, attract and please customers, compete successfully, and achieve organizational objectives. The central thrust of a company's strategy is undertaking moves to build and strengthen the company's long-term competitive position and financial performance and, ideally, gain a competitive advantage over rivals that then becomes a company's ticket to above-average profitability. A company's strategy typically evolves over time, emerging from a blend of (1) proactive and purposeful actions on the part of company managers and (2) as-needed reactions to unanticipated developments and fresh market conditions.

Closely related to the concept of strategy is the concept of a company's business model. A company's business model is management's story line for how and why the company's product offerings and competitive approaches will generate a revenue stream and have an associated cost structure that produces attractive earnings and return on investment—in effect, a company's business model sets forth the economic logic for making money in a particular business, given the company's current strategy.

A winning strategy fits the circumstances of a company's external situation and its internal resource strengths and competitive capabilities, builds competitive advantage, and boosts company performance.

Crafting and executing strategy are core management functions. Whether a company wins or loses in the marketplace is directly attributable to the caliber of that company's strategy and the proficiency with which the strategy is executed.

ASSURANCE OF LEARNING EXERCISES

1. Go to www.redhat.com and check whether the company's recent financial reports indicate that its business model is working. Is the company sufficiently profitable to validate its business model and strategy? Is its revenue stream from selling training, consulting, and engineering services growing or declining as a percentage of total revenues? Does your review of the company's recent financial performance suggest that its business model and strategy are changing? Read the company's latest statement about its business model and about why it is pursuing the subscription approach (as compared to Microsoft's approach of selling copies of its operating software directly to PC manufacturers and individuals).

2. Go to www.bestbuy.com, click on the investor relations section, and explore Best Buy's latest annual reports and 10-K filings to see if you can identify the key elements of Best Buy's strategy. Use the framework provided in Figure 1.1 to help identify the key elements of Best Buy's strategy. What type of competitive advantage does Best Buy seem to be pursuing?

3. Given what you know about the specialty coffee industry, does Starbucks' strategy as described in Illustration Capsule 1.1 seem to be well matched to industry and competitive conditions? Does the strategy seem to be keyed to a cost advantage, differentiating features, serving the unique needs of a niche, or developing resource strengths and competitive capabilities rivals can't imitate or trump (or a mixture of these)? How has Starbucks' strategy evolved (or failed to evolve) in recent years? What is there about Starbucks' strategy that can lead to sustainable competitive advantage?

4. On December 15, 2003, Levi Strauss & Company announced it would close its two last remaining apparel plants in the United States to finalize its transition from a clothing manufacturer to a marketing, sales, and design company. Beginning in 2004, all Levi's apparel was to be produced by contract manufacturers located in low-wage countries. As recently as 1990, Levi Strauss had produced 90 percent of its apparel in company-owned plants in the United States employing over 20,000 production workers. With every plant closing, Levi Strauss & Company provided severance and job retraining packages to affected workers and cash payments to small communities where its plants were located. Still, these communities struggled to recover from the loss of jobs associated with Levi Strauss's plant closings; many of the former Levi Strauss employees who took new jobs found it difficult to match their previous levels of compensation and benefits. Does Levi Strauss's strategy to outsource its manufacturing pass the moral scrutiny test? Is it ethical for a company to close plants employing over 20,000 workers and shift production to low-wage-paying contract manufacturers in foreign countries? Why or why not?

EXERCISE FOR SIMULATION PARTICIPANTS

This chapter discusses three questions that must be answered by managers in organizations of all sizes. After you have read the Participant's Guide or Player's Manual for the strategy simulation exercise that you will participate in this academic term, you and your co-managers should come up with one- or two-paragraph answers to the following three questions prior to entering your first set of decisions. While your answer to the first of the three questions can be developed from your reading of the manual, the second and third questions will require a collaborative discussion among the members of your company's management team about how you intend to manage the company you have been assigned to run.

1. Where are we now? (Is your company in a good, an average, or a weak competitive position vis-à-vis rival companies? Does your company appear to be in sound financial condition? What problems does your company have that need to be addressed?)

2. Where do we want to go? (Where would you like your company to be after the first five decision rounds? By how much would you like to increase total profits of the company by the end of the simulation exercise? What kinds of performance outcomes will signal that you and your co-managers are managing the company successfully?)

3. How are we going to get there? (Which of the basic strategic and competitive approaches discussed in Chapter 1 makes the most sense for your company to pursue? What kind of competitive advantage over rivals do you intend to try to build?)

2

Leading the Process of Crafting and Executing Strategy

LEARNING OBJECTIVES

1. Grasp why it is critical for company managers to think long and hard about where a company needs to head and why.

2. Understand the importance of setting both strategic and financial objectives.

3. Recognize that the task of crafting a company strategy draws on the entrepreneurial talents of managers at all organizational levels.

4. Understand why the strategic initiatives taken at various organizational levels must be tightly coordinated to achieve companywide performance targets.

5. Become aware of what a company must do to achieve operating excellence and to execute its strategy proficiently.

6. Understand why the strategic management process is ongoing, not an every-now-and-then task.

7. Learn what leadership skills management must exhibit to drive strategy execution forward.

8. Become aware of the role and responsibility of a company's board of directors in overseeing the strategic management process.

Crafting and executing strategy are the heart and soul of managing a business enterprise. But exactly what is involved in developing a strategy and executing it proficiently? What are the various components of the strategy-making, strategy-executing process? To what extent are company personnel—aside from top executives—involved in the process? In this chapter we present an overview of the managerial ins and outs of crafting and executing company strategies. We give special attention to management's direction-setting responsibilities—charting a strategic course, setting performance targets, and choosing a strategy capable of producing the desired outcomes. We also explain why strategy making is a task for a company's entire management team and discuss which kinds of strategic decisions tend to be made at which levels of management. The chapter concludes with a look at the roles and responsibilities of a company's board of directors in the strategy-making, strategy-executing process and how good corporate governance protects shareholder interests and promotes good management.

WHAT DOES THE STRATEGY-MAKING, STRATEGY-EXECUTING PROCESS ENTAIL?

The managerial process of crafting and executing a company's strategy consists of five interrelated and integrated phases:

1. *Developing a strategic vision* of where the company needs to head and what its future product/customer/market/technology focus should be.
2. *Setting objectives* and using them as yardsticks for measuring the company's performance and progress.
3. *Crafting a strategy to achieve the objectives* and move the company along the strategic course that management has charted.
4. *Implementing and executing the chosen strategy efficiently and effectively.*
5. *Evaluating performance and initiating corrective adjustments* in the company's long-term direction, objectives, strategy, or execution in light of actual experience, changing conditions, new ideas, and new opportunities.

Figure 2.1 displays this five-phase process. Let's examine each phase in enough detail to set the stage for the forthcoming chapters and give you a bird's-eye view of this book.

PHASE 1: DEVELOPING A STRATEGIC VISION

Very early in the strategy-making process, a company's senior managers must wrestle with the issue of what direction the company should take. Would a change in the company's present product/market/customer/technology focus likely improve the company's market position and future prospects? Deciding to commit the company to follow one

Figure 2.1   The Strategy-Making, Strategy-Executing Process

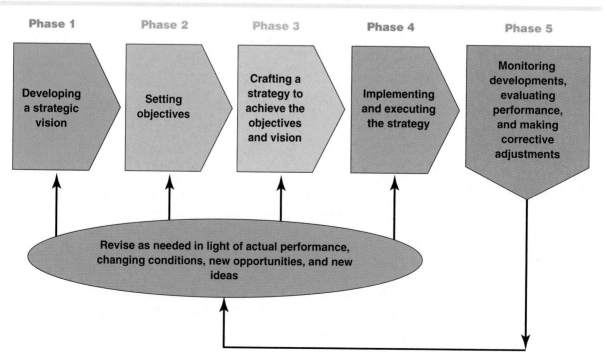

Table 2.1   Factors to Consider in Deciding on a Company's Future Direction

External Considerations	Internal Considerations
• Is the outlook for the company promising if the company sticks with its present product/market/customer/technology focus and strategic direction? • Are changes under way in the competitive landscape acting to enhance or weaken the company's prospects? • What, if any, new customer groups and/or geographic markets should the company get in position to serve? • Are there any emerging market opportunities the company ought to pursue? • Should we plan to abandon any of the markets, market segments, or customer groups we are currently serving?	• What are our ambitions for the company—what industry standing do we want the company to have? • Will our present business generate sufficient growth and profitability to please shareholders? • What resource strengths does the company have that will aid its ability to add new products/services and/or get into new businesses? • Is the company stretching its resources too thin by trying to compete in too many product categories or market arenas, some of which are unprofitable? • Is the company's technological focus too broad or too narrow?

direction versus another pushes managers to draw some carefully reasoned conclusions about whether and how to modify the company's product/market/customer/technology focus and long-term direction. A number of factors need to be considered in deciding where to head and why such a direction makes good business sense—see Table 2.1

Top management's views and conclusions about the company's direction and future product/customer/market/technology focus constitute a **strategic vision** for the company. A strategic vision delineates management's aspirations for the business, providing a panoramic view of "where we are going." A strategic vision thus points an organization in a particular direction, charts a strategic path, and molds organizational identity. A clearly articulated strategic vision communicates management's aspirations to stakeholders and helps steer the energies of company personnel in a common direction. For instance, Henry Ford's vision of a car in every garage had power because it captured the imagination of others, aided internal efforts to mobilize the Ford Motor Company's resources, and served as a reference point for gauging the merits of the company's strategic actions.

> **CORE CONCEPT**
> A *strategic vision* describes the route a company intends to take in developing and strengthening its business. It lays out the company's strategic course in preparing for the future.

Well-conceived visions are *distinctive* and *specific* to a particular organization; they avoid generic, feel-good statements like "We will become a global leader and the first choice of customers in every market we choose to serve"—which could apply to any of hundreds of organizations.[1] And they are not the product of a committee charged with coming up with an innocuous one-sentence vision that wins approval from various stakeholders. Nicely worded vision statements with no specifics about the company's product/market/customer/technology focus fall well short of what it takes for a vision to measure up. A strategic vision proclaiming management's quest "to be the market leader" or "to be the first choice of customers" or "to be the most innovative" or "to be recognized as the best company in the industry" offer scant guidance about a company's direction and what changes and challenges lie on the road ahead.

For a strategic vision to function as a valuable managerial tool, it must (1) illuminate the company's directional path and (2) provide managers with a reference point for making strategic decisions and preparing the company for the future. It must say something definitive about the company's future product/market/customer/technology focus. A good vision always needs to be beyond a company's immediate reach so as to help unleash unified actions on the part of company personnel that move the company

Table 2.2   Characteristics of an Effectively Worded Vision Statement

Graphic	Paints a picture of the kind of company that management is trying to create and the market position(s) the company is striving to stake out.
Directional	Is forward-looking; describes the strategic course that management has charted and the kinds of product/market/customer/technology changes that will help the company prepare for the future.
Focused	Is specific enough to provide managers with guidance in making decisions and allocating resources.
Flexible	Is not a once-and-for-all-time statement—the directional course that management has charted may have to be adjusted as product/market/customer/technology circumstances change.
Feasible	Is within the realm of what the company can reasonably expect to achieve in due time.
Desirable	Indicates why the direction makes good business sense and is in the long-term interests of stakeholders (especially shareowners, employees, and customers).
Easy to communicate	Is explainable in 5–10 minutes and, ideally, can be reduced to a simple, memorable slogan (like Henry Ford's famous vision of "a car in every garage").

Source: Based partly on John P. Kotter, *Leading Change* (Boston: Harvard Business School Press, 1996), p. 72.

down the path of realizing the vision. Table 2.2 lists some characteristics of an effective vision statement.

A sampling of vision statements currently in use shows a range from strong/clear to overly general/generic. A surprising number of the vision statements found on company Web sites and in annual reports are vague about the company's future product/market/customer/technology focus. Some are nice-sounding but say little. Others read like something written by a committee hoping to win the support of different stakeholders. And some are so short on specifics as to apply to most any company in any industry. Many read like a public relations statement—high-sounding words that someone came up with because it is fashionable for companies to have an official vision statement.[2] Table 2.3 provides a list of the most common shortcomings in

Table 2.3   Common Shortcomings in Company Vision Statements

Vague or incomplete	Short on specifics about where the company is headed or what the company is doing to prepare for the future.
Not forward-looking	Doesn't indicate whether or how management intends to alter the company's current product/market/customer/technology focus.
Too broad	So inclusive that the company could head in most any direction, pursue most any opportunity, or enter most any business.
Bland or uninspiring	Lacks the power to motivate company personnel or inspire shareholder confidence about the company's direction or future prospects
Not distinctive	Provides no unique company identity; could apply to companies in any of several industries (or at least several rivals operating in the same industry or market arena).
Too reliant on superlatives	Doesn't say anything specific about the company's strategic course beyond the pursuit of such lofty accolades as *best, most successful, recognized leader, global* or *worldwide leader,* or *first choice of customers.*

Sources: Based on information in Hugh Davidson, *The Committed Enterprise: How to Make Vision and Values Work* (Oxford: Butterworth-Heinemann, 2002), Chapter 2; and Michel Robert, *Strategy Pure and Simple II: How Winning Companies Dominate Their Competitors* (New York: McGraw-Hill, 1998), Chapters 2, 3, and 6.

ILLUSTRATION CAPSULE 2.1
Examples of Strategic Visions—How Well Do They Measure Up?

Vision Statement	Effective Elements	Shortcomings
Red Hat To extend our position as the most trusted Linux and open source provider to the enterprise. We intend to grow the market for Linux through a complete range of enterprise Red Hat Linux software, a powerful Internet management platform, and associated support and services.	• Directional • Focused • Feasible • Desirable • Easy to communicate	• Bland or uninspiring
UBS We are determined to be the best global financial services company. We focus on wealth and asset management, and on investment banking and securities businesses. We continually earn recognition and trust from clients, shareholders, and staff through our ability to anticipate, learn and shape our future. We share a common ambition to succeed by delivering quality in what we do. Our purpose is to help our clients make financial decisions with confidence. We use our resources to develop effective solutions and services for our clients. We foster a distinctive, meritocratic culture of ambition, performance and learning as this attracts, retains and develops the best talent for our company. By growing both our client and our talent franchises, we add sustainable value for our shareholders.	• Focused • Feasible • Desirable	• Not forward-looking • Bland or uninspiring
Caterpillar Be the global leader in customer value.	• Directional • Desirable • Easy to communicate	• Vague or incomplete • Could apply to many companies in many industries
eBay Provide a global trading platform where practically anyone can trade practically anything.	• Graphic • Flexible • Easy to communicate	• Too broad

Sources: Company documents and Web sites.

company vision statements. The one- or two-sentence vision statements most companies make available to the public, of course, provide only a glimpse of what company executives are really thinking and the strategic course they have charted—company personnel nearly always have a much better understanding of the ins and outs of where the company is headed and why than is revealed in the official vision statement. But the real purpose of a vision statement is to serve as a management tool for giving the organization a sense of direction. Like any tool, it can be used properly or improperly, either clearly conveying a company's strategic course or not.

Illustration Capsule 2.1 provides a critique of the strategic visions of several prominent companies.

How a Strategic Vision Differs from a Mission Statement

The defining characteristic of a well-conceived strategic vision is what it says about the company's *future strategic course*—"the direction we are headed and what our future product-customer-market-technology focus will be." While a company's strategic vision and its mission statement could be worded to cover much the same ground, the truth is that the mission statements of most companies say much more about the enterprise's *present business scope and purpose*—"who we are, what we do, and why we are here"—than they say about the strategic course that top management has charted. Very few mission statements are forward-looking in content or emphasis.

The distinction between a strategic vision and a mission statement is fairly clear-cut: A strategic vision portrays a company's *future* business scope ("where we are going"), whereas a company's mission typically describes its *present* business and purpose ("who we are, what we do, and why we are here").

The mission statements that one finds in company annual reports or posted on company Web sites typically provide a brief overview of the company's *present* business purpose and reasons for existing, and sometimes its geographic coverage or standing as a market leader. They may or may not single out the company's present products/services, the buyer needs it is seeking to satisfy, the customer groups it serves, or its technological and business capabilities. But rarely do company mission statements say anything about where the company is headed, the anticipated changes in its business, or the kind of company it is trying to become; hence they lack the essential forward-looking quality of a strategic vision in specifying a company's direction and *future* product-market-customer-technology focus. Consider, for example, the mission statement of Trader Joe's, a specialty grocery chain:

> The mission of Trader Joe's is to give our customers the best food and beverage values that they can find anywhere and to provide them with the information required for informed buying decisions. We provide these with a dedication to the highest quality of customer satisfaction delivered with a sense of warmth, friendliness, fun, individual pride, and company spirit.

Trader Joe's mission statement does a good job of conveying "who we are, what we do, and why we are here," but it provides no sense of "where we are headed."

The here-and-now theme that typifies so many company mission statements means that there is value in distinguishing between the forward-looking concept of a strategic vision and the company's current mission. Thus, to mirror actual practice, we will use the term *mission statement* to refer to an enterprise's description of its *present* business and why it exists. (Some companies use the term *business purpose* instead of *mission statement* in characterizing their business activities; in practice, there seems to be no meaningful difference between the terms—which one is used is a matter of preference.)

Ideally, a company mission statement is sufficiently descriptive to *identify the company's products/services and specify the buyer needs it seeks to satisfy, the customer groups or markets it is endeavoring to serve, and its approach to pleasing customers.* Not many company mission statements fully reveal *all* these facets of its business, but most company mission statements do a decent job of indicating "who we are, what we do, and why we are here." A well-conceived mission statement should also distinguish a company's business makeup from that of other enterprises in language specific enough to give the company its own identity. Occasionally, companies couch their mission in terms of making a profit; this is misguided. Profit is more correctly an *objective* and a *result* of what a company does. Moreover, earning a profit is the obvious intent of every commercial enterprise.

An example of a good mission statement with ample specifics about what the organization does is that of the Occupational Safety and Health Administration (OSHA): "to promote the safety and health of America's workers by setting and enforcing standards; providing training, outreach, and education; establishing partnerships; and encouraging continual process improvement in workplace safety and health." Google's mission statement, while short, still captures the essence of the company: "to organize the world's information and make it universally accessible and useful."

Linking the Vision/Mission with Company Values

Many companies have developed a statement of values to guide the company's pursuit of its vision/mission, strategy, and ways of operating. By **values** (or *core values,* as they are often called), we mean the beliefs, traits, and ways of doing things that management has determined should guide the pursuit of its vision and strategy, the conduct of company's operations, and the behavior of company personnel. Values, good and bad, exist in every organization. They relate to such things as fair treatment, integrity, ethical behavior, innovation, teamwork, top-notch quality, superior customer service, social responsibility, and community citizenship. Most companies have built their statements of values around four to eight traits that company personnel are expected to display and that are supposed to be mirrored in how the company conducts its business. At American Express, the core values are customer commitment, quality, integrity, teamwork, and respect for people. Toyota preaches respect for and development of its employees, teamwork, getting quality right the first time, learning, continuous improvement, and embracing change in its pursuit of low-cost, top-notch manufacturing excellence in motor vehicles.[3] DuPont stresses four values—safety, ethics, respect for people, and environmental stewardship; the first three have been in place since the company was founded 200 years ago by E. I. du Pont. Pioneering, achieving, caring, and enduring are the core values that guide decisions and actions at Abbott Laboratories, a pharmaceutical company that appeared on *Fortune*'s "Most Admired Companies" list in 2008. Abbott chose its four core values according to research suggesting these qualities were of utmost importance to the company's key stakeholders—patients, employees, and health care professionals. The company conducted a series of values workshops in 2006 that allowed more than 11,000 employees to identify regularly performed work behaviors that supported the company's values. The company further solidified the values within the organization by asking that each business unit and employee develop annual goals that embodied each of the four values.

> **CORE CONCEPT**
> A company's **values** are the beliefs, traits, and behavioral norms that company personnel are expected to display in conducting the company's business and pursuing its strategic vision and strategy.

The extent to which company values statements translate into actually living the values varies widely. At companies such as Abbott, top executives believe in the importance of grounding company operations on sound values and ways of doing business. In their view, holding company personnel accountable for displaying the stated values is a way of infusing the company with the desired character, identity, and behavioral norms—the values become the company's genetic makeup, its DNA.

At the other extreme are companies with values that act as window dressing; the values statement is merely a collection of nice words and phrases that have little discernible impact on either the behavior of company personnel or how the company operates. Such companies have values statements because they are in vogue or because they make the company look good. The now-defunct energy corporation Enron, for example, touted four corporate values—respect, integrity, communication, and excellence—but some top officials engaged in dishonest and fraudulent maneuvers that were concealed by "creative" accounting. The chasm between the company's stated values and the actions of its managers became evident during Enron's dramatic implosion and subsequent bankruptcy, along with criminal indictments, fines, or jail terms for over a dozen Enron executives.

At companies where the stated values are real rather than cosmetic, managers connect values to the pursuit of the strategic vision and mission in one of two ways. In companies with long-standing values that are deeply entrenched in the corporate culture, senior managers are careful to craft a vision, mission, and strategy that match established values; they also reiterate how the value-based behavioral norms contribute to the company's business success. In new companies or companies with weak or incomplete sets of values, top management needs to consider what values, behaviors, and business conduct should characterize the company and help drive the vision and strategy forward. Values and behaviors that complement and support the company's vision are then drafted by these executives and circulated among managers and employees for discussion and possible modification. A final values statement that incorporates the desired behaviors and traits and that connects to the vision/mission is then officially adopted. Some companies combine their vision and values into a single statement or document, circulate it to all organization members, and in many instances post the vision/mission and values statement on the company's Web site. Illustration Capsule 2.2 describes Yahoo's values, and desired behaviors intended to aid it in its mission of "connecting people to their passions, their communities, and the world's knowledge."

Communicating the Strategic Vision

Effectively communicating the strategic vision down the line to lower-level managers and employees is as important as the strategic soundness of the long-term direction top management has chosen. Frontline employees can't be expected to unite behind managerial efforts to get the organization moving in the intended direction until they understand why the strategic course that management has charted is reasonable and beneficial.

CORE CONCEPT

An effectively communicated vision is a valuable management tool for enlisting the commitment of company personnel to actions that get the company moving in the intended direction.

Winning the support of organization members for the vision nearly always means putting "where we are going and why" in writing, distributing the statement organizationwide, and having executives personally explain the vision and its rationale to as many people as feasible. Ideally, executives should present their vision for the company in a manner that reaches out and grabs people. An engaging and convincing strategic vision has enormous motivational value—for the same reason that a stone mason is more inspired by building a great cathedral for the ages than simply laying stones to create floors and walls. When managers articulate a vivid and compelling case for where the company is headed, organization members begin to say, "This is interesting and has a lot of merit. I want to be involved and do my part to make it happen." The more that a vision evokes positive support and excitement, the greater its impact in terms of arousing a committed organizational effort and getting company personnel to move in a common direction.[4] Thus, executive ability to paint a convincing and inspiring picture of a company journey and destination is an important element of effective strategic leadership.

ILLUSTRATION CAPSULE 2.2
Yahoo's Core Values

Our mission is to be the most essential global Internet service for consumers and businesses. How we pursue that mission is influenced by a set of core values—the standards that guide interactions with fellow Yahoos, the principles that direct how we service our customers, the ideals that drive what we do and how we do it. Many of our values were put into practice by two guys in a trailer some time ago; others reflect ambitions as our company grows. All of them are what we strive to achieve every day.

EXCELLENCE

We are committed to winning with integrity. We know leadership is hard won and should never be taken for granted. We aspire to flawless execution and don't take shortcuts on quality. We seek the best talent and promote its development. We are flexible and learn from our mistakes.

INNOVATION

We thrive on creativity and ingenuity. We seek the innovations and ideas that can change the world. We anticipate market trends and move quickly to embrace them. We are not afraid to take informed, responsible risk.

CUSTOMER FIXATION

We respect our customers above all else and never forget that they come to us by choice. We share a personal responsibility to maintain our customers' loyalty and trust. We listen and respond to our customers and seek to exceed their expectations.

TEAMWORK

We treat one another with respect and communicate openly. We foster collaboration while maintaining individual accountability. We encourage the best ideas to surface from anywhere within the organization. We appreciate the value of multiple perspectives and diverse expertise.

COMMUNITY

We share an infectious sense of mission to make an impact on society and empower consumers in ways never before possible. We are committed to serving both the Internet community and our own communities.

FUN

We believe humor is essential to success. We applaud irreverence and don't take ourselves too seriously. We celebrate achievement. We yodel.

WHAT YAHOO *DOESN'T* VALUE

At the end of its values statement, Yahoo makes a point of singling out 54 things that it does not value, including bureaucracy, losing, "good enough," arrogance, the status quo, following, formality, quick fixes, passing the buck, micromanaging, Monday-morning quarterbacks, 20/20 hindsight, missing the boat, playing catch-up, punching the clock, and "shoulda coulda woulda."

Source: www.yahoo.com (accessed March 24, 2008).

Expressing the Essence of the Vision in a Slogan The task of effectively conveying the vision to company personnel is sometimes made easier when management can capture the vision in a catchy, easily remembered slogan. A number of organizations have summed up their vision in a brief phrase:

> Strategic visions become real only when the vision statement is imprinted in the minds of organization members and then translated into hard objectives and strategies.

- FedEx: "Satifying worldwide demand for fast, time-definite, reliable distribution."
- Scotland Yard: "To make London the safest major city in the world."
- The Home Depot: "Helping people improve the places where they live and work."
- Charles Schwab: "To provide customers with the most useful and ethical financial services in the world."

Creating a short slogan to illuminate an organization's direction and purpose helps rally organization members to hurdle whatever obstacles lie in the company's path and to focus their attention on "where we are headed and why."

When External Change Calls for a New Strategic Direction   Sometimes there's an order-of-magnitude change in a company's environment that dramatically alters its prospects and mandates radical revision of its strategic course. Such changes come about only rarely, but they do affect almost every industry. The technology company Intel has encountered two strategic inflection points during its history:

1. In the mid-1980s, when memory chips were Intel's principal business, Japanese manufacturers intent on dominating the memory chip business began setting their prices 10 percent below the prices charged by Intel and other U.S. memory chip manufacturers. Each time U.S. companies matched the Japanese price cuts, the Japanese manufacturers responded with another 10 percent price cut. In 1985, Gordon Moore, Intel's chairman and cofounder, and Andrew Grove, Intel's CEO, jointly concluded that the best long-term solution was to abandon the memory chip business even though it accounted for 70 percent of Intel's revenue. A new vision was developed that involved committing Intel's full energies to becoming the preeminent supplier of microprocessors to the personal computing industry. Moore and Grove's new vision and strategic course for Intel produced spectacular results. More than 80 percent of the world's PCs have been made with Intel microprocessors since 1996, and Intel has become the world's most profitable chip maker.

2. In 1998, when its chief managers recognized the growing importance of the Internet, Intel refocused on becoming the preeminent building-block supplier to the Internet economy and spurring efforts to make the Internet more useful. Intel's change in vision played a major role in getting more than 1 billion computers connected to the Internet worldwide, installing millions of servers, and building an Internet infrastructure that would support trillions of dollars of e-commerce and serve as a worldwide communication medium.

As the Intel example forcefully demonstrates, when a company reaches a strategic inflection point, management has some tough decisions to make about the company's course. Often it is a question of how to sustain company success, not just how to avoid possible disaster. Responding quickly to unfolding changes in the marketplace lessens a company's chances of becoming trapped in a stagnant or declining business or letting attractive new growth opportunities slip away.

Breaking Down Resistance to a New Strategic Vision   It is particularly important for executives to provide a compelling rationale for a bold new strategic vision that takes a company in a dramatically different direction. Company personnel are prone to resist change that requires new priorities and work practices when they don't understand or accept the need for such redirection. Hence, reiterating the importance of the new vision and addressing employees' concerns about the new direction head-on become part of the task in mobilizing support for the vision. A single instance of stating the case for a new direction is not enough. Executives must repeat the reasons for the new direction often and convincingly at company gatherings and in company publications. In addition, senior managers must reinforce their pronouncements with updates about the company's latest performance and how it confirms the validity of the new vision. Unless and until the vision gains wide acceptance, it will have little effect in moving the organization down the newly chosen path.

The Payoffs of a Clear Vision Statement In sum, a well-conceived, forcefully communicated strategic vision pays off in several respects: (1) it crystallizes senior executives' own views about the firm's long-term direction; (2) it reduces the risk of rudderless decision making; (3) it is a tool for winning the support of organizational members for internal changes that will help make the vision a reality; (4) it provides a beacon for lower-level managers in forming departmental missions, setting departmental objectives, and crafting functional and departmental strategies that are in sync with the company's overall strategy; and (5) it helps an organization prepare for the future. When management is able to demonstrate significant progress in achieving these five benefits, the first step in organizational direction setting has been successfully completed.

PHASE 2: SETTING OBJECTIVES

The managerial purpose of setting **objectives** is to convert the strategic vision into specific performance targets—results and outcomes the company's management wants to achieve. Well-stated objectives are *quantifiable,* or *measurable,* and contain a *deadline for achievement.* As Bill Hewlett, cofounder of Hewlett-Packard, shrewdly observed, "You cannot manage what you cannot measure. . . . And what gets measured gets done."[5] Concrete, measurable objectives are managerially valuable because they serve as yardsticks for tracking a company's performance and progress. Indeed, the experiences of countless companies and managers teach that precisely spelling out *how much* of *what kind* of performance *by when* acts as marching orders for the entire organization and communicates to employees what level of performance is expected.[6]

> **CORE CONCEPT**
> *Objectives* are an organization's performance targets—the results and outcomes management wants to achieve. They function as yardsticks for measuring how well the organization is doing.

Such an approach definitely beats setting vague targets like "increase sales" or "reduce costs," which specify neither how much nor when, or else exhorting company personnel to "do the best they can" and then living with whatever results they deliver.

The Imperative of Setting Stretch Objectives

Ideally, managers ought to use the objective-setting exercise as a tool for *stretching an organization to perform at its full potential and deliver the best possible results.* Challenging company personnel to exert their best efforts to achieve "stretch" gains in performance pushes an enterprise to be more inventive, to exhibit more urgency in improving both its financial performance and its business position, and to be more intentional and focused in its actions.

> Setting stretch objectives is an effective tool for avoiding ho-hum results.

Stretch objectives spur exceptional performance and help build a firewall against contentment with modest gains in organizational performance. As Mitchell Leibovitz, former CEO of the auto parts and service retailer Pep Boys, once said, "If you want to have ho-hum results, have ho-hum objectives." *There's no better way to avoid ho-hum results than by setting stretch objectives and using compensation incentives to motivate organization members to achieve the stretch performance targets.*

What Kinds of Objectives to Set—The Need for a Balanced Scorecard

Two very distinct types of performance yardsticks are required: those relating to **financial performance** and those relating to **strategic performance**—outcomes that indicate a company is strengthening its marketing standing, competitive vitality, and future business prospects. Examples of commonly used **financial objectives** and **strategic objectives** include the following:

Financial Objectives	Strategic Objectives
• An *x* percent increase in annual revenues	• Winning an *x* percent market share
• Annual increases in after-tax profits of *x* percent	• Achieving lower overall costs than rivals
• Annual increases in earnings per share of *x* percent	• Overtaking key competitors on product performance or quality or customer service
• Annual dividend increases of *x* percent	• Deriving *x* percent of revenues from the sale of new products introduced within the past *x* years
• Profit margins of *x* percent	
• An *x* percent return on capital employed (ROCE) or return on equity (ROE)	• Achieving customer satisfaction rates of *x* percent
• Increased shareholder value—in the form of an upward-trending stock prices and annual dividend increases	• Consistently getting new or improved products to market ahead of rivals
• Bond and credit ratings of *x*	• Having stronger national or global sales and distribution capabilities than rivals
• Internal cash flows of *x* to fund new capital investment	

CORE CONCEPT
Financial objectives relate to the financial performance targets management has established for the organization to achieve. *Strategic objectives* relate to target outcomes that indicate a company is strengthening its market standing, competitive vitality, and future business prospects.

Achieving acceptable financial results is a must. Without adequate profitability and financial strength, a company impairs pursuit of its strategic vision and puts its long-term health and ultimate survival in serious jeopardy. Furthermore, subpar earnings and a weak balance sheet not only alarm shareholders and creditors but also put the jobs of senior executives at risk. Even so, good financial performance, by itself, is not enough. Of equal or greater importance is a company's strategic performance—outcomes that indicate whether the company's market position and competitiveness are deteriorating, holding steady, or improving.

The Case for a Balanced Scorecard: Improved Strategic Performance Fosters Better Financial Performance   A company's financial performance measures are really *lagging indicators* that reflect the results of *past* decisions and organizational activities.[7] But a company's past or current financial performance is not a reliable indicator of its future prospects—poor financial performers often turn things around and do better, while good financial performers can fall on hard times. The best and most reliable *leading indicators* of a company's future financial performance and business prospects are strategic outcomes that indicate whether the company's competitiveness and market position are stronger or weaker. For instance, if a company has set aggressive strategic objectives and is achieving them—such that its competitive strength and market position are on the rise—then there's reason to expect that its *future* financial performance will be better than its current or past performance. If a company is losing ground to competitors and its market position is slipping—outcomes that reflect weak strategic performance (and, very likely, failure to set or achieve strategic objectives)—then its ability to maintain its present profitability is highly suspect. Hence, whether a company's managers set, pursue, and achieve stretch strategic objectives tend to be a reliable leading indicator of whether its future financial performance will improve or stall.

CORE CONCEPT
A company that pursues and achieves strategic outcomes that boost its competitiveness and strength in the marketplace is in much better position to improve its future financial performance.

ILLUSTRATION CAPSULE 2.3
Examples of Company Objectives

GENERAL MOTORS

Reduce the percentage of automobiles using conventional internal combustion engines (ICE) through the development of hybrid ICEs, plug-in hybrid ICEs, range-extended electric vehicles, and hydrogen fuel cell electric engines; reduce automotive structural costs to benchmark levels of 23 percent of revenue by 2012 from 34 percent in 2005; and reduce annual U.S. labor costs by an additional $5 billion by 2011.

THE HOME DEPOT

Be the number one destination for professional contractors, whose business accounted for roughly 30 percent of 2006 sales; improve in-stock positions so customers can find and buy exactly what they need; deliver differentiated customer service and the know-how that our customers have come to expect from The Home Depot; repurchase $22.5 billion of outstanding shares during 2008; and open 55 new store locations with 5 store relocations in 2008.

YUM! BRANDS (KFC, PIZZA HUT, TACO BELL)

Open 100+ KFC restaurants in Vietnam by 2010; expand Taco Bell restaurant concept to Dubai, India, Spain and Japan during 2008 and 2009; increase number of international restaurant locations from 12,000 in 2007 to 15,000 in 2012; increase operating profit from international operations from $480 million in 2007 to $770 million in 2012; expand Pizza Hut's menu to include pasta and chicken dishes; decrease the number of company owned restaurant units in U.S. from 20% of units in 2007 to less than 10% of units by 2010; and increase the number of Taco Bell units in the U.S. by 2%–3% annually between 2008 and 2010.

AVON

Increase our beauty sales and market share; strengthen our brand image; enhance the representative experience; realize annualized cost savings of $430 million through improvements in marketing processes, sales model and organizational activities; and achieve annualized cost savings of $200 million through a strategic sourcing initiative.

Sources: Information posted on company Web sites (accessed March 27, 2008).

Consequently, a balanced scorecard for measuring company performance—one that tracks the achievement of both financial objectives and strategic objectives—is optimal.[8] Just tracking a company's financial performance overlooks the fact that what ultimately enables a company to deliver better financial results from its operations is the achievement of strategic objectives that improve its competitiveness and market strength. *The surest path to boosting company profitability quarter after quarter and year after year is to relentlessly pursue strategic outcomes that strengthen the company's market position and produce a growing competitive advantage over rivals.*

In 2006, approximately 70 percent of global companies used a balanced scorecard approach to measuring strategic and financial performance.[9] Organizations that have adopted a balanced scorecard approach to setting objectives and measuring performance include United Parcel Service (UPS), Ann Taylor Stores, the UK Ministry of Defense, Caterpillar, Daimler, Hilton Hotels, Duke University Hospital, and Siemens.[10] Illustration Capsule 2.3 provides selected strategic and financial objectives of four prominent companies.

Why Both Short-Term and Long-Term Objectives Are Needed

As a rule, a company's set of financial and strategic objectives ought to include both near-term and longer-term performance targets. Having quarterly and annual objectives focuses attention on delivering immediate performance improvements. Targets to be achieved within three to five years prompt considerations of what to do *now* to put the company in position to perform better later. Long-term objectives take on particular importance because it is generally in the best interest of shareholders for companies to be managed for optimal long-term performance. When trade-offs have to be made between achieving long-run objectives and achieving short-run objectives, long-run objectives should take precedence (unless achieving one or more short-run performance targets has overriding importance). Shareholders are seldom well-served by repeated management actions that sacrifice better long-term performance in order to make quarterly or annual targets.

<table>
<tr><td>

CORE CONCEPT

A company exhibits *strategic intent* when it relentlessly pursues an ambitious strategic objective, concentrating the full force of its resources and competitive actions on achieving that objective.

</td><td>

Strategic Intent: Relentless Pursuit of an Ambitious Long-Term Strategic Objective

Very ambitious companies often establish a long-term strategic objective that clearly signals **strategic intent** to be a winner in the marketplace, often against long odds.[11] A company's strategic intent can entail unseating the existing industry leader, becoming the dominant market share leader, delivering the best customer service of any company in the industry (or the world), or turning a new technology into products capable of changing the way people work and live. For some years, Toyota has been charging to overtake General Motors as the world's largest motor vehicle producer—a goal it achieved in 2007 when its global sales totaled 9.37 mil-

</td></tr>
</table>

lion cars and trucks compared to General Motors' 2007 sales of 8.8 million cars and trucks.[12] During the mid-1970s, United Parcel Service (UPS) management, recognizing that the world was becoming more interconnected, developed the strategic intent of becoming a leading shipper of small packages in international markets. The company made multiple mistakes as it expanded into foreign locations and failed to realize consistent returns on its heavy investments outside the United States for more than 20 years, but did not abandon its long-term strategic goal. By 2007, however, shipments of small packages had become the company's fastest growing and most profitable business. Honda, too, has engaged in strategic intent with the development of its very light jet. The company's 20-plus-year dream of producing a "Honda Civic of the sky" began in the mid-1980s. The HondaJet was expected to obtain FAA certification in 2009, with production beginning in 2010.[13]

In many cases, ambitious companies that establish exceptionally bold strategic objectives and have an unshakable commitment to achieving them lack the immediate capabilities and market grasp to achieve such lofty targets. But they pursue their strategic objective relentlessly, sometimes even obsessively. They rally the organization around efforts to make the strategic intent a reality. They go all out to marshal the resources and capabilities to close in on their strategic target (which is often global market leadership) as rapidly as they can. They craft potent offensive strategies calculated to throw rivals off balance, put them on the defensive, and force them into an ongoing game of catch-up. As a consequence, capably managed up-and-coming enterprises with strategic intents exceeding their present reach and resources are a force to be reckoned with, often proving to be more formidable competitors over time than larger, cash-rich rivals that have modest strategic objectives and market ambitions.

The Need for Objectives at All Organizational Levels

Objective setting should not stop with top management's establishing of companywide performance targets. Company objectives need to be broken down into performance targets for each of the organization's separate businesses, product lines, functional departments, and individual work units. Company performance can't reach full potential unless each organizational unit sets and pursues performance targets that contribute directly to the desired companywide outcomes and results. Objective setting is thus a top-down process that must extend to the lowest organizational levels. And it means that each organizational unit must set performance targets that support—rather than conflict with or negate—the achievement of companywide strategic and financial objectives.

PHASE 3: CRAFTING A STRATEGY

The task of crafting a strategy entails addressing a series of hows: *how* to grow the business, *how* to please customers, *how* to outcompete rivals, *how* to respond to changing market conditions, *how* to manage each functional piece of the business, *how* to develop needed competencies and capabilities, and *how* to achieve strategic and financial objectives. It also means exercising astute entrepreneurship in choosing among the various strategic alternatives—proactively searching for opportunities to do new things or to do existing things in new or better ways.[14]

The faster a company's business environment is changing, the more critical the need for its managers to be good entrepreneurs in diagnosing the direction and force of the changes under way and in responding with timely adjustments in strategy. Strategy makers have to pay attention to early warnings of future change and be willing to experiment with different ways to establish a market position. When obstacles unexpectedly appear in a company's path, it is up to management to adapt rapidly and innovatively. *Masterful strategies come partly (maybe mostly) by doing things differently from competitors where it counts—innovating more creatively, being more efficient, being more imaginative, adapting faster—rather than running with the herd.* Good strategy making is therefore inseparable from good business entrepreneurship. One cannot exist without the other.

Strategy Making Involves Managers at All Organizational Levels

A company's senior executives obviously have important strategy-making roles. The chief executive officer (CEO), as captain of the ship, carries the mantles of chief direction setter, chief objective setter, chief strategy maker, and chief strategy implementer for the total enterprise. Ultimate responsibility for *leading* the strategy-making, strategy-executing process rests with the CEO. In some enterprises the CEO or owner functions as strategic visionary and chief architect of strategy, personally deciding what the key elements of the company's strategy will be, although others may well assist with data gathering and analysis. Also, the CEO may seek the advice of other senior managers and key employees in fashioning an overall strategy and deciding on important strategic moves. A CEO-centered approach to strategy development is characteristic of small owner-managed companies and sometimes large corporations that have been founded by the present CEO or that have CEOs with strong strategic leadership skills. Larry Ellison at Oracle, Andrea Jung at Avon, Steve Jobs at Apple, and Howard Schultz at Starbucks are prominent examples of corporate CEOs who have wielded a heavy hand in shaping their company's strategy.

In most companies, however, strategy is the product of more than just the CEO's handiwork. Typically, other senior executives—business unit heads; the chief financial officer (CFO); and vice presidents for production, marketing, human resources, and other functional departments have influential strategy-making roles. Normally, a company's CFO is in charge of devising and implementing an appropriate financial strategy; the production vice president takes the lead in developing the company's production strategy; the marketing vice president orchestrates sales and marketing strategy; a brand manager is in charge of the strategy for a particular brand in the company's product lineup, and so on.

But even here it is a mistake to view strategy making as a *top* management function, the exclusive province of owner-entrepreneurs, CEOs, and other senior executives. The more that a company's operations cut across different products, industries, and geographical areas, the more that headquarters executives have little option but to delegate considerable strategy-making authority down the line to managers in charge of particular subsidiaries, geographic sales offices, distribution centers, and plants. On-the-scene managers are in the best position to evaluate the local situation and can be expected to have detailed familiarity with local customer requirements and expectations as well as with other aspects surrounding the strategic issues and choices in their arena of authority. This gives them an edge over headquarters executives in keeping the company's strategy responsive to local market and competitive conditions.

Take, for example, a company like General Electric (GE), a $173 billion corporation with operating segments ranging from financial services to aircraft engine manufacturing to television broadcasting. While top-level GE executives may well be personally involved in shaping GE's *overall* strategy and fashioning *important* strategic moves, it doesn't follow that a few senior executives at GE headquarters have either enough expertise or detailed understanding of all the relevant factors to wisely craft all the strategic initiatives for its diverse business lineup and thousands of products. They simply cannot know enough about the situation in every General Electric organizational unit to decide upon every strategy detail and direct every strategic move made in GE's worldwide organization. Rather, it takes involvement on the part of GE's whole management team—top executives; subsidiary heads; division heads; and key managers in such geographic units as sales offices, distribution centers, and plants—to craft the thousands of strategic initiatives that end up comprising the whole of GE's strategy.

While managers farther down in the managerial hierarchy obviously have a narrower, more specific strategy-making role than managers closer to the top, the important understanding here is that in most of today's companies *every manager typically has a strategy-making role—ranging from minor to major—for the area he or she heads.* Hence, any notion that an organization's strategists are at the top of the management hierarchy and that midlevel and frontline personnel merely carry out their strategic directives needs to be cast aside. In companies with wide-ranging operations, it is far more accurate to view strategy making as a *collaborative effort* involving managers (and sometimes key employees) down through the whole organizational hierarchy. A valuable strength of collaborative strategy making is that the team of people charged with crafting the strategy often include the very people who will also be charged with executing it. Giving people an influential stake in crafting the strategy they must later help execute not only builds commitment to new strategies but also enhances accountability at multiple levels of management—the excuse "It wasn't my idea to do this" won't fly.

A Company's Strategy-Making Hierarchy

It thus follows that *a company's overall strategy is a collection of strategic initiatives and actions* devised by managers and key employees up and down the whole organizational hierarchy. As an enterprise's operations become larger, more diverse, and more

Chapter 2 Leading the Process of Crafting and Executing Strategy

geographically scattered, progressively more managers and key employees at more levels in the organizational hierarchy tend to become personally engaged in crafting strategic initiatives and exercise a relevant strategy-making role. Figure 2.2 shows who is generally responsible for devising what pieces of a company's overall strategy.

In diversified, multibusiness companies where the strategies of several different businesses have to be managed, the strategy-making task involves four distinct types or levels of strategy, each of which involves different facets of the company's overall strategy:

1. *Corporate strategy* consists of initiatives to diversify into different industries, boost the combined performance of the set of businesses the company has diversified into, and figure out how to capture cross-business synergies and turn them into competitive advantage. Senior corporate executives normally have lead responsibility for devising corporate strategy and for choosing among whatever recommended actions bubble up from the organization below. Major strategic decisions are usually reviewed and approved by the company's board of directors. We will look deeper into the strategy-making process at diversified companies when we get to Chapter 8.

2. *Business strategy* concerns the actions and approaches crafted to produce successful performance in one specific line of business. Orchestrating the development of business-level strategy is the responsibility of the manager in charge of the business. The business head has at least two other strategy-related roles: (*a*) seeing that lower-level strategies are well conceived and well matched to the overall business strategy, and (*b*) getting major business-level strategic moves approved by corporate-level officers (and sometimes the board of directors) and keeping them informed of emerging strategic issues. In diversified companies, business-unit heads may have the additional obligation of making sure business-level objectives and strategy conform to corporate-level objectives and strategy themes.

3. *Functional-area strategies* concern the actions and practices employed in managing particular functions or business processes or activities within a business. A company's marketing strategy, for example, represents the managerial game plan for running the sales and marketing part of the business. A company's product development strategy represents the managerial game plan for keeping the company's product lineup in tune with what buyers are looking for. The primary role of a functional strategy is to add specifics to a company's business-level strategy. Lead responsibility for functional strategies within a business is normally delegated to the heads of the respective functions, with the general manager of the business having final approval and perhaps even exerting a strong influence over the particular pieces of the strategies.

4. *Operating strategies* concern the relatively narrow strategic initiatives and approaches for managing key operating units (plants, distribution centers, geographic units) and specific operating activities with strategic significance (advertising campaigns, supply chain activities, and Internet sales operations). Operating strategies, while of limited scope, add further detail and completeness to functional strategies and to the overall business strategy. Lead responsibility for operating strategies is usually delegated to frontline managers, subject to review and approval by higher-ranking managers.

Even though operating strategy is at the bottom of the strategy-making hierarchy, its importance should not be downplayed. A major plant that fails in its strategy to achieve production volume, unit cost, and quality targets can damage the company's

Figure 2.2   A Company's Strategy-Making Hierarchy

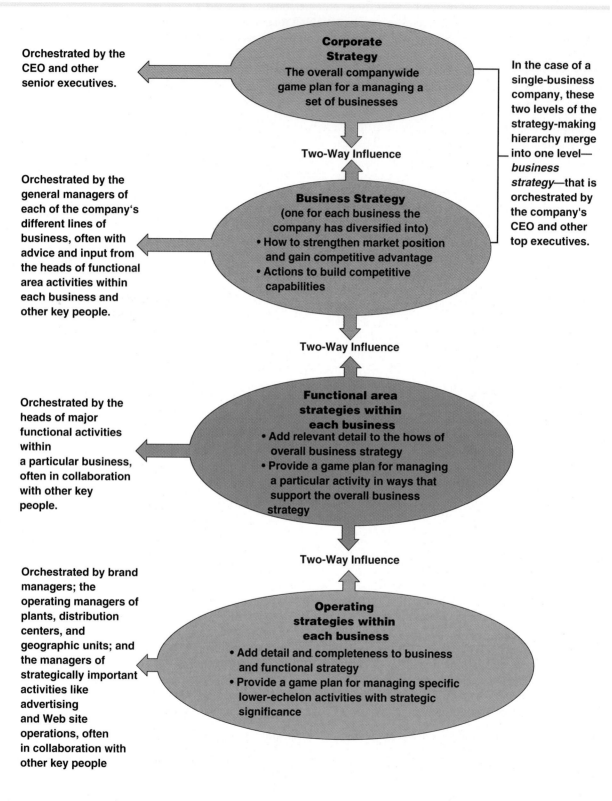

reputation for quality products and undercut the achievement of company sales and profit objectives. Frontline managers are thus an important part of an organization's strategy-making team. One cannot reliably judge the strategic importance of a given action simply by the strategy level or location within the managerial hierarchy where it is initiated.

In single-business enterprises, the corporate and business levels of strategy-making merge into one level—business strategy—because the strategy for the whole company involves only one distinct line of business. Thus, a single-business enterprise has three levels of strategy: business strategy for the company as a whole, functional-area strategies for each main area within the business, and operating strategies undertaken by lower-echelon managers. Proprietorships, partnerships, and owner-managed enterprises may have only one or two strategy-making levels since their strategy-making, strategy-executing process can be handled by just a few key people.

A Strategic Vision + Objectives + Strategy = A Strategic Plan

Developing a strategic vision and mission, setting objectives, and crafting a strategy are basic direction-setting tasks. They map out where a company is headed, the targeted strategic and financial outcomes, and the competitive moves and internal actions to be used in achieving the desired business results. Together, they constitute a **strategic plan** for coping with industry and competitive conditions, combating the expected actions of the industry's key players, and confronting the challenges and issues that stand as obstacles to the company's success.[15]

> **CORE CONCEPT**
>
> A company's *strategic plan* lays out its future direction, performance targets, and strategy.

In companies that do regular strategy reviews and develop explicit strategic plans, the strategic plan usually ends up as a written document that is circulated to most managers and perhaps selected employees. Near-term performance targets are the part of the strategic plan most often spelled out explicitly and communicated to managers and employees. A number of companies summarize key elements of their strategic plans in the company's annual report to shareholders, in postings on their Web site, or in statements provided to the business media, whereas others, perhaps for reasons of competitive sensitivity, make only vague, general statements about their strategic plans. In small, privately owned companies, it is rare for strategic plans to exist in written form. Small companies' strategic plans tend to reside in the thinking and directives of owners/executives, with aspects of the plan being revealed in meetings and conversations with company personnel, and the understandings and commitments among managers and key employees about where to head, what to accomplish, and how to proceed.

PHASE 4: IMPLEMENTING AND EXECUTING THE STRATEGY

Managing the implementation and execution of strategy is an operations-oriented, make-things-happen activity aimed at performing core business activities in a strategy-supportive manner. It is easily the most demanding and time-consuming part of the strategy management process. Converting strategic plans into actions and results tests a manager's ability to direct organizational change, motivate people, build and strengthen company competencies and competitive capabilities, create and nurture a strategy-supportive work climate, and meet or beat performance targets. Initiatives to put the strategy in place and execute it proficiently have to be launched and managed on many organizational fronts.

Management's action agenda for implementing and executing the chosen strategy emerges from assessing what the company will have to do differently or better to achieve the targeted financial and strategic performance. Each company manager has to think through the answer to the following questions: "What has to be done in my area to execute my piece of the strategic plan?" and "What actions should I take to get the process under way?" How much internal change is needed depends on how much of the strategy is new, how far internal practices and competencies deviate from what the strategy requires, and how well the present work climate/culture supports good strategy execution. Depending on the amount of internal change involved, full implementation and proficient execution of company strategy (or important new pieces thereof) can take several months to several years.

In most situations, managing the strategy execution process includes the following principal aspects:

- Staffing the organization with the needed skills and expertise, consciously building and strengthening strategy-supportive competencies and competitive capabilities, and organizing the work effort.
- Allocating ample resources to activities critical to strategic success.
- Ensuring that policies and procedures facilitate rather than impede effective execution.
- Using the best-known practices to perform core business activities and pushing for continuous improvement. Organizational units have to periodically reassess how things are being done and diligently pursue useful changes and improvements.
- Installing information and operating systems that enable company personnel to do their jobs better and quicker.
- Motivating people to pursue the target objectives energetically and, if need be, modifying their duties and job behavior to better fit the requirements of successful strategy execution.
- Tying rewards and incentives directly to the achievement of performance objectives and good strategy execution.
- Creating a company culture and work climate conducive to successful strategy execution.
- Exerting the internal leadership needed to drive implementation forward and keep improving the strategy execution process. When stumbling blocks or weaknesses are encountered, management has to see that they are addressed and rectified in timely and effective fashion.

Good strategy execution requires diligent pursuit of operating excellence. It is a job for a company's whole management team. And success hinges on the skills and cooperation of operating managers who can push needed changes in their organizational units and consistently deliver good results. Implementation of the chosen strategy can be considered successful if the company meets or beats its strategic and financial performance targets and shows good progress in achieving management's strategic vision.

PHASE 5: EVALUATING PERFORMANCE AND INITIATING CORRECTIVE ADJUSTMENTS

The fifth phase of the strategy management process—monitoring external developments, evaluating the company's progress, and making corrective adjustments—is the trigger point for deciding whether to continue or change the company's vision, objectives, strategy, and/or strategy execution methods. So long as the company's direction and strategy seem well matched to industry and competitive conditions and performance targets are being met, company executives may well decide to stay the course. Simply fine-tuning the strategic plan and continuing with efforts to improve strategy execution are sufficient.

But whenever a company encounters disruptive changes in its environment, questions need to be raised about the appropriateness of its direction and strategy. If a company experiences a downturn in its market position or persistent shortfalls in performance, then company managers are obligated to ferret out the causes—do they relate to poor strategy, poor strategy execution, or both?—and take timely corrective action. A company's direction, objectives, and strategy have to be revisited anytime external or internal conditions warrant. It is to be expected that a company will modify its strategic vision, direction, objectives, and strategy over time.

Likewise, it is not unusual for a company to find that one or more aspects of its strategy implementation and execution are not going as well as intended. Proficient strategy execution is always the product of much organizational learning. It is achieved unevenly—coming quickly in some areas and proving nettlesome in others. It is both normal and desirable to periodically assess strategy execution to determine which aspects are working well and which need improving. Successful strategy execution entails vigilantly searching for ways to improve and then making corrective adjustments whenever and wherever it is useful to do so.

> **CORE CONCEPT**
> A company's vision, objectives, strategy, and approach to strategy execution are never final; managing strategy is an ongoing process, not an every-now-and-then task.

LEADING THE STRATEGIC MANAGEMENT PROCESS

The litany for leading the process of making and executing strategy is simple enough: Craft a sound strategic plan, implement it, execute it to the fullest, adjust it as needed, and win! But the leadership challenges are significant and diverse. Exerting take-charge leadership, being a spark plug for change and action, ramrodding things through, and achieving results thrusts top executives and senior mangers in charge of business units, product categories, geographic regions, and major production and distribution facilities into a variety of leadership roles: visionary, strategist, resource acquirer, capabilities builder, motivator, and crisis solver, to mention a few. There are times when leading the strategic management process entails being a hard-nosed authoritarian, and times when it is best to be a perceptive listener and a compromising decision maker; there are times when matters are best delegated to people closest to the scene of the action, and times when being a coach is the proper role. Many occasions call for company leaders to assume a highly visible role and put in long hours guiding the process, while others entail only a brief ceremonial performance with the details delegated to subordinates.

In general, leading the strategic management process calls for the following six actions on the part of senior executives:

1. Staying on top of how well things are going.
2. Making sure the company has a good strategic plan.
3. Putting constructive pressure on organizational units to achieve good results and operating excellence.
4. Pushing corrective actions to improve both the company's strategy and how well it is being executed.
5. Leading the development of stronger core competencies and competitive capabilities.
6. Displaying ethical integrity and leading social responsibility initiatives.

Staying on Top of How Well Things Are Going

To stay on top of whether the company's direction and strategy are on track and how well the strategy execution process is going, a manager needs to develop a broad network of contacts and sources of information, both formal and informal. The regular channels include talking with key subordinates, attending presentations and meetings, talking to customers, watching the competitive reactions of rival firms, exchanging e-mail and holding telephone conversations with people in outlying locations, making onsite visits, and listening to rank-and-file employees. However, some sources of information are more trustworthy than the rest, and the views and perspectives offered by different people can vary widely. Presentations and briefings by subordinates may not represent the whole truth. Bad news or problems may be minimized or in some cases not reported at all by subordinates in hopes that they can turn things around before the shortcomings are noticed. Hence, senior managers have to make sure that they have accurate information and a feel for the existing situation. They have to confirm whether things are on track, learn what obstacles lie in the path of good financial and strategic performance, and develop a basis for determining what, if anything, they can personally do to improve the strategy management process.

CORE CONCEPT

Management by walking around (MBWA) is one of the techniques that effective leaders use to stay on top of how well things are going and to learn what issues they need to address.

One of the best ways for executives to stay on top of things is by making regular visits to the field and talking with many different people at many different levels—a technique often labeled **managing by walking around (MBWA)**. Wal-Mart executives have had a long-standing practice of spending two to three days every week visiting Wal-Mart's stores and talking with store managers and employees. Sam Walton, Wal-Mart's founder, insisted, "The key is to get out into the store and listen to what the associates have to say." Jack Welch, the highly effective CEO of General Electric (GE) from 1980 to 2001, not only spent several days each month personally visiting GE operations and talking with major customers but also arranged his schedule so that he could spend time exchanging information and ideas with GE managers from all over the world who were attending classes at the company's leadership development center near GE's headquarters. Some companies have weekly get-togethers in each division (often on Friday afternoons), attended by both executives and employees, to create a regular opportunity for tidbits of information to flow freely between down-the-line employees and executives. Many manufacturing executives make a point of strolling the factory floor to talk with workers and meeting regularly with union officials. Some managers operate out of open cubicles in big spaces populated with other personnel in open cubicles so that they can interact easily and frequently with coworkers. Jeff Bezos, Amazon.com's CEO, is noted for his practice of MBWA, firing off a battery of questions when he tours facilities and insisting that Amazon managers spend time in the trenches to prevent overly abstract thinking and disconnections from the reality of what's happening.[16]

Most managers rightly attach great importance to gathering information and opinions firsthand from people at different organizational levels about how well various aspects of the strategy-execution process are going. Such contacts give managers a feel for what progress is being made, what problems are being encountered, and whether additional resources or different approaches may be needed. Just as important, MBWA provides opportunities for managers to give encouragement, lift spirits, shift attention from the old to the new priorities, and create some excitement—all of which generate positive energy and help mobilize organizational efforts behind strategy execution.

Making Sure a Company Has a Good Strategic Plan

It is the responsibility of top executives—most especially the CEO—to ensure that a company has a sound and cohesive strategic plan. There are two things that the CEO and other top-level executives should do in leading the development of a good strategic plan. One is to *effectively communicate the company's vision, objectives, and major strategy components* to down-the-line managers and key personnel. The company's vision, mission, objectives, and overall strategy paint the white lines for strategy makers throughout the organization. *Midlevel and frontline managers cannot craft unified strategic moves without first understanding the company's long-term direction and knowing the major components of the company's strategy that their strategy-making efforts are supposed to support and enhance.* Thus, *leading* the development of a strategic plan is very much a top management *responsibility,* even though the tasks of setting objectives and formulating the details of strategy are most definitely *a team effort,* involving company personnel at the corporate and business levels on down to the associated functional and operating levels—as displayed in Figure 2.2.

When the strategizing process is effectively led by the CEO and other top executives, with lower-level strategy-making efforts taking their cues from the higher-level strategy elements they are supposed to complement and support, there's less potential for conflict between different levels in the strategy hierarchy. An absence of strong strategic leadership from the top sets the stage for some degree of strategic confusion and disunity.

A second responsibility of senior managers is leading the development of a good strategic plan. There are two things that the CEO and other top-level executives should do in leading the development of a good strategic plan. The first is to *effectively communicate the company's vision, objectives, and major strategy components to down-the-line managers and key personnel.* The greater the numbers of company personnel who know, understand, and buy into the company's long-term direction and overall strategy, the smaller the risk that organization units will go off in conflicting strategic directions. The second is to *exercise due diligence in reviewing lower-level strategies for consistency* and support of higher-level strategies. Any strategy conflicts must be addressed and resolved, either by modifying the lower-level strategies with conflicting elements or by adapting the higher-level strategy to accommodate more appealing strategy ideas and initiatives bubbling up from below. *Anything less than a unified collection of strategies weakens the overall strategy and is likely to impair company performance.*

The Importance of Corporate Intrapreneurship in the Strategy-Making Process   Keeping the organization bubbling with fresh supplies of ideas and suggestions for improvement is another key demand of strategic leadership. Managers cannot mandate innovative suggestions by simply exhorting people to "be creative." Rather, they have to foster a culture where innovative ideas and experimentation with new ways of doing things can blossom and thrive. In some companies, top management makes a regular practice of encouraging individuals and teams to develop and champion proposals for new product lines and new business ventures. The idea is to unleash the talents and energies of promising "corporate intrapreneurs," letting them try out untested business ideas and giving them the room to pursue new strategic initiatives. Executives judge which proposals merit support, give the chosen intrapreneurs the organizational and budgetary support they need, and let them run with the ball. Thus, important pieces of company strategy can originate with those intrapreneurial individuals and teams who succeed in championing a proposal through the approval stage and then end up being charged with the lead role in launching new products, overseeing the company's entry into new geographic markets, or heading up new business ventures.

At IBM, the company's chief managers found that its reward system—which focused on short-term results, fostered a managerial preoccupation with current markets, and bred an analysis-driven culture—discouraged new business development and slowed the strategy-making process to 12–18 months. To encourage corporate intrapreneurship, IBM developed a new set of policies to foster growth through emerging business opportunities. The new approach encouraged senior managers to push promising entrepreneurial business ventures proposed by subordinates into the market through experiments with existing customers. Those ideas that customers valued and that were deemed capable of generating acceptable revenues and profits went on to be marketed to new customers. Within five years, IBM's corporate intrapreneurship efforts had developed 25 new businesses; 3 of those failed, but the remaining 22 generated more than $15 billion in revenues in 2004.[17]

Organizational leaders can promote innovation and keep the strategy fresh in any of the following ways:

- *Encouraging individuals and groups to brainstorm proposals for new business ventures or improving existing products*—The leadership trick in promoting corporate intrapreneurship is to keep a sense of urgency alive in the business so that people see change and innovation as necessities.

- *Taking special pains to foster, nourish, and support people who are eager to test new business ventures and explore adding new or improved products*—People with maverick ideas or out-of-the-ordinary proposals have to be given room to operate. Above all, would-be champions who advocate radical or different ideas must not be looked on as disruptive or troublesome. The best champions and change agents are persistent, tenacious, and committed to seeing their idea through to success.

- *Ensuring that the rewards for successful champions are large and visible and that people who champion ideas for new products or business ventures that end up being discarded are not punished but rather encouraged to try again*—Encouraging lots of tries is important, since many ideas for new products and business ventures won't pan out.

- *Using all kinds of ad hoc organizational forms to support ideas and experimentation*— Forming venture teams and new business task forces to explore promising ideas, along with top management willingness to give entrepreneurial employees the latitude to work on a promising project without official authorization, are just a few of the possible organizational means a company can use to foster innovation. (*Skunkworks* is a term for a group of people who work on a project outside the usual norms or rules in an organization.)

Putting Constructive Pressure on Organizational Units to Achieve Good Results and Operating Excellence

Managers have to be out front in mobilizing organizational energy behind the drive for good financial and strategic performance and operating excellence. Part of the leadership requirement here entails nurturing a results-oriented work climate, where performance standards are high and a spirit of achievement is pervasive. If management wants to drive the strategic management process by instilling a results-oriented work climate, then senior executives have to take the lead in promoting a culture of innovation and high performance, a strong sense of involvement on the part of company personnel, emphasis on individual initiative and creativity, respect for the contribution of individuals and groups, and pride in doing things right.

Organizational leaders who succeed in creating a results-oriented work climate typically are intensely people-oriented, and they are skilled users of people-management practices that win the emotional commitment of company personnel and inspire them to do their best.[18] They understand that treating employees well generally leads to increased teamwork, higher morale, greater loyalty, and increased employee commitment to making a contribution. All of these foster an esprit de corps that energizes organizational members to contribute to the drive for a top-flight strategic plan, operating excellence and better-than-average financial performance.

While leadership efforts to instill a results-oriented culture usually accentuate the positive, there are negative reinforcers, too. Managers whose units consistently perform poorly have to be replaced. Low-performing workers and people who reject the results-oriented cultural emphasis have to be weeded out or at least moved to out-of-the-way positions. Average performers have to be candidly counseled that they have limited career potential unless they show more progress in the form of more effort, better skills, and ability to deliver better results.

Pushing Corrective Actions to Improve Both the Company's Strategy and How Well It Is Being Executed

The leadership challenge of making corrective adjustments is twofold: deciding when adjustments are needed and deciding what adjustments to make. Both decisions are a normal and necessary part of managing the strategy execution process, since no scheme for implementing and executing strategy can foresee all the events and problems that will arise.[19] There comes a time at every company when managers have to fine-tune or overhaul the approaches to strategy execution and push for better results. Clearly, when a company's strategy execution effort is not delivering good results and making measured progress toward operating excellence, it is the leader's responsibility to step forward and push corrective actions.

The *process* of making corrective adjustments involves sensing needs; gathering information; developing options and exploring their pros and cons; putting forth action proposals and partial solutions; striving for a consensus; and, finally, formally adopting an agreed-on course of action.[20] The time frame for deciding what corrective changes to initiate can vary from a few hours or days to a few months—depending on the complexity of the issue and the urgency of the matter. In a crisis, it is typical for leaders to have key subordinates gather information, identify and evaluate options, and perhaps prepare a preliminary set of recommended actions for consideration. The organizational leader then usually meets with key subordinates and personally presides over extended discussions of the proposed responses, trying to build a quick consensus among members of the executive inner circle. If no consensus emerges and action is required immediately, the burden falls on the manager in charge to choose the response and urge its support.

Leading the Development of Better Competencies and Capabilities

A company that proactively tries to strengthen its competencies and competitive capabilities not only adds power to its strategy and to its potential for winning competitive advantage but also enhances its chances for achieving good strategy execution and operating excellence. Senior management usually has to *lead* the strengthening effort because competencies and competitive capabilities are spawned by the combined efforts of different work groups, departments, and strategic allies. The tasks of developing human skills, knowledge bases, and intellectual assets and then integrating them to forge competitively advantageous competencies and capabilities is an exercise best orchestrated by senior managers who appreciate their significance and who have the clout to enforce the necessary cooperation among individuals, groups, departments, and external allies.

Aside from leading efforts to strengthen *existing* competencies and capabilities, effective strategy leadership also entails trying to anticipate changes in customer/market requirements and proactively build *new* competencies and capabilities that hold promise for building an enduring competitive edge over rivals. Senior managers are in the best position to see the need and potential of such new capabilities and then to play a lead role in the capability-building, resource-strengthening process. *Proactively building new competencies and capabilities ahead of rivals to gain a competitive edge is strategic leadership of the best kind,* but strengthening the company's resource base in reaction to newly developed capabilities of pioneering rivals occurs more frequently.

Displaying Ethical Integrity and Undertaking Social Responsibility Initiatives

For an organization to avoid the pitfalls of scandal and disgrace associated with unethical strategies and operating practices, top executives must be openly and unswervingly committed to conducting the company's business in an ethical manner and to operating according to socially redeeming values and to business principles. Leading the effort to operate the company's business in an ethically principled fashion has three pieces.

- First and foremost, the CEO and other senior executives must set an excellent example in their own ethical behavior, demonstrating character and personal integrity in their actions and decisions. The behavior of senior executives, always watched carefully, sends a clear message to company personnel regarding the real standards of personal conduct.

- Second, top executives must declare unequivocal support for high ethical standards (perhaps even expressing these standards in a company code of ethics) and take an uncompromising stand on expecting all company personnel to adhere to high ethical standards (and comply fully with the company's code of ethics).

- Third, top executives must reprimand those who have been lax in enforcing ethical compliance. Failure to act swiftly and decisively in punishing ethical misconduct is interpreted as a lack of commitment.

Undertaking Social Responsibility Initiatives   Like the observance of ethical principles, the exercise of social responsibility requires visible and forthright leadership on the part of top executives. What separates companies that make a sincere effort to be good corporate citizens from companies that are content to do only what is legally required are company leaders who believe strongly that just making a profit is not good enough. Such leaders are committed to a higher standard of performance that includes social and environmental metrics as well as financial and strategic metrics. The strength of the commitment from the top—typically a company's CEO and board of directors—ultimately determines whether a company will implement and execute a full-fledged strategy of social responsibility whereby it pursues initiatives to protect the environment, actively participate in community affairs, support charitable causes, and positively impact workforce diversity and the overall well-being of employees.

> **Companies with socially conscious strategy leaders and a core value of corporate social responsibility move beyond the rhetorical flourishes of corporate citizenship and enlist the full support of company personnel behind social responsibility initiatives**

CORPORATE GOVERNANCE: THE ROLE OF THE BOARD OF DIRECTORS IN THE STRATEGY-MAKING, STRATEGY-EXECUTING PROCESS

Although senior managers have *lead responsibility* for crafting and executing a company's strategy, it is the duty of the board of directors to exercise strong oversight and see that the five tasks of strategic management are done in a manner that benefits shareholders (in the case of investor-owned enterprises) or stakeholders (in the case of not-for-profit organizations). In watching over management's strategy-making, strategy-executing actions, a company's board of directors has four important obligations to fulfill:

1. *Be inquiring critics and oversee the company's direction, strategy, and business approaches.* Board members must ask probing questions and draw on their business acumen to make independent judgments about whether strategy proposals have been adequately analyzed and whether proposed strategic actions appear to have greater promise than alternatives.

2. *Evaluate the caliber of senior executives' strategy-making and strategy-executing skills.* The board is always responsible for determining whether the current CEO is doing a good job of strategic leadership.

3. *Institute a compensation plan for top executives that rewards them for actions and results that serve stakeholder interests, and most especially those of shareholders.* A basic principle of corporate governance is that the owners of a corporation delegate managerial control to top management in return for compensation. In their role as an *agent* of shareholders, top executives have a duty to make decisions and operate the company in accord with shareholder interests. Boards of directors must develop salary and incentive compensation plans that make it in the self-interest of executives to operate the business in a manner that benefits the owners. It is also incumbent on the board of directors to prevent management from gaining executive perks and privileges that simply line the pockets of executives. Numerous media reports have recounted instances in which boards of directors have gone along with opportunistic executive efforts to secure excessive, if not downright obscene, compensation of one kind or another (multimillion-dollar interest-free loans, personal use of corporate aircraft, lucrative severance and retirement packages, outsized stock incentive

awards, and so on). The compensation plan developed by General Electric's board of directors' compensation committee makes a significant portion of the CEO's compensation contingent on GE's financial performance and growth in its stock price. In 2007, the company's strong performance allowed GE chairman and CEO Jeffrey Immelt to receive total compensation of $9.1 million. Immelt's capabilities and track record at leading GE had regularly ranked him as one of the world's best CEOs by *Barron's* and kept GE atop *Fortune's* "Most Admired Companies" list.

4. *Oversee the company's financial accounting and financial reporting practices.* While top executives, particularly the company's CEO and CFO, are primarily responsible for seeing that the company's financial statements accurately report the results of the company's operations, board members have a fiduciary duty to protect shareholders by exercising oversight of the company's financial practices. In addition, corporate boards must ensure that generally accepted accounting principles (GAAP) are properly used in preparing the company's financial statements and determine whether proper financial controls are in place to prevent fraud and misuse of funds.

Every corporation should have a strong, independent board of directors that (1) is well informed about the company's performance, (2) guides and judges the CEO and other top executives, (3) has the courage to curb management actions they believe are inappropriate or unduly risky, (4) certifies to shareholders that the CEO is doing what the board expects, (5) provides insight and advice to management, and (6) is intensely involved in debating the pros and cons of key decisions and actions.[21] Boards of directors that lack the backbone to challenge a strong-willed or imperial CEO or that rubber-stamp most anything the CEO recommends without probing inquiry and debate abandon their duty to represent and protect shareholder interests. The whole fabric of effective corporate governance is undermined when boards of directors shirk their responsibility to maintain ultimate control over the company's strategic direction, the major elements of its strategy, the business approaches management is using to implement and execute the strategy, executive compensation, and the financial reporting process.

KEY POINTS

The managerial process of crafting and executing a company's strategy consists of five interrelated and integrated phases:

1. *Developing a strategic vision* of where the company needs to head and what its future product/customer/market/technology focus should be. This managerial step provides long-term direction, infuses the organization with a sense of purposeful action, and communicates to stakeholders what management's aspirations for the company are.

2. *Setting objectives* and using the targeted results and outcomes as yardsticks for measuring the company's performance and progress. Objectives need to spell out *how much* of *what kind* of performance *by when,* and they need to require a significant amount of organizational stretch. Measuring company performance entails setting both *financial objectives* and *strategic objectives. A balanced scorecard approach* tracks both types of objectives.

3. *Crafting a strategy to achieve the objectives* and move the company along the strategic course that management has charted. Crafting strategy is concerned principally with forming responses to changes under way in the external environment, devising competitive moves and market approaches aimed at producing sustainable competitive advantage, building competitively valuable competencies and capabilities, and uniting the strategic actions initiated in various parts of the company. The more that a company's operations cut across different products, industries, and geographical areas, the more that strategy making becomes a *collaborative effort* involving managers and company personnel at many organizational levels. The total strategy that emerges in such companies is really a collection of strategic actions and business approaches initiated partly by senior company executives, partly by the heads of major business divisions, partly by functional-area managers, and partly by operating managers on the frontlines. The larger and more diverse the operations of an enterprise, the more points of strategic initiative it has and the more managers and employees at more levels of management that have a relevant strategy-making role. A single-business enterprise has three levels of strategy—business strategy for the company as a whole, functional-area strategies for each main area within the business, and operating strategies undertaken by lower-echelon managers to flesh out strategically significant aspects for the company's business and functional area strategies. In diversified, multibusiness companies, the strategy-making task involves four distinct types or levels of strategy: corporate strategy for the company as a whole, business strategy (one for each business the company has diversified into), functional-area strategies within each business, and operating strategies. Typically, the strategy-making task is more top-down than bottom-up, with higher-level strategies serving as the guide for developing lower-level strategies.

4. *Implementing and executing the chosen strategy efficiently and effectively.* Managing the implementation and execution of strategy is an operations-oriented, make-things-happen activity aimed at shaping the performance of core business activities in a strategy-supportive manner. Management's handling of the strategy implementation process can be considered successful if things go smoothly enough that the company meets or beats its strategic and financial performance targets and shows good progress in achieving management's strategic vision.

5. *Evaluating performance and initiating corrective adjustments* in vision, long-term direction, objectives, strategy, or execution in light of actual experience, changing conditions, new ideas, and new opportunities. This phase of the strategy management process is the trigger point for deciding whether to continue or change the company's vision, objectives, strategy, and/or strategy execution methods.

A company's strategic vision plus its objectives plus its strategy equals a *strategic plan* for coping with industry and competitive conditions, outcompeting rivals, and addressing the challenges and issues that stand as obstacles to the company's success.

Successful managers have to do several things in leading the drive for good strategy execution and operating excellence. First, they stay on top of things. They keep a finger on the organization's pulse by spending considerable time outside their offices, listening and talking to organization members, coaching, cheerleading, and picking up important information. Second, they are active and visible in putting constructive pressure on the organization to achieve good results. Generally, this is best accomplished by promoting an esprit de corps that mobilizes and energizes organizational members to execute strategy in a competent fashion and deliver the targeted results. Third, they keep the organization focused on operating excellence by championing innovative ideas for improvement and promoting the use of best practices to ensure value-creating activities are performed in a first-rate fashion. Fourth, they exert their clout in developing competencies and competitive capabilities that enable better execution. Fifth, they serve as a role model in displaying high ethical standards, and they insist that company personnel conduct the company's business ethically and in a socially responsible manner. They demonstrate unequivocal and visible commitment to the ethics enforcement process. Sixth and finally, when a company's strategy execution effort is not delivering good results and the organization is not making measured progress toward operating excellence, it is the leader's responsibility to step forward and push corrective actions.

Boards of directors have a duty to shareholders to play a vigilant role in overseeing management's handling of a company's strategy-making, strategy-executing process. A company's board is obligated to (1) critically appraise and ultimately approve strategic action plans; (2) evaluate the strategic leadership skills of the CEO and others in line to succeed the incumbent CEO; (3) institute a compensation plan for top executives that rewards them for actions and results that serve stakeholder interests, most especially those of shareholders; and (4) ensure that the company issues accurate financial reports and has adequate financial controls.

ASSURANCE OF LEARNING EXERCISES

1. Using the information in Table 2.2 and Table 2.3, critique the adequacy and merit of the following vision statements, listing effective elements and shortcomings. Rank the vision statements from best to worst once you complete your evaluation.

Vision Statement	Effective Elements	Shortcomings
Wells Fargo We want to satisfy all of our customers' financial needs, help them succeed financially, be the premier provider of financial services in every one of our markets, and be known as one of America's great companies.		
Hilton Hotels Corporation Our vision is to be the first choice of the world's travelers. Hilton intends to build on the rich heritage and strength of our brands by: • Consistently delighting our customers • Investing in our team members • Delivering innovative products and services • Continuously improving performance • Increasing shareholder value • Creating a culture of pride • Strengthening the loyalty of our constituents		
The Dental Products Division of 3M Corporation Become THE supplier of choice to the global dental professional markets, providing world-class quality and innovative products. [Note: All employees of the division wear badges bearing these words, and whenever a new product or business procedure is being considered, management asks, "Is this representative of THE leading dental company?"]		

(Continued)

Vision Statement	Effective Elements	Shortcomings

H. J. Heinz Company

Be the world's premier food company, offering nutritious, superior tasting foods to people everywhere. Being the premier food company does not mean being the biggest but it does mean being the best in terms of consumer value, customer service, employee talent, and consistent and predictable growth.

Chevron

To be *the* global energy company most admired for its people, partnership and performance. Our vision means we:

- provide energy products vital to sustainable economic progress and human development throughout the world;
- are people and an organization with superior capabilities and commitment;
- are the partner of choice;
- deliver world-class performance;
- earn the admiration of all our stakeholders—investors, customers, host governments, local communities and our employees—not only for the goals we achieve but how we achieve them.

Sources: Company Web sites and annual reports.

2. Go to www.dell.com/speeches and read Michael Dell's recent speeches. Do Michael Dell's speeches provide evidence that he is an effective leader at Dell? Using evidence from his speeches, discuss whether he is concerned with (*a*) staying on top of what is happening and identifying obstacles to good strategy execution, (*b*) pushing the organization to achieve good results and operating excellence, and (*c*) displaying ethical integrity and spearheading social responsibility initiatives.

3. Go to www.dell.com/leadership and read the sections dedicated to its board of directors and corporate governance. Using evidence from these sections, discuss whether there is effective governance at Dell in regard to (*a*) a critical appraisal of strategic action plans, (*b*) evaluation of the strategic leadership skills of the CEO, (*c*) executive compensation, and (*d*) accurate financial reports and controls.

EXERCISES FOR SIMULATION PARTICIPANTS

1. Meet with your co-managers and prepare a strategic vision statement for your company. It should be no shorter than one sentence but no longer than a brief paragraph. When you are finished, check to see if your vision statement meets the conditions for an effectively worded strategic vision set forth in Table 2.2 and avoids the shortcomings set forth in Table 2.3. If not, then revise it accordingly. What would be a good slogan that captures the essence of your strategic vision and that could be used to help communicate the vision to company personnel, shareholders, and other stakeholders?

2. Write a sentence that expresses your company's strategic intent.

3. What are your company's financial objectives? What are your company's strategic objectives?

4. What are the three or four key elements of your company's strategy?

3

Evaluating a Company's External Environment

LEARNING OBJECTIVES

1. To gain command of the basic concepts and analytical tools widely used to diagnose a company's industry and competitive conditions.

2. To become adept at recognizing the factors that cause competition in an industry to be fierce, more or less normal, or relatively weak.

3. To learn how to determine whether an industry's outlook presents a company with sufficiently attractive opportunities for growth and profitability.

4. To understand why in-depth evaluation of specific industry and competitive conditions is a prerequisite to crafting a strategy well matched to a company's situation.

In the opening paragraph of Chapter 1, we said that one of the three central questions that managers must address in evaluating their company's business prospects is "What's the company's present situation?" Two facets of a company's situation are especially pertinent: (1) the industry and competitive environment in which the company operates and (2) the company's collection of resources and capabilities, its strengths and weaknesses vis-à-vis rivals, and its windows of opportunity.

Insightful analysis of a company's external and internal environment is a prerequisite for crafting a strategy that is an excellent fit with the company's situation, is capable of building competitive advantage, and holds good prospect for boosting company performance—the three criteria of a winning strategy.

As depicted in Figure 3.1, the task of crafting a company's strategy should always begin with appraisals of the company's external environment and internal environment (as a basis for deciding on a long-term strategic direction and developing a strategic vision), then proceed to an evaluation of the most promising alternative strategic options and business models, and culminate in choosing a specific strategy.

This chapter presents the concepts and analytical tools for zeroing in on a single-business company's external environment. Attention centers on the competitive arena in which a company operates, the drivers of market change, and rival companies' actions. In Chapter 4 we explore the methods of evaluating a company's internal circumstances and competitiveness.

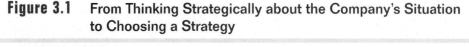

Figure 3.1 From Thinking Strategically about the Company's Situation to Choosing a Strategy

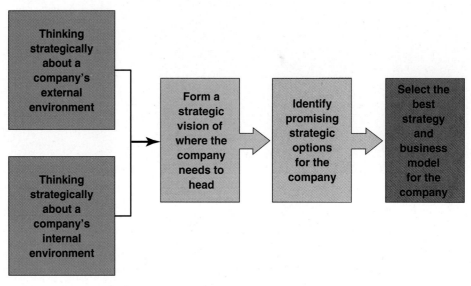

THE STRATEGICALLY RELEVANT COMPONENTS OF A COMPANY'S EXTERNAL ENVIRONMENT

All companies operate in a macroenvironment shaped by influences emanating from general economic conditions; population demographics; societal values and lifestyles; legislation and regulations; technology; and, closer to home, the industry and competitive environment in which the company operates (see Figure 3.2). Strictly speaking, a company's macroenvironment includes *all relevant factors and influences* outside the company's boundaries; by *relevant,* we mean important enough to have a bearing on the decisions the company ultimately makes about its direction, objectives, strategy, and business model. Strategically relevant influences coming from the outer ring of the macroenvironment can sometimes have a high impact on a company's business situation and have a very significant impact on the company's direction and strategy. The strategic opportunities of cigarette producers to grow their business are greatly reduced by antismoking ordinances and the growing cultural stigma attached to smoking. Motor vehicle companies must adapt their strategies (especially as concerns the fuel mileage of their vehicles) to customer concerns about gasoline prices. The demographics of an aging population and longer life expectancies are having a dramatic impact on the business prospects and strategies of health care and prescription drug companies. Companies in most all industries have to craft strategies that are responsive to environmental regulations, growing use of the Internet, and energy prices. Companies in the food processing, restaurant, sports, and fitness industries have to pay special attention to changes in lifestyles, eating habits, leisure-time preferences, and attitudes toward nutrition and fitness in fashioning their strategies.

Figure 3.2   The Components of a Company's Macroenvironment

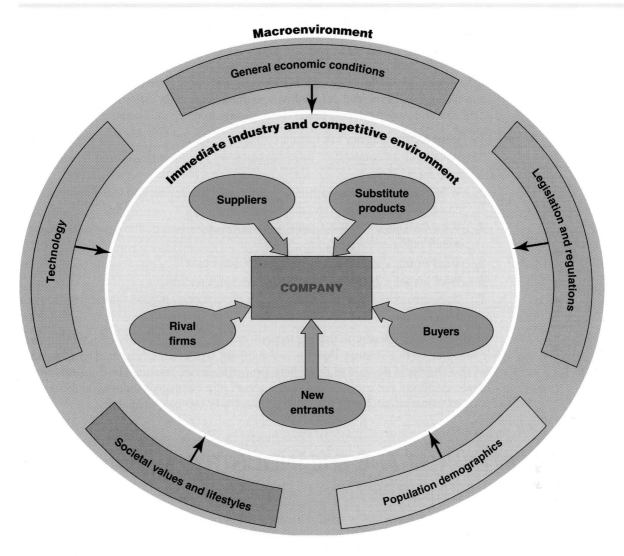

Happenings in the outer ring of the macroenvironment may occur rapidly or slowly, with or without advance warning. The impact of outer-ring factors on a company's choice of strategy can range from big to small. But even if the factors in the macroenvironment change slowly or affect a company's situation only modestly, there are enough strategically relevant outer-ring trends and events to justify a watchful eye. As company managers scan the external environment, they must be alert for potentially important outer-ring developments, assess their impact and influence, and adapt the company's direction and strategy as needed.

However, the factors and forces in a company's macroenvironment having the *biggest* strategy-shaping impact typically pertain to the company's immediate industry and competitive environment—the actions of rivals firms, buyer behavior, supplier-related considerations, and so on. Consequently, it is on a company's industry and competitive environment that we concentrate our attention in this chapter.

THINKING STRATEGICALLY ABOUT A COMPANY'S INDUSTRY AND COMPETITIVE ENVIRONMENT

To gain a deep understanding of a company's industry and competitive environment, managers do not need to gather all the information they can find and spend lots of time digesting it. Rather, the task is much more focused. Thinking strategically about a company's industry and competitive environment entails using some well-defined concepts and analytical tools to get clear answers to seven questions:

1. What are the industry's dominant economic features?
2. What kinds of competitive forces are industry members facing, and how strong is each force?
3. What forces are driving industry change and what impact will these changes have on competitive intensity and industry profitability?
4. What market positions do industry rivals occupy—who is strongly positioned and who is not?
5. What strategic moves are rivals likely to make next?
6. What are the key factors for future competitive success?
7. Does the outlook for the industry offer the company a good opportunity to earn attractive profits?

Analysis-based answers to these questions provide managers with the understanding needed to craft a strategy that fits the company's external situation. The remainder of this chapter is devoted to describing the methods of obtaining solid answers to the seven questions and explaining how the nature of a company's industry and competitive environment weighs on the strategic choices of company managers.

QUESTION 1: WHAT ARE THE INDUSTRY'S DOMINANT ECONOMIC FEATURES?

Because industries differ so significantly, analyzing a company's industry and competitive environment begins with identifying an industry's dominant economic features and gaining an an accurate and insightful view of the industry landscape. An industry's dominant economic features are defined by such factors as market size and growth rate, the number and sizes of buyers and sellers, the geographic boundaries of the market (which can extend from local to worldwide), whether sellers' products are virtually identical or highly differentiated, the pace of technological change, and the extent of vertical integration. Table 3.1 provides a convenient summary of what economic features to look at and the corresponding questions to consider in profiling an industry's landscape.

Getting a handle on an industry's distinguishing economic features not only allows managers to prepare for the analysis to come but also helps them understand the kinds of strategic moves that industry members are likely to employ. For example, in industries characterized by one product advance after another—such as the video game, computer, and pharmaceuticals industries—companies must invest in research and development (R&D) and maintain strong product innovation capabilities. An industry that has recently passed through the rapid-growth stage and is looking at single-digit percentage increases

Table 3.1 What to Consider in Identifying an Industry's Dominant Economic Features

Economic Feature	Questions to Answer
Market size and growth rate	• How big is the industry and how fast is it growing? • What does the industry's position in the product life cycle (early development, rapid growth and takeoff, early maturity and slowing growth, saturation and stagnation, decline) reveal about the industry's growth prospects?
Number of rivals	• Is the industry fragmented into many small companies or concentrated and dominated by a few large companies? • Is the industry consolidating to a smaller number of competitors?
Scope of competitive rivalry	• Is the geographic area over which most companies compete local, regional, national, multinational, or global? • Is having a presence in foreign markets becoming more important to a company's long-term competitive success?
Number of buyers	• Is market demand fragmented among many buyers? • Do some buyers have bargaining power because they purchase in large volume?
Degree of product differentiation	• Are the products of rivals becoming more differentiated or less differentiated? • Are the products of rivals becoming increasingly similar and causing heightened price competition?
Product innovation	• Is the industry characterized by rapid product innovation and short product life cycles? • How important is R&D and product innovation? • Are there opportunities to overtake key rivals by being first-to-market with next-generation products?
Demand–supply conditions	• Is a surplus of capacity pushing prices and profit margins down? • Is the industry overcrowded with competitors?
Pace of technological change	• What role does advancing technology play in this industry? • Are ongoing upgrades of facilities/equipment essential because of rapidly advancing production process technologies? • Do most industry members have or need strong technological capabilities? Why?
Vertical integration	• Do most competitors operate in only one stage of the industry (parts and components production, manufacturing and assembly, distribution, retailing), or do some competitors operate in multiple stages? • Is there any cost or competitive advantage or disadvantage associated with being fully or partially integrated?
Economies of scale	• Is the industry characterized by economies of scale in purchasing, manufacturing, advertising, shipping, or other activities? • Do companies with large-scale operations have an important cost advantage over small-scale firms?
Learning/experience curve effects	• Are certain industry activities characterized by strong learning and experience effects ("learning by doing") such that unit costs decline as a company's experience in performing the activity builds? • Do any companies have significant cost advantages because of their learning/experience in performing particular activities?

in buyer demand is likely to be experiencing a competitive shake-out and much stronger strategic emphasis on cost reduction and improved customer service.

In industries like semiconductors, strong *learning/experience effects* in manufacturing cause unit costs to decline about 20 percent each time cumulative production volume doubles. With a 20 percent experience curve effect, if the first 1 million chips cost $100 each, the unit cost would drop to $80 (80 percent of $100) when production volume reaches 2 million and then drop further to $64 (80 percent of $80) when production volume reaches 4 million.[1] The bigger the learning or experience curve effect, the bigger the cost advantage of the company with the largest cumulative production volume. Thus, when an industry is characterized by important learning/experience curve effects (or by economies of scale), industry members are strongly motivated to adopt volume-increasing strategies to capture the resulting cost-saving economies and maintain their competitiveness. Unless small-scale firms succeed in pursuing strategic options that allow them to grow sales sufficiently to remain cost-competitive with larger-volume rivals, they are unlikely to survive. The bigger the learning/experience curve effects and/or scale economies in an industry, the more imperative it becomes for competing sellers to pursue strategies to win additional sales and market share—the company with the biggest sales volume gains sustainable competitive advantage as the low-cost producer.

QUESTION 2: HOW STRONG ARE COMPETITIVE FORCES?

Competitive forces are never the same from one industry to another. Far and away the most powerful and widely used tool for systematically diagnosing the principal competitive pressures in a market and assessing the strength and importance of each is the *five-forces model of competition.*[2] This model, depicted in Figure 3.3, holds that the state of competition in an industry is a composite of competitive pressures operating in five areas of the overall market:

1. Competitive pressures associated with the market maneuvering and jockeying for buyer patronage that goes on among *rival sellers* in the industry.
2. Competitive pressures associated with the threats of new entrants.
3. Competitive pressures coming from the attempts of companies in other industries to win buyers over to their own substitute products.
4. Competitive pressures stemming from supplier bargaining power and supplier–seller collaboration.
5. Competitive pressures stemming from buyer bargaining power and seller–buyer collaboration.

The way one uses the five-forces model to determine the makeup and strength of competitive pressures in a given industry is to build the picture of competitive landscape in three steps:

- *Step 1:* Identify the *specific* competitive pressures associated with each of the five forces.
- *Step 2:* Evaluate how strong the pressures comprising each of the five forces are (fierce, strong, moderate to normal, or weak).
- *Step 3:* Determine whether the collective strength of the five competitive forces is conducive to earning attractive profits.

Figure 3.3   The Five-Forces Model of Competition: A Key Analytical Tool

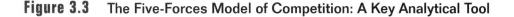

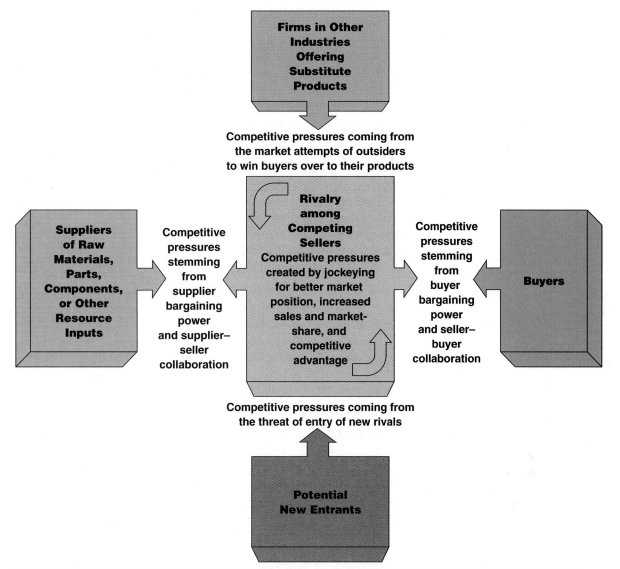

Source: Adapted from Michael E. Porter, "How Competitive Forces Shape Strategy," *Harvard Business Review* 57, no. 2 (March–April 1979), pp. 137–45; and Michael E. Porter, "The Five Competitive Forces That Shape Strategy," *Harvard Business Review* 86, no. 1 (January 2008), pp. 80–86.

Competitive Pressures Created by the Rivalry among Competing Sellers

The strongest of the five competitive forces is nearly always the market maneuvering for buyer patronage that goes on among rival sellers of a product or service. In effect, *a market is a competitive battlefield* where there's no end to the maneuvering for buyer patronage. Rival sellers employ whatever weapons they have in their business arsenal to strengthen their market positions, attract and retain buyers, and earn good profits.

The challenge for company managers is to craft a competitive strategy that, at the very least, allows the company to hold its own against rivals and that, ideally, *produces a competitive edge.* But competitive contests are ongoing and dynamic. When one firm makes a strategic move that produces good results, its rivals typically respond with offensive or defensive countermoves of their own, shifting their strategic emphasis from one combination of product attributes, marketing tactics, and capabilities to another. This pattern of action and reaction, move and countermove, adjustment and readjustment produces a continually evolving competitive landscape where the market battle ebbs and flows, sometimes takes unpredictable twists and turns, and produces winners and losers. But the winners—the current market leaders— have no guarantees of continued leadership; their market success is no more durable than the power of their strategies to fend off the strategies of ambitious challengers. In every industry, the ongoing maneuvering of rivals leads to one or another company gaining or losing momentum in the marketplace according to whether their latest strategic actions succeed or fail.[3]

Figure 3.4 shows a sampling of competitive weapons that firms can deploy in battling rivals and indicates the factors that influence the intensity of their rivalry. A brief discussion of the principal factors that influence the tempo of rivalry among industry competitors is in order:[4]

- *Rivalry intensifies when competing sellers are active in making fresh moves to improve their market standing and business performance.* One indicator of active rivalry is lively price competition, a condition that puts pressure on industry members to drive costs out of the business and threatens the survival of high-cost companies. Another indicator of active rivalry is rapid introduction of next-generation products—when one or more rivals frequently introduce new or improved products, competitors that lack good product-innovation capabilities feel considerable competitive heat to get their own new and improved products into the marketplace quickly. Other indicators of active rivalry among industry members include:

  - Whether industry members are racing to differentiate their products from rivals by offering better performance features or higher-quality or improved customer service or a wider product selection.

  - How frequently rivals resort to such marketing tactics as special sales promotions, heavy advertising, rebates, or low-interest-rate financing to drum up additional sales.

  - How actively industry members are pursuing efforts to build stronger dealer networks or establish positions in foreign markets or otherwise expand their distribution capabilities and market presence.

  - How hard companies are striving to gain a market edge over rivals by developing valuable expertise and capabilities that rivals are hard-pressed to match.

  Normally, competitive jockeying among rival sellers is active and fairly intense because competing companies are highly motivated to launch whatever fresh actions and creative market maneuvers they can think of to try to strengthen their market positions and business performance.

- *Rivalry is usually stronger when buyer demand is growing slowly and weaker when buyer demand is growing rapidly.* Rapidly expanding buyer demand

Figure 3.4   Weapons for Competing and Factors Affecting the Strength of Rivalry

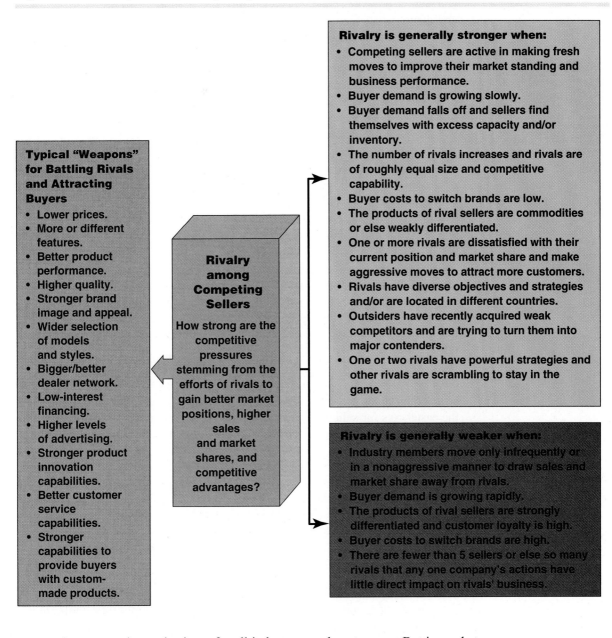

Typical "Weapons" for Battling Rivals and Attracting Buyers

- Lower prices.
- More or different features.
- Better product performance.
- Higher quality.
- Stronger brand image and appeal.
- Wider selection of models and styles.
- Bigger/better dealer network.
- Low-interest financing.
- Higher levels of advertising.
- Stronger product innovation capabilities.
- Better customer service capabilities.
- Stronger capabilities to provide buyers with custom-made products.

Rivalry among Competing Sellers

How strong are the competitive pressures stemming from the efforts of rivals to gain better market positions, higher sales and market shares, and competitive advantages?

Rivalry is generally stronger when:

- Competing sellers are active in making fresh moves to improve their market standing and business performance.
- Buyer demand is growing slowly.
- Buyer demand falls off and sellers find themselves with excess capacity and/or inventory.
- The number of rivals increases and rivals are of roughly equal size and competitive capability.
- Buyer costs to switch brands are low.
- The products of rival sellers are commodities or else weakly differentiated.
- One or more rivals are dissatisfied with their current position and market share and make aggressive moves to attract more customers.
- Rivals have diverse objectives and strategies and/or are located in different countries.
- Outsiders have recently acquired weak competitors and are trying to turn them into major contenders.
- One or two rivals have powerful strategies and other rivals are scrambling to stay in the game.

Rivalry is generally weaker when:

- Industry members move only infrequently or in a nonaggressive manner to draw sales and market share away from rivals.
- Buyer demand is growing rapidly.
- The products of rival sellers are strongly differentiated and customer loyalty is high.
- Buyer costs to switch brands are high.
- There are fewer than 5 sellers or else so many rivals that any one company's actions have little direct impact on rivals' business.

produces enough new business for all industry members to grow. But in markets where growth is sluggish or where buyer demand drops off unexpectedly, expansion-minded firms and/or firms with excess capacity often are quick to cut prices and initiate other sales-increasing tactics, thereby igniting a battle for market share that can threaten the survival of competitively weak firms.

- *Rivalry increases when buyer demand falls off and sellers find themselves with excess capacity and/or inventory.* Excess supply conditions create a "buyer's market," putting added competitive pressure on industry rivals to scramble for profitable sales levels. When a product is perishable, seasonal, or costly to hold in inventory, competitive pressures build quickly anytime one or more firms decide to cut prices and dump supplies on the market. Likewise, whenever fixed costs account for a large fraction of total cost (so that unit costs tend to be lowest at or near full capacity), firms come under significant pressure to cut prices or otherwise try to boost sales whenever they are operating below full capacity. Unused capacity imposes a significant cost-increasing penalty, because there are fewer units over which to spread fixed costs. The pressure of high fixed costs can push rival firms into price concessions, special discounts, rebates, low-interest-rate financing, and other volume-boosting tactics.

- *Rivalry is stronger in industries where the number of rivals increases and competitors are equal in size and capability.* Competitive rivalry in the quick-service restaurant industry is particularly strong, where there are numerous relatively equal-sized hamburger, deli sandwich, chicken, and taco chains. For the most part, McDonald's, Burger King, Taco Bell, KFC, Arby's, and other national fast-food chains have comparable capabilities and must compete aggressively to hold their own in the industry.

- *Rivalry increases as it becomes less costly for buyers to switch brands.* The less expensive it is for buyers to switch their purchases from the seller of one brand to the seller of another brand, the easier it is for sellers to steal customers away from rivals. But the higher the costs associated with switching brands, the less prone buyers are to make the switch. Abandoning a familiar brand may entail added time, inconvenience, or psychological costs.

- *Rivalry increases as it becomes less costly for buyers to switch brands and diminishes as buyer switching costs increase.* The less expensive it is for buyers to switch their purchases from the seller of one brand to the seller of another brand, the easier it is for sellers to steal customers away from rivals. But the higher the costs buyers incur to switch brands, the less prone they are to brand switching. Even if consumers view one or more rival brands as more attractive, they may not be inclined to switch because of the added time and inconvenience that may be involved or the psychological costs of abandoning a familiar brand. Distributors and retailers may not switch to the brands of rival manufacturers because they are hesitant to sever longstanding supplier relationships, incur any technical support costs or retraining expenses in making the switchover, go to the trouble of testing the quality and reliability of the rival brand, or devote resources to marketing the new brand (especially if the brand is lesser-known). Apple Computer, for example, has long had to struggle to convince PC users to switch from Windows-based PCs because of the time burdens and inconvenience associated with learning Apple's operating system and because so many Windows-based applications will not run on a MacIntosh due to operating system incompatibility. In short, unless buyers are dissatisfied with the brand they are presently purchasing, high switching costs can significantly weaken the rivalry among competing sellers.

- *Rivalry increases as the products of rival sellers become more standardized and diminishes as the products of industry rivals become more differentiated.* When the offerings of rivals are identical or weakly differentiated, buyers have less reason to be brand-loyal—a condition that makes it easier for rivals to convince buyers to switch to their offering. And since the brands of different sellers have comparable attributes, buyers can shop the market for the best deal and switch brands at will. On the other hand, strongly differentiated product offerings among rivals breed high brand loyalty on the part of buyers—because many buyers view the attributes of certain brands as better suited to their needs. Strong brand attachments make it tougher for sellers to draw customers away from rivals. Unless meaningful numbers of buyers are open to considering new or different product attributes being offered by rivals, the high degree of brand loyalty that accompanies strong product differentiation works against fierce rivalry among competing sellers.

- *Rivalry is more intense when industry conditions tempt competitors to use price cuts or other competitive weapons to boost unit volume.* When a product is perishable, seasonal, or costly to hold in inventory, competitive pressures build quickly anytime one or more firms decide to cut prices and dump supplies on the market. Likewise, whenever fixed costs account for a large fraction of total cost so that unit costs tend to be lowest at or near full capacity, firms come under significant pressure to cut prices or otherwise try to boost sales whenever they are operating below full capacity. Unused capacity imposes a significant cost-increasing penalty because there are fewer units over which to spread fixed costs. The pressure of high fixed costs can push rival firms into price concessions, special discounts, rebates, low-interest-rate financing, and other volume-boosting tactics.

- *Rivalry increases when one or more competitors become dissatisfied with their market position.* Firms that are losing ground or in financial trouble often initiate aggressive (perhaps even desperate) turnaround strategies that can involve price discounts, greater advertising, or merger with other rivals—such strategies can turn competitive pressures up a notch.

- *Rivalry becomes more volatile and unpredictable as the diversity of competitors increases in terms of visions, strategic intents, objectives, strategies, resources, and countries of origin.* A diverse group of sellers often contains one or more mavericks willing to try novel or rule-breaking market approaches, thus generating a livelier and less predictable competitive environment. Globally competitive markets usually boost the intensity of rivalry, especially when aggressors having lower costs or products with more attractive features are intent on gaining a strong foothold in new country markets.

- *Rivalry increases when strong companies outside the industry acquire weak firms in the industry and launch aggressive, well-funded moves to transform their newly acquired competitors into major market contenders.* A concerted effort to turn a weak rival into a market leader nearly always entails launching well-financed strategic initiatives to dramatically improve the competitor's product offering, excite buyer interest, and win a much bigger market share—actions that, if successful, put added pressure on rivals to counter with fresh strategic moves of their own.

- *When one or two companies employ powerful, successful competitive strategies, the competitive pressures on other industry members intensify significantly.* Industry members that suddenly start to lose sales and market share to offensive-minded competitors may have to scramble to stay in the game; they either have to launch effective strategic responses (which further intensifies rivalry) or be relegated to also-ran status.

- *Rivalry is usually weaker in industries made up of vast numbers of small rivals; likewise, it is often weak when there are fewer than five competitors.* When an industry is populated with so many rivals that the impact of successful moves by any one company ripple out to have little discernible impact on the businesses of its many rivals, then head-to-head rivalry turns out to be relatively weak—industry members soon learn that it is not imperative to respond every time one or another rival does something to enhance its market position. Rivalry also tends to be weak if an industry consists of just two to four sellers because each competitor soon learns that aggressive moves to grow its sales and market share have immediate adverse impact on rivals' businesses and will almost certainly provoke vigorous retaliation. Hence, there is a tendency for competition among the few to produce a live-and-let-live approach to competing because rivals see the merits of restrained efforts to wrest sales and market share from competitors as opposed to undertaking hard-hitting offensives that escalate into a profit-eroding arms race or price war. However, some caution must be exercised in concluding that rivalry is weak just because there are only a few competitors. The fierceness of the current battle between Linux and Microsoft in operating system software and between Intel and AMD in microprocessors for PCs and servers and the decades-long war between Coca-Cola and Pepsi are prime examples.

Rivalry can be characterized as *cutthroat* or *brutal* when competitors engage in protracted price wars or habitually employ other aggressive tactics that are mutually destructive to profitability. Rivalry can be considered *fierce* to *strong* when the battle for market share is so vigorous that the profit margins of most industry members are squeezed to bare-bones levels. Rivalry can be characterized as *moderate* or *normal* when the maneuvering among industry members, while lively and healthy, still allows most industry members to earn acceptable profits. Rivalry is *weak* when most companies in the industry are content with their sales growth and market shares, rarely undertake offensives to steal customers away from one another, and have comparatively attractive earnings and returns on investment.

Competitive Pressures Associated with the Threat of New Entrants

Several factors determine whether the threat of new companies entering the marketplace poses significant competitive pressure (see Figure 3.5). One factor relates to the size of the pool of likely entry candidates. As a rule, the bigger the pool of entry candidates, the stronger is the threat of potential entry. Frequently, the strongest competitive pressures associated with potential entry come not from outsiders but from current industry participants looking for growth opportunities. *Existing industry members are often strong candidates to enter market segments or geographic areas where they currently do not have a market presence.* Companies already well established in certain product categories or geographic areas often possess the resources, competencies, and competitive capabilities to hurdle the barriers of entering a different market segment or new geographic area.

A second factor concerns whether the likely entry candidates face high or low entry barriers. High barriers reduce the competitive threat of potential entry, while low barriers make entry more likely, especially if the industry is growing and offers attractive profit opportunities. The most widely encountered barriers that entry candidates must hurdle include:[5]

- *The presence of sizable economies of scale in production or other areas of operation*—When incumbent companies enjoy cost advantages associated with large-scale operations, outsiders must either enter on a large scale (a costly and perhaps risky move) or accept a cost disadvantage and consequently lower profitability.

- *Cost and resource disadvantages not related to scale of operation*—Industry incumbents can have cost advantages that stem from experience/learning curve

Figure 3.5   Factors Affecting the Threat of Entry

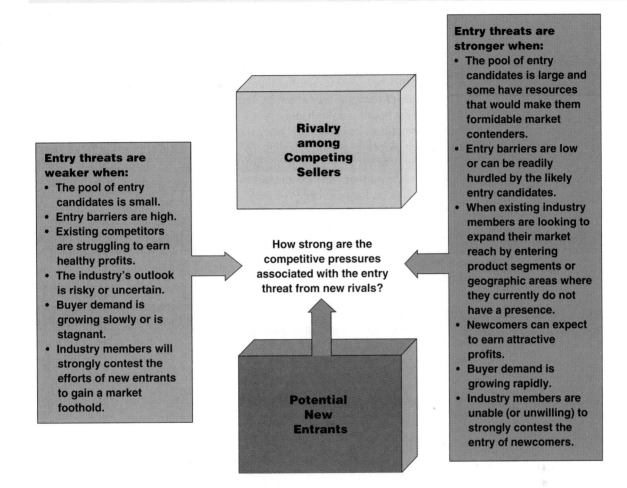

Entry threats are weaker when:
- The pool of entry candidates is small.
- Entry barriers are high.
- Existing competitors are struggling to earn healthy profits.
- The industry's outlook is risky or uncertain.
- Buyer demand is growing slowly or is stagnant.
- Industry members will strongly contest the efforts of new entrants to gain a market foothold.

Rivalry among Competing Sellers

How strong are the competitive pressures associated with the entry threat from new rivals?

Potential New Entrants

Entry threats are stronger when:
- The pool of entry candidates is large and some have resources that would make them formidable market contenders.
- Entry barriers are low or can be readily hurdled by the likely entry candidates.
- When existing industry members are looking to expand their market reach by entering product segments or geographic areas where they currently do not have a presence.
- Newcomers can expect to earn attractive profits.
- Buyer demand is growing rapidly.
- Industry members are unable (or unwilling) to strongly contest the entry of newcomers.

effects, the possession of proprietary technology, partnerships with the best and cheapest suppliers, and low fixed costs (because they have older facilities that have been mostly depreciated).

- *Strong brand preferences and high degrees of customer loyalty*—The stronger the attachment of buyers to established brands, the harder it is for a newcomer to break into the marketplace. In such cases, a new entrant must have the financial resources to spend enough on advertising and sales promotion to overcome customer loyalties and build its own clientele. Establishing brand recognition and building customer loyalty can be a slow and costly process. In addition, if it is difficult or costly for a customer to switch to a new brand, a new entrant must persuade buyers that its brand is worth the switching costs. To overcome switching-cost barriers, new entrants may have to offer buyers a discounted price or an extra margin of quality or service. Such barriers discourage new entry because they act to boost financial requirements and lower expected profit margins for new entrants.

- *High capital requirements*—The larger the total dollar investment needed to enter the market successfully, the more limited the pool of potential entrants. The most obvious capital requirements for new entrants relate to manufacturing facilities and equipment, introductory advertising and sales promotion campaigns, working capital to finance inventories and customer credit, and sufficient cash to cover start-up costs.

• *The difficulties of building a distributor/retailer network and securing adequate space on retailers' shelves*—A potential entrant can face numerous distribution channel challenges. Wholesale distributors may be reluctant to take on a product that lacks buyer recognition. It may be hard to recruit retailers and convince them to give a new brand ample display space and an adequate trial period. Potential entrants sometimes have to "buy" their way into wholesale or retail channels by cutting their prices to provide dealers and distributors with higher markups and profit margins or by giving them big advertising and promotional allowances—this restricts the pool of entry candidates to companies with deep enough financial pockets to take on the challenges of building a viable network of distributors and retailers.

• *Restrictive regulatory policies*—Government agencies can limit or even bar entry by requiring licenses and permits. Regulated industries like cable TV, telecommunications, electric and gas utilities, and radio and television broadcasting are characterized by government-controlled entry. Stringent government-mandated safety regulations and environmental pollution standards raise entry costs.

• *Tariffs and international trade restrictions*—National governments commonly use tariffs and trade restrictions (antidumping rules, local content requirements, local ownership requirements, quotas, etc.) to raise entry barriers for foreign firms and protect domestic producers from outside competition.

• *The ability and willingness of industry incumbents to launch vigorous initiatives to block a newcomer's successful entry*—Even if a potential entrant has or can acquire the needed competencies and resources to attempt entry, it must still worry about the reaction of existing firms.[6] Sometimes, there's little that incumbents can do to throw obstacles in an entrant's path. But there are times when incumbents use price cuts, increase advertising, introduce product improvements, and launch legal attacks to prevent the entrant from building a clientele. Cable TV companies have vigorously fought the entry of satellite TV into the industry by seeking government intervention to delay satellite providers in offering local stations, offering satellite customers discounts to switch back to cable, and charging satellite customer high monthly rates for cable Internet access.

CORE CONCEPT

The threat of entry is stronger when entry barriers are low, when there's a sizable pool of entry candidates, when industry growth is rapid and profit potentials are high, and when incumbent firms are unable or unwilling to vigorously contest a newcomer's entry

Whether an industry's entry barriers ought to be considered high or low depends on the resources and competencies possessed by the pool of potential entrants. Companies with sizable financial resources, proven competitive capabilities, and a respected brand name may be able to hurdle an industry's entry barriers rather easily. Small start-up enterprises may find the same entry barriers insurmountable. When Honda opted to enter the U.S. lawn-mower market in competition against Toro, Snapper, Craftsman, John Deere, and others, it was easily able to hurdle entry barriers that would have been formidable to other newcomers because it had long-standing expertise in gasoline engines and because its well-known reputation for quality and durability gave it instant credibility with homeowners. Honda had to spend relatively little on advertising to attract buyers and gain a market foothold, distributors and dealers were quite willing to handle the Honda lawn-mower line, and Honda had ample capital to build a U.S. assembly plant.

In evaluating whether the threat of additional entry is strong or weak, company managers must also look at how attractive the growth and profit prospects are for new entrants. *Rapidly growing market demand and high potential profits act as magnets, motivating potential entrants to commit the resources needed to hurdle entry barriers.*[7] When growth and profit opportunities are sufficiently attractive, entry barriers are unlikely to be an effective entry deterrent. *The best test of whether potential entry is a strong or weak competitive force in the marketplace is to ask if the industry's growth and profit prospects are strongly attractive to potential entry candidates.* The stronger the threat of entry, the more that incumbent firms must seek ways to fortify their positions against newcomers and make entry more costly or difficult.

One additional point: *The threat of entry changes as the industry's prospects grow brighter or dimmer and as entry barriers rise or fall.* For example, in the pharmaceutical industry the expiration of a key patent on a widely prescribed drug virtually guarantees that one or more drug makers will enter with generic offerings of their own. Use of the Internet for shopping is making it much easier for e-tailers to enter into competition against some of the best-known retail chains. In international markets, entry barriers for foreign-based firms fall as tariffs are lowered, as host governments open up their domestic markets to outsiders, as domestic wholesalers and dealers seek out lower-cost foreign-made goods, and as domestic buyers become more willing to purchase foreign brands.

> High entry barriers and weak entry threats today do not always translate into high entry barriers and weak entry threats tomorrow.

Competitive Pressures from the Sellers of Substitute Products

Companies in one industry come under competitive pressure from the actions of companies in a closely adjoining industry whenever buyers view the products of the two industries as good substitutes. For instance, the producers of sugar experience competitive pressures from the sales and marketing efforts of the makers of Equal, Splenda, and Sweet'N Low. Similarly, the producers of eyeglasses and contact lenses face competitive pressures from doctors who do corrective laser surgery. The makers of disc-based music players are facing such stiff competition from Apple's iPod and other brands of MP3 players that devices whose chief purpose is to play of music CDs and DVDs are fast becoming obsolete. Newspapers are struggling to maintain their relevance to subscribers who can readily turn to cable news channels for late-breaking news and use Internet sources to get information about sports results, stock quotes, and job opportunities. First-run movie theater chains are feeling competitive heat as consumers are staying home to watch movies on their big-screen, high-definition TVs, using either DVDs or movies-on-demand services. The producers of metal cans are becoming increasingly engaged in a battle with the makers of retort pouches (multi-layer packages made from polypropylene, aluminum foil, or polyester) for the business of companies producing packaged fruits, vegetables, meats, and pet foods. Retort pouches are more attractively priced than metal cans because they are less expensive to produce and ship.

Just how strong the competitive pressures are from the sellers of substitute products depends on three factors:

1. *Whether substitutes are readily available and attractively priced.* The presence of readily available and attractively priced substitutes creates competitive pressure by placing a ceiling on the prices industry members can charge.[8] When substitutes are cheaper than an industry's product, industry members come under heavy

competitive pressure to reduce their prices and find ways to absorb the price cuts with cost reductions.

2. *Whether buyers view the substitutes as being comparable or better in terms of quality, performance, and other relevant attributes.* Customers are prone to compare performance and other attributes as well as price. For example, consumers have found digital cameras to be a superior substitute for film cameras not only because digital cameras are easy to use but also because they allow people to download images to a home computer and delete bad shots without paying for film developing. Competition from good-performing substitutes unleashes competitive pressures on industry participants to incorporate new performance features and attributes that makes their product offerings more competitive.

3. *Whether the costs that buyers incur in switching to the substitutes are high or low.* High switching costs deter switching to substitutes, while low switching costs make it easier for the sellers of attractive substitutes to lure buyers to their products.[9] Typical switching costs include the inconvenience of switching to a substitute, the costs of additional equipment, the psychological costs of severing old supplier relationships, and employee retraining costs.

Figure 3.6 summarizes the conditions that determine whether the competitive pressures from substitute products are strong, moderate, or weak.

As a rule, the lower the price of substitutes, the higher their quality and performance, and the lower the user's switching costs, the more intense the competitive pressures posed by substitute products. Other market indicators of the competitive strength of substitute products include (1) whether the sales of substitutes are growing faster than the sales of the industry being analyzed (a sign that the sellers of substitutes may be drawing customers away from the industry in question), (2) whether the producers of substitutes are moving to add new capacity, and (3) whether the profits of the producers of substitutes are on the rise.

Competitive Pressures Stemming from Supplier Bargaining Power and Supplier–Seller Collaboration

Whether supplier–seller relationships represent a weak competitive force or a strong one depends on (1) whether the major suppliers can exercise sufficient bargaining power to influence the terms and conditions of supply in their favor, and (2) how closely one or more industry members collaborate with their suppliers to achieve supply chain efficiencies.

How Supplier Bargaining Power Can Create Competitive Pressures

Sometimes the actions of important suppliers bring competitive pressures to bear on the companies they are supplying. For instance, Microsoft and Intel, both of whom supply PC makers with products that most PC users consider essential, are known for using their dominant market status not only to charge PC makers premium prices but also to leverage PC makers in other ways. Microsoft pressures PC makers to position the icons for Microsoft software prominently on the screens of new computers that come with factory-loaded software. Intel tends to give PC makers who use the biggest percentages of Intel chips in their PC models top priority in filling orders for newly introduced Intel chips. Being on Intel's list of preferred customers helps a PC maker get an allocation of the first production runs of Intel's latest and greatest chips and thus get new PC models to market ahead of rivals. The ability of Microsoft and Intel

Figure 3.6   Factors Affecting the Strength of Competitive Pressures from Substitute Products

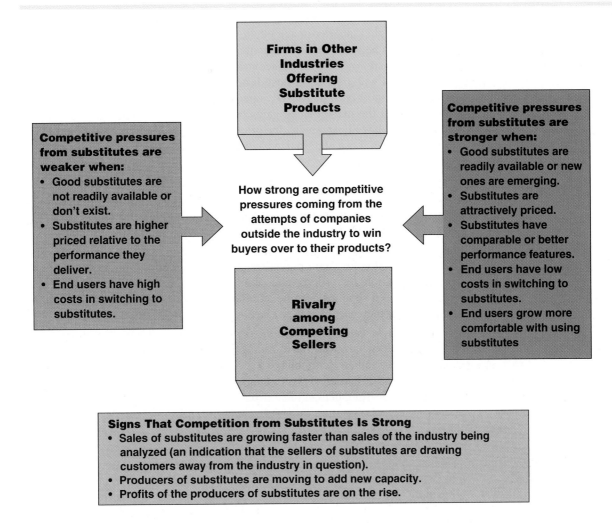

to pressure PC makers for preferential treatment of one kind or another in turn affects competition among rival PC makers.

Small-scale retailers must often contend with the power of manufacturers whose products enjoy prestigious and well-respected brand names; when a manufacturer knows that a retailer needs to stock the manufacturer's product because consumers expect to find the product on the shelves of retail stores where they shop, the manufacturer usually has some degree of pricing power and may even be able to push hard for favorable shelf displays. Motor vehicle manufacturers typically exert considerable power over the terms and conditions with which they supply new vehicles to their independent automobile dealerships. The operators of franchised units of such chains as McDonald's, Dunkin' Donuts, Pizza Hut, Sylvan Learning Centers, and Hampton Inns must frequently agree not only to source some of their supplies from the franchisor at prices and terms favorable to that franchisor but also to operate their facilities in a manner largely dictated by the franchisor.

Strong supplier bargaining power is also a competitive factor in industries where unions have been able to organize the workforces of some industry members but not others; those industry members that must negotiate wages, fringe benefits, and working conditions with powerful unions (which control the supply of labor) often find themselves with higher labor costs than their competitors with nonunion labor forces. The bigger the gap between union and nonunion labor costs in an industry, the more that unionized industry members must scramble to find ways to relieve the competitive pressure associated with their labor cost disadvantage. High labor costs are proving a huge competitive liability to unionized supermarket chains like Kroger and Safeway in trying to combat the market share gains being made by Wal-Mart in supermarket retailing—at Wal-Mart Supercenters, the prices for supermarket items tend to run 5 to 20 percent lower than those at unionized supermarket chains.

The factors that determine whether any of the suppliers to an industry are in a position to exert substantial bargaining power or leverage are fairly clear-cut:[10]

- *Whether the item being supplied is a commodity that is readily available from many suppliers at the going market price.* Suppliers have little or no bargaining power or leverage whenever industry members have the ability to source their requirements at competitive prices from any of several alternative and eager suppliers, perhaps dividing their purchases among two or more suppliers to promote lively competition for orders. The suppliers of commodity items have market power only when supplies become quite tight and industry members are so eager to secure what they need that they agree to terms more favorable to suppliers.

- *Whether a few large suppliers are the primary sources of a particular item.* The leading suppliers may well have pricing leverage unless they are plagued with excess capacity and are scrambling to secure additional orders for their products. Companies find it harder to wring concessions from major suppliers with good reputations and strong demand than from struggling suppliers striving to broaden their customer base or more fully utilize their production capacity.

- *Whether it is difficult or costly for industry members to switch their purchases from one supplier to another or to switch to attractive substitute inputs.* High switching costs signal strong bargaining power on the part of suppliers, whereas low switching costs and ready availability of good substitute inputs signal weak bargaining power. Soft drink bottlers, for example, can counter the bargaining power of aluminum can suppliers by shifting or threatening to shift to greater use of plastic containers and introducing more attractive plastic container designs.

- *Whether certain needed inputs are in short supply.* Suppliers of items in short supply have some degree of pricing power, whereas a surge in the availability of particular items greatly weakens supplier pricing power and bargaining leverage.

- *Whether certain suppliers provide a differentiated input that enhances the performance or quality of the industry's product.* The more valuable that a particular input is in terms of enhancing the performance or quality of the products of industry members or of improving the efficiency of their production processes, the more bargaining leverage its suppliers are likely to possess.

- *Whether certain suppliers provide equipment or services that deliver valuable cost-saving efficiencies to industry members in operating their production processes.* Suppliers who provide cost-saving equipment or other valuable or necessary production-related services are likely to possess bargaining leverage. Industry members that do not source from such suppliers may find themselves at a cost disadvantage and thus under competitive pressure to do so (on terms that are favorable to the suppliers).

- *Whether suppliers provide an item that accounts for a sizable fraction of the costs of the industry's product.* The bigger the cost of a particular part or component, the more opportunity for the pattern of competition in the marketplace to be affected by the actions of suppliers to raise or lower their prices.

- *Whether industry members are major customers of suppliers.* As a rule, suppliers have less bargaining leverage when their sales to members of this one industry constitute a big percentage of their total sales. In such cases, the well-being of suppliers is closely tied to the well-being of their major customers. Suppliers then have a big incentive to protect and enhance their customers' competitiveness via reasonable prices, exceptional quality, and ongoing advances in the technology of the items supplied.

- *Whether it makes good economic sense for industry members to integrate backward and self-manufacture items they have been buying from suppliers.* The make-or-buy issue generally boils down to how purchased components compare to self-manufactured components in quality and price. For instance, boat manufacturers find it cheaper to source marine engines from outside manufacturers who specialize in engine manufacturing rather than make their own engines because the quantity of engines they need is too small to justify the investment in manufacturing facilities, master the production process, and capture scale economies. Specialists in marine engine manufacturing, by supplying engines to the entire boating industry, can obtain a big enough sales volume to fully realize scale economies, become proficient in all the manufacturing techniques, and keep costs low. As a rule, suppliers are safe from the threat of self-manufacture by their customers *until* the volume of parts a customer needs becomes large enough for the customer to justify backward integration into self-manufacture.

Figure 3.7 summarizes the conditions that tend to make supplier bargaining power strong or weak.

How Collaborative Partnerships Between Industry Members and Their Suppliers Can Create Competitive Pressures

In more and more industries, industry members are forging strategic partnerships with select suppliers in efforts to (1) reduce inventory and logistics costs (e.g., through just-in-time deliveries); (2) speed the availability of next-generation components; (3) enhance the quality of the parts and components being supplied and reduce defect rates; and (4) squeeze out important cost savings for both themselves and their suppliers. Numerous Internet technology applications are now available that permit real-time data sharing, eliminate paperwork, and produce cost savings all along the supply chain. The many benefits of effective seller–supplier collaboration can translate into competitive advantage for industry members who do the best job of managing supply chain relationships.

Dell Inc. has used strategic partnering with key suppliers as a major element in its strategy to be the world's lowest-cost supplier of branded PCs, servers, and workstations. Because Dell has managed its supply chain relationships in ways that contribute to a low-cost, high-quality competitive edge in components supply, it has put enormous pressure on its PC rivals to try to imitate its supply chain management practices. Effective partnerships with suppliers on the part of one or more industry members can thus become a major source of competitive pressure for rival firms.

The more opportunities that exist for win–win efforts between a company and its suppliers, the less their relationship is characterized by who has the upper hand in

Figure 3.7   Factors Affecting the Bargaining Power of Suppliers

Supplier bargaining power is stronger when:
- Industry members incur high costs in switching their purchases to alternative suppliers.
- Needed inputs are in short supply (which gives suppliers more leverage in setting prices).
- A supplier has a differentiated input that enhances the quality or performance of sellers' products or is a valuable or critical part of sellers' production process.
- There are only a few suppliers of a particular input.
- Some suppliers threaten to integrate forward into the business of industry members and perhaps become a powerful rival.

Supplier bargaining power is weaker when:
- The item being supplied is a commodity, that is, an item readily available from many suppliers at the going market price.
- Seller switching costs to alternative suppliers are low.
- Good substitute inputs exist or new ones emerge.
- There is a surge in the availability of supplies (thus greatly weakening supplier pricing power).
- Industry members account for a big fraction of suppliers' total sales and continued high volume purchases are important to the well-being of suppliers.
- Industry members are a threat to integrate backward into the business of suppliers and to self-manufacture their own requirements.
- Seller collaboration or partnering with selected suppliers provides attractive win–win opportunities.

bargaining with the other. Collaborative partnerships between a company and a supplier tend to last so long as the relationship is producing valuable benefits for both parties. Only if a supply partner is falling behind alternative suppliers is a company likely to switch suppliers and incur the costs and trouble of building close working ties with a different supplier.

Competitive Pressures Stemming from Buyer Bargaining Power and Seller–Buyer Collaboration

Whether seller–buyer relationships represent a weak or strong competitive force depends on (1) whether some or many buyers have sufficient bargaining leverage to obtain price concessions and other favorable terms and conditions of sale, and

(2) whether strategic partnerships between certain industry members and their customers produce competitive pressures that adversely affect other industry members.

How Buyer Bargaining Power Creates Competitive Pressures   As with suppliers, the leverage that certain types of buyers have in negotiating favorable terms can range from weak to strong. Individual consumers, for example, rarely have much bargaining power in negotiating price concessions or other favorable terms with sellers. The primary exceptions involve situations in which price haggling is customary, such as the purchase of new and used motor vehicles, homes, and big-ticket items like jewelry and pleasure boats. For most consumer goods and services, individual buyers have no bargaining leverage—their option is to pay the seller's posted price, delay their purchase until prices and terms improve, or take their business elsewhere.

In contrast, large retail chains like Wal-Mart, Best Buy, Staples, and Home Depot typically have considerable negotiating leverage in purchasing products from manufacturers since retailers usually stock just two or three competing brands of a product. In addition, the strong bargaining power of major supermarket chains like Kroger and Safeway allows them to demand promotional allowances and lump-sum payments (called slotting fees) from food products manufacturers in return for stocking certain brands or putting them in the best shelf locations. Motor vehicle manufacturers have strong bargaining power in negotiating to buy original equipment tires from Goodyear, Michelin, Bridgestone/Firestone, Continental, and Pirelli not only because they buy in large quantities but also because tire makers have judged original equipment tires to be important contributors to brand awareness and brand loyalty. "Prestige" buyers have a degree of clout in negotiating with sellers because a seller's reputation is enhanced by having prestige buyers on its customer list.

Even if buyers do not purchase in large quantities or offer a seller important market exposure or prestige, they gain a degree of bargaining leverage in the following circumstances:[11]

- *If buyers' costs of switching to competing brands or substitutes are relatively low*—Buyers who can readily switch between several sellers have more negotiating leverage than buyers who have high switching costs. When the products of rival sellers are virtually identical, it is relatively easy for buyers to switch from seller to seller at little or no cost. For example, the screws, rivets, steel, and capacitors used in the production of large home appliances like washers and dryers are nearly indistinguishable products available from many sellers. The potential for buyers to easily switch from one seller to another encourages sellers to make concessions to win or retain a buyer's business.

- *If the number of buyers is small or if a customer is particularly important to a seller*—The smaller the number of buyers of the part or component being supplied, the less easy it is for suppliers to find alternative sales opportunities when a customer is lost to a competitor. The prospect of losing a customer that is not easily replaced often makes a seller more willing to grant concessions of one kind or another. In the digital camera industry, for example, the sellers of lenses and other components have little bargaining power because there are a relatively small number of digital camera makers that need their components.

- *If demand for the item being supplied is weak*—Weak or declining demand for suppliers' products creates a buyer's market; conversely, strong or rapidly growing demand for suppliers' products creates a seller's market and shifts bargaining power to suppliers.

- *If buyers of the item being supplied are well informed about the purchase they are considering*—The more information buyers have about market conditions surrounding the item being supplied and about the products, prices, and costs of alternative suppliers, the better their bargaining position. The mushrooming availability of product information on the Internet is giving added bargaining power to individuals. Buyers can easily use the Internet to compare prices and features of vacation packages, shop for the best interest rates on mortgages and loans, and find the best prices on big-ticket items such as high-definition TVs. Bargain-hunting individuals can shop around for the best deal on the Internet and use that information to negotiate a better deal from local retailers; this method is becoming commonplace in buying new and used motor vehicles. Further, the Internet has created opportunities for manufacturers, wholesalers, retailers, and sometimes individuals to join online buying groups to pool their purchasing power and approach vendors for better terms than could be gotten individually. A multinational manufacturer's geographically scattered purchasing groups can use Internet technology to pool their orders with parts and components suppliers and bargain for volume discounts. Purchasing agents at some companies are banding together at third-party websites to pool corporate purchases to get better deals or special treatment.

- *If buyers pose a credible threat of integrating backward into the business of their suppliers*—Companies like Anheuser-Busch, Coors, and Heinz have integrated backward into metal can manufacturing to gain bargaining power in obtaining the balance of their can requirements from otherwise powerful metal can manufacturers. Retailers gain bargaining power by stocking and promoting their own private-label brands alongside manufacturers' name brands.

- *If buyers have discretion in whether and when they purchase the product*—Consumers who are unhappy with the present deals offered on discretionary items such as furniture, large appliances, and home electronics may choose to delay purchases until prices and financing terms improve. If college students believe that the prices of new textbooks are too high, they can purchase used copies. Business customers who are not happy with the prices or features of such discretionary items as new manufacturing equipment or computer software upgrades can opt to delay purchase until either terms improve or next-generation products become available.

Figure 3.8 highlights the factors causing buyer bargaining power to be strong or weak.

A final point to keep in mind is that *not all buyers of an industry's product have equal degrees of bargaining power,* and some may be less sensitive than others to price, quality, or service differences. For example, apparel manufacturers confront significant bargaining power when selling to big retailers like Macy's, T. J. Maxx, or Target; but those same manufacturers can command much better prices from small owner-managed apparel boutiques.

How Collaborative Partnerships Between Certain Industry Members and Their Key Customers Can Create Competitive Pressures Partnerships between sellers and buyers are an increasingly important element of the competitive picture in *business-to-business relationships* (as opposed to business-to-consumer relationships). Many sellers that provide items to business customers have found it in their mutual interest to collaborate closely with buyers on such matters as just-in-time deliveries, order processing, electronic invoice payments, and data sharing. Wal-Mart,

Figure 3.8 Factors Affecting the Bargaining Power of Buyers

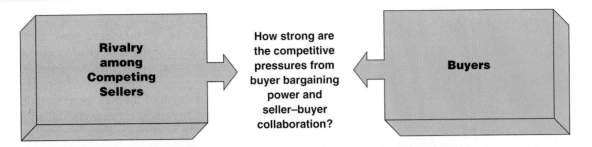

Buyer bargaining power is stronger when:
- Buyer switching costs to competing brands or substitute products are low.
- Buyers are large and can demand concessions when purchasing large quantities.
- Large volume purchases by buyers are important to sellers.
- Buyer demand is weak or declining.
- There are only a few buyers—so that each one's business is important to sellers.
- Identity of buyer adds prestige to the seller's list of customers.
- Quantity and quality of information available to buyers improves.
- Buyers have the ability to postpone purchases until later if they do not like the present deals being offered by sellers.
- Some buyers are a threat to integrate backward into the business of sellers and become important competitors.

Buyer bargaining power is weaker when:
- Buyers purchase the item infrequently or in small quantities.
- Buyer switching costs to competing brands are high.
- There is a surge in buyer demand that creates a seller's market.
- A seller's brand reputation is important to a buyer.
- A particular seller's product delivers quality or performance that is very important to buyer and that is not matched in other brands.
- Buyer collaboration or partnering with selected sellers provides attractive win–win opportunities.

for example, has entered into partnerships with manufacturers to keep merchandise in stock and to lower its inventory costs. Wal-Mart allows vendors like Procter & Gamble, Sara Lee, or Unilever to monitor store bar-code scanner data to determine when Wal-Mart's distribution centers need shipments and how big those shipments must be. In some instances, sellers ship inventory directly to each Wal-Mart store as merchandise is sold and shelves become depleted. Wal-Mart's transition from using bar codes to radio frequency identification (RFID) was welcomed by those of its suppliers who saw an opportunity to boost the sales of their products in Wal-Mart stores. RFID receivers in each Wal-Mart store or distribution center allowed suppliers to track RFID-tagged inventory by number and location. Procter & Gamble and other Wal-Mart suppliers could then connect to Wal-Mart's computer networks to watch the real-time inventory flow of the items they supplied to Wal-Mart and make just-in-time shipments to prevent inventory stockouts.

Is the Collective Strength of the Five Competitive Forces Conducive to Good Profitability?

Scrutinizing each of the five competitive forces one by one provides a powerful diagnosis of the state of competition in a given market. Once the strategist has gained an understanding of the specific competitive pressures comprising each force and determined whether these pressures constitute a strong, moderate, or weak competitive force, the next step is to evaluate the collective strength of the five forces and determine whether the state of competition is conducive to earning attractively high profits. Is the collective impact of the five competitive forces stronger than "normal"? Are some of the competitive forces sufficiently strong to undermine industry profitability? Can companies in this industry reasonably expect to earn decent profits in light of the prevailing competitive forces?

> **The stronger the forces of competition, the harder it becomes for industry members to earn attractive profits.**

Is the Industry Competitively Attractive or Unattractive?   *As a rule, the stronger the collective impact of the five competitive forces, the lower the combined profitability of industry participants.* The most extreme case of a "competitively unattractive" industry is when all five forces are producing strong competitive pressures: rivalry among sellers is vigorous, low entry barriers allow new rivals to gain a market foothold, competition from substitutes is intense, and both suppliers and customers are able to exercise considerable bargaining leverage. Fierce to strong competitive pressures coming from all five directions nearly always drive industry profitability to unacceptably low levels, frequently producing losses for many industry members and forcing some out of business. But an industry can be competitively unattractive without all five competitive forces being strong. Intense competitive pressures from just two or three of the five forces may suffice to destroy the conditions for good profitability. Unattractive competitive conditions that include strong substitutes, fierce competitive rivalry, and low buyer switching costs have created a dismal outlook for the movie rental business. In 2007, Blockbuster recorded a net loss of $85 million on revenues of $5.5 billion, while the industry runner-up, Movie Gallery, filed bankruptcy in October 2007 after recording losses for three consecutive years. Movie Gallery lost an additional $70 million by the end of 2007, and its shares were delisted by the NASDAQ in 2008.

In contrast, when the collective impact of the five competitive forces is moderate to weak, an industry is competitively attractive in the sense that industry members can reasonably expect to earn good profits and a nice return on investment. The ideal competitive environment for earning superior profits is one in which both suppliers and customers are in weak bargaining positions, there are no good substitutes, high barriers block further entry, and rivalry among present sellers generates only moderate competitive pressures. Weak competition is the best of all possible worlds for also-ran companies because even they can usually eke out a decent profit—if a company can't earn adequate profits when competition is weak, then its business outlook is indeed grim.

In most industries, the collective strength of the five competitive forces is somewhere near the middle of the two extremes of very intense and very weak, typically ranging from slightly stronger than normal to slightly weaker than normal, and typically allowing well-managed companies with sound strategies to earn attractive profits.

Matching Company Strategy to Competitive Conditions   Working
through the five-forces model step by step not only aids strategy makers in assessing whether the intensity of competition allows good profitability but also promotes

sound strategic thinking about how to better match company strategy to the specific competitive character of the marketplace. Effectively matching a company's strategy to prevailing competitive conditions has two aspects:

1. Pursuing avenues that shield the firm from as many of the different competitive pressures as possible.
2. Initiating actions calculated to shift competition in the company's favor, put added competitive pressure on rivals, and perhaps even define the business model for the industry.

> A company's strategy is increasingly effective the more it provides some insulation from competitive pressures and shifts the competitive battle in the company's favor.

But making headway on these two fronts first requires identifying competitive pressures, gauging the relative strength of each of the five competitive forces, and gaining a deep enough understanding of the state of competition in the industry to know which strategy buttons to push.

QUESTION 3: WHAT FORCES ARE DRIVING INDUSTRY CHANGE AND WHAT IMPACTS WILL THEY HAVE?

While it is critical to understand the nature and intensity of competitive forces in an industry, it is just as important to understand that general industry conditions and an industry's overall outlook are fluid and subject to change. All industries are affected by new developments and ongoing trends that gradually or speedily produce new industry conditions important enough to require a strategic response from participating firms. The popular hypothesis that industries go through a life cycle of takeoff, rapid growth, early maturity and slowing growth, market saturation, and eventual stagnation or decline helps explain industry change—but there are more causes of industry change than an industry's normal progression through the life cycle.[12] Just what are the other drivers of industry change? Might they be even stronger drivers of change than progression through the life cycle? And don't strategy makers need to be alert to all the drivers of industry change, as well as to their likely impacts on industry and competitive conditions, in order to craft company strategies that will fit future industry circumstances?

The Concept of Driving Forces

The important thing to understand about industry change is that it occurs because agents of change are working to entice or pressure certain industry participants (competitors, customers, suppliers) to alter their actions in important ways.[13] The most powerful of the change agents are called **driving forces** because they have the biggest influences in reshaping the industry landscape and altering competitive conditions. Some driving forces originate in the outer ring of the company's macroenvironment (see Figure 3.2), but most originate in the company's more immediate industry and competitive environment.

Driving-forces analysis has three steps: (1) identifying what the driving forces are; (2) assessing whether the drivers of change are, on the whole, acting to make the industry more or less attractive; and (3) determining what strategy changes are needed to prepare for the impacts of the driving forces. All three steps merit further discussion.

> **CORE CONCEPT**
> Industry conditions change because important forces are *driving* industry participants (competitors, customers, or suppliers) to alter their actions; the *driving forces* in an industry are the *major underlying causes* of changing industry and competitive conditions—they have the biggest influence on how the industry landscape will be altered.

Identifying an Industry's Driving Forces

Many developments can affect an industry powerfully enough to qualify as driving forces. Some drivers of change are unique, but most fall into one of the following categories (these 14 driving forces are summarized in Table 3.2):[14]

- *Changes in an industry's long-term growth rate*—Shifts in industry growth up or down are a driving force for industry change, affecting the balance between industry supply and buyer demand, entry and exit, and the character and strength of competition. An upsurge in buyer demand triggers a race among established firms and newcomers to capture the new sales opportunities; ambitious companies with trailing market shares may see the upturn in demand as a golden opportunity to launch offensive strategies to broaden their customer base and move up several notches in the industry standings. A slowdown in the rate at which buyer demand is growing nearly always intensifies rivalry because growth-oriented companies may try to launch aggressive initiatives to take sales and market share away from rivals. If industry sales suddenly turn flat or begin to shrink after years of rising at double-digit levels, competition is certain to intensify. Stagnating sales usually prompt both competitively weak and growth-oriented companies to sell their business operations to those industry members who elect to stick it out; as demand for the industry's product continues to shrink, the remaining industry members may be forced to close inefficient plants and retrench to a smaller production base. Thus, either a higher or lower rate of industry growth acts to produce new industry conditions, transform the competitive landscape, and trigger strategy changes on the part of some industry members.

- *Increasing globalization*—Competition begins to shift from primarily a regional or national focus to an international or global focus when industry members begin

Table 3.2 The Most Common Driving Forces

1. Changes in the long-term industry growth rate
2. Increasing globalization
3. Emerging new Internet capabilities and applications
4. Changes in who buys the product and how they use it
5. Product innovation
6. Technological change and manufacturing process innovation
7. Marketing innovation
8. Entry or exit of major firms
9. Diffusion of technical know-how across more companies and more countries
10. Changes in cost and efficiency
11. Growing buyer preferences for differentiated products instead of standardized commodity product (or for a more standardized product instead of strongly differentiated products)
12. Reductions in uncertainty and business risk
13. Regulatory influences and government policy changes
14. Changing societal concerns, attitudes, and lifestyles

seeking out customers in foreign markets or when production activities begin to migrate to countries where costs are lowest. Globalization of competition really starts to take hold when one or more ambitious companies precipitate a race for worldwide market leadership. Globalization can also be precipitated by the blossoming of consumer demand in more and more countries and by the actions of government officials to reduce trade barriers or open up once-closed markets to foreign competitors, as is occurring in many parts of Europe, Latin America, and Asia. Significant differences in labor costs among countries give manufacturers a strong incentive to locate plants for labor-intensive products in low-wage countries and use these plants to supply market demand across the world. Wages in China, India, Vietnam, Mexico, and Brazil, for example, are about one-fourth those in the United States, Germany, and Japan. The forces of globalization are sometimes such a strong driver that companies find it highly advantageous, if not necessary, to spread their operating reach into more and more country markets. Globalization is very much a driver of industry change in such industries as credit cards, cell phones, digital cameras, golf and ski equipment, motor vehicles, steel, petroleum, personal computers, video games, public accounting, and textbook publishing.

- *Emerging new Internet capabilities and applications*—Since the late 1990s, the Internet has woven its way not only into everyday business operations but also into the social fabric of life all across the world. Growing acceptance of Internet shopping and file sharing, the emergence of high-speed connections and Voice over Internet Protocol (VoIP) technology, and an ever-growing series of Internet applications have been major drivers of change in industry after industry. Mounting consumer preferences for buying or sharing music files have profoundly reshaped the music industry and affected traditional brick-and-mortar music retailers. Widespread use of e-mail has forever eroded the revenues of fax services and governmental postal services worldwide. Online course offerings at universities are beginning to revolutionize higher education. Companies are increasingly using online technology to (1) collaborate closely with suppliers and streamline their supply chains and (2) revamp internal operations and squeeze out cost savings. The ability of companies to reach consumers via the Internet increases the number of rivals a company faces and often escalates rivalry by pitting pure online sellers against combination brick-and-click sellers against pure brick-and-mortar sellers. The Internet of the future will feature faster speeds, dazzling applications, and over a billion connected gadgets performing an array of functions, thus driving further industry and competitive changes. But Internet-related impacts vary from industry to industry. The challenges here are to assess precisely how emerging Internet developments are altering a particular industry's landscape and to factor these impacts into the strategy-making equation.

- *Changes in who buys the product and how they use it*—Shifts in buyer demographics and the ways products are used can alter competition by affecting how customers perceive value, how customers make purchasing decisions, and where customers purchase the product. Apple's iPod and other brands of MP3 players have transformed how music is bought and played; album sales in the United States, for example, declined from 785.1 million units in 2000 to 500.5 million units in 2007, whereas there were an estimated 840 million downloads of single digital recordings in 2007. The explosion of features and functions being incorporated into cell phones and their enormous popularity with cell phone users is causing all kinds of waves in telecommunications, video games, and digital photography. Longer life expectancies and growing percentages of relatively well-to-do retirees are driving big changes in buyer demographics in such industries as health care, prescription drugs, recreational living, and vacation travel.

- *Product innovation*—Industry conditions and the competitive landscape are always affected by rivals racing to be first to introduce one new product or product enhancement after another. An ongoing stream of product innovations tends to alter the pattern of competition in an industry by attracting more first-time buyers, rejuvenating industry growth, and/or creating wider or narrower product differentiation. Successful product introductions strengthen the market positions of the innovating companies, usually at the expense of companies that stick with their old products or that are slow to follow with their own versions of the new product. Product innovation has been a key driving force in such industries as cell phones, big-screen televisions, digital cameras, golf clubs, video games, toys, and prescription drugs.

- *Technological change and manufacturing process innovation*—Advances in technology can dramatically alter an industry's landscape, making it possible to produce new and better products at lower cost and opening up whole new industry frontiers. For instance, Voice over Internet Protocol (VoIP) has spawned low-cost, Internet-based phone networks that have begun competing with traditional telephone companies worldwide (whose higher-cost technology depends on hard-wire connections via overhead and underground telephone lines). LCD and plasma screen technology and high-definition technology are transforming the television industry. Satellite radio technology has made it possible for satellite radio companies with their largely commercial-free programming to draw millions of listeners away from traditional radio stations whose revenue streams from commercials are dependent on audience size. Technological developments can also produce competitively significant changes in capital requirements, minimum efficient plant sizes, distribution channels and logistics, and experience/learning curve effects. In the steel industry, ongoing advances in electric arc minimill technology (which involve recycling scrap steel to make new products) have allowed steelmakers with state-of-the-art minimills to gradually expand into the production of more and more steel products and steadily take sales and market share from higher-cost integrated producers (which make steel from scratch using iron ore, coke, and traditional blast furnace technology). Nucor Corporation, the leader of the minimill technology revolution in the United States, began operations in 1970 and has ridden the wave of technological advances in minimill technology to become the biggest U.S. steel producer, with 2007 revenues of nearly $16.6 billion. In a space of 30 years, advances in minimill technology have changed the face of the steel industry worldwide.

- *Marketing innovation*—When firms are successful in introducing *new ways* to market their products, they can spark a burst of buyer interest, widen industry demand, increase product differentiation, and lower unit costs—any or all of which can alter the competitive positions of rival firms and force strategy revisions.

- *Entry or exit of major firms*—The entry of one or more foreign companies into a geographic market once dominated by domestic firms nearly always shakes up competitive conditions. Likewise, when an established domestic firm from another industry attempts entry either by acquiring other companies or by launching its own start-up venture, it usually applies its skills and resources in some innovative fashion that pushes competition in new directions. Entry by a major firm thus often produces a new ball game, not only with new key players but also with new rules for competing. Similarly, the exit of a major firm changes the competitive structure by reducing the number of market leaders (perhaps increasing the dominance of the leaders who remain) and causing a rush to capture the exiting firm's customers.

- *Diffusion of technical know-how across more companies and more countries*—As knowledge about how to perform a particular activity or execute a particular manufacturing technology spreads, the competitive advantage held by firms originally possessing this know-how erodes. Knowledge diffusion can occur through scientific journals, trade publications, on-site plant tours, word of mouth among suppliers and customers, employee migration, and Internet sources. In recent years, rapid technology transfer across national boundaries has been a prime factor in causing industries to become more globally competitive.

- *Changes in cost and efficiency*—Widening or shrinking differences in the costs among key competitors tend to dramatically alter the state of competition. Advances in fluorescent lightbulb technology and light-emitting diode (LED) technology have enabled manufacturers to produce energy-efficient fluorescent-based spiral lightbulbs and LED lighting products that last several times longer than traditional incandescent bulbs. While the prices of compact fluorescent and LED bulbs are several times greater than incandescent bulbs, they are proving to be far cheaper to use because of their longer lives (as much as eight years between replacements) and the considerable energy savings (as much as $50 over the life of the bulb). As a consequence, sales of incandescent bulbs were on the decline while sales of compact fluorescent and LED bulbs were growing rapidly. When sharply rising prices for crude oil in 2007–2008 caused big jumps in gasoline prices, automakers scrambled to boost the fuel efficiency of their car and truck models—sales of fuel-efficient vehicles like Toyota's popular hybrid Prius rose while sales of gas-guzzling SUVs fell off dramatically. Declining costs to produce PCs have enabled price cuts and spurred PC sales (especially lower-priced models) by making them more affordable to low-income households worldwide.

- *Growing buyer preferences for differentiated products instead of a commodity product (or for a more standardized product instead of strongly differentiated products)*—When buyer tastes and preferences start to diverge, sellers can win a loyal following with product offerings that stand apart from those of rival sellers. In recent years, beer drinkers have grown less loyal to a single brand and have begun to drink a variety of domestic and foreign beers; as a consequence, beer manufacturers have introduced a host of new brands. Buyer preferences for motor vehicles are becoming increasingly diverse, with few models generating sales of more than 250,000 units annually. When a shift from standardized to differentiated products occurs, the driver of change is the contest among rivals to cleverly outdifferentiate one another.

  However, buyers sometimes decide that a standardized, budget-priced product suits their requirements as well as or better than a premium-priced product with lots of snappy features and personalized services. Pronounced shifts toward greater product standardization usually spawn lively price competition and force rival sellers to drive down their costs to maintain profitability. The lesson here is that competition is driven partly by whether the market forces in motion are acting to increase or decrease product differentiation.

- *Reductions in uncertainty and business risk*—Emerging industries are typically characterized by uncertainty over such issues as potential market size, how much time and money will be needed to surmount technological problems, and what distribution channels and buyer segments to emphasize. Emerging industries tend to attract only risk-taking entrepreneurial companies. Over time, however, if the business model of industry pioneers proves profitable and market demand for the product appears durable, more conservative firms are usually enticed to enter the market. Often, these later entrants are large, financially strong firms looking to invest in attractive growth industries.

Lower business risks and less industry uncertainty also affect competition in international markets. In the early stages of a company's entry into foreign markets, conservatism prevails—firms limit their downside exposure by using less risky strategies like exporting, licensing, joint marketing agreements, or joint ventures with local companies to accomplish entry. Then, as experience accumulates and perceived risk levels decline, companies move more boldly and more independently, making acquisitions, constructing their own plants, putting in their own sales and marketing capabilities to build strong competitive positions in each country market, and beginning to link the strategies in each country to create a more globalized strategy.

- *Regulatory influences and government policy changes*—Governments can drive competitive changes by opening their domestic markets to foreign participation or closing them to protect domestic companies. (Note that this driving force is spawned by forces in a company's macroenvironment.) Government incentives to attract companies to locate plants in their communities can impact competitive conditions. Several southern U.S. states created lucrative incentive packages that induced a number of foreign automakers to build new multibillion-dollar plants employing thousands of workers in their states; these plants, which mostly have nonunion workforces, now provide formidable competition for the unionized plants operated by Ford, General Motors, and Chrysler. In contrast, the National Do Not Call Registry, established in 2003, made it difficult for telemarketers to generate new customers. For example, Scholastic Inc., the world's largest publisher and distributor of children's books (including the Harry Potter and Baby-Sitters Club series), had for years relied on telemarketing to sign up new book club members; when its telemarketing campaigns were hampered by the restrictions imposed by the federal Do Not Call legislation, Scholastic turned to Internet-based marketing approaches to generate new customers. But when the Internet campaigns failed to keep Scholastic's book club subscriber base from eroding and resulted in direct-to-home operating losses of nearly $3 million in 2005, $13 million in 2006, and more than $29 million in 2007, Scholastic management concluded in 2008 that the marketplace changes brought about by the Do Not Call legislation had irreparably harmed the book club industry and made it wise to divest its book club business.

- *Changing societal concerns, attitudes, and lifestyles*—Emerging social issues and changing attitudes and lifestyles can be powerful instigators of industry change. (As with the preceding driving force, this driving force springs from factors at work in a company's macroenvironment.) Growing antismoking sentiment has emerged as a major driver of change in the tobacco industry. Concerns about high gasoline prices are causing lifestyle changes in both vehicle purchases and driving habits. Consumer concerns about salt, sugar, chemical additives, saturated fat, cholesterol, carbohydrates, and nutritional value have forced food producers to revamp food-processing techniques, redirect R&D efforts, and compete in developing nutritious, good-tasting products. Safety concerns have driven product design changes in the automobile, toy, and outdoor power equipment industries, to mention a few. Increased interest in physical fitness has spawned new industries in exercise equipment, biking, outdoor apparel, sports gyms and recreation centers, vitamin and nutrition supplements, and medically supervised diet programs. Social concerns about air and water pollution have forced industries to incorporate expenditures for controlling pollution into their cost structures. Shifting societal concerns, attitudes, and lifestyles alter the pattern of competition, usually favoring those players that respond quickly and creatively with products targeted to the new trends and conditions.

The large number of different *potential driving forces* explains why it is too simplistic to view industry change only in terms of moving through the different stages in an industry's life cycle and why a full understanding of all types of change drivers is a fundamental part of industry analysis. However, while many forces of change may be at work in a given industry, no more than three or four are likely to be true driving forces powerful enough to qualify as the *major determinants* of why and how the industry is changing. Thus, company strategists must resist the temptation to label every change they see as a driving force; the analytical task is to evaluate the forces of industry and competitive change carefully enough to separate major factors from minor ones.

Assessing the Impact of the Driving Forces

Just identifying the driving forces is not sufficient, however. The second, and more important, step in driving-forces analysis is to determine whether the prevailing driving forces are, on the whole, acting to make the industry environment more or less attractive. Answers to three questions are needed here:

1. Are the driving forces collectively acting to cause demand for the industry's product to increase or decrease?
2. Are the driving forces acting to make competition more or less intense?
3. Will the combined impacts of the driving forces lead to higher or lower industry profitability?

Getting a handle on the collective impact of the driving forces usually requires looking at the likely effects of each force separately, since the driving forces may not all be pushing change in the same direction. For example, two driving forces may be acting to spur demand for the industry's product while one driving force may be working to curtail demand. Whether the net effect on industry demand is up or down hinges on which driving forces are the more powerful. The analyst's objective here is to get a good grip on what external factors are shaping industry change and what difference these factors will make.

> An important part of driving forces analysis is to determine whether the collective impact of the driving forces will be to increase or decrease market demand, make competition more or less intense, and lead to higher or lower industry profitability.

Making Strategy Adjustments to Take the Impact of the Driving Forces into Account

The third step of driving-forces analysis—where the real payoff for strategy-making comes—is for managers to draw some conclusions about what strategy adjustments will be needed to deal with the impacts of the driving

> Driving forces analysis, when done properly, pushes company managers to think about what's around the corner and what the company needs to be doing to get ready for it.

> The real payoff of driving forces analysis is to help managers understand what strategy changes are needed to prepare for the impacts of the driving forces.

forces. The real value of doing driving forces analysis is to gain better understanding of what strategy adjustments will be needed to cope with the drivers of industry change and the impacts they are likely to have on market demand, competitive intensity, and industry profitability. In short, the strategy-making challenge that flows from driving-forces analysis is what to do to prepare for the industry and competitive changes being wrought by the driving forces. Indeed, without understanding the forces driving industry change and the impacts these forces will have on the character of the industry environment and on the company's business over the next one to three years, managers are ill-prepared to craft a strategy tightly matched to emerging conditions. So driving-forces analysis is not something to take lightly; it has practical value and is basic to the task of thinking strategically about where the industry is headed and how to prepare for the anticipated changes.

QUESTION 4: WHAT MARKET POSITIONS DO RIVALS OCCUPY—WHO IS STRONGLY POSITIONED AND WHO IS NOT?

CORE CONCEPT

Strategic group mapping is a technique for displaying the different market or competitive positions that rival firms occupy in the industry.

Since competing companies commonly sell in different price/quality ranges, emphasize different distribution channels, incorporate product features that appeal to different types of buyers, have different geographic coverage, and so on, it stands to reason that some companies enjoy stronger or more attractive market positions than other companies. Understanding which companies are strongly positioned and which are weakly positioned is an integral part of analyzing an industry's competitive structure. The best technique for revealing the market positions of industry competitors is **strategic group mapping**.[15] This analytical tool is useful for comparing the market positions of each firm separately or for grouping them into like positions when an industry has so many competitors that it is not practical to examine each one in depth.

Using Strategic Group Maps to Assess the Market Positions of Key Competitors

CORE CONCEPT

A *strategic group* is a cluster of industry rivals that have similar competitive approaches and market positions.

A **strategic group** consists of those industry members with similar competitive approaches and positions in the market.[16] Companies in the same strategic group can resemble one another in any of several ways: they may have comparable product-line breadth, sell in the same price/quality range, emphasize the same distribution channels, use essentially the same product attributes to appeal to similar types of buyers, depend on identical technological approaches, or offer buyers similar services and technical assistance.[17] An industry contains only one strategic group when all sellers pursue essentially identical strategies and have comparable market positions. At the other extreme, an industry may contain as many strategic groups as there are competitors when each rival pursues a distinctively different competitive approach and occupies a substantially different market position.

The procedure for constructing a *strategic group map* is straightforward:

- Identify the competitive characteristics that differentiate firms in the industry; typical variables are price/quality range (high, medium, low); geographic coverage (local, regional, national, global); degree of vertical integration (none, partial, full); product-line breadth (wide, narrow); use of distribution channels (one, some, all); and degree of service offered (no-frills, limited, full).
- Plot the firms on a two-variable map using pairs of these differentiating characteristics.
- Assign firms that fall in about the same strategy space to the same strategic group.
- Draw circles around each strategic group, making the circles proportional to the size of the group's share of total industry sales revenues.

This produces a two-dimensional diagram like the one for the world automobile industry in Illustration Capsule 3.1.

Several guidelines need to be observed in mapping the positions of strategic groups in the industry's overall strategy space.[18] First, the two variables selected as axes for the map should *not* be highly correlated; if they are, the circles on the map will fall along a diagonal and strategy makers will learn nothing more about the relative positions of competitors than they would by considering just one of the variables. For instance, if companies with broad product lines use multiple distribution channels while companies with narrow lines use a single distribution channel, then looking at broad versus narrow product lines reveals just as much about who is positioned where as looking at single versus multiple distribution channels; that is, one of the variables is redundant. Second, the variables chosen as axes for the map should expose big differences in how rivals position themselves to compete in the marketplace. This, of course, means analysts must identify the characteristics that differentiate rival firms and use these differences as variables for the axes and as the basis for deciding which firm belongs in which strategic group. Third, the variables used as axes don't have to be either quantitative or continuous; rather, they can be discrete variables or defined in terms of distinct classes and combinations. Fourth, drawing the sizes of the circles on the map proportional to the combined sales of the firms in each strategic group allows the map to reflect the relative sizes of each strategic group. Fifth, if more than two good competitive variables can be used as axes for the map, several maps can be drawn to give different exposures to the competitive positioning relationships present in the industry's structure. Because there is not necessarily one best map for portraying how competing firms are positioned in the market, it is advisable to experiment with different pairs of competitive variables.

What Can Be Learned from Strategic Group Maps?

Strategic group maps are revealing in several respects. The most important has to do with which rivals are similarly positioned and are thus close rivals and which are distant rivals. Generally speaking, *the closer strategic groups are to each other on the map, the stronger the cross-group competitive rivalry tends to be.* Although firms in the same strategic group are the closest rivals, the next closest rivals are in the immediately adjacent groups.[19] Often, firms in strategic groups that are far apart on the map hardly compete at all. For instance, BMW's car lineup, customer base, and pricing points are much too different from those of Mazda, Suzuki, and Ford to justify calling them close competitors of

Strategic group maps reveal which companies are close competitors and which are distant competitors.

ILLUSTRATION CAPSULE 3.1
Comparative Market Positions of Selected Automobile Manufacturers: A Strategic Group Map Application

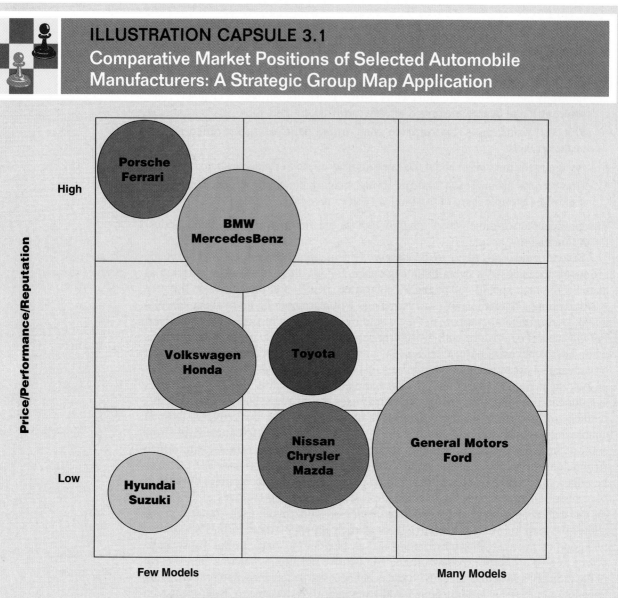

Model Variety (compact, full-size, SUVs, trucks)

Note: Circles are drawn roughly proportional to the total revenues of manufacturers included in each strategic group.

BMW. For the same reason, Timex is not a meaningful competitive rival of Rolex, and Holiday Inn Express is not a close competitor of such luxury hotel chains as Ritz-Carlton and Four Seasons.

The second thing to be gleaned from strategic group mapping is that *not all positions on the map are equally attractive.* Two reasons account for why some positions can be more attractive than others:

1. *Prevailing competitive pressures and industry driving forces favor some strategic groups and hurt others.*[20] Discerning which strategic groups are advantaged and disadvantaged requires scrutinizing the map in light of what has also been learned

from the prior analysis of competitive forces and driving forces. Quite often the strength of competition varies from group to group—there's little reason to believe that all firms in an industry feel the same types or degrees of competitive pressure, since their strategies and market positions may well differ in important respects. For instance, the battle among Ford, Nissan, Hyundai, Toyota, and Honda for customers looking for low-cost, fuel-efficient vehicles is of a different character than the competition among Mercedes, BMW, and Porsche whose models appeal to upper-income buyers more interested in vehicle styling, performance, and brand image cachet. Likewise, the competitive battle between Wal-Mart and Target is more fierce than the rivalry among the flagship stores of couture brands such as Gucci, Chanel, Fendi, Louis Vuitton, Prada, and Versace. Furthermore, industry driving forces may be acting to grow the demand for the products of firms in some strategic groups and shrink the demand for the products of firms in other strategic groups—as is the case in the news industry, where Internet news services and cable news networks are gaining ground at the expense of newspapers and network television. The industry driving forces of emerging Internet capabilities and applications; changes in who buys the product and how they use it; and changing societal concerns, attitudes, and lifestyles are making it increasingly difficult for traditional media to increase audiences and attract new advertisers.

Firms in strategic groups that are being adversely impacted by intense competitive pressures or driving forces may try to shift to a more favorably situated group. But shifting to a different position on the map can prove difficult when entry barriers for the target strategic group are high. Moreover, attempts to enter a new strategic group nearly always increase competitive pressures in the target strategic group. If certain firms are known to be trying to change their competitive positions on the map, then attaching arrows to the circles showing the targeted direction helps clarify the picture of competitive maneuvering among rivals.

2. *The profit potential of different strategic groups varies due to the strengths and weaknesses in each group's market position.* The profit prospects of firms in different strategic groups can vary from good to ho-hum to poor because of differing growth rates for the principal buyer segments served by each group, differing degrees of competitive rivalry within strategic groups, differing degrees of exposure to competition from substitute products outside the industry, and differing degrees of supplier or customer bargaining power from group to group.

Thus, part of strategic group map analysis always entails drawing conclusions about where on the map is the "best" place to be and why. Which companies/strategic groups are destined to prosper because of their positions? Which companies/strategic groups seem destined to struggle because of their positions? And equally important, how might firms in poorly positioned strategic groups reposition themselves to improve their prospects for good financial performance?

QUESTION 5: WHAT STRATEGIC MOVES ARE RIVALS LIKELY TO MAKE NEXT?

Unless a company pays attention to what competitors are doing and knows their strengths and weaknesses, it ends up flying blind into competitive battle. As in sports, scouting the opposition is essential. *Competitive intelligence* about rivals' strategies, their latest actions and announcements, their resource strengths and weaknesses, the efforts being made to improve their situation, and the thinking and leadership styles of their executives is valuable for predicting or anticipating the strategic moves competitors are likely to make next. Good information allows a company to prepare defensive countermoves, to craft its own strategic moves with some confidence about what market maneuvers to expect from rivals, and to exploit any openings that arise from competitors' missteps or strategy flaws.

> Good scouting reports on rivals provide a valuable assist in anticipating what moves rivals are likely to make next and outmaneuvering them in the marketplace.

Identifying Competitors' Strategies and Resource Strengths and Weaknesses

Keeping close tabs on a competitor's strategy entails monitoring what the rival is doing in the marketplace and what its management is saying in company press releases, Web postings (especially the presentations management has recently made to securities analysts), and such public documents as annual reports and 10-K filings. (Figure 1.1 in Chapter 1 indicates what to look for in identifying a company's strategy.) Company personnel may be able to pick up useful information from a rival's exhibits at trade shows and from conversations with a rival's customers, suppliers, and former employees.[21] Many companies have a competitive intelligence unit that sifts through the available information to construct up-to-date strategic profiles of rivals—their current strategies, resource strengths and competitive capabilities, and competitive shortcomings. Such profiles are typically updated regularly and made available to managers and other key personnel.

Those who gather competitive intelligence on rivals, however, can sometimes cross the fine line between honest inquiry and unethical or even illegal behavior. For example, calling rivals to get information about prices, the dates of new product introductions, or wage and salary levels is legal, but misrepresenting one's company affiliation during such calls is unethical. Pumping rivals' representatives at trade shows is ethical only if one wears a name tag with accurate company affiliation indicated. Avon Products at one point secured information about its biggest rival, Mary Kay Cosmetics (MKC), by having its personnel search through the garbage bins outside MKC's headquarters.[22] When MKC officials learned of the action and sued, Avon claimed it did nothing illegal, since a 1988 Supreme Court case had ruled that trash left on public property (in this case, a sidewalk) was anyone's for the taking. Avon even produced a videotape of its removal of the trash at the MKC site. Avon won the lawsuit—but Avon's action, while legal, scarcely qualifies as ethical.

In sizing up competitors, it makes sense for company strategists to make three assessments:

1. Which competitor has the best strategy? Which competitors appear to have flawed or weak strategies?

2. Which competitors are poised to gain market share, and which ones seem destined to lose ground?

3. Which competitors are likely to rank among the industry leaders five years from now? Do one or more up-and-coming competitors have powerful strategies and sufficient resource capabilities to overtake the current industry leader?

The industry's *current* major players are generally easy to identify, but today's market leaders don't automatically become tomorrow's. Some of the industry's largest firms may be plagued with weaknesses that are causing them to lose ground, while the superior strategies and capabilities of up-and-coming companies may likely soon place them in the position of industry leader. In evaluating which competitors are favorably or unfavorably positioned to gain market ground, company strategists need to focus on why there is potential for some rivals to do better or worse than other rivals. Usually, a competitor's prospects are a function of whether it is in a strategic group that is being favored or hurt by competitive pressures and driving forces, whether its strategy has resulted in competitive advantage or disadvantage, and whether its resources and capabilities are well suited for competing on the road ahead.

Predicting Rivals' Next Moves

Predicting the next strategic moves of competitors is the hardest yet most useful part of competitor analysis. Good clues about what actions a specific company is likely to undertake can often be gleaned from how well it is faring in the marketplace, the problems or weaknesses it needs to address, and how much pressure it is under to improve its financial performance. Content rivals are likely to continue their present strategy with only minor fine-tuning. Ailing rivals can be performing so poorly that fresh strategic moves are virtually certain. Ambitious rivals looking to move up in the industry ranks are strong candidates for launching new strategic offensives to pursue emerging market opportunities and exploit the vulnerabilities of weaker rivals.

Since the moves a competitor is likely to make are generally predicated on the views their executives have about the industry's future and their beliefs about their firm's situation, it makes sense to closely scrutinize not only company executives' past actions and leadership styles but also their public pronouncements about where the industry is headed, what it will take to be successful, and what their firm's situation is. Information from the grapevine about what rivals are doing can also be analyzed. Other considerations in trying to predict what strategic moves rivals are likely to make next include the following:

> Managers who fail to study competitors closely risk being caught napping when rivals make fresh and perhaps bold strategic moves.

- Which rivals badly need to increase their unit sales and market share? What strategic options are they most likely to pursue: lowering prices, adding new models and styles, expanding their dealer networks, entering additional geographic markets, boosting advertising to build better brand-name awareness, acquiring a weaker competitor, or placing more emphasis on direct sales via their Web site?
- Which rivals have a strong incentive, along with the resources, to make major strategic changes, perhaps moving to a different position on the strategic group map? Which rivals are probably locked in to pursuing the same basic strategy with only minor adjustments?
- Which rivals are good candidates to be acquired? Which rivals may be looking to make an acquisition and are financially able to do so?
- Which rivals are likely to enter new geographic markets?
- Which rivals are strong candidates to expand their product offerings and enter new product segments where they do not currently have a presence?

To succeed in predicting a competitor's next moves, company strategists need to have a good feel for each rival's situation, how its managers think, and what the rival's best strategic options are. Doing the necessary detective work can be tedious and time-consuming, but scouting competitors well enough to anticipate their next moves allows managers to prepare effective countermoves (perhaps even beat a rival to the punch) and to take rivals' probable actions into account in crafting their own best course of action.

QUESTION 6: WHAT ARE THE KEY FACTORS FOR FUTURE COMPETITIVE SUCCESS?

CORE CONCEPT

Key success factors are the product attributes, competencies, competitive capabilities, and market achievements with the greatest impact on future competitive success in the marketplace.

An industry's **key success factors (KSFs)** are those competitive factors that most affect industry members' ability to prosper in the marketplace—the particular strategy elements, product attributes, resources, competencies, competitive capabilities, and market achievements that spell the difference between being a strong competitor and a weak competitor—and sometimes between profit and loss. KSFs by their very nature are so important to future competitive success that *all firms* in the industry must pay close attention to them or risk becoming an industry also-ran. To indicate the significance of KSFs another way, how well a company's product offering, resources, and capabilities measure up against an industry's KSFs determines just how financially and competitively successful that company will be. Identifying KSFs, in light of the prevailing and anticipated industry and competitive conditions, is therefore always a top priority analytical and strategy-making consideration. Company strategists need to understand the industry landscape well enough to separate the factors most important to competitive success from those that are less important.

In the bottled water industry, the KSFs are access to distribution (to get the company's brand stocked and favorably displayed in retail outlets where bottled water is sold), image (the product's name and the attractiveness of its packaging are deciding factors in choosing a brand for many consumers), low-cost production capabilities, and sufficient sales volume to achieve scale economies in marketing expenditures. In the ready-to-wear apparel industry, the KSFs are appealing designs and color combinations, low-cost manufacturing, a strong network of retailers or company-owned stores, distribution capabilities that allow stores to keep the best-selling items in stock, and advertisements that effectively convey the brand's image. These attributes and capabilities apply to all brands of apparel ranging from private-label brands sold by discounters to premium-priced ready-to-wear brands sold by upscale department stores. Key success factors thus vary from industry to industry, and even from time to time within the same industry, as driving forces and competitive conditions change. Table 3.3 lists the most common types of industry key success factors.

An industry's key success factors can usually be deduced through identifying the industry's dominant economic characteristics, assessing what competition is like, considering the impacts of the driving forces, comparing the market positions of industry

Table 3.3   Common Types of Industry Key Success Factors (KSFs)

Technology-related KSFs	• Expertise in a particular technology or in scientific research (important in pharmaceuticals, Internet applications, mobile communications, and most other high-tech industries) • Proven ability to improve production processes (important in industries where advancing technology opens the way for higher manufacturing efficiency and lower production costs)
Manufacturing-related KSFs	• Ability to achieve scale economies and/or capture experience curve effects (important to achieving low production costs) • Quality control know-how (important in industries where customers insist on product reliability) • High utilization of fixed assets (important in capital-intensive/high-fixed-cost industries) • Access to attractive supplies of skilled labor • High labor productivity (important for items with high labor content) • Low-cost product design and engineering (reduces manufacturing costs) • Ability to manufacture or assemble products that are customized to buyer specifications
Distribution-related KSFs	• A strong network of wholesale distributors/dealers • Strong direct sales capabilities via the Internet and/or having company-owned retail outlets • Ability to secure favorable display space on retailer shelves
Marketing-related KSFs	• Breadth of product line and product selection • A well-known and well-respected brand name • Fast, accurate technical assistance • Courteous, personalized customer service • Accurate filling of buyer orders (few back orders or mistakes) • Customer guarantees and warranties (important in mail-order and online retailing, big-ticket purchases, new product introductions) • Clever advertising
Skills and capability–related KSFs	• A talented workforce (superior talent is important in professional services like accounting and investment banking) • National or global distribution capabilities • Product innovation capabilities (important in industries where rivals are racing to be first-to-market with new product attributes or performance features) • Design expertise (important in fashion and apparel industries) • Short delivery time capability • Supply chain management capabilities • Strong e-commerce capabilities—a user-friendly Web site and/or skills in using Internet technology applications to streamline internal operations
Other types of KSFs	• Overall low costs (not just in manufacturing) so as to be able to meet customers' expectations of low prices • Convenient locations (important in many retailing businesses) • Ability to provide fast, convenient after-the-sale repairs and service • A strong balance sheet and access to financial capital (important in newly emerging industries with high degrees of business risk and in capital-intensive industries) • Patent protection

members, and forecasting the likely next moves of key rivals. In addition, the answers to three questions help identify an industry's KSFs:

1. On what basis do buyers of the industry's product choose between the competing brands of sellers? That is, what product attributes are crucial?

2. Given the nature of competitive rivalry and the competitive forces prevailing in the marketplace, what resources and competitive capabilities does a company need to have to be competitively successful?

3. What shortcomings are almost certain to put a company at a significant competitive disadvantage?

CORE CONCEPT

A sound strategy incorporates the intent to stack up well on all of the industry's key success factors and to excel on one or two KSFs.

Only rarely are there more than five or six key factors for future competitive success. And even among these, two or three usually outrank the others in importance. Managers should therefore resist the temptation to label a factor that has only minor importance a KSF. To compile a list of every factor that matters even a little bit defeats the purpose of concentrating management attention on the factors truly critical to long-term competitive success.

Correctly diagnosing an industry's KSFs raises a company's chances of crafting a sound strategy. The goal of company strategists should be to design a strategy aimed at stacking up well on all of the industry's current and future KSFs and trying to be *distinctively better* than rivals on one (or possibly two) of the KSFs. Indeed, companies that stand out or excel on a particular KSF are likely to enjoy a stronger market position—*being distinctively better than rivals on one or two key success factors tends to translate into competitive advantage.* Hence, using the industry's KSFs as *cornerstones* for the company's strategy and trying to gain sustainable competitive advantage by excelling at one particular KSF is a fruitful competitive strategy approach.[23]

QUESTION 7: DOES THE OUTLOOK FOR THE INDUSTRY OFFER THE COMPANY A GOOD OPPORTUNITY TO EARN ATTRACTIVE PROFITS?

The final step in evaluating the industry and competitive environment is to use the preceding analysis to decide whether the outlook for the industry presents the company with a sufficiently attractive business opportunity. The important factors on which to base such a conclusion include:

*   The industry's growth potential.
*   Whether powerful competitive forces are squeezing industry profitability to subpar levels and whether competition appears destined to grow stronger or weaker.
*   Whether industry profitability will be favorably or unfavorably affected by the prevailing driving forces.
*   The degrees of risk and uncertainty in the industry's future.
*   Whether the industry as a whole confronts severe problems—regulatory or environmental issues, stagnating buyer demand, industry overcapacity, mounting competition, and so on.
*   The company's competitive position in the industry vis-à-vis rivals. (Being a well-entrenched leader or strongly positioned contender in a lackluster industry may present adequate opportunity for good profitability; however, having to fight a

steep uphill battle against much stronger rivals may hold little promise of eventual market success or good return on shareholder investment, even though the industry environment is attractive.)

- The company's potential to capitalize on the vulnerabilities of weaker rivals (perhaps converting a relatively unattractive *industry* situation into a potentially rewarding *company* opportunity).

- Whether the company has sufficient competitive strength to defend against or counteract the factors that make the industry unattractive.

As a general proposition, *if an industry's overall profit prospects are above average, the industry environment is basically attractive; if industry profit prospects are below average, conditions are unattractive.* However, it is a mistake to think of a particular industry as being equally attractive or unattractive to all industry participants and all potential entrants. Attractiveness is relative, not absolute, and conclusions one way or the other have to be drawn from the perspective of a particular company. Industries attractive to insiders may be unattractive to outsiders. Industry environments unattractive to weak competitors may be attractive to strong competitors. A favorably positioned company may survey a business environment and see a host of opportunities that weak competitors cannot capture.

> **CORE CONCEPT**
> The degree to which an industry is attractive or unattractive is not the same for all industry participants and all potential entrants; the attractiveness of the opportunities an industry presents depends heavily on whether a company has the resource strengths and competitive capabilities to capture them.

When a company decides an industry is fundamentally attractive and presents good opportunities, a strong case can be made that it should invest aggressively to capture the opportunities it sees and to improve its long-term competitive position in the business. When a strong competitor concludes that an industry is relatively unattractive, it may elect to simply protect its present position, invest cautiously if at all, and look for opportunities in other industries. A competitively weak company in an unattractive industry may see its best option as finding a buyer, perhaps a rival, to acquire its business.

KEY POINTS

Thinking strategically about a company's external situation involves probing for answers to the following seven questions:

1. *What are the industry's dominant economic features?* Industries differ significantly on such factors as market size and growth rate, the number and relative sizes of both buyers and sellers, the geographic scope of competitive rivalry, the degree of product differentiation, the speed of product innovation, demand–supply conditions, the extent of vertical integration, and the extent of scale economies and experience/learning curve effects. In addition to setting the stage for the analysis to come, identifying an industry's economic features also promotes understanding of the kinds of strategic moves that industry members are likely to employ.

2. *What kinds of competitive forces are industry members facing, and how strong is each force?* The strength of competition is a composite of five forces: (1) competitive pressures stemming from the competitive maneuvering among industry rivals,

(2) competitive pressures associated with the market inroads being made by the sellers of substitutes, (3) competitive pressures associated with the threat of new entrants into the market, (4) competitive pressures stemming from supplier bargaining power and supplier–seller collaboration, and (5) competitive pressures stemming from buyer bargaining power and seller–buyer collaboration. The nature and strength of the competitive pressures associated with these five forces have to be examined force by force to identify the specific competitive pressures they each comprise and to decide whether these pressures constitute a strong or weak competitive force. The next step in competition analysis is to evaluate the collective strength of the five forces and determine whether the state of competition is conducive to good profitability. Working through the five-forces model step by step not only aids strategy makers in assessing whether the intensity of competition allows good profitability but also promotes sound strategic thinking about how to better match company strategy to the specific competitive character of the marketplace. Effectively matching a company's strategy to the particular competitive pressures and competitive conditions that exist has two aspects: (1) pursuing avenues that shield the firm from as many of the prevailing competitive pressures as possible, and (2) initiating actions calculated to produce sustainable competitive advantage, thereby shifting competition in the company's favor, putting added competitive pressure on rivals, and perhaps even defining the business model for the industry.

3. *What forces are driving changes in the industry, and what impact will these changes have on competitive intensity and industry profitability?* Industry and competitive conditions change because forces are in motion that create incentives or pressures for change. The first phase is to identify the forces that are driving change in the industry; the most common driving forces include changes in the long-term industry growth rate, globalization of competition in the industry, emerging Internet capabilities and applications, changes in buyer composition, product innovation, technological change and manufacturing process innovation, marketing innovation, entry or exit of major firms, diffusion of technical know-how, changes in cost and efficiency, growing buyer preferences for differentiated versus standardized products (or vice versa), reductions in uncertainty and business risk, regulatory influences and government policy changes, and changing societal and lifestyle factors. The second phase of driving-forces analysis is to determine whether the driving forces, taken together, are acting to make the industry environment more or less attractive. Are the driving forces causing demand for the industry's product to increase or decrease? Are the driving forces acting to make competition more or less intense? Will the driving forces lead to higher or lower industry profitability?

4. *What market positions do industry rivals occupy—who is strongly positioned and who is not?* Strategic group mapping is a valuable tool for understanding the similarities, differences, strengths, and weaknesses inherent in the market positions of rival companies. Rivals in the same or nearby strategic groups are close competitors, whereas companies in distant strategic groups usually pose little or no immediate threat. The lesson of strategic group mapping is that some positions on the map are more favorable than others. The profit potential of different strategic groups varies due to strengths and weaknesses in each group's market position. Often, industry driving forces and competitive pressures favor some strategic groups and hurt others.

5. *What strategic moves are rivals likely to make next?* This analytical step involves identifying competitors' strategies, deciding which rivals are likely to be strong contenders and which are likely to be weak, evaluating rivals' competitive options, and predicting their next moves. Scouting competitors well enough to anticipate their actions can help a company prepare effective countermoves (perhaps even beating a rival to the punch) and allows managers to take rivals' probable actions into account in designing their own company's best course of action. Managers who fail to study competitors risk being caught unprepared by the strategic moves of rivals.

6. *What are the key factors for future competitive success?* An industry's key success factors (KSFs) are the particular strategy elements, product attributes, competitive capabilities, and business outcomes that spell the difference between being a strong competitor and a weak competitor—and sometimes between profit and loss. KSFs by their very nature are so important to competitive success that *all firms* in the industry must pay close attention to them or risk becoming an industry also-ran. Correctly diagnosing an industry's KSFs raises a company's chances of crafting a sound strategy. The goal of company strategists should be to design a strategy aimed at stacking up well on all of the industry KSFs and trying to be *distinctively better* than rivals on one (or possibly two) of the KSFs. Indeed, using the industry's KSFs as *cornerstones* for the company's strategy and trying to gain sustainable competitive advantage by excelling at one particular KSF is a fruitful competitive strategy approach.

7. *Does the outlook for the industry present the company with sufficiently attractive prospects for profitability?* If an industry's overall profit prospects are above average, the industry environment is basically attractive; if industry profit prospects are below average, conditions are unattractive. Conclusions regarding industry attractive are a major driver of company strategy. When a company decides an industry is fundamentally attractive, a strong case can be made that it should invest aggressively to capture the opportunities it sees and to improve its long-term competitive position in the business. When a strong competitor concludes an industry is relatively unattractive, it may elect to simply protect its present position, investing cautiously if at all and looking for opportunities in other industries. A competitively weak company in an unattractive industry may see its best option as finding a buyer, perhaps a rival, to acquire its business. On occasion, an industry that is unattractive overall is still very attractive to a favorably situated company with the skills and resources to take business away from weaker rivals.

A competently conducted industry and competitive analysis generally tells a clear, easily understood story about the company's external environment. Different analysts can have different judgments about competitive intensity, the impacts of driving forces, how industry conditions will evolve, how good the outlook is for industry profitability, and the degree to which the industry environment offers the company an attractive business opportunity. However, while no method can guarantee a single conclusive diagnosis about the state of industry and competitive conditions and an industry's future outlook, this doesn't justify shortcutting hard-nosed strategic analysis and relying instead on opinion and casual observation. Managers become better strategists when they know what questions to pose and what tools to use. This is why this chapter has concentrated on suggesting the right questions to ask, explaining concepts and analytical approaches, and indicating the kinds of things to look for. There's no substitute for doing cutting-edge strategic thinking about a company's external situation—anything less weakens managers' ability to craft strategies that are well matched to industry and competitive conditions.

ASSURANCE OF LEARNING EXERCISES

1. Using your favorite Internet search engine, do some research on competitive forces and driving forces that are at work in the snack food industry. Draw a five-forces diagram for the snack food industry and briefly discuss the nature and strength of each of the five competitive forces. Make a list of the driving forces operating in the snack foods industry and draw some conclusions about whether the likely impact of these driving forces on snack foods companies will be favorable or unfavorable.

2. Refer back to the strategic group map in Illustration Capsule 3.1: Who are Toyota's closest competitors? Between which two strategic groups is competition the strongest? Why do you think no automobile manufacturers are positioned in the upper right corner of the map? Which company/strategic group faces the weakest competition from the members of other strategic groups?

3. Using the information provided in Table 3.2 and your knowledge as a casual dining patron, what are the key success factors for restaurants such as Outback Steakhouse or Carrabba's Italian Grill? Your list should contain no more than six industry key success factors. In deciding on your list, it's important to distinguish between factors critical to success in the industry and factors that enhance a company's overall well-being.

EXERCISES FOR SIMULATION PARTICIPANTS

1. Which of the five competitive forces is creating the strongest competitive pressures for your company?

2. What are the "weapons of competition" that rival companies in your industry can use to gain sales and market share? Refer back to Figure 3.4 to help you identify the various competitive factors.

3. What are the factors affecting the intensity of rivalry in the industry in which your company is competing. Use Figure 3.4 and the accompanying discussion to help you pinpoint the specific factors most affecting competitive intensity. Would you characterize the rivalry and jockeying for better market position, increased sales, and market share among the companies in your industry as fierce, very strong, strong, moderate, or relatively weak? Why?

4. Are there any driving forces in the industry in which your company is competing? What impact will these driving forces have? Will they cause competition to be more or less intense? Will they act to boost or squeeze profit margins? List at least two actions your company should consider taking in order to combat any negative impacts of the driving forces.

5. Draw a strategic group map showing the market positions of the companies in your industry. Which companies do you believe are in the most attractive position on the map? Which companies are the most weakly positioned? Which companies do you believe are likely to try to move to a different position on the strategic group map?

6. What do you see as the key factors for being a successful competitor in your industry? List at least three KSFs.

Evaluating a Company's Resources and Competitive Position

LEARNING OBJECTIVES

1. Understand how to evaluate a company's internal situation and capabilities and identify the resource strengths capable of becoming the cornerstone of the company's strategic approach.

2. Grasp how and why activities performed internally by a company and those performed externally by its suppliers and forward channel allies determine a company's cost structure and ability to compete successfully.

3. Learn how to evaluate a company's competitive strength relative to key rivals.

4. Understand the role and importance of industry and competitive analysis and internal situation analysis in identifying strategic issues company managers must address.

In Chapter 3 we described how to use the tools of industry and competitive analysis to assess a company's external environment and lay the groundwork for matching a company's strategy to its external situation. In this chapter we discuss the techniques of evaluating a company's resource capabilities, relative cost position, and competitive strength versus rivals, so as to lay the groundwork for matching the company's strategy to its internal situation. The analytical spotlight for assessing a company's situation will be trained on five questions:

1. How well is the company's present strategy working?

2. What are the company's resource strengths and weaknesses, and its external opportunities and threats?

3. Are the company's prices and costs competitive with those of rivals?

4. Is the company competitively stronger or weaker than key rivals?

5. What strategic issues and problems merit front-burner managerial attention?

In probing for answers to these questions, four analytical tools—SWOT analysis, value chain analysis, benchmarking, and competitive strength assessment—will be used. All four are valuable techniques for revealing a company's competitiveness and for helping company managers match their strategy to the company's own particular circumstances.

QUESTION 1: HOW WELL IS THE COMPANY'S PRESENT STRATEGY WORKING?

In evaluating how well a company's present strategy is working, a manager has to start with what the strategy is. Figure 4.1 shows the key components of a single-business company's strategy. The first thing to pin down is the company's competitive approach. Is the company striving to be a low-cost leader *or* stressing ways to differentiate its product offering from rivals? Is the company's competitive approach tied to resource strengths and capabilities that allow it to deliver value to customers in ways that are unmatched by rivals? Is it concentrating its efforts on serving a broad spectrum of customers *or* a narrow market niche? Another strategy-defining consideration is the firm's competitive scope within the industry—what

Figure 4.1   Identifying the Components of a Single-Business Company's Strategy

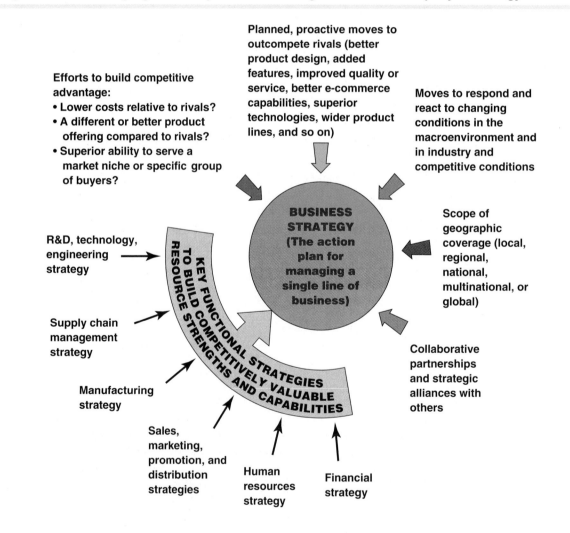

its geographic market coverage is and whether it operates in just a single stage of the industry's production/distribution chain or is vertically integrated across several stages. Another good indication of the company's strategy is whether the company has made moves recently to improve its competitive position and performance—for instance, by cutting prices, improving design, stepping up advertising, entering a new geographic market (domestic or foreign), or merging with a competitor. The company's functional strategies in research and development (R&D), production, marketing, finance, human resources, information technology (IT), and so on further characterize company strategy.

While there's merit in evaluating the strategy from a *qualitative* standpoint (its completeness, internal consistency, rationale, and relevance), the best *quantitative* evidence of how well a company's strategy is working comes from its results. The two best empirical indicators are (1) whether the company is achieving its stated financial and strategic objectives, and (2) whether the company is an above-average industry performer. Persistent shortfalls in meeting company performance targets and weak performance relative to rivals are reliable warning signs that the company suffers from poor strategy making, less-than-competent strategy execution, or both. Other indicators of how well a company's strategy is working include:

- Whether the firm's sales are growing faster, slower, or about the same pace as the market as a whole, thus resulting in a rising, eroding, or stable market share.
- Whether the company is acquiring new customers at an attractive rate as well as retaining existing customers.
- Whether the firm's profit margins are increasing or decreasing and how well its margins compare to rival firms' margins.
- Trends in the firm's net profits and return on investment, and how these compare to the same trends for other companies in the industry.
- Whether the company's overall financial strength and credit rating are improving or on the decline.
- Whether the company can demonstrate continuous improvement in such internal performance measures as days of inventory, employee productivity, unit cost, defect rate, scrap rate, misfilled orders, delivery times, warranty costs, and so on.
- How shareholders view the company based on trends in the company's stock price and shareholder value (relative to the stock price trends at other companies in the industry).
- The firm's image and reputation with its customers.
- How well the company stacks up against rivals on technology, product innovation, customer service, product quality, delivery time, price, getting newly developed products to market quickly, and other relevant factors on which buyers base their choice of brands.

The stronger a company's current overall performance, the less likely the need for radical changes in strategy. The weaker a company's financial performance and market standing, the more its current strategy must be questioned. Weak performance is almost always a sign of weak strategy, weak execution, or both.

> **The stronger a company's financial performance and market position, the more likely it has a well-conceived, well-executed strategy.**

Table 4.1 provides a compilation of the financial ratios most commonly used to evaluate a company's financial performance and balance sheet strength.

Table 4.1 Key Financial Ratios: How to Calculate Them and What They Mean

Ratio	How Calculated	What It Shows
Profitability ratios		
1. Gross profit margin	$$\frac{\text{Revenues} - \text{Cost of goods sold}}{\text{Revenues}}$$	Shows the percentage of revenues available to cover operating expenses and yield a profit. Higher is better, and the trend should be upward.
2. Operating profit margin (or return on sales)	$$\frac{\text{Revenues} - \text{Operating expenses}}{\text{Revenues}}$$ or $$\frac{\text{Operating income}}{\text{Revenues}}$$	Shows the profitability of current operations without regard to interest charges and income taxes. Higher is better, and the trend should be upward.
3. Net profit margin (or net return on sales)	$$\frac{\text{Profits after taxes}}{\text{Revenues}}$$	Shows after-tax profits per dollar of sales. Higher is better, and the trend should be upward.
4. Return on total assets	$$\frac{\text{Profits after taxes} + \text{Interest}}{\text{Total assets}}$$	A measure of the return on total investment in the enterprise. Interest is added to after-tax profits to form the numerator, since total assets are financed by creditors as well as by stockholders. Higher is better, and the trend should be upward.
5. Return on stockholder's equity	$$\frac{\text{Profits after taxes}}{\text{Total stockholders' equity}}$$	Shows the return stockholders are earning on their investment in the enterprise. A return in the 12–15 percent range is average, and the trend should be upward.
6. Earnings per share	$$\frac{\text{Profits after taxes}}{\text{Number of shares of common stock outstanding}}$$	Shows the earnings for each share of common stock outstanding. The trend should be upward, and the bigger the annual percentage gains, the better.
Liquidity ratios		
1. Current ratio	$$\frac{\text{Current assets}}{\text{Current liabilities}}$$	Shows a firm's ability to pay current liabilities using assets that can be converted to cash in the near term. Ratio should definitely be higher than 1.0; ratios of 2 or higher are better still.
2. Quick ratio (or acid-test ratio)	$$\frac{\text{Current assets} - \text{Inventory}}{\text{Current liabilities}}$$	Shows a firm's ability to pay current liabilities without relying on the sale of its inventories.
3. Working capital	Current assets − Current liabilities	Bigger amounts are better because the company has more internal funds available to (1) pay its current liabilities on a timely basis and (2) finance inventory expansion, additional accounts receivable, and a larger base of operations without resorting to borrowing or raising more equity capital.
Leverage ratios		
1. Debt-to-assets ratio	$$\frac{\text{Total debt}}{\text{Total assets}}$$	Measures the extent to which borrowed funds have been used to finance the firm's operations. Low fractions or ratios are better—high fractions indicate overuse of debt and greater risk of bankruptcy.

(Continued)

Ratio	How Calculated	What It Shows
2. Long-term debt-to-capital ratio	$$\frac{\text{Long-term debt}}{\text{Long-term debt} + \text{Total stockholders' equity}}$$	An important measure of creditworthiness and balance sheet strength. Indicates the percentage of capital investment which has been financed by creditors and bondholders. Fractions or ratios below .25 or 25% are usually quite satisfactory since monies invested by stockholders account for 75% or more of the company's total capital. The lower the ratio, the greater the capacity to borrow additional funds. Debt-to-capital ratios above 50% and certainly above 75% indicate a heavy and perhaps excessive reliance on debt, lower creditworthiness, and weak balance sheet strength.
3. Debt-to-equity ratio	$$\frac{\text{Total debt}}{\text{Total stockholders' equity}}$$	Should usually be less than 1.0. High ratios (especially above 1.0) signal excessive debt, lower creditworthiness, and weaker balance sheet strength.
4. Long-term debt-to-equity ratio	$$\frac{\text{Long-term debt}}{\text{Total stockholders' equity}}$$	Shows the balance between debt and equity in the firm's *long-term* capital structure. Low ratios indicate greater capacity to borrow additional funds if needed.
5. Times-interest-earned (or coverage) ratio	$$\frac{\text{Operating income}}{\text{Interest expenses}}$$	Measures the ability to pay annual interest charges. Lenders usually insist on a minimum ratio of 2.0, but ratios above 3.0 signal better creditworthiness.

Activity ratios

Ratio	How Calculated	What It Shows
1. Days of inventory	$$\frac{\text{Inventory}}{\text{Cost of goods sold} \div 365}$$	Measures inventory management efficiency. Fewer days of inventory are usually better.
2. Inventory turnover	$$\frac{\text{Cost of goods sold}}{\text{Inventory}}$$	Measures the number of inventory turns per year. Higher is better.
3. Average collection period	$$\frac{\text{Accounts receivable}}{\text{Total sales} \div 365}$$ or $$\frac{\text{Accounts receivable}}{\text{Average daily sales}}$$	Indicates the average length of time the firm must wait after making a sale to receive cash payment. A shorter collection time is better.

Other important financial measures

Ratio	How Calculated	What It Shows
1. Dividend yield on common stock	$$\frac{\text{Annual dividends per share}}{\text{Current market price per share}}$$	A measure of the return to owners received in the form of dividends.
2. Price/earnings (P/E) ratio	$$\frac{\text{Current market price per share}}{\text{Earnings per share}}$$	P/E ratios above 20 indicate strong investor confidence in a firm's outlook and earnings growth; firms whose future earnings are at risk or likely to grow slowly typically have ratios below 12.
3. Dividend payout ratio	$$\frac{\text{Annual dividends per share}}{\text{Earnings per share}}$$	Indicates the percentage of after-tax profits paid out as dividends.
4. Internal cash flow	$\text{After-tax profits} + \text{Depreciation}$	A quick and rough estimate of the cash a company's business is generating after payment of operating expenses, interest, and taxes. Such amounts can be used for dividend payments or funding capital expenditures.

QUESTION 2: WHAT ARE THE COMPANY'S RESOURCE STRENGTHS AND WEAKNESSES AND ITS EXTERNAL OPPORTUNITIES AND THREATS?

SWOT analysis is a simple but powerful tool for sizing up a company's resource capabilities and deficiencies, its market opportunities, and the external threats to its future well-being.

Appraising a company's resource strengths and weaknesses and its external opportunities and threats, commonly known as **SWOT analysis,** provides a good overview of whether the company's overall situation is fundamentally healthy or unhealthy. Just as important, a first-rate SWOT analysis provides the basis for crafting a strategy that capitalizes on the company's resources, aims squarely at capturing the company's best opportunities, and defends against the threats to its well-being.

Identifying Company Resource Strengths, Competencies, and Competitive Capabilities

A *resource strength* is something a company is good at doing or an attribute that enhances its competitiveness in the marketplace. Resource strengths can take any of several forms:

- *A skill, an area of specialized expertise, or a competitively important capability*—skills in keeping operating costs low, proven capabilities in creating and introducing innovative products, skills in creating a cost-efficient supply chain, expertise in getting new products to market quickly, and expertise in providing consistently good customer service.
- *Valuable physical assets*—attractive real estate locations, ownership of valuable natural resource deposits, and state-of-the-art plants, equipment, and distribution facilities.
- *Valuable human assets and intellectual capital*—an experienced and capable workforce, talented employees in key areas, cutting-edge technological knowledge, collective learning embedded in the organization, or proven managerial know-how.[1]
- *Valuable organizational assets*—proven quality control systems, proprietary technology, key patents, state-of-the-art systems for doing business via the Internet, a cadre of highly trained customer service representatives, a strong network of distributors or retail dealers, sizable amounts of cash and marketable securities, and a strong balance sheet and credit rating (thus giving the company access to additional financial capital).
- *Valuable intangible assets*—a powerful or well-known brand name or strong buyer loyalty.
- *An achievement or attribute that puts the company in a position of market advantage*—low overall costs relative to competitors, market share leadership, a superior product, a wider product line than rivals, wide geographic coverage, or award-winning customer service.
- *Competitively valuable alliances or cooperative ventures*—fruitful partnerships with suppliers that reduce costs and/or enhance product quality and performance; alliances or joint ventures that provide access to valuable technologies, specialized know-how, or geographic markets.

A company's resource strengths represent its *competitive assets* and determine whether its competitive power in the marketplace will be impressively strong or disappointingly weak. A company that is well-endowed with potent resource strengths and competitive capabilities normally has considerable competitive power—especially when its management team skillfully utilizes the company's resources in ways that build sustainable competitive advantage. Companies with modest on weak competitive assets nearly always are relegated to a trailing position in the industry.[2]

Assessing a Company's Competencies and Capabilities—What Activities Does It Perform Well?   One of the most important aspects of appraising a company's resource strengths has to do with its competence level in performing key pieces of its business—such as supply chain management, R&D, production, distribution, sales and marketing, and customer service. Which activities does it perform especially well? Are there any activities it performs better than rivals? A company's proficiency in conducting different facets of its operations can range from merely a competence in performing an activity to a core competence to a distinctive competence:

1.   A **competence** is something an organization is good at doing. It is nearly always the product of experience, representing an accumulation of learning and the buildup of proficiency in performing an internal activity. Usually a company competence originates with deliberate efforts to develop the organizational ability to do something, however imperfectly or inefficiently. Such efforts involve selecting people with the requisite knowledge and skills, upgrading or expanding individual abilities as needed, and then molding the efforts and work products of individuals into a cooperative effort to create organizational ability. Then, as experience builds, such that the company gains proficiency in performing the activity consistently well and at an acceptable cost, the ability evolves into a true competence and company capability. Some competencies relate to specific skills and expertise (like just-in-time inventory control, low-cost manufacturing know-how, picking good locations for new stores, designing an unusually appealing and user-friendly Web site); they spring from proficiency in a single discipline or function and may be performed in a single department or organizational unit. Other competencies, however, are inherently multidisciplinary and cross-functional—they are the result of effective collaboration among people with different expertise working in different organizational units. A competence in continuous product innovation, for example, comes from teaming the efforts of people and groups with expertise in market research, new product R&D, design and engineering, cost-effective manufacturing, and market testing.

> **CORE CONCEPT**
> A *competence* is an activity that a company has learned to perform well.

2.   A **core competence** is a proficiently performed internal activity that is *central* to a company's strategy and competitiveness. A core competence is a more valuable resource strength than a competence because of the well-performed activity's core role in the company's strategy and the contribution it makes to the company's success in the marketplace. A core competence can relate to any of several aspects of a company's business: expertise in integrating multiple technologies to create families of new products, know-how in creating and operating systems for cost-efficient supply chain management, the capability to speed new or next-generation products to market, good after-sale service capabilities, skills in manufacturing a high-quality product at a low cost, or the capability to fill customer orders accurately and swiftly. A company may have more than one core competence in its

> **CORE CONCEPT**
> A *core competence* is a *competitively important* activity that a company performs better than other internal activities.

resource portfolio, but rare is the company that can legitimately claim more than two or three core competencies. Most often, *a core competence is knowledge-based, residing in people and in a company's intellectual capital rather than in its assets on the balance sheet.* Moreover, a core competence is more likely to arise from cross-department combinations of knowledge and expertise than from a single department or work group. 3M Corporation has a core competence in product innovation—3M's record of introducing new products goes back several decades, and new product introduction is central to the company's strategy of growing its business. MySpace, a subsidiary of News Corporation, has a core competence in anticipating features that will appeal to Internet users who join social networking sites. The ability of Internet users to share information, photos, videos, Karaoke-type audio recordings, and interesting news stories with friends and others made MySpace the world's largest social networking site as of 2008, with more than 117 million unique visitors each month. Ben & Jerry's Homemade, which was acquired by Unilever in 2000, has a core competence in creating unusual flavors of ice cream and marketing them with catchy names like Chunky Monkey, Imagine Whirled Peace, Chubby Hubby, Dublin Mudslide, Pfish Food, Karamel Sutra, Turtle Soup, Vermonty Python, and Fossil Fuel.

3. A **distinctive competence** is a competitively valuable activity that a company *performs better than its rivals.* A distinctive competence thus signifies even greater proficiency than a core competence. But what is especially important about a distinctive competence is that the company enjoys *competitive superiority in performing that activity*—a distinctive competence represents a level of proficiency that rivals do not have. Because a distinctive competence represents uniquely strong capability relative to rival companies, it qualifies as a *competitively superior resource strength* with competitive advantage potential. This is particularly true when the distinctive competence enables a company to deliver standout value to customers (in the form of lower costs and prices or better product performance or superior service). Toyota has worked diligently over several decades to establish a distinctive competence in low-cost, high-quality manufacturing of motor vehicles; its "lean production" system is far superior to that of any other automaker, and the company is pushing the boundaries of its production advantage with a new type of assembly line—called the Global Body Line—that costs 50 percent less to install and can be changed to accommodate a new model for 70 percent less than its previous production system.[3] Starbucks' distinctive competence in creating innovative coffee drinks and an inviting store ambience has propelled it to the forefront among coffee retailers.

> **CORE CONCEPT**
>
> A *distinctive competence* is a competitively important activity that a company performs better than its rivals—it thus represents *a competitively superior resource strength.*

The conceptual differences between a competence, a core competence, and a distinctive competence draw attention to the fact that a company's resource strengths and competitive capabilities are not all equal.[4] Some competencies and competitive capabilities merely enable market survival because most rivals have them—indeed, not having a competence or capability that rivals have can result in competitive disadvantage. If an apparel company does not have the competence to produce its apparel items very cost-efficiently, it is unlikely to survive given the intense price competition in the apparel industry. Every Web retailer requires a basic competence in designing an appealing and user-friendly Web site.

Core competencies are *competitively* more important resource strengths than competencies because they add power to the company's strategy and have a bigger positive impact on its market position and profitability. Distinctive competencies are even more competitively important. A distinctive competence is a competitively potent resource strength for three reasons: (1) it gives a company competitively valuable capability that is unmatched by rivals, (2) it has potential for being the cornerstone of the company's strategy, and (3) it can produce a competitive edge in the marketplace since it represents a level of proficiency that is superior to rivals. It is always easier for a company to build competitive advantage when it has a distinctive competence in performing an activity important to market success, when rival companies do not have offsetting competencies, and when it is costly and time-consuming for rivals to imitate the competence. A distinctive competence is thus potentially the mainspring of a company's success—unless it is trumped by more powerful resources of rivals.

What Is the Competitive Power of a Resource Strength?   Most telling about a company's resource strengths is how powerful they are in the marketplace. The competitive power of a resource strength is measured by how many of the following four tests it can pass:[5]

1. *Is the resource really competitively valuable?* All companies possess a collection of resources and competencies—some have the potential to contribute to a competitive advantage, while others may not. Apple's Mac OS X operating system is by most accounts a world beater (compared to Windows Vista), but Apple has struggled to convert its resource strength in operating system design into competitive success in the global PC market.

2. *Is the resource strength rare—is it something rivals lack?* Companies have to guard against pridefully believing that their core competencies are distinctive competencies or that their brand name is more powerful than the brand names of rivals. Who can really say whether Coca-Cola's consumer marketing prowess is better than PepsiCo's or whether the Mercedes-Benz brand name is more powerful than that of BMW or Lexus? Although many retailers claim to be quite proficient in product selection and in-store merchandising, a number run into trouble in the marketplace because they encounter rivals whose competencies in product selection and in-store merchandising are equal to or better than theirs.

3. *Is the resource strength hard to copy?* The more difficult and more expensive it is to imitate a company's resource strength, the greater its potential competitive value. Resources tend to be difficult to copy when they are unique (a fantastic real estate location, patent protection); when they must be built over time (a brand name, a strategy-supportive organizational culture); and when they carry big capital requirements (a cost-effective plant to manufacture cutting-edge microprocessors). Wal-Mart's competitors have failed miserably in their attempts over the past two decades to match its state-of-the-art distribution capabilities.

4. *Can the resource strength be trumped by substitute resource strengths and competitive capabilities?* Resources that are competitively valuable, rare, and costly to imitate lose their ability to offer competitive advantage if rivals possess equivalent substitute resources. For example, manufacturers relying on automation to gain a cost-based advantage in production activities may find their technology-based advantage nullified by rivals' use of low-wage offshore manufacturing. Resources can contribute to a competitive advantage only when resource substitutes don't exist.

In-depth understanding of the competitive power of company resource strengths enables managers to consider the merits of boosting existing strengths and/or striving to develop altogether new competencies and capabilities that could prove competitively valuable.

In addition, management may determine that it doesn't possess a resource that independently passes all four tests listed above with high marks, but does have a *bundle of resources* that can be leveraged to develop a core competence. Although Callaway Golf Company's engineering capabilities and market research capabilities are matched relatively well by rivals Cobra Golf and Ping Golf, it has bundled good product development resources, technological know-how, and understanding of golfers and the golfing marketplace to remain the largest seller of golf equipment for more than a decade. Callaway's unique bundle of resource strengths qualifies as a distinctive competence and is the basis of the company's competitive advantage.

Competitively Valuable Resource Strengths and Competencies Call for the Use of a Resource-Based Strategy   Companies that possess competitively valuable resource strengths and competencies typically deploy these resources and capabilities in a manner that boosts the competitive power of their overall strategy and bolsters their position in the marketplace. **Resource-based strategies** attempt to exploit company resources in a manner that offers value to customers in ways rivals are unable to match. Indeed, the whole point of a resource-based strategy is to deliberately develop and deploy competencies and capabilities that add to a company's competitive power in the marketplace and make its overall strategy more potent in battling rivals. For example, a company pursuing a broad low-cost strategy might invest in superefficient distribution centers that give it the capability to distribute its products at a lower cost than rivals. Wal-Mart's distribution efficiency is one factor in its being able to underprice rivals. Over a period of more than a decade, Dell has put considerable time and money into cultivating relationships with its key suppliers that give it exceptionally low inventory carrying costs (as well as access to low-cost, quality components for its PC models). Many Dell plants operate with only several hours' inventory of certain parts and components because the suppliers have online access to Dell's daily production schedule and make frequent deliveries (sometimes every two hours) of the precise components that particular work stations on the floor of Dell's assembly plants need to build each PC to a customer's specifications. Resource strengths and competitive capabilities can also facilitate differentiation in the marketplace. Because Fox News and CNN can devote more air time to breaking news stories and get reporters on the scene quicker than ABC, NBC, and CBS can, many viewers turn to the cable networks when a major news event occurs.

Resource-based strategies can also be directed at eroding or at least neutralizing the competitive potency of a particular rival's resource strengths by identifying and developing substitute resources that accomplish the purpose. For example, Amazon.com lacks a big network of retail stores to compete with those operated by rival Barnes & Noble, but Amazon's much larger book inventory (as compared to any retail store), coupled with its vast selection of other products and short delivery times, is more attractive to many busy consumers than visiting a big-box bookstore. In other words, Amazon has carefully and consciously developed competitively valuable online resource capabilities that have proved to be effective substitutes for competing head-to-head against Barnes & Noble's retail stores and those of other brick-and-mortar retailers without having to invest in hundreds of brick-and-mortar retail stores of its own. Whereas many cosmetics companies sell their products through department stores and specialty retailers, Avon and Mary

Kay Cosmetics have substituted for the lack of a retail dealer network by assembling a direct sales force numbering in the hundreds of thousands—their sales associates can personally demonstrate products to interested buyers in their homes or at parties, take orders on the spot, and deliver the items to buyers' homes.[6]

Identifying Company Resource Weaknesses, Missing Capabilities, and Competitive Deficiencies

A *resource weakness,* or *competitive deficiency,* is something a company lacks or does poorly (in comparison to others) or a condition that puts it at a disadvantage in the marketplace. A company's resource weaknesses can relate to (1) inferior or unproven skills, expertise, or intellectual capital in competitively important areas of the business; (2) deficiencies in competitively important physical, organizational, or intangible assets; or (3) missing or competitively inferior capabilities in key areas. *Internal weaknesses are thus shortcomings in a company's complement of resources and represent competitive liabilities.* Nearly all companies have competitive liabilities of one kind or another. Whether a company's resource weaknesses make it competitively vulnerable depends on how much they matter in the marketplace and whether they are offset by resource strengths that substitute for missing capabilities.

Table 4.2 lists the kinds of factors to consider in compiling a company's resource strengths and weaknesses. Sizing up a company's complement of resource capabilities and deficiencies is akin to constructing a *strategic balance sheet,* where resource strengths represent *competitive assets* and resource weaknesses represent *competitive liabilities.* Obviously, the ideal condition is for the company's competitive assets to outweigh its competitive liabilities by an ample margin—a 50–50 balance is definitely not the desired condition!

> **CORE CONCEPT**
> A company's resource strengths represent competitive assets; its resource weaknesses represent competitive liabilities.

Identifying a Company's External Market Opportunities

Market opportunity is a big factor in shaping a company's strategy. Indeed, managers can't properly tailor strategy to the company's situation without first identifying its market opportunities and appraising the growth and profit potential each one holds. (See Table 4.2, under "Potential Market Opportunities.") Depending on the prevailing circumstances, a company's opportunities can be plentiful or scarce, fleeting or lasting, and can range from wildly attractive (an absolute must to pursue) to marginally interesting (because the growth and profit potential are questionable) to unsuitable (because there's not a good match with the company's resource strengths and capabilities).

While stunningly big opportunities sometimes appear fairly frequently in volatile, fast-changing markets (typically due to important technological developments or rapidly shifting consumer preferences), they are nonetheless hard to see in advance. The more volatile and thus unpredictable that market conditions are, the more limited is a company's ability to spot important opportunities much ahead of rivals—there are simply too many variables in play for managers to peer into the fog of the future, identify one or more upcoming opportunities, and get a jump on rivals in pursuing it.[7] In mature markets, unusually attractive market opportunities emerge sporadically, often after long periods of relative calm. But future market conditions here may be less foggy, thus facilitating good market reconnaissance and making emerging opportunities easier for industry members to detect. But in both volatile and stable markets, the rise of a

Table 4.2   What to Look for in Identifying a Company's Strengths, Weaknesses, Opportunities, and Threats

Potential Resource Strengths and Competitive Capabilities	Potential Resource Weaknesses and Competitive Deficiencies
<ul><li>A powerful strategy</li><li>Core competencies in _____</li><li>A distinctive competence in _____</li><li>A product that is strongly differentiated from those of rivals</li><li>Competencies and capabilities that are well matched to industry key success factors</li><li>A strong financial condition; ample financial resources to grow the business</li><li>Strong brand-name image/company reputation</li><li>An attractive customer base</li><li>Economy of scale or learning/experience curve advantages over rivals</li><li>Proprietary technology/superior technological skills/important patents</li><li>Superior intellectual capital relative to key rivals</li><li>Cost advantages over rivals</li><li>Strong advertising and promotion</li><li>Product innovation capabilities</li><li>Proven capabilities in improving production processes</li><li>Good supply chain management capabilities</li><li>Good customer service capabilities</li><li>Better product quality relative to rivals</li><li>Wide geographic coverage and/or strong global distribution capability</li><li>Alliances/joint ventures with other firms that provide access to valuable technology, competencies, and/or attractive geographic markets</li></ul>	<ul><li>No clear strategic direction</li><li>Resources that are not well matched to industry key success factors</li><li>No well-developed or proven core competencies</li><li>A weak balance sheet, burdened with too much debt</li><li>Higher overall unit costs relative to key competitors</li><li>Weak or unproven product innovation capabilities</li><li>A product/service with ho-hum attributes or features inferior to those of rivals</li><li>Too narrow a product line relative to rivals</li><li>Weak brand image or reputation</li><li>Weak dealer networks; lack of adequate global distribution capability</li><li>Behind on product quality, R&D, and/or technological know-how</li><li>In the wrong strategic group</li><li>Losing market share because . . .</li><li>Lack of management depth</li><li>Inferior intellectual capital relative to leading rivals</li><li>Subpar profitability because . . .</li><li>Plagued with internal operating problems or obsolete facilities</li><li>Behind rivals in e-commerce capabilities</li><li>Short on financial resources to grow the business and pursue promising initiatives</li><li>Too much underutilized plant capacity</li></ul>
Potential Market Opportunities	**Potential External Threats to a Company's Prospects**
<ul><li>Openings to win market share from rivals</li><li>Sharply rising buyer demand for the industry's product</li><li>Serving additional customer groups or market segments</li><li>Expanding into new geographic markets</li><li>Expanding the company's product line to meet a broader range of customer needs</li><li>Utilizing existing company skills or technological know-how to enter new product lines or new businesses</li><li>Online sales</li><li>Integrating forward or backward</li><li>Falling trade barriers in attractive foreign markets</li><li>Acquiring rival firms or companies with attractive technological expertise or capabilities</li><li>Entering into alliances or joint ventures to expand the firm's market coverage or boost its competitive capability</li><li>Openings to exploit emerging new technologies</li></ul>	<ul><li>Increasing intensity of competition among industry rivals—may squeeze profit margins</li><li>Slowdowns in market growth</li><li>Likely entry of potent new competitors</li><li>Loss of sales to substitute products</li><li>Growing bargaining power of customers or suppliers</li><li>A shift in buyer needs and tastes away from the industry's product</li><li>Adverse demographic changes that threaten to curtail demand for the industry's product</li><li>Vulnerability to unfavorable industry driving forces</li><li>Restrictive trade policies on the part of foreign governments</li><li>Costly new regulatory requirements</li></ul>

golden opportunity is almost never under the control of a single company or manufactured by company executives—rather, it springs from the simultaneous alignment of several external factors. For instance, in China the recent upsurge in demand for motor vehicles was spawned by a convergence of many factors—increased disposable income, rising middle-class aspirations, a major government road-building program, the demise of employer-provided housing, and easy credit.[8] But golden opportunities are nearly always seized rapidly—and the companies that seize them are usually those that have been staying alert with diligent market reconnaissance and preparing themselves to capitalize on shifting market conditions by patiently assembling an arsenal of competitively valuable resources. New market opportunities are most easily seized by companies possessing talented personnel, technical know-how, valuable strategic partnerships, and a war chest of cash to finance aggressive action when the time comes.[9]

In evaluating a company's market opportunities and ranking their attractiveness, managers have to guard against viewing every *industry* opportunity as a *company* opportunity. Not every company is equipped with the resources to successfully pursue each opportunity that exists in its industry. Some companies are more capable of going after particular opportunities than others, and a few companies may be hopelessly outclassed. *The market opportunities most relevant to a company are those that match up well with the company's financial and organizational resource capabilities, offer the best growth and profitability, and present the most potential for competitive advantage.*

> A company is well advised to pass on a particular industry opportunity unless the company has or can acquire the resources to capture it.

Identifying the External Threats to Profitability

Often, certain factors in a company's external environment pose *threats* to its profitability, competitive well-being, and growth prospects. Threats can stem from the emergence of cheaper or better technologies, rivals' introduction of new or improved products, the entry of lower-cost foreign competitors into a company's market stronghold, new regulations that are more burdensome to a company than to its competitors, vulnerability to a rise in interest rates, the potential of a hostile takeover, unfavorable demographic shifts, adverse changes in foreign exchange rates, political upheaval in a foreign country where the company has facilities, and the like. (See Table 4.2, under "Potential External Threats to a Company's Prospects.")

External threats may pose no more than a moderate degree of adversity (all companies confront some threatening elements in the course of doing business), or they may be so imposing as to make a company's situation and outlook quite tenuous. On rare occasions, market shocks can give birth to a *sudden-death* threat that throws a company into a battle to survive. Many of the world's major airlines have been plunged into unprecedented financial crisis because of a combination of factors: rising prices for jet fuel; slower-than-expected growth in passenger traffic (which resulted in having too many empty seats on too many flights); mounting competition from low-fare carriers; shifting traveler preferences for low fares as opposed to lots of in-flight amenities; and out-of-control labor costs. It is management's job to identify the threats to the company's prospects and to evaluate what strategic actions can be taken to neutralize or lessen their impact.

What Can Be Learned from a SWOT Analysis?

SWOT analysis involves more than making four lists. The two most important parts of SWOT analysis are *drawing conclusions* from the SWOT listings about the company's

Simply making lists of a company's strengths, weaknesses, opportunities, and threats is not enough; the payoff from SWOT analysis comes from the conclusions about a company's situation and the implications for strategy improvement that flow from the four lists.

overall situation, and *translating these conclusions into strategic actions* to better match the company's strategy to its resource strengths and market opportunities, to correct the important weaknesses, and to defend against external threats. Figure 4.2 shows the three steps of SWOT analysis.

Just what story the SWOT listings tell about the company's overall situation is often revealed in the answers to the following sets of questions:

- Does the company have an attractive set of resource strengths? Does it have any strong core competencies or a distinctive competence? Are the company's strengths and capabilities well matched to the industry key success factors? Do they add adequate power to the company's strategy, or are more or different strengths needed? Will the company's current strengths and capabilities matter in the future?

- How serious are the company's weaknesses and competitive deficiencies? Are they mostly inconsequential and readily correctable, or could one or more prove fatal if not remedied soon? Are some of the company's weaknesses in areas that relate to the industry's key success factors? Are there any weaknesses that, if uncorrected,

Figure 4.2   The Three Steps of SWOT Analysis: Identify, Draw Conclusions, Translate into Strategic Action

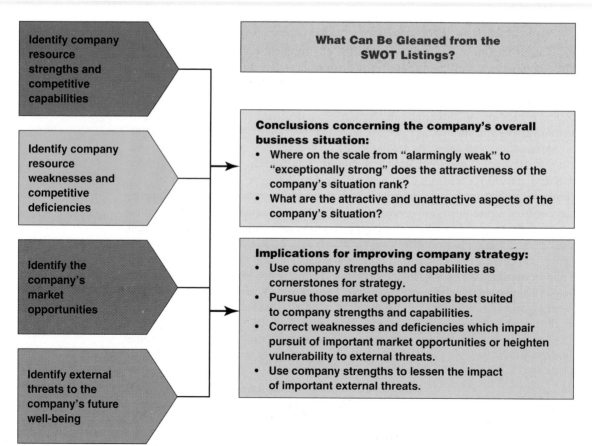

would keep the company from pursuing an otherwise attractive opportunity? Does the company have important resource gaps that need to be filled for it to move up in the industry rankings and/or boost its profitability?

- Do the company's resource strengths and competitive capabilities (its competitive assets) outweigh its resource weaknesses and competitive deficiencies (its competitive liabilities) by an attractive margin?

- Does the company have attractive market opportunities that are well suited to its resource strengths and competitive capabilities? Does the company lack the resources and capabilities to pursue any of the most attractive opportunities?

- Are the threats alarming, or are they something the company appears able to deal with and defend against?

- All things considered, how strong is the company's overall situation? Where on a scale of 1 to 10 (where 1 is alarmingly weak and 10 is exceptionally strong) should the firm's position and overall situation be ranked? What aspects of the company's situation are particularly attractive? What aspects are of the most concern?

The final piece of SWOT analysis is to translate the diagnosis of the company's situation into actions for improving the company's strategy and business prospects. The following questions point to implications the SWOT listings have for strategic action:

- Which competitive capabilities need to be strengthened immediately (so as to add greater power to the company's strategy and boost sales and profitability)? Do new types of competitive capabilities need to be put in place to help the company better respond to emerging industry and competitive conditions? Which resources and capabilities need to be given greater emphasis, and which merit less emphasis? Should the company emphasize leveraging its existing resource strengths and capabilities, or does it need to create new resource strengths and capabilities?

- What actions should be taken to reduce the company's competitive liabilities? Which weaknesses or competitive deficiencies are in urgent need of correction?

- Which market opportunities should be top priority in future strategic initiatives (because they are good fits with the company's resource strengths and competitive capabilities, present attractive growth and profit prospects, and/or offer the best potential for securing competitive advantage)? Which opportunities should be ignored, at least for the time being (because they offer less growth potential or are not suited to the company's resources and capabilities)?

- What should the company be doing to guard against the threats to its well-being?

A company's resource strengths should generally form the cornerstones of strategy because they represent the company's best chance for market success.[10] As a rule, strategies that place heavy demands on areas where the company is weakest or has unproven ability are suspect and should be avoided. If a company doesn't have the resources and competitive capabilities around which to craft an attractive strategy, managers need to take decisive remedial action either to upgrade existing organizational resources and capabilities and add others as needed or to acquire them through partnerships or strategic alliances with firms possessing the needed expertise. Plainly, managers have to look toward correcting competitive weaknesses that make the company vulnerable, hold down profitability, or disqualify it from pursuing an attractive opportunity.

At the same time, sound strategy making requires sifting through the available market opportunities and aiming strategy at capturing those that are most attractive and suited to the company's circumstances. Rarely does a company have the resource depth to pursue all available market opportunities simultaneously without spreading itself too thin. How much attention to devote to defending against external threats to the company's market position and future performance hinges on how vulnerable the company is, whether there are attractive defensive moves that can be taken to lessen their impact, and whether the costs of undertaking such moves represent the best use of company resources.

QUESTION 3: ARE THE COMPANY'S PRICES AND COSTS COMPETITIVE?

The higher a company's costs are above those of close rivals, the more competitively vulnerable it becomes.

Company managers are often stunned when a competitor cuts its price to "unbelievably low" levels or when a new market entrant comes on strong with a very low price. The competitor may not, however, be *dumping* (an economic term for selling below cost), buying its way into the market with a superlow price, or waging a desperate move to gain sales—it may simply have substantially lower costs. One of the most telling signs of whether a company's business position is strong or precarious is whether its prices and costs are competitive with industry rivals. For a company to compete successfully, its costs must be *in line* with those of close rivals.

Price–cost comparisons are especially critical in a commodity-product industry where the value provided to buyers is the same from seller to seller, price competition is typically the ruling market force, and lower-cost companies have the upper hand. But even in industries where products are differentiated and competition centers on the different attributes of competing brands as much as on price, rival companies have to keep their costs *in line* and make sure that any added costs they incur—and any price premiums they charge—create ample value that buyers are willing to pay extra for. While some cost disparity is justified so long as the products or services of closely competing companies are sufficiently differentiated, a high-cost firm's market position becomes increasingly vulnerable the more its costs exceed those of close rivals.

Two analytical tools are particularly useful in determining whether a company's prices and costs are competitive: value chain analysis and benchmarking.

The Concept of a Company Value Chain

CORE CONCEPT

A company's *value chain* identifies the primary activities that create customer value and the related support activities.

Every company's business consists of a collection of activities undertaken in the course of designing, producing, marketing, delivering, and supporting its product or service. All of the various activities that a company performs internally combine to form a **value chain**—so called because the underlying intent of a company's activities is to do things that ultimately *create value for buyers*. A company's value chain also includes an allowance for profit because a markup over the cost of performing the firm's value-creating activities is customarily part of the price (or total cost) borne by buyers—unless an enterprise succeeds in creating and delivering sufficient value to buyers to produce an attractive profit, it can't survive for long.

As shown in Figure 4.3 (on page 118), a company's value chain consists of two broad categories of activities: (1) the *primary activities* that are foremost in creating value for customers, (2) and the requisite *support activities* that facilitate and enhance the performance of the primary activities.[11] For example, the primary value-creating activities for a maker of bakery goods include supply chain management, recipe development and testing, mixing and baking, packaging, sales and marketing, and distribution; related support activities include quality control, human resource management, and administration. A wholesaler's primary activities and costs deal with merchandise selection and purchasing, inbound shipping and warehousing from suppliers, and outbound distribution to retail customers. The primary activities for a department store retailer include merchandise selection and buying, store layout and product display, advertising, and customer service; its support activities include site selection, hiring and training, and store maintenance, plus the usual assortment of administrative activities. A hotel chain's primary activities and costs are in site selection and construction, reservations, operation of its hotel properties (check-in and check-out, maintenance and housekeeping, dining and room service, and conventions and meetings), and managing its lineup of hotel locations; principal support activities include accounting, hiring and training hotel staff, advertising, building a brand and reputation, and general administration. Supply chain management is a crucial activity for Nissan, L. L. Bean, and PetSmart but is not a value chain component at Google or Bank of America. Sales and marketing are dominant activities at Procter & Gamble and Sony but have minor roles at oil drilling companies and natural gas pipeline companies. Thus, what constitutes primary and secondary activities varies according to the specific nature of a company's business, meaning that you should view the listing of the primary and support activities in Figure 4.3 as illustrative rather than definitive.

A Company's Primary and Secondary Activities Identify the Major Components of Its Cost Structure   Segregating a company's operations into different types of primary and secondary activities is the first step in understanding its cost structure. Each activity in the value chain gives rise to costs and ties up assets. Assigning the company's operating costs and assets to each individual activity in the chain provides cost estimates and capital requirements—a process that accountants call *activity-based cost accounting*. Quite often, there are links between activities such that the manner in which one activity is done can affect the costs of performing other activities. For instance, how a product is designed has a huge impact on the number of different parts and components, their respective manufacturing costs, and the expense of assembly.

The combined costs of all the various activities in a company's value chain define the company's internal cost structure. Further, the cost of each activity contributes to whether the company's overall cost position relative to rivals is favorable or unfavorable. The tasks of value chain analysis and benchmarking are to develop the data for comparing a company's costs activity-by-activity against the costs of key rivals and to learn which internal activities are a source of cost advantage or disadvantage. A company's relative cost position is a function of how the overall costs of the activities it performs in conducting business compare to the overall costs of the activities performed by rivals.

Why the Value Chains of Rival Companies Often Differ

A company's value chain reflects the evolution of its own particular business and internal operations, the technology and operating practices it employs, its strategy, the approaches it is using to execute its strategy, and the underlying economics of the activities themselves.[12] Because these factors differ from company to company (even among companies in the same industry), the value chains of rival companies sometimes differ substantially—a condition that complicates the task of assessing rivals'

Figure 4.3   A Representative Company Value Chain

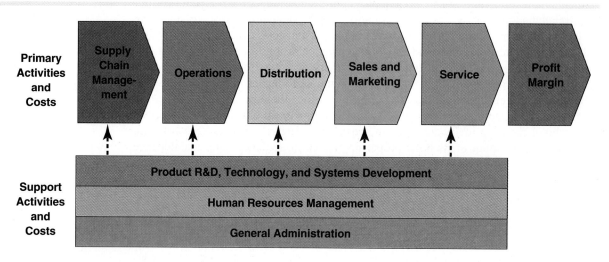

PRIMARY ACTIVITIES

- **Supply Chain Management**—Activities, costs, and assets associated with purchasing fuel, energy, raw materials, parts and components, merchandise, and consumable items from vendors; receiving, storing, and disseminating inputs from suppliers; inspection; and inventory management.

- **Operations**—Activities, costs, and assets associated with converting inputs into final product form (production, assembly, packaging, equipment maintenance, facilities, operations, quality assurance, environmental protection).

- **Distribution**—Activities, costs, and assets dealing with physically distributing the product to buyers (finished goods warehousing, order processing, order picking and packing, shipping, delivery vehicle operations, establishing and maintaining a network of dealers and distributors).

- **Sales and Marketing**—Activities, costs, and assets related to sales force efforts, advertising and promotion, market research and planning, and dealer/distributor support.

- **Service**—Activities, costs, and assets associated with providing assistance to buyers, such as installation, spare parts delivery, maintenance and repair, technical assistance, buyer inquiries, and complaints.

SUPPORT ACTIVITIES

- **Product R&D, Technology, and Systems Development**—Activities, costs, and assets relating to product R&D, process R&D, process design improvement, equipment design, computer software development, telecommunications systems, computer-assisted design and engineering, database capabilities, and development of computerized support systems.

- **Human Resources Management**—Activities, costs, and assets associated with the recruitment, hiring, training, development, and compensation of all types of personnel; labor relations activities; and development of knowledge-based skills and core competencies.

- **General Administration**—Activities, costs, and assets relating to general management, accounting and finance, legal and regulatory affairs, safety and security, management information systems, forming strategic alliances and collaborating with strategic partners, and other "overhead" functions.

Source: Based on the discussion in Michael E. Porter, *Competitive Advantage* (New York: Free Press, 1985), pp. 37–43.

relative cost positions. For instance, music retailers like Blockbuster and F.Y.E., which purchase CDs from recording studios and wholesale distributors and sell them in their own retail store locations, have different value chains and different cost structures than rival online music stores like Apple's iTunes Store and Yahoo! Music, which sell downloadable files directly to music shoppers. Competing companies may differ in their degrees of vertical integration.

The operations component of the value chain for a manufacturer that *makes* all of its own parts and components and assembles them into a finished product differs from the operations of a rival producer that *buys* the needed parts and components from outside suppliers and only performs assembly operations. Likewise, there is legitimate reason to expect value chain and cost differences between a company that is pursuing a low-cost/low-price strategy and a rival that is positioned on the high end of the market. The costs of certain activities along the low-cost company's value chain should indeed be relatively low, whereas the high-end firm may understandably be spending relatively more to perform those activities that create the added quality and extra features of its products.

Moreover, cost and price differences among rival companies can have their origins in activities performed by suppliers or by distribution channel allies involved in getting the product to end users. Suppliers or wholesale/retail dealers may have excessively high cost structures or profit margins that jeopardize a company's cost-competitiveness even though its costs for internally performed activities are competitive. For example, when determining Michelin's cost-competitiveness vis-à-vis Goodyear and Bridgestone in supplying replacement tires to vehicle owners, we have to look at more than whether Michelin's tire manufacturing costs are above or below Goodyear's and Bridgestone's. Let's say that a motor vehicle owner looking for a new set of tires has to pay $400 for a set of Michelin tires and only $350 for a set of Goodyear or Bridgestone tires. The $50 difference can stem not only from Michelin's higher manufacturing costs (reflecting, perhaps, the added costs of Michelin's strategic efforts to build a better-quality tire with more performance features) but also from (1) differences in what the three tire makers pay their suppliers for materials and tire-making components, and (2) differences in the operating efficiencies, costs, and markups of Michelin's wholesale–retail dealer outlets versus those of Goodyear and Bridgestone.

The Value Chain System for an Entire Industry

As the tire industry example makes clear, a company's value chain is embedded in a larger system of activities that includes the value chains of its suppliers and the value chains of whatever distribution channel allies it uses in getting its product or service to end users.[13] Suppliers' value chains are relevant because suppliers perform activities and incur costs in creating and delivering the purchased inputs used in a company's own value-creating activities. The costs, performance features, and quality of these inputs influence a company's own costs and product differentiation capabilities. Anything a company can do to help its suppliers drive down the costs of their value chain activities or improve the quality and performance of the items being supplied can enhance its own competitiveness—a powerful reason for working collaboratively with suppliers in managing supply chain activities.[14]

The value chains of forward channel partners and/or the customers to whom a company sells are relevant because (1) the costs and margins of a company's distributors and retail dealers are part of the price the ultimate consumer pays, and (2) the activities that distribution allies perform affect customer satisfaction. For these reasons, companies normally work closely

> A company's cost-competitiveness depends not only on the costs of internally performed activities (its own value chain) but also on costs in the value chains of its suppliers and forward channel allies.

with their forward channel allies (who are their direct customers) to perform value chain activities in mutually beneficial ways. For instance, motor vehicle manufacturers work closely with their local automobile dealers to keep the retail prices of their vehicles competitive with rivals' models and to ensure that owners are satisfied with dealers' repair and maintenance services. Some aluminum can producers have constructed plants next to beer breweries and deliver cans on overhead conveyors directly to the breweries' can-filling lines; this has resulted in significant savings in production scheduling, shipping, and inventory costs for both container producers and breweries.[15] Many automotive parts suppliers have built plants near the auto assembly plants they supply to facilitate just-in-time deliveries, reduce warehousing and shipping costs, and promote close collaboration on parts design and production scheduling. Irrigation equipment companies; suppliers of grape-harvesting and winemaking equipment; and firms making barrels, wine bottles, caps, corks, and labels all have facilities in the California wine country to be close to the nearly 700 winemakers they supply.[16] The lesson here is that a company's value chain activities are often closely linked to the value chains of their suppliers and the forward allies or customers to whom they sell.

As a consequence, *accurately assessing a company's competitiveness from the perspective of the consumers who ultimately use its products or services thus requires that company managers understand an industry's entire value chain system for delivering a product or service to customers, not just the company's own value chain.* A typical industry value chain that incorporates the value chains of suppliers and forward channel allies (if any) is shown in Figure 4.4. However, industry value chains vary significantly by industry. The primary value chain activities in the pulp and paper industry (timber farming, logging, pulp mills, and papermaking) differ from the primary value chain activities in the home appliance industry (parts and components manufacture, assembly, wholesale distribution, retail sales). The value chain for the soft drink industry (processing of basic ingredients and syrup manufacture, bottling and can filling, wholesale distribution, advertising, and retail merchandising) differs from that for the computer software industry (programming, disk loading, marketing, distribution). Producers of bathroom and kitchen faucets depend heavily on the activities of wholesale distributors and building supply retailers in winning sales to

Figure 4.4   Representative Value Chain for an Entire Industry

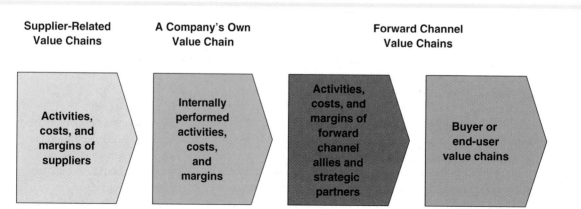

Source: Based in part on the single-industry value chain displayed in Michael E. Porter, *Competitive Advantage* (New York: Free Press, 1985), p. 35.

ILLUSTRATION CAPSULE 4.1
Estimated Value Chain Costs for Recording and Distributing Music CDs through Traditional Music Retailers

The following table presents the representative costs and markups associated with producing and distributing a music CD retailing for $15 in brick-and-mortar music stores.

Value Chain Activities and Costs in Producing and Distributing a CD		
1. Record company direct production costs:		$2.40
Artists and repertoire	$0.75	
Pressing of CD and packaging	1.65	
2. Royalties		.99
3. Record company marketing expenses		1.50
4. Record company overhead		1.50
5. Total record company costs		6.39
6. Record company's operating profit		1.86
7. Record company's selling price to distributor/wholesaler		8.25
8. Average wholesale distributor markup to cover distribution activities and profit margins		1.50
9. Average wholesale price charged to retailer		9.75
10. Average retail markup over wholesale cost		5.25
11. Average price to consumer at retail		$15.00

Source: Developed by the authors from information in "Fight the Power," a case study prepared by Adrian Aleyne, Babson College, 1999 and other sources.

homebuilders and do-it-yourselfers but producers of papermaking machines internalize their distribution activities by selling directly to the operators of paper plants. Illustration Capsule 4.1 shows representative costs for various activities performed by the producers and marketers of music CDs.

Activity-Based Cost Accounting: A Tool for Determining the Costs of Value Chain Activities

Once the major value chain activities are identified, the next step in evaluating a company's cost-competitiveness involves using the company's cost accounting system to determine the costs of performing specific value chain activities, using what accountants call activity-based costing.[17] *Traditional accounting* identifies costs according to broad categories of expenses—wages and salaries, employee benefits, supplies, maintenance, utilities, travel, depreciation, R&D, interest, general administration, and so on. But activity-based cost accounting involves establishing expense categories for specific value chain activities and assigning costs to the activity responsible for creating the cost. An illustrative example is shown in Table 4.3. Perhaps 25 percent of the companies that have explored the feasibility of activity-based costing have adopted this accounting approach.

Table 4.3   The Difference between Traditional Cost Accounting and Activity-Based Cost Accounting: An Example from Air Conditioner Manufacturing

Traditional Cost Accounting Categories for Air Conditioner Manufacturing		Cost of Performing Specific Air Conditioner Manufacturing Activities Using Activity-Based Cost Accounting	
Wages and benefits	$2,786,900	Operating production machinery	$ 435,400
Computers and software	731,405	Maintaining product and customer data	132,500
Product transportation	319,800	Moving parts from warehouse to assembly area	1,500,400
Energy	170,600	Production-run setup for seven model types	723,300
Facility and vehicle rent	165,870	Production scheduling for seven model types	24,800
Business and training travel	66,000	Receiving and handling raw materials	877,100
Miscellaneous	65,480	Shipping finished goods to customers	561,000
Depreciation	48,200	Customer service (communications with customers concerning design changes and production status)	144,220
Advertising	40,000		
Office and utilities	4,465	Total costs	$4,398,720
Total costs	$4,398,720		

Source: Developed from information in Heather Nachtmann and Mohammad Hani Al-Rifai, "An Application of Activity Based Costing in the Air Conditioner Manufacturing Industry," *Engineering Economics* 40 (2004), pp. 221–36.

The degree to which a company's costs should be disaggregated into specific activities depends on how valuable it is to develop cross-company cost comparisons for narrowly defined activities as opposed to broadly defined activities. Generally speaking, cost estimates are needed at least for each broad category of primary and secondary activities, but finer classifications may be needed if a company discovers that it has a cost disadvantage vis-à-vis rivals and wants to pin down the exact source or activity causing the cost disadvantage. It can also be necessary to develop cost estimates for activities performed in the competitively relevant portions of suppliers' and customers' value chains—which requires going to outside sources for reliable cost information.

Once a company has developed good cost estimates for each of the major activities in its value chain and perhaps has cost estimates for subactivities within each primary/secondary value chain activity, then it is ready to see how its costs for these activities compare with the costs of rival firms. This is where benchmarking comes in.

Benchmarking: A Tool for Assessing Whether a Company's Value Chain Activities Are Competitive

CORE CONCEPT

Benchmarking is a potent tool for learning which companies are best at performing particular activities and then using their techniques (or best practices) to improve the cost and effectiveness of a company's own internal activities.

Many companies today are **benchmarking** their costs of performing a given activity against competitors' costs (and/or against the costs of a noncompetitor that efficiently and effectively performs much the same activity in another industry). *Benchmarking is a tool that allows a company to determine whether the manner in which it performs particular functions and activities represents industry "best practices" when both cost and effectiveness are taken into account.*

Benchmarking entails comparing how different companies perform various value chain activities—how materials are purchased, how suppliers are paid, how inventories are managed, how products are assembled, how fast the company can get new products to market, how the quality control function is performed, how customer orders are filled and shipped, how employees are trained, how payrolls are processed, and how maintenance is performed—and then making cross-company comparisons of the costs of these activities.[18] The objectives of benchmarking are to identify the best practices in performing an activity, to learn how other companies have actually achieved lower costs or better results in performing benchmarked activities, and to take action to improve a company's competitiveness whenever benchmarking reveals that its costs and results of performing an activity are not on a par with what other companies (either competitors or non-competitors) have achieved.

Xerox became one of the first companies to use benchmarking when, in 1979, Japanese manufacturers began selling midsize copiers in the United States for $9,600 each—less than Xerox's production costs.[19] Xerox management suspected its Japanese competitors were dumping, but it sent a team of line managers to Japan, including the head of manufacturing, to study competitors' business processes and costs. With the aid of Xerox's joint venture partner in Japan, Fuji-Xerox, who knew the competitors well, the team found that Xerox's costs were excessive due to gross inefficiencies in the company's manufacturing processes and business practices. The findings triggered a major internal effort at Xerox to become cost-competitive and prompted Xerox to begin benchmarking 67 of its key work processes against companies identified as employing the best practices. Xerox quickly decided not to restrict its benchmarking efforts to its office equipment rivals but to extend them to any company regarded as "world class" in performing *any activity* relevant to Xerox's business. Other companies quickly picked up on Xerox's approach. Toyota managers got their idea for just-in-time inventory deliveries by studying how U.S. supermarkets replenished their shelves. Southwest Airlines reduced the turnaround time of its aircraft at each scheduled stop by studying pit crews on the auto racing circuit. Over 80 percent of Fortune 500 companies reportedly use benchmarking for comparing themselves against rivals on cost and other competitively important measures.

The tough part of benchmarking is not whether to do it, but rather how to gain access to information about other companies' practices and costs. Sometimes benchmarking can be accomplished by collecting information from published reports, trade groups, and industry research firms and by talking to knowledgeable industry analysts, customers, and suppliers. Sometimes field trips to the facilities of competing or noncompeting companies can be arranged to observe how things are done, compare practices and processes, and perhaps exchange data on productivity and other cost components. However, such companies, even if they agree to host facilities tours and answer questions, are unlikely to share competitively sensitive cost information. Furthermore, comparing one company's costs to another's costs may not involve comparing apples to apples if the two companies employ different cost accounting principles to calculate the costs of particular activities.

However, a third and fairly reliable source of benchmarking information has emerged. The explosive interest of companies in benchmarking costs and identifying best practices has prompted consulting organizations (e.g., Accenture, A. T. Kearney, The Benchmarking Exchange, Towers Perrin, and Best Practices, LLC) and several councils and associations (e.g., APQC, the Qualserve Benchmarking Clearinghouse, and the Strategic Planning Institute's Council on Benchmarking) to gather benchmarking data, distribute information about best practices, and provide comparative cost data without identifying the names of particular companies. Independent reporting that disguises the names of individual companies protects competitively sensitive data

> Benchmarking the costs of company activities against rivals provides hard evidence of whether a company is cost-competitive.

ILLUSTRATION CAPSULE 4.2
Benchmarking and Ethical Conduct

Because discussions between benchmarking partners can involve competitively sensitive data, conceivably raising questions about possible restraint of trade or improper business conduct, many benchmarking organizations urge all individuals and organizations involved in benchmarking to abide by a code of conduct grounded in ethical business behavior. One of the most widely used codes of conduct is the one developed by APQC (formerly the American Productivity and Quality Center) and advocated by the Qualserve Benchmarking Clearinghouse; it is based on the following principles and guidelines:

- Avoid discussions or actions that could lead to or imply an interest in restraint of trade, market and/or customer allocation schemes, price fixing, dealing arrangements, bid rigging, or bribery. Don't discuss costs with competitors if costs are an element of pricing.

- Refrain from the acquisition of trade secrets from another by any means that could be interpreted as improper, including the breach of any duty to maintain secrecy. Do not disclose or use any trade secret that may have been obtained through improper means or that was disclosed by another in violation of duty to maintain its secrecy or limit its use.

- Be willing to provide your benchmarking partner with the same type and level of information that you request from that partner.

- Communicate fully and early in the relationship to clarify expectations, avoid misunderstanding, and establish mutual interest in the benchmarking exchange.

- Be honest and complete.

- The use or communication of a benchmarking partner's name with the data obtained or practices observed requires the prior permission of the benchmarking partner.

- Honor the wishes of benchmarking partners regarding how the information that is provided will be handled and used.

- In benchmarking with competitors, establish specific ground rules up front. For example, "We don't want to talk about things that will give either of us a competitive advantage, but rather we want to see where we both can mutually improve or gain benefit."

- Check with legal counsel if any information gathering procedure is in doubt. If uncomfortable, do not proceed. Alternatively, negotiate and sign a specific nondisclosure agreement that will satisfy the attorneys representing each partner.

- Do not ask competitors for sensitive data or cause benchmarking partners to feel they must provide data to continue the process.

- Use an ethical third party to assemble and "blind" competitive data, with inputs from legal counsel in direct competitor sharing. (Note: When cost is closely linked to price, sharing cost data can be considered to be the same as sharing price data.)

- Any information obtained from a benchmarking partner should be treated as internal, privileged communications. If "confidential" or proprietary material is to be exchanged, then a specific agreement should be executed to specify the content of the material that needs to be protected, the duration of the period of protection, the conditions for permitting access to the material, and the specific handling requirements necessary for that material.

Source: APQC, www.apqc.org, and the Qualserve Benchmarking Clearinghouse, www.awwa.org (accessed April 30, 2008).

and lessens the potential for unethical behavior on the part of company personnel in gathering their own data about competitors. Illustration Capsule 4.2 presents a widely recommended code of conduct for engaging in benchmarking.

Strategic Options for Remedying a Cost Disadvantage

Value chain analysis and benchmarking can reveal a great deal about a firm's cost-competitiveness. Examining the costs of a company's own value chain activities and comparing them to rivals' indicates who has how much of a cost advantage or disadvantage and which cost components are responsible. Such information is vital in strategic actions to eliminate a cost disadvantage or create a cost advantage. One of the fundamental insights of value chain analysis and benchmarking is that *a company's competitiveness on cost depends on how efficiently it manages its value chain activities relative to how well competitors manage theirs.*[20] There are three main areas in a company's overall value chain where important differences in the costs of competing firms can occur: a company's own activity segments, suppliers' part of the industry value chain, and the forward channel portion of the industry chain.

Remedying an Internal Cost Disadvantage   When a company's cost disadvantage stems from performing internal value chain activities at a higher cost than key rivals, managers can pursue any of several strategic approaches to restore cost parity:[21]

1. Implement the use of best practices throughout the company, particularly for high-cost activities.

2. Try to eliminate some cost-producing activities altogether by revamping the value chain. Examples include cutting out low-value-added activities or bypassing the value chains and associated costs of distribution allies and marketing directly to end users (the approach used by Dell in PCs and by airlines that encourage passengers to purchase tickets directly from airline Web sites instead of from travel agents).

3. Relocate high-cost activities (e.g., manufacturing) to geographic areas (e.g., Asia, Latin America, Eastern Europe) where they can be performed more cheaply.

4. See if certain internally performed activities can be outsourced from vendors or performed by contractors more cheaply than they can be done in-house.

5. Invest in productivity-enhancing, cost-saving technological improvements (robotics, flexible manufacturing techniques, state-of-the-art electronic networking).

6. Find ways to detour around the activities or items where costs are high—computer chip makers regularly design around the patents held by others to avoid paying royalties; automakers have substituted lower-cost plastic and rubber for metal at many exterior body locations.

7. Redesign the product and/or some of its components to facilitate speedier and more economical manufacture or assembly.

8. Try to make up the internal cost disadvantage by reducing costs in the supplier or forward channel portions of the industry value chain—usually a last resort.

Remedying a Supplier-Related Cost Disadvantage   Supplier-related cost disadvantages can be attacked by pressuring suppliers for lower prices, switching to lower-priced substitute inputs, and collaborating closely with suppliers to identify mutual cost-saving opportunities.[22] For example, just-in-time deliveries from suppliers can lower a company's inventory and internal logistics costs and may also allow its suppliers to economize on their warehousing, shipping, and production scheduling costs—a win–win outcome for both. In a few instances, companies may find that it is cheaper to integrate backward into the business of high-cost suppliers and make the item in-house instead of buying it from outsiders. If a company strikes out in wringing savings out of its high-cost supply chain activities, then it must resort to finding cost savings either in-house or in the forward channel portion of the industry value chain to offset its supplier-related cost disadvantage.

Remedying a Cost Disadvantage Associated with Activities Performed by Forward Channel Allies   There are three main ways to combat a cost disadvantage in the forward portion of the industry value chain:

1.   Pressure dealer-distributors and other forward channel allies to reduce their costs and markups so as to make the final price to buyers more competitive with the prices of rivals.

2.   Work closely with forward channel allies to identify win–win opportunities to reduce costs. For example, a chocolate manufacturer learned that by shipping its bulk chocolate in liquid form in tank cars instead of 10-pound molded bars, it could not only save its candy-bar-manufacturing customers the costs associated with unpacking and melting but also eliminate its own costs of molding bars and packing them.

3.   Change to a more economical distribution strategy, including switching to cheaper distribution channels (perhaps direct sales via the Internet) or perhaps integrating forward into company-owned retail outlets.

If these efforts fail, the company can either try to live with the cost disadvantage or pursue cost-cutting earlier in the value chain system.

Translating Proficient Performance of Value Chain Activities into Competitive Advantage

> Performing value chain activities in ways that give a company the capabilities to either outmatch the competencies and capabilities of rivals or else beat them on costs are two good ways to secure competitive advantage.

A company that does a *first-rate job* of managing its value chain activities *relative to competitors* stands a good chance of achieving sustainable competitive advantage. As shown in Figure 4.5, a company can outmanage rivals in performing value chain activities in either or both of two ways: (1) by astutely developing core competencies and maybe a distinctive competence that rivals don't have or can't quite match and that are instrumental in helping it deliver attractive value to customers, and/or (2) by simply doing an overall better job than rivals of lowering its combined costs of performing all the various value chain activities, such that it ends up with a low-cost advantage over rivals.

The first of these two approaches begins with management efforts to build more organizational expertise in performing certain competitively important value chain activities, deliberately striving to develop competencies and capabilities that add power to its strategy and competitiveness. If management begins to make selected competencies and capabilities cornerstones of its strategy and continues to invest resources in building greater and greater proficiency in performing them, then one (or maybe several) of the targeted competencies/capabilities may rise to the level of a core competence. Later, following additional organizational learning and investments in gaining still greater proficiency, a core competence could evolve into a distinctive competence, giving the company superiority over rivals in performing an important value chain activity. Such superiority, if it gives the company significant competitive clout in the marketplace, can produce an attractive competitive edge over rivals and, more important, prove difficult for rivals to match or offset with competencies and capabilities of their own making. *As a general rule, it is substantially harder for rivals to achieve "best in industry" proficiency in performing a key value chain activity than it is for them to clone the features and attributes of a hot-selling product or service.*[23] This is especially true when a company with a distinctive competence avoids becoming

Figure 4.5   Translating Company Performance of Value Chain Activities into Competitive Advantage

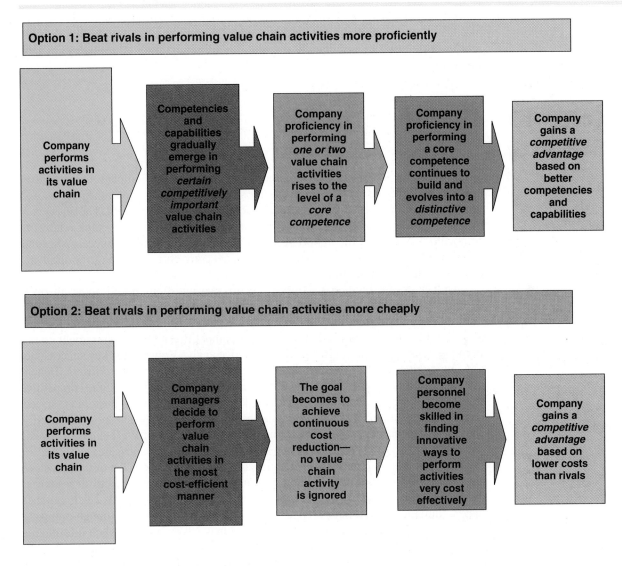

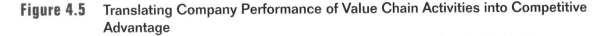

complacent and works diligently to maintain its industry-leading expertise and capability. GlaxoSmithKline, one of the world's most competitively capable pharmaceutical companies, has built its business position around expert performance of a few competitively crucial activities: extensive R&D to achieve first discovery of new drugs, a carefully constructed approach to patenting, skill in gaining rapid and thorough clinical clearance through regulatory bodies, and unusually strong distribution and sales-force capabilities.[24] FedEx's astute management of its value chain has produced unmatched competencies and capabilities in overnight package delivery.

The second approach to building competitive advantage entails determined management efforts to be cost-efficient in performing value chain activities. Such efforts have to be ongoing and persistent, and they have to involve each and every value chain activity. The goal must be continuous cost reduction, not a one-time or on-again/off-again effort.

Companies whose managers are truly committed to low-cost performance of value chain activities and succeed in engaging company personnel to discover innovative ways to drive costs out of the business have a real chance of gaining a durable low-cost edge over rivals. It is not as easy as it seems to imitate a company's low-cost practices. Companies like Wal-Mart, Dell, Nucor Steel, Southwest Airlines, Toyota, and French discount retailer Carrefour have been highly successful in managing their value chains in a low-cost manner.

QUESTION 4: IS THE COMPANY COMPETITIVELY STRONGER OR WEAKER THAN KEY RIVALS?

Using value chain analysis and benchmarking to determine a company's competitiveness on price and cost is necessary but not sufficient. A more comprehensive assessment needs to be made of the company's overall competitive strength. The answers to two questions are of particular interest: First, how does the company rank relative to competitors on each of the important factors that determine market success? Second, all things considered, does the company have a net competitive advantage or disadvantage versus major competitors?

An easy-to-use method for answering the two questions posed above involves developing quantitative strength ratings for the company and its key competitors on each industry key success factor and each competitively pivotal resource capability. Much of the information needed for doing a competitive strength assessment comes from previous analyses. Industry and competitive analysis reveals the key success factors and competitive capabilities that separate industry winners from losers. Benchmarking data and scouting key competitors provide a basis for judging the competitive strength of rivals on such factors as cost, key product attributes, customer service, image and reputation, financial strength, technological skills, distribution capability, and other competitively important resources and capabilities. SWOT analysis reveals how the company in question stacks up on these same strength measures.

Step 1 in doing a competitive strength assessment is to make a list of the industry's key success factors and most telling measures of competitive strength or weakness (6 to 10 measures usually suffice). Step 2 is to rate the firm and its rivals on each factor. Numerical rating scales (e.g., from 1 to 10) are best to use, although ratings of stronger ($+$), weaker ($-$), and about equal ($=$) may be appropriate when information is scanty and assigning numerical scores conveys false precision. Step 3 is to sum the strength ratings on each factor to get an overall measure of competitive strength for each company being rated. Step 4 is to use the overall strength ratings to draw conclusions about the size and extent of the company's net competitive advantage or disadvantage and to take specific note of areas of strength and weakness.

Table 4.4 provides two examples of competitive strength assessment, using the hypothetical ABC Company against four rivals. The first example employs an *unweighted rating system*. With unweighted ratings, each key success factor/competitive strength measure is assumed to be equally important (a rather dubious assumption). Whichever company has the highest strength rating on a given measure has an implied competitive edge on that factor; the size of its edge is mirrored in the margin of difference between its rating and the ratings assigned to rivals—a rating of 9 for one company versus ratings of 5, 4, and 3, respectively, for three other companies indicates a bigger advantage than a rating of 9 versus ratings of 8, 7, and 6. Summing a

Table 4.4 Illustrations of Unweighted and Weighted Competitive Strength Assessments

A. Sample of an Unweighted Competitive Strength Assessment

Key Success Factor/Strength Measure	Strength Rating (Scale: 1 = Very weak; 10 = Very strong)				
	ABC Co.	Rival 1	Rival 2	Rival 3	Rival 4
Quality/product performance	8	5	10	1	6
Reputation/image	8	7	10	1	6
Manufacturing capability	2	10	4	5	1
Technological skills	10	1	7	3	8
Dealer network/distribution capability	9	4	10	5	1
New product innovation capability	9	4	10	5	1
Financial resources	5	10	7	3	1
Relative cost position	5	10	3	1	4
Customer service capabilities	5	7	10	1	4
Unweighted overall strength rating	**61**	**58**	**71**	**25**	**32**

B. Sample of a Weighted Competitive Strength Assessment
(Rating scale: 1 = Very weak; 10 = Very strong)

Key Success Factor/Strength Measure	Importance Weight	ABC Co.		Rival 1		Rival 2		Rival 3		Rival 4	
		Strength Rating	Score	Strength Rating	Score	Strength Rating	Score	Strength Rating	Score	Strength Rating	Score
Quality/product performance	0.10	8	0.80	5	0.50	10	1.00	1	0.10	6	0.60
Reputation/image	0.10	8	0.80	7	0.70	10	1.00	1	0.10	6	0.60
Manufacturing capability	0.10	2	0.20	10	1.00	4	0.40	5	0.50	1	0.10
Technological skills	0.05	10	0.50	1	0.05	7	0.35	3	0.15	8	0.40
Dealer network/distribution capability	0.05	9	0.45	4	0.20	10	0.50	5	0.25	1	0.05
New product innovation capability	0.05	9	0.45	4	0.20	10	0.50	5	0.25	1	0.05
Financial resources	0.10	5	0.50	10	1.00	7	0.70	3	0.30	1	0.10
Relative cost position	0.30	5	1.50	10	3.00	3	0.90	1	0.30	4	1.20
Customer service capabilities	0.15	5	0.75	7	1.05	10	1.50	1	0.15	4	0.60
Sum of importance weights	**1.00**										
Weighted overall strength rating		61	**5.95**	58	**7.70**	71	**6.85**	25	**2.10**	32	**3.70**

company's ratings on all the measures produces an overall strength rating. The higher a company's overall strength rating, the stronger its overall competitiveness versus rivals. The bigger the difference between a company's overall rating and the scores of *lower-rated* rivals, the greater its implied *net competitive advantage.* Conversely, the bigger the difference between a company's overall rating and the scores of *higher-rated* rivals, the greater its implied *net competitive disadvantage.* Thus, ABC's total score of 61 (see the top half of Table 4.4) signals a much greater net competitive advantage over Rival 4 (with a score of 32) than over Rival 1 (with a score of 58) but indicates a moderate net competitive disadvantage against Rival 2 (with an overall score of 71).

A weighted competitive strength analysis is conceptually stronger than an unweighted analysis because of the inherent weakness in assuming that all the strength measures are equally important.

However, a better method is a *weighted rating system* (shown in the bottom half of Table 4.4) because the different measures of competitive strength are unlikely to be equally important. In an industry where the products/services of rivals are virtually identical, for instance, having low unit costs relative to rivals is nearly always the most important determinant of competitive strength. In an industry with strong product differentiation, the most significant measures of competitive strength may be brand awareness, amount of advertising, product attractiveness, and distribution capability. In a weighted rating system, each measure of competitive strength is assigned a weight based on its perceived importance in shaping competitive success. A weight could be as high as 0.75 (maybe even higher) in situations where one particular competitive variable is overwhelmingly decisive, or a weight could be as low as 0.20 when two or three strength measures are more important than the rest. Lesser competitive strength indicators can carry weights of 0.05 or 0.10. No matter whether the differences between the importance weights are big or little, *the sum of the weights must add up to 1.0.*

Weighted strength ratings are calculated by rating each competitor on each strength measure (using the 1 to 10 rating scale) and multiplying the assigned rating by the assigned weight (a rating of 4 times a weight of 0.20 gives a weighted rating, or score, of 0.80). Again, the company with the highest rating on a given measure has an implied competitive edge on that measure, with the size of its edge reflected in the difference between its rating and rivals' ratings. The weight attached to the measure indicates how important the edge is. Summing a company's weighted strength ratings for all the measures yields an overall strength rating. Comparisons of the weighted overall strength scores indicate which competitors are in the strongest and weakest competitive positions and who has how big a net competitive advantage over whom.

Note in Table 4.4 that the unweighted and weighted rating schemes produce different orderings of the companies. In the weighted system, ABC Company drops from second to third in strength, and Rival 1 jumps from third into first because of its high strength ratings on the two most important factors. Weighting the importance of the strength measures can thus make a significant difference in the outcome of the assessment.

Interpreting the Competitive Strength Assessments

High competitive strength ratings signal a strong competitive position and possession of competitive advantage; low ratings signal a weak position and competitive disadvantage.

Competitive strength assessments provide useful conclusions about a company's competitive situation. The ratings show how a company compares against rivals, factor by factor or capability by capability, thus revealing where it is strongest and weakest, and against whom. Moreover, the overall competitive strength scores indicate how all the different factors add up—whether the company is at a net competitive advantage or disadvantage against each rival. The firm with the largest overall competitive strength rating enjoys the strongest competitive position, with the size of its net competitive advantage reflected by how much its score exceeds the scores of rivals.

In addition, the strength ratings provide guidelines for designing wise offensive and defensive strategies. For example, consider the ratings and weighted scores in the bottom half of Table 4.4. If ABC Co. wants to go on the offensive to win additional sales and market share, such an offensive probably needs to be aimed directly at winning customers away from Rivals 3 and 4 (which have lower overall strength scores) rather than Rivals 1 and 2 (which have higher overall strength scores). Moreover, while ABC has high ratings for technological skills (a 10 rating), dealer network/distribution capability (a 9 rating), new product innovation capability (a 9 rating), quality/product performance (an 8 rating), and reputation/image (an 8 rating), these strength measures have low importance weights—meaning that ABC has strengths in areas that don't translate into much competitive clout in the marketplace. Even so, it outclasses Rival 3 in all five areas, plus it enjoys lower costs than Rival 3 (ABC has a 5 rating on relative cost position versus a 1 rating for Rival 3)—and relative cost position carries the highest importance weight of all the strength measures. ABC also has greater competitive strength than Rival 3 as concerns customer service capabilities (which carries the second-highest importance weight). Hence, because ABC's strengths are in the very areas where Rival 3 is weak, ABC is in good position to attack Rival 3—it may well be able to persuade a number of Rival 3's customers to switch their purchases over to ABC's product.

But in mounting an offensive to win customers away from Rival 3, ABC should note that Rival 1 has an excellent relative cost position—its rating of 10, combined with the importance weight of 0.30 for relative cost, means that Rival 1 has meaningfully lower costs in an industry where low costs are competitively important. Rival 1 is thus strongly positioned to retaliate against ABC with lower prices if ABC's strategy offensive ends up drawing customers away from Rival 1. Moreover, Rival 1's very strong relative cost position vis-à-vis all the other companies arms it with the ability to use its lower-cost advantage to underprice all of its rivals and gain sales and market share at their expense. If ABC wants to defend against its vulnerability to potential price-cutting by Rival 1, then it needs to aim a portion of its strategy at lowering its costs.

> A company's competitive strength scores pinpoint its strengths and weaknesses against rivals and point directly to the kinds of offensive/defensive actions it can use to exploit its competitive strengths and reduce its competitive vulnerabilities.

The point here is that a competitively astute company should use the strength scores in deciding what strategic moves to make—what strengths to exploit in winning business away from rivals and which competitive weaknesses to try to correct. When a company has important competitive strengths in areas where one or more rivals are weak, it makes sense to consider offensive moves to exploit rivals' competitive weaknesses. When a company has important competitive weaknesses in areas where one or more rivals are strong, it makes sense to consider defensive moves to curtail its vulnerability.

QUESTION 5: WHAT STRATEGIC ISSUES AND PROBLEMS MERIT FRONT-BURNER MANAGERIAL ATTENTION?

The final and most important analytical step is to zero in on exactly what strategic issues that company managers need to address—and resolve—for the company to be more financially and competitively successful in the years ahead. This step involves drawing on the results of both industry and competitive analysis and the evaluations of the company's own competitiveness. The task here is to get a clear fix on exactly what strategic and competitive challenges confront the company, which of the company's competitive shortcomings need fixing, what obstacles stand in the way of improving the company's competitive position in the marketplace, and what specific problems merit front-burner attention by company managers. *Pinpointing the precise things that management needs to worry about sets the agenda for deciding what actions to take next to improve the company's performance and business outlook.*

> Zeroing in on the strategic issues a company faces and compiling a "worry list" of problems and roadblocks creates a strategic agenda of problems that merit prompt managerial attention.

The "worry list" of issues and problems that have to be wrestled with can include such things as *how* to stave off market challenges from new foreign competitors, *how* to combat the price discounting of rivals, *how* to reduce the company's high costs and pave the way for price reductions, *how* to sustain the company's present rate of growth in light of slowing buyer demand, *whether* to expand the company's product line, *whether* to correct the company's competitive deficiencies by acquiring a rival company with the missing strengths, *whether* to expand into foreign markets rapidly or cautiously, *whether* to reposition the company and move to a different strategic group, *what to do* about growing buyer interest in substitute products, and *what to do* to combat the aging demographics of the company's customer base. The worry list thus always centers on such concerns as "how to . . . ," "what to do about . . . ," and "whether to . . ."—the purpose of the worry list is to identify the specific issues/ problems that management needs to address, not to figure out what specific actions to take. Deciding what to do—which strategic actions to take and which strategic moves to take—comes later (when it is time to craft the strategy and choose among the various strategic alternatives).

> Actually deciding upon a strategy and what specific actions to take is what comes *after* developing the list of strategic issues and problems that merit front-burner management attention.

If the items on the worry list are relatively minor—which suggests the company's strategy is mostly on track and reasonably well matched to the company's overall situation, company managers seldom need to go much beyond fine-tuning of the present strategy. If, however, the issues and problems confronting the company are serious and indicate the present strategy is not well suited for the road ahead, the task of crafting a better strategy has got to go to the top of management's action agenda.

> A good strategy must contain ways to deal with all the strategic issues and obstacles that stand in the way of the company's financial and competitive success in the years ahead.

KEY POINTS

There are five key questions to consider in analyzing a company's own particular competitive circumstances and its competitive position vis-à-vis key rivals:

1. *How well is the present strategy working?* This involves evaluating the strategy from a qualitative standpoint (completeness, internal consistency, rationale, and suitability to the situation) and also from a quantitative standpoint (the strategic and financial results the strategy is producing). The stronger a company's current overall performance, the less likely the need for radical strategy changes. The weaker a company's performance and/or the faster the changes in its external situation

(which can be gleaned from industry and competitive analysis), the more its current strategy must be questioned.

2. *What are the company's resource strengths and weaknesses, and its external opportunities and threats?* A SWOT analysis provides an overview of a firm's situation and is an essential component of crafting a strategy tightly matched to the company's situation. The two most important parts of SWOT analysis are (1) drawing conclusions about what story the compilation of strengths, weaknesses, opportunities, and threats tells about the company's overall situation, and (2) acting on those conclusions to better match the company's strategy to its resource strengths and market opportunities, to correct the important weaknesses, and to defend against external threats. A company's resource strengths, competencies, and competitive capabilities are strategically relevant because they are the most logical and appealing building blocks for strategy; resource weaknesses are important because they may represent vulnerabilities that need correction. External opportunities and threats come into play because a good strategy necessarily aims at capturing a company's most attractive opportunities and at defending against threats to its well-being.

3. *Are the company's prices and costs competitive?* One telling sign of whether a company's situation is strong or precarious is whether its prices and costs are competitive with those of industry rivals. Value chain analysis and benchmarking are essential tools in determining whether the company is performing particular functions and activities cost-effectively, learning whether its costs are in line with competitors, and deciding which internal activities and business processes need to be scrutinized for improvement. Value chain analysis teaches that how competently a company manages its value chain activities relative to rivals is a key to building a competitive advantage based on either better competencies and competitive capabilities or lower costs than rivals.

4. *Is the company competitively stronger or weaker than key rivals?* The key appraisals here involve how the company matches up against key rivals on industry key success factors and other chief determinants of competitive success and whether and why the company has a competitive advantage or disadvantage. Quantitative competitive strength assessments, using the method presented in Table 4.4, indicate where a company is competitively strong and weak, and provide insight into the company's ability to defend or enhance its market position. As a rule a company's competitive strategy should be built around its competitive strengths and should aim at shoring up areas where it is competitively vulnerable. When a company has important competitive strengths in areas where one or more rivals are weak, it makes sense to consider offensive moves to exploit rivals' competitive weaknesses. When a company has important competitive weaknesses in areas where one or more rivals are strong, it makes sense to consider defensive moves to curtail its vulnerability.

5. *What strategic issues and problems merit front-burner managerial attention?* This analytical step zeros in on the strategic issues and problems that stand in the way of the company's success. It involves using the results of both industry and competitive analysis and company situation analysis to identify a "worry list" of issues to be resolved for the company to be financially and competitively successful in the years ahead. The worry list always centers on such concerns as "how to . . . ," "what to do about . . . ," and "whether to . . ."—the purpose of the worry list is to identify the specific issues/problems that management needs to address. Actually

deciding on a strategy and what specific actions to take is what comes after the list of strategic issues and problems that merit front-burner management attention is developed.

Good company situation analysis, like good industry and competitive analysis, is a valuable precondition for good strategy making. A competently done evaluation of a company's resource capabilities and competitive strengths exposes strong and weak points in the present strategy and how attractive or unattractive the company's competitive position is and why. Managers need such understanding to craft a strategy that is well suited to the company's competitive circumstances.

ASSURANCE OF LEARNING EXERCISES

1. Review the information in Illustration Capsule 4.1 concerning the costs of the different value chain activities associated with recording and distributing music CDs through traditional brick-and-mortar retail outlets. Then answer the following questions:

   a. Does the growing popularity of downloading music from the Internet give rise to a new music industry value chain that differs considerably from the traditional value chain? Explain why or why not.

   b. What costs would be cut out of the traditional value chain or bypassed in the event recording studios sell downloadable files of artists' recordings direct to online buyers?

   c. What happens to the traditional value chain if more and more consumers use peer-to-peer file-sharing software to download music from the Internet rather than purchase CDs or downloadable files?

2. Using the information in Table 4.1 and the financial statement information for Avon Products below, calculate the following ratios for Avon for both 2006 and 2007:

   a. Gross profit margin
   b. Operating profit margin
   c. Net profit margin
   d. Times-interest-earned (coverage) ratio
   e. Return on shareholders' equity
   f. Return on assets
   g. Debt-to-equity ratio
   h. Long-term debt-to-capital ratio
   i. Days of inventory
   j. Inventory turnover ratio
   k. Average collection period

Based on these ratios, did Avon's financial performance improve, weaken, or remain about the same from 2006 to 2007?

Consolidated Statements of Income for Avon Products, Inc., 2006–2007 (in millions, except per share data)

	Years ended December 31	
	2007	2006
Total revenue	$ 9,938.7	$ 8,763.9
Costs, expenses and other:		
Cost of sales	3,941.2	3,416.5
Selling, general, and administrative expenses	5,124.8	4,586.0
Operating profit	872.7	761.4
Interest expense	112.2	99.6
Interest income	(42.2)	(55.3)
Other expense, net	6.6	13.6
Total other expenses	76.6	57.9
Income before taxes and minority interest	796.1	703.5
Income taxes	262.8	223.4
Income before minority interest	533.3	480.1
Minority interest	(2.6)	(2.5)
Net income	$ 530.7	$ 477.6
Earnings per share:		
Basic	$ 1.22	$ 1.07
Diluted	$ 1.21	$ 1.06
Weighted-average shares outstanding:		
Basic	433.47	447.40
Diluted	436.89	449.16

Consolidated Balance Sheets for Avon Products, Inc.
(in millions, except per share data)

	Years ended December 31	
	2007	2006
Assets		
Current assets		
Cash, including cash equivalents of $492.3 and $825.1	$ 963.4	$ 1,198.9
Accounts receivable (less allowances of $141.1 and $119.1)	840.4	700.4
Inventories	1,041.8	900.3
Prepaid expenses and other	669.8	534.8
Total current assets	3,515.4	3,334.4

(Continued)

	Years ended December 31	
	2007	**2006**
Property, plant and equipment, at cost		
Land	71.8	65.3
Buildings and improvements	972.7	910.0
Equipment	1,317.9	1,137.0
	2,362.4	2,112.3
Less accumulated depreciation	(1,084.2)	(1,012.1)
	1,278.2	1,100.2
Other assets	922.6	803.6
Total assets	$ 5,716.2	$ 5,238.2
Liabilities and Shareholders' Equity		
Current liabilities		
Debt maturing within one year	$ 929.5	$ 615.6
Accounts payable	800.3	655.8
Accrued liabilities	1,221.3	1,044.6
Income taxes	102.3	209.2
Total current liabilities	3,053.4	2,525.2
Long-term debt	1,167.9	1,170.7
Other liabilities (including minority interest of $38.2 and $37.0)	783.3	751.9
Total liabilities	$ 5,004.6	$ 4,447.8
Shareholders' Equity		
Common stock, par value $0.25 — authorized 1,500 shares; issued 736.3 and 732.7 shares	184.7	183.5
Additional paid-in capital	1,724.6	1,549.8
Retained earnings	3,586.5	3,396.8
Accumulated other comprehensive loss	(417.0)	(656.3)
Treasury stock, at cost—308.6 and 291.4 shares	(4,367.2)	(3,683.4)
Total shareholders' equity	$ 711.6	$ 790.4
Total liabilities and shareholders' equity	$ 5,716.2	$ 5,238.2

Source: Avon Products Inc. 2007 10-K.

EXERCISES FOR SIMULATION PARTICIPANTS

1. What hard evidence can you cite that indicates your company's strategy is working fairly well (or perhaps not working so well, if your company's performance is lagging that of rival companies)?

2. What resource strengths and resource weaknesses does your company have? What external market opportunities for growth and increased profitability exist for your company? What external threats to your company's future well-being and profitability do you and your co-managers see? What does the preceding SWOT

analysis indicate about your company's present situation and future prospects—where on the scale from "exceptionally strong" to "alarmingly weak" does the attractiveness of your company's situation rank?

3. Does your company have any core competencies? If so, what are they?

4. What are the key elements of your company's value chain? Refer to Figure 4.3 in developing your answer.

5. Using the methodology presented in Table 4.4, do a weighted competitive strength assessment for your company and two other companies that you and your co-managers consider to be very close competitors.

5

The Five Generic Competitive Strategies

Which One to Employ?

LEARNING OBJECTIVES

1. Gain command of how each of the five generic competitive strategies lead to competitive advantage and deliver superior value to customers.

2. Learn why some of the five generic strategies work better in certain kinds of industry and competitive conditions than in others.

3. Learn the major avenues for achieving a competitive advantage based on lower costs.

4. Learn the major avenues for developing a competitive advantage based on differentiating a company's product or service offering from the offerings of rivals in ways that better satisfy buyer needs and preferences.

This chapter describes the five *basic competitive strategy options*—which of the five to employ is a company's first and foremost choice in crafting an overall strategy and beginning its quest for competitive advantage. A company's **competitive strategy** *deals exclusively with the specifics of management's game plan for competing successfully—its specific efforts to please customers, its offensive and defensive moves to counter the maneuvers of rivals, its responses to whatever market conditions prevail at the moment, its initiatives to strengthen its market position, and its approach to securing a competitive advantage vis-à-vis rivals.* A company achieves competitive advantage whenever it has some type of edge over rivals in attracting buyers and coping with competitive forces. There are many routes to competitive advantage, but they all involve giving buyers what they perceive as superior value compared to the offerings of rival sellers

Superior value can mean a good product at a lower price; a superior product that is worth paying more for; or a best-value offering that represents an attractive combination of price, features, quality, service, and other appealing attributes. Delivering superior value—whatever form it takes—nearly always requires performing value chain activities differently than rivals and building competencies and resource capabilities that are not readily matched.

> **CORE CONCEPT**
> A *competitive strategy* concerns the specifics of management's game plan for competing successfully and securing a competitive advantage over rivals.

> **CORE CONCEPT**
> The objective of competitive strategy is to knock the socks off rival companies by doing a better job of satisfying buyer needs and preferences.

THE FIVE GENERIC COMPETITIVE STRATEGIES

There are countless variations in the competitive strategies that companies employ, mainly because each company's strategic approach entails custom-designed actions to fit its own circumstances and industry environment. The chances are remote that any two companies—even companies in the same industry—will employ strategies that are exactly alike in every detail. Managers at different companies always have a slightly different spin on how to best align their company's strategy with market conditions; moreover, they have different notions of how they intend to outmaneuver rivals and what strategic options make the most sense for their particular company. However, when one strips away the details to get at the real substance, the biggest and most important differences among competitive strategies boil down to (1) whether a company's market target is broad or narrow, and (2) whether the company is pursuing a competitive advantage linked to low costs or product differentiation. Five distinct competitive strategy approaches stand out:[1]

1. *A low-cost provider strategy*—striving to achieve lower overall costs than rivals and appealing to a broad spectrum of customers, usually by underpricing rivals.

2. *A broad differentiation strategy*—seeking to differentiate the company's product offering from rivals' in ways that will appeal to a broad spectrum of buyers.

3. *A best-cost provider strategy*—giving customers more value for the money by incorporating good-to-excellent product attributes at a lower cost than rivals; the target is to have the lowest (best) costs and prices compared to rivals offering products with comparable attributes.

4. *A focused (or market niche) strategy based on low costs*—concentrating on a narrow buyer segment and outcompeting rivals by having lower costs than rivals and thus being able to serve niche members at a lower price.

5. *A focused (or market niche) strategy based on differentiation*—concentrating on a narrow buyer segment and outcompeting rivals by offering niche members customized attributes that meet their tastes and requirements better than rivals' products.

Each of these five generic competitive approaches stakes out a different market position, as shown in Figure 5.1. Each involves distinctively different approaches to competing and operating the business. The remainder of this chapter explores the ins and outs of the five generic competitive strategies and how they differ.

LOW-COST PROVIDER STRATEGIES

CORE CONCEPT

A low-cost leader's basis for competitive advantage is lower overall costs than competitors. Successful low-cost leaders are exceptionally good at finding ways to drive costs out of their businesses.

Striving to be the industry's overall low-cost provider is a powerful competitive approach in markets with many price-sensitive buyers. A company achieves low-cost leadership when it becomes the industry's lowest-cost provider rather than just being one of perhaps several competitors with comparatively low costs. A low-cost provider's strategic target is meaningfully lower costs than rivals—but not necessarily the absolutely lowest cost possible. In striving for a cost advantage over rivals, managers must take care to include features and services that buyers consider essential—*even if it is priced lower than competing products, a product offering that is too frills-free sabotages the attractiveness of the company's product and can turn*

Figure 5.1 The Five Generic Competitive Strategies: Each Stakes Out a Different Market Position

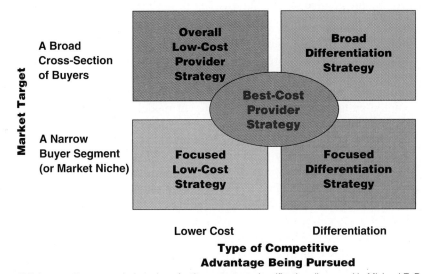

Source: This is an author-expanded version of a three-strategy classification discussed in Michael E. Porter, *Competitive Strategy* (New York: Free Press, 1980), pp. 35–40.

buyers off. For maximum effectiveness, companies employing a low-cost provider strategy need to achieve their cost advantage in ways difficult for rivals to copy or match. If rivals find it relatively easy or inexpensive to imitate the leader's low-cost methods, then the leader's advantage will be too short-lived to yield a valuable edge in the marketplace.

A company has two options for translating a low-cost advantage over rivals into attractive profit performance. Option 1 is to use the lower-cost edge to underprice competitors and attract price-sensitive buyers in great enough numbers to increase total profits. Option 2 is to maintain the present price, be content with the present market share, and use the lower-cost edge to earn a higher profit margin on each unit sold, thereby raising the firm's total profits and overall return on investment.

The Two Major Avenues for Achieving a Cost Advantage

To achieve a low-cost edge over rivals, a firm's cumulative costs across its overall value chain must be lower than competitors' cumulative costs—and the means of achieving the cost advantage must be durable. There are two ways to accomplish this:[2]

1. Perform value chain activities more cost-effectively than rivals.
2. Revamp the firm's overall value chain to eliminate or bypass some cost-producing activities altogether.

Let's look at each of the two approaches to securing a cost advantage.

Cost-Efficient Management of Value Chain Activities   For a company to do a more cost-efficient job of managing its value chain than rivals, managers must launch a concerted, ongoing effort to ferret out cost-saving opportunities in every part of the value chain. No activity can escape cost-saving scrutiny, and all company personnel must be expected to use their talents and ingenuity to come up with innovative and effective ways to keep costs down. All avenues for performing value chain activities at a lower cost than rivals have to be explored. Attempts to outmanage rivals on cost commonly involve such actions as:

1. *Striving to capture all available economies of scale.* Economies of scale stem from an ability to lower unit costs by increasing the scale of operation—there are many occasions when a large plant is more economical to operate than a small or medium-size plant, or when a large distribution warehouse is more cost-efficient than a small one. Often, manufacturing economies can be achieved by using common parts and components in different models and/or by cutting back on the number of models offered (especially slow-selling ones) and then scheduling longer production runs for fewer models. In global industries, making separate products for each country market instead of selling a mostly standard product worldwide tends to boost unit costs because of lost time in model changeover, shorter production runs, and inability to reach the most economic scale of production for each country model.

2. *Taking full advantage of experience/learning curve effects.* The cost of performing an activity can decline over time as the learning and experience of company personnel builds. Experience/learning economies can stem from debugging and mastering newly introduced technologies, using the experiences and suggestions of workers to install more efficient plant layouts and assembly procedures, and the added speed and effectiveness that accrues from repeatedly picking sites for and building new plants, retail outlets, or distribution centers. Aggressively managed low-cost providers pay diligent attention to capturing the benefits of learning and experience and to keeping these benefits proprietary to whatever extent possible.

3. *Trying to operate facilities at full capacity.* Whether a company is able to operate at or near full capacity has a big impact on unit costs when its value chain contains activities associated with substantial fixed costs. Higher rates of capacity utilization allow depreciation and other fixed costs to be spread over a larger unit volume, thereby lowering fixed costs per unit. The more capital-intensive the business, or the higher the percentage of fixed costs as a percentage of total costs, the more important that full-capacity operation becomes, because there's such a stiff unit-cost penalty for underutilizing existing capacity.

4. *Pursuing efforts to boost sales volumes and thus spread such costs as research and development (R&D), advertising, and selling and administrative costs out over more units.* The more units a company sells, the more it lowers its unit costs for R&D, sales and marketing, and administrative overhead. PepsiCo and Anheuser-Busch can afford to spend $2.7 million on a 30-second Super Bowl ad because the cost of such an ad can be spread out over the hundreds of millions of units they sell. In contrast, a small company with a sales volume of only 1 million units would find the $2.7 million cost of a Super Bowl ad prohibitive—just one ad would raise costs over $2.00 per unit even if the ad was unusually effective and caused sales volume to jump 25 percent, to 1.25 million units.

5. *Improving supply chain efficiency.* Partnering with suppliers to streamline the ordering and purchasing process, to reduce inventory carrying costs via just-in-time inventory practices, to economize on shipping and materials handling, and to ferret out other cost-saving opportunities is a much-used approach to cost reduction. A company with a core competence (or better still a distinctive

competence) in cost-efficient supply chain management can sometimes achieve a sizable cost advantage over less adept rivals.

6. *Substituting the use of low-cost for high-cost raw materials or component parts.* If certain raw materials and parts cost too much, a company can either substitute lower-cost items or maybe even design the high-cost components out of the product altogether.

7. *Using online systems and sophisticated software to achieve operating efficiencies.* Sharing data with suppliers—from the latest customer orders to detailed forecasts of components requirements—and using enterprise resource planning (ERP) or manufacturing execution system (MES) software can greatly reduce production times and labor costs. Southwest Airlines developed software enabling it to schedule flights and assign flight crews cost-effectively. MTD—a global manufacturer of lawn mowers, garden tractors, and other outdoor power equipment—implemented ERP and MES systems to track critical supply chain activities. Within the first six months of adopting the software systems, MTD management was able to cut $6 million from annual operating expenses by reducing costly supply chain inefficiencies.

8. *Adopting labor-saving operating methods.* There are numerous ways for a company to economize on labor costs—installing labor-saving technology, shifting production from geographic areas where labor costs are high to those where labor costs are low, avoiding the use of union labor where possible (so as to detour costly union work rules that can stifle productivity and union demands for above-market pay scales and costly fringe benefits), and using incentive compensation systems that promote high labor productivity.

9. *Using the company's bargaining power vis-à-vis suppliers to gain concessions.* Many large enterprises (e.g., Wal-Mart, Home Depot, the world's major motor vehicle producers) have used their bargaining clout in purchasing large volumes to wrangle good prices from suppliers. Having greater buying power than rivals can translate to an important cost advantage.

10. *Being alert to the cost advantages of outsourcing and vertical integration.* Outsourcing the performance of certain value chain activities can be more economical than performing them in-house if outside specialists, by virtue of their expertise and volume, can perform the activities at lower cost. Indeed, outsourcing has in recent years become a widely used cost-reduction approach. However, there can be times when integrating into the activities of either suppliers or distribution channel allies can allow an enterprise to detour suppliers or buyers who have an adverse impact on costs because of their considerable bargaining power.

In addition to the above means of trying to perform value chain activities more efficiently than rivals, a company can also achieve important cost savings by deliberately opting for an inherently economical strategy. For instance, a company can aid its efforts to win a durable cost advantage over rivals by:

- Stripping frills and features from its product offering that do not have much value to customers.

- Having lower specifications for purchased materials, parts, and components than do rivals. Thus, a maker of personal computers can use the cheapest hard drives, microprocessors, monitors, DVD drives, and other components that it can find so as to end up with lower production costs than rival PC makers.

- Distributing the company's product only through low-cost distribution channels and avoiding high-cost distribution channels.
- Choosing to use the most economical method for delivering customer orders (even if it results in longer delivery times).

Deliberately incorporating strategy elements that keep costs low can greatly assist a company's drive to be the industry's low-cost provider.

Revamping the Value Chain to Curb or Eliminate Unnecessary Activities
Dramatic cost advantages can emerge from finding innovative ways to cut back on or entirely bypass certain cost-producing value chain activities. There are two primary ways companies can achieve a cost advantage by reconfiguring their value chains:

- *Bypassing the activities and costs of distributors and dealers by selling direct to customers.* Selling direct can involve (1) having the company's own direct sales force (which adds the costs of maintaining and supporting a sales force but which may be cheaper than accessing customers through distributors and dealers), and/or (2) conducting sales operations at the company's Web site (sales costs at a company's Web site may be a substantially less than those incurred by selling through distributor-dealer channels). Costs in the wholesale/retail portions of the value chain frequently represent 35–50 percent of the price final consumers pay. There are several prominent examples where companies have instituted a sell-direct approach to cutting costs out of the value chain. Software developers are increasingly using the Internet to market and deliver their products directly to buyers; allowing customers to download software directly from the Internet eliminates the costs of producing and packaging CDs and cuts out the host of activities, costs, and markups associated with shipping and distributing software through wholesale and retail channels. By cutting all these costs and activities out of the value chain, software developers have the pricing room to boost their profit margins and still sell their products below levels that retailers would have to charge. The major airlines now sell most of their tickets directly to passengers via their Web sites, ticket counter agents, and telephone reservation systems, allowing them to save hundreds of millions of dollars in commissions once paid to travel agents.
- *Replacing certain value chain activities with faster and cheaper online technology.* Internet technology applications have become powerful and pervasive tools for conducting business and reengineering company and industry value chains. For instance, Internet technology has revolutionized supply chain management, turning many time-consuming and labor-intensive activities into paperless transactions performed instantaneously. Company procurement personnel can—with only a few mouse clicks within one seamless system—check materials inventories against incoming customer orders, check suppliers' stocks, check the latest prices for parts and components at auction and e-sourcing Web sites, and check FedEx or UPS delivery schedules. Various e-procurement software packages streamline the purchasing process by eliminating much of the manual handling of data and by substituting electronic communication for paper documents such as requests for quotations, purchase orders, order acceptances, and shipping notices. There is software that permits the relevant details of incoming customer orders to be instantly shared with the suppliers of needed parts and components. All this facilitates just-in-time deliveries of parts and components and matching the production of parts

and components to assembly plant requirements and production schedules, cutting out unnecessary activities and producing savings for both suppliers and manufacturers. Retailers can install online systems that relay data from cash register sales at the checkout counter back to manufacturers and their suppliers. Manufacturers can use online systems to collaborate closely with parts and components suppliers in designing new products and shortening the time it takes to get them into production. Online systems allow warranty claims and product performance problems involving supplier components to be instantly relayed to the relevant suppliers so that corrections can be expedited. Substituting the use of online systems for activities once performed manually has the further effect of breaking down corporate bureaucracies and reducing overhead costs. The whole back-office data management process (order processing, invoicing, customer accounting, and other kinds of transaction costs) can be handled fast, accurately, and with less paperwork and fewer personnel. New online video conferencing technology is currently allowing companies to slice huge sums from their travel budgets by having company personnel at different geographic locations participate in online meetings rather than traveling to meet face-to-face; online meetings, which can now be conducted very effectively, not only are very cost-effective but they facilitate faster decision-making and boost the productivity of company personnel (by eliminating wasteful travel time).

- *Streamlining operations by eliminating low-value-added or unnecessary work steps and activities.* Examples include using computer-assisted design (CAD) techniques, standardizing parts and components across models and styles, having suppliers collaborate to combine parts and components into modules so that products can be assembled in fewer steps, and shifting to an easy-to-manufacture product design. At Wal-Mart, some items supplied by manufacturers are delivered directly to retail stores rather than being routed through Wal-Mart's distribution centers and delivered by Wal-Mart trucks; in other instances, Wal-Mart unloads incoming shipments from manufacturers' trucks arriving at its cross-docked distribution centers directly onto outgoing Wal-Mart trucks headed to particular stores without ever moving the goods into the distribution center. Many supermarket chains have greatly reduced in-store meat butchering and cutting activities by shifting to meats that are cut and packaged at the meat-packing plant and then delivered in ready-to-sell form.

- *Relocating facilities so as to curb the need for shipping and handling activities.* Having suppliers locate facilities adjacent to the company's plant or locating the company's plants or warehouses near customers can help curb or eliminate shipping and handling costs.

- *Offering a frills-free product.* Deliberately restricting the company's product offering to the essentials can help a company cut costs associated with snazzy attributes and a full lineup of options and extras. Activities and costs can also be eliminated by incorporating fewer performance and quality features into the product and by offering buyers fewer services. Stripping extras like first-class seating, meals, and reserved seating is a favorite technique of budget airlines like Southwest Airlines, Ryanair (Europe), easyJet (Europe), and Gol (Brazil).

- *Offering a limited product line.* Pruning slow-selling items from the product lineup and being content to meet the needs of most buyers rather than all buyers can eliminate activities and costs associated with numerous product versions and wide selection.

ILLUSTRATION CAPSULE 5.1
How Wal-Mart Managed Its Value Chain to Achieve a Huge Low-Cost Advantage over Rival Supermarket Chains

Wal-Mart has achieved a substantial cost and pricing advantage over rival supermarket chains by both revamping portions of the grocery retailing value chain and by outmanaging its rivals in efficiently performing various value chain activities. Its cost advantage stems from a series of initiatives and practices:

- Instituting extensive information-sharing with vendors via online systems that relay sales at its checkout counters directly to suppliers of the items, thereby providing suppliers with real-time information on customer demand and preferences (creating an estimated 6 percent cost advantage). It is standard practice at Wal-Mart to collaborate extensively with vendors on all aspects of the purchasing and store delivery process to squeeze out mutually beneficial cost savings. Procter & Gamble, Wal-Mart's biggest supplier, went so far as to integrate its enterprise resource planning (ERP) system with Wal-Mart's.

- Pursuing global procurement of some items and centralizing most purchasing activities so as to leverage the company's buying power (creating an estimated 2.5 percent cost advantage).

- Investing in state-of-the-art automation at its distribution centers, efficiently operating a truck fleet that makes daily deliveries to Wal-Mart's stores, and putting assorted other cost-saving practices into place at its headquarters, distribution centers, and stores (resulting in an estimated 4 percent cost advantage).

- Striving to optimize the product mix and achieve greater sales turnover (resulting in about a 2 percent cost advantage).

- Installing security systems and store operating procedures that lower shrinkage rates (producing a cost advantage of about 0.5 percent).

- Negotiating preferred real estate rental and leasing rates with real estate developers and owners of its store sites (yielding a cost advantage of 2 percent).

- Managing and compensating its workforce in a manner that produces lower labor costs (yielding an estimated 5 percent cost advantage).

Altogether, these value chain initiatives give Wal-Mart an approximately 22 percent cost advantage over Kroger, Safeway, and other leading supermarket chains. With such a sizable cost advantage, Wal-Mart has been able to underprice its rivals and become the world's leading supermarket retailer in little more than a decade.

Source: Developed by the authors from information at www.wal-mart.com (accessed September 15, 2004) and in Marco Iansiti and Roy Levien, "Strategy as Ecology," *Harvard Business Review* 82, no. 3 (March 2004), p. 70.

Illustration Capsule 5.1 describes how Wal-Mart has managed its value chain in the retail grocery portion of its business to achieve a dramatic cost advantage over rival supermarket chains and become the world's biggest grocery retailer.

Examples of Companies That Revamped Their Value Chains to Reduce Costs   Nucor Corporation, the most profitable steel producer in the United States and one of the largest steel producers worldwide, drastically revamped the value chain process for manufacturing steel products by using relatively inexpensive electric arc furnaces where scrap steel and directly reduced iron ore are melted and then sent to a continuous caster and rolling mill to be shaped into steel bars, steel beams, steel plate, and sheet steel. Using electric arc furnaces to make new steel products by recycling scrap steel eliminated many of the expensive steps in making steel products from scratch. For instance, Nucor's value chain approach makes the use of coal, coke, and iron ore unnecessary; cuts investment in facilities and equipment (eliminating coke ovens, blast furnaces, basic oxygen furnaces, and ingot casters); and requires only a modest number of employees. As a consequence, Nucor was able to make steel with a far lower capital investment and far lower operating costs than traditional steel mills using iron ore, coke, and coal to make pig iron and then running the pig iron through a variety of capital- and labor-intensive processes to eventually end up with steel products in a variety of shapes and thicknesses. Nucor's low-cost value chain approach has made it one of the lowest-cost producers of steel in the world, enabled Nucor to outcompete traditional steel companies using make-it-from-scratch technology, and earn attractive profits for its shareholders. Nucor has reported profits for every quarter in every year since 1966—a remarkable accomplishment in a mature and cyclical industry notorious for poor profitability.

Southwest Airlines has reconfigured the traditional value chain of commercial airlines to lower costs and thereby offer dramatically lower fares to passengers. Its mastery of fast turnarounds at the gates (about 25 minutes versus 45 minutes for rivals) allows its planes to fly more hours per day. This translates into being able to schedule more flights per day with fewer aircraft, allowing Southwest to generate more revenue per plane on average than rivals. Southwest does not offer in-flight meals, assigned seating, baggage transfer to connecting airlines, or first-class seating and service, thereby eliminating all the cost-producing activities associated with these features. The company's fast and user-friendly online reservation system facilitates e-ticketing and reduces staffing requirements at telephone reservation centers and airport counters. Its use of automated check-in equipment reduces staffing requirements for terminal check-in.

The Keys to Success in Achieving Low-Cost Leadership

To succeed with a low-cost provider strategy, company managers have to scrutinize each cost-creating activity and determine what factors cause costs to be high or low. Then they have to use this knowledge to keep the unit costs of each activity low, exhaustively pursuing cost efficiencies throughout the value chain. They have to be proactive in restructuring the value chain to eliminate nonessential work steps and low-value activities. Normally, low-cost producers work diligently to create cost-conscious corporate cultures that feature broad employee participation in continuous cost improvement efforts and limited perks and frills for executives. They strive to operate with exceptionally small corporate staffs to keep administrative costs to a minimum. Many successful low-cost leaders also use benchmarking to keep close tabs on how their costs compare with rivals and firms performing comparable activities in other industries.

> Success in achieving a low-cost edge over rivals comes from outmanaging rivals in performing value chain activities cost-effectively and eliminating or curbing nonessential value chain activities

But while low-cost providers are champions of frugality, they are usually aggressive in investing in resources and capabilities that promise to drive costs out of the business. Wal-Mart, one of the foremost practitioners of low-cost leadership, employs state-of-the-art technology throughout its operations—its distribution facilities are an automated showcase, it uses online systems to order goods from suppliers and manage inventories, it equips its stores with cutting-edge sales-tracking and checkout systems, and it sends daily point-of-sale data to 4,000 vendors. Wal-Mart's information and communications systems and capabilities are more sophisticated than those of virtually any other retail chain in the world.

Other companies noted for their successful use of low-cost provider strategies include Lincoln Electric in arc welding equipment, Briggs & Stratton in small gasoline engines, Bic in ballpoint pens, Black & Decker in power tools, and General Electric and Whirlpool in major home appliances.

When a Low-Cost Provider Strategy Works Best

A competitive strategy predicated on low-cost leadership is particularly powerful when:

1. *Price competition among rival sellers is especially vigorous.* Low-cost providers are in the best position to compete offensively on the basis of price, to use the appeal of lower price to grab sales (and market share) from rivals, to remain profitable in the face of strong price competition, and to survive price wars.

2. *The products of rival sellers are essentially identical and supplies are readily available from any of several eager sellers.* Commodity-like products and/or ample supplies set the stage for lively price competition; in such markets, it is less efficient, higher-cost companies whose profits get squeezed the most.

3. *There are few ways to achieve product differentiation that have value to buyers.* When the differences between brands do not matter much to buyers, buyers are nearly always sensitive to price differences and shop the market for the best price.

4. *Most buyers use the product in the same ways.* With common user requirements, a standardized product can satisfy the needs of buyers, in which case low selling price, not features or quality, becomes the dominant factor in causing buyers to choose one seller's product over another's.

5. *Buyers incur low costs in switching their purchases from one seller to another.* Low switching costs give buyers the flexibility to shift purchases to lower-priced sellers having equally good products or to attractively priced substitute products. A low-cost leader is well positioned to use low price to induce its customers not to switch to rival brands or substitutes.

6. *Buyers are large and have significant power to bargain down prices.* Low-cost providers have partial profit-margin protection in bargaining with high-volume buyers, since powerful buyers are rarely able to bargain price down past the survival level of the next most cost-efficient seller.

7. *Industry newcomers use introductory low prices to attract buyers and build a customer base.* The low-cost leader can use price cuts of its own to make it harder for a new rival to win customers; the pricing power of the low-cost provider acts as a barrier for new entrants.

> A low-cost provider is in the best position to win the business of price-sensitive buyers, set the floor on market price, and still earn a profit.

As a rule, the more price-sensitive buyers are, the more appealing a low-cost strategy becomes. A low-cost company's ability to set the industry's price floor and still earn a profit erects protective barriers around its market position.

The Pitfalls of a Low-Cost Provider Strategy

Perhaps the biggest pitfall of a low-cost provider strategy is getting carried away with price cutting and ending up with lower, rather than higher, profitability. A low-cost/low-price advantage results in superior profitability only if (1) prices are cut by less than the size of the cost advantage or (2) the added gains in unit sales are large enough to bring in a bigger total profit despite lower margins per unit sold. A company with a 5 percent cost advantage cannot cut prices 20 percent, end up with a volume gain of only 10 percent, and still expect to earn higher profits!

A second big pitfall is not emphasizing avenues of cost advantage that can be kept proprietary or that relegate rivals to playing catch-up. The value of a cost advantage depends on its sustainability. Sustainability, in turn, hinges on whether the company achieves its cost advantage in ways difficult for rivals to copy or match.

A third pitfall is becoming too fixated on cost reduction. Low cost cannot be pursued so zealously that a firm's offering ends up being too features-poor to generate buyer appeal. Furthermore, a company driving hard to push its costs down has to guard against misreading or ignoring increased buyer interest in added features or service, declining buyer sensitivity to price, or new developments that start to alter how buyers use the product. A low-cost zealot risks losing market ground if buyers start opting for more upscale or features-rich products.

> A low-cost provider's product offering must always contain enough attributes to be attractive to prospective buyers—low price, by itself, is not always appealing to buyers

Even if these mistakes are avoided, a low-cost competitive approach still carries risk. Cost-saving technological breakthroughs or the emergence of still-lower-cost value chain models can nullify a low-cost leader's hard-won position. The current leader may have difficulty in shifting quickly to the new technologies or value chain approaches because heavy investments lock it in (at least temporarily) to its present value chain approach.

BROAD DIFFERENTIATION STRATEGIES

Differentiation strategies are attractive whenever buyers' needs and preferences are too diverse to be fully satisfied by a standardized product or by sellers with identical capabilities. A company attempting to succeed through differentiation must study buyers' needs and behavior carefully to learn what buyers consider important, what they think has value, and what they are willing to pay for.[3] Then the company has to incorporate buyer-desired attributes into its product or service offering that will clearly set it apart from rivals. Competitive advantage results once a sufficient number of buyers become strongly attached to the differentiated attributes.

> **CORE CONCEPT**
> The essence of a broad differentiation strategy is to be unique in ways that are valuable to a wide range of customers.

Successful differentiation allows a firm to do one or more of the following:

- Command a premium price for its product.
- Increase unit sales (because additional buyers are won over by the differentiating features).
- Gain buyer loyalty to its brand (because some buyers are strongly attracted to the differentiating features and bond with the company and its products).

Differentiation enhances profitability whenever the extra price the product commands outweighs the added costs of achieving the differentiation. Company differentiation strategies fail when buyers don't value the brand's uniqueness and/or when a company's approach to differentiation is easily copied or matched by its rivals.

Types of Differentiation Themes

Companies can pursue differentiation from many angles: a unique taste (Dr Pepper, Listerine); multiple features (Microsoft Vista, Microsoft Office); wide selection and one-stop shopping (Home Depot, Amazon.com); superior service (FedEx); spare parts availability (Caterpillar guarantees 48-hour spare parts delivery to any customer anywhere in the world or else the part is furnished free); engineering design and performance (Mercedes, BMW); prestige and distinctiveness (Rolex); product reliability (Johnson & Johnson in baby products); quality manufacture (Karastan in carpets, Michelin in tires, Toyota and Honda in automobiles); technological leadership (3M Corporation in bonding and coating products); a full range of services (Charles Schwab in stock brokerage); a complete line of products (Campbell's soups); and top-of-the-line image and reputation (Ralph Lauren and Starbucks).

Easy-to-copy differentiating features cannot produce sustainable competitive advantage; differentiation based on competencies and capabilities tends to be more sustainable.

The most appealing approaches to differentiation are those that are hard or expensive for rivals to duplicate. Indeed, resourceful competitors can, in time, clone almost any product or feature or attribute. If Coca-Cola introduces a vanilla-flavored soft drink, so can Pepsi; if Ford offers a 50,000-mile bumper-to-bumper warranty on its new vehicles, so can Nissan and General Motors. If Apple introduces a cell phone with a variety of advanced Internet features, so can Nokia, Samsung, and Research in Motion (the maker of the popular BlackBerry models). As a rule, differentiation yields a longer-lasting and more profitable competitive edge when it is based on product innovation, technical superiority, product quality and reliability, comprehensive customer service, and unique competitive capabilities. Such differentiating attributes are generally tougher and take longer for rivals to match, and buyers widely perceive them as having value.

Where along the Value Chain to Create the Differentiating Attributes

Differentiation is not something hatched in marketing and advertising departments, nor is it limited to the catchalls of quality and service. Differentiation opportunities can exist in activities all along an industry's value chain; possibilities include the following:

- *Supply chain activities* that ultimately spill over to affect the performance or quality of the company's end product. Starbucks gets high ratings on its coffees partly because it has strict specifications on the coffee beans purchased from suppliers.
- *Product R&D activities* that aim at improved product designs and performance features, expanded end uses and applications, more frequent first-on-the-market victories, wider product variety and selection, added user safety, greater recycling capability, or enhanced environmental protection.
- *Production R&D and technology-related activities* that permit custom-order manufacture at an efficient cost; make production methods safer for the environment; or improve product quality, reliability, and appearance. Many manufacturers have developed flexible manufacturing systems that allow different models and product versions to be made on the same assembly line. Being able to provide buyers with made-to-order products can be a potent differentiating capability.
- *Manufacturing activities* that reduce product defects, prevent premature product failure, extend product life, allow better warranty coverage, improve economy of use, result in more end-user convenience, or enhance product appearance. The quality edge enjoyed by Japanese automakers stems partly from their distinctive competence in performing assembly-line activities.
- *Distribution and shipping activities* that allow for fewer warehouse and on-the-shelf stockouts, quicker delivery to customers, more accurate order filling, and/or lower shipping costs.
- *Marketing, sales, and customer service activities* that result in superior technical assistance to buyers, faster maintenance and repair services, more and better product information provided to customers, more and better training materials for end users, better credit terms, quicker order processing, or greater customer convenience.

Managers need keen understanding of the sources of differentiation and the activities that drive uniqueness to evaluate various differentiation approaches and design durable ways to set their product offering apart from those of rival brands.

The Four Best Routes to Competitive Advantage via a Broad Differentiation Strategy

While it is easy enough to grasp that a successful differentiation strategy must entail creating buyer value in ways unmatched by rivals, the big issue in crafting a differentiation strategy is which of four basic routes to take in delivering unique buyer value via a broad differentiation strategy. Usually, building a sustainable competitive advantage via differentiation involves pursuing one of four basic routes to delivering superior value to buyers. One route is to *incorporate product attributes and user features that lower the buyer's overall costs of using the company's product.* Making a company's product more economical for a buyer to use can be done by reducing the buyer's raw materials waste (providing cut-to-size components), reducing a buyer's inventory requirements (providing just-in-time deliveries), increasing maintenance intervals and product reliability so as to lower a buyer's repair and maintenance costs, using online systems to reduce a buyer's procurement and order processing costs, and providing free technical support. Rising costs for gasoline have dramatically spurred the efforts of motor vehicle manufacturers worldwide to introduce models with better fuel economy.

A second route is to *incorporate features that raise product performance.*[4] This can be accomplished with attributes that provide buyers greater reliability, durability, convenience, or ease of use. Other performance-enhancing options include making the company's product or service cleaner, safer, quieter, or more maintenance-free than rival brands. Cell phone manufacturers are in a race to introduce next-generation phones with a more appealing, trendsetting set of user features and options.

> **CORE CONCEPT**
> A differentiator's basis for competitive advantage is either a product/service offering whose attributes differ significantly from the offerings of rivals or a set of capabilities for delivering customer value that rivals don't have.

A third route to a differentiation-based competitive advantage is to *incorporate features that enhance buyer satisfaction in noneconomic or intangible ways.* Toyota's Prius appeals to environmentally conscious motorists who wish to help reduce global carbon dioxide emissions. Rolls-Royce, Ralph Lauren, Gucci, Tiffany, Cartier, and Rolex have differentiation-based competitive advantages linked to buyer desires for status, image, prestige, upscale fashion, superior craftsmanship, and the finer things in life. L. L. Bean makes its mail-order customers feel secure in their purchases by providing an unconditional guarantee with no time limit: "All of our products are guaranteed to give 100 percent satisfaction in every way. Return anything purchased from us at any time if it proves otherwise. We will replace it, refund your purchase price, or credit your credit card, as you wish."

The fourth route is *to deliver value to customers by differentiating on the basis of competencies and competitive capabilities that rivals don't have or can't afford to match.*[5] The importance of cultivating competencies and capabilities that add power to a company's resource strengths and competitiveness comes into play here. Core and/or distinctive competencies may give a company unique capabilities that deliver important value to customers and help set the company apart from its rivals. There are numerous examples of companies that have differentiated themselves on the basis of capabilities. Japanese automakers can adapt faster to changing consumer preferences for one vehicle style versus another because they have the capabilities to bring new models to market faster than American and European automakers. Apple's competencies in product innovation produced the iPod and the iPhone, both of which have been immensely popular with consumers and put Apple very much in the spotlight. Samsung's competencies and capabilities in liquid crystal display (LCD) technology have made it a global leader in LCD TVs with screen sizes of 27-inches and larger.

The Importance of Perceived Value and Signaling Value

Buyers seldom pay for value they don't perceive, no matter how real the unique extras may be.[6] Thus, the price premium commanded by a differentiation strategy reflects both *the value actually delivered* to the buyer and *the value perceived* by the buyer (even if not actually delivered). Actual and perceived value can differ whenever buyers have trouble assessing what their experience with the product will be. Incomplete knowledge on the part of buyers often causes them to judge value according to such signals as price (where price connotes quality); packaging; the extent of ad campaigns (i.e., how well-known the product is); ad content and image; the quality of brochures and sales presentations; the seller's facilities; the seller's list of customers; the firm's market share; the length of time the firm has been in business; and the professionalism, appearance, and personality of the seller's employees. Such signals of value may be as important as actual value (1) when the nature of differentiation is subjective or hard to quantify, (2) when buyers are making a first-time purchase, (3) when repurchase is infrequent, and (4) when buyers are unsophisticated.

When a Differentiation Strategy Works Best

Differentiation strategies tend to work best in market circumstances where:

- *Buyer needs and uses of the product are diverse.* Diverse buyer preferences present competitors with a bigger window of opportunity to do things differently and set themselves apart with product attributes that appeal to particular buyers. For instance, the diversity of consumer preferences for menu selection, ambience, pricing, and customer service gives restaurants exceptionally wide latitude in creating a differentiated product offering. Other companies having many ways to strongly differentiate themselves from rivals include the publishers of magazines, the makers of motor vehicles, and the manufacturers of cabinetry and countertops.

- *There are many ways to differentiate the product or service and many buyers perceive these differences as having value.* There's plenty of room for retail apparel competitors to stock different styles and quality of apparel merchandise but very little room for the makers of paper clips or copier paper or sugar to set their products apart. Likewise, the sellers of different brands of gasoline or aspirin or plastic cups have little differentiation opportunity compared to the sellers of watches or magazines or patio furniture or breakfast cereal. Unless different buyers have distinguishably different preferences for certain features and product attributes, profitable differentiation opportunities are very restricted.

- *Few rival firms are following a similar differentiation approach.* The best differentiation approaches involve trying to appeal to buyers on the basis of attributes that rivals are not emphasizing. A differentiator encounters less head-to-head rivalry when it goes its own separate way in creating uniqueness and does not try to outdifferentiate rivals on the very same attributes—when many rivals are all claiming "Ours tastes better than theirs" or "Ours gets your clothes cleaner than theirs," the most likely result is weak brand differentiation and *strategy overcrowding*—where competitors end up chasing much the same buyers with much the same product offerings.

- *Technological change is fast-paced and competition revolves around rapidly evolving product features.* Rapid product innovation and frequent introductions of next-version products not only provide space for companies to pursue separate differentiating paths but also heighten buyer interest. In video game hardware and video games, golf equipment, PCs, cell phones, and MP3 players, competitors are locked into an ongoing battle to set themselves apart by introducing the best next-generation products—companies that fail to come up with new and improved products and distinctive performance features quickly lose out in the marketplace. In network TV broadcasting in the United States, NBC, ABC, CBS, Fox, and several others are always scrambling to develop a lineup of TV shows that will win higher audience ratings and pave the way for charging higher advertising rates and boosting ad revenues.

The Pitfalls of a Differentiation Strategy

Differentiation strategies can fail for any of several reasons. *A differentiation strategy is always doomed when competitors are able to quickly copy most or all of the appealing product attributes a company comes up with.* Rapid imitation means that no rival achieves differentiation, since whenever one firm introduces some aspect of uniqueness that strikes the fancy of buyers, fast-following copycats quickly reestablish similarity. This is why a firm must search out sources of uniqueness that are time-consuming or burdensome for rivals to match if it hopes to use differentiation to win a competitive edge over rivals.

CORE CONCEPT
Any differentiating feature that works well is a magnet for imitators.

A second pitfall is that the company's differentiation strategy produces a ho-hum market reception because buyers see little value in the unique attributes of a company's product. Thus, even if a company sets the attributes of its brand apart from the brands of rivals, its strategy can fail because of trying to differentiate on the basis of something that does not deliver adequate value to buyers (such as lowering a buyer's cost to use the product or enhancing a buyer's well-being). Anytime many potential buyers look at a company's differentiated product offering and conclude "So what," the company's differentiation strategy is in deep trouble—buyers will likely decide the product is not worth the extra price and sales will be disappointingly low.

The third big pitfall of a differentiation strategy is overspending on efforts to differentiate the company's product offering, thus eroding profitability. Company efforts to achieve differentiation nearly always raise costs. The trick to profitable differentiation is either to keep the costs of achieving differentiation below the price premium the differentiating attributes can command in the marketplace (thus increasing the profit margin per unit sold) or to offset thinner profit margins per unit by selling enough additional units to increase total profits. If a company goes overboard in pursuing costly differentiation efforts and then unexpectedly discovers that buyers are unwilling to pay a sufficient price premium to cover the added costs of differentiation, it ends up saddled with unacceptably thin profit margins or even losses. The need to contain differentiation costs is why many companies add little touches of differentiation that add to buyer satisfaction but are inexpensive to institute. Upscale restaurants often provide valet parking. Ski resorts provide skiers with complimentary coffee or hot apple cider at the base of the lifts in the morning and late afternoon. FedEx, UPS, and many catalog and online retailers allow customers to track packages in transit via the Internet. Some hotels and motels provide free continental breakfasts, exercise facilities, and in-room coffeemaking amenities. Publishers are using their Web sites to deliver supplementary educational materials to the buyers of their textbooks. Laundry detergent and soap manufacturers offer both scented and scent-free products.

Other common pitfalls and mistakes in crafting a differentiation strategy include:[7]

- *Overdifferentiating so that product quality or service levels exceed buyers' needs.* Even if buyers like the differentiating extras, they may not find them sufficiently valuable for their purposes to pay extra to get them. Many shoppers shy away from buying top-of-the-line items because they have no particular interest in all the bells and whistles, and believe that a less deluxe model or style makes better economic sense.
- *Trying to charge too high a price premium.* Even if buyers view certain extras or deluxe features as nice to have, they may still conclude that the added cost is excessive relative to the value they deliver. A differentiator must guard against turning off would-be buyers with what is perceived as price gouging. Normally, the bigger the price premium for the differentiating extras, the harder it is to keep buyers from switching to the lower-priced offerings of competitors.
- *Being timid and not striving to open up meaningful gaps in quality or service or performance features vis-à-vis the products of rivals.* Tiny differences between rivals' product offerings may not be visible or important to buyers. If a company wants to generate the fiercely loyal customer following needed to earn superior profits and open up a differentiation-based competitive advantage over rivals, then its strategy must result in strong rather than weak product differentiation. In markets where differentiators do no better than achieve weak product differentiation (because the attributes of rival brands are fairly similar in the minds of many buyers), customer loyalty to any one brand is weak, the costs of brand switching are fairly low, and no one company has enough of a market edge that it can get by with charging a price premium over rival brands.

A low-cost provider strategy can defeat a differentiation strategy when buyers are satisfied with a basic product and don't think extra attributes are worth a higher price.

BEST-COST PROVIDER STRATEGIES

CORE CONCEPT
The competitive advantage of a best-cost provider is lower costs than rivals in incorporating upscale attributes, putting the company in a position to underprice rivals whose products have similar upscale attributes.

Best-cost provider strategies aim at giving customers *more value for the money.* The objective is to deliver superior value to buyers by satisfying their expectations on key quality/features/performance/service attributes and beating their expectations on price (given what rivals are charging for much the same attributes). *A company achieves best-cost status from an ability to incorporate attractive or upscale attributes at a lower cost than rivals.* The attractive attributes can take the form of appealing features, good-to-excellent product performance or quality, or attractive customer service. If a company has the resource strengths and competitive capabilities to incorporate these upscale attributes into its product offering *at a lower cost than rivals,* then it enjoys best-cost status—it is the low-cost provider *of an upscale product.*

Being a best-cost provider is different from being a low-cost provider because the additional upscale features entail additional costs (that a low-cost provider can avoid by offering buyers a basic product with few frills). As Figure 5.1 indicates, best-cost provider strategies stake out a middle ground between pursuing a low-cost advantage and a differentiation advantage and between appealing to the broad market as a whole and a narrow market niche. From a competitive positioning standpoint, best-cost strategies are thus a *hybrid,* balancing a strategic emphasis on low cost against a strategic emphasis on differentiation (upscale features delivered at a price that constitutes superior value).

The competitive advantage of a best-cost provider is its capability to include upscale attributes at a lower cost than rivals whose products have comparable attributes. A best-cost provider can use its low-cost advantage to underprice rivals whose products have similar upscale attributes—it is usually not difficult to entice customers away from rivals charging a higher price for an item with highly comparable features, quality, performance, and/or customer service attributes. To achieve competitive advantage with a best-cost provider strategy, it is critical that a company have the resources and capabilities to incorporate upscale attributes at a lower cost than rivals. In other words, it must be able to (1) incorporate attractive features at a lower cost than rivals whose products have similar features, (2) manufacture a product of good-to-excellent quality at a lower cost than rivals, (3) develop a product that delivers good-to-excellent performance at a lower cost than rivals, or (4) provide attractive customer service at a lower cost than rivals who provide comparably attractive customer service. What makes a best-cost provider strategy so appealing is being able to incorporate upscale attributes at a lower cost than rivals and then using the company's low-cost advantage to underprice rivals whose products have similar upscale attributes.

The target market for a best-cost provider is value-conscious buyers—buyers who are looking for appealing extras at an appealingly low price. Value-hunting buyers (as distinct from buyers looking only for bargain-basement prices) often constitute a sizable part of the overall market. Normally, value-conscious buyers are willing to pay a fair price for extra features, but they shy away from paying top dollar for items having all the bells and whistles. It is the desire to cater to *value-conscious buyers* as opposed to *budget-conscious buyers* that sets a best-cost provider apart from a low-cost provider—the two strategies aim at distinguishably different market targets.

When a Best-Cost Provider Strategy Is Appealing

A best-cost provider strategy is very well-suited for markets where buyer diversity makes product differentiation the norm and where many buyers are also sensitive to price and value. This is because a best-cost provider can position itself near the middle of the market with either a medium-quality product at a below-average price or a high-quality product at an average or slightly higher price. Often, substantial numbers of buyers prefer midrange products rather than the cheap, basic products of low-cost producers or the expensive products of top-of-the-line differentiators. But unless a company has the resources, know-how, and capabilities to incorporate upscale product or service attributes at a lower cost than rivals, adopting a best-cost strategy is ill-advised—a winning strategy must always be matched to a company's resource strengths and capabilities.

Illustration Capsule 5.2 describes how Toyota has applied the principles of a best-cost provider strategy in producing and marketing its Lexus brand.

The Big Risk of a Best-Cost Provider Strategy

A company's biggest vulnerability in employing a best-cost provider strategy is getting squeezed between the strategies of firms using low-cost and high-end differentiation strategies. Low-cost providers may be able to siphon customers away with the appeal of a lower price (despite their less-appealing product attributes). High-end differentiators may be able to steal customers away with the appeal of better product attributes (even though their products carry a higher price tag). Thus, to be successful, a best-cost provider must offer buyers *significantly* better product attributes in order to justify a price above what low-cost leaders are charging. Likewise, it has to achieve significantly lower costs in providing upscale features so that it can outcompete high-end differentiators on the basis of a *significantly* lower price.

Toyota Motor Company is widely regarded as a low-cost provider among the world's motor vehicle manufacturers. Despite its emphasis on product quality, Toyota has achieved low-cost leadership because it has developed considerable skills in efficient supply chain management and low-cost assembly capabilities, and because its models are positioned in the low-to-medium end of the price spectrum, where high production volumes are conducive to low unit costs. But when Toyota decided to introduce its new Lexus models to compete in the luxury-car market, it employed a classic best-cost provider strategy. Toyota took the following four steps in crafting and implementing its Lexus strategy:

- Designing an array of high-performance characteristics and upscale features into the Lexus models so as to make them comparable in performance and luxury to other high-end models and attractive to Mercedes, BMW, Audi, Jaguar, Cadillac, and Lincoln buyers.

- Transferring its capabilities in making high-quality Toyota models at low cost to making premium-quality Lexus models at costs below other luxury-car makers. Toyota's supply chain capabilities and low-cost assembly know-how allowed it to incorporate high-tech performance features and upscale quality into Lexus models at substantially less cost than comparable Mercedes and BMW models.

- Using its relatively lower manufacturing costs to underprice comparable Mercedes and BMW models. Toyota believed that with its cost advantage it could price attractively equipped Lexus cars low enough to draw price-conscious buyers away from Mercedes and BMW. Toyota's pricing policy also allowed it to induce Toyota, Honda, Ford, or GM owners desiring more luxury to switch to a Lexus. Lexus's pricing advantage over Mercedes and BMW was sometimes quite significant. For example, in 2008 the Lexus RX 350, a midsized SUV, carried a sticker price in the $37,000–$48,000 range (depending on how it was equipped), whereas variously equipped Mercedes ML 350 SUVs had price tags in the $42,000–$85,000 range and a BMW X5 SUV could range anywhere from $46,000 to $75,000, depending on the optional equipment chosen.

- Establishing a new network of Lexus dealers, separate from Toyota dealers, dedicated to providing a level of personalized, attentive customer service unmatched in the industry.

Lexus's best-cost provider strategy allowed it to become the number one selling luxury car brand worldwide in 2000—a distinction that it held through 2007 and may well to continue to hold.

FOCUSED (OR MARKET NICHE) STRATEGIES

What sets focused strategies apart from low-cost leadership or broad differentiation strategies is concentrated attention on a narrow piece of the total market. The target segment, or niche, can be defined by geographic uniqueness, by specialized requirements in using the product, or by special product attributes that appeal only to niche members. Community Coffee, the largest family-owned specialty coffee retailer in the United States, has a geographic focus on the state of Louisiana and communities across the Gulf of Mexico. Community Coffee holds only a 1.1 percent share of the national coffee market, but it has recorded sales in excess of $100 million and has won a 50 percent share of the coffee business in the 11-state region where it is distributed. Other examples of firms that concentrate on a well-defined market niche keyed to a particular product or buyer segment include Animal Planet and the History Channel (in cable TV); Porsche (in sports cars); Bandag (a specialist in truck tire recapping that promotes its recaps aggressively at more than 1,000 truck stops); CGA Inc. (a specialist in providing insurance to cover the cost of lucrative hole-in-one prizes at golf tournaments); and Match.com (the world's largest online dating service). Microbreweries, local bakeries, bed-and-breakfast inns, and local owner-managed retail boutiques are all good examples of enterprises that have scaled their operations to serve narrow or local customer segments.

A Focused Low-Cost Strategy

A focused strategy based on low cost aims at securing a competitive advantage by serving buyers in the target market niche at a lower cost and a lower price than rival competitors. This strategy has considerable attraction when a firm can lower costs significantly by limiting its customer base to a well-defined buyer segment. The avenues to achieving a cost advantage over rivals also serving the target market niche are the same as for low-cost leadership—outmanage rivals in keeping the costs of value chain activities contained to a bare minimum and search for innovate ways to reconfigure the firm's value chain and bypass or reduce certain value chain activities. The only real difference between a low-cost provider strategy and a focused low-cost strategy is the size of the buyer group that a company is trying to appeal to—the former involves a product offering that appeals broadly to most buyer groups and market segments, whereas the latter involves meeting the needs of only those buyers in a narrow market segment.

Focused low-cost strategies are fairly common. Producers of private-label goods are able to achieve low costs in product development, marketing, distribution, and advertising by concentrating on making generic items similar to name-brand merchandise and selling directly to retail chains wanting a low-priced store brand. The Perrigo Company has become a leading manufacturer of over-the-counter health care products, with 2007 sales of more than $1.4 billion, by focusing on producing private-label brands for retailers such as Wal-Mart, CVS, Walgreens, Rite Aid, and Safeway. Motel 6 has used a low-cost strategy in catering to budget-conscious travelers who just want to pay for a clean, no-frills place to spend the night. Illustration Capsule 5.3 describes how Vizio's low costs and focus on big-box retailers allowed it to become a major seller of flat-panel TVs in the United States in less than five years from its start-up.

A Focused Differentiation Strategy

A focused strategy keyed to differentiation aims at securing a competitive advantage with a product offering carefully designed to appeal to the unique preferences and needs of a narrow, well-defined group of buyers (as distinguished from a broad differentiation strategy aimed at many buyer groups and market segments). Successful use of a focused differentiation strategy depends on the existence of a buyer segment that is looking for special product attributes or seller capabilities and on a firm's ability to stand apart from rivals competing in the same target market niche.

Companies like Godiva Chocolates, Chanel, Gucci, Rolls-Royce, Häagen-Dazs, and W. L. Gore (the maker of Gore-Tex) employ successful differentiation-based focused strategies targeted at upscale buyers wanting products and services with world-class attributes. Indeed, most markets contain a buyer segment willing to pay a big price premium for the very finest items available, thus opening the strategic window for some competitors to pursue differentiation-based focused strategies aimed at the very top of the market pyramid. Ferrari markets its 1,500 cars sold in North America each year to a list of just 20,000 highly affluent car enthusiasts. Only those in the highest echelon of this exclusive group were contacted by Ferrari for a chance to put their names on the waiting list for one of the 20 $1.1 million FXX models planned for sale in North America.

Another successful focused differentiator is Trader Joe's, a 300-store, 11-state chain that is a combination gourmet deli and food warehouse. Customers shop Trader Joe's as much for entertainment as for conventional grocery items—the store stocks out-of-the-ordinary culinary treats like raspberry salsa, salmon burgers, and jasmine fried rice, as well as the standard goods normally found in supermarkets. What sets Trader Joe's apart is not just its unique combination of food novelties and competitively priced grocery items but also its capability to turn an otherwise mundane grocery excursion into a whimsical treasure hunt that is just plain fun.

ILLUSTRATION CAPSULE 5.3
Vizio's Focused Low-Cost Strategy

California-based Vizio Inc. designs flat-panel LCD and plasma TVs that range in size from 20 to 52 inches and are sold only by big-box discount retailers such as Wal-Mart, Sam's Club, Costco Wholesale, Best Buy, and Circuit City. If you've shopped for a flat-panel TV recently, you've probably noticed that Vizio is among the lowest-priced brands and that its picture quality is surprising good considering the price. The company is able to keep its cost low by only designing TVs and then sourcing its production to a limited number of contract manufacturers in Taiwan. In fact, 80 percent of its production is handled by a company called AmTran Technology. Such a dependence on a supplier can place a buyer in a precarious situation, making them vulnerable to price increases or product shortages, but Vizio has countered this possible threat by making AmTran a major stockholder. AmTran Technology owns a 23 percent stake in Vizio and earns about 80 percent of its revenues from its sales of televisions to Vizio. This close relationship with its major supplier and its focus on a single product category sold through limited distribution channels allows it to offer its customers deep price discounts.

Vizio's first major account was landed in 2003 when it approached Costco buyers with a 46-inch plasma TV whose wholesale price was half that of the next-lowest-price competitor. Within two months, Costco was carrying Vizio flat-panel TVs in 320 of its warehouse stores in the United States. In October 2007, Vizio approached buyers for Sam's Club with a 20-inch LCD TV that could be sold at retail for under $350. The price and quality of the 20-inch TV led Sam's Club buyers to place an order for 20,000 TVs for a March 2008 delivery. At year-end 2007, Vizio was the third largest seller of flat-panel TVs in the United States, with a market share of 12.4 percent and within one-tenth of a percentage point of matching number two Sony's 12.5 percent market share. Vizio recorded revenues of $2 billion in 2007 and was the industry's most profitable seller of TVs. Vizio management expected to challenge Samsung for the title of market share leader in 2008, which had a market share of 14.2 percent in 2007.

Source: Christopher Lawton, Yukari Iwatani Kane, and Jason Dean, "Picture Shift: U.S. Upstart Takes On TV Giants in Price War," *Wall Street Journal,* April 15, 2008, p. A1.

Illustration Capsule 5.4 describes Progressive Insurance's focused differentiation strategy.

When a Focused Low-Cost or Focused Differentiation Strategy Is Attractive

A focused strategy aimed at securing a competitive edge based on either low cost or differentiation becomes increasingly attractive as more of the following conditions are met:

- The target market niche is big enough to be profitable and offers good growth potential.
- Industry leaders do not see that having a presence in the niche is crucial to their own success—in which case focusers can often escape battling head-to-head against some of the industry's biggest and strongest competitors.
- It is costly or difficult for multisegment competitors to put capabilities in place to meet the specialized needs of buyers comprising the target market niche and at the same time satisfy the expectations of their mainstream customers.
- The industry has many different niches and segments, thereby allowing a focuser to pick a competitively attractive niche suited to its resource strengths and capabilities. Also, with more niches there is more room for focusers to avoid each other in competing for the same customers.

ILLUSTRATION CAPSULE 5.4
Progressive Insurance's Focused Differentiation Strategy in Auto Insurance

Progressive Insurance has fashioned a strategy in auto insurance focused on people with a record of traffic violations who drive high-performance cars, drivers with accident histories, motorcyclists, teenagers, and other high-risk categories of drivers that most auto insurance companies steer away from. Progressive discovered that some of these high-risk drivers are affluent and pressed for time, making them less sensitive to paying premium rates for their car insurance. Management learned that it could charge such drivers high enough premiums to cover the added risks, plus it differentiated Progressive from other insurers by expediting the process of obtaining insurance. Progressive pioneered the low-cost direct sales model of allowing customers to purchase insurance online and over the phone.

Progressive also studied the market segments for insurance carefully enough to discover that some motorcycle owners were not especially risky (middle-aged suburbanites who sometimes commuted to work or used their motorcycles mainly for recreational trips with their friends). Progressive's strategy allowed it to become a leader in the market for luxury-car insurance for customers who appreciated Progressive's streamlined approach to doing business.

In further differentiating and promoting Progressive's policies, management created teams of roving claims adjusters who would arrive at accident scenes to assess claims and issue checks for repairs on the spot. Progressive introduced 24-hour claims reporting, now an industry standard. In addition, it developed a sophisticated pricing system so that it could quickly and accurately assess each customer's risk and weed out unprofitable customers.

By being creative and excelling at the nuts and bolts of its business, Progressive has won a 7.6 percent share of the $150 billion market for auto insurance and has the highest underwriting margins in the auto-insurance industry.

Sources: **www.progressiveinsurance.com;** Ian C. McMillan, Alexander van Putten, and Rita Gunther McGrath, "Global Gamesmanship," *Harvard Business Review* 81, no. 5 (May 2003), p. 68; *Fortune,* May 16, 2005, p. 34; and "Motorcyclists Age, Affluence Trending Upward," *BestWire,* July 24, 2007

- Few, if any, other rivals are attempting to specialize in the same target segment—a condition that reduces the risk of segment overcrowding.
- The focuser has a reservoir of customer goodwill and loyalty (accumulated from having catered to the specialized needs and preferences of niche members over many years) that it can draw on to help stave off the ambitious challengers looking to horn in on its business.

The advantages of focusing a company's entire competitive effort on a single market niche are considerable, especially for small and medium-sized companies that may lack the breadth and depth of resources to tackle going after a broad customer base with a something-for-everyone lineup of models, styles, and product selection. By focusing its attention on online auctions—at one time a small niche in the overall auction business—eBay made a huge name for itself and attractive profits for shareholders. Google has capitalized on its specialized expertise in Internet search engines to become one of the most spectacular growth companies of the past 10 years. Two hippie entrepreneurs, Ben Cohen and Jerry Greenfield, built Ben & Jerry's Homemade Ice Cream into an impressive business by focusing their energies and resources solely on the superpremium segment of the ice cream business.

The Risks of a Focused Low-Cost or Focused Differentiation Strategy

Focusing carries several risks. One is the chance that competitors will find effective ways to match the focused firm's capabilities in serving the target niche—perhaps by coming up with products or brands specifically designed to appeal to buyers in the target niche or by developing expertise and capabilities that offset the focuser's strengths. In the lodging business, large chains like Marriott and Hilton have launched multibrand strategies that allow them to compete effectively in several lodging segments simultaneously. Marriott has flagship hotels with a full complement of services and amenities that allow it to attract travelers and vacationers going to major resorts; it has J. W. Marriot and Ritz-Carlton hotels that provide deluxe comfort and service to business and leisure travelers; it has a Courtyard by Marriott and SpringHill Suites brands for business travelers looking for moderately priced lodging; it has Marriott Residence Inns and TownePlace Suites designed as a "home away from home" for travelers staying five or more nights; and it has 520 Fairfield Inn locations that cater to travelers looking for quality lodging at an affordable price. Similarly, Hilton has a lineup of brands (Conrad Hotels, Doubletree Hotels, Embassy Suite Hotels, Hampton Inns, Hilton Hotels, Hilton Garden Inns, and Homewood Suites) that enable it to compete in multiple segments and compete head-to-head against lodging chains that operate in only a single segment. Multibrand strategies are attractive to large companies like Marriott and Hilton precisely because they enable a company to enter a market niche and siphon business away from companies that employ a focus strategy.

A second risk of employing a focus strategy is the potential for the preferences and needs of niche members to shift over time toward the product attributes desired by the majority of buyers. An erosion of the differences across buyer segments lowers entry barriers into a focuser's market niche and provides an open invitation for rivals in adjacent segments to begin competing for the focuser's customers. A third risk is that the segment may become so attractive it is soon inundated with competitors, intensifying rivalry and splintering segment profits.

THE CONTRASTING FEATURES OF THE FIVE GENERIC COMPETITIVE STRATEGIES: A SUMMARY

Choosing the generic competitive strategy to serve as the framework on which to build the rest of the company's strategy is not a trivial matter. Each of the five generic competitive strategies positions the company differently in its market and competitive environment. Each establishes a central theme for how the company will endeavor to outcompete rivals. Each creates some boundaries or guidelines for maneuvering as market circumstances unfold. Each points to different ways of experimenting and tinkering with the basic strategy—for example, employing a low-cost provider strategy means experimenting with ways that costs can be cut and value chain activities can be streamlined, whereas a broad differentiation strategy means exploring ways to add new differentiating features or to perform value chain activities differently. Each entails differences in terms of product line, production emphasis, marketing emphasis, and means of sustaining the strategy—as shown in Table 5.1.

Thus, a choice of which generic strategy to employ spills over to affect several aspects of how the business will be operated and the manner in which value chain activities must be managed. Deciding which generic strategy to employ is perhaps the most important strategic commitment a company makes—it tends to drive the rest of the company's strategic actions.

One of the big dangers in crafting a competitive strategy is that managers, torn between the pros and cons of the various generic strategies, will opt for *stuck-in-the-middle strategies* that represent compromises between lower costs and greater differentiation and between broad and narrow market appeal. Compromise or

Table 5.1 Distinguishing Features of the Five Generic Competitive Strategies

	Low-Cost Provider	Broad Differentiation	Best-Cost Provider	Focused Low-Cost Provider	Focused Differentiation
Strategic target	• A broad cross-section of the market	• A broad cross-section of the market	• Value-conscious buyers	• A narrow market niche where buyer needs and preferences are distinctively different	• A narrow market niche where buyer needs and preferences are distinctively different
Basis of competitive advantage	• Lower overall costs than competitors	• Ability to offer buyers something attractively different from competitors	• Ability to give customers more value for the money	• Lower overall cost than rivals in serving niche members	• Attributes that appeal specifically to niche members
Product line	• A good basic product with few frills (acceptable quality and limited selection)	• Many product variations, wide selection; emphasis on differentiating features	• Items with appealing attributes; assorted upscale features	• Features and attributes tailored to the tastes and requirements of niche members	• Features and attributes tailored to the tastes and requirements of niche members
Production emphasis	• A continuous search for cost reduction without sacrificing acceptable quality and essential features	• Build in whatever differentiating features buyers are willing to pay for; strive for product superiority	• Build in upscale features and appealing attributes at lower cost than rivals	• A continuous search for cost reduction while incorporating features and attributes matched to niche member preferences	• Custom-made products that match the tastes and requirements of niche members
Marketing emphasis	• Try to make a virtue out of product features that lead to low cost	• Tout differentiating features • Charge a premium price to cover the extra costs of differentiating features	• Tout delivery of best value • Either deliver comparable features at a lower price than rivals or else match rivals on prices and provide better features	• Communicate attractive features of a budget-priced product offering that fits niche buyers' expectations	• Communicate how product offering does the best job of meeting niche buyers' expectations
Keys to sustaining the strategy	• Economical prices/good value • Strive to manage costs down, year after year, in every area of the business	• Stress constant innovation to stay ahead of imitative competitors • Concentrate on a few key differentiating features	• Unique expertise in simultaneously managing costs down while incorporating upscale features and attributes	• Stay committed to serving the niche at lowest overall cost; don't blur the firm's image by entering other market segments or adding other products to widen market appeal	• Stay committed to serving the niche better than rivals; don't blur the firm's image by entering other market segments or adding other products to widen market appeal

middle-ground strategies rarely produce sustainable competitive advantage or a distinctive competitive position—well-executed best-cost provider strategies are the only exception. Usually, companies with compromise strategies end up with a middle-of-the-pack industry ranking—they have average costs, some but not a lot of product differentiation relative to rivals, an average image and reputation, and little prospect of industry leadership. Having a competitive edge over rivals is the single most dependable contributor to above-average company profitability. Hence only if a company makes a strong and unwavering commitment to one of the five generic competitive strategies does it stand much chance of achieving the sustainable competitive advantage that such strategies can deliver if properly executed.

KEY POINTS

Early in the process of crafting a strategy, company managers have to decide which of the five basic competitive strategies to employ—overall low-cost, broad differentiation, best-cost, focused low-cost, or focused differentiation.

In employing a low-cost provider strategy, a company must do a better job than rivals of cost-effectively managing value chain activities and/or it must find innovative ways to eliminate or bypass cost-producing activities. Low-cost provider strategies work particularly well when the products of rival sellers are virtually identical or very weakly differentiated and supplies are readily available from eager sellers, when there are not many ways to differentiate that have value to buyers, when many buyers are price sensitive and shop the market for the lowest price, and when buyer switching costs are low.

Broad differentiation strategies seek to produce a competitive edge by incorporating attributes and features that set a company's product/service offering apart from rivals in ways that buyers consider valuable and worth paying for. Successful differentiation allows a firm to (1) command a premium price for its product, (2) increase unit sales (because additional buyers are won over by the differentiating features), and/or (3) gain buyer loyalty to its brand (because some buyers are strongly attracted to the differentiating features and bond with the company and its products). Differentiation strategies work best in markets with diverse buyer preferences where there are big windows of opportunity to strongly differentiate a company's product offering from those of rival brands, in situations where few other rivals are pursuing a similar differentiation approach, and in circumstances where companies are racing to bring out the most appealing next-generation product. A differentiation strategy is doomed when competitors are able to quickly copy most or all of the appealing product attributes a company comes up with, when a company's differentiation efforts meet with a ho-hum or so what market reception, or when a company erodes profitability by overspending on efforts to differentiate its product offering.

Best-cost provider strategies combine a strategic emphasis on low cost with a strategic emphasis on more than minimal quality, service, features, or performance. The aim is to create competitive advantage by giving buyers more value for the money—an approach that entails matching close rivals on key quality/service/features/performance attributes and beating them on the costs of incorporating such attributes into the product or service. A best-cost provider strategy works best in markets where buyer diversity makes product differentiation the norm and where many buyers are also sensitive to price and value.

A focus strategy delivers competitive advantage either by achieving lower costs than rivals in serving buyers comprising the target market niche or by developing specialized ability to offer niche buyers an appealingly differentiated offering than meets their needs better than rival brands. A focused strategy based on either low cost or differentiation becomes increasingly attractive when the target market niche is big enough to be profitable and offers good growth potential, when it is costly or difficult for multisegment competitors to put capabilities in place to meet the specialized needs of the target market niche and at the same time satisfy the expectations of their mainstream customers, when there are one or more niches that present a good match with a focuser's resource strengths and capabilities, and when few other rivals are attempting to specialize in the same target segment.

Deciding which generic strategy to employ is perhaps the most important strategic commitment a company makes—it tends to drive the rest of the strategic actions a company decides to undertake and it sets the whole tone for the pursuit of a competitive advantage over rivals.

ASSURANCE OF LEARNING EXERCISES

1. Best Buy is the largest consumer electronics retailer in the United States; its sales in 2007 reached nearly $36 billion. The company competes aggressively on price with rivals such as Circuit City, Costco Wholesale, Sam's Club, Wal-Mart, and Target, but it is also known by consumers for its first-rate customer service. Best Buy customers have commented that the retailer's sales staff is exceptionally knowledgeable about the products they sell and can direct them to the exact location of difficult-to-find items. Best Buy customers also appreciate that demonstration models of PC monitors, MP3 players, and other electronics are fully powered and ready for in-store use. Best Buy's Geek Squad tech support and installation services are additional customer service features that are valued by many customers. How would you characterize Best Buy's competitive strategy? Should it be classified as a low-cost provider strategy? A differentiation strategy? A best-cost strategy? Explain your answer.

2. Stihl is the world's leading manufacturer and marketer of chain saws, with annual sales exceeding $2 billion. With innovations dating to its 1929 invention of the gasoline-powered chain saw, the company holds over 1,000 patents related to chain saws and outdoor power tools. The company's chain saws, leaf blowers, and hedge trimmers sell at price points well above competing brands and are sold only by its network of 8,000 independent dealers. The company boasts in its advertisements that its products are rated number one by consumer magazines and are *not* sold at Lowe's or The Home Depot. How does Stihl's choice of distribution channels and advertisements contribute to its differentiation strategy?

3. Explore BMW's Web site (www.bmw.com) and see if you can identify at least three ways in which the company seeks to differentiate itself from rival automakers. Is there reason to believe that BMW's differentiation strategy has been successful in producing a competitive advantage? Why or why not?

EXERCISES FOR SIMULATION PARTICIPANTS

1. Which one of the five generic competitive strategies best characterizes your company's strategic approach to competing successfully?
2. Which rival companies appear to be employing a low-cost provider strategy?
3. Which rival companies appear to be employing a broad differentiation strategy?
4. Which rival companies appear to be employing a best-cost provider strategy?
5. Which rival companies appear to be employing some type of focus strategy?

CHAPTER

6

Supplementing the Chosen Competitive Strategy

Other Important Business
Strategy Choices

LEARNING OBJECTIVES

1. Gain an understanding of how strategic alliances and collaborative partnerships can bolster a company's competitive capabilities and resource strengths.

2. Become aware of the strategic benefits of mergers and acquisitions.

3. Understand when a company should consider using a vertical integration strategy to extend its operations to more stages of the overall industry value chain.

4. Understand the conditions that favor farming out certain value chain activities to vendors and strategic allies.

5. Recognize how and why different types of market situations shape business strategy choices.

6. Understand when being a first-mover or a fast-follower or a late-mover can lead to competitive advantage.

> Strategies for taking the hill won't necessarily hold it.
>
> **— Amar Bhide**

> Successful business strategy is about actively shaping the game you play, not just playing the game you find.
>
> **—Adam M. Brandenburger and Barry J. Nalebuff**

> The sure path to oblivion is to stay where you are.
>
> **— Bernard Fauber**

> Strategy is all about combining choices of what to do and what not to do into a system that creates the requisite fit between what the environment needs and what the company does.
>
> **— Costas Markides**

Once a company has settled on which of the five generic strategies to employ, attention turns to what other *strategic actions* it can take to complement its competitive approach and maximize the power of its overall strategy. As discussed in earlier chapters, a company's overall business strategy includes not only the details of its competitive strategy to deliver value to customers in a unique way (and the related functional-area and operating-level strategies) but also any other strategic initiatives that can embellish its competitive capabilities and resource strengths and promote sustainable competitive advantage. Several measures to enhance a company's strategy have to be considered:

- Whether entering into strategic alliances and/or partnerships can enhance a company's competitive capabilities and resource strengths.

- Whether to bolster the company's market position via merger or acquisitions.

- Whether to integrate backward or forward into more stages of the industry value chain.

- Which value chain activities, if any, should be outsourced.

- How best to tailor the company's strategy to such industry conditions as rapid growth, slow growth, market stagnation, rapid-fire change and market turbulence, and industry fragmentation.

- When to undertake strategic moves—whether it is advantageous to be a first-mover or a fast-follower or a late-mover.

The chapter contains sections discussing the pros and cons of each of these strategy-enhancing measures.

STRATEGIC ALLIANCES AND PARTNERSHIPS

Companies in all types of industries and in all parts of the world have elected to form strategic alliances and partnerships to complement their own strategic initiatives and strengthen their competitiveness in domestic and international markets. This is an about-face from times past, when the vast majority of companies were content to go it alone, confident that they already had or could independently develop whatever resources and know-how were needed to be successful in their markets. But globalization of the world economy; revolutionary advances in technology across a broad front; and untapped opportunities in national markets in Asia, Latin America, and Europe have made strategic partnerships of one kind or another integral to competing on a broad geographic scale.

Many companies now find themselves thrust into two very demanding competitive races: (1) *the global race to build a market presence in many different national markets* and join the ranks of companies recognized as global market leaders, and (2) *the race to seize opportunities on the frontiers of advancing technology* and build the resource strengths and business capabilities to compete successfully in the industries and product markets of the future.[1] Even the largest and most financially sound companies have concluded that simultaneously running the races for global market leadership and for a stake in the industries of the future requires more diverse and expansive skills, resources, technological expertise, and competitive capabilities than they can assemble and manage alone. Such companies, along with others that are missing the resources and competitive capabilities needed to pursue promising opportunities, have determined that the fastest way to fill the gap is often to form alliances with enterprises having the desired strengths. Consequently, these companies form strategic alliances or partnerships in which two or more companies jointly work to achieve mutually beneficial strategic outcomes. Thus, a **strategic alliance** is a formal agreement between two or more separate companies in which there is strategically relevant collaboration of some sort, joint contribution of resources, shared risk, shared control, and mutual dependence. Often, alliances involve joint marketing, joint sales or distribution, joint production, design collaboration, joint research, or projects to jointly develop new technologies or products. The relationship between the partners may be contractual or merely collaborative; the arrangement commonly stops short of formal ownership ties between the partners (although there are a few strategic alliances where one or more allies have minority ownership in certain of the other alliance members). Five factors make an alliance "strategic," as opposed to just a convenient business arrangement:[2]

> **CORE CONCEPT**
>
> *Strategic alliances* are collaborative arrangements where two or more companies join forces to achieve mutually beneficial strategic outcomes. The competitive attraction of alliances is in allowing companies to bundle competencies and resources that are more valuable in a joint effort than when kept separate.

1. It is critical to the company's achievement of an important objective.
2. It helps build, sustain, or enhance a core competence or competitive advantage.
3. It helps block a competitive threat.
4. It helps open up important new market opportunities.
5. It mitigates a significant risk to a company's business.

Strategic cooperation is a much-favored, indeed necessary, approach in industries where new technological developments are occurring at a furious pace along many different paths and where advances in one technology spill over to affect others (often blurring industry boundaries). Whenever industries are experiencing high-velocity technological advances in many areas simultaneously, firms find it virtually essential to have cooperative relationships with other enterprises to stay on the leading edge of technology and product performance even in their own area of specialization.

Companies in many different industries all across the world have made strategic alliances a core part of their overall strategy; U.S. companies alone announced nearly 68,000 alliances from 1996 through 2003.[3] In the personal computer (PC) industry, alliances are pervasive because the different components of PCs and the software to run them are supplied by so many different companies—one set of companies provides the microprocessors, another group makes the circuit boards, another the monitors, another the disk drives, another the memory chips, and so on. Moreover, their facilities are scattered across the United States, Japan, Taiwan, Singapore, Malaysia, and parts of Europe. Strategic alliances among companies in the various parts of the PC industry facilitate the close cross-company collaboration required on next-generation product development, logistics, production, and the timing of new product releases.

Since 2003, Samsung, a global electronics company headquartered in South Korea, has entered into more than 30 major strategic alliances involving such companies as Sony, Nokia, Intel, Microsoft, Dell, Toshiba, Lowe's, IBM, Hewlett-Packard, and Disney Automation; the alliances involved joint investments, technology transfer arrangements, joint R&D projects, and agreements to supply parts and components—all of which facilitated Samsung's strategic efforts to globalize its business and secure it position as a leader in the worldwide electronics industry. Microsoft collaborates very closely with independent software developers to ensure that their programs will run on the next-generation versions of Windows. Genentech, a leader in biotechnology and human genetics, has a partnering strategy to increase its access to novel biotherapeutics products and technologies and has formed R&D alliances with over 30 companies to boost its prospects for developing new cures for various diseases and ailments. United Airlines, American Airlines, Continental, Delta, and Northwest created an alliance to form Orbitz, an Internet travel site that enabled them to compete head-to-head against Expedia and Travelocity and, further, to give them more economical access to travelers and vacationers shopping online for airfares, rental cars, lodging, cruises, and vacation packages.

Intel and wireless telephone provider Clearwire launched a strategic alliance in 2004 to create an advanced Wi-Fi technology that would allow portable PC users to link to the Internet via cellular telephone signals. In 2008, Intel and Clearwire were in negotiations with Google, Time Warner, Comcast, and Sprint to expand Clearwire's WiMAX network in the United States. WiMAX, a fourth-generation Wi-Fi technology, allowed people to browse the Internet at speeds as great as 10 times faster than other cellular Wi-Fi technologies. Intel planned to support the WiMAX alliance with the launch of laptop computers equipped with WiMAX wireless cards by late 2008. The appeal of the partnership for Time Warner and Comcast was the ability to bundle the sale of wireless services to its cable customers, while Clearwire and Sprint hoped that settling on a common technology would make WiMAX the dominant wireless Internet format. Google's interest in the alliance was to strengthen its lead in desktop search on wireless devices.

Toyota has forged long-term strategic partnerships with many of its suppliers of automotive parts and components, both to achieve lower costs and to improve the quality and reliability of its vehicles. In 2008, when Chrysler found itself unable to build hybrid SUVs and trucks using its Two Mode technological innovation (because it lacked the economies of scale necessary to produce proprietary components at a reasonable cost), it entered into a strategic alliance with Nissan whereby Nissan would build Chrysler vehicles with the hybrid technology and Chrysler would take over the production of certain Nissan truck models. Chrysler also entered into an alliance with China's Chery Automobile Company to expand Chrysler's line of small cars with a Chery-produced model. Johnson & Johnson and Merck entered into an alliance to market Pepcid AC; Merck developed the stomach distress remedy, and Johnson & Johnson functioned as marketer—the alliance made Pepcid products the best-selling remedies for acid indigestion and heartburn.

Company use of alliances is quite widespread.

Studies indicate that large corporations are commonly involved in 30 to 50 alliances and that a number have hundreds of alliances. One recent study estimated that about 35 percent of corporate revenues in 2003 came from activities involving strategic alliances, up from 15 percent in 1995.[4]

Another study reported that the typical large corporation relied on alliances for 15 to 20 percent of its revenues, assets, or income.[5] Companies that have formed a host of alliances have a need to manage their alliances like a portfolio—terminating those that no longer serve a useful purpose or that have produced meager results, forming promising new alliances, and restructuring certain existing alliances to correct performance problems and/or redirect the collaborative effort.[6]

Why and How Strategic Alliances Are Advantageous

The best alliances are highly selective, focusing on particular value chain activities and on obtaining a particular competitive benefit. They tend to enable a firm to build on its strengths and to learn.

The most common reasons why companies enter into strategic alliances are to expedite the development of promising new technologies or products, to overcome deficits in their own technical and manufacturing expertise, to bring together the personnel and expertise needed to create desirable new skill sets and capabilities, to improve supply chain efficiency, to gain economies of scale in production and/or marketing, and to acquire or improve market access through joint marketing agreements.[7] Manufacturers frequently pursue alliances with parts and components suppliers to gain the efficiencies of better supply chain management and to speed new products to market. By joining forces in components production and/or final assembly, companies may be able to realize cost savings not achievable with their own small volumes. Allies can learn much from one another in performing joint research, sharing technological know-how, and collaborating on complementary new technologies and products—sometimes enough to enable them to pursue other new opportunities on their own.[8] In industries where technology is advancing rapidly, alliances are all about fast cycles of learning, staying abreast of the latest developments, and gaining quick access to the latest round of technological know-how. In bringing together firms with different skills and knowledge bases, alliances open up learning opportunities that help partner firms better leverage their own resource strengths.[9]

There are several other instances in which companies find strategic alliances particularly valuable. A company that is racing for *global market leadership* needs alliances to:

- *Get into critical country markets quickly* and accelerate the process of building a potent global market presence.
- *Gain inside knowledge about unfamiliar markets and cultures through alliances with local partners.* For example, U.S., European, and Japanese companies wanting to build market footholds in the fast-growing Chinese market have pursued

partnership arrangements with Chinese companies to help in getting products through the tedious and typically corrupt customs process; to help guide them through the maze of government regulations; to supply knowledge of local markets; to provide guidance on adapting their products to better match the buying preferences of Chinese consumers; to set up local manufacturing capabilities; and to assist in distribution, marketing, and promotional activities. The Chinese government has long required foreign companies operating in China to have a state-owned Chinese company as a minority or maybe even 50 percent partner—only recently has it backed off this requirement for foreign companies operating in selected parts of the Chinese economy.

- *Access valuable skills and competencies* that are concentrated in particular geographic locations (such as software design competencies in the United States, fashion design skills in Italy, and efficient manufacturing skills in Japan and China).

A company that is racing to *stake out a strong position in an industry of the future* needs alliances to:

- *Establish a stronger beachhead* for participating in the target industry.
- *Master new technologies and build new expertise and competencies* faster than would be possible through internal efforts.
- *Open up broader opportunities* in the target industry by melding the firm's own capabilities with the expertise and resources of partners.

Capturing the Benefits of Strategic Alliances

The extent to which companies benefit from entering into alliances and partnerships seems to be a function of six factors:[10]

1. *Picking a good partner*—A good partner not only has the desired expertise and capabilities but also shares the company's vision about the purpose of the alliance. Experience indicates that it is generally wise to avoid a partnership in which there is strong potential of direct competition—agreements to jointly market each other's products hold much potential for conflict unless the products are complements rather than substitutes and unless there is good chemistry among key personnel. Experience also indicates that alliances between strong and weak companies rarely work, because the alliance is unlikely to provide the strong partner with useful resources or skills, plus there's a greater chance of the alliance producing mediocre results.

2. *Being sensitive to cultural differences*—Unless the outsider exhibits respect for the local culture and local business practices, productive working relationships are unlikely to emerge.

3. *Recognizing that the alliance must benefit both sides*—Information must be shared as well as gained, and the relationship must remain forthright and trustful. Many alliances fail because one or both partners grow unhappy with what they are learning. Also, if either partner plays games with information or tries to take advantage of the other, the resulting friction can quickly erode the value of further collaboration.

4. *Ensuring that both parties live up to their commitments*—Both parties have to deliver on their commitments for the alliance to produce the intended benefits.

The division of work has to be perceived as fairly apportioned, and the caliber of the benefits received on both sides has to be perceived as adequate.

5. *Structuring the decision-making process so that actions can be taken swiftly when needed*—In many instances, the fast pace of technological and competitive changes dictates an equally fast decision-making process. If the parties get bogged down in discussion or in gaining internal approval from higher-ups, the alliance can turn into an anchor of delay and inaction.

6. *Managing the learning process and then adjusting the alliance agreement over time to fit new circumstances*—One of the keys to long-lasting success is adapting the nature and structure of the alliance to be responsive to shifting market conditions, emerging technologies, and changing customer requirements. Wise allies are quick to recognize the merit of an evolving collaborative arrangement, where adjustments are made to accommodate changing market conditions and to overcome whatever problems arise in establishing an effective working relationship. Most alliances encounter troubles of some kind within a couple of years—those that are flexible enough to evolve are better able to recover.

Most alliances that aim at sharing technology or providing market access turn out to be temporary, fulfilling their purpose after a few years because the benefits of mutual learning have occurred and because the businesses of both partners have developed to the point where they are ready to go their own ways. In such cases, it is important for each partner to learn thoroughly and rapidly about the other partner's technology, business practices, and organizational capabilities and then transfer valuable ideas and practices into its own operations promptly. Although long-term alliances sometimes prove mutually beneficial, most partners don't hesitate to terminate the alliance and go it alone when the payoffs run out.

Alliances are more likely to be long-lasting when (1) they involve collaboration with suppliers or distribution allies and each party's contribution involves activities in different portions of the industry value chain, or (2) both parties conclude that continued collaboration is in their mutual interest, perhaps because new opportunities for learning are emerging or perhaps because further collaboration will allow each partner to extend its market reach beyond what it could accomplish on its own.

Why Many Alliances Are Unstable or Break Apart

The stability of an alliance depends on how well the partners work together, their success in responding and adapting to changing internal and external conditions, and their willingness to renegotiate the bargain if circumstances so warrant. A successful alliance requires real in-the-trenches collaboration, not merely an arm's-length exchange of ideas. Unless partners place a high value on the skills, resources, and contributions each brings to the alliance and the cooperative arrangement results in valuable win–win outcomes, it is doomed. A surprisingly large number of alliances never live up to expectations. In 2007, a *Harvard Business Review* article reported that even though the number of strategic alliances increases by about 25 percent annually, about 60 to 70 percent continue to fail each year.[11]

The high divorce rate among strategic allies has several causes—diverging objectives and priorities, an inability to work well together (the alliance between Disney and Pixar is a classic example of an alliance coming apart because of clashes between high-level executives), changing conditions that render the purpose of the alliance obsolete, the emergence of more attractive technological paths, and marketplace rivalry between one or more allies.[12] Experience indicates that *alliances stand a reasonable chance of helping a company reduce competitive disadvantage, but very rarely have they proved a strategic option for gaining a durable competitive edge over rivals.*

The Strategic Dangers of Relying Heavily on Alliances and Partnerships

The Achilles' heel of alliances and cooperative strategies is a dependence on other companies for *essential* expertise and capabilities. To be a market leader (and perhaps even a serious market contender), a company must ultimately develop its own capabilities in areas where internal strategic control is pivotal to protecting its competitiveness and building competitive advantage. Moreover, some alliances hold only limited potential because the partner guards its most valuable skills and expertise; in such instances, acquiring or merging with a company possessing the desired know-how and resources is a better solution.

MERGER AND ACQUISITION STRATEGIES

Mergers and acquisitions are much-used strategic options—for example, the total worldwide value of mergers and acquisitions completed between 2002 and late 2007 approached $16 trillion.[13] Mergers and acquisitions are especially well-suited for situations in which alliances and partnerships do not go far enough in providing a company with access to needed resources and capabilities.[14] Ownership ties are more permanent than partnership ties, allowing the operations of the merger/acquisition participants to be tightly integrated and creating more in-house control and autonomy. A *merger* is a pooling of equals, with the newly created company often taking on a new name. An *acquisition* is a combination in which one company, the acquirer, purchases and absorbs the operations of another, the acquired. The difference between a merger and an acquisition relates more to the details of ownership, management control, and financial arrangements than to strategy and competitive advantage. The resources, competencies, and competitive capabilities of the newly created enterprise end up much the same whether the combination is the result of acquisition or merger.

> Combining the operations of two companies, via merger or acquisition, is an attractive strategic option for achieving operating economies, strengthening the resulting company's competencies and competitiveness, and opening up avenues of new market opportunity.

Many mergers and acquisitions are driven by strategies to achieve any of five strategic objectives:[15]

1. *To create a more cost-efficient operation out of the combined companies*—When a company acquires another company in the same industry, there's usually enough overlap in operations that certain inefficient plants can be closed or distribution activities partly combined and downsized (when nearby centers serve some of the same geographic areas) or sales-force and marketing activities combined and downsized (when each company has salespeople calling on the same customer). The combined companies may also be able to reduce supply chain costs because of buying in greater volume from common suppliers and from closer collaboration with supply chain partners. Likewise, it is usually feasible to squeeze out cost savings in administrative activities, again by combining and downsizing such administrative activities as finance and accounting, information technology, human resources, and so on. Delta Air Lines and Northwest Airlines entered into a merger agreement in 2008 that would create the world's largest airline and

hopefully give the new company a reasonable chance of survival in the troubled airline industry. Both companies had emerged from bankruptcy in 2007 and, at the time of the merger announcement, were still struggling to keep costs low and earn profits as fuel costs soared. The merger was expected to allow the new airline to cut $1 billion from its annual operating costs by eliminating redundant activities and improving aircraft utilization. In addition, the merger would allow the new airline to narrow the size of its fleet and retire many older fuel-hungry planes. Quite a number of acquisitions are undertaken with the objective of transforming two or more otherwise high-cost companies into one lean competitor with average or below-average costs.

2. *To expand a company's geographic coverage*—One of the best and quickest ways to expand a company's geographic coverage is to acquire rivals with operations in the desired locations. And if there is some geographic overlap, then a side benefit is being able to reduce costs by eliminating duplicate facilities in those geographic areas where undesirable overlap exists. Banks like Wells Fargo, Bank of America, Wachovia, and SunTrust have pursued geographic expansion by making a series of acquisitions over the years, enabling them to establish a market presence in an ever-growing number of states and localities. Many companies use acquisitions to expand internationally—food-products companies like Nestlé, Kraft, Unilever, and Procter & Gamble—all racing for global market leadership—have made acquisitions an integral part of their strategies to widen their geographic reach.

3. *To extend the company's business into new product categories*—Many times a company has gaps in its product line that need to be filled. Acquisition can be a quicker and more potent way to broaden a company's product line than going through the exercise of introducing a company's own new product to fill the gap. PepsiCo's Frito-Lay division acquired Flat Earth, a maker of fruit and vegetable crisps, to broaden its lineup of snacks that appeal to health-conscious consumers. Coca-Cola added to its lineup of healthy beverages with the $4.1 billion acquisition of Glacéau in 2007. Glacéau is the maker of VitaminWater, which is the leading enhanced-water brand in the United States.

4. *To gain quick access to new technologies or other resources and competitive capabilities*—Making acquisitions to bolster a company's technological know-how or to fill resource holes is a favorite of companies racing to establish a position in an industry or product category about to be born. Making acquisitions aimed at filling meaningful gaps in technological expertise allows a company to bypass a time-consuming and perhaps expensive R&D effort (which might not succeed). Cisco Systems purchased over 75 technology companies between 2000 and 2008 to give it more technological reach and product breadth, thereby buttressing its standing as the world's biggest supplier of systems for building the infrastructure of the Internet. Intel has made over 300 acquisitions in the past five or so years to broaden its technological base, obtain the resource capabilities to produce and market a variety of Internet-related and electronics-related products, and make it less dependent on supplying microprocessors for PCs.

5. *To try to invent a new industry and lead the convergence of industries whose boundaries are being blurred by changing technologies and new market opportunities*—A company's management may conclude that two or more distinct industries are converging into one and decide to establish a strong position in the consolidating markets by bringing together the resources and products of several different companies. Microsoft TV has made a series of acquisitions that have enabled it to

launch Internet Protocol Television (IPTV). Microsoft TV allows broadband users to use their home computers or Xbox game consoles to download live programming, video on demand, pictures, and music. News Corporation has also prepared for the convergence of media services with the purchase of satellite TV companies to complement its media holdings in TV broadcasting (the Fox network, and TV stations in various countries); cable TV (Fox News, Fox Sports, and FX); filmed entertainment (Twentieth Century Fox and Fox Studios); and newspaper, magazine, and book publishing. Most recently, News Corp. acquired Dow Jones, the publisher of *The Wall Street Journal,* to further extend its media business holdings.

Numerous companies have employed an acquisition strategy to catapult themselves from the ranks of the unknown into positions of market leadership. During the 1990s, North Carolina National Bank (NCNB) pursued a series of acquisitions to transform itself into a major regional bank in the Southeast. But NCNB's strategic vision was to become a bank with offices across most of the United States; it therefore changed its name to NationsBank. In 1998, NationsBank acquired Bank of America for $66 billion and also adopted its name. In 2004, Bank of America acquired Fleet Boston Financial for $48 billion. Bank of America spent $35 billion in 2005 to acquire MBNA, a leading credit card company, and acquired U.S. Trust Corporation and LaSalle Bank in 2007. In 2008, Bank of America had a network of 6,150 branch banks in 31 states and the District of Columbia, and held deposits of more than $800 billion. It ranked as the largest U.S. bank in terms of shareholders' equity and market capitalization, the second largest U.S. bank in total assets (more than $1.7 trillion in 2007), and the second most profitable U.S. bank, with 2007 net income of nearly $15 billion. Illustration Capsule 6.1 describes how Clear Channel Communications has used acquisitions to build a leading global position in outdoor advertising and radio broadcasting.

Why Mergers and Acquisitions Sometimes Fail to Produce Anticipated Results

All too frequently, mergers and acquisitions do not produce the hoped-for outcomes.[16] Cost savings may prove smaller than expected. Gains in competitive capabilities may take substantially longer to realize or, worse, may never materialize at all. Efforts to mesh the corporate cultures can stall due to formidable resistance from organization members. Managers and employees at the acquired company may argue forcefully for continuing to do certain things the way they were done prior to the acquisition. Key employees at the acquired company can quickly become disenchanted and leave; the morale of company personnel who remain can drop to disturbingly low levels because they disagree with newly instituted changes. Differences in management styles and operating procedures can prove hard to resolve. The managers appointed to oversee the integration of a newly acquired company can make mistakes in deciding what activities to leave alone and what activities to meld into their own operations and systems.

A number of previously applauded mergers/acquisitions have yet to live up to expectations or have proved to be spectacular failures—the merger of AOL and Time Warner, the merger of Daimler-Benz and Chrysler, Ford's acquisition of Jaguar and Land Rover, and Boston Scientific's acquisition of Guidant Corporation are prime examples. The AOL–Time Warner merger proved to be a disaster, partly because AOL's once-rapid growth had evaporated, partly because of a huge clash of corporate cultures, and partly because most of the expected benefits from industry convergence never materialized. Ford paid a handsome price to acquire Jaguar but was

ILLUSTRATION CAPSULE 6.1
Clear Channel Communications: Using Mergers and Acquisitions to Become a Global Market Leader

In 2008, Clear Channel Communications was among the worldwide leaders in radio broadcasting and outdoor advertising. Clear Channel owned and operated more than 1,000 radio stations in the United States and operated an additional 240 radio stations in Australia, New Zealand, and Mexico. Clear Channel's total number of outdoor advertising displays across the world exceeded 850,000 in 2008. The company, which was founded in 1972 by Lowry Mays and Billy Joe McCombs, got its start by acquiring an unprofitable country-music radio station in San Antonio, Texas. Over the next 10 years, Mays learned the radio business and slowly bought other radio stations in a variety of states. Going public in 1984 helped the company raise the equity capital needed to continue acquiring radio stations in additional geographic markets.

When the Federal Communications Commission loosened the rules regarding the ability of one company to own both radio and TV stations in the late 1980s, Clear Channel broadened its strategy and began acquiring small, struggling TV stations. By 1998, Clear Channel had used acquisitions to build a leading position in radio and television stations. Domestically, it owned, programmed, or sold airtime for 69 AM radio stations, 135 FM stations, and 18 TV stations in 48 local markets in 24 states. Clear Channel's big move was to begin expanding internationally, chiefly by acquiring interests in radio station properties in a variety of countries.

In 1997, Clear Channel used acquisitions to establish a major position in outdoor advertising. Its first acquisition was Phoenix-based Eller Media Company, an outdoor advertising company with over 100,000 billboard facings. This was quickly followed by additional acquisitions of outdoor advertising companies, the most important of which were ABC Outdoor in Milwaukee, Wisconsin; Paxton Communications (with operations in Tampa and Orlando, Florida); Universal Outdoor; the More Group,

with outdoor operations and 90,000 displays in 24 countries; and the Ackerley Group.

Then in October 1999, Clear Channel made a major move by acquiring AM-FM Inc. and changed its name to Clear Channel Communications; the AM-FM acquisition gave Clear Channel operations in 32 countries, including 830 radio stations, 19 TV stations, and more than 425,000 outdoor displays.

Additional acquisitions were completed during the 2000–2003 period. The emphasis was on buying radio, TV, and outdoor advertising properties with operations in many of the same local markets, which made it feasible to (1) cut costs by sharing facilities and staffs, (2) improve programming, and (3) sell advertising to customers in packages for all three media simultaneously. Packaging ads for two or three media not only helped Clear Channel's advertising clients distribute their messages more effectively but also allowed the company to combine its sales activities and have a common sales force for all three media, achieving significant cost savings and boosting profit margins. But in 2000 Clear Channel broadened its media strategy by acquiring SFX Entertainment, one of the world's largest promoters, producers, and presenters of live entertainment events.

In 2006, Clear Channel management recognized that the company's outdoor advertising and radio businesses were by far the company's most profitable businesses and began a search for buyers of its lesser-performing businesses. The company spun off its live entertainment business in 2006 and entered into an agreement to sell its 56 television stations in 2007. In 2008, it was seeking a buyer for 288 of its 1,005 radio stations that operated in small markets. Its remaining 717 radio stations all operated in the top 100 markets in the United States. In 2008, Clear Channel's outdoor advertising business owned and operated more than 200,000 billboards in the United States and 687,000 outdoor displays in 50 other countries.

Sources: **www.clearchannel.com** (accessed May 2008), and *BusinessWeek,* October 19, 1999, p. 56.

---

not able to make the Jaguar brand a major factor in the luxury-car segment in competition against Mercedes, BMW, and Lexus. In 2008, Ford sold Jaguar to India's Tata Motors. In the same deal, Ford also sold its Land Rover division to Tata because of disappointingly low sales volumes—Land Rover was another failed acquisition Ford made to broaden its lineup of models and boost sales volumes. The combination of the engineering expertise of Daimler-Benz and Chrysler's styling and design capabilities was expected to address each of the two merger partners' shortcomings. Daimler-Benz, maker of the Mercedes-Benz brand of vehicles, had long been known for its superior quality and performance, but stodgy styling, while Chrysler had a long tradition of producing beautifully styled vehicles with dismal defect rates and engineering imperfections. The 1998 merger, which formed DaimlerChrysler, did in fact help Daimler-Benz improve its styling, but it also resulted in the esteemed Mercedes brand recording its lowest reliability ratings in the company's history. Chrysler was spun off in 2007, and the now-separate companies are simply called Daimler and Chrysler. Similarly, Boston Scientific's $25 billion acquisition of Guidant Corporation in 2006 has yet to prove successful. At the time of the acquisition, Guidant was a leader in the $10 billion market for pacemakers and other medical devices to treat cardiac disease with 2005 earnings of $355 million. The lofty price paid for Guidant was funded by $6.5 billion in loans and an equity issue that increased outstanding Boston Scientific shares by 80 percent. The addition of $300 million in interest expense to service Boston Scientific's long-term debt contributed to its 2007 net loss of $495 million.

VERTICAL INTEGRATION STRATEGIES: OPERATING ACROSS MORE STAGES OF THE INDUSTRY VALUE CHAIN

Vertical integration extends a firm's competitive and operating scope within the same industry. It involves expanding the firm's range of activities backward into sources of supply and/or forward toward end users. Thus, if a manufacturer invests in facilities to produce certain component parts that it formerly purchased from outside suppliers, it remains in essentially the same industry as before. The only change is that it has operations in two stages of the industry value chain. For example, paint manufacturer Sherwin-Williams remains in the paint business even though it has integrated forward into retailing by operating more than 3,300 retail stores that market its paint products directly to consumers.

Vertical integration strategies can aim at *full integration* (participating in all stages of the industry value chain) or *partial integration* (building positions in selected stages of the industry's total value chain). A firm can pursue vertical integration by starting its own operations in other stages in the industry's activity chain or by acquiring a company already performing the activities it wants to bring in-house.

The Advantages of a Vertical Integration Strategy

The two best reasons for investing company resources in vertical integration are to strengthen the firm's competitive position and to boost its profitability.[17] Vertical integration has no real payoff profitwise or strategywise unless it produces sufficient cost savings/profit increases to justify the extra investment, adds materially to a company's technological and competitive strengths, and/or helps differentiate the company's product offering.

CORE CONCEPT
A vertical integration strategy has appeal *only* if it significantly strengthens a firm's competitive position.

Integrating Backward to Achieve Greater Competitiveness   It is harder than one might think to generate cost savings or boost profitability by integrating backward into activities such as parts and components manufacture (which could otherwise be purchased from suppliers with specialized expertise in making these parts and components). For backward integration to be a viable and profitable strategy, a company must be able to (1) achieve the same scale economies as outside suppliers and (2) match or beat suppliers' production efficiency with no drop-off in quality. Neither outcome is a slam dunk. To begin with, a company's in-house requirements are often too small to reach the optimum size for low-cost operation—for instance, if it takes a minimum production volume of 1 million units to achieve mass-production economies and a company's in-house requirements are just 250,000 units, then it falls way short of being able to capture the scale economies of outside suppliers (who may readily find buyers for 1 million or more units). Furthermore, matching the production efficiency of suppliers is fraught with problems when suppliers have considerable production experience of their own, when the technology they employ has elements that are hard to master, and/or when substantial R&D expertise is required to develop next-version parts and components or keep pace with advancing technology in parts/components production.

But that being said, there are still occasions when a company can improve its cost position and competitiveness by performing a broader range of value chain activities in-house rather than having certain of these activities performed by outside suppliers. The best potential for being able to reduce costs via a backward integration strategy exists in situations where suppliers have outsize profit margins, where the item being supplied is a major cost component, and where the requisite technological skills are easily mastered or can be gained by acquiring a supplier with the desired technological know-how. Furthermore, when a company has proprietary know-how that it wants to keep from rivals, then in-house performance of value chain activities related to this know-how is beneficial even if such activities could be performed by outsiders.

Backward vertical integration can produce a differentiation-based competitive advantage when a company ends up with a better-quality product/service offering, improves the caliber of its customer service, or in other ways enhances the performance of its final product. On occasion, integrating into more stages along the industry value chain can add to a company's differentiation capabilities by allowing it to build or strengthen its core competencies, better master key skills or strategy-critical technologies, or add features that deliver greater customer value. Other potential advantages of backward integration include sparing a company the uncertainty of being dependent on suppliers for crucial components or support services and lessening a company's vulnerability to powerful suppliers inclined to raise prices at every opportunity. Panera Bread has been quite successful with a backward vertical integration strategy that involves internally producing fresh dough for company-owned and franchised bakery-cafés to use in making baguettes, pastries, bagels, and other types of bread—the company has earned substantial profits from producing both these items internally rather than having these supplied by outsiders. Furthermore, Panera Bread's vertical integration strategy makes good competitive sense because it helps lower store operating costs and facilitates consistent product quality at the company's 1,185 U.S. locations.

Integrating Forward to Enhance Competitiveness   The strategic impetus for forward integration is to gain better access to end users and better market visibility. In many industries, independent sales agents, wholesalers, and retailers handle competing brands of the same product; having no allegiance to any one company's brand, they tend to push whatever sells and earns them the biggest profits. An independent insurance agency, for example, represents a number of different insurance companies—in trying to find the best match between a customer's insurance requirements and the policies of alternative insurance companies, there's plenty of opportunity for independent agents to end up promoting the policies of certain insurance companies ahead of other insurance companies. An insurance company may conclude, therefore, that it is better off integrating forward and setting up its own local sales offices with its own local agents to promote the company's insurance policies exclusively. Likewise, a tire manufacturer may find it better to integrate forward into tire retailing than to use independent distributors and retailers that stock multiple brands. A number of houseware and apparel manufacturers have integrated forward into retailing so as to move seconds, overstocked items, and slow-selling merchandise through their own branded factory outlet stores. Some producers have opted to integrate forward into retailing by selling directly to customers at the company's Web site. Bypassing regular wholesale/retail channels in favor of direct sales and Internet retailing can have appeal if it lowers distribution costs, produces a relative cost advantage over certain rivals, and results in lower selling prices to end users.

The Disadvantages of a Vertical Integration Strategy

Vertical integration has some substantial drawbacks, however.[18] It boosts a firm's capital investment in the industry, increasing business risk (what if industry growth and profitability go sour?) and boosting a company's vested interests in sticking with its vertically integrated value chain (what if some aspects of its technology and production facilities become obsolete before they are worn out or fully depreciated?). Vertically integrated companies that have invested heavily in a particular technology or in parts/components manufacture are often slow to embrace technological advances or more efficient production methods compared to partially integrated or nonintegrated firms. This is because less integrated firms can pressure suppliers to provide only the latest and best parts and components (even going so far as to shift their purchases from one supplier to another if need be), whereas a vertically integrated firm that is saddled with older technology or facilities that make items it no longer needs is looking at the high costs of premature abandonment. Second, integrating forward or backward locks a firm into relying on its own in-house activities and sources of supply (which later may prove more costly than outsourcing) and potentially results in less flexibility in accommodating shifting buyer preferences or a product design that doesn't include parts and components that it makes in-house. *In today's world of close working relationships with suppliers and efficient supply chain management systems, very few businesses can make a case for integrating backward into the business of suppliers to ensure a reliable supply of materials and components or to reduce production costs.* The best materials and components suppliers stay abreast of advancing technology and are adept in boosting their efficiency and keeping their costs and prices as low as possible. A company that pursues a vertical integration strategy and tries to produce many parts and components in-house is likely to find itself hard-pressed to keep up with technological advances and cutting-edge production practices for each part and component used in making its product.

Third, vertical integration poses all kinds of capacity-matching problems. In motor vehicle manufacturing, for example, the most efficient scale of operation for making axles is different from the most economic volume for radiators, and different yet again for both engines and transmissions. Building the capacity to produce just the right number of axles, radiators, engines, and transmissions in-house—and doing so at the lowest unit costs for each—is much easier said than done. If internal capacity for making transmissions is deficient, the difference has to be bought externally. Where internal capacity for radiators proves excessive, customers need to be found for the surplus. And if by-products are generated—as occurs in the processing of many chemical products—they require arrangements for disposal. Consequently, integrating across several production stages in ways that achieve the lowest feasible costs is not as easy as it might seem.

Fourth, integration forward or backward often calls for radical changes in skills and business capabilities. Parts and components manufacturing, assembly operations, wholesale distribution and retailing, and direct sales via the Internet are different businesses with different key success factors. Managers of a manufacturing company should consider carefully whether it makes good business sense to invest time and money in developing the expertise and merchandising skills to integrate forward into wholesaling and retailing. Many manufacturers learn the hard way that company-owned wholesale/retail networks present many headaches, fit poorly with what they do best, and don't always add the kind of value to their core business they thought they would. Selling to customers via the Internet poses still another set of problems—it is usually easier to use the Internet to sell to business customers than to consumers.

Finally, integrating backward into parts and components manufacture can impair a company's operations when it comes to changing out the use of certain parts and components. It is one thing to design out a component made by a supplier and another to design out a component being made in-house (which can mean laying off employees and writing off the associated investment in equipment and facilities). Companies that alter designs and models frequently in response to shifting buyer preferences often find outsourcing the needed parts and components to be cheaper and less complicated than producing them in-house. Most of the world's automakers, despite their expertise in automotive technology and manufacturing, have concluded that purchasing many of their key parts and components from manufacturing specialists results in higher quality, lower costs, and greater design flexibility than does the vertical integration option.

Weighing the Pros and Cons of Vertical Integration

All in all, a strategy of vertical integration can have both important strengths and weaknesses. The tip of the scales depends on (1) whether vertical integration can enhance the performance of strategy-critical activities in ways that lower cost, build expertise, protect proprietary know-how, or increase differentiation; (2) the impact of vertical integration on investment costs, flexibility and response times, and the administrative costs of coordinating operations across more value chain activities; and (3) whether the integration substantially enhances a company's competitiveness and profitability. *Vertical integration strategies have merit according to which capabilities and value chain activities truly need to be performed in-house and which can be performed better or cheaper by outsiders.* Absent solid benefits, integrating forward or backward is not likely to be an attractive strategy option.

OUTSOURCING STRATEGIES: NARROWING THE BOUNDARIES OF THE BUSINESS

CORE CONCEPT
Outsourcing involves farming out certain value chain activities to outside vendors.

Outsourcing involves a conscious decision to abandon or forgo attempts to perform certain value chain activities internally and instead to farm them out to outside specialists and strategic allies. The two big reasons for outsourcing are (1) that outsiders can often perform certain activities better or cheaper and (2) that outsourcing allows a firm to focus its entire energies on those activities at the center of its expertise (its core competencies) and that are the most critical to its competitive and financial success.

The current interest of many companies in making outsourcing a key component of their overall strategy and their approach to supply chain management represents a big departure from the way that companies used to deal with their suppliers and vendors. In years past, it was common for companies to maintain arm's-length relationships with suppliers and outside vendors, insisting on items being made to precise specifications and negotiating long and hard over price.[19] Although a company might place orders with the same supplier repeatedly, there was no expectation that this would be the case; price usually determined which supplier was awarded an order, and companies used the threat of switching suppliers to get the lowest possible prices. To enhance their bargaining power and to make the threat of switching credible, it was standard practice for companies to source key parts and components from several suppliers as opposed to dealing with only a single supplier. But today, most companies are abandoning such approaches in favor of forging alliances and strategic partnerships with a small number of highly capable suppliers. Collaborative relationships are replacing contractual, purely price-oriented relationships because companies have discovered that many of the advantages of performing value chain activities in-house can be captured and many of the disadvantages avoided by forging close, long-term cooperative partnerships with able suppliers and vendors and tapping into the expertise and capabilities that they have painstakingly developed.

When Outsourcing Strategies Are Advantageous

Outsourcing pieces of the value chain to narrow the boundaries of a firm's business makes strategic sense whenever:

- *An activity can be performed better or more cheaply by outside specialists.* Many PC makers, for example, have abandoned in-house assembly of their PC models, opting to outsource assembly activities from contract specialists that assemble several brands of PCs—such contract assemblers are able to perform assembly activities at lower cost because their larger-scale operations (1) enable them to purchase PC components in bigger volume and typically at lower costs and (2) provide maximum access to scale economies. Similarly, Nikon—by outsourcing the shipment of digital cameras to UPS—gained the capability to deliver its cameras to retailers in the United States, Latin America, and the Caribbean in as little as two days after an order was placed even though Nikon's camera production was located at facilities in Japan, Korea, and Indonesia.

> **CORE CONCEPT**
> A company should generally *not* perform any value chain activity internally that can be performed more efficiently or effectively by outsiders—the chief exception is when a particular activity is strategically crucial and internal control over that activity is deemed essential.

- *The activity is not crucial to the firm's ability to achieve sustainable competitive advantage and won't hollow out its core competencies, capabilities, or technical know-how.* Outsourcing of maintenance services, data processing and data storage, fringe benefit management, Web site operations, and similar administrative support activities to specialists has become commonplace. Colgate-Palmolive, for instance, has been able to reduce its information technology operational costs by more than 10 percent per year through an outsourcing agreement with IBM. A number of companies have begun outsourcing their call center operations to foreign-based contractors who have access to lower-cost labor supplies and can employ lower-paid call center personnel to respond to customer inquiries or requests for technical support.

- *It reduces the company's risk exposure to changing technology and/or changing buyer preferences.* When a company outsources certain parts, components, and services, its suppliers must bear the burden of incorporating state-of-the-art technologies and/or undertaking redesigns and upgrades to accommodate a company's plans to introduce next-generation products. If what a supplier provides falls out of favor with buyers or is designed out of next-generation products, it is the supplier's business that suffers rather than a company's own internal operations.

- *It improves a company's ability to innovate.* Collaborative partnerships with world-class suppliers who have cutting-edge intellectual capital and are early adopters of the latest technology give a company access to ever better parts and components—such supplier-driven innovations, when incorporated into a company's own product offering, fuel a company's ability to introduce its own new and improved products.

- *It streamlines company operations in ways that improve organizational flexibility and cuts the time it takes to get new products into the marketplace.* Outsourcing gives a company the flexibility to switch suppliers in the event that its present supplier falls behind competing suppliers. To the extent that its suppliers can speedily get next-generation parts and components into production, then a company can get its own next-generation product offerings into the marketplace quicker. Moreover, seeking out new suppliers with the needed capabilities already in place is frequently quicker, easier, less risky, and cheaper than hurriedly retooling internal operations to replace obsolete capabilities or try to install and master new technologies.

- *It allows a company to assemble diverse kinds of expertise speedily and efficiently.* A company can nearly always gain quicker access to first-rate capabilities and expertise by partnering with suppliers who already have them in place than it can by trying to build them from scratch with its own company personnel.

- *It allows a company to concentrate on its core business, leverage its key resources, and do even better what it already does best.* A company is better able to build and develop its own competitively valuable competencies and capabilities when it concentrates its full resources and energies on performing those activities internally that it can perform better than outsiders and/or that it needs to have under its direct control. Coach, for example, devotes its energy to designing new styles of handbags and leather accessories, opting to outsource handbag production to 40 contract manufacturers in 15 countries. Hewlett-Packard, IBM, and others have sold manufacturing plants to suppliers and then contracted to purchase the output. Starbucks finds purchasing coffee beans from independent growers far more advantageous than trying to integrate backward into the coffee-growing business.

The Big Risk of an Outsourcing Strategy

The biggest danger of outsourcing is that a company will farm out too many or the wrong types of activities and thereby hollow out its own capabilities.[20] In such cases, a company loses touch with the very activities and expertise that over the long run determine its success. But most companies are alert to this danger and take actions to protect against being held hostage by outside suppliers. Cisco Systems guards against loss of control and protects its manufacturing expertise by designing the production methods that its contract manufacturers must use. Cisco keeps the source code for its designs proprietary, thereby controlling the initiation of all improvements and safeguarding its innovations from imitation. Further, Cisco uses the Internet to monitor the factory operations of contract manufacturers around the clock; it can therefore know immediately when problems arise and decide whether to get involved.

BUSINESS STRATEGY CHOICES FOR SPECIFIC MARKET SITUATIONS

As we began emphasizing back in Chapter 3, a good strategy is always well matched to (1) prevailing industry and competitive conditions and (2) a company's own internal resource strengths and weaknesses. We saw in Chapter 3 that a good fit between strategy and the external situation of a company requires an assessment of the industry's driving forces, competitive forces, and key success factors, but there's more to be revealed about matching strategy to specific kinds of industry conditions. This section looks at the various options for matching a company's strategy to six commonly encountered types of market conditions:

- Freshly emerging markets.
- Rapidly growing markets.
- Mature, slow-growth markets.
- Stagnant or declining markets.
- Turbulent markets characterized by rapid-fire change.
- Fragmented markets comprised of a large number of relatively small sellers.

Competing in Emerging Markets

An emerging market is one in the formative stage. Examples include Voice over Internet Protocol (VoIP) telephone communications, online education, e-book publishing, solar energy production, genetic engineering, and nanoelectronics. Many companies striving to establish a strong foothold in a freshly emerging market are start-up enterprises that are busily engaged in perfecting technology, gearing up operations, and trying to broaden distribution and gain buyer acceptance. Important product design issues or technological problems may still have to be worked out. The business models and strategies of companies in an emerging marketplace are unproved—they may look promising but may or may not ever result in attractive profitability.

The Unique Characteristics of an Emerging Market   Competing in emerging markets presents managers with some unique strategy-making challenges:[21]

- Because the market is in its infancy, there's usually much speculation about how it will function, how fast it will grow, and how big it will get. The little historical information available is virtually useless in making sales and profit projections. There's lots of guesswork about how rapidly buyers will be attracted and how much they will be willing to pay. For example, there is much uncertainty about how many users of traditional telephone service will be inclined to switch over to VoIP technology and how rapidly any such switchovers will occur.
- In many cases, much of the technological know-how underlying the products of emerging industries is proprietary and closely guarded, having been developed in-house by pioneering firms. In such cases, patents and unique technical expertise are key factors in securing competitive advantage. In other cases, numerous companies have access to the requisite technology and may be racing to perfect it, often in collaboration with others. In still other instances, there can be competing technological approaches, with much uncertainty over whether multiple technologies will end up competing alongside one another or whether one approach will ultimately win out because of lower costs or better performance—such a battle

is currently under way in the emerging market for hydrogen fuel cell engines for automobiles. General Motors has pioneered one design, while Volkswagen, Honda, Toyota, Ford, Daimler, and BMW have developed their own slightly different fuel cell designs.

- Just as there may be uncertainties surrounding an emerging industry's technology, there may also be no consensus regarding which product attributes will prove decisive in winning buyer favor. Rivalry therefore centers on each firm's efforts to get the market to ratify its own strategic approach to technology, product design, marketing, and distribution. Such rivalry can result in wide differences in product quality and performance from brand to brand.

- Since in an emerging industry all buyers are first-time users, the marketing task is to induce initial purchase and to overcome customer concerns about product features, performance reliability, and conflicting claims of rival firms.

- Many potential buyers expect first-generation products to be rapidly improved, so they delay purchase until technology and product design mature and second- or third-generation products appear on the market.

- Entry barriers tend to be relatively low, even for entrepreneurial start-up companies. Large, well-known, opportunity-seeking companies with ample resources and competitive capabilities are likely to enter if the industry has promise for explosive growth or if its emergence threatens their present business. For instance, many traditional local telephone companies, seeing the potent threat of wireless communications technology and VoIP, have opted to enter the mobile communications business and begin offering landline customers a VoIP option.

- Strong learning/experience curve effects may be present, allowing significant price reductions as volume builds and costs fall.

- Sometimes firms have trouble securing ample supplies of raw materials and components (until suppliers gear up to meet the industry's needs).

- Undercapitalized companies, finding themselves short of funds to support needed R&D and get through several lean years until the product catches on, end up merging with competitors or being acquired by financially strong outsiders looking to invest in a growth market.

CORE CONCEPT

Companies in an emerging industry have wide latitude in experimenting with different strategic approaches.

Strategy Options for Emerging Industries   The lack of established rules of the game gives industry participants considerable freedom to experiment with a variety of different strategic approaches. Competitive strategies keyed either to low cost or differentiation are usually viable. Focusing makes good sense when resources and capabilities are limited and the industry has too many technological frontiers or too many buyer segments to pursue at once. Broad or focused differentiation strategies keyed to technological or product superiority typically offer the best chance for early competitive advantage.

In addition to choosing a competitive strategy, companies in an emerging industry usually have to fashion a strategy containing one or more of the following elements:[22]

1. Push to perfect the technology, improve product quality, and develop additional attractive performance features. Out-innovating the competition is often one of the best avenues to industry leadership.

2. Consider merging with or acquiring another firm to gain added expertise and pool resource strengths.

3. As technological uncertainty clears and a dominant technology emerges, try to capture any first-mover advantages by adopting it quickly. However, while there's merit in trying to be the industry standard-bearer on technology and to pioneer the dominant product design, firms have to beware of betting too heavily on their own preferred technological approach or product design—especially when there are many competing technologies, R&D is costly, and technological developments can quickly move in surprising new directions.

4. Acquire or form alliances with companies that have related or complementary technological expertise as a means of helping outcompete rivals on the basis of technological superiority.

5. Pursue new customer groups, new user applications, and entry into new geographical areas (perhaps using strategic partnerships or joint ventures if financial resources are constrained).

6. Make it easy and cheap for first-time buyers to try the industry's first-generation product.

7. As the product becomes familiar to a wide portion of the market, shift the advertising emphasis from creating product awareness to increasing frequency of use and building brand loyalty.

8. Use price cuts to attract the next layer of price-sensitive buyers into the market.

9. Form strategic alliances with key suppliers whenever effective supply chain management provides important access to specialized skills, technological capabilities, and critical materials or components.

Young companies in emerging industries face four strategic hurdles: (1) raising the capital to finance initial operations until sales and revenues take off, profits appear, and cash flows turn positive; (2) developing a strategy to ride the wave of industry growth (what market segments and competitive advantages to go after); (3) managing the rapid expansion of facilities and sales in a manner that positions them to contend for industry leadership; and (4) defending against competitors trying to horn in on their success.[23] Up-and-coming companies can help their cause by selecting knowledgeable members for their boards of directors and by hiring entrepreneurial managers with experience in guiding young businesses through the start-up and takeoff stages. *A firm that develops solid resource capabilities, an appealing business model, and a good strategy has a golden opportunity to shape the rules and establish itself as the recognized industry front-runner.*

But strategic efforts to win the early race for growth and market-share leadership in an emerging industry have to be balanced against the longer-range need to build a durable competitive edge and a defendable market position.[24] The initial front-runners in a fast-growing emerging industry that shows signs of good profitability will almost certainly have to defend their positions against opportunity-seeking competitors trying to horn in on their success. Well-financed outsiders can be counted on to enter with aggressive offensive strategies once industry sales take off, the perceived risk of investing in the industry lessens, and the success of current industry members becomes apparent. Sometimes a rush of new entrants, attracted by the growth and profit potential, overcrowds the market and forces industry consolidation to a smaller number of players. Resource-rich latecomers, aspiring to industry leadership, may become major players by acquiring and merging the operations of weaker competitors and then using their own perhaps considerable brand-name recognition to draw customers and build market share. Hence, the strategies of the early leaders must be aimed at competing for the long haul and making a point of developing the resources, capabilities, and market recognition needed to sustain early successes and stave off competition from capable, ambitious newcomers.

Competing in Rapidly Growing Markets

In a fast-growing market, a company needs a strategy predicated on growing faster than the market average so that it can boost its market share and improve its competitive standing vis-à-vis rivals.

Companies that have the good fortune to be in an industry growing at double-digit rates have a golden opportunity to achieve double-digit revenue and profit growth. If market demand is expanding 20 percent annually, then a company can grow 20 percent annually simply by doing little more than contentedly riding the tide—it simply has to be aggressive enough to secure enough new customers to realize a 20 percent gain in sales, not a particularly impressive strategic feat. What is more interesting, however, is to craft a strategy that enables sales to grow at 25 or 30 percent when the overall market is growing by 20 percent. Should a company's strategy deliver sales growth of only 12 percent in a market growing at 20 percent, then it is actually losing ground in the marketplace—a condition that signals a weak strategy and a less appealing product offering. The point here is that, in a rapidly growing market, a company must aim its strategy at producing gains in revenue that exceed the market average; otherwise, the best it can hope for is to maintain its market standing (if it is able to boost sales at a rate equal to the market average) and its market standing may indeed erode if its sales rise by less than the market average.

To be able to grow at a pace exceeding the market average, a company generally must have a strategy that incorporates one or more of the following elements:

- *Driving down costs per unit so as to enable price reductions that attract droves of new customers.* Charging a lower price always has strong appeal in markets where customers are price-sensitive, and lower prices can help push up buyers' demand by drawing new customers into the marketplace. But since rivals can lower their prices also, a company must really be able to drive its unit costs down *faster than rivals,* such that it can use its low-cost advantage to underprice rivals. The makers of Global Positioning System (GPS) navigation devices are aggressively pursuing cost reductions to make their products more affordable for a wider range of end uses and consumers.

- *Pursuing rapid product innovation, both to set a company's product offering apart from rivals and to incorporate attributes that appeal to growing numbers of customers.* Differentiation strategies, when keyed to product attributes that draw in large numbers of new customers, help bolster a company's reputation for product superiority and lay the foundation for sales gains in excess of the overall rate of market growth. If the market is one where technology is advancing rapidly and product life cycles are short, then it becomes especially important to be first-to-market with next-generation products. But product innovation strategies require competencies in R&D and new product development and design, plus organizational agility in getting new and improved products to market quickly. At the same time they are pursuing cost reductions, the makers of GPS navigation devices are pursuing all sorts of product improvements to enhance performance and functionality and drive sales up at an even faster clip.

- *Gaining access to additional distribution channels and sales outlets.* Pursuing wider distribution access so as to reach more potential buyers is a particularly good strategic approach for realizing above-average sales gains. But usually this requires a company to be a first-mover in positioning itself in new distribution channels and forcing rivals into playing catch-up.

- *Expanding the company's geographic coverage.* Expanding into areas, either domestic or foreign, where the company does not have a market presence can also be an effective way to reach more potential buyers and pave the way for gains in sales that outpace the overall market average.

- *Expanding the product line to add models/styles that appeal to a wider range of buyers.* Offering buyers a wider selection can be an effective way to draw new customers in numbers sufficient to realize above-average sales gains. Makers of MP3 players and mobile phones are adding new models to stimulate buyer demand; McDonald's has added new coffee drinks and other menu selections to build store traffic. Marketers of VoIP technology are rapidly introducing a wider variety of plans to broaden their appeal to customers with different calling habits and needs.

Competing in Slow-Growth, Mature Markets

A market is said to be *mature* when nearly all potential buyers are already users of the industry's products and growth in market demand closely parallels that of the economy as a whole. In a mature market, demand consists mainly of replacement sales to existing users, with growth hinging on the industry's abilities to attract the few remaining new buyers and to convince existing buyers to up their usage. Consumer goods industries that are mature typically have a growth rate under 5 percent—roughly equal to the growth of the customer base or overall economy.

How Slowing Growth Alters Market Conditions An industry's transition to maturity does not begin on an easily predicted schedule. Industry maturity can be forestalled by technological advances, product innovations, or other driving forces that keep rejuvenating market demand. Nonetheless, when growth rates do slacken, the onset of market maturity usually produces fundamental changes in the industry's competitive environment:[25]

1. *Slowing growth in buyer demand generates more head-to-head competition for market share.* Firms that want to continue on a rapid-growth track start looking for ways to take customers away from competitors. Outbreaks of price cutting, increased advertising, and other aggressive tactics to gain market share are common.

2. *Buyers become more sophisticated, often driving a harder bargain on repeat purchases.* Since buyers have experience with the product and are familiar with competing brands, they are better able to evaluate different brands and can use their knowledge to negotiate a better deal with sellers.

3. *Competition often produces a greater emphasis on cost and service.* As sellers all begin to offer the product attributes buyers prefer, buyer choices increasingly depend on which seller offers the best combination of price and service.

4. *Firms have a topping-out problem in adding new facilities.* Reduced rates of industry growth mean slowdowns in capacity expansion for manufacturers—adding too much plant capacity at a time when growth is slowing can create oversupply conditions that adversely affect manufacturers' profits well into the future. Likewise, retail chains that specialize in the industry's product have to cut back on the number of new stores being opened to keep from saturating localities with too many stores.

5. *Product innovation and new end-use applications are harder to come by.* Producers find it increasingly difficult to create new product features, find further uses for the product, and sustain buyer excitement.

6. *International competition increases.* Growth-minded domestic firms start to seek out sales opportunities in foreign markets. Some companies, looking for ways to cut costs, relocate plants to countries with lower wage rates. Greater product standardization and diffusion of technological know-how reduce entry barriers and make it possible for enterprising foreign companies to become serious market contenders in more countries. Industry leadership passes to companies that succeed in building strong competitive positions in most of the world's major geographic markets and in winning the biggest global market shares.

7. *Industry profitability falls temporarily or permanently.* Slower growth, increased competition, more sophisticated buyers, and occasional periods of overcapacity put pressure on industry profit margins. Weaker, less-efficient firms are usually the hardest hit.

8. *Stiffening competition induces a number of mergers and acquisitions among former competitors, driving industry consolidation to a smaller number of larger players.* Inefficient firms and firms with weak competitive strategies can achieve respectable results in a fast-growing industry with booming sales. But the intensifying competition that accompanies industry maturity exposes competitive weakness and throws second- and third-tier competitors into a survival-of-the-fittest contest.

Strategies That Fit Conditions in Slow-Growth, Mature Markets   As the new competitive character of industry maturity begins to hit full force, any of several strategic moves can strengthen a firm's competitive position: pruning the product line, improving value chain efficiency, trimming costs, increasing sales to present customers, acquiring rival firms, expanding internationally, and strengthening capabilities.[26]

Pruning Marginal Products and Models   A wide selection of models, features, and product options sometimes has competitive value during the growth stage, when buyers' needs are still evolving. But such variety can become too costly as price competition stiffens and profit margins are squeezed. Maintaining many product versions works against achieving design, parts inventory, and production economies at the manufacturing levels and can increase inventory stocking costs for distributors and retailers. In addition, the prices of slow-selling versions may not cover their true costs. Pruning marginal products from the line opens the door for cost savings and permits more concentration on items whose margins are highest and/or where a firm has a competitive advantage. General Motors has been cutting slow-selling models and brands from its lineup of offerings—it has eliminated the entire Oldsmobile division. Similarly, Ford is said to be considering the elimination of the Mercury brand from its lineup of vehicle offerings. Textbook publishers are discontinuing publication of those books that sell only a few thousand copies annually (where profits are marginal at best) and are instead focusing their resources on texts that are more widely adopted and generate sales of at least 5,000 copies per edition.

Improving Value Chain Efficiency   Efforts to reinvent the industry value chain can have a fourfold payoff: lower costs, better product or service quality, greater capability to turn out multiple or customized product versions, and shorter design-to-market cycles. Manufacturers can mechanize high-cost activities, redesign production lines to improve labor efficiency, build flexibility into the assembly process so that customized product versions can be easily produced, and increase use of advanced technology (robotics, computerized controls, and automated assembly). Suppliers of parts and components, manufacturers, and distributors can collaboratively deploy online systems and product coding techniques to streamline activities and achieve cost savings all along the value chain—from supplier-related activities all the way through distribution, retailing, and customer service.

Trimming Costs   Stiffening price competition gives firms extra incentive to drive down unit costs. Company cost-reduction initiatives can cover a broad front. Some of the most frequently pursued options are pushing suppliers for better prices, implementing tighter supply chain management practices, cutting low-value activities out of the value chain, developing more economical product designs, reengineering internal processes using e-commerce technology, and shifting to more economical distribution arrangements.

Increasing Sales to Present Customers   In a mature market, growing by taking customers away from rivals may not be as appealing as expanding sales to existing customers. Strategies to increase purchases by existing customers can involve adding more sales promotions, providing complementary items and ancillary services, and finding more ways for customers to use the product. Wal-Mart, for example, has boosted average sales per customer by adding dry-cleaning services, optical centers, in-store restaurants, gasoline sales, and tire and battery service centers.

Acquiring Rival Firms at Bargain Prices   Sometimes a firm can acquire the facilities and assets of struggling rivals quite cheaply. Bargain-priced acquisitions can help create a low-cost position if they also present opportunities for greater operating efficiency. In addition, an acquired firm's customer base can provide expanded market coverage and opportunities for greater scale economies. The most desirable acquisitions are those that will significantly enhance the acquiring firm's competitive strength.

Expanding Internationally   As its domestic market matures, a firm may seek to enter foreign markets where attractive growth potential still exists and competitive pressures are not so strong. Many multinational companies are expanding into such emerging markets as China, India, Brazil, Argentina, and the Philippines, where the long-term growth prospects are quite attractive. Strategies to expand internationally also make sense when a domestic firm's skills, reputation, and product are readily transferable to foreign markets. For example, even though the U.S. market for beverages is mature, Coca-Cola has remained a growth company by upping its efforts to penetrate emerging markets where sales of bottled water, soft drinks, fruit juices, and energy drinks are expanding rapidly.

Building New or More Flexible Capabilities   The stiffening pressures of competition in a maturing or already mature market can often be combated by strengthening the company's resource base and competitive capabilities. This can mean adding new competencies or capabilities, deepening existing competencies to make them harder to imitate, or striving to make core competencies more adaptable to changing customer requirements and expectations. Microsoft has responded to challenges by such competitors as Google and Linux by expanding its competencies in search engine software and revamping its entire approach to programming next-generation operating systems.

ILLUSTRATION CAPSULE 6.2
PepsiCo's Strategy for Growing Rapidly in Mature, Slow-Growth Markets

PepsiCo's net revenues of approximately $40 billion in 2007 made it the world's largest snack and beverage company. The company's business lineup in 2008 included Frito-Lay salty snacks, Quaker Chewy granola bars, Pepsi soft drink products, Tropicana orange juice, Lipton Brisk tea, Gatorade, Propel, SoBe, Aquafina, Flat Earth, Naked Juice, and many other regularly consumed products. PepsiCo's ability to achieve growth in industries long characterized by low-single-digit growth rates is a result of the impressive strategies crafted by its CEO, Indra Nooyi, and the company's other chief managers.

In 2008, the company's primary strategic priorities were keyed to developing "good-for-you" snacks and beverages, strengthening its position in international markets, and acquiring small, rapidly growing snack food and beverage companies. PepsiCo was able to increase sales in the United States through the introduction of new beverages such as Amp Energy, SoBe Adrenaline Rush, flavored varieties of Aquafina, and new flavors of Gatorade and Propel Fitness Water. The company had also hired the former director of the Mayo Clinic endocrinology department to develop new snacks that would appeal to health-conscious consumers. New snacks like SunChips and acquisitions of brands such as Flat Earth fruit and vegetable crisps and Stacy's Simply Naked pita chips helped healthy snacks and beverages account for 30 percent of PepsiCo's 2007 revenues. The company hoped to make its good-for-you products account for 50 percent of its revenues, with more product innovations and additional acquisitions of grains, nuts, and fruit snack brands.

International markets were also critical to PepsiCo's growth in revenues and earnings. International sales increased by 22 percent in 2007, which was triple the rate of domestic sales growth. The company's fastest growth occurred in markets such as Russia, the Middle East, and Turkey, where both its traditional and its good-for-you snacks and beverages achieved double-digit sales gains. Healthy products such as juices, water, tea, and energy drinks made up more than half of PepsiCo's beverage sales in Russia in 2007. The company planned to increase the percentage of healthy snacks in all country markets where it competed, since most consumers around the world wished to reduce their consumption of saturated fats, cholesterol, trans fats, and simple carbohydrates.

An equally important component of PepsiCo's strategy for competing in mature markets involved divesting marginal products from its lineup of businesses and brands. Shortly after Nooyi joined PepsiCo as head of mergers and acquisitions in 1994, it became clear to PepsiCo's top managers that the company's restaurant brands—Pizza Hut, Taco Bell, and KFC—had to go. The fast-food industry was saturated with too many locations, real estate was becoming more expensive, and a price war was under way, with all of the major chains boasting 99-cent value menus. The spin-off of PepsiCo's restaurant businesses reduced the company's revenues by a third but got the company out of a low-margin, capital-intensive business that was a drag on its overall return on investment.

Source: Betsy Morris, "What Makes Pepsi Great?" *Fortune,* March 3, 2008, pp. 55–66; and PepsiCo's 2007 annual report.

Chevron has developed a best-practices discovery team and a best-practices resource map to enhance the speed and effectiveness with which it is able to transfer efficiency improvements from one oil refinery to another.

Illustration Capsule 6.2 describes how PepsiCo has achieved double-digit growth in revenues and earnings while competing in the mature soft drink and snack food industries.

Mistakes Companies Make in Mature Markets   Perhaps the biggest strategic mistake a company can make as an industry matures is steering a middle course between low cost, differentiation, and focusing—blending efforts to achieve low cost with efforts to incorporate differentiating features and efforts to focus on a limited target market. Such strategic compromises typically leave the firm *stuck in the middle* with a fuzzy strategy, too little commitment to winning a competitive advantage, an average image with buyers, and little chance of springing into the ranks of the industry leaders.

Other strategic pitfalls include being slow to mount a defense against stiffening competitive pressures, concentrating more on protecting short-term profitability than on building or maintaining long-term competitive position, waiting too long to respond to price cutting by rivals, overexpanding in the face of slowing growth, overspending on advertising and sales promotion efforts in a losing effort to combat the growth slowdown, failing to invest in product or process innovations that could help the company maintain growth despite slowing industry growth, and failing to pursue cost reductions soon enough or aggressively enough.[27]

Competing in Stagnant or Declining Markets

Many firms operate in industries where demand is growing more slowly than the economywide average or is even declining. The demand for an industry's product can decline for any of several reasons: (1) advancing technology gives rise to better-performing substitute products (slim LCD monitors displace bulky CRT monitors; MP3 players replace portable CD players; wrinkle-free fabrics replace the need for laundry/dry-cleaning services) or lower costs (cheaper synthetics replace expensive leather); (2) the customer group shrinks (mountain biking); (3) lifestyles and buyer tastes change (smoking cigarettes and wearing dress hats go out of vogue); (4) the prices of complementary products rise (higher gasoline prices drive down purchases of gas-guzzling vehicles).[28] The most attractive declining industries are those in which sales are eroding only slowly, there are pockets of stable or even growing demand, and some market niches present good profit opportunities. But in some stagnant or declining industries, decaying buyer demand precipitates a desperate competitive battle among industry members for the available business, replete with price discounting, costly sales promotions, growing amounts of idle plant capacity, and fast-eroding profit margins. It matters greatly whether buyer demand falls gradually or sharply, and whether competition proves to be fierce or moderate.

Businesses competing in stagnant or declining industries have to make a fundamental strategic choice—whether to remain committed to the industry for the long term despite the industry's dim prospects or whether to pursue an end-game strategy to withdraw gradually or quickly from the market. Deciding to stick with the industry despite eroding market demand can have considerable merit. Stagnant demand by itself is not enough to make an industry unattractive. Market demand may be decaying slowly. Some segments of the market may still present good profit opportunities. Cash flows from operations may still remain strongly positive. Strong competitors may well be able to grow and boost profits by taking market share from weaker competitors.[29] Furthermore, the acquisition or exit of weaker firms creates opportunities for the remaining companies to capture greater market share. Hence, striving to become the market leader and be one of the few remaining companies in a declining industry can lead to above-average profitability even though overall market demand is stagnant or eroding. On the other hand, if the market environment of a declining industry is characterized by bitter warfare for customers and lots of overcapacity, such that companies are plagued with heavy operating losses, then an early exit makes much more strategic sense.

> It is erroneous to assume that companies in a declining industry are doomed to suffer falling revenues and profits.

If a company decides to stick with a declining industry—because top management is encouraged by the remaining opportunities and/or sees merit in striving for market share leadership (or even just being one of the few remaining companies in the industry), then its three best strategic alternatives are usually the following:[30]

1. *Pursue a focused strategy aimed at the fastest-growing or slowest-decaying market segments within the industry.* Stagnant or declining markets, like other markets, are composed of numerous segments or niches. Frequently, one or more of these segments is growing rapidly (or at least decaying much more slowly), despite stagnation in the industry as a whole. An astute competitor who zeroes in on fast-growing segments and does a first-rate job of meeting the needs of buyers comprising these segments can often escape stagnating sales and profits and even gain decided competitive advantage. For instance, both Abercrombie & Fitch and American Eagle Outfitters have achieved success by focusing on the growing teen segment of the otherwise stagnant market for ready-to-wear apparel; revenue growth and profit margins are substantially higher for trendy apparel than is the case with other segments of the ready-to-wear apparel industry. Companies that focus on the one or two most attractive market segments in a declining business may well decide to ignore the other segments altogether—withdrawing from them entirely or at least gradually or rapidly disinvesting in them. But the key is to *move aggressively* to establish a strong position in the most attractive parts of the stagnant or declining industry.

2. *Stress differentiation based on quality improvement and product innovation.* Either enhanced quality or innovation can rejuvenate demand by creating important new growth segments or inducing buyers to trade up. Successful product innovation opens up an avenue for competing that bypasses meeting or beating rivals' prices. Differentiation based on successful innovation has the additional advantage of being difficult and expensive for rival firms to imitate. The New Covent Garden Food Company has met with success by introducing packaged fresh soups for sale in major supermarkets, where the typical soup offerings are canned or dry mixes. Procter & Gamble rejuvenated sales of its toothbrushes with its new line of Crest battery-powered spin toothbrushes, and it revitalized interest in tooth care products with a series of product innovations related to teeth whitening. Bread makers are countering the decline in sales of their bleached-flour white breads by introducing all kinds of whole-grain breads (which have far more nutritional value).

3. *Strive to drive costs down and become the industry's low-cost leader.* Companies in stagnant industries can improve profit margins and return on investment by pursuing innovative cost reduction year after year. Potential cost-saving actions include (*a*) cutting marginally beneficial activities out of the value chain; (*b*) outsourcing functions and activities that can be performed more cheaply by outsiders; (*c*) redesigning internal business processes to exploit cost-reducing e-commerce technologies; (*d*) consolidating underutilized production facilities; (*e*) adding more distribution channels to ensure the unit volume needed for low-cost production; (*f*) closing low-volume, high-cost retail outlets; and (*g*) pruning marginal products from the firm's offerings. Japan-based Asahi Glass (a low-cost producer of flat glass), PotashCorp and IMC Global (two low-cost leaders in potash production), Safety Components International (a low-cost producer of air bags for motor vehicles), Alcan Aluminum, and Nucor Steel have all been successful in driving costs down in competitively tough and largely stagnant industry environments.

These three strategic themes are not mutually exclusive.[31] Introducing innovative versions of a product can create a fast-growing market segment. Similarly, relentless pursuit of greater operating efficiencies permits price reductions that create price-conscious growth segments. Note that all three themes are spin-offs of the five generic competitive strategies, adjusted to fit the circumstances of a tough industry environment.

End-Game Strategies for Declining Industries   An *end-game strategy* can take either of two paths: (1) a *slow-exit strategy* that involves a gradual phasing down of operations coupled with an objective of getting the most cash flow from the business even if it means sacrificing market position or profitability, and (2) a *fast-exit* or *sell-out-quickly strategy* to disengage from the industry during the early stages of the decline and recover as much of the company's investment as possible for deployment elsewhere.[32]

A Slow-Exit Strategy   With a slow-exit strategy, *the key objective is to generate the greatest possible harvest of cash from the business for as long as possible.* Management either eliminates or severely curtails new investment in the business. Capital expenditures for new equipment are put on hold or given low financial priority (unless replacement needs are unusually urgent); instead, efforts are made to stretch the life of existing equipment and make do with present facilities as long as possible. Old plants with high costs may be retired from service. The operating budget is chopped to a rock-bottom level. Promotional expenses may be cut gradually, quality reduced in not-so-visible ways, nonessential customer services curtailed, and maintenance of facilities held to a bare minimum. The resulting increases in cash flow (and perhaps even bottom-line profitability and return on investment) compensate for whatever declines in sales might be experienced. Withering buyer demand is tolerable if sizable amounts of cash can be reaped in the interim. If and when cash flows dwindle to meager levels as sales volumes decay, the business can be sold or, if no buyer can be found, closed.

A Fast-Exit Strategy   The challenge of a sell-out-quickly strategy is to find a buyer willing to pay an agreeable price for the company's business assets. Buyers may be scarce since there's a tendency for investors to shy away from purchasing a stagnant or dying business. And even if willing buyers appear, they will be in a strong bargaining position once it's clear that the industry's prospects are permanently waning. How much prospective buyers will pay is usually a function of how rapidly they expect the industry to decline, whether they see opportunities to rejuvenate demand (at least temporarily), whether they believe that costs can be cut enough to still produce attractive profit margins or cash flows, whether there are pockets of stable demand where buyers are not especially price-sensitive, and whether they believe that fading market demand will weaken competition (which could enhance profitability) or trigger strong competition for the remaining business (which could put pressure on profit margins). Thus, the expectations of prospective buyers will tend to drive the price they are willing to pay for the business assets of a company wanting to sell out quickly.

Competing in Turbulent, Fast-Changing Markets

Many companies operate in industries characterized by rapid technological change, short product life cycles, the entry of important new rivals, lots of competitive maneuvering by rivals, and fast-evolving customer requirements and expectations—all occurring in a manner that creates swirling market conditions. Since news of this or that important competitive development arrives daily, it is an imposing task just to monitor and assess developing events. High-velocity change is plainly the prevailing condition in computer/server hardware and software, video games, networking, wireless telecommunications, medical equipment, biotechnology, prescription drugs, and online retailing.

Ways to Cope with Rapid Change   The central strategy-making challenge in a turbulent market environment is managing change.[33] As illustrated in Figure 6.1, a company can assume any of three strategic postures in dealing with high-velocity change:[34]

- *It can react to change.* The company can respond to a rival's new product with a better product. It can counter an unexpected shift in buyer tastes and buyer demand by redesigning or repackaging its product, or shifting its advertising emphasis to different product attributes. Reacting is a defensive strategy and is therefore unlikely to create fresh opportunity, but it is nonetheless a necessary component in a company's arsenal of options.

- *It can anticipate change.* The company can make plans for dealing with the expected changes and follow its plans as changes occur (fine-tuning them as may be needed). Anticipation entails looking ahead to analyze what is likely to occur and then preparing and positioning for that future. It entails studying buyer behavior, buyer needs, and buyer expectations to get insight into how the market will evolve, then lining up the necessary production and distribution capabilities ahead of time. Like reacting to change, anticipating change is still fundamentally defensive in that forces outside the enterprise are in the driver's seat. Anticipation, however, can open up new opportunities and thus is a better way to manage change than just pure reaction.

- *It can lead change.* Leading change entails initiating the market and competitive forces that others must respond to—it is an offensive strategy aimed at putting a company in the driver's seat. Leading change means being first to market with an important new product or service. It means being the technological leader, rushing next-generation products to market ahead of rivals, and having products whose features and attributes shape customer preferences and expectations. It means proactively seeking to shape the rules of the game.

> A sound way to deal with turbulent market conditions is to try to lead change with proactive strategic moves while at the same time trying to anticipate and prepare for upcoming changes and being quick to react to unexpected developments.

As a practical matter, a company's approach to managing change should, ideally, incorporate all three postures (though not in the same proportion). The best-performing companies in high-velocity markets consistently seek to lead change with proactive strategies that often entail the flexibility to pursue any of several strategic options, depending on how the market actually evolves. Even so, an environment of relentless change makes it incumbent on any company to anticipate and prepare for the future and to react quickly to unpredictable or uncontrollable new developments.

Strategy Options for Fast-Changing Markets   Competitive success in fast-changing markets tends to hinge on a company's ability to improvise, experiment, adapt, reinvent, and regenerate as market and competitive conditions shift rapidly and sometimes unpredictably.[35] The company has to constantly reshape

Figure 6.1   Meeting the Challenge of High-Velocity Change

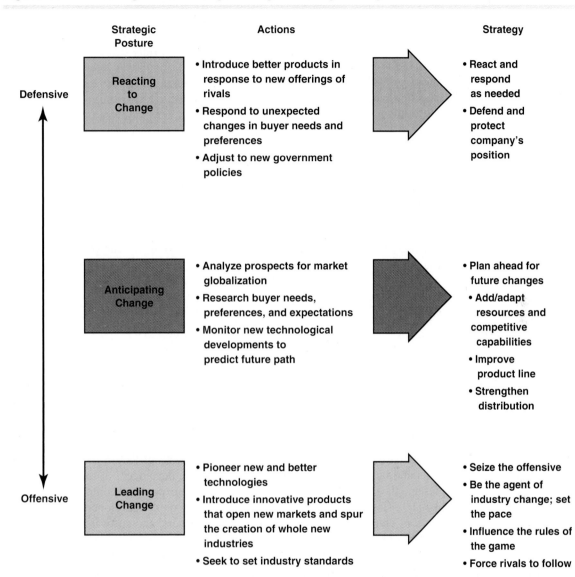

Source: Adapted from Shona L. Brown and Kathleen M. Eisenhardt, *Competing on the Edge. Strategy as Structured Chaos* (Boston, MA: Harvard Business School Press, 1998) p. 5.

its strategy and its basis for competitive advantage. While the process of altering offensive and defensive moves every few months or weeks to keep the overall strategy closely matched to changing conditions is inefficient, the alternative—a fast-obsolescing strategy—is worse. The following five strategic moves seem to offer the best payoffs:

1. *Invest aggressively in R&D to stay on the leading edge of technological know-how.* Translating technological advances into innovative new products

(and remaining close on the heels of whatever advances and features are pioneered by rivals) is a necessity in industries where technology is the primary driver of change. But it is often desirable to focus the R&D effort on a few critical areas, not only to avoid stretching the company's resources too thin but also to deepen the firm's expertise, master the technology, fully capture learning curve effects, and become the dominant leader in a particular technology or product category.[36] When a fast-evolving market environment entails many technological areas and product categories, competitors have little choice but to employ some type of focus strategy and concentrate on being the leader in a particular product/technology category.

2. *Keep the company's products and services fresh and exciting enough to stand out in the midst of all the change that is taking place.* One of the risks of rapid change is that products and even companies can get lost in the shuffle. The marketing challenge here is to keep the firm's products and services in the limelight and, further, to keep them innovative and well matched to the changes that are occurring in the marketplace.

3. *Develop quick-response capability.* Because no company can predict all of the changes that will occur, it is crucial to have the organizational capability to be able to react quickly, improvising if necessary. This means shifting resources internally, adapting existing competencies and capabilities, creating new competencies and capabilities, and not falling far behind rivals. Companies that are habitual late-movers are destined to be industry also-rans.

4. *Rely on strategic partnerships with outside suppliers and with companies making tie-in products.* In many high-velocity industries, technology is branching off to create so many new technological paths and product categories that no company has the resources and competencies to pursue them all. Specialization (to promote the necessary technical depth) and focus (to preserve organizational agility and leverage the firm's expertise) are desirable strategies. Companies build their competitive position not just by strengthening their own internal resource base but also by partnering with those suppliers making state-of-the-art parts and components and by collaborating closely with both the developers of related technologies and the makers of tie-in products. For example, personal computer companies like Dell, Hewlett-Packard, and Acer rely heavily on the developers and manufacturers of chips, monitors, hard drives, DVD players, and software for innovative advances in PCs. None of the PC makers have done much in the way of integrating backward into parts and components because they have learned that the most effective way to provide PC users with a state-of-the-art product is to outsource the latest, most advanced components from technologically sophisticated suppliers who make it their business to stay on the cutting edge of their specialization and who can achieve economies of scale by mass-producing components for many PC assemblers. An outsourcing strategy also allows a company the flexibility to replace suppliers that fall behind on technology or product features or that cease to be competitive on price. The managerial challenge here is to strike a good balance between building a rich internal resource base that, on the one hand, keeps the firm from being at the mercy of its suppliers and allies and, on the other hand, maintains organizational agility by relying on the resources and expertise of capable (and perhaps best-in-world) outsiders.

5. *Initiate fresh actions every few months, not just when a competitive response is needed.* In some sense, change is partly triggered by the passage of time rather than

visible sellers. Others remain atomistic because it is inherent in the nature of their businesses. And still others remain stuck in a fragmented state because existing firms lack the resources or ingenuity to employ a strategy powerful enough to drive industry consolidation.

Strategy Options for Competing in a Fragmented Market   In fragmented industries, firms generally have the strategic freedom to pursue broad or narrow market targets and low-cost or differentiation-based competitive advantages. Many different strategic approaches can exist side by side (unless the industry's product is highly standardized or a commodity—like concrete blocks, sand and gravel, or paperboard boxes). Fragmented industry environments are usually ideal for focusing on a well-defined market niche—a particular geographic area or buyer group or product type. In an industry that is fragmented due to highly diverse buyer tastes or requirements, focusing usually offers more competitive advantage potential than trying to come up with a product offering that has broad market appeal.

Some of the most suitable strategy options for competing in a fragmented industry include:

- *Constructing and operating "formula" facilities*—This strategic approach is frequently employed in restaurant and retailing businesses operating at multiple locations. It involves constructing standardized outlets in favorable locations at minimum cost and then operating them cost-effectively. This is a favorite approach for locally owned fast-food enterprises and convenience stores that have multiple locations serving a geographically limited market area. Major fast-food companies like Yum! Brands—the parent of Pizza Hut, Taco Bell, KFC, Long John Silver's, and A&W restaurants—and big convenience store retailers like 7-Eleven have, of course, perfected the formula facilities strategy.

- *Becoming a low-cost operator*—When price competition is intense and profit margins are under constant pressure, companies can stress no-frills operations featuring low overhead, high-productivity/low-cost labor, lean capital budgets, and dedicated pursuit of total operating efficiency. Successful low-cost producers in a fragmented industry can play the price-discounting game and still earn profits above the industry average. Many e-tailers compete on the basis of bargain prices; so do budget motel chains like Econo Lodge, Super 8, and Days Inn.

- *Specializing by product type*—When a fragmented industry's products include a range of styles or services, a strategy to focus on one product or service category can be effective. Some firms in the furniture industry specialize in only one furniture type such as brass beds, rattan and wicker, lawn and garden, or early American. In auto repair, companies specialize in transmission repair, body work, or speedy oil changes.

- *Specializing by customer type*—A firm can stake out a market niche in a fragmented industry by catering to those customers who are interested in low prices, unique product attributes, customized features, carefree service, or other extras. A number of restaurants cater to take-out customers; others specialize in fine dining, and still others cater to the sports bar crowd. Bed-and-breakfast inns cater to a particular type of traveler/vacationer (and also focus on a very limited geographic area).

- *Focusing on a limited geographic area*—Even though a firm in a fragmented industry can't win a big share of total industrywide sales, it can still try to dominate a local or regional geographic area. Concentrating company efforts on a limited

ILLUSTRATION CAPSULE 6.3
Just Play Golf's Strategy in the Fragmented Market for Golf Accessories

The golf accessory industry is highly fragmented—there are hundreds of companies that manufacture and market items such as ball markers, divot tools, cleats and spikes, towels, tees, training aids, instructional books and videos, pull carts, range finders, travel bags, and head covers. The window of opportunity for employing a focus strategy is big. The Club Caddy, a simple clip that attaches to a golf club and allows a golfer to place a club on the ground in an upright position, came onto the market in 2007. The Club Caddy is manufactured and marketed by Just Play Golf Inc. and was developed by company founder David Jones after playing golf at a South Carolina resort in 1995. On a day when the ground was exceptionally wet, the pro shop asked Jones to keep his cart on the paved path and not drive on the turf. Jones never seemed to hit a shot near the cart path and found himself frequently walking to his ball, carrying his putter and the one or two clubs he might need to hit the shot to the green. As he kept picking up clubs from the ground and wiping the dampness from the grips, he felt there should be a market for some type of product that would allow a golfer to place clubs down without the grips making contact with the wet ground. Six months later, Jones awoke at 3:00 a.m. with an idea for the Club Caddy clear in his mind. He ran to the dining room table with pencil and paper and began drawing the concept for his new golf accessory. Over the next eleven years, Jones spent about $25,000 to patent the Club Caddy and bring it to market, with its modest sales made mostly to local golfing buddies.

Jones's access to broad distribution for the Club Caddy didn't come until 2007, after he appeared on a reality television program produced by The Golf Channel called *Fore Inventors Only.* By this time, David Jones had invested about all he could in the Club Caddy, but he took the additional risk of asking for a $300 advance on his salary to travel to Orland, Florida, to audition for the program. Jones was among more than 1,000 inventors who were each given three minutes to make their pitch. The Club Caddy was one of 103 inventions selected to compete on the reality television series. The prize included shelf space at all 74 Golfsmith retail stores throughout North America for one year, a fully developed infomercial produced by The Golf Channel, and $50,000 worth of airtime for commercials on The Golf Channel.

The inventors' products were evaluated by a panel of judges made up of former PGA Tour player Fulton Allen, *Golf for Women* magazine editor Stina Sternberg, and golf instructor Billy Harmon. The three judges narrowed the list to five inventions, which were voted on by viewers as the best new golf product. Jones's Club Caddy won the competition with 30 percent of the vote. By 2008, Jones's new company, Just Play Golf Inc., had expanded retail distribution of the Club Caddy to several large retail stores in addition to Golfsmith, had signed a nonexclusive license with a large distributor to make the product available to a broader range of U.S. retailers, and had been contacted by retailers outside the United States for distribution of the Club Caddy in international markets.

Source: Information provided by Just Play Golf Inc. personnel; Chris Gay, "Inventor Hopes to Swing Vote," *Augusta Chronicle,* July 7, 2007, p. C1; Jeremy Friedman, "Champion Crowned on Fore Inventors," www.thegolfchannel.com, September 5, 2007; and Stan Awtrey, "Invention Stands Up to Competition; Winning Device Lets Clubs Be Placed Upright," *Atlanta Journal-Constitution,* September 6, 2007, p. 3D.

territory can produce greater operating efficiency, speed delivery and customer services, promote strong brand awareness, and permit saturation advertising, while avoiding the diseconomies of stretching operations out over a much wider area. Several locally owned banks, drugstores, and sporting goods retailers successfully operate multiple locations within a limited geographic area. Numerous local restaurant operators have pursued operating economies by opening anywhere from 4 to 10 restaurants (each with each its own distinctive theme and menu) scattered across a single metropolitan area like Chicago or Denver or Houston.

Illustration Capsule 6.3 describes how a start-up company in the fragmented golf accessory industry has employed a product-niche type of focus strategy.

TIMING STRATEGIC MOVES—TO BE AN EARLY MOVER OR A LATE MOVER?

When to make a strategic move is often as crucial as *what* move to make. Certain market environments reward first-movers with competitive advantage, while in other markets it is more advantageous to be a late-mover.[39] Consequently, it is important for company strategists to be aware of what conditions favor being a first-mover, a fast-follower, or a late-mover.

CORE CONCEPT
Because of first-mover advantages and disadvantages, competitive advantage can spring from *when* a move is made as well as from *what* move is made.

When Being a First-Mover Leads to Competitive Advantage

Being first to initiate a strategic move can have a high payoff when (1) pioneering helps build a firm's image and reputation with buyers; (2) early commitments to new technologies, new-style components, new or emerging distribution channels, and so on can produce an absolute cost advantage over rivals; (3) first-time customers remain strongly loyal to pioneering firms in making repeat purchases; and (4) moving first constitutes a preemptive strike, making imitation extra hard or unlikely. The bigger the first-mover advantages, the more attractive making the first move becomes.[40] In e-commerce, companies that were first with a new technology, network solution, or business model—like Amazon.com, Yahoo, eBay, and Priceline.com—enjoyed lasting first-mover advantages in gaining the visibility and reputation needed to remain market leaders. However, other first-movers such as Xerox in fax machines, eToys (an online toy retailer), Webvan and Peapod (in online groceries), and scores of other dot-com companies never converted their first-mover status into any sort of competitive advantage (or even a business that was able to survive for that matter). Sometimes markets are slow to accept the innovative product offering of a first-mover; sometimes, a fast-follower with greater resources and marketing muscle can easily overtake the first-mover (as Microsoft was able to do when it introduced Internet Explorer against Netscape, the pioneer of Internet browsers with a lion-sized market share); and sometimes furious technological change or product innovation makes a first-mover vulnerable to quickly appearing next-generation technology or products. Hence, just being a first-mover by itself is seldom enough to win a sustainable competitive advantage.[41]

To sustain any advantage that may initially accrue to a pioneer, a first-mover needs to be a fast learner and continue to move aggressively to capitalize on any initial pioneering advantage. It helps immensely if the first-mover has deep financial pockets, important competencies and competitive capabilities, and astute managers. If a first-mover's skills, know-how, and actions are easily copied or even surpassed, then fast-followers and even late-movers can catch or overtake the first-mover in a relatively short period. What makes being a first-mover strategically important is not being the first company to do something but rather being the first competitor to put together the precise combination of features, customer value, and sound revenue/cost/profit economics that gives it an edge over rivals in the battle for market leadership.[42] If the marketplace quickly takes to a first-mover's innovative product offering, a first-mover must have large-scale production, marketing, and distribution capabilities if it is to stave off fast-followers who possess these capabilities. If technology is advancing at a

ILLUSTRATION CAPSULE 6.4
Amazon.com's First-Mover Advantage in Online Retailing

Amazon.com's path to becoming the world's largest online retailer began in 1994 when Jeff Bezos, a Manhattan hedge fund analyst at the time, noticed that the number of Internet users was increasing by 2,300 percent annually. Bezos saw the tremendous growth as an opportunity to sell products that would be demanded by a large number of Internet users and could be easily shipped. Bezos launched the online bookseller Amazon.com in 1995. The start-up's revenues soared to $148 million in 1997, $610 million in 1998, and $1.6 billion in 1999. The business plan Bezos hatched while on a cross-country trip with his wife in 1994 made him *Time*'s Person of the Year in 1999.

Amazon.com's early entry into online retailing had delivered a first-mover advantage, but between 2000 and 2008, Bezos undertook a series of additional strategic initiatives to solidify the company's number one ranking in the industry. Bezos undertook a massive building program in the late 1990s that added five new warehouses and fulfillment centers totaling $300 million. The additional warehouse space was added years before it was needed, but Bezos wanted to ensure that, as demand continued to grow,

the company could continue to offer its customers the best selection, the lowest prices, and the cheapest and most convenient delivery. The company also expanded its product line to include sporting goods, tools, toys, grocery items, electronics, and digital music downloads. Amazon.com's 2007 revenues of $14.8 billion accounted for 6 percent of the $136 billion U.S. online retail market and made it number 177 on *Fortune*'s list of America's 500 largest corporations. Also, Jeff Bezos's shares in Amazon.com made him the 110th wealthiest person in the world, with an estimated net worth of $8.2 billion.

Not all of Bezos's efforts to maintain a first-mover advantage in online retailing were a success. Bezos commented in a 2008 *Fortune* article profiling the company, "We were investors in every bankrupt, 1999-vintage e-commerce startup. Pets.com, living.com, kozmo.com. We invested in a lot of high-profile flameouts." He went on to specify that although the ventures were a "waste of money," they didn't take Amazon away from its own mission. Bezos also suggested that gaining advantage as a first-mover is "taking a million tiny steps—and learning quickly from your missteps."

Source: Josh Quittner, "How Jeff Bezos Rules the Retail Space," *Fortune,* May 5, 2008, pp. 126–34.

torrid pace, a first-mover cannot hope to sustain its lead without having strong capabilities in R&D, design, and new product development, along with the financial strength to fund these activities.

Illustration Capsule 6.4 describes how Amazon.com achieved a first-mover advantage in online retailing.

Blue Ocean Strategy: A Powerful First-Mover Approach

A *blue ocean strategy* seeks to gain a dramatic and durable competitive advantage by *abandoning efforts to beat out competitors in existing markets and, instead, inventing a new industry or distinctive market segment that renders existing competitors largely irrelevant and allows a company to create and capture altogether new demand.*[43] This strategy views the business universe as consisting of two distinct types of market space. One is where industry boundaries are defined and accepted, the competitive rules of the game are well understood by all industry members, and companies try to outperform rivals by capturing a bigger share of existing demand; in such markets, lively competition constrains a company's prospects for rapid growth and superior profitability since rivals move quickly to either imitate or counter the successes of competitors. The second type of market space is where the industry does not really exist yet, is untainted by competition, and offers wide open opportunity for profitable and rapid growth if a company can come up with a product offering and strategy that allows it to create new demand rather than fight over existing demand. A terrific example of blue ocean market space is the online auction industry that eBay created and now dominates.

Another company that has employed a blue ocean strategy is Cirque du Soleil, which increased its revenues by 22 times during the 1993–2003 period in the circus business, an industry that had been in long-term decline for 20 years. How did Cirque du Soleil pull this off against legendary industry leader Ringling Bros. and Barnum & Bailey? By reinventing the circus: creating a distinctively different market space for its performances (Las Vegas night clubs and theater-type settings), and pulling in a whole new group of customers—adults and corporate clients—who were noncustomers of traditional circuses and were willing to pay several times more than the price of a conventional circus ticket to have an "entertainment experience" featuring sophisticated clowns and star-quality acrobatic acts in a comfortable tentlike atmosphere. Cirque du Soleil studiously avoided the use of animals not only because of costs but also because of concerns over the treatment of circus animals; Cirque do Soleil's market research led management to conclude that the lasting allure of the traditional circus came down to just three factors: the clowns, classic acrobatic acts, and a tentlike stage. As of 2007, Cirque du Soleil was presenting 15 different shows each with its own theme and story line, was performing before audiences of about 10 million people annually, and had performed 250 engagements in 100 cities since its formation in 1984.

Other examples of companies that have achieved competitive advantages by creating blue ocean market spaces include Starbucks in the coffee shop industry, The Home Depot in big-box retailing of hardware and building supplies, Dollar General in extreme discount retailing, and FedEx in overnight package delivery. Companies that create blue ocean market spaces can usually sustain their initially won competitive advantage without encountering major competitive challenge for 10 to 15 years because of high barriers to imitation and the strong brand-name awareness that a blue ocean strategy can produce.

When Being a Late-Mover Can Be Advantageous

There are instances when there are actually *advantages* to being an adept follower rather than a first-mover. Late-mover advantages (or *first-mover disadvantages*) arise in four instances:

- When pioneering leadership is more costly than imitating followership and only negligible learning/experience curve benefits accrue to the leader—a condition that allows a follower to end up with lower costs than the first-mover.
- When the products of an innovator are somewhat primitive and do not live up to buyer expectations, thus allowing a clever follower to win disenchanted buyers away from the leader with better-performing products.
- When the demand side of the marketplace is skeptical about the benefits of a new technology or product being pioneered by a first-mover.
- When rapid market evolution (due to fast-paced changes in either technology or buyer needs and expectations) gives fast-followers and maybe even cautious late-movers the opening to leapfrog a first-mover's products with more attractive next-version products.

Deciding Whether to Be an Early Mover
or a Late Mover

In weighing the pros and cons of being a first-mover versus a fast-follower versus a late-mover, it matters whether the race to market leadership in a particular industry is a marathon or a sprint. In marathons, a slow-mover is not unduly penalized—first-mover advantages can be fleeting, and there's ample time for fast-followers and sometimes even late-movers to play catch-up.[44] Thus, the speed at which the pioneering innovation is likely to catch on matters considerably as companies struggle with whether to pursue a particular emerging market opportunity aggressively (as a first-mover or fast-follower) or cautiously (as a late-mover). For instance, it took 18 months for 10 million users to sign up for Hotmail, 5.5 years for worldwide mobile phone use to grow from 10 million to 100 million, and close to 10 years for the number of at-home broadband subscribers to grow to 100 million worldwide. The lesson here is that there is a market-penetration curve for every emerging opportunity; typically, the curve has an inflection point at which all the pieces of the business model fall into place, buyer demand explodes, and the market takes off. The inflection point can come early on a fast-rising curve (like use of e-mail) or farther up on a slow-rising curve (like use of broadband). Any company that seeks competitive advantage by being a first-mover thus needs to ask some hard questions:

- Does market takeoff depend on the development of complementary products or services that currently are not available?
- Is new infrastructure required before buyer demand can surge?
- Will buyers need to learn new skills or adopt new behaviors? Will buyers encounter high switching costs?
- Are there influential competitors in a position to delay or derail the efforts of a first-mover?

When the answer to any of these questions is yes, then a company must be careful not to pour too many resources into getting ahead of the market opportunity—the battle for market leadership is likely going to be more of a 10-year marathon than a short-lived contest.

Being first off the starting block turns out to be competitively important only when pioneering early introduction of a technology or product delivers clear and substantial benefits to early adopters and buyers, thus winning their immediate support, perhaps giving the pioneer a reputational head-start advantage, and forcing competitors to quickly follow the pioneer's lead. In the remaining instances where the race for industry leadership is more of a marathon, the companies that end up capturing and dominating new-to-the-world markets are almost never the pioneers that gave birth to them—there is time for a company to marshal the needed resources and to ponder its best time and method of entry.[45] Plus, being a late-mover into industries of the future has the advantages of being less risky and skirting the costs of pioneering.

But while a company is right to be cautious about quickly entering virgin territory where all kinds of risks abound, rarely does a company have much to gain from consistently being a late-mover whose main concern is avoiding the mistakes of first-movers. Companies that are habitual late-movers regardless of the circumstances, while often able to survive, can find themselves scrambling to keep pace with more progressive and innovative rivals. For a habitual late-mover to catch up, it must count on first-movers to be slow learners and complacent in letting their lead dwindle. It also has to hope that buyers will be slow to gravitate to the products of first-movers, again giving it time to catch up. And it has to have competencies and capabilities that are sufficiently strong to allow it to close the gap fairly quickly once it makes its move. Counting on all first-movers to stumble or otherwise be easily overtaken is usually a bad bet that puts a late-mover's competitive position at risk.

KEY POINTS

Many companies are using strategic alliances and collaborative partnerships to help them in the race to build a global market presence or be a leader in the industries of the future. Strategic alliances are an attractive, flexible, and often cost-effective means by which companies can gain access to missing technology, expertise, and business capabilities.

Mergers and acquisitions are another attractive strategic option for strengthening a firm's competitiveness. When the operations of two companies are combined via merger or acquisition, the new company's competitiveness can be enhanced in any of several ways—lower costs; stronger technological skills; more or better competitive capabilities; a more attractive lineup of products and services; wider geographic coverage; and/or greater financial resources with which to invest in R&D, add capacity, or expand into new areas.

Vertically integrating forward or backward makes strategic sense only if it strengthens a company's position via either cost reduction or creation of a differentiation-based advantage. Otherwise, the drawbacks of vertical integration (increased investment, greater business risk, increased vulnerability to technological changes, and less flexibility in making product changes) are likely to outweigh any advantages.

Outsourcing pieces of the value chain formerly performed in-house can enhance a company's competitiveness whenever an activity (1) can be performed better or more cheaply by outside specialists; (2) is not crucial to the firm's ability to achieve sustainable competitive advantage and won't hollow out its core competencies, capabilities, or technical know-how; (3) reduces the company's risk exposure to changing technology and/or changing buyer preferences; (4) streamlines company operations in ways that improve organizational flexibility, cut cycle time, speed decision making, and reduce coordination costs; and/or (5) allows a company to concentrate on its core business and do what it does best.

Crafting a strategy tightly matched to a company's external situation thus involves an understanding of competitive forces, driving forces, key success factors, and other unique industry conditions. For example, it is important for decision makers to consider the basic type of industry environment (emerging, rapid-growth, mature/slow-growth, stagnant/declining, high-velocity/turbulent, fragmented) and what strategic options and strategic postures are usually best suited to the specific type of environment.

The timing of strategic moves also has relevance in the quest for competitive advantage. Company managers are obligated to carefully consider the advantages or disadvantages that attach to being a first-mover versus a fast-follower versus a wait-and-see late-mover.

A blue ocean offensive strategy seeks to gain a dramatic and durable competitive advantage by abandoning efforts to beat out competitors in existing markets and, instead, inventing a new industry or distinctive market segment that renders existing competitors largely irrelevant and allows a company to create and capture altogether new demand.

ASSURANCE OF LEARNING EXERCISES

1. Use your favorite search engine to identify at least two companies in different industries that have outsourced certain activities to specialized vendors. Identify what value chain activities the companies have chosen to outsource and evaluate whether any of the outsourcing arrangements seem likely to threaten any of the companies' competitive capabilities.

2. Using your university library's subscription to Lexis-Nexis, EBSCO, or a similar database (or an Internet search engine), perform a search on *acquisition strategy.* Identify at least two companies in different industries that are using acquisitions to strengthen their market positions. How have these acquisitions enhanced the acquiring companies' resource strengths and competitive capabilities?

3. Go to www.bridgestone.co.jp/english/info and click on the Data Library link to review information about Bridgestone Corporation's tire and raw materials operations. To what extent is the company vertically integrated? What segments of the industry value chain has the company chosen to perform? What are the benefits and liabilities of Bridgestone's vertical integration strategy?

4. Listed below are ten industries. Classify each one as (*a*) emerging, (*b*) rapid-growth, (*c*) mature/slow-growth, (*d*) stagnant/declining, (*e*) high-velocity/turbulent, and (*f*) fragmented. Do research on the Internet, if needed, to locate information on industry conditions and reach a conclusion on what classification to assign each of the following:

    a. Network television
    b. Dry-cleaning industry
    c. Beef industry
    d. Camera film and film-developing industry
    e. Wine, beer, and liquor retailing
    f. Watch industry
    g. Mobile phone industry
    h. Recorded music industry (DVDs, CDs, MP3s)
    i. Computer software industry
    j. Petroleum industry

EXERCISES FOR SIMULATION PARTICIPANTS

1. Does your company have the option to merge with or acquire other companies? If so, which rival companies would you like to acquire or merge with?

2. Is your company vertically integrated? Explain.

3. Is your company able to engage in outsourcing? If so, what do you see as the pros and cons of outsourcing?

4. What options for being a first-mover does your company have? Do any of these first-mover options hold competitive advantage potential?

5. Is your company facing the prospects of slowing market growth? If so, which, if any, of the strategic options discussed above in the section entitled Strategies for Competing in Slow-Growth, Mature Markets seem most promising for your company?

Strategies for Competing in Foreign Markets

LEARNING OBJECTIVES

1. Develop an understanding of why companies that have achieved competitive advantage in their domestic market may opt to enter foreign markets.

2. Learn how and why differing market conditions in different countries influence a company's strategy for competing in foreign markets.

3. Gain familiarity with the major strategic options for entering and competing in foreign markets.

4. Understand the principal approaches used by multinational companies in building competitive advantage in foreign markets.

5. Gain an understanding of the unique characteristics of competing in emerging markets.

Any company that aspires to industry leadership in the 21st century must think in terms of global, not domestic, market leadership. The world economy is globalizing at an accelerating pace as countries previously closed to foreign companies open up their markets, as the Internet shrinks the importance of geographic distance, and as ambitious growth-minded companies race to build stronger competitive positions in the markets of more and more countries. Companies in industries that are already globally competitive or in the process of becoming so are under the gun to come up with a strategy for competing successfully in foreign markets. This chapter focuses on strategy options for expanding beyond domestic boundaries and competing in the markets of either a few or a great many countries. The spotlight will be on four strategic issues unique to competing multinationally:

1. Whether to customize the company's offerings in each different country market to more precisely match the tastes and preferences of local buyers or to offer a mostly standardized product worldwide.

2. Whether to employ essentially the same basic competitive strategy in all countries or modify the strategy country by country.

3. Where to locate the company's production facilities, distribution centers, and customer service operations so as to realize the greatest location advantages.

4. How to efficiently transfer the company's resource strengths and capabilities from one country to another in an effort to secure competitive advantage.

In the process of exploring these issues, we will introduce such concepts as multicountry competition; global competition; and cross-country differences in cultural, demographic, and market conditions. The chapter also includes sections on strategy options for entering and competing in foreign markets; the importance of locating operations in the most advantageous countries; and the special circumstances of competing in such emerging markets as China, India, Brazil, Russia, and Eastern Europe.

WHY COMPANIES EXPAND INTO FOREIGN MARKETS

A company may opt to expand outside its domestic market for any of four major reasons:

1. *To gain access to new customers*—Expanding into foreign markets offers potential for increased revenues, profits, and long-term growth and becomes an especially attractive option when a company's home markets are mature. Firms like Cisco Systems, Dell, Sony, Nokia, Avon, and Toyota, which are racing for global leadership in their respective industries, are moving rapidly and aggressively to extend their market reach into all corners of the world.

2. *To achieve lower costs and enhance the firm's competitiveness*—Many companies are driven to sell in more than one country because domestic sales volume is not large enough to fully capture manufacturing economies of scale or learning/experience curve effects and thereby substantially improve the firm's cost-competitiveness. The relatively small size of country markets in Europe explains why companies like Michelin, BMW, and Nestlé long ago began selling their products all across Europe and then moved into markets in North America and Latin America.

3. *To capitalize on its core competencies*—A company may be able to leverage its competencies and capabilities into a position of competitive advantage in foreign markets as well as just domestic markets. Nokia's competencies and capabilities in mobile phones have propelled it to global market leadership in the wireless telecommunications business. Wal-Mart is capitalizing on its considerable expertise in discount retailing to expand into China, Latin America, Japan, South Korea, and the United Kingdom; specifically, Wal-Mart executives believe the company has tremendous growth opportunities in China.

4. *To spread its business risk across a wider market base*—A company spreads business risk by operating in a number of different foreign countries rather than depending entirely on operations in its domestic market. Thus, if the economies of certain Asian countries turn down for a period of time, a company with operations across much of the world may be sustained by buoyant sales in Latin America or Europe.

In a few cases, companies in industries based on natural resources (e.g., oil and gas, minerals, rubber, and lumber) often find it necessary to operate in the international arena because attractive raw material supplies are located in foreign countries.

The Difference between Competing Internationally and Competing Globally

Typically, a company will start to compete internationally by entering just one or maybe a select few foreign markets. Competing on a truly global scale comes later, after the company has established operations on several continents and is racing against rivals for global market leadership. Thus, there is a meaningful distinction between the competitive scope of a company that operates in a few foreign countries (with perhaps modest ambitions to enter several more country markets) and a company that markets its products in 50 to 100 countries and is expanding its operations into additional country markets annually. The former is most accurately termed an *international competitor* while the latter qualifies as a *global competitor.* In the discussion that follows, we'll continue to make a distinction between strategies for competing internationally and strategies for competing globally.

FACTORS THAT SHAPE STRATEGY CHOICES IN FOREIGN MARKETS

There are four important factors that shape a company's strategic approach to competing in foreign markets: (1) the degree to which there are important cross-country differences in cultural, demographic, and market conditions; (2) whether opportunities exist to gain competitive advantage based on whether a company's activities are located in some countries rather than in others; (3) the risks of adverse shifts in currency exchange rates; and (4) the extent to which the policies of foreign governments lead to more favorable business environments in some countries than in other countries.

Cross-Country Differences in Cultural, Demographic, and Market Conditions

Regardless of a company's motivation for expanding outside its domestic markets, the strategies it uses to compete in foreign markets must be situation-driven. Cultural, demographic, and market conditions vary significantly among the countries of the world.[1] Cultures and lifestyles are the most obvious areas in which countries differ; market demographics and income levels are close behind. Consumers in Spain do not have the same tastes, preferences, and buying habits as consumers in Norway; buyers differ yet again in Greece, Chile, New Zealand, and Taiwan. Less than 20 percent of the populations of Brazil, India, and China have annual purchasing power equivalent to $25,000. Middle-class consumers represent a much smaller portion of the population in these and other emerging countries than in North America, Japan, and much of Western Europe—China's middle class numbers about 125 million out of a population of 1.3 billion.[2] Sometimes product designs suitable in one country are inappropriate in another—for example, in the United States electrical devices run on 110-volt systems, but in some European countries the standard is a 220–240-volt system, necessitating the use of different electrical designs and components. In parts of Asia refrigerators are a status symbol and may be placed in the living room, leading to preferences for stylish designs and colors—in India bright blue and red are popular colors. In other Asian countries household space is constrained and many refrigerators are only four feet high so that the top can be used for storage. In Italy most people use automatic washing machines, but there is a strongly entrenched cultural preference for hanging the clothes out to dry—the widespread belief that sun-dried clothes are fresher virtually shuts down any opportunities for appliance makers to market clothes dryers in Italy.

Similarly, market growth varies from country to country. In emerging markets like India, China, Brazil, and Malaysia, market growth potential is far higher than in the more mature economies of Britain, Denmark, Canada, and Japan. In automobiles, for example, the potential for market growth is explosive in China, where 2007 sales of new vehicles amounted to less than 9 million in a country with 1.3 billion people. In India there are efficient, well-developed national channels for distributing trucks, scooters, farm equipment, groceries, personal care items, and other packaged products to the country's 3 million retailers, whereas in China distribution is primarily local and there is no national network for distributing most products. The marketplace is intensely competitive in some countries and only moderately so in others. Industry driving forces may be one thing in Spain, quite another in Canada, and different yet again in Turkey or Argentina or South Korea.

One of the biggest concerns of companies competing in foreign markets is whether to customize their offerings in each different country market to match the tastes and preferences of local buyers or whether to offer a mostly standardized product worldwide. While closely matching products to local tastes makes them more appealing to local buyers, customizing a company's products country by country may have the effect of raising production and distribution costs due to the greater variety of designs and components, shorter production runs, and the complications of added inventory handling and distribution logistics. Greater standardization of a global company's product offering, on the other hand, can lead to scale economies and learning/experience curve effects, thus contributing to the achievement of a low-cost advantage. *The tension between the market pressures to localize a company's product offerings country by country and the competitive pressures to lower costs is one of the big strategic issues that participants in foreign markets have to resolve.*

Aside from the basic cultural and market differences among countries, a company also has to pay special attention to location advantages that stem from country-to-country variations in manufacturing and distribution costs, the risks of adverse shifts in exchange rates, and the economic and political demands of host governments.

Gaining Competitive Advantage Based on Where Activities Are Located

Differences in wage rates, worker productivity, inflation rates, energy costs, tax rates, government regulations, and the like create sizable variations in manufacturing costs from country to country. Plants in some countries have major manufacturing cost advantages because of lower input costs (especially labor), relaxed government regulations, the proximity of suppliers, or unique natural resources. In such cases, the low-cost countries become principal production sites, with most of the output being exported to markets in other parts of the world. Companies that build production facilities in low-cost countries (or that source their products from contract manufacturers in these countries) have a competitive advantage over rivals with plants in countries where costs are higher. The competitive role of low manufacturing costs is most evident in low-wage countries like China, India, Pakistan, Cambodia, Vietnam, Mexico, Brazil, Guatemala, the Philippines, and several countries in Africa that have become production havens for manufactured goods with high labor content (especially textiles and apparel). Labor costs in China were estimated to be about $0.70 an hour in 2006 versus $2.75 in Mexico, $4.91 in Brazil, $6.29 in Hungary, $7.65 in Portugal, $23.82 in the United States, $25.74 in Canada, $34.21 in Germany, and $41.05 in Norway.[3] China is fast becoming the manufacturing capital of the world—virtually all of the world's major manufacturing companies now have facilities in China, and China attracted $69.5 billion in foreign direct investment in 2006, an amount greater than any other country in the world. Likewise, concerns about short delivery times and low shipping costs make some countries better locations than others for establishing distribution centers.

The quality of a country's business environment also offers locational advantages—the governments of some countries are anxious to attract foreign investments and go all out to create a business climate that outsiders will view as favorable. A good example is Ireland, which has one of the world's most pro-business environments. Ireland offers companies very low corporate tax rates, has a government that is responsive to the needs of industry, and aggressively recruits high-tech manufacturing facilities and multinational companies. Ireland's policies were a major factor in Intel's decision to locate a $2.5 billion chip manufacturing plant in Ireland that employs over 4,000 people. Another locational advantage is the clustering of suppliers of components and capital equipment; infrastructure suppliers (universities, vocational training providers, research enterprises); trade associations; and makers of complementary products in a geographic area—such clustering can be an important source of cost savings in addition to facilitating close collaboration with key suppliers.

The Risks of Adverse Exchange Rate Shifts

The volatility of exchange rates greatly complicates the issue of geographic cost advantages. Currency exchange rates often move up or down 20 to 40 percent annually. Changes of this magnitude can either totally wipe out a country's low-cost advantage or transform a former high-cost location into a competitive-cost location. For instance, in the mid-1980s, when the dollar was strong relative to the Japanese yen (meaning that $1 would purchase, say, 125 yen as opposed to only 100 yen), Japanese heavy-equipment maker Komatsu was able to undercut U.S.-based Caterpillar's prices by as much as 25 percent, causing Caterpillar to lose sales and market share. But starting in 1985, when exchange rates began to shift and the dollar grew steadily weaker against the yen (meaning that $1 was worth fewer and fewer yen and that a Komatsu product made in Japan at a cost of 20 million yen translated into costs of many more dollars than before), Komatsu had to raise its prices to U.S. buyers six times over two years. With its competitiveness against Komatsu restored because of the weaker dollar and Komatsu's higher prices, Caterpillar regained sales and market share. *The lesson of fluctuating exchange rates is that companies that export goods to foreign countries always gain in competitiveness when the currency of the country in which the goods are manufactured is weak. Exporters are disadvantaged when the currency of the country where goods are being manufactured grows stronger.* Sizable long-term shifts in exchange rates thus shuffle the global cards of which rivals have the upper hand in the marketplace and which countries represent the low-cost manufacturing location.

> **CORE CONCEPT**
> Companies with manufacturing facilities in a particular country are more cost-competitive in exporting goods to world markets when the local currency is weak (or declines in value relative to other currencies); their competitiveness erodes when the local currency grows stronger relative to the currencies of the countries to which the locally made goods are being exported.

As a further illustration of the risks associated with fluctuating exchange rates, consider the case of a U.S. company that has located manufacturing facilities in Brazil (where the currency is reals—pronounced *ray-alls*) and that exports most of the Brazilian-made goods to markets in the European Union (where the currency is euros). To keep the numbers simple, assume that the exchange rate is 2.5 Brazilian reals for 1 euro and that the product being made in Brazil has a manufacturing cost of 2.5 Brazilian reals (or 1 euro). Now suppose that for some reason the exchange rate shifts from 2.5 reals per euro to 3 reals per euro (meaning that the real has declined in value and that the euro is stronger). Making the product in Brazil is now more cost-competitive because a Brazilian good costing 2.5 reals to produce has fallen to only 0.8 euros at the new exchange rate. If, in contrast, the value of the Brazilian real grows stronger in relation to the euro—resulting in an exchange rate of 2 reals to 1 euro—the same good costing 2.5 reals to produce now has a cost of 1.5 euros. Clearly, the attraction of manufacturing a good in Brazil and selling it in Europe is far greater when the euro is strong (an exchange rate of 1 euro for 3 Brazilian reals) than when the euro is weak (an exchange rate of 1 euro for only 2 Brazilian reals).

Insofar as U.S.-based manufacturers are concerned, declines in the value of the U.S. dollar against foreign currencies act to reduce or eliminate whatever cost advantage foreign manufacturers might have over U.S. manufacturers and can even prompt foreign companies to establish production plants in the United States. Likewise, a weak euro enhances the cost-competitiveness of companies manufacturing goods in Europe for export to foreign markets; a strong euro versus other currencies weakens the cost-competitiveness of European plants that manufacture goods for export. The growing strength of the euro relative to the U.S. dollar has encouraged a number of European manufacturers such as Volkswagen, Fiat, and Airbus to shift production from European factories to new facilities in the United States. Also, the weakening dollar caused Chrysler to discontinue its contract manufacturing agreement with a Austrian firm for assembly of minivans and Jeeps sold in Europe. Beginning in 2008, Chrysler's vehicles sold in Europe were exported from its factories in Illinois and Missouri. The weak dollar was also a factor in Ford's and GM's recent decisions to begin exporting U.S.-made vehicles to China and Latin America.

It is important to note that *currency exchange rates are rather unpredictable, swinging first one way and then another way, so the competitiveness of any company's facilities in any country is partly dependent on whether exchange rate changes over time have a favorable or unfavorable cost impact.* Companies producing goods in one country for export abroad always improve their cost-competitiveness when the country's currency grows weaker relative to currencies of the countries to which the goods are being exported, and they find their cost-competitiveness eroded when the local currency grows stronger. On the other hand, domestic companies that are under pressure from lower-cost imported goods become more cost-competitive when their currency grows weaker in relation to the currencies of the countries where the imported goods are made—in other words, a U.S. manufacturer views a weaker U.S. dollar as a *favorable exchange rate shift* because such shifts help make its costs more competitive versus those of foreign rivals.

CORE CONCEPT

Fluctuating exchange rates pose significant risks to a company's competitiveness in foreign markets. Exporters win when the currency of the country where goods are being manufactured grows weaker, and they lose when the currency grows stronger. Domestic companies under pressure from lower-cost imports are benefited when their government's currency grows weaker in relation to the countries where the imported goods are being made.

The Impact of Host Government Policies on the Local Business Climate

National governments enact all kinds of measures affecting business conditions and the operation of foreign companies in their markets. They may set local content requirements on goods made inside their borders by foreign-based companies, have rules and policies that protect local companies from foreign competition, put restrictions on exports to ensure adequate local supplies, regulate the prices of imported and locally produced goods, enact deliberately burdensome procedures and requirements for imported goods to pass customs inspection, and impose tariffs or quotas on the imports of certain goods. Until 2001, when it joined the World Trade Organization, China imposed a 100 percent tariff on motor vehicle imports. The European Union imposes quotas on textile and apparel imports from China, as a measure to protect European producers in southern Europe. India has a long history of utilizing excise taxes of as much as 50 percent on newly purchased products to protect its domestic producers. However, such duties were lowered to 8 to 14 percent in 2008 to help boost consumer demand to further accelerate India's overall economic growth rate.

National governments also vary in the degree to which they impose burdensome tax structures and regulatory requirements upon foreign companies doing business within their borders. In 2008, for example, China raised the tax on purchases of SUVs (most all of which were made outside China) from 20 percent to 40 percent. Sometimes outsiders face a web of regulations regarding technical standards, product certification, prior approval of capital spending projects, withdrawal of funds from the country, and required minority (sometimes majority) ownership of foreign company operations by local companies or investors. Some national governments tend to be hostile to or suspicious of foreign companies operating within their borders. Some governments provide subsidies and low-interest loans to domestic companies to help them compete against foreign-based companies. On the other hand, a number of national governments, anxious to obtain new plants and jobs, offer foreign companies a helping hand in the form of subsidies, privileged market access, and technical assistance. Hence, in deciding which foreign country markets to participate in and which ones to avoid, companies carefully weigh local government politics and policies toward business in general, and foreign companies in particular,.

> Companies desirous of expanding their participation in foreign markets tend to put most of their energies and resources into those country markets not only where market opportunities are attractive but also where the business climate is favorable.

THE CONCEPTS OF MULTICOUNTRY COMPETITION AND GLOBAL COMPETITION

There are important differences in the patterns of international competition from industry to industry.[4] At one extreme is **multicountry competition,** in which there's so much cross-country variation in market conditions and in the companies contending for leadership that the market contest among rivals in one country is localized and not closely connected to the market contests in other countries. The standout features of multicountry competition are that (1) buyers in different countries are attracted to different product attributes, (2) sellers vary from country to country, and (3) industry conditions and competitive forces in each national market differ in important respects. Take the banking industry in Italy, Brazil, and Japan as an example—the requirements and expectations of banking customers vary among the three countries, the lead banking competitors in Italy differ from those in Brazil or in Japan, and the competitive battle among the leading banks in Italy is unrelated to the rivalry in Brazil or Japan. Thus, with multicountry competition, rival firms battle for national championships and winning in one country does not necessarily signal the ability to fare well in other countries. In multicountry competition, the power of a company's strategy and resource capabilities in one country may not enhance its competitiveness to the same degree in other countries where it operates. Moreover, any competitive advantage a company secures in one country is largely confined to that country; the spillover effects to other countries are minimal to nonexistent. Industries characterized by multicountry competition include radio and TV broadcasting, consumer banking, life insurance, apparel, metals fabrication, many types of food products (coffee, cereals, breads, canned goods, frozen foods), and retailing.

At the other extreme is **global competition,** in which prices and competitive conditions across country markets are strongly linked and the term global or world market has true meaning. In a globally competitive industry, much the same group of rival companies competes in many different countries, but especially so in countries where sales volumes are large and where

> **CORE CONCEPT**
> *Multicountry competition* exists when competition in one national market is localized and not closely connected to competition in another national market. When competition in each country differs in important respects, there is no global market but rather a collection of self-contained country markets.

> **CORE CONCEPT**
> *Global competition* exists when competitive conditions across national markets are linked strongly enough to form a true international market and when leading competitors compete head to head in many different countries.

having a competitive presence is strategically important to building a strong global position in the industry. Thus, a company's competitive position in one country both affects and is affected by its position in other countries. In global competition, a firm's overall competitive advantage grows out of its entire worldwide operations; the competitive advantage it creates at its home base is supplemented by advantages growing out of its operations in other countries (having plants in low-wage countries, being able to transfer expertise from country to country, having the capability to serve customers who also have multinational operations, and brand-name recognition in many parts of the world). Rival firms in globally competitive industries vie for worldwide leadership. Global competition exists in motor vehicles, television sets, tires, mobile phones, personal computers, copiers, watches, digital cameras, bicycles, and commercial aircraft.

An industry can have segments that are globally competitive and segments in which competition is country by country.[5] In the hotel/motel industry, for example, the low- and medium-priced segments are characterized by multicountry competition—competitors mainly serve travelers within the same country. In the business and luxury segments, however, competition is more globalized. Companies like Nikki, Marriott, Sheraton, and Hilton have hotels at many international locations, use worldwide reservation systems, and establish common quality and service standards to gain marketing advantages in serving businesspeople and other travelers who make frequent international trips. In lubricants, the marine engine segment is globally competitive—ships move from port to port and require the same oil everywhere they stop. Brand reputations in marine lubricants have a global scope, and successful marine engine lubricant producers (Exxon Mobil, BP, and Shell) operate globally. In automotive motor oil, however, multicountry competition dominates—countries have different weather conditions and driving patterns, production of motor oil is subject to limited scale economies, shipping costs are high, and retail distribution channels differ markedly from country to country. Thus, domestic firms—like Quaker State and Pennzoil in the United States and Castrol in Great Britain—can be leaders in their home markets without competing globally.

It is also important to recognize that an industry can be in transition from multicountry competition to global competition. In a number of today's industries—beer and major home appliances are prime examples—leading domestic competitors have begun expanding into more and more foreign markets, often acquiring local companies or brands and integrating them into their operations. As some industry members start to build global brands and a global presence, other industry members find themselves pressured to follow the same strategic path—especially if establishing multinational operations results in important scale economies and a powerhouse brand name. As the industry consolidates to fewer players, such that many of the same companies find themselves in head-to-head competition in more and more country markets, global competition begins to replace multicountry competition.

At the same time, consumer tastes in a number of important product categories are converging across the world. Less diversity of tastes and preferences opens the way for companies to create global brands and sell essentially the same products in most countries of the world. Even in industries where consumer tastes remain fairly diverse, companies are learning to use "custom mass production" to economically create different versions of a product and thereby satisfy the tastes of people in different countries.

In addition to taking the obvious cultural and political differences between countries into account, a company has to shape its strategic approach to competing in foreign markets according to whether its industry is characterized by multicountry competition, global competition, or a transition from one to the other.

STRATEGY OPTIONS FOR ENTERING AND COMPETING IN FOREIGN MARKETS

There are a host of generic strategic options for a company that decides to expand outside its domestic market and compete internationally or globally:

1. *Maintain a national (one-country) production base and export goods to foreign markets,* using either company-owned or foreign-controlled forward distribution channels.

2. *License foreign firms to use the company's technology or to produce and distribute the company's products.*

3. *Employ a franchising strategy.*

4. *Use strategic alliances or joint ventures with foreign companies as the primary vehicle for entering foreign markets* and perhaps also use alliances as an ongoing strategic arrangement aimed at maintaining or strengthening competitiveness.

5. *Follow a multicountry strategy,* varying the company's strategic approach (perhaps a little, perhaps a lot) from country to country in response to differing local market and competitive conditions and differing buyer tastes and preferences.

6. *Follow a global strategy,* using essentially the same competitive strategy approach in all country markets where the company has a presence.

The following sections discuss these six strategic options in more detail.

Export Strategies

Using domestic plants as a production base for exporting goods to foreign markets is an excellent initial strategy for pursuing international sales. It is a conservative way to test the international waters. The amount of capital needed to begin exporting is often quite minimal; existing production capacity may well be sufficient to make goods for export. With an export strategy, a manufacturer can limit its involvement in foreign markets by contracting with foreign wholesalers experienced in importing to handle the entire distribution and marketing function in their countries or regions of the world. If it is more advantageous to maintain control over these functions, however, a manufacturer can establish its own distribution and sales organizations in some or all of the target foreign markets. Either way, a home-based production and export strategy helps the firm minimize its direct investments in foreign countries. Such strategies are commonly favored by Chinese, Korean, and Italian companies—products are designed and manufactured at home and then distributed through local channels in the importing countries; the primary functions performed abroad relate chiefly to establishing a network of distributors and perhaps conducting sales promotion and brand awareness activities.

Whether an export strategy can be pursued successfully over the long run hinges on the relative cost-competitiveness of the home-country production base. In some industries, firms gain additional scale economies and learning/experience curve benefits from centralizing production in one or several giant plants whose output capability exceeds demand in any one country market; obviously, a company must export to capture such economies. However, an export strategy is vulnerable when (1) manufacturing costs in the home country are substantially higher than in foreign countries where rivals have plants, (2) the costs of shipping the product to distant foreign markets are relatively high, or (3) adverse shifts occur in currency exchange rates. Unless an exporter can both keep its production and shipping costs competitive with rivals and successfully hedge against unfavorable changes in currency exchange rates, its success will be limited.

Licensing Strategies

Licensing makes sense when a firm with valuable technical know-how or a unique patented product has neither the internal organizational capability nor the resources to enter foreign markets. Licensing also has the advantage of avoiding the risks of committing resources to country markets that are unfamiliar, politically volatile, economically unstable, or otherwise risky. By licensing the technology or the production rights to foreign-based firms, the firm does not have to bear the costs and risks of entering foreign markets on its own, yet it is able to generate income from royalties. The big disadvantage of licensing is the risk of providing valuable technological know-how to foreign companies and thereby losing some degree of control over its use; monitoring licensees and safeguarding the company's proprietary know-how can prove quite difficult in some circumstances. But if the royalty potential is considerable and the companies to whom the licenses are being granted are both trustworthy and reputable, then licensing can be an attractive option. Many software and pharmaceutical companies use licensing strategies.

Franchising Strategies

While licensing works well for manufacturers and owners of proprietary technology, franchising is often better suited to the global expansion efforts of service and retailing enterprises. McDonald's, Yum! Brands (the parent of A&W, Pizza Hut, KFC, Long John Silver's, and Taco Bell), The UPS Store, 7-Eleven, and Hilton Hotels have all used franchising to build a presence in foreign markets. Franchising has much the same advantages as licensing. The franchisee bears most of the costs and risks of establishing foreign locations; a franchisor has to expend only the resources to recruit, train, support, and monitor franchisees. The big problem a franchisor faces is maintaining quality control; foreign franchisees do not always exhibit strong commitment to consistency and standardization, especially when the local culture does not stress the same kinds of quality concerns. Another problem that can arise is whether to allow foreign franchisees to make modifications in the franchisor's product offering so as to better satisfy the tastes and expectations of local buyers. Should McDonald's allow its franchised units in Japan to modify Big Macs to suit Japanese tastes? Should the franchised Pizza Hut units in China be permitted to substitute spices that appeal to Chinese consumers? Or should the same menu offerings be rigorously and unvaryingly required of all franchisees worldwide?

Strategic Alliances and Joint Ventures with Foreign Partners

Cross-border alliances have proved to be popular and viable vehicles for companies to edge their way into the markets of foreign countries.

Strategic alliances, joint ventures, and other cooperative agreements with foreign companies are a favorite and potentially fruitful means for entering a foreign market or strengthening a firm's competitiveness in world markets.[6] Historically, export-minded firms in industrialized nations sought alliances with firms in less-developed countries to import and market their products locally—such arrangements were often necessary to win approval for entry from the host country's government. Restrictions on investment in China by its government prior to the country's 2001 entry into the World Trade

Organization helped create about 10,000 joint ventures annually in China between 1998 and 2001. However, as those restrictions were lifted, the number of wholly foreign-owned enterprises in China grew from about 10,000 per year prior to 2001 to 30,000 per year between 2003 and 2007. Even with fewer restrictions on foreign investment, many U.S. and European companies have continued to ally with Chinese companies in their efforts to enter the market, with the number of new joint ventures created between 2002 and 2007 ranging from 7,000 to 12,000.[7]

Both Japanese and American companies are actively forming alliances with European companies to strengthen their ability to compete in the 27-nation European Union and to capitalize on the opening up of Eastern European markets. Companies in Europe, Latin America, and Asia are, of course, particularly interested in strategic partnerships that will strengthen their ability to gain a foothold in the U.S. market. In general, companies intent on international expansion commonly look to alliances and joint ventures as a means of strengthening their ability to compete across a wider geographical area.

However, cooperative arrangements between domestic and foreign companies have strategic appeal for reasons besides gaining better access to attractive country markets.[8] A second big appeal of cross-border alliances is to capture economies of scale in production and/or marketing. By joining forces in producing components, assembling models, and marketing their products, companies can realize cost savings not achievable with their own small volumes. A third motivation for entering into a cross-border alliance is to fill gaps in technical expertise and/or knowledge of local markets (buying habits and product preferences of consumers, local customs, and so on). Allies learn much from one another in performing joint research, sharing technological know-how, studying one another's manufacturing methods, and understanding how to tailor sales and marketing approaches to fit local cultures and traditions. Indeed, one of the win-win benefits of an alliance is to learn from the skills, technological know-how, and capabilities of alliance partners and implant the knowledge and know-how of these partners in personnel throughout the company.

A fourth motivation for cross-border alliances is to share distribution facilities and dealer networks, thus mutually strengthening their access to buyers. A fifth benefit is that cross-border allies can direct their competitive energies more toward mutual rivals and less toward one another; teaming up may help them close the gap on leading companies. A sixth driver of cross-border alliances comes into play when companies desiring to enter a new foreign market conclude that alliances with local companies are an effective way to establish working relationships with key officials in the host-country government.[9] And, finally, alliances can be a particularly useful way for companies across the world to gain agreement on important technical standards—they have been used to arrive at standards for assorted PC devices, Internet-related technologies, high-definition televisions, and mobile phones.

What makes cross-border alliances an attractive strategic means of gaining the above types of benefits (as compared to acquiring or merging with foreign-based companies to gain much the same benefits) is that entering into alliances and strategic partnerships to gain market access and/or expertise of one kind or another allows a company to preserve its independence (which is not the case with a merger) and avoid using perhaps scarce financial resources to fund acquisitions. Furthermore, an alliance offers the flexibility to readily disengage once its purpose has been served or if the benefits prove elusive, whereas an acquisition is a more permanent sort of arrangement (although the acquired company can, of course, be divested).[10]

Illustration Capsule 7.1 provides five examples of cross-border strategic alliances.

> Cross-border alliances enable a growth-minded company to widen its geographic coverage and strengthen its competitiveness in foreign markets while, at the same time, offering flexibility and allowing a company to retain some degree of autonomy and operating control.

ILLUSTRATION CAPSULE 7.1
Five Examples of Cross-Border Strategic Alliances

1. Cisco, the worldwide leader in networking components, entered into a strategic alliance with the Finnish telecommunications firm Nokia Siemens Networks to develop communications networks capable of transmitting data either across the Internet or by mobile technologies. Nokia Siemens Networks itself was created through a 2006 international joint venture between German-based Siemens AG and the Finnish communications giant Nokia. The Cisco–Nokia Siemens alliance was created to better position both companies for convergence among Internet technologies and wireless communication devices that was expected to dramatically change how both computer networks and wireless telephones would be used.

2. Verio, a subsidiary of Japan-based NTT Communications and one of the leading global providers of Web hosting services and IP data transport, operates with the philosophy that in today's highly competitive and challenging technology market, companies must gain and share skills, information, and technology with technology leaders across the world. Believing that no company can be all things to all customers in the Web hosting industry, Verio executives have developed an alliance-oriented business model that combines the company's core competencies with the skills and products of best-of-breed technology partners. Verio's strategic partners include Accenture, Cisco Systems, Microsoft, Sun Microsystems, Oracle, Arsenal Digital Solutions (a provider of worry-free tape backup, data restore, and data storage services), Internet Security Systems (a provider of firewall and intrusion detection systems), and Mercantec (which develops storefront and shopping cart software). Verio management believes that its portfolio of strategic alliances allows it to use innovative, best-of-class technologies in providing its customers with fast, efficient, accurate data transport and a complete set of Web hosting services. An independent panel of 12 judges recently selected Verio as the winner of the Best Technology Foresight Award for its efforts in pioneering new technologies.

3. A 2003 strategic alliance between British oil producer BP and Russian oil and gas producer Alfa, Access, Renova (AAR) has produced Russia's third largest crude oil producer. The strategic alliance provided BP with access to AAR's vast oil reserves and allowed AAR access to BP's assets in Russia, including BP's retail refined gasoline network. The addition of BP's oil field production expertise increased the field production by 250 percent between 2003 and 2007. BP's exploration and drilling capabilities also contributed to the development new greenfield projects that were expected to come online in 2009.

4. Toyota and First Automotive Works, China's biggest automaker, entered into an alliance in 2002 to make luxury sedans, sport-utility vehicles, and minivehicles for the Chinese market. The intent was to make as many as 400,000 vehicles annually by 2010, an amount equal to the number that Volkswagen, the company with the largest share of the Chinese market, was making as of 2002. The alliance envisioned a joint investment of about $1.2 billion. At the time of the announced alliance, Toyota was lagging behind Honda, General Motors, and Volkswagen in setting up production facilities in China. Capturing a bigger share of the Chinese market was seen as crucial to Toyota's success in achieving its strategic objective of having a 15 percent share of the world's automotive market by 2010.

5. European Aeronautic Defence and Space (EADS) was formed by an alliance of aerospace companies from Britain, Spain, Germany, and France that included British Aerospace, Daimler-Benz Aerospace, and Aerospatiale. The objective of the alliance was to create a European aircraft company capable of competing with U.S.-based Boeing Corporation. The alliance has proved highly successful, infusing its commercial airline division, Airbus, with the know-how and resources to compete head-to-head with Boeing for world leadership in large commercial aircraft (over 100 passengers). The company also established an alliance with U.S. military aircraft manufacturer Northrop Grumman to develop a highly sophisticated refueling tanker based on the A330 airliner for the U.S. Air Force. As of 2008, the U.S. government was still evaluating competing bids from EADS/Northrop Grumman and Boeing, but the alliance had yielded contracts to produce the tanker for the United Kingdom, Australia, Saudi Arabia, and the United Arab Emirates.

Sources: Company Web sites and press releases; Yves L. Doz and Gary Hamel, *Alliance Advantage: The Art of Creating Value through Partnering* (Boston, MA: Harvard Business School Press, 1998).

The Risks of Strategic Alliances with Foreign Partners   Alliances and joint ventures with foreign partners have their pitfalls, however. Cross-border allies typically have to overcome language and cultural barriers and figure out how to deal with diverse (or perhaps conflicting) operating practices. The communication, trust-building, and coordination costs are high in terms of management time.[11] It is not unusual for there to be little personal chemistry among some of the key people on whom success or failure of the alliance depends—the rapport such personnel need to work well together may never emerge. And even if allies are able to develop productive personal relationships, they can still have trouble reaching mutually agreeable ways to deal with key issues or resolve differences. There is a natural tendency for allies to struggle to collaborate effectively in competitively sensitive areas, thus spawning suspicions on both sides about forthright exchanges of information and expertise. Occasionally, the egos of corporate executives can clash—an alliance between Northwest Airlines and KLM Royal Dutch Airlines resulted in a bitter feud among both companies' top officials (who, according to some reports, refused to speak to each other).[12] Plus there is the thorny problem of getting alliance partners to sort through issues and reach decisions fast enough to stay abreast of rapid advances in technology or fast-changing market conditions.

It requires many meetings of many people working in good faith to iron out what is to be shared, what is to remain proprietary, and how the cooperative arrangements will work. Often, once the bloom is off the rose, partners discover they have conflicting objectives and strategies, deep differences of opinion about how to proceed, and/or important differences in corporate values and ethical standards. Tensions build up, working relationships cool, and the hoped-for benefits never materialize.[13]

Even if the alliance becomes a win–win proposition for both parties, there is the danger of becoming overly dependent on foreign partners for essential expertise and competitive capabilities. If a company is aiming for global market leadership and needs to develop capabilities of its own, then at some juncture cross-border merger or acquisition may have to be substituted for cross-border alliances and joint ventures. One of the lessons about cross-border alliances is that they are more effective in helping a company establish a beachhead of new opportunity in world markets than they are in enabling a company to achieve and sustain global market leadership. Global market leaders, while benefiting from alliances, usually must guard against becoming overly dependent on the assistance they get from alliance partners—otherwise they are not masters of their own destiny.

> Strategic alliances are more effective in helping establish a beachhead of new opportunity in world markets than in achieving and sustaining global leadership.

When a Cross-Border Alliance May Be Unnecessary   Experienced multinational companies that market in 50 to 100 or more countries across the world find less need for entering into cross-border alliances than do companies in the early stages of globalizing their operations.[14] Multinational companies make it a point to develop senior managers who understand how "the system" works in different countries, plus they can avail themselves of local managerial talent and know-how by simply hiring experienced local managers. If a multinational enterprise with considerable experience in entering the markets of different countries wants to detour the hazards of allying with local businesses, it can simply assemble a capable management team consisting of both senior managers with considerable international experience and local managers. The role of its own in-house managers with international business savvy is to transfer technology, business practices, and the corporate culture into the company's operations in the new country market and to serve as conduits for the flow of information between the corporate office and local operations. The role of local managers is to contribute needed understanding of the local market conditions, local buying habits, and local ways of doing business and, often, to head up local operations.

Hence, one cannot automatically presume that a company needs the wisdom and resources of a local partner to guide it through the process of successfully entering the markets of foreign countries. Indeed, experienced multinationals often discover that local partners do not always have adequate local market knowledge—much of the so-called experience of local partners can predate the emergence of current market trends and conditions, and sometimes their operating practices can be archaic.[15]

Choosing between a Localized Multicountry Strategy and a Global Strategy

The issue of whether to vary the company's competitive approach to fit specific market conditions and buyer preferences in each host country or whether to employ essentially the same strategy in all countries is perhaps the foremost strategic issue that companies must address when they operate in two or more foreign markets. Figure 7.1 shows a company's options for resolving this issue.

Think-Local, Act-Local Approaches to Strategy-Making   The bigger the differences in buyer tastes, cultural traditions, and market conditions in different countries, the stronger the case for a "think-local, act-local" approach to strategy making, where a company tailors its product offerings and perhaps its basic competitive strategy to fit buyer tastes and market conditions in each country where it opts to compete. The strength of employing a set of *localized* or *multicountry strategies* is that the company's actions and business approaches are deliberately crafted to accommodate the differing tastes and expectations of buyers in each country and to stake out the most attractive market positions vis-à-vis local competitors. A think-local, act-local approach means giving local managers considerable strategy-making latitude. It means having plants produce different product versions for different local markets, and adapting marketing and distribution to fit local customs and cultures. The bigger the country-to-country variations, the more that a company's overall strategy is a collection of its localized country strategies rather than a common or "global" strategy.[16]

> **CORE CONCEPT**
>
> A *localized or multicountry strategy* is one where a company varies its product offering and competitive approach from country to country in response to important cross-country variations in buyer preferences and market conditions.

A think-local, act-local approach to strategy making is essential when there are significant country-to-country differences in customer preferences and buying habits; when there are significant cross-country differences in distribution channels and marketing methods; when host governments enact regulations requiring that products sold locally meet strict manufacturing specifications or performance standards; and when the trade restrictions of host governments are so diverse and complicated that they preclude a uniform, coordinated worldwide market approach. With localized strategies, a company often has different product versions for different countries and sometimes sells them under different brand names. Castrol, a specialist in oil lubricants, has over 3,000 different formulas of lubricants, many of which have been tailored for different climates, vehicle types and uses, and equipment applications that characterize different country markets. In the food products industry, it is common for companies to vary the ingredients in their products and sell the localized versions under local brand names in order to cater to country-specific tastes and eating preferences. After an unsuccessful launch of the Dasani bottled water brand in Europe, Coca-Cola found that it

Figure 7.1 A Company's Strategic Options for Dealing with Cross-Country Variations in Buyer Preferences and Market Conditions

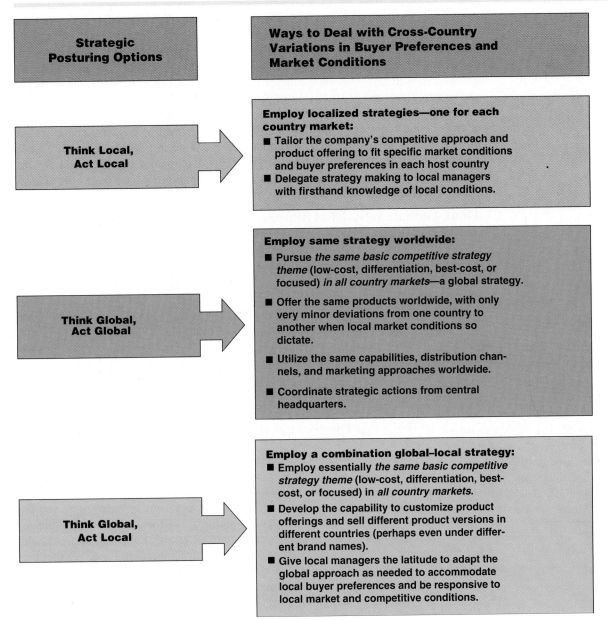

Strategic Posturing Options	Ways to Deal with Cross-Country Variations in Buyer Preferences and Market Conditions
Think Local, Act Local	**Employ localized strategies—one for each country market:** ■ Tailor the company's competitive approach and product offering to fit specific market conditions and buyer preferences in each host country ■ Delegate strategy making to local managers with firsthand knowledge of local conditions.
Think Global, Act Global	**Employ same strategy worldwide:** ■ Pursue *the same basic competitive strategy theme* (low-cost, differentiation, best-cost, or focused) *in all country markets*—a global strategy. ■ Offer the same products worldwide, with only very minor deviations from one country to another when local market conditions so dictate. ■ Utilize the same capabilities, distribution channels, and marketing approaches worldwide. ■ Coordinate strategic actions from central headquarters.
Think Global, Act Local	**Employ a combination global–local strategy:** ■ Employ essentially *the same basic competitive strategy theme* (low-cost, differentiation, best-cost, or focused) in *all country markets*. ■ Develop the capability to customize product offerings and sell different product versions in different countries (perhaps even under different brand names). ■ Give local managers the latitude to adapt the global approach as needed to accommodate local buyer preferences and be responsive to local market and competitive conditions.

was best to adapt its strategy for competing in the bottled water industry to local market conditions. European consumers' preference for spring water rather than purified water forced Coca-Cola into a strategy of acquiring local brands rather than entering foreign markets with a global brand.[17] Deutsche Telekom markets broadband services, land-based telephone systems, wireless telephone services, and information and communication services to millions of customers in about 50 countries around the world.

The company employs a localized, multicountry strategy, with its broadband and land-based telephone systems marketed only in Germany. Its information and communication services are marketed primarily to government agencies throughout Europe and manufacturers located in about 40 countries. Deutsche Telekom's T-Mobile wireless service is marketed in nine European countries and the United States.

Think-local, act-local strategies do have two big drawbacks: (1) They hinder transfer of a company's competencies and resources across country boundaries (since the strategies in different host countries can be grounded in varying competencies and capabilities), and (2) they do not promote building a single, unified competitive advantage—especially one based on low cost. Companies employing highly localized or multicountry strategies face big hurdles in achieving low-cost leadership *unless* they find ways to customize their products and *still* be in position to capture scale economies and learning/experience curve effects. Companies like Dell and Toyota, because they have mass customization production capabilities, have been able to cost-effectively adapt their product offerings to local buyer tastes.

Think-Global, Act-Global Approaches to Strategy Making

While multicountry or localized strategies are best suited for industries where multicountry competition dominates and a fairly high degree of local responsiveness is competitively imperative, global strategies are best suited for globally competitive industries. A *global strategy* is one in which the company's approach is predominantly the same in all countries—it sells the same products under the same brand names everywhere, uses much the same distribution channels in all countries, and competes on the basis of the same capabilities and marketing approaches worldwide. A "think-global, act-global" strategic theme prompts company managers to integrate and coordinate the company's strategic moves worldwide and to expand into most if not all nations where there is significant buyer demand. It puts considerable strategic emphasis on building a *global* brand name and aggressively pursuing opportunities to transfer ideas, new products, and capabilities from one country to another.[18] Indeed, with a think-global, act-global approach to strategy making, a company's operations in each country can be viewed as experiments that result in learning and in capabilities that may merit transfer to other country markets.

> **CORE CONCEPT**
>
> A *global strategy* is one where a company employs the same basic competitive approach in all countries where it operates, sells much the same products everywhere, strives to build global brands, and coordinates its strategic moves worldwide.

Whenever country-to-country differences are small enough to be accommodated within the framework of a global strategy, a global strategy is preferable to localized strategies because a company can more readily unify its operations and focus on building a strong *global* brand image.

Moreover, with a global strategy a company is better able to concentrate its full resources on achieving a sustainable low-cost or differentiation-based competitive advantage over rivals, putting itself in better position to contend strongly for world market leadership.[19] Figure 7.2 summarizes the basic differences between a localized or multicountry strategy and a global strategy.

Think-Global, Act-Local Approaches to Strategy Making

Often a company can accommodate cross-country variations in buyer tastes, local customs, and market conditions with a "think-global, act-local" approach to developing strategy. This middle-ground approach entails using the same basic competitive theme (low-cost, differentiation, best-cost, or focused) in each country but allowing local mangers the latitude to (1) incorporate whatever country-specific variations in product attributes are needed to best satisfy local buyers and (2) make whatever adjustments in production, distribution, and marketing are needed to be responsive to local

Figure 7.2   How a Localized or Multicountry Strategy Differs from a Global Strategy

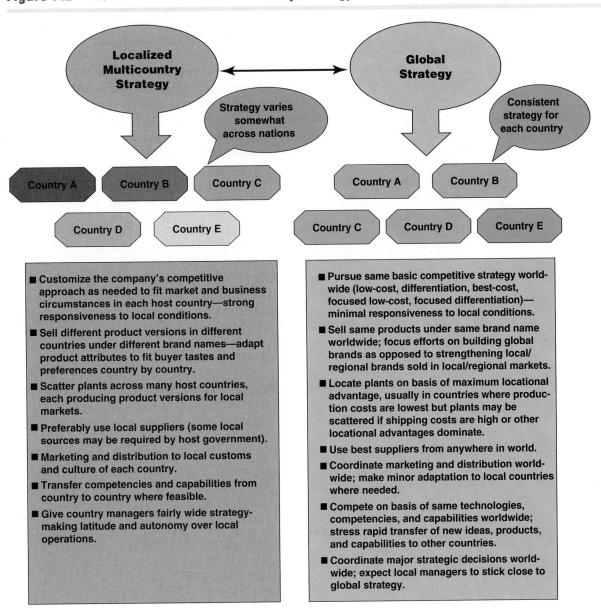

market conditions and compete successfully against local rivals. Slightly different product versions sold under the same brand name may suffice to satisfy local tastes, and it may be feasible to accommodate these versions rather economically in the course of designing and manufacturing the company's product offerings. Philip Morris International markets brands such as Marlboro, Chesterfield, Parliament, and Virginia Slims worldwide. However, the company also makes different versions of Marlboro cigarettes available in different parts of the world to better meet the somewhat different preferences and habits of smokers in each market. The company's Marlboro Mix 9 is a high-nicotine, clove-infused cigarette sold in Indonesia, where smokers prefer powerful, sweet-smelling cigarettes. It's Marlboro Intense was formulated for the Turkish market, while its smooth-tasting Marlboro Filter Plus caters to the tastes of smokers in South Korea, Russia, Kazakhstan, and Ukraine.

As a rule, most companies that operate multinationally endeavor to employ as global a strategy as customer needs and market conditions permit. Ford Motor Company and General Motors have each operated successfully with localized strategies for more than 80 years but have recently begun moving toward more globalized multicountry strategies. General Motors began an initiative in 2004 to insist that its worldwide units share basic parts and work together to design vehicles that can be sold, with modest variations, anywhere around the world; by reducing the types of radios used in its cars and trucks from 270 to 50, it expected to save 40 percent in radio costs. The company continues to produce many country- or region-specific brands such as Opel in Europe and Africa, Holden in Australia, and Vauxhall in the United Kingdom. However, beginning in 2006, GM's Opel brand in Europe and its Saturn brand in North America began sharing models. The 2008 Saturn Sky, Astra, Aura, and Vue all shared identical platforms with Opel models sold in Europe. GM also began executing a think-global, act-local approach in China. GM planned to export 15,000 Buick Enclave SUVs produced in the United States to China and was considering importing its popular four-cylinder Buick Excelle sold in China to the U.S. market. GM planned to equip the U.S. version of the Excelle with an engine slightly larger than that of the Chinese version.

Whirlpool has been globalizing its low-cost leadership strategy in home appliances for nearly 20 years, striving to standardize parts and components and move toward worldwide designs for as many of its appliance products as possible. But it has found it necessary to continue producing significantly different versions of refrigerators, washing machines, and cooking appliances for consumers in different regions of the world because the needs and tastes of local buyers for appliances of different sizes and designs have not converged sufficiently to permit standardization. Illustration Capsule 7.2 describes how three companies localize their strategies for competing in country markets across the world.

THE QUEST FOR COMPETITIVE ADVANTAGE IN FOREIGN MARKETS

There are three important ways in which a firm can gain competitive advantage (or offset domestic disadvantages) by expanding outside its domestic market.[20] First, it can use location to lower costs or achieve greater product differentiation. Second, it can transfer competitively valuable competencies and capabilities from its domestic markets to foreign markets. And, third, it can use cross-border coordination in ways that a domestic-only competitor cannot.

Using Location to Build Competitive Advantage

Location-based advantages range from access to low-cost labor to obtaining low corporate tax rates in pro-business countries to improving innovation by locating activities in countries with unusually large pools of talented and skilled employees.[21]

ILLUSTRATION CAPSULE 7.2
Multicountry Strategies at Electronic Arts, Coca-Cola, and BP

ELECTRONIC ARTS' MULTICOUNTRY STRATEGY IN VIDEO GAMES

Electronic Arts (EA), the world's largest independent developer and marketer of video games, designs games that are suited to the differing tastes of game players in different countries and also designs games in multiple languages. EA has two major design studios—one in Vancouver, British Columbia, and one in Los Angeles—and smaller design studios in San Francisco, Orlando, London, and Tokyo. This dispersion of design studios helps EA design games that are specific to different cultures—for example, the London studio took the lead in designing the popular FIFA Soccer game to suit European tastes and to replicate the stadiums, signage, and team rosters; the U.S. studio took the lead in designing games involving NFL football, NBA basketball, and NASCAR racing. No other game software company had EA's ability to localize games or to launch games on multiple platforms in multiple countries in multiple languages. EA's The Sims was the best-selling PC game series of all time, with more than 100 million copies sold worldwide between 2000 and 2008. The Sims was published in 22 languages and sold in 60 countries.

COCA-COLA'S MULTICOUNTRY STRATEGY IN BEVERAGES

Coca-Cola strives to meet the demands of local tastes and cultures, offering 300 brands in some 200 countries. Its network of bottlers and distributors is distinctly local, and the company's products and brands are formulated to cater to local tastes. The ways in which Coca-Cola's local operating units bring products to market, the packaging that is used, and the advertising messages that are employed are all intended to match the local culture and fit in with local business practices. Many of the ingredients and supplies for Coca-Cola's products are sourced locally.

BP'S MULTICOUNTRY STRATEGY IN THE GASOLINE AND SERVICE STATION BUSINESS

Country differences in requirements for gasoline formulations mean that most oil producers employ think-local, act-local strategies to some extent. Government requirements for gasoline additives that help reduce carbon monoxide, smog, and other emissions are almost never the same from country to country. BP uses localized strategies in its gasoline and service station business segment because of these cross-country formulation differences and because of customer familiarity with local brand names. For example, the company markets gasoline in the United States under its BP and Arco brands, but it markets gasoline in Germany, Belgium, Poland, Hungary, and the Czech Republic under the Aral brand. Aral has been among Germany's most well-known gasoline brands and service station chains for more than 70 years. In 1937, Aral ran 8,000 gas stations in Germany and held a 25 percent share of the German market for gasoline sales. Over the next 30 years, the company continued to expand its chain of service stations to 11,000 locations. BP acquired Aral in 2002 and, as part of its think-local, act-local strategy, converted its 630 BP gas stations in Germany to Aral stations.

Sources: www.ea.com, www.cocacola.com, and www.bp.com (accessed September 2004 and July 2008).

To use location to build competitive advantage, a company must consider two issues: (1) whether to concentrate each activity it performs in a few select countries or to disperse performance of the activity to many nations, and (2) in which countries to locate particular activities.[22]

When to Concentrate Activities in a Few Locations   Companies tend to concentrate their activities in a limited number of locations in the following circumstances:

- *When the costs of manufacturing or other activities are significantly lower in some geographic locations than in others*—For example, much of the world's athletic footwear is manufactured in Asia (China and Malaysia) because of low labor costs; much of the production of motherboards for PCs is located in Taiwan because of both low costs and the high-caliber technical skills of the Taiwanese labor force.

- *When there are significant scale economies*—The presence of significant economies of scale in components production or final assembly means that a company can gain major cost savings from operating a few super-efficient plants as opposed to a host of small plants scattered across the world. Achieving low-cost provider status often requires a company to have the largest worldwide manufacturing share (as distinct from brand share or market share), with production centralized in one or a few world-scale plants. Some companies even use such plants to manufacture units sold under the brand names of rivals to further boost production-related scale economies. Chinese makers of apparel, footwear, housewares, toys, sporting goods, and parts for computers and peripherals have used their large manufacturing share and low labor costs to establish a low-cost advantage. Marketing and distribution economies associated with multinational operations can also yield scale economies necessary for low-cost leadership.

> Companies that compete multinationally can pursue competitive advantage in world markets by locating their value chain activities in whatever nations prove most advantageous.

- *When there is a steep learning curve associated with performing an activity in a single location*—In some industries learning/experience curve effects in parts manufacture or assembly are so great that a company establishes one or two large plants from which it serves the world market. The key to riding down the learning curve is to concentrate production in a few locations to increase the accumulated volume at a plant (and thus the experience of the plant's workforce) as rapidly as possible.

- *When certain locations have superior resources, allow better coordination of related activities, or offer other valuable advantages*—A research unit or a sophisticated production facility may be situated in a particular nation because of its pool of technically trained personnel. Samsung became a leader in memory chip technology by establishing a major R&D facility in Silicon Valley and transferring the know-how it gained back to headquarters and its plants in South Korea. Also, parts manufacturing plants may be geographically concentrated and clustered around final assembly plants where just-in-time inventory practices yield big cost savings and/or where an assembly firm has long-term partnering arrangements with its key suppliers.

When to Disperse Activities Across Many Locations

There are several instances when dispersing activities is more advantageous than concentrating them. Buyer-related activities—such as distribution to dealers, sales and advertising, and after-sale service—usually must take place close to buyers. This means physically locating the capability to perform such activities in every country market where a global firm has major customers (unless buyers in several adjoining countries can be served quickly from a nearby central location). For example, firms that make mining and oil-drilling equipment maintain operations in many international locations to support customers' needs for speedy equipment repair and technical assistance. The four biggest public accounting firms have numerous international offices to service the foreign operations of their multinational corporate clients. A global competitor that effectively disperses its buyer-related activities can gain a service-based competitive edge in world markets over rivals whose buyer-related activities are more concentrated—this is one reason the Big Four public accounting firms

(PricewaterhouseCoopers, KPMG, Deloitte & Touche, and Ernst & Young) have been so successful relative to regional and national firms. Dispersing activities to many locations is also competitively advantageous when high transportation costs, diseconomies of large size, and trade barriers make it too expensive to operate from a central location. Many companies distribute their products from multiple locations to shorten delivery times to customers. In addition, it is strategically advantageous to disperse activities to hedge against the risks of fluctuating exchange rates; supply interruptions (due to strikes, mechanical failures, and transportation delays); and adverse political developments. Such risks are greater when activities are concentrated in a single location.

Using Cross-Border Transfers of Competencies and Capabilities to Build Competitive Advantage

One of the best ways for a company with valuable competencies and resource strengths to grow sales and profits is to use its considerable resource strengths to enter additional country markets. Transferring competencies, capabilities, and resource strengths from country to country may also contribute to the development of broader or deeper competencies and capabilities—ideally helping a company achieve dominating depth in some competitively valuable area. Dominating depth in a competitively valuable capability, resource, or value chain activity is a strong basis for sustainable competitive advantage over other international or global competitors, and especially so over domestic-only competitors. A one-country customer base is often too small to support the resource buildup needed to achieve such depth; this is particularly true when the market is just emerging and sophisticated resources have not been required.

Whirlpool, the leading global manufacturer of home appliances, with 72 plants and technology centers in 17 countries and sales in 170 countries, has used the Internet to create a global information technology platform that allows the company to transfer key product innovations and production processes across regions and brands quickly and effectively. Wal-Mart is slowly but forcefully expanding its operations with a strategy that involves transferring its considerable domestic expertise in distribution and discount retailing to store operations recently established in China, Japan, Latin America, and the United Kingdom. Its status as the largest, most resource-deep, and most sophisticated user of distribution-retailing know-how has served it well in building its foreign sales and profitability. But Wal-Mart is not racing madly to position itself in many foreign markets; rather, it is establishing a strong presence in select country markets and learning how to be successful in these before tackling entry into other countries well suited to its business model.

However, cross-border resource transfers are not a guaranteed recipe for success. Philips Consumer Electronics sells more flat-panel TVs and DVD/Blu-ray players and recorders in Europe than any other company. Philips has worldwide sales of about 27 billion euros, but as of 2007 Philips had lost money for 19 consecutive years in its U.S. consumer electronics business. In the United States, the company's televisions and DVD recorders (sold under the Magnavox and Philips brands) are slow sellers. Philips has been notoriously slow in introducing new products into the U.S. market, struggling to change its image as a low-end brand and convince U.S. electronics retailers to stock the Philips brand.

Using Cross-Border Coordination to Build Competitive Advantage

International and global competitors are able to coordinate activities across different countries to build competitive advantage.[23] If a firm learns how to assemble its product more efficiently at, say, its Brazilian plant, the accumulated expertise can be quickly communicated via the Internet to assembly plants in other world locations. Knowledge gained in marketing a company's product in Great Britain can readily be exchanged with company personnel in New Zealand or Australia. A global or international manufacturer can shift production from a plant in one country to a plant in another to take advantage of exchange rate fluctuations, to enhance its leverage with host-country governments, and to respond to changing wage rates, components shortages, energy costs, or changes in tariffs and quotas. Production schedules can be coordinated worldwide; shipments can be diverted from one distribution center to another if sales rise unexpectedly in one place and fall in another.

Multinational companies can use online systems to involve their best design and engineering personnel (wherever they are located) in collectively coming up with next-generation products. Efficiencies can also be achieved by shifting workloads from where they are unusually heavy to locations where personnel are underutilized. Whirlpool's efforts to link its product R&D and manufacturing operations in North America, Latin America, Europe, and Asia allowed it to accelerate the discovery of innovative appliance features, coordinate the introduction of these features in the appliance products marketed in different countries, and create a cost-efficient worldwide supply chain. Whirlpool's conscious efforts to integrate and coordinate its various operations around the world have helped it become a low-cost producer and also speed product innovations to market, thereby giving Whirlpool an edge over rivals in designing and rapidly introducing innovative and attractively priced appliances worldwide.

Furthermore, a multinational company that consistently incorporates the same differentiating attributes in its products worldwide has enhanced potential to build a global brand name with significant power in the marketplace. The reputation for quality that Honda established worldwide first in motorcycles and then in automobiles gave it competitive advantage in positioning Honda lawn mowers at the upper end of the U.S. outdoor power equipment market—the Honda name gave the company immediate credibility with U.S. buyers of power equipment and enabled it to become an instant market contender without all the fanfare and cost of a multimillion-dollar ad campaign to build brand awareness.

STRATEGIES TO COMPETE IN THE MARKETS OF EMERGING COUNTRIES

Companies racing for global leadership have to consider competing in emerging markets like China, India, Brazil, Indonesia, Thailand, Poland, Russia, and Mexico—countries where the business risks are considerable but where the opportunities for growth are huge, especially as their economies develop and living standards climb toward levels in the industrialized world.[24] With the world now comprising more than 6 billion people—fully one-third of whom are in India and China, and hundreds of millions more in other less-developed countries in Asia and Latin America—a

ILLUSTRATION CAPSULE 7.3
Yum! Brands' Strategy for Becoming the Leading Food Service Brand in China

In 2007, Yum! Brands operated more than 35,000 restaurants in more than 110 countries. Its best-known brands were KFC, Taco Bell, Pizza Hut, A&W, and Long John Silver's. Its fastest revenue growth in 2007 came from its 3,100 restaurants in China, which recorded revenues of $2.1 billion and operating profits of $375 million during the year. KFC was the largest quick-service chain in China, with 2,140 units in 2007, while Pizza Hut was the largest casual dining chain, with nearly 1,000 units. Yum! Brands planned to open at least 425 new restaurant locations annually in China, including new Pizza Hut Home delivery units and East Dawning units, which had a menu offering traditional Chinese food. All of Yum! Brands' menu items for China were developed in its R&D facility in Shanghai.

In addition to adapting its menu to local tastes and adding new units at a rapid pace, Yum! Brands also adapted the restaurant ambiance and decor to appeal to local consumer preferences and behavior. The company changed its KFC store formats to provide educational displays that supported parents' priorities for their children and to make KFC a fun place for children to visit. The typical KFC outlet in China averaged two birthday parties per day.

In 2008, Yum! Brands operated 60 KFC, Taco Bell, Pizza Hut, A&W, and Long John Silver's restaurants for every 1 million Americans. The company's 3,100 units in China represented only 2 restaurants per 1 million people in China. Yum! Brands' management believed that its strategy keyed to continued expansion in the number of units in China and additional menu refinements would allow its operating profits from restaurants located in China to account for 40 percent of systemwide operating profits by 2017.

Sources: Yum! Brands 2007 10-K report; information posted at www.yum.com.

company that aspires to world market leadership (or to sustained rapid growth) cannot ignore the market opportunities or the base of technical and managerial talent such countries offer. For example, in 2008 China was the world's second largest economy (behind the United States), measured by purchasing power. In 2003, its population of 1.3 billion people consumed nearly 33 percent of the world's annual cotton production, 51 percent of the world's pork, 35 percent of all cigarettes, 23 percent of televisions, 20 percent of cell phones, and 18 percent of all washing machines. China is also the world's largest consumer of many commodities—accounting for 50 percent of the world's demand for cement, 33 percent of all steel produced, 31 percent of worldwide coal production, and over 25 percent of the world's aluminum purchases. China's growth in demand for consumer goods had put it on track to become the second largest market for motor vehicles by 2010 and the world's largest market for luxury goods by 2014.[25] Thus, no company that aspires to global market leadership can afford to ignore the strategic importance of establishing competitive market positions in China, India, other parts of the Asia-Pacific region, Latin America, and Eastern Europe. Illustration Capsule 7.3 describes Yum! Brands' strategy to boost its sales and market share in China.

Tailoring products to fit conditions in an emerging country market like China, however, often involves more than making minor product changes and becoming more familiar with local cultures.[26] Ford's attempt to sell a Ford Escort in India at a price of $21,000—a luxury-car price, given that India's best-selling Maruti-Suzuki model sold at the time for $10,000 or less, and that fewer than 10 percent of Indian households have annual purchasing power greater than $20,000—met with a less-than-enthusiastic market response. McDonald's has had to offer vegetable burgers in parts of Asia and to rethink its prices, which are often high by local standards and affordable only by the well-to-do. Kellogg has struggled to introduce its cereals successfully because consumers in many less-developed countries do not eat cereal for breakfast—changing habits is difficult and expensive. In several emerging countries, Coca-Cola has found that advertising its world image does not strike a chord with the local populace in a number of emerging-country markets. Single-serving packages of detergents, shampoos, pickles, cough syrup, and cooking oils are very popular in India because they allow buyers to conserve cash by purchasing only what they need immediately. Thus, many companies find that trying to employ a strategy akin to that used in the markets of developed countries is hazardous.[27] Experimenting with some, perhaps many, local twists is usually necessary to find a strategy combination that works.

Strategy Options for Emerging-Country Markets

The following are options for tailoring a company's strategy to fit the sometimes unusual or challenging circumstances presented in emerging-country markets:

- *Prepare to compete on the basis of low price.* Consumers in emerging markets are often highly focused on price, which can give low-cost local competitors the edge unless a company can find ways to attract buyers with bargain prices as well as better products.[28] For example, when Unilever entered the market for laundry detergents in India, it realized that 80 percent of the population could not afford the brands it was selling to affluent consumers there (or the brands it was selling in wealthier countries). To compete against a very low-priced detergent made by a local company, Unilever came up with a low-cost formula that was not harsh to the skin, constructed new low-cost production facilities, packaged the detergent (named Wheel) in single-use amounts so that it could be sold very cheaply, distributed the product to local merchants by hand carts, and crafted an economical marketing campaign that included painted signs on buildings and demonstrations near stores. The new brand quickly captured $100 million in sales and was the number one detergent brand in India in 2008, measured by dollar sales. Unilever later replicated the strategy with low-priced packets of shampoos and deodorants in India and in South America with a detergent brand named Ala.

- *Be prepared to modify aspects of the company's business model or strategy to accommodate local circumstances (but not so much that the company loses the advantage of global scale and global branding).*[29] For instance, when Dell entered China, it discovered that individuals and businesses were not accustomed to placing orders through the Internet. (In contrast, in North America, over 50 percent of Dell's sales in 2002–2007 were online.) To adapt, Dell modified its direct sales model to rely more heavily on phone and fax orders and decided to be patient in getting Chinese customers to place Internet orders. Further, because numerous Chinese government departments and state-owned enterprises insisted that hardware vendors make their bids through distributors and systems integrators (as opposed to dealing directly with Dell salespeople, as did large enterprises in other countries), Dell opted to use third parties in marketing its products to this buyer segment (although it did sell through its own sales force where it could). But Dell was careful not to abandon those parts of its business model that gave it a competitive edge over rivals. When McDonald's moved into Russia in the 1990s, it was forced to alter its practice of obtaining needed supplies from outside vendors because capable local suppliers were not available; to supply its Russian outlets and stay true to its core principle of serving consistent-quality fast food, McDonald's set up its own vertically integrated supply chain—cattle were imported from Holland, and russet potatoes were imported from the United States.

McDonald's management also worked with a select number of Russian bakers for its bread; brought in agricultural specialists from Canada and Europe to improve the management practices of Russian farmers; built its own 100,000-square-foot McComplex to produce hamburger, French fries, ketchup, mustard, and Big Mac sauce; and set up a trucking fleet to move supplies to restaurants.

- *Try to change the local market to better match the way the company does business elsewhere.*[30] A multinational company often has enough market clout to drive major changes in the way a local market operates. When Hong Kong–based STAR launched its first satellite TV channel in 1991, it generated profound impacts on the TV marketplace in India. The Indian government lost its monopoly on TV broadcasts. Several other satellite TV channels aimed at Indian audiences quickly emerged. The excitement of additional TV channels in India triggered a boom in TV manufacturing in India. When Japan's Suzuki entered India in 1981, it triggered a quality revolution among Indian auto parts manufacturers. Local parts and components suppliers teamed up with Suzuki's vendors in Japan and worked with Japanese experts to produce higher-quality products. Over the next two decades, Indian companies became proficient in making top-notch parts and components for vehicles, won more prizes for quality than companies in any country other than Japan, and broke into the global market as suppliers to many automakers in Asia and other parts of the world. Mahindra and Mahindra, one of India's premier automobile manufacturers, has been recognized by a number of organizations for its product quality. Among its most noteworthy awards was its number one ranking by J. D. Power Asia Pacific in 2007 for new vehicle overall quality.

- *Stay away from those emerging markets where it is impractical or uneconomic to modify the company's business model to accommodate local circumstances.*[31] The Home Depot expanded into Mexico in 2001 and China in 2006, but it has avoided entry into other emerging countries because its value proposition of good quality, low prices, and attentive customer service relies on (1) good highways and logistical systems to minimize store inventory costs, (2) employee stock ownership to help motivate store personnel to provide good customer service, and (3) high labor costs for housing construction and home repairs to encourage homeowners to engage in do-it-yourself projects. Relying on these factors in the U.S. and Canadian markets has worked spectacularly for Home Depot, but Home Depot has found that it cannot count on these factors in nearby Latin America.

> Profitability in emerging markets rarely comes quickly or easily—new entrants have to adapt their business models and strategies to local conditions and be patient in earning a profit.

Company experiences in entering developing markets like China, India, Russia, and Brazil indicate that profitability seldom comes quickly or easily. Building a market for the company's products can often turn into a long-term process that involves reeducation of consumers, sizable investments in advertising and promotion to alter tastes and buying habits, and upgrades of the local infrastructure (the supplier base, transportation systems, distribution channels, labor markets, and capital markets). In such cases, a company must be patient, work within the system to improve the infrastructure, and lay the foundation for generating sizable revenues and profits once conditions are ripe for market takeoff.

Defending against Global Giants: Strategies for Local Companies in Emerging Markets

If opportunity-seeking, resource-rich multinational companies are looking to enter emerging markets, what strategy options can local companies use to survive? As it turns out, the prospects for local companies facing global giants are by no means grim.

Studies of local companies in developing markets have disclosed five strategies that have proved themselves in defending against globally competitive multinationals:[32]

1. *Develop business models that exploit shortcomings in local distribution networks or infrastructure.* In many instances, the extensive collection of resources possessed by multinationals is of little help in building a presence in emerging markets. The lack of well-established wholesaler and distributor networks, telecommunication systems, consumer banking, or media necessary for advertising make it difficult for multinationals to migrate business models proved in developed markets to emerging countries. Such markets sometimes favor local companies whose managers are familiar with the local language and culture and are skilled in selecting large numbers of conscientious employees to carry out labor-intensive tasks. Grupo Elektra is an electronics, furniture, and household goods retailer in Mexico that has overcome a void in Mexico's credit-reporting system that maintains few records on middle- and low-income consumers. To make financing available to its customers, Elektra has launched its own bank and placed a branch inside each store. Since credit reports are not available for most of its customers, its loan officers make their lending decisions after visiting the homes of applicants and determining if the applicant's standard of living appears consistent with the amount of household income stated on their loan application. The system has helped Elektra grow at a compound annual rate of 133 percent between 2002 and 2007. In addition, Grupo Elektra's Banco Azteca had a loan repayment rate of 90 percent in 2006.

    Shanda, a Chinese producer of massively multiplayer online role-playing games (MMORPGs), has overcome China's lack of an established credit card network by selling prepaid access cards through local merchants. The company's focus on online games also addresses shortcomings in China's software piracy laws. Emerge Logistics has used its understanding of China's extensive government bureaucracy and fragmented network of delivery services to deliver goods for multinationals doing business in China. Many foreign firms have found it difficult to get their goods to market, since the average Chinese trucking company owns only one or two trucks. An India-based electronics company has been able to carve out a market niche for itself by developing an all-in-one business machine designed especially for India's 1.2 million small shopkeepers that tolerates the frequent power outages in that country.[33]

2. *Utilize keen understanding of local customer needs and preferences to create customized products or services.* In many emerging markets, multinationals find it difficult to attract the business of customers unable to pay global prices. When emerging markets are largely made up of customers who are satisfied with local standard or near-global standard products, a good strategy option is to concentrate on customers who prefer a local touch and to accept the loss of customers attracted to global brands.[34] In many cases, a local company enjoys a significant cost advantage over global rivals (perhaps because of simpler product design or lower operating and overhead costs), allowing it to compete on the basis of price. Also, a local company may be able to astutely exploit its local orientation—its familiarity with local preferences, its expertise in traditional products, its long-standing customer relationships.

    A small Middle Eastern cell phone manufacturer competes successfully against industry giants Nokia, Samsung, and Motorola by selling a model designed especially for Muslims—it is loaded with the Koran, alerts people at prayer times, and is equipped with a compass that points them toward Mecca. Shenzhen-based Tencent has become the leader in instant messaging in China, with a 70 to 80 percent share of the market in 2006, through its unique understanding of Chinese behavior and culture. Chinese consumers are among the most frequent users of instant messaging and use cybercommunities to express their individuality. The company generated more than $375 million in revenues in 2006 by allowing its 220 million QQ instant messengers to customize their digital avatars used during messaging and chat sessions with an extensive array of outfits and accessories (including digital cars). Users were allowed to download QQ for free but were required to pay 1–2 yuan (about 15–30 cents) for each accessory.

3. *Take advantage of low-cost labor and other competitively important local work-force qualities.* Local companies that lack the technological capabilities possessed by multinational entrants to emerging markets may be able to rely on low-cost labor or knowledge of the capabilities of the local labor force to offset any cost disadvantage. Focus Media is China's largest outdoor advertising firm and has relied on access to China's low-cost labor to update its 130,000 liquid crystal displays (LCDs) and billboards in 90 cities. While multinationals operating in China use electronically networked screens that allow messages to be changed remotely, Focus uses an army of employees who ride to each display by bicycle to change advertisements with programming contained on a USB flash drive or DVD. Indian information technology firms such as Infosys Technologies and Satyam Computer Services have been able to keep personnel costs lower than multinational competitors EDS and Accenture because of their familiarity with local labor markets. While multinationals have focused recruiting efforts in urban centers like Bangalore and Delhi and have subsequently helped to drive up engineering and computer science salaries in such cities, local companies have shifted recruiting efforts to second-tier cities that are unfamiliar to foreign firms.

4. *Use acquisition and rapid growth strategies to better defend against expansion-minded multinationals.* With the growth potential of emerging markets such as China, India, and Brazil obvious to the world, local companies must attempt to develop scale as quickly as possible to defend against the stronger multinationals' arsenal of resources. Most successful regional companies in emerging markets have pursued mergers and acquisitions at a rapid-fire pace to build a nationwide presence. Acquisitions allow small firms to broaden product offerings and achieve the economies of scale necessary to compete against global rivals. For example, Focus Media built its network of 130,000 LCDs in China through multiple acquisitions and, by 2006, held a 2-to-1 advantage over Clear Channel Communications in terms of total number of displays in China. Chinese baby-related products manufacturer and marketer Goodbaby had defended itself against foreign entrants by setting up company offices in 35 cities to establish broad distribution across China. In 2008, Goodbaby's 1,500 products that included strollers, baby monitors, bicycles, and toys were sold in more than 4,000 retail locations in throughout China.

5. *Transfer company expertise to cross-border markets and initiate actions to contend on a global level.* When a company has resource strengths and capabilities suitable for competing in other country markets, launching initiatives to transfer its expertise to cross-border markets becomes a viable strategic option.[35] Televisa, Mexico's largest media company, used its expertise in Spanish culture and linguistics to become the world's most prolific producer of Spanish-language soap operas. Jollibee Foods, a family-owned company with 56 percent of the fast-food business in the Philippines, combated McDonald's entry first by upgrading service and delivery standards and then by using its expertise in seasoning hamburgers with garlic and soy sauce and making noodle and rice meals with fish to open outlets catering to Asian residents in Hong Kong, the Middle East, and California.

ILLUSTRATION CAPSULE 7.4
How Ctrip Successfully Defended against Multinationals to Become China's Largest Online Travel Agency

Ctrip has used a business model tailored to the Chinese travel market, its access to low-cost labor, and its unique understanding of customer preferences and buying habits to build scale rapidly and defeat foreign rivals such as Expedia and Travelocity in becoming the largest travel agency in China. The company was founded in 1999 with a focus on business travelers, since corporate travel accounts for the majority of China's travel bookings. The company also placed little emphasis on online transactions since, at the time, there was no national ticketing system in China, most hotels did not belong to a national or global chain, and most consumers preferred paper tickets to electronic tickets. To overcome this infrastructure shortcoming, the company established its own central database of 5,600 hotels located throughout China and flight information for all major airlines operating in China. Ctrip set up a call center of 3,000 representatives that could use its proprietary database to provide travel information for up to 100,000 customers per day. Because most of its transactions were not done over the Internet, the company hired couriers in all major cities in China to ride by bicycle or scooter to collect payments and deliver tickets to Ctrip's corporate customers. Ctrip also initiated a loyalty program that provided gifts and incentives to the administrative personnel who arranged travel for business executives. In 2006, more than 70 percent of Ctrip's bookings came from off-line reservations made by business customers.

Sources: Based on information in Arindam K. Bhattacharya and David C. Michael, "How Local Companies Keep Multinationals at Bay," *Harvard Business Review* 86, no. 3 (March 2008), pp. 85–95.

If a local company in an emerging market has transferable resources and capabilities, it can sometimes launch successful initiatives to meet the pressures for globalization head-on and start to compete on a global level itself.[36] When General Motors (GM) decided to outsource the production of radiator caps for all of its North American vehicles, Sundaram Fasteners of India pursued the opportunity; it purchased one of GM's radiator cap production lines, moved it to India, and became GM's sole supplier of radiator caps in North America—at 5 million units a year. As a participant in GM's supplier network, Sundaram learned about emerging technical standards, built its capabilities, and became one of the first Indian companies to achieve QS 9000 certification, a quality standard that GM now requires for all suppliers. Sundaram's acquired expertise in quality standards enabled it then to pursue opportunities to supply automotive parts in Japan and Europe. Haier became the leader in the appliance industry in China through its low-cost manufacturing capabilities and its intimate understanding of consumer needs. Rather than producing only traditional washing machines and dryers, Haier produced small appliances that met just about any type of consumer need. For example, the company produces a tiny washer that cleans a single set of clothes that has become very popular in regions of China where humidity is very high and people tend to change clothes often. Haier has transferred its expertise in producing low-cost specialty appliances to meet the unique needs of consumers in Europe and North America. Haier's air conditioners, wine cellars, mini refrigerators, beer keg cooler/dispensers, and other compact appliances—which can be found in the United States at The Home Depot, Best Buy, and Wal-Mart—are best-sellers in their categories.

Illustration Capsule 7.4 discusses how a travel agency in China used a combination of these five strategies to become that country's largest travel consolidator and online travel agent.

KEY POINTS

Most issues in competitive strategy that apply to domestic companies apply also to companies that compete internationally. But there are four strategic issues unique to competing across national boundaries:

1. Whether to customize the company's offerings in each different country market to match the tastes and preferences of local buyers or offer a mostly standardized product worldwide.

2. Whether to employ essentially the same basic competitive strategy in all countries or modify the strategy country by country to fit the specific market conditions and competitive circumstances it encounters.

3. Where to locate the company's production facilities, distribution centers, and customer service operations so as to realize the greatest locational advantages.

4. How to efficiently transfer the company's resource strengths and capabilities from one country to another in an effort to secure competitive advantage.

Strategy options for competing in world markets include maintaining a national (one-country) production base and exporting goods to foreign markets, licensing foreign firms to use the company's technology or produce and distribute the company's products, employing a franchising strategy, using strategic alliances or other collaborative partnerships to enter a foreign market or strengthen a firm's competitiveness in world markets, following a multicountry strategy, or following a global strategy.

Strategic alliances with foreign partners have appeal from several angles: gaining wider access to attractive country markets, allowing capture of economies of scale in production and/or marketing, filling gaps in technical expertise and/or knowledge of local markets, saving on costs by sharing distribution facilities and dealer networks, helping gain agreement on important technical standards, and helping combat the impact of alliances that rivals have formed.

Multicountry competition refers to situations where competition in one national market is largely independent of competition in another national market—there is no "international market," just a collection of self-contained country (or maybe regional) markets. Global competition exists when competitive conditions across national markets are linked strongly enough to form a true world market and when leading competitors compete head-to-head in many different countries.

Once a company has chosen to establish international operations, it has three basic options: (1) a think-local, act-local approach to crafting a strategy; (2) a think-global, act-global approach to crafting a strategy; and (3) a combination think-global, act-local approach. A *think-local, act-local* strategy is appropriate for industries where multicountry competition dominates; a localized approach to strategy making calls for a company to vary its product offering and competitive approach from country to country in order to accommodate differing buyer preferences and market conditions. A *think-global, act-global* approach works best in markets that are globally competitive or beginning to globalize; global strategies involve employing the same basic competitive approach (low-cost, differentiation, best-cost, focused) in all country markets and marketing essentially the same products under the same brand names in all countries where the company operates. A *think-global, act-local* approach can be used when it is feasible for a company to employ essentially the same basic competitive strategy in all markets but still customize its product offering and some aspect of its operations to fit local market circumstances.

There are three ways in which a firm can gain competitive advantage (or offset domestic disadvantages) in global markets. One way involves locating various value chain activities among nations in a manner that lowers costs or achieves greater product differentiation. A second way involves efficient and effective transfer of competitively valuable competencies and capabilities from its domestic markets to foreign markets. A third way draws on a multinational or global competitor's ability to deepen or broaden its resource strengths and capabilities and to coordinate its dispersed activities in ways that a domestic-only competitor cannot.

Companies racing for global leadership have to consider competing in emerging markets like China, India, Brazil, Indonesia, and Mexico—countries where the business risks are considerable but the opportunities for growth are huge. To succeed in these markets, companies often have to (1) compete on the basis of low price, (2) be prepared to modify aspects of the company's business model or strategy to accommodate local circumstances (but not so much that the company loses the advantage of global scale and global branding), and/or (3) try to change the local market to better match the way the company does business elsewhere. Profitability is unlikely to come quickly or easily in emerging markets, typically because of the investments needed to alter buying habits and tastes and/or the need for infrastructure upgrades. And there may be times when a company should simply stay away from certain emerging markets until conditions for entry are better suited to its business model and strategy.

Local companies in emerging country markets can seek to compete against multinational companies by (1) developing business models that exploit shortcomings in local distribution networks or infrastructure, (2) utilizing understanding of local customer needs and preferences to create customized products or services, (3) taking advantage of low-cost labor and other competitively important qualities of the local workforce, (4) using economies of scope and scale to better defend against expansion-minded multinationals, or (5) transferring company expertise to cross-border markets and taking initiatives to compete on a global level themselves.

ASSURANCE OF LEARNING EXERCISES

1. Harley-Davidson has chosen to compete in various country markets in Europe and Asia using an export strategy. Read the sections of its latest annual report at www.harley-davidson.com related to its international operations. Why has the company avoided developing production facilities outside the United States?

2. Log on to www.ford.co.uk and review the information provided under the Vehicles and Company pull-down menus. Given this information and what you know about Ford's operations in North America, does it appear that Ford is pursuing a global strategy or a localized multicountry strategy? Support your answer.

3. The Hero Group is among the 10 largest corporations in India, with 19 business segments and annual revenues of $3.19 billion in fiscal 2005–2006. Many of the corporation's business units have used strategic alliances with foreign partners to compete in new product and geographic markets. Review the company's statements concerning its alliances and international business operations at www.herogroup.com/alliance.htm and prepare a two-page report that outlines the Hero Group's successful use of international strategic alliances.

4. Assume you are in charge of developing the strategy for a multinational company selling products in some 50 different countries around the world. One of the issues you face is whether to employ a multicountry strategy or a global strategy.

   a. If your company's product is personal computers, do you think it would make better strategic sense to employ a multicountry strategy or a global strategy? Why?

   b. If your company's product is dry soup mixes and canned soups, would a multicountry strategy seem to be more advisable than a global strategy? Why?

   c. If your company's product is washing machines, would it seem to make more sense to pursue a multicountry strategy or a global strategy? Why?

   d. If your company's product is basic work tools (hammers, screwdrivers, pliers, wrenches, saws), would a multicountry strategy or a global strategy seem to have more appeal? Why?

EXERCISES FOR SIMULATION PARTICIPANTS

The questions below are for simulation participants whose companies operate in an international or global market arena. If your company competes only in a single country, then skip the questions in this section.

1. Is the international market arena in which your company competes characterized by multicountry competition or global competition? Explain.

2. Which of the strategies for competing in foreign markets is your company employing?

3. Which one of the following best describes the strategic approach your company is taking in trying to compete successfully?

- Think local, act local
- Think global, act local
- Think global, act global

Explain your answer.

4. To what extent, if any, have you and your co-managers adapted your company's strategy to take shifting exchange rates into account? In other words, have you undertaken any actions to try to minimize the impact of adverse shifts in exchange rates?

5. To what extent, if any, have you and your co-managers adapted your company's strategy to take geographic differences in import tariffs or import duties into account?

8 Diversification

Strategies for Managing a Group of Businesses

LEARNING OBJECTIVES

1. Understand when and how business diversification can enhance shareholder value.

2. Gain an understanding of how related diversification strategies can produce cross-business strategic fits capable of delivering competitive advantage.

3. Become aware of the merits and risks of corporate strategies keyed to unrelated diversification.

4. Gain command of the analytical tools for evaluating a company's diversification strategy.

5. Become familiar with a company's five main corporate strategy options after it has diversified.

In this chapter, we move up one level in the strategy-making hierarchy, from strategy making in a single-business enterprise to strategy making in a diversified enterprise. Because a diversified company is a collection of individual businesses, the strategy-making task is more complicated. In a one-business company, managers have to come up with a plan for competing successfully in only a single industry environment—the result is what we labeled in Chapter 2 as *business strategy* (or *business-level strategy*). But in a diversified company, the strategy-making challenge involves assessing multiple industry environments and developing a *set* of business strategies, one for each industry arena in which the diversified company operates. And top executives at a diversified company must still go one step further and devise a companywide or *corporate strategy* for improving the attractiveness and performance of the company's overall business lineup and for making a rational whole out of its diversified collection of individual businesses.

In most diversified companies, corporate-level executives delegate considerable strategy-making authority to the heads of each business, usually giving them the latitude to craft a business strategy suited to their particular industry and competitive circumstances and holding them accountable for producing good results. But the task of crafting a diversified company's overall or corporate strategy falls squarely in the lap of top-level executives and involves four distinct facets:

1. *Picking new industries to enter and deciding on the means of entry*—The first concerns in diversifying are what new industries to get into and whether to enter by starting a new business from the ground up, acquiring a company already in the target industry, or forming a joint venture or strategic alliance with another company. A company can diversify narrowly into a few industries or broadly into many industries. The choice of whether to enter an industry via (*a*) a start-up operation; (*b*) a joint venture; or (*c*) an acquisition of an established leader, an up-and-coming company, or a troubled company with turnaround potential shapes what position the company will initially stake out for itself.

2. *Initiating actions to boost the combined performance of the businesses the firm has entered*—As positions are created in the chosen industries, corporate strategists typically zero in on ways to strengthen the long-term competitive positions and profits of the businesses the firm has invested in. Corporate parents can help their business subsidiaries by providing financial resources, by supplying missing skills, or technological

know-how or managerial expertise to better perform key value chain activities, and by providing new avenues for cost reduction. They can also acquire another company in the same industry and merge the two operations into a stronger business, or acquire new businesses that strongly complement existing businesses. Typically, a diversified company will pursue rapid-growth strategies in its most promising businesses, initiate turnaround efforts in weak-performing businesses with potential, and divest businesses that are no longer attractive or that don't fit into management's long-range plans.

3. *Pursuing opportunities to leverage cross-business value chain relationships and strategic fits into competitive advantage*—A company that diversifies into businesses with competitively important value chain matchups (pertaining to technology, supply chain logistics, production, overlapping distribution channels, or common customers) gains competitive advantage potential not open to a company that diversifies into businesses whose value chains are totally unrelated. Capturing this competitive advantage potential requires that corporate strategists spend considerable time trying to capitalize on such cross-business opportunities as transferring skills or technology from one business to another, reducing costs via sharing use of common facilities and resources, and utilizing the company's well-known brand names and distribution muscle to grow the sales of newly acquired products.

4. *Establishing investment priorities and steering corporate resources into the most attractive business units*—A diversified company's different businesses are usually not equally attractive from the standpoint of investing additional funds. It is incumbent on corporate management to (*a*) decide on the priorities for investing capital in the company's different businesses, (*b*) channel resources into areas where earnings potentials are higher and away from areas where they are lower, and (*c*) divest business units that are chronically poor performers or are in an increasingly unattractive industry. Divesting poor performers and businesses in unattractive industries frees up unproductive investments either for redeployment to promising business units or for financing attractive new acquisitions.

The demanding and time-consuming nature of these four tasks explains why corporate executives generally refrain from becoming immersed in the details of crafting and implementing business-level strategies, preferring instead to delegate lead responsibility for business strategy to the heads of each business unit.

In the first portion of this chapter we describe the various means a company can use to become diversified and explore the pros and cons of related versus unrelated diversification strategies. The second part of the chapter looks at how to evaluate the attractiveness of a diversified company's business lineup, decide whether it has a good diversification strategy, and identify ways to improve its performance. In the chapter's concluding section, we survey the strategic options open to already-diversified companies.

WHEN TO DIVERSIFY

So long as a company has its hands full trying to capitalize on profitable growth opportunities in its present industry, there is no urgency to pursue diversification. The big risk of a single-business company, of course, is having all of the firm's eggs in one industry basket. If demand for the industry's product is eroded by the appearance of alternative technologies, substitute products, or fast-shifting buyer preferences, or if the industry becomes competitively unattractive and unprofitable, then a company's prospects can quickly dim. Consider, for example, what growing use of debit cards and online bill payment have done to the check printing business; what iPods, other brands of digital music players, and online music stores have done to the business outlook for the retailers of music CDs; and what cell phone companies and marketers of Voice over Internet Protocol (VoIP) have done to the revenues of such once-dominant long-distance providers as AT&T, British Telecommunications, and Japan's NTT.

Thus, diversifying into new industries always merits strong consideration whenever a single-business company encounters diminishing market opportunities and stagnating sales in its principal business—most landline-based telecommunications companies across the world are quickly diversifying their product offerings to include wireless and VoIP services. In addition, there are four other instances in which a company becomes a prime candidate for diversifying:[1]

1. When it spots opportunities for expanding into industries whose technologies and products complement its present business.
2. When it can leverage existing competencies and capabilities by expanding into businesses where these same resource strengths are key success factors and valuable competitive assets.
3. When diversifying into closely related businesses opens new avenues for reducing costs.
4. When it has a powerful and well-known brand name that can be transferred to the products of other businesses and thereby used as a lever for driving up the sales and profits of such businesses.

The decision to diversify presents wide-open possibilities. A company can diversify into closely related businesses or into totally unrelated businesses. It can diversify its present revenue and earning base to a small extent (such that new businesses account for less than 15 percent of companywide revenues and profits) or to a major extent (such that new businesses produce 30 or more percent of revenues and profits). It can move into one or two large new businesses or a greater number of small ones. It can achieve multibusiness/multi-industry status by acquiring an existing company already in a business/industry it wants to enter, starting up a new business subsidiary from scratch, or forming a joint venture with one or more companies to enter new businesses.

BUILDING SHAREHOLDER VALUE: THE ULTIMATE JUSTIFICATION FOR DIVERSIFYING

Diversification must do more for a company than simply spread its business risk across various industries. In principle, diversification cannot be considered a success unless it results in *added shareholder value*—value that shareholders cannot capture on their own by purchasing stock in companies in different industries or investing in mutual funds so as to spread their investments across several industries.

For there to be reasonable expectations that a company's diversification efforts can produce added value, a move to diversify into a new business must pass three tests:[2]

1. *The industry attractiveness test*—The industry to be entered must be attractive enough to yield consistently good returns on investment. Whether an industry is attractive depends chiefly on the presence of industry and competitive conditions that are conducive to earning as good or better profits and return on investment as the company is earning in its present business(es). It is hard to justify diversifying into an industry where profit expectations are *lower* than in the company's present businesses.

2. *The cost-of-entry test*—The cost to enter the target industry must not be so high as to erode the potential for good profitability. A catch-22 can prevail here, however. The more attractive an industry's prospects are for growth and good long-term profitability, the more expensive it can be to get into. Entry barriers for start-up companies are likely to be high in attractive industries; were barriers low, a rush of new entrants would soon erode the potential for high profitability. And buying a well-positioned company in an appealing industry often entails a high acquisition cost that makes passing the cost-of-entry test less likely. For instance, suppose that the price to purchase a company is $3 million and that the company is earning after-tax profits of $200,000 on an equity investment of $1 million (a 20 percent annual return). Simple arithmetic requires that the profits be tripled if the purchaser (paying $3 million) is to earn the same 20 percent return. Building the acquired firm's earnings from $200,000 to $600,000 annually could take several years—and require additional investment on which the purchaser would also have to earn a 20 percent return. Since the owners of a successful and growing company usually demand a price that reflects their business's profit prospects, it's easy for such an acquisition to fail the cost-of-entry test.

3. *The better-off test*—Diversifying into a new business must offer potential for the company's existing businesses and the new business to perform better together under a single corporate umbrella than they would perform operating as independent, stand-alone businesses. For example, let's say that company A diversifies by purchasing company B in another industry. If A and B's consolidated profits in the years to come prove no greater than what each could have earned on its own, then A's diversification won't provide its shareholders with added value. Company A's shareholders could have achieved the same $1 + 1 = 2$ result by merely purchasing stock in company B. Shareholder value is not created by diversification unless it produces a $1 + 1 = 3$ effect where sister businesses *perform better together* as part of the same firm than they could have performed as independent companies.

> **CORE CONCEPT**
> Creating added value for shareholders via diversification requires building a multibusiness company where the whole is greater than the sum of its parts.

Diversification moves that satisfy all three tests have the greatest potential to grow shareholder value over the long term. Diversification moves that can pass only one or two tests are suspect.

STRATEGIES FOR ENTERING NEW BUSINESSES

The means of entering new businesses can take any of three forms: acquisition, internal start-up, or joint ventures with other companies.

Acquisition of an Existing Business

Acquisition is the most popular means of diversifying into another industry. Not only is it quicker than trying to launch a brand-new operation, but it also offers an effective way to hurdle such entry barriers as acquiring technological know-how, establishing supplier relationships, becoming big enough to match rivals' efficiency and unit costs, having to spend large sums on introductory advertising and promotions, and securing adequate distribution. Buying an ongoing operation allows the acquirer to move directly to the task of building a strong market position in the target industry rather than getting bogged down in going the internal start-up route and trying to develop the knowledge, resources, scale of operation, and market reputation necessary to become an effective competitor within a few years.

The big dilemma an acquisition-minded firm faces is whether to pay a premium price for a successful company or to buy a struggling company at a bargain price.[3] If the buying firm has little knowledge of the industry but ample capital, it is often better off purchasing a capable, strongly positioned firm—unless the price of such an acquisition is prohibitive and flunks the cost-of-entry test. However, when the acquirer sees promising ways to transform a weak firm into a strong one and has the resources, the know-how, and the patience to do it, a struggling company can be the better long-term investment.

Internal Start-Up

Achieving diversification through *internal start-up* involves building a new business subsidiary from scratch. This entry option takes longer than the acquisition option and poses some hurdles. A newly formed business unit not only has to overcome entry barriers but also has to invest in new production capacity, develop sources of supply, hire and train employees, build channels of distribution, grow a customer base, and so on. Generally, forming a start-up subsidiary to enter a new business has appeal only when (1) the parent company already has in-house most or all of the skills and resources it needs to piece together a new business and compete effectively; (2) there is ample time to launch the business; (3) internal entry has lower costs than entry via acquisition; (4) the targeted industry is populated with many relatively small firms such that the new start-up does not have to compete head-to-head against larger, more powerful rivals; (5) adding new production capacity will not adversely impact the supply–demand balance in the industry; and (6) incumbent firms are likely to be slow or ineffective in responding to a new entrant's efforts to crack the market.[4]

> The biggest drawbacks to entering an industry by forming an internal start-up are the costs of over-coming entry barriers and the extra time it takes to build a strong and profitable competitive position.

Joint Ventures

Joint ventures entail forming a new corporate entity owned by two or more companies, where the purpose of the joint venture is to pursue a mutually attractive opportunity. The terms and conditions of a joint venture concern joint operation of a mutually owned business, which tends to make the arrangement more definitive and perhaps more durable than a strategic alliance—in a strategic alliance, the arrangement between the partners is one of limited collaboration for a limited purpose and a partner can choose to simply walk away or reduce its commitment to collaborating at any time.

A joint venture to enter a new business can be useful in at least three types of situations.[5] First, a joint venture is a good vehicle for pursuing an opportunity that is too complex, uneconomical, or risky for one company to pursue alone. Second, joint ventures make sense when the opportunities in a new industry require a broader range of competencies and know-how than a company can marshal. Many of the opportunities in satellite-based telecommunications, biotechnology, and network-based systems that blend hardware, software, and services call for the coordinated development of complementary innovations and tackling an intricate web of financial, technical, political, and regulatory factors simultaneously. In such cases, pooling the resources and competencies of two or more companies is a wiser and less risky way to proceed.

Third, companies sometimes use joint ventures to diversify into a new industry when the diversification move entails having operations in a foreign country—several governments require foreign companies operating within their borders to have a local partner that has minority, if not majority, ownership in the local operations. Aside from fulfilling host government ownership requirements, companies usually seek out a local partner with expertise and other resources that will aid the success of the newly established local operation.

However, as discussed in Chapters 6 and 7, partnering with another company—in the form of either a joint venture or a collaborative alliance—has significant drawbacks due to the potential for conflicting objectives, disagreements over how to best operate the venture, culture clashes, and so on. Joint ventures are generally the least durable of the entry options, usually lasting only until the partners decide to go their own ways.

CHOOSING THE DIVERSIFICATION PATH: RELATED VERSUS UNRELATED BUSINESSES

Once a company decides to diversify, its first big strategy decision is whether to diversify into related businesses, unrelated businesses, or some mix of both (see Figure 8.1). **Related businesses** are those whose value chains possess competitively valuable cross-business relationships that present opportunities for the businesses to perform better under the same corporate umbrella than they could by operating as stand-alone entities. The big appeal of related diversification is to build shareholder value by leveraging these cross-business relationships into competitive advantage, thus allowing the company as a whole to perform better than just the sum of its individual businesses. **Unrelated businesses** are those whose value chain activities are so dissimilar that no competitively valuable cross-business relationships are present.

The next two sections explore the ins and outs of related and unrelated diversification.

THE CASE FOR DIVERSIFYING INTO RELATED BUSINESSES

A related diversification strategy involves building the company around businesses whose value chains possess competitively valuable strategic fits, as shown in Figure 8.2. **Strategic fit** exists whenever one or more activities comprising the value chains of different businesses are sufficiently similar as to present opportunities for:[6]

- Transferring competitively valuable expertise, technological know-how, or other capabilities from one business to another.

Figure 8.1 Strategy Alternatives for a Company Looking to Diversify

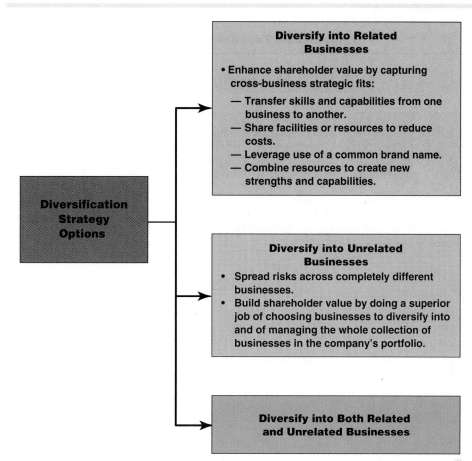

Combining the related value chain activities of separate businesses into a single operation to achieve lower costs. For instance, it is often feasible to manufacture the products of different businesses in a single plant or use the same warehouses for shipping and distribution or have a single sales force for the products of different businesses (because they are marketed to the same types of customers).

Exploiting common use of a well-known and potent brand name. For example, Yamaha's name in motorcycles gave it instant credibility and recognition in entering the personal watercraft business, allowing it to achieve a significant market share without spending large sums on advertising to establish a brand identity for the WaveRunner. Apple's reputation for producing easy-to-operate computers was a competitive asset that facilitated the company's diversification into digital music players. Sony's name in consumer electronics made it easier for it to enter the market for video games with its PlayStation console and lineup of PlayStation video games.

Cross-business collaboration to create competitively valuable resource strengths and capabilities.

> **CORE CONCEPT**
>
> **Strategic fit** exists when the value chains of different businesses present opportunities for cross-business resource transfer, lower costs through combining the performance of related value chain activities, cross-business use of a potent brand name, and cross-business collaboration to build new or stronger competitive capabilities.

Figure 8.2   Related Businesses Possess Related Value Chain Activities and Competitively Valuable Strategic Fits

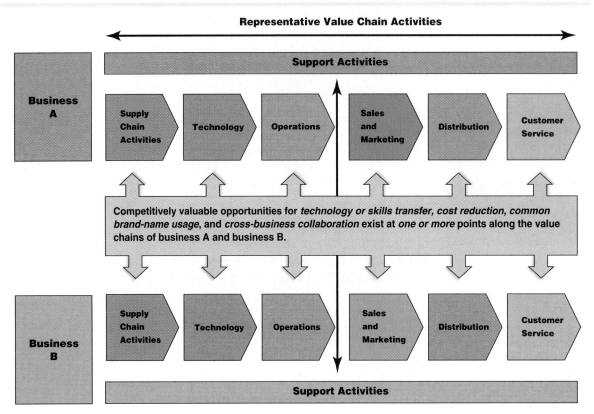

Related diversification thus has strategic appeal from several angles. It allows a firm to reap the competitive advantage benefits of skills transfer, lower costs, a powerful brand name, and/or stronger competitive capabilities and still spread investor risks over a broad business base. Furthermore, the relatedness among the different businesses provides sharper focus for managing diversification and a useful degree of strategic unity across the company's various business activities.

Identifying Cross-Business Strategic Fits along the Value Chain

Cross-business strategic fits can exist anywhere along the value chain: in R&D and technology activities, in supply chain activities and relationships with suppliers, in manufacturing, in sales and marketing, in distribution activities, or in administrative support activities.[7]

Strategic Fits in R&D and Technology Activities   Diversifying into businesses where there is potential for sharing common technology, exploiting the full range of business opportunities associated with a particular technology and its derivatives, or transferring technological know-how from one business to another has considerable appeal. Businesses with technology-sharing benefits can perform better together than apart because of potential cost savings in R&D and potentially shorter times in getting new products to market; also, technological advances in one business can lead to increased sales for both. Technological innovations have been the driver behind the efforts of cable TV companies to diversify into high-speed Internet access (via the use of cable modems) and, further, to explore providing local and long-distance telephone service to residential and commercial customers via either a single wire or VoIP technology.

Strategic Fits in Supply Chain Activities   Businesses that have supply chain strategic fits can perform better together because of the potential for skills transfer in procuring materials, greater bargaining power in negotiating with common suppliers, the benefits of added collaboration with common supply chain partners, and/or added leverage with shippers in securing volume discounts on incoming parts and components. Dell's strategic partnerships with leading suppliers of microprocessors, circuit boards, disk drives, memory chips, flat-panel displays, wireless capabilities, long-life batteries, and other PC-related components have been an important element of the company's strategy to diversify into servers, data storage devices, networking components, and LCD TVs—products that include many components common to PCs and that can be sourced from the same strategic partners that provide Dell with PC components.

Manufacturing-Related Strategic Fits   Cross-business strategic fits in manufacturing-related activities can represent an important source of competitive advantage in situations where a diversifier's expertise in quality manufacture and cost-efficient production methods can be transferred to another business. When Emerson Electric diversified into the chain-saw business, it transferred its expertise in low-cost manufacturing to its newly acquired Beaird-Poulan business division; the transfer drove Beaird-Poulan's new strategy—to be the low-cost provider of chain-saw products—and fundamentally changed the way Beaird-Poulan chain saws were designed and manufactured. Another benefit of production-related value chain match-ups is the ability to consolidate production into a smaller number of plants and significantly reduce overall production costs. When snowmobile maker Bombardier diversified into motorcycles, it was able to set up motorcycle assembly lines in the same manufacturing facility where it was assembling snowmobiles. When Smucker's acquired Procter & Gamble's Jif peanut butter business, it was able to combine the manufacture of its own Smucker's peanut butter products with those of Jif—plus, it gained greater leverage with vendors in purchasing its peanut supplies.

Distribution-Related Strategic Fits   Businesses with closely related distribution activities can perform better together than apart because of potential cost savings in sharing the same distribution facilities or using many of the same wholesale distributors and retail dealers to access customers. When Conair Corporation acquired Allegro Manufacturing's travel bag and travel accessory business in 2007, it was able to consolidate its own distribution centers for hair dryers and curling irons with those of Allegro, thereby generating cost savings for both businesses. Likewise, since Conair products and Allegro's neck rests, ear plugs, luggage tags, and toiletry kits were sold by the same types of retailers (discount stores, supermarket chains, and drugstore chains), Conair was able to convince many of the retailers not carrying Allegro products to take on the line.

Strategic Fits in Sales and Marketing Activities Various cost-saving opportunities spring from diversifying into businesses with closely related sales and marketing activities. The same distribution centers can be utilized for warehousing and shipping the products of different businesses. When the products are sold directly to the same customers, sales costs can often be reduced by using a single sales force and avoiding having two different salespeople call on the same customer. The products of related businesses can be promoted at the same Web site, and included in the same media ads and sales brochures. After-sale service and repair organizations for the products of closely related businesses can often be consolidated into a single operation. There may be opportunities to reduce costs by consolidating order processing and billing and using common promotional tie-ins (cents-off couponing, free samples and trial offers, seasonal specials, and the like). When global power-tool maker Black & Decker acquired Vector Products, it was able to use its own global sales force and distribution facilities to sell and distribute the newly acquired Vector power inverters, vehicle battery chargers, and rechargeable spotlights because the types of customers that carried its power tools (discounters like Wal-Mart and Target, home centers, and hardware stores) also stocked the types of products produced by Vector.

A second category of benefits arises when different businesses use similar sales and marketing approaches; in such cases, there may be competitively valuable opportunities to transfer selling, merchandising, advertising, and product differentiation skills from one business to another. Procter & Gamble's product lineup includes Folgers coffee, Tide laundry detergent, Crest toothpaste, Ivory soap, Charmin toilet tissue, Gillette razors and blades, Duracell batteries, Oral-B toothbrushes, and Head & Shoulders shampoo. All of these have different competitors and different supply chain and production requirements, but they all move through the same wholesale distribution systems, are sold in common retail settings to the same shoppers, are advertised and promoted in much the same ways, and require the same marketing and merchandising skills.

Strategic Fits in Managerial and Administrative Support Activities Often, different businesses require comparable types managerial know-how, thereby allowing know-how in one line of business to be transferred to another. At General Electric (GE), managers who were involved in GE's expansion into Russia were able to expedite entry because of information gained from GE managers involved in expansions into other emerging markets. The lessons GE managers learned in China were passed along to GE managers in Russia, allowing them to anticipate that the Russian government would demand that GE build production capacity in the country rather than enter the market through exporting or licensing. In addition, GE's managers in Russia were better able to develop realistic performance expectations and make tough upfront decisions since experience in China and elsewhere warned them (1) that there would likely be increased short-term costs during the early years of start-up and (2) that if GE committed to the Russian market for the long term and aided the country's economic development it could eventually expect to be given the freedom to pursue profitable penetration of the Russian market.[8]

Likewise, different businesses can often use the same administrative and customer service infrastructure. For instance, an electric utility that diversifies into natural gas, water, appliance sales and repair services, and home security services can use the same customer data network, the same customer call centers and local offices, the same billing and customer accounting systems, and the same customer service infrastructure to support all of its products and services.

ILLUSTRATION CAPSULE 8.1
Related Diversification at Darden Restaurants, L'Oréal, and Johnson & Johnson

See if you can identify the value chain relationships that make the businesses of the following companies related in competitively relevant ways. In particular, you should consider whether there are cross-business opportunities for (1) skills/technology transfer (2) combining related value chain activities to achieve lower costs, (3) leveraging use of a well-respected brand name, and/or (4) cross-business collaboration to create new resource strengths and capabilities.

DARDEN RESTAURANTS

- Olive Garden restaurant chain (Italian-themed).
- Red Lobster restaurant chain (seafood-themed).
- Longhorn Steakhouse chain (steak-themed).
- Seasons 52 chain (a sophisticated wine bar and grill featuring fresh, flavorful natural foods).
- Bahama Breeze restaurant chain (Caribbean-themed).

L'ORÉAL

- Maybelline, Lancôme, Helena Rubenstein, Kiehl's, Garnier, and Shu Uemura cosmetics.
- L'Oréal and Soft Sheen/Carson hair care products.

- Redken, Matrix, L'Oréal Professional, and Kérastase Paris professional hair care and skin care products.
- Ralph Lauren and Giorgio Armani fragrances.
- Biotherm skin care products.
- La Roche–Posay and Vichy Laboratories dermo-cosmetics.

JOHNSON & JOHNSON

- Baby products (powder, shampoo, oil, lotion).
- Band-Aids and other first-aid products.
- Women's health and personal care products (Stayfree, Carefree, Sure & Natural).
- Neutrogena and Aveeno skin care products.
- Nonprescription drugs (Tylenol, Motrin, Pepcid AC, Mylanta, Monistat).
- Prescription drugs.
- Prosthetic and other medical devices.
- Surgical and hospital products.
- Accuvue contact lenses.

Sources: Company Web sites, annual reports, and 10-K reports.

Illustration Capsule 8.1 lists the businesses of three companies that have pursued a strategy of related diversification.

Strategic Fit, Economies of Scope, and Competitive Advantage

What makes related diversification an attractive strategy is the opportunity to convert cross-business strategic fits into a competitive advantage over business rivals whose operations do not offer comparable strategic-fit benefits. The greater the relatedness among a diversified company's sister businesses, the bigger a company's window for converting strategic fits into competitive advantage via (1) skills transfer, (2) combining related value chain activities to achieve lower costs, (3) leveraging use of a well-respected brand name, and/or (4) cross-business collaboration to create new resource strengths and capabilities.

Economies of Scope: A Path to Competitive Advantage One of the most important competitive advantages that a related diversification strategy can produce is lower costs than competitors. Related businesses often present opportunities to eliminate or reduce the costs of performing certain value chain activities; such cost savings are termed **economies of scope**—a concept distinct from *economies of scale.* Economies of *scale* are cost savings that accrue directly from a larger-sized operation; for example, unit costs may be lower in a large plant than in a small plant, lower in a large distribution center than in a small one, lower for large-volume purchases of components than for small-volume purchases. Economies of *scope,* however, stem directly from cost-saving strategic fits along the value chains of related businesses. Such economies are open only to a multibusiness enterprise and are the result of a related diversification strategy that allows sister businesses to share technology, perform R&D together, use common manufacturing or distribution facilities, share a common sales force or distributor/dealer network, use the same established brand name, and/or share the same administrative infrastructure. *The greater the cross-business economies associated with cost-saving strategic fits, the greater the potential for a related diversification strategy to yield a competitive advantage based on lower costs than rivals.*

From Competitive Advantage to Added Profitability and Gains in Shareholder Value   The competitive advantage potential that flows from economies of scope and the capture of other strategic-fit benefits is what enables a company pursuing related diversification to achieve $1 + 1 = 3$ financial performance and the hoped-for gains in shareholder value. The strategic and business logic is compelling: Capturing strategic fits along the value chains of its related businesses gives a diversified company a clear path to achieving competitive advantage over undiversified competitors and competitors whose own diversification efforts don't offer equivalent strategic-fit benefits.[9] Such competitive advantage potential provides a company with a dependable basis for earning profits and a return on investment that exceed what the company's businesses could earn as stand-alone enterprises. Converting the competitive advantage potential into greater profitability is what fuels $1 + 1 = 3$ gains in shareholder value—the necessary outcome for satisfying the better-off test and proving the business merit of a company's diversification effort.

There are three things to bear in mind here. One, capturing cross-business strategic fits via a strategy of related diversification builds shareholder value in ways that shareholders cannot undertake by simply owning a portfolio of stocks of companies in different industries. Two, the capture of cross-business strategic-fit benefits is possible only via a strategy of related diversification. Three, the benefits of cross-business strategic fits are not automatically realized when a company diversifies into related businesses; *the benefits materialize only after management has successfully pursued internal actions to capture them.*

THE CASE FOR DIVERSIFYING INTO UNRELATED BUSINESSES

An unrelated diversification strategy discounts the merits of pursuing cross-business strategic fits and, instead, focuses squarely on entering and operating businesses in industries that allow the company as a whole to grow its revenues and earnings. Companies that pursue a strategy of unrelated diversification generally exhibit a willingness to diversify into *any industry* where senior managers see *opportunity* to realize

Figure 8.3 Unrelated Businesses Have Unrelated Value Chains and No Strategic Fits

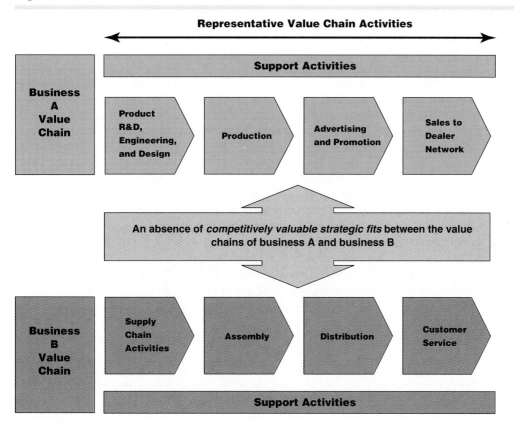

consistently good financial results—*the basic premise of unrelated diversification is that any company or business that can be acquired on good financial terms and that has satisfactory growth and earnings potential represents a good acquisition and a good business opportunity.* Such companies are frequently labeled *conglomerates* because their business interests range broadly across diverse industries.

With a strategy of unrelated diversification, the emphasis is on satisfying the attractiveness and cost-of-entry tests and each business's prospects for good financial performance. As indicated in Figure 8.3, there's no deliberate effort to satisfy the better-off test in the sense of diversifying only into businesses having strategic fits with the firm's other businesses. Thus, with an unrelated diversification strategy, company managers spend much time and effort screening acquisition candidates and evaluating the pros and cons of keeping or divesting existing businesses, using such criteria as:

- Whether the business can meet corporate targets for profitability and return on investment.
- Whether the business is in an industry with attractive growth potential.
- Whether the business is big enough to contribute *significantly* to the parent firm's bottom line.
- Whether the business has burdensome capital requirements (associated with replacing out-of-date plants and equipment, growing the business, and/or providing working capital).

- Whether the business is plagued with chronic union difficulties and labor problems.
- Whether there is industry vulnerability to recession, inflation, high interest rates, tough government regulations concerning product safety or the environment, and other potentially negative factors.

Companies that pursue unrelated diversification nearly always enter new businesses by acquiring an established company rather than by forming a start-up subsidiary within their own corporate structures. The premise of acquisition-minded corporations is that growth by acquisition can deliver enhanced shareholder value through upward-trending corporate revenues and earnings and a stock price that *on average* rises enough year after year to amply reward and please shareholders. Three types of acquisition candidates are usually of particular interest: (1) businesses that have bright growth prospects but are short on investment capital are highly coveted acquisition targets for cash-rich companies scouting for good market opportunities, (2) undervalued companies that can be acquired at a bargain price, and (3) struggling companies whose operations can be turned around with the aid of the parent company's financial resources and managerial know-how.

A key issue in unrelated diversification is how wide a net to cast in building a portfolio of unrelated businesses. In other words, should a company pursuing unrelated diversification seek to have few or many unrelated businesses? How much business diversity can corporate executives successfully manage? A reasonable way to resolve the issue of how much diversification comes from answering two questions: "What is the least diversification it will take to achieve acceptable growth and profitability?" and "What is the most diversification that can be managed, given the complexity it adds?"[10] The optimal amount of diversification usually lies between these two extremes.

Illustration Capsule 8.2 lists the businesses of three companies that have pursued unrelated diversification. Such companies are frequently labeled *conglomerates* because their business interests range broadly across diverse industries.

The Merits of an Unrelated Diversification Strategy

A strategy of unrelated diversification has appeal from several angles:

1. Business risk is scattered over a set of truly *diverse* industries. In comparison to related diversification, unrelated diversification more closely approximates *pure* diversification of financial and business risk because the company's investments are spread over businesses whose technologies and value chain activities bear no close relationship and whose markets are largely disconnected.[11]

2. The company's financial resources can be employed to maximum advantage by (*a*) investing in *whatever industries* offer the best profit prospects (as opposed to considering only opportunities in industries with related value chain activities) and (*b*) diverting cash flows from company businesses with lower growth and profit prospects to acquiring and expanding businesses with higher growth and profit potentials.

3. To the extent that corporate managers are exceptionally astute at spotting bargain-priced companies with big upside profit potential, shareholder wealth can be enhanced by buying distressed businesses at a low price, turning their operations around fairly quickly with infusions of cash and managerial know-how supplied by the parent company, and then riding the crest of the profit increases generated by the newly acquired businesses.

ILLUSTRATION CAPSULE 8.2
Unrelated Diversification at General Electric, Fortune Brands, and United Technologies

The defining characteristic of unrelated diversification is few competitively valuable cross-business relationships. Peruse the business group listings for General Electric, Fortune Brands, and United Technologies and see if you can confirm why these three companies have unrelated diversification strategies.

GENERAL ELECTRIC

- Major household appliances (refrigerators, dishwashers, ranges, cooking tops, ovens, microwaves, clothes washers and dryers).
- Jet engines and aviation services.
- Lighting products and lighting controls.
- Oil and gas equipment.
- Locomotive engines, rail traffic control and dispatch systems, and signaling products.
- Monitoring and video surveillance systems, building access and control systems, and fire detection and security systems for businesses and homes.
- Water treatment systems and water treatment chemicals.
- Rechargeable lithium-ion batteries.
- Advanced materials (engineering thermoplastics, silicon-based products and technology platforms, and fused quartz and ceramics).
- Capital management services and financial products for businesses and consumers, including all types of business loans, operating leases, real estate and equipment financing programs, inventory financing, health care financial services, asset management services, business and consumer credit cards, personal loans and debt consolidation services, home equity loans, commercial insurance, and identity theft protection services.
- Trailer rentals, along with online fleet management and maintenance software.
- Electric power generation equipment and systems, including wind turbines, gas turbines, nuclear power plant equipment, and equipment for fossil-fuel-generating plants.
- Electrical distribution equipment, including power transformers, high-voltage breakers, distribution transformers and breakers, capacitors, relays, regulators, substation equipment, and metering products.
- X-ray and advanced imaging products, medical diagnostic technologies and equipment, patient monitoring systems, disease research, drug discovery, and biopharmaceuticals.
- Media and entertainment—GE's NBC Universal business unit owned and operated the NBC television network, a Spanish-language network (Telemundo), several news and entertainment networks (CNBC, MSNBC, Bravo, Sci-Fi Channel, USA Network), Universal Studios, various television production operations, a group of television stations, and several theme parks.

FORTUNE BRANDS

- Premium spirits—Jim Beam, Maker's Mark, Knob Creek, Canadian Club, and 10 other brands.
- Titleist, Footjoy, Cobra, and Pinnacle golf products.
- Home and hardware businesses, including Moen faucets, Therma Tru doors, Simonton windows, Master Lock security hardware, Master Brand kitchen and bath cabinetry, Waterloo tool storage products, and 10 other home and hardware businesses.

UNITED TECHNOLOGIES

- Pratt & Whitney aircraft engines.
- Carrier heating and air-conditioning equipment.
- Otis elevators and escalators.
- Sikorsky military and commercial helicopters.
- Hamilton Sunstrand aerospace systems.
- UTC fire detection and security systems.

Sources: Company Web sites and 2007 10-K reports.

4. Company profitability may prove somewhat more stable over the course of economic upswings and downswings because market conditions in all industries don't move upward or downward simultaneously—in a broadly diversified company, there's a chance that market downtrends in some of the company's businesses

will be partially offset by cyclical upswings in its other businesses, thus producing somewhat less earnings volatility. (In practice, however, there is no convincing evidence that the consolidated profits of firms with unrelated diversification strategies are more stable or less subject to reversal in periods of recession and economic stress than the profits of firms with related diversification strategies.)

Unrelated diversification certainly merits consideration when a firm is trapped in or overly dependent on an endangered or unattractive industry, especially when it has no competitively valuable resources or capabilities it can transfer to an adjacent industry. A case can also be made for unrelated diversification when a company has a strong preference for spreading business risks widely and not restricting itself to investing in a family of closely related businesses.

Building Shareholder Value via Unrelated Diversification   Given the absence of cross-business strategic fits with which to capture added competitive advantage, the task of building shareholder value via unrelated diversification ultimately hinges on the business acumen of corporate executives. To succeed in using a strategy of unrelated diversification to produce companywide financial results above and beyond what the businesses could generate operating as stand-alone entities, corporate executives must:

- Do a superior job of diversifying into new businesses that can produce consistently good earnings and returns on investment (thereby satisfying the attractiveness test).
- Do an excellent job of negotiating favorable acquisition prices (thereby satisfying the cost-of-entry test).
- Do such a good job overseeing the firm's business subsidiaries and contributing to how they are managed—by providing expert problem-solving skills, creative strategy suggestions, and high-caliber decision-making guidance to the heads of the various business subsidiaries—that the subsidiaries perform at a higher level than they would otherwise be able to do through the efforts of the business-unit heads alone (a possible way to satisfy the better-off test).
- Be shrewd in identifying when to shift resources out of businesses with dim profit prospects and into businesses with above-average prospects for growth and profitability.
- Be good at discerning when a business needs to be sold (because it is on the verge of confronting adverse industry and competitive conditions and probable declines in long-term profitability) and also finding buyers who will pay a price higher than the company's net investment in the business (so that the sale of divested businesses will result in capital gains for shareholders rather than capital losses).

To the extent that corporate executives are able to craft and execute a strategy of unrelated diversification that produces enough of the above outcomes to result in a stream of dividends and capital gains for stockholders greater than a $1 + 1 = 2$ outcome, a case can be made that shareholder value has truly been enhanced.

The Drawbacks of Unrelated Diversification

Unrelated diversification strategies have two important negatives that undercut the pluses: very demanding managerial requirements and limited competitive advantage potential.

Demanding Managerial Requirements   Successfully managing a set of fundamentally different businesses operating in fundamentally different industry and competitive environments is an exceptionally challenging proposition for corporate-level managers. It is difficult because key executives at the corporate level, while perhaps having personally worked in one or two of the company's businesses, rarely have the time and expertise to be sufficiently familiar with all the circumstances surrounding each of the company's businesses to be in a position to give high-caliber guidance to business-level managers. Indeed, the greater the number of businesses a company is in and the more diverse they are, the harder it is for corporate managers to (1) stay abreast of what's happening in each industry and each subsidiary and thus judge whether a particular business has bright prospects or is headed for trouble, (2) know enough about the issues and problems facing each subsidiary to pick business-unit heads having the requisite combination of managerial skills and know-how, (3) be able to tell the difference between those strategic proposals of business-unit managers that are prudent and those that are risky or unlikely to succeed, and (4) know what to do if a business unit stumbles and its results suddenly head downhill.[12]

> **CORE CONCEPT**
> The two biggest drawbacks to unrelated diversification are the difficulties of competently managing many different businesses and being without the added source of competitive advantage that cross-business strategic fit provides.

In a company like General Electric or United Technologies (see Illustration Capsule 8.2) or Tyco International (which acquired over 1,000 companies between 1994 and 2001), corporate executives are constantly scrambling to stay on top of fresh industry developments and the strategic progress and plans of each subsidiary, often depending on briefings by business-level managers for many of the details. As a rule, the more unrelated businesses that a company has diversified into, the more corporate executives depend on briefings from business-unit heads and "managing by the numbers"—that is, keeping a close track on the financial and operating results of each subsidiary and assuming that the heads of the various subsidiaries have most everything under control so long as the latest key financial and operating measures look good. Managing by the numbers works if the heads of the various business units are capable and consistently meet their numbers. The problem comes when things start to go awry in a business despite the best effort of business-unit managers; in that case corporate management has to get deeply involved in turning around a business it does not know all that much about—as the former chairman of a Fortune 500 company advised, "Never acquire a business you don't know how to run." Because every business tends to encounter rough sledding, a good way to gauge the merits of acquiring a company in an unrelated industry is to ask, "If the business got into trouble, is corporate management likely to know how to bail it out?" When the answer is no (or even a qualified yes or maybe), growth via acquisition into unrelated businesses is a chancy strategy.[13] Just one or two unforeseen problems or big strategic mistakes (like misjudging the importance of certain competitive forces or the impact of driving forces or key success factors, not recognizing that a newly acquired business has some serious resource deficiencies and/or competitive shortcomings, or being too optimistic about turning around a struggling subsidiary) can cause a precipitous drop in corporate earnings and crash the parent company's stock price.

Hence, competently overseeing a set of widely diverse businesses can turn out to be much harder than it sounds. In practice, comparatively few companies have proved that they have top management capabilities that are up to the task. There are far more companies whose corporate executives have failed at delivering consistently good financial results with an unrelated diversification strategy than there are companies with corporate executives who have been successful.[14] It is simply very difficult for

Relying solely on the expertise of corporate executives to wisely manage a set of unrelated businesses is *a much weaker foundation for enhancing shareholder value* than is a strategy of related diversification where corporate performance can be boosted by competitively valuable cross-business strategic fits.

corporate executives to achieve $1 + 1 = 3$ gains in shareholder value based on their expertise in (*a*) picking which industries to diversify into and which companies in these industries to acquire, (*b*) shifting resources from low-performing businesses into high-performing businesses, and (*c*) giving high-caliber decision-making guidance to the general managers of their business subsidiaries. The odds are that the result of unrelated diversification will be $1 + 1 = 2$ or less.

Limited Competitive Advantage Potential   The second big negative is that *unrelated diversification offers no potential for competitive advantage beyond what each individual business can generate on its own.* Unlike a related diversification strategy, there are no cross-business strategic fits to draw on for reducing costs, beneficially transferring skills and technology, leveraging use of a powerful brand name, or collaborating to build mutually beneficial competitive capabilities and thereby *adding to any competitive advantage possessed by individual businesses.* Yes, a cash-rich corporate parent pursuing unrelated diversification can provide its subsidiaries with the capital and maybe even the managerial know-how to help resolve problems in particular business units, but otherwise it has little to offer in the way of enhancing the competitive strength of its individual business units. *Without the competitive advantage potential of strategic fits, consolidated performance of an unrelated group of businesses stands to be little or no better than the sum of what the individual business units could achieve if they were independent.*

COMBINATION RELATED–UNRELATED DIVERSIFICATION STRATEGIES

There's nothing to preclude a company from diversifying into both related and unrelated businesses. Indeed, in actual practice the business makeup of diversified companies varies considerably. Some diversified companies are really *dominant-business enterprises*—one major "core" business accounts for 50 to 80 percent of total revenues and a collection of small related or unrelated businesses accounts for the remainder. Some diversified companies are *narrowly diversified* around a few (two to five) related or unrelated businesses. Others are *broadly diversified* around a wide-ranging collection of related businesses, unrelated businesses, or a mixture of both. And a number of multibusiness enterprises have diversified into unrelated areas but have a collection of related businesses within each area—thus giving them a business portfolio consisting of *several unrelated groups of related businesses.* There's ample room for companies to customize their diversification strategies to incorporate elements of both related and unrelated diversification, as may suit their own risk preferences and strategic vision.

The various corporate strategy initiatives that help identify management's approach to building shareholder value through diversification are shown in Figure 8.4. Having a clear fix on the company's current corporate strategy sets the stage for evaluating how good the strategy is and proposing strategic moves to boost the company's performance.

Figure 8.4   Identifying a Diversified Company's Strategy

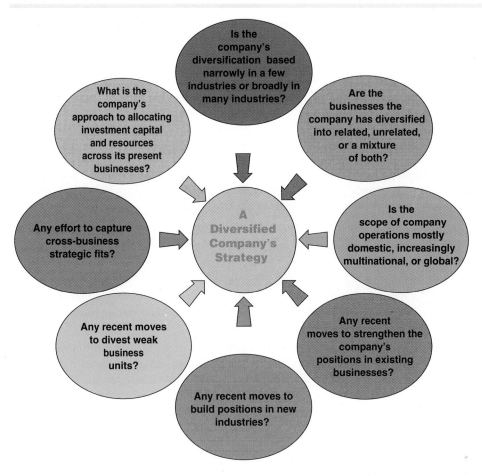

EVALUATING THE STRATEGY OF A DIVERSIFIED COMPANY

Strategic analysis of diversified companies builds on the concepts and methods used for single-business companies. But there are some additional aspects to consider and a couple of new analytical tools to master. The procedure for evaluating the pluses and minuses of a diversified company's strategy and deciding what actions to take to improve the company's performance involves six steps:

1. Assessing the attractiveness of the industries the company has diversified into, both individually and as a group.

2. Assessing the competitive strength of the company's business units and determining how many are strong contenders in their respective industries.

3. Checking the competitive advantage potential of cross-business strategic fits among the company's various business units.

4. Checking whether the firm's resources fit the requirements of its present business lineup.

5. Ranking the performance prospects of the businesses from best to worst and determine what the corporate parent's priority should be in allocating resources to its various businesses.

6. Crafting new strategic moves to improve overall corporate performance.

The core concepts and analytical techniques underlying each of these steps merit further discussion.

Step 1: Evaluating Industry Attractiveness

A principal consideration in evaluating a diversified company's business makeup and the caliber of its strategy is the attractiveness of the industries in which it has business operations. Answers to several questions are required:

1. *Does each industry the company has diversified into represent a good business for the company to be in?* Ideally, each industry in which the firm operates will pass the attractiveness test.

2. *Which of the company's industries are most attractive and which are least attractive?* Comparing the attractiveness of the industries and ranking them from most to least attractive is a prerequisite to wise allocation of corporate resources across the various businesses.

3. *How appealing is the whole group of industries in which the company has invested?* The answer to this question points to whether the group of industries holds promise for attractive growth and profitability. A company whose revenues and profits come chiefly from businesses in relatively unattractive industries probably needs to look at divesting businesses in unattractive industries and entering industries that qualify as highly attractive.

The more attractive the industries (both individually and as a group) a diversified company is in, the better its prospects for good long-term performance.

Calculating Industry Attractiveness Scores for Each Industry into Which the Company Has Diversified A simple and reliable analytical tool involves calculating quantitative industry attractiveness scores, which can then be used to gauge each industry's attractiveness, rank the industries from most to least attractive, and make judgments about the attractiveness of all the industries as a group.

The following measures are typically used to gauge an industry's attractiveness:

- *Market size and projected growth rate*—Big industries are more attractive than small industries, and fast-growing industries tend to be more attractive than slow-growing industries, other things being equal.

- *The intensity of competition*—Industries where competitive pressures are relatively weak are more attractive than industries where competitive pressures are strong.

- *Emerging opportunities and threats*—Industries with promising opportunities and minimal threats on the near horizon are more attractive than industries with modest opportunities and imposing threats.

- *The presence of cross-industry strategic fits*—The more the industry's value chain and resource requirements match up well with the value chain activities of other industries in which the company has operations, the more attractive the industry is to a firm pursuing related diversification. However, cross-industry strategic fits may be of no consequence to a company committed to a strategy of unrelated diversification.

- *Resource requirements*—Industries having resource requirements within the company's reach are more attractive than industries where capital and other resource requirements could strain corporate financial resources and organizational capabilities.

- *Seasonal and cyclical factors*—Industries where buyer demand is relatively steady year-round and not unduly vulnerable to economic ups and downs tend to be more attractive than industries where there are wide swings in buyer demand within or across years. However, seasonality may be a plus for a company that is in several seasonal industries, if the seasonal highs in one industry correspond to the lows in another industry, thus helping even out monthly sales levels.

- *Social, political, regulatory, and environmental factors*—Industries with significant problems in such areas as consumer health, safety, or environmental pollution or that are subject to intense regulation are less attractive than industries where such problems are not burning issues.

- *Industry profitability*—Industries with healthy profit margins and high rates of return on investment are generally more attractive than industries where profits have historically been low or unstable.

- *Industry uncertainty and business risk*—Industries with less uncertainty on the horizon and lower overall business risk are more attractive than industries whose prospects for one reason or another are quite uncertain, especially when the industry has formidable resource requirements.

After settling on a set of attractiveness measures that suit a diversified company's circumstances, each attractiveness measure is assigned a weight reflecting its relative importance in determining an industry's attractiveness—it is weak methodology to assume that the various attractiveness measures are equally important. The intensity of competition in an industry should nearly always carry a high weight (say, 0.20 to 0.30). Strategic-fit considerations should be assigned a high weight in the case of companies with related diversification strategies; but, for companies with an unrelated diversification strategy, strategic fits with other industries may be given a low weight or even dropped from the list of attractiveness measures altogether. Seasonal and cyclical factors generally are assigned a low weight (or maybe even eliminated from the analysis) unless a company has diversified into industries strongly characterized by seasonal demand and/or heavy vulnerability to cyclical upswings and downswings. The importance weights must add up to 1.0.

Next, each industry is rated on each of the chosen industry attractiveness measures, using a rating scale of 1 to 10 (where a *high* rating signifies *high* attractiveness and a *low* rating signifies *low* attractiveness). *Keep in mind here that the more intensely competitive an industry is, the lower the attractiveness rating for that industry.* Likewise, the higher the capital and resource requirements associated with being in a particular industry, the lower the attractiveness rating. And an industry subject to stringent pollution control regulations or that causes societal problems (like cigarettes or alcoholic beverages) should usually be given a low attractiveness rating. Weighted attractiveness scores are then calculated by multiplying the industry's rating on each measure by the corresponding weight. For example, a rating of 8 times a weight of 0.25 gives a

Table 8.1   Calculating Weighted Industry Attractiveness Scores

Industry Attractiveness Measure	Importance Weight	Industry A Rating/ Score	Industry B Rating/ Score	Industry C Rating/ Score	Industry D Rating/ Score
Market size and projected growth rate	0.10	8/0.80	5/0.50	2/0.20	3/0.30
Intensity of competition	0.25	8/2.00	7/1.75	3/0.75	2/0.50
Emerging opportunities and threats	0.10	2/0.20	9/0.90	4/0.40	5/0.50
Cross-industry strategic fits	0.20	8/1.60	4/0.80	8/1.60	2/0.40
Resource requirements	0.10	9/0.90	7/0.70	5/0.50	5/0.50
Seasonal and cyclical influences	0.05	9/0.45	8/0.40	10/0.50	5/0.25
Societal, political, regulatory, and environmental factors	0.05	10/0.50	7/0.35	7/0.35	3/0.15
Industry profitability	0.10	5/0.50	10/1.00	3/0.30	3/0.30
Industry uncertainty and business risk	0.05	5/0.25	7/0.35	10/0.50	1/0.05
Sum of the assigned weights	1.00				
Overall weighted industry attractiveness scores		**7.20**	**6.75**	**5.10**	**2.95**

[Rating scale: 1 = Very unattractive to company; 10 = Very attractive to company]

weighted attractiveness score of 2.00. The sum of the weighted scores for all the attractiveness measures provides an overall industry attractiveness score. This procedure is illustrated in Table 8.1.

Interpreting the Industry Attractiveness Scores   Industries with a score much below 5.0 probably do not pass the attractiveness test. If a company's industry attractiveness scores are all above 5.0, it is probably fair to conclude that the group of industries the company operates in is attractive as a whole. But the group of industries takes on a decidedly lower degree of attractiveness as the number of industries with scores below 5.0 increases, especially if industries with low scores account for a sizable fraction of the company's revenues.

For a diversified company to be a strong performer, a substantial portion of its revenues and profits must come from business units with relatively high attractiveness scores. It is particularly important that a diversified company's principal businesses be in industries with a good outlook for growth and above-average profitability. Having a big fraction of the company's revenues and profits come from industries with slow growth, low profitability, or intense competition tends to drag overall company performance down. Business units in the least attractive industries are potential candidates for divestiture, unless they are positioned strongly enough to overcome the unattractive aspects of their industry environments or they are a strategically important component of the company's business makeup.

The Difficulties of Calculating Industry Attractiveness Scores   There are two hurdles to using this method of evaluating industry attractiveness. One is deciding on appropriate weights for the industry attractiveness measures. Not only may different analysts have different views about which weights are appropriate for the different attractiveness measures, but different weightings may also be appropriate for different companies—based on their strategies, performance targets, and financial circumstances. For instance, placing a low weight on industry resource requirements may be justifiable for a cash-rich company, whereas a high weight may be more appropriate for a financially strapped company. The second hurdle is gaining sufficient command of the industry to assign accurate and objective ratings. Generally, a company can come up with the statistical data needed to compare its industries on such factors as market size, growth rate, seasonal and cyclical influences, and industry profitability. Cross-industry fits and resource requirements are also fairly easy to judge. But the attractiveness measure where judgment weighs most heavily is that of intensity of competition. It is not always easy to conclude whether competition in one industry is stronger or weaker than in another industry because of the different types of competitive influences that prevail and the differences in their relative importance. In the event that the available information is too skimpy to confidently assign a rating value to an industry on a particular attractiveness measure, then it is usually best to use a score of 5, which avoids biasing the overall attractiveness score either up or down.

But despite the hurdles, calculating industry attractiveness scores is a systematic and reasonably reliable method for ranking a diversified company's industries from most to least attractive—numbers like those shown for the four industries in Table 8.1 help pin down the basis for judging which industries are more attractive and to what degree.

Step 2: Evaluating Business-Unit Competitive Strength

The second step in evaluating a diversified company is to appraise how strongly positioned its business units are in their respective industries. Doing an appraisal of each business unit's strength and competitive position in its industry not only reveals its chances for industry success but also provides a basis for ranking the units from competitively strongest to competitively weakest and sizing up the competitive strength of all the business units as a group.

Calculating Competitive Strength Scores for Each Business Unit
Quantitative measures of each business unit's competitive strength can be calculated using a procedure similar to that for measuring industry attractiveness. The following factors are useful in quantifying the competitive strengths of a diversified company's business subsidiaries:

- *Relative market share*—A business unit's *relative market share* is defined as the ratio of its market share to the market share held by the largest rival firm in the industry, with market share measured in unit volume, not dollars. For instance, if business A has a market-leading share of 40 percent and its largest rival has 30 percent, A's relative market share is 1.33. (Note that only business units that are market share leaders in their respective industries can have relative market shares greater than 1.0.) If business B has a 15 percent market share and B's largest rival has 30 percent, B's relative market share is 0.5. *The further below 1.0 a business unit's relative market share is, the weaker its competitive strength and market position vis-à-vis rivals.* A 10 percent market share, for example, does not signal much competitive strength if the leader's share is 50 percent (a 0.20 relative market share), but a 10 percent share is actually quite strong if the leader's share is only 12 percent (a 0.83 relative market share)—this why a company's relative market share is a better measure of competitive strength than a company's market share based on either dollars or unit volume.

> Using relative market share to measure competitive strength is analytically superior to using straight-percentage market share.

- *Costs relative to competitors' costs*—Business units that have low costs relative to key competitors' costs tend to be more strongly positioned in their industries than business units struggling to maintain cost parity with major rivals. Assuming that the prices charged by industry rivals are about the same, there's reason to expect that business units with higher relative market shares have lower unit costs than competitors with lower relative market shares because their greater unit sales volumes offer the possibility of economies from larger-scale operations and the benefits of any learning/experience curve effects. Another indicator of low cost can be a business unit's supply chain management capabilities. The only time when a business unit's competitive strength may not be undermined by having higher costs than rivals is when it has incurred the higher costs to strongly differentiate its product offering and its customers are willing to pay premium prices for the differentiating features.

- *Ability to match or beat rivals on key product attributes*—A company's competitiveness depends in part on being able to satisfy buyer expectations with regard to features, product performance, reliability, service, and other important attributes.

- *Ability to benefit from strategic fits with sister businesses*—Strategic fits with other businesses within the company enhance a business unit's competitive strength and may provide a competitive edge.

- *Ability to exercise bargaining leverage with key suppliers or customers*—Having bargaining leverage signals competitive strength and can be a source of competitive advantage.

- *Caliber of alliances and collaborative partnerships with suppliers and/or buyers*—Well-functioning alliances and partnerships may signal a potential competitive advantage vis-à-vis rivals and thus add to a business's competitive strength. Alliances with key suppliers are often the basis for competitive strength in supply chain management.

- *Brand image and reputation*—A strong brand name is a valuable competitive asset in most industries.

- *Competitively valuable capabilities*—Business units recognized for their technological leadership, product innovation, or marketing prowess are usually strong competitors in their industry. Skills in supply chain management can generate valuable cost or product differentiation advantages. So can unique production capabilities. Sometimes a company's business units gain competitive strength because of their knowledge of customers and markets and/or their proven managerial capabilities. *An important thing to look for here is how well a business unit's competitive assets match industry key success factors.* The more a business unit's resource strengths and competitive capabilities match the industry's key success factors, the stronger its competitive position tends to be.

- *Profitability relative to competitors*—Business units that consistently earn above-average returns on investment and have bigger profit margins than their rivals usually have stronger competitive positions. Moreover, above-average profitability signals competitive advantage, while below-average profitability usually denotes competitive disadvantage.

After settling on a set of competitive-strength measures that are well matched to the circumstances of the various business units, weights indicating each measure's importance need to be assigned. A case can be made for using different weights for different business units whenever the importance of the strength measures differs significantly from business to business, but otherwise it is simpler just to go with a single set of weights and avoid the added complication of multiple weights. As before, the

Table 8.2 Calculating Weighted Competitive Strength Scores for a Diversified Company's Business Units

Competitive Strength Measure	Importance Weight	Business A in Industry A Rating/ Score	Business B in Industry B Rating/ Score	Business C in Industry C Rating/ Score	Business D in Industry D Rating/ Score
Relative market share	0.15	10/1.50	1/0.15	6/0.90	2/0.30
Costs relative to competitors' costs	0.20	7/1.40	2/0.40	5/1.00	3/0.60
Ability to match or beat rivals on key product attributes	0.05	9/0.45	4/0.20	8/0.40	4/0.20
Ability to benefit from strategic fits with sister businesses	0.20	8/1.60	4/0.80	4/0.80	2/0.60
Bargaining leverage with suppliers/ buyers; caliber of alliances	0.05	9/0.45	3/0.15	6/0.30	2/0.10
Brand image and reputation	0.10	9/0.90	2/0.20	7/0.70	5/0.50
Competitively valuable capabilities	0.15	7/1.05	2/0.30	5/0.75	3/0.45
Profitability relative to competitors	0.10	5/0.50	1/0.10	4/0.40	4/0.40
Sum of the assigned weights	1.00				
Overall weighted competitive strength scores		**7.85**	**2.30**	**5.25**	**3.15**

[Rating scale: 1 = Very weak; 10 = Very strong]

importance weights must add up to 1.0. Each business unit is then rated on each of the chosen strength measures, using a rating scale of 1 to 10 (where a *high* rating signifies competitive *strength* and a *low* rating signifies competitive *weakness*). In the event that the available information is too skimpy to confidently assign a rating value to a business unit on a particular strength measure, then it is usually best to use a score of 5, which avoids biasing the overall score either up or down. Weighted strength ratings are calculated by multiplying the business unit's rating on each strength measure by the assigned weight. For example, a strength score of 6 times a weight of 0.15 gives a weighted strength rating of 0.90. The sum of weighted ratings across all the strength measures provides a quantitative measure of a business unit's overall market strength and competitive standing. Table 8.2 provides sample calculations of competitive strength ratings for four businesses.

Interpreting the Competitive Strength Scores Business units with competitive strength ratings above 6.7 (on a scale of 1 to 10) are strong market contenders in their industries. Businesses with ratings in the 3.3–6.7 range have moderate competitive strength vis-à-vis rivals. Businesses with ratings below 3.3 are in competitively weak market positions. If a diversified company's business units all have competitive strength scores above 5.0, it is fair to conclude that its business units are all fairly strong market contenders in their respective industries. But as the number of business units with scores below 5.0 increases, there's reason to question whether the company can perform well with so many businesses in relatively weak competitive positions. This concern takes on even more importance when business units with low scores account for a sizable fraction of the company's revenues.

Figure 8.5   A Nine-Cell Industry Attractiveness–Competitive Strength Matrix

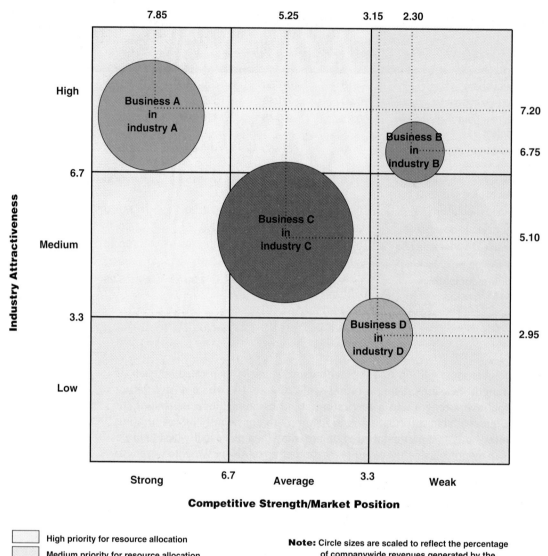

Using a Nine-Cell Matrix to Simultaneously Portray Industry Attractiveness and Competitive Strength   The industry attractiveness and business strength scores can be used to portray the strategic positions of each business in a diversified company. Industry attractiveness is plotted on the vertical axis, and competitive strength on the horizontal axis. A nine-cell grid emerges from dividing the vertical axis into three regions (high, medium, and low attractiveness) and the horizontal axis into three regions (strong, average, and weak competitive strength). As shown in Figure 8.5, high attractiveness is associated with scores of 6.7 or greater on a rating scale of 1 to 10, medium attractiveness to scores of 3.3 to 6.7, and low attractiveness to scores below 3.3.

Likewise, high competitive strength is defined as a score greater than 6.7, average strength as scores of 3.3 to 6.7, and low strength as scores below 3.3. *Each business unit is plotted on the nine-cell matrix according to its overall attractiveness score and strength score, and then shown as a "bubble."* The size of each bubble is scaled to what percentage of revenues the business generates relative to total corporate revenues. The bubbles in Figure 8.5 were located on the grid using the four industry attractiveness scores from Table 8.1 and the strength scores for the four business units in Table 8.2.

The locations of the business units on the attractiveness–strength matrix provide valuable guidance in deploying corporate resources to the various business units. In general, *a diversified company's prospects for good overall performance are enhanced by concentrating corporate resources and strategic attention on those business units having the greatest competitive strength and positioned in highly attractive industries—* specifically, businesses in the three cells in the upper left portion of the attractiveness-strength matrix, where industry attractiveness and competitive strength/market position are both favorable. The general strategic prescription for businesses falling in these three cells (for instance, business A in Figure 8.5) is "grow and build," with businesses in the high–strong cell standing first in line for resource allocations by the corporate parent.

Next in priority come businesses positioned in the three diagonal cells stretching from the lower left to the upper right (businesses B and C in Figure 8.5). Such businesses usually merit medium or intermediate priority in the parent's resource allocation ranking. However, some businesses in the medium-priority diagonal cells may have brighter or dimmer prospects than others. For example, a small business in the upper right cell of the matrix (like business B), despite being in a highly attractive industry, may occupy too weak a competitive position in its industry to justify the investment and resources needed to turn it into a strong market contender and shift its position leftward in the matrix over time. If, however, a business in the upper right cell has attractive opportunities for rapid growth and a good potential for winning a much stronger market position over time, it may merit a high claim on the corporate parent's resource allocation ranking and be given the capital it needs to pursue a grow-and-build strategy—the strategic objective here would be to move the business leftward in the attractiveness–strength matrix over time.

Businesses in the three cells in the lower right corner of the matrix (like business D in Figure 8.5) typically are weak performers and have the lowest claim on corporate resources. Most such businesses are good candidates for being divested (sold to other companies) or else managed in a manner calculated to squeeze out the maximum cash flows from operations—the cash flows from low-performing/low-potential businesses can then be diverted to financing expansion of business units with greater market opportunities. In exceptional cases where a business located in the three lower right cells is nonetheless fairly profitable (which it might be if it is in the low–average cell) or has the potential for good earnings and return on investment, the business merits retention and the allocation of sufficient resources to achieve better performance.

The nine-cell attractiveness–strength matrix provides clear, strong logic for why a diversified company needs to consider both industry attractiveness and business strength in allocating resources and investment capital to its different businesses. A good case can be made for concentrating resources in those businesses that enjoy higher degrees of attractiveness and competitive strength, being very selective in making investments in businesses with intermediate positions on the grid, and withdrawing resources from businesses that are lower in attractiveness and strength unless they offer exceptional profit or cash flow potential.

Step 3: Checking the Competitive Advantage Potential of Cross-Business Strategic Fits

While this step can be bypassed for diversified companies whose business are all unrelated (since, by design, no strategic fits are present), a high potential for converting strategic fits into competitive advantage is central to concluding just how good a company's related diversification strategy is. Checking the competitive advantage potential of cross-business strategic fits involves searching for and evaluating how much benefit a diversified company can gain from value chain matchups that present (1) opportunities to combine the performance of certain activities, thereby reducing costs and capturing economies of scope; (2) opportunities to transfer skills, technology, or intellectual capital from one business to another, thereby leveraging use of existing resources; (3) opportunities to share use of a well-respected brand name; and (4) opportunities for sister businesses to collaborate in creating valuable new competitive capabilities (such as enhanced supply chain management capabilities, quicker first-to-market capabilities, or greater product innovation capabilities).

Figure 8.6 illustrates the process of comparing the value chains of sister businesses and identifying competitively valuable cross-business strategic fits. *But more than just strategic fit identification is needed. The real test is what competitive value can be generated from these fits.* To what extent can cost savings be realized? How much competitive value will come from cross-business transfer of skills, technology, or intellectual capital? Will transferring a potent brand name to the products of sister businesses grow sales significantly? Will cross-business collaboration to create or strengthen competitive capabilities lead to significant gains in the marketplace or in financial performance? Absent significant strategic fits and dedicated company efforts to capture the benefits, one has to be skeptical about the potential for a diversified company's businesses to perform better together than apart.

Step 4: Checking for Resource Fit

The businesses in a diversified company's lineup need to exhibit good **resource fit.** Resource fit exists when (1) businesses add to a company's overall resource strengths and (2) a company has adequate resources to support its entire group of businesses without spreading itself too thin. One important dimension of resource fit concerns whether a diversified company can generate the internal cash flows sufficient to fund the capital requirements of its businesses, pay its dividends, meet its debt obligations, and otherwise remain financially healthy.

Financial Resource Fits: Cash Cows versus Cash Hogs   Different businesses have different cash flow and investment characteristics. For example, business units in rapidly growing industries are often **cash hogs**—so labeled because the cash flows they are able to generate from internal operations aren't big enough to fund their expansion. To keep pace with rising buyer demand, rapid-growth businesses frequently need sizable annual capital investments—for new facilities and equipment, for new product development or technology improvements, and for additional working

Figure 8.6   Identifying the Competitive Advantage Potential of Cross-Business Strategic Fits

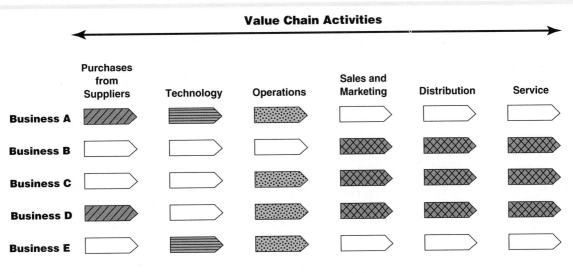

Opportunity to combine purchasing activities, gain more leverage with suppliers, and realize supply chain economies

Opportunity to share technology, transfer technical skills, combine R&D

Opportunity to combine sales and marketing activities, use common distribution channels, leverage use of a common brand name, and/or combine after-sale service activities

Opportunities for cross-bussiness collaboration to create new competitive capabilities

No strategic-fit opportunities

capital to support inventory expansion and a larger base of operations. A business in a fast-growing industry becomes an even bigger cash hog when it has a relatively low market share and is pursuing a strategy to become an industry leader. Because a cash hog's financial resources must be provided by the corporate parent, corporate managers have to decide whether it makes good financial and strategic sense to keep pouring new money into a business that continually needs cash infusions.

In contrast, business units with leading market positions in mature industries may, however, be **cash cows**—businesses that generate substantial cash surpluses over what is needed to adequately fund their operations. Market leaders in slow-growth industries often generate sizable positive cash flows *over and above what is needed for growth and reinvestment* because their industry-leading positions tend to give them the sales volumes and reputation to earn attractive profits and because the slow-growth nature of their industry often entails relatively modest annual investment requirements. Cash cows, though not always attractive from a growth standpoint, are valuable businesses from a financial resource perspective. The surplus cash flows they generate can be used to pay corporate dividends, finance acquisitions, and provide funds for investing in the company's promising cash hogs. It makes good

CORE CONCEPT

A *cash cow* business generates cash flows over and above its internal requirements, thus providing a corporate parent with funds for investing in cash hog businesses, financing new acquisitions, or paying dividends.

financial and strategic sense for diversified companies to keep cash cows healthy, fortifying and defending their market position so as to preserve their cash-generating capability over the long term and thereby have an ongoing source of financial resources to deploy elsewhere. The cigarette business is one of the world's biggest cash cows.

Viewing a diversified group of businesses as a collection of cash flows and cash requirements (present and future) is a major step forward in understanding what the financial ramifications of diversification are and why having businesses with good financial resource fit is so important. For instance, *a diversified company's businesses exhibit good financial resource fit when the excess cash generated by its cash cows is sufficient to fund the investment requirements of promising cash hogs.* Ideally, investing in promising cash hogs over time results in growing the hogs into self-supporting *star businesses* that have strong or market-leading competitive positions in attractive, high-growth markets and high levels of profitability. Star businesses are often the cash cows of the future—when the markets of star businesses begin to mature and their growth slows, their competitive strength should produce self-generated cash flows more than sufficient to cover their investment needs. The "success sequence" is thus cash hog to young star (but perhaps still a cash hog) to self-supporting star to cash cow.

If, however, a cash hog has questionable promise (either because of low industry attractiveness or a weak competitive position), then it becomes a logical candidate for divestiture. Pursuing an aggressive invest-and-expand strategy for a cash hog with an uncertain future seldom makes sense because it requires the corporate parent to keep pumping more capital into the business with only a dim hope of eventually turning the cash hog into a future star and realizing a good return on its investments. Such businesses are a financial drain and fail the resource-fit test because they strain the corporate parent's ability to adequately fund its other businesses. Divesting a less-attractive cash hog is usually the best alternative unless (1) it has valuable strategic fits with other business units or (2) the capital infusions needed from the corporate parent are modest relative to the funds available and there's a decent chance of growing the business into a solid bottom-line contributor yielding a good return on invested capital.

Other Tests of Resource Fit   Aside from cash flow considerations, there are two other factors to consider in determining whether the businesses comprising a diversified company's portfolio exhibit good resource fit from a financial perspective:

- *Does the business adequately contribute to achieving companywide performance targets?* A business has good financial fit when it contributes to the achievement of corporate performance objectives (growth in earnings per share, above-average return on investment, recognition as an industry leader, etc.) and when it materially enhances shareholder value via helping drive increases in the company's stock price. A business exhibits poor financial fit if it soaks up a disproportionate share of the company's financial resources, makes subpar or inconsistent bottom-line contributions, is unduly risky and failure would jeopardize the entire enterprise, or remains too small to make a material earnings contribution even though it performs well.

- *Does the company have adequate financial strength to fund its different businesses and maintain a healthy credit rating?* A diversified company's strategy fails the resource-fit test when its financial resources are stretched across so many businesses that its credit rating is impaired. Severe financial strain sometimes occurs when a company borrows so heavily to finance new acquisitions that it has to trim way back on capital expenditures for existing businesses and use the big majority of its financial resources to meet interest obligations and to pay down debt. Time

Warner, Royal Ahold, and AT&T, for example, have found themselves so financially overextended that they have had to sell off some of their business units to raise the money to pay down burdensome debt obligations and continue to fund essential capital expenditures for the remaining businesses.

- *Does the company have (or can it develop) the specific resource strengths and competitive capabilities needed to be successful in each of its businesses?*[15] Sometimes the resource strengths a company has accumulated in its core or mainstay business prove to be a poor match with the key success factors and competitive capabilities needed to succeed in one or more businesses it has diversified into. For instance, LVMH, a multibusiness company in France, discovered that the company's resources and managerial skills were quite well suited for parenting luxury goods businesses including Louis Vuitton, Christian Dior, Givenchy, Fendi, Dom Perignon, Moët & Chandon, and Hennessy but not for parenting art auctions and radio stations; as a consequence, LVMH decided to divest its art auctioning and radio broadcasting businesses after those businesses had run up significant operating losses and proved to be a drain on the corporate treasury. Another company with businesses in restaurants and retailing decided that its resource capabilities in site selection, controlling operating costs, management selection and training, and supply chain logistics would enable it to succeed in the hotel business and in property management; but what management missed was that these businesses had some significantly different key success factors—namely, skills in controlling property development costs, maintaining low overheads, product branding (hotels), and ability to recruit a sufficient volume of business to maintain high levels of facility utilization.[16] Thus, a mismatch between the company's resource strengths and the key success factors in a particular business can be serious enough to warrant divesting an existing business or not acquiring a new business. In contrast, when a company's resources and capabilities are a good match with the key success factors of industries it is not presently in, it makes sense to take a hard look at acquiring companies in these industries and expanding the company's business lineup.

- *Are recently acquired businesses acting to strengthen a company's resource base and competitive capabilities or are they causing its competitive and managerial resources to be stretched too thin?* A diversified company has to guard against overtaxing its resource strengths and managerial capabilities, a condition that can arise (1) when it goes on an acquisition spree and management is called on to assimilate and oversee many new businesses very quickly or (2) when it lacks sufficient resource and managerial depth to do a creditable job of transferring skills and competences from one of its businesses to another. The broader the diversification, the greater the concern about whether the company has sufficient managerial depth to cope with the diverse range of operating problems its wide business lineup presents. And the more a company's diversification strategy is tied to transferring its existing know-how or technologies to new businesses, the more it has to develop a big enough and deep enough resource pool to supply these businesses with sufficient capability to create competitive advantage.[17] Otherwise its strengths end up being spread too thin across many businesses and the opportunity for competitive advantage slips through the cracks.

A Cautionary Note about Transferring Resources from One Business to Another Hitting a home run in one business doesn't mean that a company can easily enter a new business with similar resource requirements and hit a second home run.[18] Noted British retailer Marks & Spencer—despite possessing a range of impressive resource capabilities (ability to choose excellent store locations, a supply chain that gives it both low costs and high merchandise quality, loyal employees, an excellent reputation with consumers, and strong management expertise) that have made it one of Britain's premier retailers for 100 years—has failed repeatedly in its efforts to diversify into department store retailing in the United States. Even though Philip Morris (now named Altria) had built powerful consumer marketing capabilities in its cigarette and beer businesses, it floundered in soft drinks and ended up divesting its acquisition of 7UP after several frustrating years of competing against strongly entrenched and resource-capable rivals like Coca-Cola and PepsiCo. Then in 2002 it decided to divest its Miller Brewing business—despite its long-standing marketing successes in cigarettes and in its Kraft Foods subsidiary—because it was unable to grow Miller's market share in head-to-head competition against the considerable marketing prowess of Anheuser-Busch.

Step 5: Ranking the Performance Prospects of Business Units and Assigning a Priority for Resource Allocation

Once a diversified company's strategy has been evaluated from the perspective of industry attractiveness, competitive strength, strategic fit, and resource fit, the next step is to rank the performance prospects of the businesses from best to worst and determine which businesses merit top priority for resource support and new capital investments by the corporate parent.

The most important considerations in judging business-unit performance are sales growth, profit growth, contribution to company earnings, and return on capital invested in the business. Sometimes, cash flow is a big consideration. Information on each business's past performance can be gleaned from a company's financial records. While past performance is not necessarily a good predictor of future performance, it does signal whether a business already has good to excellent performance or has problems to overcome.

Furthermore, the industry attractiveness/business strength evaluations provide a solid basis for judging a business's prospects. Normally, strong business units in attractive industries have significantly better prospects than weak businesses in unattractive industries. And, normally, the revenue and earnings outlook for businesses in fast-growing industries is better than for businesses in slow-growing industries—one important exception is when a business in a slow-growing industry has the competitive strength to draw sales and market share away from its rivals and thus achieve much faster growth than the industry as whole. As a rule, the prior analyses, taken together, signal which business units are likely to be strong performers on the road ahead and which are likely to be laggards. And it is a short step from ranking the prospects of business units to drawing conclusions about whether the company as a whole is capable of strong, mediocre, or weak performance in upcoming years.

The rankings of future performance generally determine what priority the corporate parent should give to each business in terms of resource allocation. *Business subsidiaries with the brightest profit and growth prospects and solid strategic and resource fits generally should head the list for corporate resource support.* More specifically, corporate executives must be diligent in steering resources out of low-opportunity areas into high-opportunity areas. Divesting marginal businesses is one of the best ways of freeing unproductive assets for redeployment. Surplus funds from cash cows also can be used to finance the range of chief strategic and financial options

Figure 8.7   The Chief Strategic and Financial Options for Allocating a Diversified Company's Financial Resources

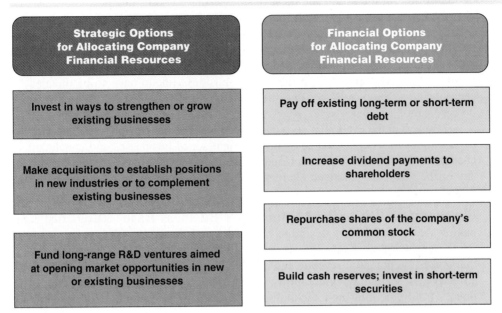

shown in Figure 8.7. Ideally, a company will have enough funds to do what is needed, both strategically and financially. If not, strategic uses of corporate resources should usually take precedence unless there is a compelling reason to strengthen the firm's balance sheet or divert financial resources to pacify shareholders.

Step 6: Crafting New Strategic Moves to Improve Overall Corporate Performance

The diagnosis and conclusions flowing from the five preceding analytical steps set the agenda for crafting strategic moves to improve a diversified company's overall performance. Corporate strategy options once a company has diversified boil down to five broad categories of actions (see Figure 8.7):

1. Sticking closely with the existing business lineup and pursuing the opportunities these businesses present.
2. Broadening the company's business scope by making new acquisitions in new industries.
3. Divesting some businesses and retrenching to a narrower base of business operations.
4. Restructuring the company's business lineup with a combination of divestitures and new acquisitions to put a whole new face on the company's business makeup.
5. Pursuing multinational diversification and striving to globalize the operations of several of the company's business units.

Sticking Closely with the Existing Business Lineup   The option of sticking with the current business lineup makes sense when the company's present businesses offer attractive growth opportunities and can be counted on to generate good earnings and cash flows. As long as the company's set of existing businesses puts it in good position for the future and these businesses have good strategic and/or resource fits, then rocking the boat with major changes in the company's business mix is usually unnecessary. Corporate executives can concentrate their attention on getting the best performance from each of its businesses, steering corporate resources into those areas of greatest potential and profitability. The specifics of "what to do" to wring better performance from the present business lineup have to be dictated by each business's circumstances and the preceding analysis of the corporate parent's diversification strategy.

However, in the event that corporate executives are not entirely satisfied with the opportunities they see in the company's present set of businesses and conclude that changes in the company's direction and business makeup are in order, they can opt for any of the four other strategic alternatives shown in Figure 8.8 and described in the following sections.

Broadening a Diversified Company's Business Base

Diversified companies sometimes find it desirable to build positions in new industries, whether related or unrelated. There are several motivating factors. One is sluggish growth that makes the potential revenue and profit boost of a newly acquired business look attractive. A second is vulnerability to seasonal or recessionary influences or to threats from emerging new technologies. A third is the potential for transferring resources and capabilities to other related or complementary businesses. A fourth is rapidly changing conditions in one or more of a company's core businesses brought on by technological, legislative, or new product innovations that alter buyer requirements and preferences. For instance, the passage of legislation in the United States allowing banks, insurance companies, and stock brokerages to enter one another's businesses spurred a raft of acquisitions and mergers to create full-service financial enterprises capable of meeting the multiple financial needs of customers. Citigroup, already the largest U.S. bank with a global banking franchise, acquired Salomon Smith Barney to position itself in the investment banking and brokerage business and acquired insurance giant Travelers Group to enable it to offer customers insurance products.

A fifth, and often very important, motivating factor for adding new businesses is to complement and strengthen the market position and competitive capabilities of one or more of its present businesses. Procter & Gamble's 2005 acquisition of Gillette strengthened and extended P&G's reach into personal care and household products—Gillette's businesses included Oral-B toothbrushes, Gillette razors and razor blades, Duracell batteries, Braun shavers and small appliances (coffeemakers, mixers, hair dryers, and electric toothbrushes), and toiletries (Right Guard, Foamy, Soft & Dry, White Rain, and Dry Idea). Unilever, a leading maker of food and personal care products, expanded its business lineup by acquiring SlimFast, Ben & Jerry's Homemade Ice Cream, and Bestfoods (whose brands included Knorr's soups, Hellman's mayonnaise, Skippy peanut butter, and Mazola cooking oils). Unilever saw these businesses as giving it more clout in competing against such other diversified food and household products companies as Nestlé, Kraft, Procter & Gamble, Campbell Soup, and General Mills. Cisco Systems built itself into a worldwide leader in networking systems for the Internet by making 130 technology-based acquisitions from 1993 to 2008 that extended its market reach from routing and switching into IP telephony, home networking, wireless LAN, storage networking, network security, broadband, and optical and broadband systems.

Figure 8.8 A Company's Five Main Strategic Alternatives after It Diversifies

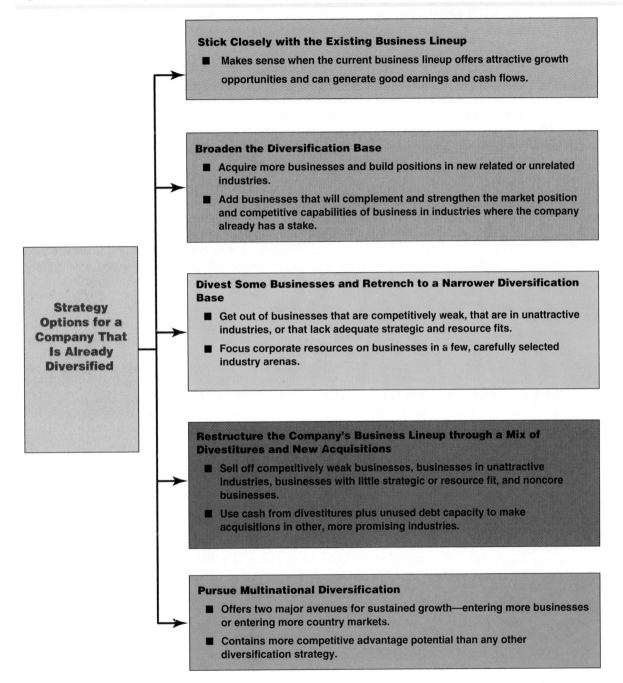

Stick Closely with the Existing Business Lineup
- Makes sense when the current business lineup offers attractive growth opportunities and can generate good earnings and cash flows.

Broaden the Diversification Base
- Acquire more businesses and build positions in new related or unrelated industries.
- Add businesses that will complement and strengthen the market position and competitive capabilities of business in industries where the company already has a stake.

Divest Some Businesses and Retrench to a Narrower Diversification Base
- Get out of businesses that are competitively weak, that are in unattractive industries, or that lack adequate strategic and resource fits.
- Focus corporate resources on businesses in a few, carefully selected industry arenas.

Restructure the Company's Business Lineup through a Mix of Divestitures and New Acquisitions
- Sell off competitively weak businesses, businesses in unattractive industries, businesses with little strategic or resource fit, and noncore businesses.
- Use cash from divestitures plus unused debt capacity to make acquisitions in other, more promising industries.

Pursue Multinational Diversification
- Offers two major avenues for sustained growth—entering more businesses or entering more country markets.
- Contains more competitive advantage potential than any other diversification strategy.

Strategy Options for a Company That Is Already Diversified

Illustration Capsule 8.3 describes how Johnson & Johnson has used acquisitions to diversify far beyond its well-known Band-Aid and baby care businesses and become a major player in pharmaceuticals, medical devices, and medical diagnostics.

Divesting Some Businesses and Retrenching to a Narrower Diversification Base A number of diversified firms have had difficulty managing a diverse group of businesses and have elected to get out of some of them. Retrenching

ILLUSTRATION CAPSULE 8.3
Managing Diversification at Johnson & Johnson: The Benefits of Cross-Business Strategic Fits

Johnson & Johnson (J&J), once a consumer products company known for its Band-Aid line and its baby care products, has evolved into a $61 billion diversified enterprise consisting of some 250-plus operating companies organized into three divisions: pharmaceuticals, medical devices and diagnostics, and consumer health care products. Over the past decade J&J has made acquisitions totaling more than $50 billion; about 10 to 15 percent of J&J's annual growth in revenues has come from acquisitions. Much of the company's recent growth has been in the pharmaceutical division, which in 2007 accounted for 41 percent of J&J's revenues and 48 percent of its operating profits.

While each of J&J's business units sets its own strategies and operates with its own finance and human resource departments, corporate management strongly encourages cross-business cooperation and collaboration, believing that many of the advances in 21st-century medicine will come from applying advances in one discipline to another. J&J's drug-coated stent grew out of a discussion between a drug researcher and a researcher in the company's stent business. The innovative product helps prevent infection after cardiatric procedures. (When stents are inserted to prop open arteries following angioplasty, the drug coating helps prevent infection.) A gene technology database compiled by the company's gene research lab was shared with personnel from the diagnostics division, who developed a test that the drug researchers used to predict which patients would most benefit from an experimental cancer therapy. J&J's liquid Band-Aid product (a liquid coating applied to hard-to-cover places like fingers and knuckles) is based on a material used in a wound-closing product sold by the company's hospital products company. In 2007, scientists from three separate business units were working toward the development of an absorbable patch that would stop bleeding on contact. The development of the instant clotting patch was expected to save the lives of thousands of accident victims since uncontrolled bleeding was the number one cause of death due to injury.

J&J's corporate management maintains that close collaboration among people in its diagnostics, medical devices, and pharmaceuticals businesses—where numerous cross-business strategic fits exist—gives J&J an edge on competitors, most of whom cannot match the company's breadth and depth of expertise.

Sources: Amy Barrett, "Staying on Top," *BusinessWeek,* May 5, 2003, pp. 60–68; Johnson & Johnson 2007 annual report; and www.jnj.com (accessed July 25, 2008).

Focusing corporate resources on a few core and mostly related businesses avoids the mistake of diversifying so broadly that resources and management attention are stretched too thin.

to a narrower diversification base is usually undertaken when top management concludes that its diversification strategy has ranged too far afield and that the company can improve long-term performance by concentrating on building stronger positions in a smaller number of core businesses and industries. Hewlett-Packard spun off its testing and measurement businesses into a stand-alone company called Agilent Technologies so that it could better concentrate on its PC, workstation, server, printer and peripherals, and electronics businesses.

But there are other important reasons for divesting one or more of a company's present businesses. Sometimes divesting a business has to be considered because market conditions in a once-attractive industry have badly deteriorated. A business can become a prime candidate for divestiture because it lacks adequate strategic or resource fit, because it is a cash hog with questionable long-term potential, or because it is weakly positioned in its industry with little prospect that the corporate parent can realize a decent return on its investment in the business. Sometimes a company acquires businesses that, down the road, just do not work out as expected even though management has tried all it can think of to make them profitable. Subpar performance by some business units is bound to occur, thereby raising questions of whether to divest them or keep them and attempt a turnaround. Other business units, despite adequate financial performance, may not mesh as well with the rest of the firm as was originally thought.

On occasion, a diversification move that seems sensible from a strategic-fit stand-point turns out to be a poor *cultural fit*.[19] Several pharmaceutical companies had just this experience. When they diversified into cosmetics and perfume, they discovered their personnel had little respect for the "frivolous" nature of such products compared to the far nobler task of developing miracle drugs to cure the ill. The absence of shared values and cultural compatibility between the medical research and chemical-compounding expertise of the pharmaceutical companies and the fashion/marketing orientation of the cosmetics business was the undoing of what otherwise was diversification into businesses with technology-sharing potential, product-development fit, and some overlap in distribution channels.

Time Warner's 2000 merger with America Online (AOL) proved to be a dismal failure—its planned convergence of Time Warner Entertainment's movies, music, magazine content, and cable network programming with AOL's Internet platform and Time Warner Cable's broadband capabilities never materialized; the cultures of the three divisions prevented the capture of strategic-fit benefits; and shareholder value eroded by nearly 80 percent. After struggling for more than seven years to make a success of its diversification, Time Warner management spun off its Time Warner Cable operations into an independent business and began evaluating offers from buyers interested in purchasing AOL.

Tyco International began a restructuring program in 2004 to narrow its diversification base from more than 2,000 separate businesses with operations in over 100 countries. Much of Tyco's diversification came during the 1994–2001 tenure of CEO Dennis Kozlowski, who made over 1,000 acquisitions, totaling approximately $63 billion. The company's far-flung diversification included businesses in electronics, electrical components, fire and security systems, health care products, valves, undersea telecommunications systems, plastics, and adhesives. Tyco's corporate restructuring was capped with the 2007 spin-off of its electronics and health care businesses; once completed, the restructuring reduced the size of the company from approximately $40 billion in revenues and $70 billion in assets in 2001 to $18 billion in revenues and $33 billion in assets in 2007.

There's evidence indicating that pruning businesses and narrowing a firm's diversification base improves corporate performance.[20] But corporate parents often end up selling off unwanted or under-performing businesses too late and at too low a price, sacrificing shareholder value.[21] A useful guide to determine whether or when to divest a business subsidiary is to ask, "If we were not in this business today, would we want to get into it now?"[22] When the answer is no or probably not, divestiture should be considered. Another signal that a business should become a divestiture candidate is whether it is worth more to another company than to the present parent; in such cases, shareholders would be well served if the company sells the business and collects a premium price from the buyer for whom the business is a valuable fit.[23]

> Diversified companies need to divest low-performing businesses or businesses that don't fit in order to concentrate on expanding existing businesses and entering new ones where opportunities are more promising.

The Two Options for Divesting a Business: Selling It or Spinning It Off as an Independent Company Selling a business outright to another company is far and away the most frequently used option for divesting a business. But sometimes a business selected for divestiture has ample resource strengths to compete successfully on its own. In such cases, a corporate parent may elect to spin the unwanted business off as a financially and managerially independent company, either by selling shares to the investing public via an initial public offering or by distributing shares in the new company to existing shareholders of the corporate parent. When a corporate parent decides to spin off one of its businesses as a separate company, there's the issue of whether or not to retain partial ownership. Retaining partial ownership makes sense when the business to be divested has a hot product or technological capabilities that give it good profit prospects. When Bank of America elected to divest its CTC Consulting business unit, which made independent investment recommendations to clients with extreme wealth, it elected to retain an ownership interest in the business so as to provide Bank of America shareholders a way of participating in whatever future market success that CTC might have on its own. Investors expected CTC Consulting to perform better as an independent company since it would no longer be burdened by the conflict of interest that resulted from its corporate affiliation with a financial institution that offered its own investment products. In 2005, Cendant announced it would split its diversified businesses into four separate publicly traded companies—one for vehicle rental services (which consisted of Avis and Budget car rental companies); one for real estate and mortgage services (which included Century 21, Coldwell Banker, ERA, Sotheby's International Realty, and NRT—a residential real estate brokerage company); one for hospitality and lodging (consisting of such hotels and motel chains as Wyndam, Ramada, Days Inn, Howard Johnson, Travelodge, AmeriHost Inn, and Knights Inn, plus an assortment of timeshare resort properties); and one for travel (consisting of various travel agencies, online ticket and vacation travel sites like Orbitz and Cheap Tickets, and vacation rental operations handling some 55,000 villas and condos). Cendant said the reason for the split-up was that shareholders would realize more value from operating the businesses independently—a clear sign that Cendant's diversification strategy had failed to deliver added shareholder value and that the parts were worth more than the whole. Similarly, IAC/InterActive, which operated a host of Internet properties such as Ask.com and Match.com, spun off several businesses in 2008 because of lackluster performance and challenging industry conditions. The company's spin-off of its Lending Tree mortgage loan service unit, a timeshare-exchange business, Ticketmaster, and the Home Shopping Network yielded $1.3 billion that management planned to use to support investments in remaining businesses and fund a share buyback plan intended to help boost the company's dramatically declining stock price.

Selling a business outright requires finding a buyer. This can prove hard or easy, depending on the business. As a rule, a company selling a troubled business should not ask, "How can we pawn this business off on someone, and what is the most we can get for it?"[24] Instead, it is wiser to ask, "For what sort of company would this business be a good fit, and under what conditions would it be viewed as a good deal?" Enterprises for which the business is a good fit are likely to pay the highest price. Of course, if a buyer willing to pay an acceptable price cannot be found, then a company must decide whether to keep the business until a buyer appears; spin it off as a separate company; or, in the case of a crisis-ridden business that is losing substantial sums, simply close it down and liquidate the remaining assets. Liquidation is obviously a last resort.

CORE CONCEPT

Restructuring involves divesting some businesses and acquiring others so as to put a whole new face on the company's business lineup.

Restructuring a Company's Business Lineup through a Mix of Divestitures and New Acquisitions   Restructuring strategies involve divesting some businesses and acquiring others so as to put a whole new face on the company's business lineup. Performing radical surgery on a company's group of businesses is an appealing strategy alternative when its financial performance is being squeezed or eroded by:

- Too many businesses in slow-growth, declining, low-margin, or otherwise unattractive industries (a condition indicated by the number and size of businesses with industry attractiveness ratings below 5 and located on the bottom half of the attractiveness–strength matrix—see Figure 8.5).

- Too many competitively weak businesses (a condition indicated by the number and size of businesses with competitive strength ratings below 5 and located on the right half of the attractiveness–strength matrix).

- Ongoing declines in the market shares of one or more major business units that are falling prey to more market-savvy competitors.

- An excessive debt burden with interest costs that eat deeply into profitability.

- Ill-chosen acquisitions that haven't lived up to expectations.

Restructuring can also be mandated by the emergence of new technologies that threaten the survival of one or more of a diversified company's important businesses or by the appointment of a new CEO who decides to redirect the company. On occasion, restructuring can be prompted by special circumstances—like when a firm has a unique opportunity to make an acquisition so big and important that it has to sell several existing business units to finance the new acquisition or when a company needs to sell off some businesses in order to raise the cash for entering a potentially big industry with wave-of-the-future technologies or products.

Candidates for divestiture in a corporate restructuring effort typically include not only weak or up-and-down performers or those in unattractive industries but also business units that lack strategic fit with the businesses to be retained, businesses that are cash hogs or that lack other types of resource fit, and businesses incompatible with the company's revised diversification strategy (even though they may be profitable or in an attractive industry). As businesses are divested, corporate restructuring generally involves aligning the remaining business units into groups with the best strategic fits and then redeploying the cash flows from the divested business to either pay down debt or make new acquisitions to strengthen the parent company's business position in the industries it has chosen to emphasize.[25]

Over the past decade, corporate restructuring has become a popular strategy at many diversified companies, especially those that had diversified broadly into many different industries and lines of business. For instance, between 1994 and 2005 Ingersoll Rand radically restructured its business lineup by divesting its automotive components and mining components business units that accounted for 56 percent of its total revenues. During the same period, Ingersoll Rand made acquisitions of new businesses that went on to account for 52 percent of its 2005 total revenues. In 2007, the company executed the $6.2 billion sale of its road development, Bobcat, and utility equipment businesses and completed a variety of small acquisitions. Its corporate restructuring continued into 2008, with its $9.5 billion acquisition of Trane, a maker of heating and air-conditioning products. Trane had just undergone its own restructuring one year earlier when American Standard divested its legacy plumbing fixture business, spun off an automotive braking unit, and changed its name to Trane to reflect its new focus on heating and air-conditioning.

PerkinElmer used a series of divestitures and new acquisitions to transform itself from a supplier of low-margin services sold to the government agencies into an innovative high-tech company with operations in over 125 countries and businesses in four industry groups—life sciences (drug research and clinical screening), optoelectronics, medical instruments, and fluid control and containment services (for customers in aerospace, power generation, and semiconductors). In 2005, PerkinElmer took a second restructuring step by divesting its entire fluid control and containment business group so that it could concentrate on its higher growth health sciences and optoelectronics businesses; the company's CEO said, "While fluid services is an excellent business, it does not fit with our long-term strategy."[26]

During Jack Welch's first four years as CEO of General Electric (GE), the company divested 117 business units, accounting for about 20 percent of GE's assets; these divestitures, coupled with several important acquisitions, resulted in GE having 14 major business divisions and led to Welch's challenge to the managers of GE's divisions to become number one or number two in their industry. Ten years after Welch became CEO, GE was a different company, having divested operations worth $9 billion, made new acquisitions totaling $24 billion, and cut its workforce by 100,000 people. Then, during the 1990–2001 period, GE continued to reshuffle its business lineup, acquiring over 600 new companies, including 108 in 1998 and 64 during a 90-day period in 1999. Most of the new acquisitions were in Europe, Asia, and Latin America and were aimed at transforming GE into a truly global enterprise. In 2003, GE's new CEO, Jeffrey Immelt, began a further restructuring of GE's business lineup with three initiatives: (1) spending $10 billion to acquire British-based Amersham and extend GE's Medical Systems business unit into diagnostic pharmaceuticals and biosciences, thereby creating a $15 billion business designated as GE Healthcare; (2) acquire the entertainment assets of debt-ridden French media conglomerate Vivendi Universal Entertainment (Universal Studios, five Universal theme parks, USA Network, Sci-Fi Channel, the Trio cable channel, and Spanish-language broadcaster Telemundo) and integrate its operations into GE's NBC division (the owner of NBC, 29 television stations, and cable networks CNBC, MSNBC, and Bravo), thereby creating a broad-based $13 billion media business positioned to compete against Walt Disney, Time Warner, Fox, and Viacom; and (3) beginning a withdrawal from the insurance business by divesting several companies in its insurance division and preparing to spin off its remaining life and mortgage insurance businesses through an initial public offering (IPO) for a new company called Genworth Financial. In 2008, Jeffrey Immelt announced that GE would spin off its Industrial division, which included GE appliances, lighting, and various industrial businesses.

In a study of the performance of the 200 largest U.S. corporations from 1990 to 2000, McKinsey & Company found that those companies that actively managed their business portfolios through acquisitions and divestitures created substantially more shareholder value than those that kept a fixed lineup of businesses.[27] Illustration Capsule 8.4 discusses how VF Corporation shareholders have benefited through the company's large-scale restructuring program.

Pursuing Multinational Diversification

The distinguishing characteristics of a multinational diversification strategy are a *diversity of businesses* and a *diversity of national markets*.[28] Such diversity makes multinational diversification a particularly challenging and complex strategy to conceive and execute. Managers have to develop business strategies for each industry (with as many multinational variations as conditions in each country market dictate). Then they have to pursue and manage opportunities for cross-business and cross-country collaboration and strategic coordination in ways calculated to result in competitive advantage and enhanced profitability.

Moreover, the geographic operating scope of individual businesses within a diversified multinational company (DMNC) can range from one country only to several countries to many countries to global. Thus, each business unit within a DMNC often competes in a somewhat different combination of geographic markets than the other businesses do—adding another element of strategic complexity, and perhaps an element of opportunity.

ILLUSTRATION CAPSULE 8.4
The Corporate Restructuring Strategy That Made VF the Star of the Apparel Industry

VF Corporation's corporate restructuring—which included a mix of divestitures and acquisitions—has provided its shareholders with returns that are more than five times greater than shareholder returns provided by competing apparel manufacturers. In fact, VF delivered a total shareholder return of 110 percent between 1998 and 2007, and its 2007 revenues of $7 billion and annual revenue growth and earnings growth of 16 percent and 14 percent, respectively, made it number 335 on *Fortune*'s list of 500 largest U.S. companies. The company's corporate restructuring began in 2000 when it divested its slow-growing businesses, including its namesake Vanity Fair brand of lingerie and sleepwear. The company's $136 million acquisition of North Face in 2000 was the first in the series of many acquisitions of "lifestyle brands" that connected with the way people lived, worked, and played. Since the acquisition and turnaround of North Face, VF has spent $2.8 billion to acquire 18 additional businesses. New apparel brands acquired by VF Corporation include Vans skateboard shoes, Nautica, John Varvatos, 7 For All Mankind

sportswear, Reef surf wear, and Lucy athletic wear. The company also acquired a variety of apparel companies specializing in apparel segments such as uniforms for professional baseball and football teams and law enforcement.

VF Corporation's acquisitions came after years of researching each company and developing a relationship with an acquisition candidate's chief managers before closing the deal. The company made a practice of leaving management of acquired companies in place, while bringing in new managers only when necessary talent and skills were lacking. In addition, companies acquired by VF were allowed to keep long-standing traditions that shaped culture and spurred creativity. For example, the Vans headquarters in Cypress, California, retained its halfpipe and concrete floor so that its employees could skateboard to and from meetings.

In 2007, VF Corporation was the most profitable apparel firm in the industry, with net earnings of $591 million. The company expected new acquisitions that would push the company's revenues to $11 billion by 2012.

Sources: Suzanne Kapner, "How a 100-Year Old Apparel Firm Changed Course," *Fortune,* April 9, 2008, online edition; and www.vf.com (accessed July 24, 2008).

Illustration Capsule 8.5 on the next page shows the scope of four prominent DMNCs.

The Appeal of Multinational Diversification: More Opportunities for Sustained Growth and Maximum Competitive Advantage Potential Despite their complexity, multinational diversification strategies have great appeal. They contain *two major avenues* for growing revenues and profits: One is to grow by entering additional businesses, and the other is to grow by extending the operations of existing businesses into additional country markets. Moreover, a strategy of multinational diversification also contains five attractive paths to competitive advantage, *all of which can be pursued simultaneously:*

1. *Full capture of economies of scale and learning/experience curve effects.* In some businesses, the volume of sales needed to realize full economies of scale and/ or benefit fully from learning/experience curve effects is rather sizable, often exceeding the volume that can be achieved operating within the boundaries of a single country market, especially a small one. *The ability to drive down unit costs by expanding sales to additional country markets is one reason why a diversified multinational may seek to acquire a business and then rapidly expand its operations into more and more foreign markets.*

ILLUSTRATION CAPSULE 8.5
The Global Scope of Four Prominent Diversified Multinational Corporations

Company	Global Scope	Businesses into Which the Company Has Diversified
Sony	Operations in more than 100 countries and sales offices in more than 200 countries	• Televisions, VCRs, DVD players, Walkman radios and digital music players, clock radios, digital cameras and camcorders, car audio and GPS systems, mobile phones, Vaio PCs, Blu-ray technology products; PlayStation game consoles, portable video game players, video game software; Columbia, Epic, and Sony Classical prerecorded music; Columbia TriStar motion pictures; syndicated television programs; entertainment complexes, semiconductors, and financial services (insurance and banking)
Nestlé	Factories in 80 countries and sales offices in more than 200 countries	• Beverages (Nescafé and Taster's Choice coffees, Nestea, 72 brands of bottled waters including Perrier, San Pellegrino, Acqua Panna, Arrowhead, Deer Park, and Poland Springs); milk and dairy products (including Carnation, Coffee Mate, Milkmaid, Nestlé ice cream and yogurt, Dreyer's/Edy's ice creams and frozen yogurt); infant foods (including Gerber and 16 other brands); nutritional foods (PowerBar, Jenny Craig, and 8 other brands); pet foods (Friskies, Alpo, Fancy Feast, Purina, Beneful, ProPlan, and 7 other brands); Stouffer's, Lean Cuisine, Hot Pockets, and Buitoni food products and prepared dishes; Nestlé, Toll House, and Buitoni refrigerated products; Maggi soups; chocolate and confectionery products (Nestlé Crunch, Smarties, Polo, Butterfinger, KitKat); and pharmaceuticals (Alcon ophthalmic products, Galderma dermatological products)
Siemens	Operations in 160 countries and sales offices in more than 190 countries	• Electrical power generation, transmission, and distribution equipment and products; manufacturing automation systems; industrial motors, machinery, and tools; plant construction and maintenance services; telephones, VoIP and WiMax devices; PCs, mainframes, computer network products, consulting services; mass transit and light rail systems, rail cars, locomotives, lighting products (bulbs, lamps, automotive lighting, theater and television lighting systems); semiconductors; fire safety systems; industrial water treatment products; heating and ventilation systems; and financial, procurement, and logistics services.
Samsung	Operations in more than 60 countries and sales in more than 200 countries	• Personal computers, hard disk drives, CD/DVD drives for PCs, monitors, printers, fax machines, memory chips, televisions; DVD players; digital music players; cell phones and various other telecommunications products, home appliances (washing machines, dryers, refrigerators, air conditioners, cooking appliances), optical fibers, fiber-optic cables, and fiber-optic connectors.

Sources: Company annual reports and Web sites.

2. *Opportunities to capitalize on cross-business economies of scope.* Diversifying into related businesses offering economies of scope can drive the development of a low-cost advantage over less diversified rivals. For example, a DMNC that uses mostly the same distributors and retail dealers worldwide can diversify into new businesses using these same worldwide distribution channels at relatively little incremental expense. The cost savings of piggybacking distribution activities can be substantial. Moreover, with more business selling more products in more countries, a DMNC acquires more bargaining leverage in its purchases from suppliers and more bargaining leverage with retailers in securing attractive display

space for its products. Consider, for example, the competitive power that Sony derived from these very sorts of economies of scope when it decided to diversify into the video game business with its PlayStation product line. Sony had in-place capability to go after video game sales in all country markets where it presently did business in other electronics product categories (TVs, computers, DVD players, VCRs, radios, and CD players, and camcorders). And it had the marketing clout and brand-name credibility to persuade retailers to give Sony's PlayStation products prime shelf space and visibility. These strategic-fit benefits helped Sony quickly overtake longtime industry leaders Nintendo and Sega and defend its market leadership against Microsoft's new Xbox.

3. *Opportunities to transfer competitively valuable resources both from one business to another and from one country to another.* A company pursuing related diversification can gain a competitive edge over less diversified rivals by transferring competitively valuable resources from one business to another; a multinational company can gain competitive advantage over rivals with narrower geographic coverage by transferring competitively valuable resources from one country to another. But a strategy of multinational diversification enables simultaneous pursuit of both sources of competitive advantage.

4. *Ability to leverage use of a well-known and competitively powerful brand name.* Diversified multinational companies whose businesses have brand names that are well known and respected across the world possess a valuable strategic asset with competitive advantage potential. For example, Sony's well-established global brand-name recognition gives it an important marketing and advertising advantage over rivals with lesser-known brands. When Sony goes into a new marketplace with the stamp of the Sony brand on its product families, it can command prominent display space with retailers. It can expect to win sales and market share simply on the confidence that buyers place in products carrying the Sony name. While Sony may spend money to make consumers aware of the availability of its new products, it does not have to spend nearly as much on achieving brand recognition and market acceptance as would a lesser-known competitor looking at the marketing and advertising costs of entering the same new product/business/country markets and trying to go head-to-head against Sony. Further, if Sony moves into a new country market for the first time and does well selling Sony PlayStations and video games, it is easier to sell consumers in that country Sony TVs, digital cameras, PCs, MP3 players, and so on—plus, the related advertising costs are likely to be less than they would be without having already established the Sony brand strongly in the minds of buyers.

5. *Ability to capitalize on opportunities for cross-business and cross-country collaboration and strategic coordination.*[29] A multinational diversification strategy allows competitively valuable cross-business and cross-country coordination of certain value chain activities. For instance, by channeling corporate resources directly into a combined R&D/technology effort for all related businesses, as opposed to letting each business unit fund and direct its own R&D effort however it sees fit, a DMNC can merge its expertise and efforts *worldwide* to advance core technologies, expedite cross-business and cross-country product improvements, speed the development of new products that complement existing products, and pursue promising technological avenues to create altogether new businesses—all significant contributors to competitive advantage and better corporate performance.[30] Honda has been very successful in building R&D expertise in gasoline

engines and transferring the resulting technological advances to its businesses in automobiles, motorcycles, outboard engines, snow blowers, lawn mowers, garden tillers, and portable power generators. Further, a DMNC can reduce costs through cross-business and cross-country coordination of purchasing and procurement from suppliers, from collaborative introduction and shared use of e-commerce technologies and online sales efforts, and from coordinated product introductions and promotional campaigns. Firms that are less diversified and less global in scope have less such cross-business and cross-country collaborative opportunities.

The Combined Effects of These Advantages Is Potent   A strategy of diversifying into *related* industries and then competing *globally* in each of these industries thus has great potential for being a winner in the marketplace because of the long-term growth opportunities it offers and the multiple corporate-level competitive advantage opportunities it contains. *Indeed, a strategy of multinational diversification contains more competitive advantage potential (above and beyond what is achievable through a particular business's own competitive strategy) than any other diversification strategy.* The strategic key to maximum competitive advantage is for a DMNC to concentrate its diversification efforts in those industries where there are resource-sharing and resource-transfer opportunities and where there are important economies of scope and brand name benefits. The more a company's diversification strategy yields these kinds of strategic-fit benefits, the more powerful a competitor it becomes and the better its profit and growth performance is likely to be.

CORE CONCEPT

A strategy of multinational diversification has more built-in potential for competitive advantage than any other diversification strategy.

KEY POINTS

The purpose of diversification is to build shareholder value. Diversification builds shareholder value when a diversified group of businesses can perform better under the auspices of a single corporate parent than they would as independent, stand-alone businesses—the goal is to achieve not just a $1 + 1 = 2$ result but rather to realize important $1 + 1 = 3$ performance benefits. Whether getting into a new business has potential to enhance shareholder value hinges on whether a company's entry into that business can pass the attractiveness test, the cost-of-entry test, and the better-off test.

Entry into new businesses can take any of three forms: acquisition, internal start-up, or joint venture/strategic partnership. Each has its pros and cons, but acquisition is the most frequently used; internal start-up takes the longest to produce home-run results, and joint venture/strategic partnership, though used second most frequently, is the least durable.

There are two fundamental approaches to diversification—into related businesses and into unrelated businesses. The rationale for *related* diversification is *strategic:* Diversify into businesses with strategic fits along their respective value chains, capitalize on strategic-fit relationships to gain competitive advantage, and then use competitive advantage to achieve the desired $1 + 1 = 3$ impact on shareholder value.

The basic premise of unrelated diversification is that any business that has good profit prospects and can be acquired on good financial terms is a good business to diversify into. Unrelated diversification strategies surrender the competitive advantage potential of strategic fit in return for such advantages as (1) spreading business risk over a variety of industries and (2) providing opportunities for financial gain (if candidate acquisitions have undervalued assets, are bargain-priced and have good upside potential given the right management, or need the backing of a financially strong parent to capitalize on attractive opportunities). However, the greater the number of businesses a company has diversified into and the more diverse these businesses are, the harder it is for corporate executives to select capable managers to run each business, know when the major strategic proposals of business units are sound, or decide on a wise course of recovery when a business unit stumbles.

Analyzing how good a company's diversification strategy is a six-step process:

Step 1: *Evaluate the long-term attractiveness of the industries into which the firm has diversified.* Industry attractiveness needs to be evaluated from three angles: the attractiveness of each industry on its own, the attractiveness of each industry relative to the others, and the attractiveness of all the industries as a group.

Step 2: *Evaluate the relative competitive strength of each of the company's business units.* Again, quantitative ratings of competitive strength are preferable to subjective judgments. The purpose of rating the competitive strength of each business is to gain clear understanding of which businesses are strong contenders in their industries, which are weak contenders, and the underlying reasons for their strength or weakness. The conclusions about industry attractiveness can be joined with the conclusions about competitive strength by drawing an industry attractiveness–competitive strength matrix that helps identify the prospects of each business and what priority each business should be given in allocating corporate resources and investment capital.

Step 3: *Check for cross-business strategic fits.* A business is more attractive strategically when it has value chain relationships with sister business units that offer potential to (1) realize economies of scope or cost-saving efficiencies; (2) transfer technology, skills, know-how, or other resource capabilities from one business to another; (3) leverage use of a well-known and trusted brand name; and (4) build new or stronger resource strengths and competitive capabilities via cross-business collaboration. Cross-business strategic fits represent a significant avenue for producing competitive advantage beyond what any one business can achieve on its own.

Step 4: *Check whether the firm's resource strengths fit the resource requirements of its present business lineup.* Resource fit exists when (1) businesses add to a company's resource strengths, either financially or strategically, (2) a company has the resources to adequately support the resource requirements of its businesses as a group without spreading itself too thin, and (3) there are close matches between a company's resources and industry key success factors. One important test of financial resource fit involves determining whether a company has ample cash cows and not too many cash hogs.

Step 5: *Rank the performance prospects of the businesses from best to worst and determine what the corporate parent's priority should be in allocating resources to its various businesses.* The most important considerations in judging business-unit performance are sales growth, profit growth, contribution to company earnings, and the return on capital invested in the business. Sometimes, cash flow generation is a big consideration. Normally, strong business units in attractive industries have significantly better performance prospects than weak businesses or businesses in unattractive industries. Business subsidiaries with the brightest profit and growth prospects and solid strategic and resource fits generally should head the list for corporate resource support.

Step 6: *Crafting new strategic moves to improve overall corporate performance.* This step entails using the results of the preceding analysis as the basis for devising actions to strengthen existing businesses, make new acquisitions, divest weak-performing and unattractive businesses, restructure the company's business lineup, expand the scope of the company's geographic reach multinationally or globally, and otherwise steer corporate resources into the areas of greatest opportunity. Once a company has diversified, corporate management's task is to manage the collection of businesses for maximum long-term performance. There are five different strategic paths for improving a diversified company's performance: (1) sticking with the existing business lineup, (2) broadening the firm's business base by diversifying into additional businesses, (3) retrenching to a narrower diversification base by divesting some of its present businesses, (4) restructuring the company's business lineup with a combination of divestitures and new acquisitions to put a whole new face on the company's business makeup, and (5) pursuing multinational diversification and striving to globalize the operations of several of the company's business units.

ASSURANCE OF LEARNING EXERCISES

1. See if you can identify the value chain relationships that make Outback Steakhouse's different restaurant businesses (listed below) related in competitively relevant ways. In particular, you should consider whether there are cross-business opportunities for (*a*) skills/technology transfer, (*b*) combining related value chain activities to achieve lower costs, and/or (*c*) leveraging use of a well-respected brand name.

   - Outback Steakhouse
   - Carrabba's Italian Grill
   - Roy's Restaurant (Hawaiian fusion cuisine)
   - Bonefish Grill (market-fresh fine seafood)
   - Fleming's Prime Steakhouse & Wine Bar
   - Lee Roy Selmon's (Southern comfort food)
   - Cheeseburger in Paradise
   - Blue Coral Seafood & Spirits (fine seafood)

2. Go to Unilever's Web site (www.unilever.com) and peruse the company's lineup of brands and businesses. Is Unilever's strategy best characterized as one of related diversification, unrelated diversification, or a combination of related and unrelated diversification? Be prepared to justify and explain your answer in terms of the extent to which the value chains of Unilever's different businesses seem to have competitively valuable cross-business relationships.

3. Go to the Web site of the diversified luxury goods company LVMH (www.lvmh. com) and peruse the company's lineup of luxury brands and businesses. Is LVMH's strategy best characterized as one of related diversification, unrelated diversification, or a combination of related and unrelated diversification? Do you see any

competitively valuable cross-business relationships at LVMH? Might the expertise of LVMH's corporate executives in managing a portfolio of luxury brands be valuable to each of the business/brands and also act to help build added value for LVMH shareholders? Why or why not?

4. The defining characteristic of unrelated diversification is few competitively valuable cross-business relationships. Peruse the business group listings for Lancaster Colony below and see if you can confirm why it is pursuing an unrelated diversification strategy.

   - Specialty food products: Cardini, Marzetti, Girard's, and Pheiffer salad dressings; Chatham Village croutons; Jack Daniels mustards; Inn Maid noodles; and Romanoff caviar
   - Candle-lite brand candles marketed to retailers and private-label customer chains
   - Glassware, plasticware, coffee urns, and matting products marketed to the food service and lodging industries

   If you need additional information about Lancaster Colony's business lineup to determine its strategy to answer the question, visit the company's Web site (www. lancastercolony.com).

5. The Walt Disney Company is in the following businesses:
   - Theme parks
   - Disney Cruise Line
   - Resort properties
   - Movie, video, and theatrical productions (for both children and adults)
   - Television broadcasting (ABC, Disney Channel, Toon Disney, Classic Sports Network, ESPN and ESPN2, E!, Lifetime, and A&E networks)
   - Radio broadcasting (Disney Radio)
   - Musical recordings and sales of animation art
   - Anaheim Mighty Ducks NHL franchise
   - Anaheim Angels Major League Baseball franchise (25 percent ownership)
   - Books and magazine publishing
   - Interactive software and Internet sites
   - The Disney Store retail shops

   Based on the above list, would you say that Walt Disney's business lineup reflects a strategy of related diversification, unrelated diversification, or a combination of related and unrelated diversification? Be prepared to justify and explain your answer in terms of the extent to which the value chains of Disney's different businesses seem to have competitively valuable cross-business relationships.

6. The Jarden Corporation has recently acquired a number of businesses that include:
   - Sunbeam and Oster small appliances
   - Völkl and K2 ski equipment
   - Mr. Coffee coffemakers
   - Rival, VillaWare, and Crock-Pot cookware
   - Shakespeare and Penn fishing rods and reels
   - Marmot and ExOfficio outdoor apparel
   - Coleman camping equipment

- Rawlins sporting goods
- Hoyle playing cards
- Ball jars (used for home canning)
- Bionaire and Holmes humidifiers, fans, and other home comfort products
- Healthometer scales
- Jarden zinc and electroplated products
- First Alert alarm systems

Based on the above list, would you say that Jarden's acquisition strategy involves the pursuit of related diversification, unrelated diversification, or a combination of both? Explain.

7. General Electric recently organized its broadly diversified lineup of products and services into the following six business groups:

- GE Commercial Finance: commercial and consumer finance (loans, operating leases, financing programs and financial services provided to corporations, retailers, and consumers in 35 countries)—revenues of $34.3 billion in 2007.
- GE Healthcare: medical imaging and information technologies, medical diagnostics, patient monitoring systems, disease research, drug discovery and biopharmaceuticals—revenues of $17 billion in 2007.
- GE Industrial: consumer appliances, lighting, and electrical equipment; industrial automation hardware and software, controls, sensors, and security systems—revenues of $17.7 billion in 2007.
- GE Infrastructure: jet engines for military and civil aircraft, freight and passenger locomotives, motorized systems for mining trucks and drills, and gas turbines for marine and industrial applications, electric power generation equipment, power transformers, high-voltage breakers, distribution transformers and breakers, capacitors, relays, regulators, substation equipment, metering products, water treatment and purification—revenues of $57.9 billion in 2007.
- GE Money: credit cards, consumer personal loans, automobile loans, mortgage loans—revenues of $25 billion in 2007.
- NBC Universal: owns and operates the NBC television network, a Spanish-language network (Telemundo), several news and entertainment networks (CNBC, MSNBC, Bravo, Sci-Fi Channel, Sleuth, USA Network), Universal Pictures, Universal Studios Home Entertainment, various television production operations, several special interest Internet sites; a group of television stations, and theme parks—revenues of $15.4 billion in 2007.

a. Is GE's diversified business lineup best characterized as unrelated diversification or a combination of related and unrelated diversification?

b. Is GE more accurately categorized as a dominant business-enterprise or a broadly diversified conglomerate or something else?

c. Do you see any strategic-fit opportunities in GE's business lineup? Are these strategic-fit opportunities, if any, more within each of the six business groupings or do they cut across the six business groupings? Explain.

EXERCISES FOR SIMULATION PARTICIPANTS

1. If your company can diversify into multiple products/businesses, are the diversification opportunities best characterized as related or unrelated? Explain. If the diversification opportunities are related, what precisely are the strategic-fit relationships that are available for capture?

2. Irrespective of whether your company has the option to diversify into other products/businesses, what specific resources does your company have that would make it attractive to diversify into related businesses? List as many resource strengths as you think are transferable to other businesses and also indicate what kinds of strategic-fit benefits could be captured with these resource strengths.

3. Assuming your company has the option to diversify into other products or businesses of your choosing, would you prefer to pursue a strategy of related or unrelated diversification? Why?

9

Ethical Business Strategies, Social Responsibility, and Environmental Sustainability

LEARNING OBJECTIVES

1. Understand why business conduct is judged according to the ethical standards of society at large rather than a special set of ethical standards for businesses only.

2. Understand the principal drivers of unethical strategies and business behavior.

3. Learn why unethical business conduct can be very costly for a company's shareholders.

4. Become familiar with the various approaches to managing a company's ethical conduct.

5. Gain an understanding of the concepts of corporate social responsibility, corporate citizenship, and environmental sustainability.

6. Become familiar with both the moral case and the business case for ethical business conduct and socially responsible business behavior.

When morality comes up against profit, it is seldom profit that loses.

—Shirley Chisholm
Former Congresswoman

But I'd shut my eyes in the sentry box so I didn't see nothing wrong.

—Rudyard Kipling
"The Shut-Eye Sentry"

Corporations are economic entities, to be sure, but they are also social institutions that must justify their existence by their overall contribution to society.

—Henry Mintzberg, Robert Simons, and Kunal Basu
Professors

Integrity violations are no-brainers. In such cases, you don't need to hesitate for a moment before firing someone or fret about it either. Just do it, and make sure the organization knows why, so that the consequences of breaking the rules are not lost on anyone.

—Jack Welch
Former CEO, General Electric

There is one and only one social responsibility of business—to use its resources and engage in activities designed to increase its profits so long as it stays within the rules of the game, which is to say engages in free and open competition, without deception or fraud.

—Milton Friedman
Nobel Prize–winning Economist

Clearly, a company has a responsibility to make a profit and grow the business—in capitalistic or market economies, management's fiduciary duty to create value for shareholders is not a matter for serious debate. Just as clearly, a company and its personnel also have a duty to obey the law and play by the rules of fair competition. But does a company have a duty to operate according to the ethical norms of the societies in which it operates—should it be held to some standard of ethical conduct? And does it have a duty or obligation to contribute to the betterment of society independent of the needs and preferences of the customers it serves? Should a company display a social conscience and devote a portion of its resources to bettering society? Should a company alter its business practices to help protect the environment and sustain the world's natural resources?

The focus of this chapter is to examine what link, if any, there should be between a company's efforts to craft and execute a winning strategy and its duties to (1) conduct its activities in an ethical manner; (2) demonstrate socially responsible behavior by being a committed corporate citizen and directing corporate resources to the betterment of employees, the communities in which it operates, and society as a whole; and (3) limit its strategic initiatives to those that meet the needs of consumers without depleting resources needed by future generations.

WHAT DO WE MEAN BY *BUSINESS ETHICS?*

> **CORE CONCEPT**
>
> *Business ethics* concerns the application of general ethical principles and standards to the actions and decisions of companies and the conduct of company personnel.

Business ethics is the application of ethical principles and standards to business behavior.[1] Ethical principles in business are not materially different from ethical principles in general because business actions have to be judged in the context of society's standards of right and wrong. There is not a special set of ethical standards or guidelines that businesspeople can decide to apply to their own conduct. If dishonesty is considered to be unethical and immoral, then dishonest behavior in business—whether it relates to customers, suppliers, employees, or shareholders—qualifies as equally unethical and immoral. If being ethical entails not deliberately harming others, then recalling a defective or unsafe product is ethically necessary and failing to undertake such a recall or correct the problem in future shipments of the product is likewise unethical. If society deems bribery to be unethical, then it is unethical for company personnel to make payoffs to government officials to facilitate business transactions or bestow gifts and other favors on prospective customers to win or retain their business. In short, ethical behavior in business situations requires adhering to generally accepted norms about conduct that determine whether an action is right or wrong. As a consequence, company managers have an obligation—indeed, a duty—to observe ethical norms when crafting and executing strategy.

How and Why Ethical Standards Impact the Tasks of Crafting and Executing Strategy

Many companies have acknowledged their ethical obligations in official codes and values statements. In the United States, for example, the Sarbanes-Oxley Act, passed in 2002, requires that companies whose stock is publicly traded have a code of ethics or else explain in writing to the Securities and Exchange Commission (SEC) why they do not. But there's a big difference between having a code of ethics that serves merely as public window dressing and having ethical standards that truly paint the white lines for a company's actual strategy and business conduct.[2] *The litmus test of a company's code of ethics is the extent to which it is embraced in crafting strategy and in operating the business day to day.*

It is up to senior executives to walk the talk and make a point of considering two sets of questions whenever a new strategic initiative is under review:

- Is what we are proposing to do fully compliant with our code of ethical conduct? Is there anything here that could be considered ethically objectionable?

- Is it apparent that this proposed action is in harmony with our core values? Are any conflicts or concerns evident?

Unless questions of this nature are posed—either in open discussion or by force of habit in the minds of strategy makers—then there's room for strategic initiatives to become disconnected from the company's code of ethics and stated core values. If a company's executives believe strongly in living up to the company's stated core values, there's a good chance they will unhesitatingly reject strategic initiatives and operating approaches that don't measure up. However, in companies with window-dressing ethics and core values, any strategy-ethics-values linkage stems mainly from a desire to avoid the risks of embarrassment and of possible disciplinary action should strategy makers be held accountable for approving a strategic initiative that is deemed by society to be unethical or perhaps illegal.

While most company managers are usually careful to ensure that a company's strategy is legal, the available evidence indicates they are not always so careful to ensure that all elements of their strategies and operating activities are within the bounds of what is generally deemed ethical. In recent years, there have been revelations of ethical misconduct on the part of managers at such companies as Enron, Tyco International, HealthSouth, Rite Aid, Citicorp, Bristol-Myers Squibb, Adelphia, Royal Dutch/Shell, the Italy-based food products company Parmalat, the Mexican oil giant Pemex, Marsh & McLennan and other insurance brokers, several leading brokerage houses and investment banking firms, and a host of mutual fund companies. In 2005, four global companies—Samsung and Hynix Semiconductor in South Korea, Infineon Technologies in Germany, and Micron Technology in the United States—pleaded guilty to conspiring to fix the prices of dynamic random access memory (DRAM) chips sold to such companies as Dell, Apple, and Hewlett-Packard. Alstom SA, a giant France-based engineering firm and maker of power plant turbines and high-speed trains and subway cars, has been accused by French and Swiss prosecutors of using a Swiss slush fund to pay $500 million in bribes to foreign officials to win contracts abroad during 2001–2008; executives at Siemens AG of Germany, one of Alstom's competitors, have been charged by German authorities with paying bribes of about $2 billion to win large contracts in 12 foreign countries during 2000–2006. Much of the crisis in residential real estate that emerged in the United States in 2007–2008 stemmed from consciously unethical strategies at certain banks and mortgage companies to boost the fees they earned on processing home mortgage applications by deliberately lowering lending standards and finding ways to secure mortgage approvals for home buyers who lacked sufficient income to make their monthly mortgage payments. Once these lenders earned their fees on the so-called subprime loans (a term used for high-risk mortgage loans made to home buyers with dubious qualifications to repay the loans), they secured the assistance of investment banking firms to bundle those and other mortgages into collateralized debt obligations (CDOs), found means of having the CDOs assigned triple-A bond ratings, and auctioned them to unsuspecting investors, who later suffered huge losses when the high-risk borrowers began to default on their loan payments and foreclosure procedures had to be initiated (government authorities later forced some of the firms that auctioned off these CDOs to repurchase them at the auction price and bear the losses themselves).

The consequences of crafting strategies that cannot pass the test of moral scrutiny are manifested in sharp drops in stock prices that cost shareholders billions of dollars, devastating public relations hits, sizable fines, and criminal indictments and convictions of company executives. The fallout from recent business scandals has resulted in heightened management attention to legal and ethical considerations in crafting strategy.

WHERE DO ETHICAL STANDARDS COME FROM—ARE THEY UNIVERSAL OR DEPENDENT ON LOCAL NORMS AND SITUATIONAL CIRCUMSTANCES?

Notions of right and wrong, fair and unfair, moral and immoral, ethical and unethical are present in all societies, organizations, and individuals. But there are three schools of thought about the extent to which the ethical standards travel across cultures and whether multinational companies can apply the same set of ethical standards in any and all of the locations where they operate.

The School of Ethical Universalism

According to the school of **ethical universalism,** some concepts of what is right and what is wrong are *universal* and transcend most cultures, societies, and religions.[3] For instance, being truthful (or not lying or not being deliberately deceitful) strikes a chord of what's right in the peoples of all nations. Likewise, demonstrating integrity of character, not cheating, and treating people with dignity and respect are concepts that resonate with people of most cultures and religions. In most societies, people believe that companies should not pillage or degrade the environment in the course of conducting their operations. In most societies, people would concur that it is unethical to knowingly expose workers to toxic chemicals and hazardous materials or to sell products known to be unsafe or harmful to the users. *To the extent there is common moral agreement about right and wrong actions and behaviors across multiple cultures and countries, there exists a set of universal ethical standards to which all societies, all companies, and all individuals can be held accountable.*

Ethical norms considered universal by many ethicists include honesty, trustworthiness, respecting the rights of others, practicing the Golden Rule (i.e., treat others as you would like to be treated), exercising due diligence in product safety, and not acting in a manner that harms others or pillages the environment. These universal ethical principles or norms put limits on what actions and behaviors fall inside the boundaries of what is right and which ones fall outside; they set forth the traits and behaviors that a virtuous person is supposed to believe in and to display.[4] Adherents of the school of ethical universalism maintain that the conduct of personnel at companies operating in a variety of country markets and cultural circumstances can be judged against this set of universal ethical standards.

The strength of ethical universalism is that it draws on the collective views of multiple societies and cultures to put some clear boundaries on business behavior no matter what country market or culture a company or its personnel are operating in. This means that in those instances where basic moral standards really do not vary significantly according to local cultural beliefs, traditions, religious convictions, or time and circumstance, a multinational company can develop a code of ethics that it applies more or less evenly across its worldwide operations.[5] It can avoid the slippery slope that comes from having different ethical standards for different company personnel depending on where in the world they are working.

The School of Ethical Relativism

But apart from select universal basics—honesty, trustworthiness, fairness, a regard for worker safety, and respect for the environment—there are meaningful variations in what societies generally agree to be right and wrong in the conduct of business activities. Divergent religious beliefs, historic traditions, social customs, and prevailing political and economic doctrines (whether a country leans more toward a capitalistic market economy or one heavily dominated by socialistic or communistic principles) frequently produce ethical norms that vary from one country to another. The school of **ethical relativism** holds that when there are cross-country or cross-cultural differences in what is deemed ethical or unethical in business situations, it is appropriate for local moral standards to take precedence over what the ethical standards may be elsewhere—for instance, in a company's home market.

The thesis is that whatever a culture thinks is right or wrong really is right or wrong for that culture.[6] Consider the following examples.

The Use of Underage Labor   In industrialized nations, the use of child workers is considered taboo; social activists are adamant that child labor is unethical and that companies should neither employ children under the age of 18 as full-time nor source any products from foreign suppliers that employ underage workers. Many countries have passed legislation forbidding the use of underage labor or, at a minimum, regulating the employment of people under 18. However, in India, Bangladesh, Botswana, Sri Lanka, Ghana, Somalia, Turkey, and 100-plus other countries, it is customary to view children as potential, even necessary, workers. Many poverty-stricken families cannot subsist without the income earned by young family members; sending their children to school instead of having them work is not a realistic option. In 2006, the International Labor Organization estimated that 191 million children ages 5 to 14 were working around the world.[7] If such children are not permitted to work—due to pressures imposed by activist groups in industrialized nations—they may be forced to take lower-wage jobs in "hidden" parts of the economy, to go out on the street begging, or even to traffic in drugs or engage in prostitution.[8] So if all businesses succumb to the protests of activist groups and government organizations that, based on their values and beliefs, loudly proclaim that underage labor is unethical, then have either businesses or the protesting groups really done something good on behalf of society in general?

The Payment of Bribes and Kickbacks   A particularly thorny issue facing multinational companies is the degree of cross-country variability in paying bribes.[9] In many countries in Eastern Europe, Africa, Latin America, and Asia, it is customary to pay bribes to government officials in order to win a government contract, obtain a license or permit, or facilitate an administrative ruling.[10] Senior managers in China often use their power to obtain kickbacks and offer bribes when they purchase materials or other products for their companies.[11] In some developing nations, it is difficult for any company, foreign or domestic, to move goods through customs without paying off low-level officials.[12] Some people stretch to justify the payment of bribes and kickbacks on grounds that bribing government officials to get goods through customs or giving kickbacks to customers to retail their business or win an order is simply a payment for services rendered, in the same way that people tip for service at restaurants.[13] But even though it is a clever and pragmatic rationalization, this argument rests on moral quicksand.

Companies that forbid the payment of bribes and kickbacks in their codes of ethical conduct and that are serious about enforcing this prohibition face a particularly vexing problem in those countries where bribery and kickback payments have been entrenched as a local custom for decades and are not considered unethical by the local population.[14] Refusing to pay bribes or kickbacks (so as to comply with the company's code of ethical conduct) is very often tantamount to losing business. Frequently, the sales and profits are lost to more unscrupulous companies, with the result that both ethical companies and ethical individuals are penalized. On the other hand, the payment of bribes or kickbacks not only undercuts enforcement of and adherence to the company's code of ethics but can also risk breaking the law. U.S. companies are prohibited by the Foreign Corrupt Practices Act (FCPA) from paying bribes to government officials, political parties, political candidates, or others in all countries where they do business; the FCPA requires U.S. companies with foreign operations to adopt accounting practices that ensure full disclosure of a company's transactions so that illegal payments can be detected. The 35 member countries of the Organization for Economic Cooperation and Development (OECD) in 1997 adopted a convention to combat bribery in international business transactions; the Anti-Bribery Convention obligated the countries to criminalize the bribery of foreign public officials, including payments made to political parties and party officials. However, so far there has been only token enforcement of the OECD convention and the payment of bribes in global business transactions remains a common practice in many countries.

Ethical Relativism Equates to Multiple Sets of Ethical Standards   The existence of varying ethical norms such as those cited above explains why the adherents of ethical relativism maintain that there are few absolutes when it comes to business ethics and thus few ethical absolutes for consistently judging a company's conduct in various countries and markets. Indeed, the thesis of ethical relativists is that while there are sometimes general moral prescriptions that apply in most every society and business circumstance, there are plenty of situations where ethical norms must be contoured to fit the local customs, traditions, and the notions of fairness shared by the parties involved. They argue that a "one-size-fits-all" template for judging the ethical appropriateness of business actions and the behaviors of company personnel simply does not exist—in other words, ethical problems in business cannot be fully resolved without appealing to the shared convictions of the parties in question.[15] European and American managers may want to impose standards of business conduct that give heavy weight to such core human rights as personal freedom, individual security, political participation, the ownership of property, and the right to subsistence as well as the obligation to respect the dignity of each human person, provide a safe workplace, and respect the environment; managers in China have a much weaker commitment to these kinds of human rights. Japanese managers may prefer ethical standards that show respect for the collective good of society. Muslim managers may wish to apply ethical standards compatible with the teachings of Mohammed. Individual companies may want to give explicit recognition to the importance of company personnel living up to the company's own espoused values and business principles. Clearly, there is merit in the school of ethical relativism's view that what is deemed right or wrong, fair or unfair, moral or immoral, ethical or unethical in business situations depends partly on the context of each country's local customs, religious traditions, and societal norms. Hence, there is a kernel of truth in the argument that businesses need some room to tailor their ethical standards to fit local situations. A company has to be cautious about exporting its home-country values and ethics to foreign countries where it operates—"photocopying" ethics is disrespectful of other cultures and neglects the important role of moral free space.

> Under ethical relativism, there can be no one-size-fits-all set of authentic ethical norms against which to gauge the conduct of company personnel.

Pushed to Extremes, Ethical Relativism Breaks Down   While the ethically relativist rule of "When in Rome, do as the Romans do" appears reasonable, it nonetheless presents a big problem—when the envelope starts to be pushed, as will inevitably be the case, *it is tantamount to rudderless ethical standards.* Consider, for instance, the following example: In 1992, the owners of the SS *United States,* an aging luxury ocean liner constructed with asbestos in the 1940s, had the liner towed to Turkey, where a contractor had agreed to remove the asbestos for $2 million (versus a far higher cost in the United States, where asbestos removal safety standards were much more stringent).[16] When Turkish officials blocked the asbestos removal because of the dangers to workers of contracting cancer, the owners had the liner towed to the Black Sea port of Sevastopol, in the Crimean Republic, where the asbestos removal standards were quite lax and where a contractor had agreed to remove more than 500,000 square feet of carcinogenic asbestos for less than $2 million. There are no moral grounds for arguing that exposing workers to carcinogenic asbestos is ethically correct, irrespective of what a country's law allows or the value the country places on worker safety.

A company that adopts the principle of ethical relativism and holds company personnel to local ethical standards necessarily assumes that what prevails as local morality is an adequate guide to ethical behavior. This can be ethically dangerous—it leads to the conclusion that if a country's culture is accepting of bribery or environmental degradation or exposing workers to dangerous conditions (toxic chemicals or bodily harm), then so much the worse for honest people and protection of the environment and safe working conditions. Such a position is morally unacceptable. Even though bribery of government officials in China is a common practice, when Lucent Technologies found that managers in its Chinese operations had bribed government officials, it fired the entire senior management team.[17]

> Managers in multinational enterprises have to figure out how to navigate the gray zone that arises when operating in two cultures with two sets of ethics.

Moreover, from a global markets perspective, ethical relativism results in a maze of conflicting ethical standards for multinational companies wanting to address the very real issue of what ethical standards to enforce companywide. It is a slippery slope indeed to resolve such ethical diversity without any kind of higher-order moral compass. Imagine, for example, that a multinational company says it is okay for company personnel to pay bribes and kickbacks in countries where such payments are customary but not okay in countries where they are considered unethical or illegal. Or that the company says it is fine to use child labor in its plants in those countries where underage labor is acceptable but not fine to employ child labor at the remainder of its plants. Having thus adopted conflicting ethical standards for operating in different countries, company managers have little moral basis for enforcing ethical standards companywide—rather, the clear message to employees would be that the company has no ethical standards or principles of its own. This is scarcely strong moral ground to stand on.

Ethics and Integrative Social Contracts Theory

Social contract theory provides a middle position between the opposing views of universalism (that the same set of ethical standards should apply everywhere) and relativism (that ethical standards vary according to local custom).[18] According to **integrative social contracts theory,** the ethical standards a company should try to uphold are governed both by (1) a limited number of universal ethical principles that are widely recognized as putting legitimate ethical boundaries on actions and behavior in *all* situations and (2) the circumstances of local cultures, traditions, and shared values that further prescribe what constitutes ethically permissible behavior and what does not. *The uniform agreements about what is morally right and wrong form a contract with society, or "social contract," that is binding on all individuals, groups, organizations, and businesses in terms of establishing right and wrong and in drawing the line between ethical and unethical behaviors.* But these universal ethical principles or norms nonetheless still leave some "moral free space" for the people in a particular country (or local culture or even a company) to make specific interpretations of what other actions may or may not be permissible within the bounds defined by universal ethical principles. Hence, while firms, industries, professional associations, and other business-relevant groups are "contractually obligated"

CORE CONCEPT

According to *integrative social contracts theory,* universal ethical principles or norms based on the collective views of multiple cultures and societies combine to form a "social contract" that all individuals in all situations have a duty to observe. Within the boundaries of this social contract, local cultures or groups can specify other impermissible actions; however, universal ethical norms always take precedence over local ethical norms.

to society to observe universal ethical norms, they have the discretion to go beyond these universal norms and specify other behaviors that are out of bounds and place further limitations on what is considered ethical. Both the legal and medical professions have standards regarding what kinds of advertising are ethically permissible and what kinds are not. Food producers are beginning to establish ethical guidelines for judging what is and is not appropriate advertising for food products that are inherently unhealthy and may cause dietary or obesity problems for people who eat them regularly or consume them in large quantities. Likewise, fast-food chains and restaurants are beginning to exhibit ethical concerns about the calorie content and nutritional value of their menu offerings.

The strength of integrative social contracts theory is that it accommodates the best parts of ethical universalism and ethical relativism. It is indisputable that cultural differences impact how business is conducted in various parts of the world and that these cultural differences sometimes give rise to different ethical norms. But it is just as indisputable that some ethical norms are more authentic or universally applicable than others, meaning that in many instances of cross-country differences one side may be more "ethically correct" than another. In circumstances where local ethical norms are more permissive, resolving the conflict between universal, or "first-order," ethical norms and local, or "second-order," ethical norms *requires* adhering to universal ethical norms and overriding local ethical norms. A good example is the payment of bribes and kickbacks. Yes, bribes and kickbacks seem to be common in some countries, but does this justify paying them? Just because bribery flourishes in a country does not mean that it is an authentic or legitimate ethical norm. Virtually all of the world's major religions (Buddhism, Christianity, Confucianism, Hinduism, Islam, Judaism, Sikhism, and Taoism) and all moral schools of thought condemn bribery and corruption.[19] Bribery is commonplace in India, but, in one set of interviews, Indian CEOs whose companies constantly engaged in payoffs indicated their disgust for the practice and expressed no illusions about its impropriety.[20] Therefore, a multinational company might reasonably conclude that the right ethical standard is one of refusing to condone bribery and kickbacks on the part of company personnel no matter what the local custom is and no matter what the sales consequences are.

Granting an automatic preference to local ethical norms presents vexing problems to multinational company managers when the ethical standards followed in a foreign country are lower than those in its home country or are in conflict with the company's code of ethics. Sometimes—as with bribery and kickbacks—there can be no compromise on what is ethically permissible and what is not. *This is precisely what integrative social contracts theory maintains: Adherence to universal or first-order ethical norms should always take precedence over local or second-order norms.* Consequently, integrative social contracts theory offers managers in multinational companies some valuable guidance in dealing with different ethical standards in different countries: those parts of the company's code of ethics that involve universal ethical norms must be enforced worldwide, but *within these boundaries* ethical diversity is acceptable and there is room for company personnel to observe the moral and ethical standards of host country cultures. Such an accommodation of the second-order ethical norms in various countries detours the somewhat scary case of a self-righteous multinational company trying to operate as the standard-bearer of moral truth and imposing its interpretation of its code of ethics worldwide no matter what. And it avoids the equally scary case for a company's ethical conduct to be no higher than local ethical norms in situations where local ethical norms permit practices that are generally considered immoral or when local norms clearly conflict with a company's code of ethical conduct. But even with the guidance provided by integrative social contracts theory, there are many instances where cross-country differences in ethical norms create "gray areas" where it is tough to draw a line in the sand between right and wrong decisions, actions, and business practices.

THE THREE CATEGORIES OF MANAGEMENT MORALITY

Three categories of managers stand out with regard to ethical and moral principles in business affairs:[21]

- *The moral manager*—Moral managers are dedicated to high standards of ethical behavior, both in their own actions and in their expectations of how the company's business is to be conducted. They see themselves as stewards of ethical behavior and believe it is important to exercise ethical leadership. Moral managers may well be ambitious and have a powerful urge to succeed, but they pursue success in business within the confines of both the letter and the spirit of what is ethical and legal—they typically regard the law as an ethical minimum and have a habit of operating well above what the law requires.

- *The immoral manager*—Immoral managers have no regard for so-called ethical standards in business and pay no attention to ethical principles in making decisions and conducting the company's business. Their philosophy is that good business-people cannot spend time watching out for the interests of others and agonizing over "the ethically correct thing to do." In the minds of immoral managers, nice guys come in second and the competitive nature of business requires that you either trample on others or get trampled yourself. They believe what really matters is single-minded pursuit of their own best interests—they are living examples of self-serving greed, caring only about their own or their organization's gains and successes. Immoral managers may even be willing to short-circuit legal and regulatory requirements if they think they can escape detection. And they are always on the lookout for legal loopholes and creative ways to get around rules and regulations that block or constrain actions they deem in their own or their company's self-interest. Immoral managers are thus the bad guys—they have few scruples, little or no integrity, and are willing to do most anything they believe they can get away with. It doesn't bother them much to be seen by others as wearing the black hats.

- *The amoral manager*—Amoral managers appear in two forms: the intentionally amoral manager and the unintentionally amoral manager. Intentionally amoral managers are of the strong opinion that business and ethics are not to be mixed. They are not troubled by failing to factor ethical considerations into their decisions and actions because it is perfectly legitimate for businesses to do anything they wish so long as they stay within legal and regulatory bounds—in other words, if particular actions and behaviors are legal and comply with existing regulations, then they qualify as permissible and should not be seen as unethical. Intentionally amoral managers view the observance of high ethical standards (doing more than what is required by law) as too Sunday-schoolish for the tough competitive world of business, even though observing some higher ethical considerations may be appropriate in life outside of business. Their concept of right and wrong tends to be lawyer-driven—"How much can we get by with?" and "Can we go ahead even if it is borderline?" Like immoral managers, intentionally amoral managers hold firmly to the view that anything goes, but differ from immoral managers in that they acknowledge that business actions and behaviors must comply with prevailing legal and regulatory requirements.

Unintentionally amoral managers do not pay much attention to the concept of business ethics either, but for different reasons. They are simply casual about, careless about, or inattentive to the fact that certain kinds of business decisions or company activities are unsavory or may have deleterious effects on others—in short, they go about their jobs as best they can without giving serious thought to the ethical dimension of decisions and business actions. They are ethically unconscious when it comes to business matters, partly or mainly because they have just never stopped to consider whether and to what extent business decisions or company actions sometimes spill over to create adverse impacts on others. Unintentionally amoral managers may even see themselves as people of integrity and as personally ethical. But their behaviors and actions send the message to subordinates that businesses ought to be able to do whatever the current legal and regulatory framework allows them to do without being shackled by ethical considerations.

By some accounts, the population of managers is distributed among all three types in a bell-shaped curve, with immoral managers and moral managers occupying the two tails of the curve, and the amoral managers (especially the intentionally amoral managers) occupying the broad middle ground.[22] Furthermore, within the population of managers, there is experiential evidence that while the average manager may be amoral most of the time, he or she may slip into a moral or immoral mode on occasion, given impinging factors and circumstances.

CORE CONCEPT

Amoral managers believe that businesses ought to be able to do whatever current laws and regulations allow them to do without being shackled by ethical considerations—they think that what is permissible and what is not is governed entirely by prevailing laws and regulations, not by societal concepts of right and wrong.

Evidence of Managerial Immorality in the Global Business Community

There is considerable evidence that a sizable majority of managers are either amoral or immoral. Recent issues of the *Global Corruption Report* sponsored by Berlin-based Transparency International present credible evidence that corruption among public officials and in business transactions is widespread across the world. Table 9.1 shows some of the countries where corruption is believed to be lowest and highest. This same report also presents data showing the perceived likelihood that companies in large exporting countries are paying bribes to win business in the markets of such countries as Argentina, Brazil, Colombia, Hungary, India, Indonesia, Mexico, Morocco, Nigeria, the Philippines, Poland, Russia, South Africa, South Korea, and Thailand. Bribery seems to occur most often in (1) public works contracts and construction, (2) the arms and defense industry, and (3) the oil and gas industry. Corruption, of course, extends beyond just bribes and kickbacks; price-fixing, securities fraud, and efforts to skirt regulations relating to the payment of minimum wages, use of child labor, and environmental protection are three other areas where unethical behavior is common.

A global business community that is apparently so populated with unethical business practices and managerial immorality leaves scant basis for concluding that most companies ground their strategies on exemplary ethical principles or that company managers diligently try to ingrain ethical behavior into company personnel. And as many business school professors have noted, there are considerable numbers of amoral business students in our classrooms. So efforts to root out shady and corrupt business practices and implant high ethical principles into the managerial

TABLE 9.1   Corruption Perceptions Index (CPI), Selected Countries, 2007

Country	2007 CPI Score*	High–Low Range	Number of Surveys Used	Country	2007 CPI Score*	High–Low Range	Number of Surveys Used
Finland	9.4	9.2–9.6	6	Taiwan	5.7	5.4–6.1	9
New Zealand	9.4	9.2–9.6	6	Italy	5.2	4.7–5.7	6
Denmark	9.4	9.2–9.6	6	Malaysia	5.1	4.5–5.7	9
Singapore	9.3	9.0–9.5	9	South Africa	5.1	4.9–5.5	9
Sweden	9.3	9.1–9.4	6	South Korea	5.1	4.7–5.5	9
Iceland	9.2	8.3–9.6	6	Turkey	4.1	3.8–4.5	7
Netherlands	9.0	8.8–9.2	6	Romania	3.7	3.4–4.1	8
Switzerland	9.0	8.8–9.4	6	Brazil	3.5	3.2–4.0	7
Canada	8.7	8.3–9.1	6	China	3.5	3.0–4.2	9
Norway	8.7	8.0–9.2	6	India	3.5	3.3–3.7	10
Australia	8.6	8.1–9.0	8	Mexico	3.5	3.3–3.8	7
United Kingdom	8.4	7.9–8.9	6	Saudi Arabia	3.4	2.7–3.9	4
Hong Kong	8.3	7.6–8.8	8	Thailand	3.3	2.9–3.7	9
Germany	7.8	7.3–8.4	6	Argentina	2.9	2.6–3.2	7
Japan	7.5	7.1–8.0	8	Vietnam	2.6	2.4–2.9	9
France	7.3	6.9–7.8	6	Pakistan	2.4	2.0–2.8	7
United States	7.2	6.5–7.6	8	Russia	2.3	2.1–2.6	8
Chile	7.0	6.5–7.4	7	Nigeria	2.2	2.0–2.4	8
Spain	6.7	6.2–7.0	6	Venezuela	2.0	1.9–2.1	7
Israel	6.1	5.6–6.7	6	Somalia	1.4	1.1–1.7	4
United Arab Emirates	5.7	4.8–6.5	5	Myanmar	1.4	1.1–1.7	4

Note: The CPI scores range between 10 (highly clean) and 0 (highly corrupt); the data were collected between 2006 and 2007 and represent a composite of 14 polls and surveys from 12 independent institutions. The CPI score represents the perceptions of the degree of corruption as seen by businesspeople, academics, and risk analysts. CPI scores were reported for 180 countries.

Source: Transparency International, *2008 Global Corruption Report,* www.globalcorruptionreport.org (accessed July 30, 2008), pp. 296–302.

process of crafting and executing strategy is unlikely to produce an ethically strong global business climate anytime soon, barring perhaps further scandals resulting in a major effort to address and correct the ethical laxness of company managers.

DRIVERS OF UNETHICAL STRATEGIES AND BUSINESS BEHAVIOR

The apparent pervasiveness of immoral and amoral businesspeople is one obvious reason why ethical principles are an ineffective moral compass in business dealings and why companies may resort to unethical strategic behavior. But apart from the thinking that "the business of business is business, not ethics," three other main drivers of unethical business behavior also stand out:[23]

- Faulty oversight by top management and the board of directors that implicitly allows the overzealous pursuit of personal gain, wealth, and other self-interests.
- Heavy pressures on company managers to meet or beat performance targets.
- A company culture that puts profitability and "good" business performance ahead of ethical behavior.

Overzealous Pursuit of Personal Gain, Wealth, and Self-Interest

People who are obsessed with wealth accumulation, greed, power, status, and other self-interests often push ethical principles aside in their quest for personal gain. Driven by their ambitions, they exhibit few qualms in skirting the rules or doing whatever is necessary to achieve their goals. A general disregard for business ethics can prompt all kinds of unethical strategic maneuvers and behaviors at companies. Top executives, directors, and majority shareholders at cable-TV company Adelphia Communications ripped off the company for amounts totaling well over $1 billion, diverting hundreds of millions of dollars to fund their Buffalo Sabres hockey team, build a private golf course, and buy timber rights—among other things—and driving the company into bankruptcy. Their actions, which represent one of the biggest instances of corporate looting and self-dealing in American business, took place despite the company's public pontifications about the principles it would observe in trying to care for customers, employees, stockholders, and the local communities where it operated. Andrew Fastow, Enron's chief financial officer (CFO), set himself up as the manager of one of Enron's off-the-books partnerships and as the part-owner of another, allegedly earning extra compensation of $30 million for his owner-manager roles in the two partnerships; Enron's board of directors agreed to suspend the company's conflict-of-interest rules designed to protect the company from this very kind of executive self-dealing.

According to a civil complaint filed by the Securities and Exchange Commission (SEC), the chief executive officer (CEO) of Tyco International, a well-known $35.6 billion manufacturing and services company, conspired with the company's CFO to steal more than $170 million, including a company-paid $2 million birthday party for the CEO's wife held on Sardinia, an island off the coast of Italy; a $7 million Park Avenue apartment for his wife; and secret low-interest and interest-free loans to fund private businesses and investments and purchase lavish artwork, yachts, estate jewelry, and vacation homes in New Hampshire, Connecticut, Massachusetts, and Utah. The CEO allegedly lived rent-free in a $31 million Fifth Avenue apartment that Tyco purchased in his name, directed millions of dollars of charitable contributions in his own name using Tyco funds, diverted company funds to finance his personal businesses and investments, and sold millions of dollars of Tyco stock back to Tyco itself through Tyco subsidiaries located in offshore bank-secrecy jurisdictions. Tyco's CEO and CFO were further charged with conspiring to reap more than $430 million from sales of stock, using questionable accounting to hide their actions, and engaging in deceptive accounting practices to distort the company's financial condition from 1995 to 2002. At the trial on the charges filed by the SEC, the prosecutor told the jury in his opening statement, "This case is about lying, cheating and stealing. These people didn't win the jackpot—they stole it." Defense lawyers countered that "every single transaction . . . was set down in detail in Tyco's books and records" and that the authorized and disclosed multimillion-dollar compensation packages were merited by the company's financial performance and stock price gains. The two Tyco executives were convicted and sentenced to jail.

Ten prominent Wall Street securities firms in 2003 paid $1.4 billion to settle charges that they knowingly issued misleading stock research to investors in an effort to prop up the stock prices of client corporations. A host of mutual-fund firms made under-the-table arrangements to regularly buy and sell stock for their accounts at special after-hours trading prices that disadvantaged long-term investors and had to pay nearly $2.0 billion in fines and restitution when their unethical practices were discovered by authorities during 2002–2003. Salomon Smith Barney, Goldman Sachs, Credit Suisse First Boston, and several other financial firms were assessed close to $2 billion in fines and restitution for the unethical manner in which they contributed to the scandals at Enron and WorldCom (now MCI) and for the shady practice of allocating shares of hot stocks to a select list of corporate executives who either steered or were in a position to steer investment banking business their way.

Heavy Pressures on Company Managers to Meet or Beat Earnings Targets

Performance expectations of Wall Street analysts and investors may create enormous pressure on management to do whatever it takes to sustain the company's reputation for delivering good financial performance. Executives at high-performing companies know that investors will see the slightest sign of a slowdown in earnings growth as a red flag and drive down the company's stock price. In addition, slowing growth or declining profits could lead to a downgrade of the company's credit rating if it has used lots of debt to finance its growth. The pressure to watch the scoreboard and "never miss a quarter"—so as not to upset the expectations of Wall Street analysts and fickle stock market investors—prompts managers to cut costs wherever savings show up immediately, squeeze extra sales out of early deliveries, and engage in other short-term maneuvers to make the numbers. As the pressure builds to "meet or beat the numbers," company personnel start stretching the rules further and further, until the limits of ethical conduct are overlooked.[24]

Several top executives at WorldCom (now MCI), a company built with scores of acquisitions in exchange for WorldCom stock, allegedly concocted a fraudulent $11 billion accounting scheme to hide costs and inflate revenues and profit over several years; the scheme was said to have helped the company keep its stock price propped up high enough to make additional acquisitions, support its nearly $30 billion debt load, and allow executives to cash in on their lucrative stock options. At Qwest Communications, a company created by the merger of a go-go telecom start-up and U.S. West (one of the regional Bell companies), management was charged with scheming to improperly book $2.4 billion in revenues from a variety of sources and deals, thereby inflating the company's profits and making it appear that the company's strategy to create a telecommunications company of the future was on track when, in fact, it was faltering badly behind the scenes. Top-level Qwest executives were dismissed and in 2004 new management agreed to $250 million in fines for all the misdeeds.

At Bristol-Myers Squibb, the world's fifth largest drug maker, management apparently engaged in a series of numbers-game maneuvers to meet earnings targets, including such actions as:

- Offering special end-of-quarter discounts to induce distributors and local pharmacies to stock up on certain prescription drugs—a practice known as "channel stuffing."
- Issuing last-minute price increase alerts to spur purchases and beef up operating profits.
- Setting up excessive reserves for restructuring charges and then reversing some of the charges as needed to bolster operating profits.
- Making repeated asset sales small enough that the gains could be reported as additions to operating profit rather than being flagged as one-time gains.

Such numbers games were said to be a common "earnings management" practice at Bristol-Myers and, according to one former executive, "sent a huge message across the organization that you make your numbers at all costs."[25]

Company executives often feel pressured to hit financial performance targets because their compensation depends heavily on the company's performance. During the late 1990s, it became fashionable for boards of directors to grant lavish bonuses, stock option awards, and other compensation benefits to executives for meeting specified performance targets. So outlandishly large were these rewards that executives had strong personal incentives to bend the rules and engage in behaviors that allowed the targets to be met. Much of the accounting hocus-pocus at the root of recent corporate scandals has entailed situations in which executives benefited enormously from misleading accounting or other shady activities that allowed them to hit the numbers and receive incentive awards ranging from $10 million to $100 million. At Bristol-Myers Squibb, for example, the pay-for-performance link spawned strong rules-bending incentives. About 94 percent of one top executive's $18.5 million in total compensation in 2001 came from stock-option grants, a bonus, and long-term incentive payments linked to corporate performance; about 92 percent of a second executive's $12.9 million of compensation was incentive-based.[26]

The fundamental problem with a "make the numbers and move on" syndrome is that a company doesn't really create additional value for customers or improve its competitiveness in the marketplace—these outcomes are the most reliable drivers of higher profits and added shareholder value. Cutting ethical corners or stooping to downright illegal actions in the name of profits first carries exceptionally high risk for shareholders—the steep stock price decline and tarnished brand image that accompany the discovery of scurrilous behavior leaves shareholders with a company worth much less than before—and the rebuilding task can be arduous, taking both considerable time and resources.

Company Cultures That Put the Bottom Line Ahead of Ethical Behavior

When a company's culture spawns an ethically corrupt or amoral work climate, people have a company-approved license to ignore "what's right" and engage in most any behavior or employ most any strategy they think they can get away with.[27] At such companies, ethically immoral or amoral people are given free rein and otherwise honorable people may succumb to the many opportunities around them to engage in unethical practices. A perfect example of a company culture gone awry on ethics is Enron.[28]

Enron's leaders encouraged company personnel to focus on the current bottom line and to be innovative and aggressive in figuring out what could be done to grow current revenues and earnings. Employees were expected to pursue opportunities to the utmost in the electric utility industry, which was undergoing a loosening of regulation. Enron executives viewed the company as a laboratory for innovation; the company hired the best and brightest people and pushed them to be creative, look at problems and opportunities in new ways, and exhibit a sense of urgency in making things happen. Employees were encouraged to make a difference and do their part in creating an entrepreneurial environment where creativity flourished, people could achieve their full potential, and everyone had a stake in the outcome. Enron employees got the message—pushing the limits and meeting one's numbers were viewed as survival skills. Enron's annual "rank and yank" formal evaluation process—in which the 15 to 20 percent lowest-ranking employees were let go or encouraged to seek other employment—made it abundantly clear that what counted were bottom-line results and being the "mover-and-shaker" in the marketplace. The name of the game at Enron became devising clever ways to boost revenues and earnings, even if it sometimes meant operating outside established policies and without the knowledge of superiors. In fact, outside-the-lines behavior was celebrated if it generated profitable new business. Enron's energy contracts and its trading and hedging activities grew increasingly more complex and diverse as employees pursued first one avenue and then another to help keep Enron's financial performance looking good.

As a consequence of Enron's well-publicized successes in creating new products and businesses and leveraging the company's trading and hedging expertise into new market arenas, Enron came to be regarded as an exceptionally innovative company. It was ranked by its corporate peers as the most innovative U.S. company for three consecutive years in *Fortune* magazine's annual surveys of the most admired companies. A high-performance/high-rewards climate came to pervade the Enron culture, as the best workers (determined by who produced the best bottom-line results) received impressively large incentives and bonuses (amounting to as much as $1 million for traders and even more for senior executives). On Car Day at Enron, an array of luxury sports cars arrived for presentation to the most successful employees. Understandably, employees wanted to be seen as part of Enron's star team and partake in the benefits that being one of Enron's best and smartest employees entailed. The high monetary rewards, the ambitious and hard-driving people whom the company hired and promoted, and the competitive, results-oriented culture combined to give Enron a reputation not only for trampling competitors at every opportunity but also for internal ruthlessness. The company's super-aggressiveness and win-at-all-costs mind-set nurtured a culture that gradually and then more rapidly fostered the erosion of ethical standards, eventually making a mockery of the company's stated values of integrity and respect. When it became evident in the fall of 2001 that Enron was a house of cards propped up by deceitful accounting and a myriad of unsavory practices, the company imploded in a matter of weeks—the biggest bankruptcy of all time cost investors $64 billion in losses (between August 2000, when the stock price was at its five-year high, and November 2001), and Enron employees lost their retirement assets, which were almost totally invested in Enron stock.

More recently, a team investigating an ethical scandal at oil giant Royal Dutch/Shell Group that resulted in the payment of $150 million in fines found that an ethically flawed culture was a major contributor to why managers made rosy forecasts that they couldn't meet and why top executives engaged in maneuvers to mislead investors by overstating Shell's oil and gas reserves by 25 percent (equal to 4.5 billion barrels of oil). The investigation revealed that top Shell executives knew that a variety of internal practices, together with unrealistic and unsupportable estimates submitted by overzealous and bonus-conscious managers in Shell's exploration and production group, were being used to overstate reserves. An e-mail written by Shell's top executive for exploration and production (who was caught up in the ethical misdeeds and later forced to resign) said, "I am becoming sick and tired of lying about the extent of our reserves issues and the downward revisions that need to be done because of our far too aggressive/optimistic bookings."[29]

WHY ETHICAL STRATEGIES MATTER

Company managers may formulate strategies that are ethical in all respects, or they may decide to employ strategies that, for one reason or another, have unethical or at least gray-area components. Senior executives with strong ethical convictions are normally proactive in insisting that all aspects of company strategy fall within ethical boundaries. But at companies whose senior executives are either immoral or amoral, shady strategies and unethical or borderline business practices may well be used, especially if their managers are clever at devising schemes to keep ethically questionable actions hidden from view.

There are two reasons why a company's strategy should be ethical: (1) a strategy that is unethical in whole or in part is morally wrong and reflects badly on the character of the company personnel involved, and (2) an ethical strategy is good business and in the best interest of shareholders.

The Moral Case for an Ethical Strategy

Managers do not dispassionately assess what strategic course to steer. Ethical strategy making generally begins with managers who themselves have strong character (i.e., who are honest, have integrity, and truly care about how they conduct the company's business). Managers with high ethical principles and standards are usually advocates of a corporate code of ethics and strong ethics compliance, and they are typically genuinely committed to certain corporate values and business principles. They walk the talk in displaying the company's stated values. They understand there's a big difference between adopting values statements and codes of ethics that serve merely as window dressing and those that truly paint the white lines for a company's actual strategy and business conduct. As a consequence, ethically strong managers consciously opt for strategic actions that can pass moral scrutiny—they display no tolerance for strategies with ethically controversial components.

The Business Case for an Ethical Strategy

There are solid business reasons to adopt ethical strategies even if most company managers are not of strong moral character and personally committed to high ethical standards. Pursuing unethical strategies not only damages a company's reputation but can also have costly consequences that are wide ranging. Some of the costs are readily visible; others are hidden and difficult to track down—as shown in Figure 9.1. The costs of fines and penalties and any declines in the stock price are easy enough to calculate. The administrative cleanup (or Level 2) costs are usually buried in the general costs of doing business and can be difficult to ascribe to any one ethical misdeed. Level 3 costs can be quite difficult to quantify but can sometimes be the most devastating—the Enron debacle left Arthur Andersen's reputation in shreds and led to the once-revered accounting firm's almost immediate demise. It remains to be seen whether Merck, once one of the world's most respected pharmaceutical firms, can survive the revelation that senior management deliberately concealed that its Vioxx painkiller, which the company pulled off the market in September 2004, was tied to much greater risk of heart attack and strokes—some 20 million people in the United States had taken Vioxx over the years, and Merck executives had reason to suspect as early as 2000 (and perhaps earlier) that Vioxx had dangerous side effects.[30]

APPROACHES TO MANAGING A COMPANY'S ETHICAL CONDUCT

A company can take can take any of four basic approaches with regard to ethical conduct:[32]

- The unconcerned or nonissue approach.
- The damage control approach.
- The compliance approach.
- The ethical culture approach.

The differences in these four approaches are discussed briefly below and summarized in Table 9.2.

The Unconcerned or Nonissue Approach

The unconcerned approach is prevalent at companies whose executives are immoral and unintentionally amoral. Senior executives at companies using this approach subscribe to the view that notions of right and wrong in matters of business are defined entirely by the prevailing laws and government regulations. They maintain that trying to enforce ethical standards above and beyond what is legally required is a nonissue because businesses are entitled to conduct their affairs in whatever manner they wish so long as they comply with the letter of what is legally required. Hence, there is no need to spend valuable management time trying to prescribe and enforce standards of conduct that go above and beyond legal and regulatory requirements. In companies where senior managers are immoral, the prevailing view may well be that under-the-table dealing can be good business if it can be kept hidden or if it can be justified on grounds that others are doing it too. Companies in this mode usually engage in most any business practices they believe they can get away with, and the strategies they employ may include elements that are either borderline from a legal perspective or ethically shady.

The Damage Control Approach

Damage control is favored at companies whose managers are intentionally amoral but who are wary of scandal and adverse public relations fallout that could cost them their jobs or tarnish their careers. Companies using this approach, not wanting to raise doubts about their commitment to ethical business conduct, will often adopt a code of ethics for window-dressing purposes. But it quickly becomes understood that the code exists mainly as nice words on paper—employees quickly get the message that rule bending is tolerated and may even be rewarded if the company benefits from their actions.

Company executives that practice the damage control approach are prone to look the other way when shady or borderline behavior occurs. They may even condone questionable actions that help the company reach earnings targets or bolster its market standing—such as pressuring customers to stock up on the company's product (channel stuffing), making under-the-table payments to win new business, or stonewalling the recall of products claimed to be unsafe. But they are usually careful to do such things in a manner that lessens the risks of exposure or damaging consequences. This generally includes making token gestures

> The main objective of the damage control approach is to protect against adverse publicity and any damaging consequences brought on by headlines in the media, outside investigation, threats of litigation, punitive government action, or angry or vocal stakeholders.

Table 9.2   **Four Approaches to Managing Business Ethics**

	Unconcerned or Nonissue Approach	Damage Control Approach	Compliance Approach	Ethical Culture Approach
Underlying beliefs	• The business of business is business, not ethics • Ethics has no place in the conduct of business • Companies should not be morally accountable for their actions	• Need to make a token gesture in the direction of ethical standards (a code of ethics)	• Company must be committed to ethical standards and monitoring ethics performance • Unethical behavior must be prevented and punished if discovered • Important to have a reputation for high ethical standards	• Ethics is basic to the culture • Behaving ethically must be a deeply held corporate value and become a "way of life" • Everyone is expected to walk the talk
Ethics management approaches	• There's no need to make decisions concerning business ethics—if its legal, it is okay • No intervention regarding the ethical component of decisions is needed	• Act to protect against the dangers of unethical strategies and behavior • Ignore unethical behavior or allow it to go unpunished unless the situation is extreme and requires action	• Establish a clear, comprehensive code of ethics • Prevent unethical behavior • Provide ethics training for all personnel • Have formal ethics compliance procedures, an ethics compliance office, and a chief ethics officer	• Ethical behavior is ingrained and reinforced as part of the culture • Much reliance on co-worker peer pressure—"that's not how we do things here" • Everyone is an ethics watchdog—whistle-blowing is required • Ethics heroes are celebrated; ethics stories are told
Challenges	• Financial consequences can become unaffordable • Some stakeholders are alienated	• Credibility problems with stakeholders can arise • The company is susceptible to ethical scandal • The company has a sub-par ethical reputation—executives and company personnel don't walk the talk	• Organizational members come to rely on the existing rules for moral guidance—fosters a mentality of what is not forbidden is allowed • Rules and guidelines proliferate • The locus of moral control resides in the code and in the ethics compliance system rather than in an individual's own moral responsibility for ethical behavior	• New employees must go through strong ethics induction program • Formal ethics management systems can be underutilized • Relying on peer pressures and cultural norms to enforce ethical standards can result in eliminating some or many of the compliance trappings and, over time, induce moral laxness

Source: Adapted from Gedeon J. Rossouw and Leon J. van Vuuren, "Modes of Managing Morality: A Descriptive Model of Strategies for Managing Ethics," *Journal of Business Ethics* 46, no. 4 (September 2003), pp. 392–93.

to police compliance with codes of ethics and relying heavily on all sorts of spin to help extricate the company or themselves from claims that the company's strategy has unethical components or that company personnel have engaged in unethical practices.

The Compliance Approach

Anywhere from light to forceful compliance is favored at companies whose managers (1) lean toward being somewhat amoral but are highly concerned about having ethically upstanding reputations or (2) are moral and see strong compliance methods as the best way to impose and enforce ethical rules and high ethical standards. Companies that adopt a compliance mode usually do some or all of the following to display their commitment to ethical conduct: make the code of ethics a visible and regular part of communications with employees, implement ethics training programs, appoint a chief ethics officer, have ethics committees to give guidance on ethics matters, institute formal procedures for investigating alleged ethics violations, conduct ethics audits to measure and document compliance, and/or try to deter violations by setting up ethics hotlines for anonymous callers to use in reporting possible violations. Ethics code violators at these companies are disciplined and sometimes subjected to public reprimand and punishment (including dismissal), thereby sending a clear signal to company personnel that complying with ethical standards needs to be taken seriously.

The driving force behind the company's commitment to eradicate unethical behavior normally stems from a desire to avoid the cost and damage associated with unethical conduct or else a quest to gain favor from stakeholders (especially ethically conscious customers, employees, and investors) for having a highly regarded reputation for ethical behavior. One of the weaknesses of the compliance approach is that moral control resides in the company's code of ethics and in the ethics compliance system rather than in (1) the strong peer pressures for ethical behavior that come from ingraining a highly ethical corporate culture and (2) an individual's own moral responsibility for ethical behavior.[33]

The Ethical Culture Approach

At some companies, top executives believe that high ethical principles must be deeply ingrained in the corporate culture and function as guides for "how we do things around here." A company using the ethical culture approach seeks to gain employee buy-in to the company's ethical standards, business principles, and corporate values. The ethical principles embraced in the company's code of ethics and/or in its statement of corporate values are seen as integral to the company's identity, self-image, and ways of operating. The strength of the ethical culture approach depends heavily on the ethical integrity of the executives who create and nurture the culture—it is incumbent on them to determine how high the bar is to be set and to exemplify ethical standards in their own decisions and behavior. Further, it is essential that the strategy be ethical in all respects and that company personnel execute the strategy in an ethical manner. Such strong commitment to ethical business conduct is what creates an ethical work climate and a workplace where displaying integrity is the norm.

Many of the ethical enforcement mechanisms used in the compliance approach are also employed in the ethical culture mode, but one other is added—strong peer pressure from coworkers to observe ethical norms. Thus, responsibility for ethics compliance is widely dispersed throughout all levels of management and the rank and file. Stories of former and current moral heroes are kept in circulation, and the deeds of company personnel who display ethical values and are dedicated to walking the talk are celebrated at internal company events. The message that ethics matters—and matters a lot—resounds loudly and clearly throughout the organization and in its strategy and decisions.

However, one of the challenges to overcome in the ethical culture approach is relying too heavily on peer pressure and cultural norms to enforce ethics compliance rather than on an individual's own moral responsibility for ethical behavior—absent unrelenting peer pressure or strong internal compliance systems, there is a danger that over time company personnel may become lax about ethical standards. Compliance procedures need to be an integral part of the ethical culture approach to help send the message that management takes the observance of ethical norms seriously and that behavior that falls outside ethical boundaries will have negative consequences. Illustration Capsule 9.2 discusses General Electric's approach to building a culture that combines demands for high performance with expectations for ethical conduct.

Why Companies Change Their Ethics Management Approach

Regardless of the approach they have used to managing ethical conduct, a company's executives may sense they have exhausted a particular mode's potential for managing ethics and that they need to become more forceful in their approach to ethics management. Such changes typically occur when the company's ethical failures have made the headlines and created an embarrassing situation for company officials or when the business climate changes. For example, the number of recent highly publicized corporate scandals, coupled with aggressive enforcement of anticorruption legislation (such as the Sarbanes-Oxley Act of 2002 which penalizes lax corporate governance and illicit accounting practices), has prompted numerous executives and boards of directors to clean up their acts in accounting and financial reporting, review their ethical standards, and tighten up ethics compliance procedures. Intentionally amoral managers using the unconcerned or nonissue approach to ethics management may see less risk in shifting to the damage control approach (or, for appearance's sake, maybe a "light" compliance mode). Senior managers who have employed the damage control mode may be motivated by bad experiences to mend their ways and shift to a compliance mode. In the wake of so many embarrassing corporate scandals, companies in the compliance mode may move closer to the ethical culture approach.

SOCIAL RESPONSIBILITY AND CORPORATE CITIZENSHIP STRATEGIES

That businesses have an obligation to be good citizens and foster the betterment of society, a much-debated topic in the past 40 years, took root in the 19th century when progressive companies began, in the aftermath of the industrial revolution, to provide workers with housing and other amenities. The notion that corporate executives should

ILLUSTRATION CAPSULE 9.2
How General Electric's Top Management Built a Culture That Fuses High Performance with High Integrity

Jack Welch and his successor as General Electric's CEO, Jeffrey Immelt, have fostered a culture built on high ethical standards. The company's heavy reliance on financial controls and performance-based reward systems—which are necessary because of GE's broad multinational diversification—could easily tempt managers at all levels to cut corners, engage in unethical sales tactics, inaccurately record revenues or expenses, or participate in corrupt practices prevalent in the many emerging markets where GE competes. Welch, Immelt, and GE's other top managers clearly recognize that, absent a strong ethical culture, there would be little to deter the company's thousands of managers across the globe to pursue all types of unethical behavior that would, on the surface, boost performance.

GE's top management was not so naive as to believe that it had successfully hired only moral managers with the highest personal expectations for ethical behavior, but was well aware that many among its managerial ranks were either intentionally or unintentionally amoral. The first step in establishing an ethical culture at GE was for its top management to forcefully communicate the company's principles that should guide decision making. Jeffrey Immelt begins and ends each annual meeting of the company's 220 officers and 600 senior managers with a recitation of the company's fundamental ethical principles. Immelt and GE's other managers are careful to not violate these principles themselves or give implied consent for others to skirt these principles, since human nature makes subordinates at all levels ever vigilant for the signs of hypocrisy in the actions of higher-ups. The importance of walking the talk justifies GE's "one strike and you're out" standard for its top management. For example, a high-level manager in an emerging market was terminated for failing to conduct required diligence on a third-party vendor known for its shady business practices, including the payment of bribes to local officials. Another executive was fired from GE for agreeing to a large and important Asian customer's request to falsify supplier documents that were used by regulatory agencies.

With so many ethical standards prevailing in the more than 100 countries where GE operates, the company has turned to global ethical standards rather than allow local cultures to shape business behavior. The company's global standards cover such topics as how to best evaluate suppliers' environmental records and working conditions in its manufacturing businesses and how to avoid money-laundering schemes or aiding and abetting financial services customers engaged in tax evasion or accounting fraud. Operating-level managers were formally responsible for ensuring ethical compliance in their divisions and were required to submit quarterly tracking reports to GE's corporate offices on key indicators such as spills, accident rates, and violation notices. Managers of operating units falling in the bottom quartile on such quarterly assessments were required to submit plans for improving the ethical shortcomings. GE also evaluated the ethical performance of its 4,000 managers who were responsible for profit centers or were key contributors on business teams.

GE's approach to culture building also included instilling such principles into the behavior of the company's 300,000-plus employees with no managerial responsibility. Employees are provided training to help them understand the company's ethical principles and how those principles can help them make decisions in the ethical gray areas that arise while making everyday decisions. GE also allows employees to lodge complaints about ethics compliance anonymously; those complaints are evaluated by more than 500 employees around the world with either full-time or part-time ombudsperson capacity. About 20 percent of the 1,500 concerns lodged annually lead to serious discipline. Hourly employees are also included in annual assessments of ethical performance and are rewarded through bonuses, promotions, or recognition for identifying or resolving ethical issues at the operating level.

Source: Based on the discussion of GE's culture-building process by the company's former legal counsel found in Ben W. Heineman Jr., "Avoiding Integrity Land Mines," *Harvard Business Review* 85, no. 4 (April 2007), pp. 100–108.

balance the interests of all stakeholders—shareholders, employees, customers, suppliers, the communities in which they operated, and society at large—began to blossom in the 1960s. Some years later, a group of chief executives of America's 200 largest corporations, calling themselves the Business Roundtable, took a strong stance and forcefully advocated that corporations conduct their business in a manner that benefited all

stakeholders; the Roundtable's "Statement on Corporate Responsibility,"
written in 1981, said:

> Balancing the shareholder's expectations of maximum return against other pri-
> orities is one of the fundamental problems confronting corporate management.
> The shareholder must receive a good return but the legitimate concerns of other
> constituencies (customers, employees, communities, suppliers and society at
> large) also must have the appropriate attention. . . . [Leading managers] believe
> that by giving enlightened consideration to balancing the legitimate claims of all
> its constituents, a corporation will best serve the interest of its shareholders.[34]

Today, corporate social responsibility is a concept that resonates in
Western Europe, the United States, Canada, and such developing nations as
Brazil and India.

What Do We Mean by *Social Responsibility* and *Corporate Citizenship?*

The essence of socially responsible business behavior is that a company should balance strategic actions to benefit shareholders against the *duty* to be a good corporate
citizen. Company managers must display a *social conscience* in operating the business
and specifically take into account how management decisions and company actions
affect the well-being of employees, local communities, the environment, and society at
large. Acting in a socially responsible manner thus encompasses more than just complying with the laws and regulations of the countries in which it operates, participating in community service projects, and donating monies to charities and other worthy
social causes. Demonstrating social responsibility also entails undertaking actions that
earn trust and respect from all stakeholders—operating in an honorable and ethical
manner, striving to make the company a great place to work, demonstrating genuine
respect for the environment, and trying to make a difference in bettering society. As
depicted in Figure 9.2, the menu for demonstrating a social conscience and choosing
specific ways to exercise social responsibility includes:

- *Efforts to employ an ethical strategy and observe ethical principles in operating
  the business*—A sincere commitment to observing ethical principles is necessary
  here simply because unethical strategies and conduct are incompatible with the
  concept of good corporate citizenship and socially responsible business behavior.
- *Making charitable contributions, donating money and the time of company personnel to community service endeavors, supporting various worthy organizational
  causes, and reaching out to make a difference in the lives of the disadvantaged*—
  Some companies fulfill their corporate citizenship and community outreach obligations by spreading their efforts over a multitude of charitable and community
  activities; for instance, Microsoft and Johnson & Johnson support a broad variety
  of community, art, social welfare, and environmental programs. Others prefer to
  focus their energies more narrowly. McDonald's, for example, concentrates on
  sponsoring the Ronald McDonald House program (which provides a home away
  from home for the families of seriously ill children receiving treatment at nearby
  hospitals), preventing child abuse and neglect, and participating in local community service activities. British Telecom gives 1 percent of its profits directly
  to communities, largely for education—teacher training, in-school workshops,
  and digital technology. Leading prescription drug maker GlaxoSmithKline and

Figure 9.2 Demonstrating a Social Conscience: The Five Components of Socially Responsible Business Behavior

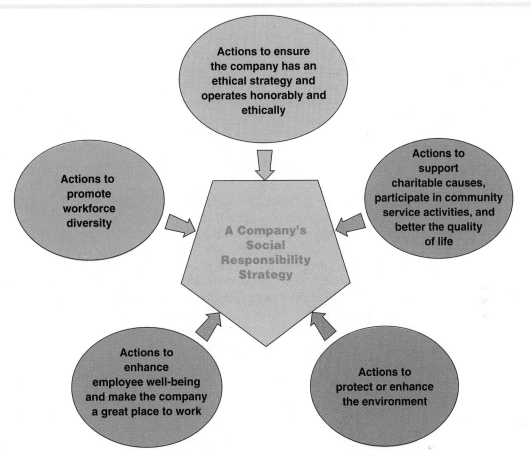

Source: Adapted from material in Ronald Paul Hill, Debra Stephens, and Iain Smith, "Corporate Social Responsibility: An Examination of Individual Firm Behavior," *Business and Society Review* 108, no. 3 (September 2003), p. 348.

other pharmaceutical companies either donate or heavily discount medicines for distribution in the least-developed nations. Companies frequently reinforce their philanthropic efforts by encouraging employees to support charitable causes and participate in community affairs, often through programs to match employee contributions.

• *Actions to protect or enhance the environment and, in particular, to minimize or eliminate any adverse impact on the environment stemming from the company's own business activities*—Social responsibility as it applies to environmental protection means doing more than what is legally required. From a social responsibility perspective, companies have an obligation to be stewards of the environment. This means using the best available science and technology to achieve higher-than-required environmental standards. Even more ideally, it means putting time and money into improving the environment in ways that extend past a company's own industry boundaries—such as participating in recycling projects, adopting energy conservation practices, and supporting efforts to clean up local water supplies. Retailers such as Home Depot and Wal-Mart in the United States and B&Q in the United Kingdom have begun pressuring their suppliers to adopt stronger environmental protection practices.[35]

- *Actions to create a work environment that enhances the quality of life for employees and makes the company a great place to work*—Numerous companies go beyond providing the ordinary kinds of compensation and exert extra efforts to enhance the quality of life for their employees, both at work and at home. This can include varied and engaging job assignments, career development programs and mentoring, rapid career advancement, appealing compensation incentives, ongoing training to ensure future employability, added decision-making authority, onsite day care, flexible work schedules for single parents, workplace exercise facilities, special leaves to care for sick family members, work-at-home opportunities, gender pay equity, showcase plants and offices, special safety programs, and the like.

- *Actions to build a workforce that is diverse with respect to gender, race, national origin, and perhaps other aspects that different people bring to the workplace*—Most large companies in the United States have established workforce diversity programs, and some go the extra mile to ensure that their workplaces are attractive to ethnic minorities and inclusive of all groups and perspectives. The pursuit of workforce diversity can be good business—Johnson & Johnson, Pfizer, and Coca-Cola believe that a reputation for workforce diversity makes recruiting employees easier (talented employees from diverse backgrounds often seek out such companies). And at Coca-Cola, where strategic success depends on getting people all over the world to become loyal consumers of the company's beverages, efforts to build a public persona of inclusiveness for people of all races, religions, nationalities, interests, and talents has considerable strategic value. Multinational companies are particularly inclined to make workforce diversity a visible strategic component; they recognize that respecting individual differences and promoting inclusiveness resonate well with people all around the world. At growing numbers of companies the diversity initiative extends to suppliers—sourcing items from small businesses owned by women or ethnic minorities.

The particular combination of socially responsible endeavors a company elects to pursue defines its **social responsibility strategy.**

Some companies use the terms *corporate social responsibility* and *corporate citizenship* interchangeably, but there's a body of thought that only companies pursuing discretionary activities in the pursuit of bettering society can be described as good corporate citizens. Adherents of corporate citizenship theories suggest that corporations, as citizens of the communities in which they operate, have an obligation to contribute to society, particularly in areas where governments have chosen not to focus or where government efforts have fallen short.[36]

Environmental Sustainability Strategies: A New and Growing Priority

A rapidly growing number of companies are expanding their exercise of social responsibility and corporate citizenship to include the impact of their strategies and operations on future generations and the well-being of the planet. Corporate strategies aimed at operating in an environmentally sustainable fashion entail deliberate and concerted actions to operate the company's business in a manner that protects and maybe even enhances natural resources and ecological support systems, guards against outcomes that will ultimately endanger the planet, and is therefore sustainable for centuries.

Sustainability initiatives undertaken by companies are frequently directed at improving the company's "Triple-P" performance—people, planet, and profit.[37] Unilever, a diversified producer of processed foods, personal care, and home cleaning products, is among the many committed corporations pursuing sustainable business practices. The company tracks 11 sustainable agricultural indicators in its processed foods business and has launched a variety of programs to improve the environmental performance of its suppliers. Examples of such programs include special low-rate financing for tomato suppliers choosing to switch to water-conserving irrigation systems and training programs in India that have allowed contract cucumber growers to reduce pesticide use by 90 percent, while improving yields by 78 percent. Unilever has also reengineered many internal processes to improve the company's overall performance on sustainability measures. For example, the company's factories have reduced water usage by 50 percent and manufacturing waste by 14 percent through the implementation of sustainability initiatives. Unilever has also redesigned packaging for many of its products to conserve natural resources and reduce the volume of consumer waste. The company's Suave shampoo bottles in the United States were reshaped to save almost 150 tons of plastic resin per year, which is the equivalent of 15 million fewer empty bottles making it to landfills annually. Also, the width of Unilever's Lipton soup cartons was reduced to save 154 tons of cardboard per year. Since 40 percent of Unilever's sales are made to consumers in developing countries, the company also is committed to addressing societal needs of consumers in those countries. Examples of the company's social performance include free laundries in poor neighborhoods in developing countries, start-up assistance for women-owned microbusinesses in India, and free drinking water provided to villages in Ghana.

Sometimes cost savings and improved profitability are drivers of environmental sustainability strategies. DuPont's sustainability initiatives regarding energy usage have resulted in energy conservation savings of more than $2 billion between 1990 and 2005. Procter & Gamble's Swiffer cleaning system, one of the company's best-selling new products, was developed as a sustainable product; not only does the Swiffer system have an earth-friendly design, but it also outperforms less-ecological alternatives. Although most consumers probably aren't aware that the Swiffer mop reduces demands on municipal water sources, saves electricity that would be needed to heat mopwater, and doesn't add to the amount of detergent making its way into waterways and waste-treatment facilities, they are attracted to purchasing Swiffer mops because they prefer Swiffer's disposable cleaning sheets to filling and refilling a mop bucket and wringing out a wet mop until the floor is clean.

Many environmentally conscious companies now make a point of citing the beneficial outcomes of their sustainability strategies in press releases and issue special sustainability reports for consumers and investors to review. Just as investment firms some years ago created mutual funds made up of companies passing some threshold of social responsibility, they are now creating mutual funds comprised of companies that are pursuing potent sustainability strategies in order to attract funds from environmentally and socially aware investors. The Dow Jones Sustainability World Index consists of the top 10 percent of the 2,500 companies listed in the Dow Jones World

CORE CONCEPT
A company's environmental sustainability strategy consists of its deliberate actions to meet the current needs of customers, suppliers, shareholders, employees, and other stakeholders in a manner that protects the environment, provides for the longevity of natural resources, maintains ecological support systems for future generations, and guards against ultimate endangerment of the planet.

Table 9.3   Companies with Exceptional Commitments to Sustainability

Name	Market Sector	Country
BMW	Automobiles & Parts	Germany
Australia & New Zealand Banking Group	Banks	Australia
Norsk Hydro	Basic Resources	Norway
Akzo Nobel	Chemicals	Netherlands
Holcim	Construction & Materials	Switzerland
Sodexho	Travel & Leisure	France
Statoil	Oil & Gas	Norway
Land Securities Group	Financial Services	United Kingdom
Unilever	Food & Beverage	Netherlands
Novo Nordisk	Health Care	Denmark
TNT	Industrial Goods & Services	Netherlands
Allianz	Insurance	Germany
Pearson	Media	United Kingdom
Philips Electronics	Personal & Household Goods	Netherlands
Marks & Spencer	Retail	United Kingdom
Intel Corp.	Technology	United States
BT Group Plc	Telecommunications	United Kingdom
CEMIG	Utilities	Brazil

Sources: Dow Jones Indexes, STOXX Limited, and SAM Group; http://www.sustainability-indexes.com/07_htmle/indexes/djsiworld_supersectorleaders_07.html (accessed August 1, 2008).

Index in terms of economic performance, environmental performance, and social performance. Table 9.3 shows companies with exceptional commitments to sustainability (judged according to their being designated as worldwide supersector leaders in the Dow Jones Sustainability World Index for 2007/2008). However, achieving a prominent ranking in sustainability indexes is no guarantee that a company will outperform industry rivals when it comes to social responsibility. For example, BP's $8 billion investment in alternative energy sources and its strong involvement in community and environmental groups had allowed it to be consistently ranked near the top among sustainability indexes, but between 2005 and 2007, the company was fined for safety violations at an Ohio refinery, was investigated by the U.S. Department of Justice for suspected manipulation of oil prices, had a major oil pipeline leak in Alaska, and was hit with a refinery explosion in Texas that claimed the lives of 15 employees.[38]

Crafting Social Responsibility and Sustainability Strategies

While striving to be socially responsible and to engage in environmentally sustainable business practices entails choosing from the menu outlined in the preceding sections and Figure 9.2, there's plenty of room for every company to make its own statement about what charitable contributions to make, what kinds of community service projects to emphasize, what environmental actions to support, how to make the company a good place to work, where and how workforce diversity fits into the picture, and what else it will do to support worthy causes and projects that benefit society.

A company may choose to focus its social responsibility strategy on generic social issues, but social responsibility strategies keyed to points of intersection between a company and society may also contribute to a company's competitive advantage.[39] Almost all activities performed by a company (such as hiring practices, emissions, and waste disposal) have either a positive effect on society or a negative one. In addition, society affects the competitive environment in which companies operate—society provides a company with labor and transportation infrastructure, sets the rules that govern competition, determines the demand for a company's products or services, and shapes the availability of supporting industries. Social responsibility strategies that focus on these points of intersection between society and the company's ability to execute various value chain activities or better serve customer needs provide social benefits as well as build competitive advantage. For example, while carbon emissions may be a generic social issue for a financial institution such as Wells Fargo, Toyota's social responsibility strategy aimed at reducing carbon emissions has produced both competitive advantage and environmental benefits. Toyota's Prius hybrid electric/gasoline automobile is not only among the least polluting automobiles but also the best-selling hybrid vehicle in the United States. The Prius has earned the company the loyalty of fuel-conscious buyers and given Toyota a green image.

> Business leaders who want their companies to be regarded as exemplary corporate citizens not only must see that their companies operate ethically but also must personally display a social conscience in making decisions that affect employees, the environment, the communities in which they operate, and society at large.

However, unless a company's social responsibility initiatives become part of the way it operates its business every day, the initiatives are unlikely to be fully effective. As an executive at Royal Dutch/Shell put it, corporate social responsibility "is not a cosmetic; it must be rooted in our values. It must make a difference to the way we do business."[40] A few companies have integrated social responsibility and/or environmental sustainability objectives into their missions and overall performance targets—they see social performance and environmental metrics as an essential component of judging the company's overall future performance. Some 2,500 companies around the world are issuing annual social responsibility reports (much like an annual report) that set forth their commitments and the progress they are making for all the world to see and evaluate.[41]

Green Mountain Coffee Roasters' commitment to protect the welfare of coffee growers and their families (in particular, making sure they receive a fair price) also intersects with the company's competitively important value chain activities. In its dealings with suppliers at small farmer cooperatives in Peru, Mexico, and Sumatra, Green Mountain pays "fair-trade" prices for coffee beans (in 2002, the fair-trade prices per pound of coffee were a minimum of $1.26 for conventional coffee and $1.41 for organically grown, versus market prices of 24 to 50 cents). Green Mountain also purchases about 25 percent of its coffee direct from farmers so as to cut out intermediaries and see that farmers realize a higher price for their efforts—coffee is the world's second most heavily traded commodity after oil, requiring the labor of some 20 million people, most of whom live at the poverty level.[42] At Marriott, the company's social agenda includes providing 180 hours of paid classroom and on-the-job training to the chronically unemployed. Ninety percent of the graduates from the job training program take jobs with Marriott and about two-thirds of those remain with Marriott for more than a year. Patagonia encourages customers to return worn-out cotton, fleece, and nylon clothing items so that the fibers can be recycled into fabrics for new clothing items.

> Social responsibility strategies that have the effect of both providing valuable social benefits and fulfilling customer needs in a superior fashion can lead to competitive advantage. Corporate social agendas that address generic social issues may help boost a company's reputation but are unlikely to improve its competitive strength in the marketplace.

Whole Foods Market's social responsibility strategy is evident in almost every segment of its company value chain and is a big part of its differentiation strategy. The company's procurement policies encourage stores to purchase fresh fruits and vegetables from local farmers and screen processed food items for more than 100 common ingredients that the company considers unhealthy or environmentally unsound. Spoiled food items are sent to regional composting centers rather than landfills, and all cleaning products used in Whole Foods stores are biodegradable. The company also has created the Animal Compassion Foundation to develop natural and humane ways of raising farm animals and has converted all of its vehicles to run on biofuels.

However, not all companies choose to link their corporate social agendas to their own business or industry. Chick-Fil-A, an Atlanta-based fast-food chain with over 1,200 outlets in 38 states, has a charitable foundation that supports 14 foster homes and a summer camp for some 1,800 campers from 22 states and several foreign countries.[43] Toys "R" Us supports initiatives addressing the issues of child labor and fair labor practices around the world. Levi Strauss & Company has made AIDS prevention and awareness a major component of its social agenda for a number of years. The company and the Levi Strauss Foundation have supported the Syringe Access Fund (which makes sterile syringes available to intravenous drug users in the United States) and Preventoons (cartoons directed at children between the ages 8 and 10 that discuss how to best prevent the transmission of the AIDS virus). The Preventoons were distributed to more than 20,000 teachers in Argentina and Uruguay to use in their classrooms.

It is common for companies engaged in natural resource extraction, electric power production, forestry and paper products, motor vehicles, and chemicals production to place more emphasis on addressing environmental concerns than, say, software and electronics firms or apparel manufacturers. Companies whose business success is heavily dependent on high employee morale or attracting and retaining the best and brightest employees are somewhat more prone to stress the well-being of their employees and foster a positive, high-energy workplace environment that elicits the dedication and enthusiastic commitment of employees, thus putting real meaning behind the claim "Our people are our greatest asset." Ernst & Young, one of the four largest global accounting firms, stresses its "People First" workforce diversity strategy, which is all about respecting differences, fostering individuality, and promoting inclusiveness so that its 105,000 employees in 140 countries can feel valued, engaged, and empowered in developing creative ways to serve the firm's clients.

Thus, while the strategies and actions of all socially responsible companies have a sameness in the sense of drawing on the five categories of socially responsible behavior shown in Figure 9.2, each company's version of being socially responsible is unique.

The Moral Case for Corporate Social Responsibility and Environmentally Sustainable Business Practices

The moral case for why businesses should actively promote the betterment of society and act in a manner that benefits all of the company's stakeholders—not just the interests of shareholders—boils down to "It's the right thing to do." In today's social and political climate, most business leaders can be expected to acknowledge that socially responsible actions and environmental sustainability are important and that businesses have a duty to be good corporate citizens. But there is a complementary school of thought that business operates on the basis of an implied social contract with the members of society. According to this contract, society grants a business the right to conduct its business affairs and agrees not to unreasonably restrain its pursuit of a fair profit for the goods or services it sells. In return for this "license to operate," a business is obligated to act as a responsible citizen and do its fair share to promote the general welfare. Such a view clearly puts a moral burden on a company to take corporate citizenship into consideration and to do what's best for shareholders within the confines of discharging its duties to operate honorably, provide good working conditions to employees, be a good environmental steward, and display good corporate citizenship.

The Business Case for Socially Responsible Behavior and Environmentally Sustainable Business Practices

Whatever the merits of the moral case for socially responsible business behavior and environmentally sustainable business practices, it has long been recognized that it is in the enlightened self-interest of companies to be good citizens and devote some of their energies and resources to the betterment of employees, the communities in which they operate, and society in general. In short, there are several reasons why the exercise of social responsibility is good business:

- *It generates internal benefits (particularly as concerns employee recruiting, workforce retention, employee morale, and training costs)*—Companies with deservedly good reputations for contributing time and money to the betterment of society are better able to attract and retain employees compared to companies with tarnished reputations. Some employees just feel better about working for a company committed to improving society.[44] This can contribute to lower turnover and better worker productivity. Other direct and indirect economic benefits include lower costs for staff recruitment and training. For example, Starbucks is said to enjoy much lower rates of employee turnover because of its full benefits package for both full-time and part-time employees, management efforts to make Starbucks a great place to work, and the company's socially responsible practices. When a U.S. manufacturer of recycled paper, taking eco-efficiency to heart, discovered how to increase its fiber recovery rate, it saved the equivalent of 20,000 tons of waste paper—a factor that helped the company become the industry's lowest-cost producer.[45] Various benchmarking and measurement mechanisms have shown that workforce diversity initiatives promote the success of companies that stay behind them. Making a company a great place to work pays dividends in recruiting talented workers, more creativity and energy on the part of workers, higher worker productivity, and greater employee commitment to the company's business mission/vision and success in the marketplace.

- *It reduces the risk of reputation-damaging incidents and can lead to increased buyer patronage*—Firms may well be penalized by employees, consumers, and shareholders for actions that are not considered socially responsible. When a major oil company suffered damage to its reputation on environmental and social grounds, the CEO repeatedly said that the most negative impact the company suffered—and the one that made him fear for the future of the company—was that bright young graduates were no longer attracted to work for the company.[46] Consumer, environmental, and human rights activist groups are quick to criticize businesses whose behavior they consider to be out of line, and they are adept at getting their message into the media and onto the Internet. Pressure groups can generate widespread adverse publicity, promote boycotts, and influence like-minded or sympathetic buyers to avoid an offender's products. Research has shown that product boycott announcements are associated with a decline in a company's stock price.[47] For many years, Nike received stinging criticism for not policing sweatshop conditions in the Asian factories of its contractors, causing Nike CEO Phil Knight to observe that "Nike has become synonymous with slave wages, forced overtime, and arbitrary abuse." In 1997, Nike began an extensive effort to monitor conditions in the 800 overseas factories from which it outsourced its shoes; Knight said, "Good shoes come from good factories and good factories have good labor relations."[48] Nonetheless, Nike has continually been plagued by complaints from human rights activists that its monitoring procedures are flawed and that it is not doing enough to correct the plight of factory workers. In contrast, to the extent that a company's socially responsible behavior wins applause from consumers and fortifies its reputation, the company may win additional patronage; Whole Foods Market, Patagonia, Chick-Fil-A, Starbucks, and Green Mountain Coffee Roasters have definitely expanded their customer bases because of their visible and well-publicized activities as socially conscious companies. More and more companies are recognizing the strategic value of social responsibility strategies that reach out to people of all cultures and demographics—in the United States, women are said to having buying power of $3.7 trillion, retired and disabled people close to $4.1 trillion, Hispanics nearly $600 billion, African Americans some $500 billion, and Asian Americans about $255 billion.[49] In sum, reaching out in ways that appeal to such groups can pay off at the cash register. Some observers and executives are convinced that a strong, visible social responsibility strategy gives a company an edge in differentiating itself from rivals and in appealing to those consumers who prefer to do business with companies that are solid corporate citizens. Yet there is only limited evidence that consumers go out of their way to patronize socially responsible companies if it means paying a higher price or purchasing an inferior product.[50]

> The higher the public profile of a company or brand, the greater the scrutiny of its activities and the higher the potential for it to become a target for pressure group action.

- *It is in the best interest of shareholders*—Well-conceived social responsibility strategies and strategies to promote environmental sustainability work to the advantage of shareholders in several ways. Socially responsible business behavior and environmentally sustainable business practices help avoid or preempt legal and regulatory actions that could prove costly and otherwise burdensome. Increasing numbers of mutual funds and pension benefit managers are restricting their stock purchases to companies that meet social responsibility criteria. According to one survey, one out of every eight dollars under professional management in the United States involved socially responsible investing.[51] Moreover, the growth in socially responsible investing and identifying socially responsible companies has led to a substantial increase in the number of companies that publish formal reports on their social and environmental activities.[52] The stock prices of companies that rate high on social and environmental performance criteria have been found to perform 35 to 45 percent better than the average of the 2,500 companies comprising the Dow Jones Global Index.[53] A two-year study of leading companies found that improving environmental compliance and developing environmentally friendly products can enhance earnings per share, profitability, and the likelihood of winning contracts.[54] Nearly 100 studies have examined the relationship between corporate citizenship and corporate financial performance over the past 30 years; the majority point to a positive relationship. Of the 80 studies that examined whether a company's social performance is a good predictor of its financial performance, 42 concluded yes, 4 concluded no, and the remainder reported mixed or inconclusive

> There's little hard evidence indicating shareholders are disadvantaged in any meaningful way by a company's actions to be socially responsible and to engage in environmentally sustainable business practices.

findings.[55] To the extent that socially responsible behavior is good business, then, a social responsibility strategy that packs some punch and is more than rhetorical flourish turns out to be in the best interest of shareholders.

In sum, companies that take social responsibility and environmental sustainability seriously can improve their business reputations and operational efficiency while also reducing their risk exposure and encouraging loyalty and innovation. Overall, companies that take special pains to protect the environment (beyond what is required by law), are active in community affairs, and are generous supporters of charitable causes and projects that benefit society are more likely to be seen as good investments and as good companies to work for or do business with. Shareholders are likely to view the business case for social responsibility as a strong one, even though they certainly have a right to be concerned whether the time and money their company spends to carry out its social responsibility strategy outweighs the benefits and reduces the bottom line by an unjustified amount.

Companies are, of course, sometimes rewarded for bad behavior—a company that is able to shift environmental and other social costs associated with its activities onto society as a whole can reap large short-term profits. The major cigarette producers for many years were able to earn greatly inflated profits by shifting the health-related costs of smoking onto others and escaping any responsibility for the harm their products caused to consumers and the general public. Numerous companies will, of course, try to evade paying for the social harms of their operations for as long as they can. Calling a halt to such actions usually hinges on (1) the effectiveness of activist social groups in publicizing the adverse consequences of a company's social irresponsibility and marshaling public opinion for something to be done, (2) the enactment of legislation or regulations to correct the inequity, and (3) widespread actions on the part of socially conscious buyers to take their business elsewhere.

KEY POINTS

Ethics involves concepts of right and wrong, fair and unfair, moral and immoral. Beliefs about what is ethical serve as a moral compass in guiding the actions and behaviors of individuals and organizations. Ethical principles in business are not materially different from ethical principles in general.

There are three schools of thought about ensuring a commitment to ethical standards for companies with international operations:

- According to the *school of ethical universalism,* the same standards of what's ethical and what's unethical resonate with peoples of most societies regardless of local traditions and cultural norms; hence, common ethical standards can be used to judge the conduct of personnel at companies operating in a variety of country markets and cultural circumstances.

- According to the *school of ethical relativism* different societal cultures and customs have divergent values and standards of right and wrong—thus, what is ethical or unethical must be judged in the light of local customs and social mores and can vary from one culture or nation to another.

- According to *integrative social contracts theory,* universal ethical principles or norms based on the collective views of multiple cultures and societies combine to form a "social contract" that all individuals in all situations have a duty to observe. Within the boundaries of this social contract, local cultures can specify other impermissible actions; however, universal ethical norms always take precedence over local ethical norms.

Three categories of managers stand out with regard to their prevailing beliefs in and commitments to ethical and moral principles in business affairs: the moral manager; the immoral manager, and the amoral manager. By some accounts, the population of managers is said to be distributed among all three types in a bell-shaped curve, with immoral managers and moral managers occupying the two tails of the curve, and the amoral managers, especially the intentionally amoral managers, occupying the broad middle ground.

The moral case for social responsibility boils down to a simple concept: It's the right thing to do. The business case for social responsibility holds that it is in the enlightened self-interest of companies to be good citizens and devote some of their energies and resources to the betterment of such stakeholders as employees, the communities in which they operate, and society in general.

The apparently large numbers of immoral and amoral businesspeople are one obvious reason why some companies resort to unethical strategic behavior. Three other main drivers of unethical business behavior also stand out:

- Overzealous or obsessive pursuit of personal gain, wealth, and other selfish interests.
- Heavy pressures on company managers to meet or beat earnings targets.
- A company culture that puts profitability and good business performance ahead of ethical behavior.

The stance a company takes in dealing with or managing ethical conduct at any given time can take any of four basic forms:

- The unconcerned or nonissue approach.
- The damage control approach.
- The compliance approach.
- The ethical culture approach.

The idea of *corporate social responsibility* calls for companies to find balance between (1) their *economic responsibilities* to reward shareholders with profits, (2) *legal responsibilities* to comply with the laws of countries where they operate, (3) *ethical responsibilities* to abide by society's norms of what is moral and just, and (4) *philanthropic responsibilities* to contribute to the noneconomic needs of society. The menu of actions and behavior for demonstrating social responsibility includes:

- Employing an ethical strategy and observing ethical principles in operating the business.
- Making charitable contributions, donating money and the time of company personnel to community service endeavors, supporting various worthy organizational causes, and making a difference in the lives of the disadvantaged. Corporate commitments are further reinforced by encouraging employees to support charitable and community activities.

- Protecting or enhancing the environment and, in particular, striving to minimize or eliminate any adverse impact on the environment stemming from the company's own business activities.

- Creating a work environment that makes the company a great place to work.

- Employing a workforce that is diverse with respect to gender, race, national origin, and perhaps other aspects that different people bring to the workplace.

There's ample room for every company to tailor its social responsibility strategy to fit its core values and business mission, thereby making its own statement about "how we do business and how we intend to fulfill our duties to all stakeholders and society at large."

Some companies use the terms *corporate social responsibility* and *corporate citizenship* interchangeably, but typically, corporate citizenship places expectations on companies to go beyond consistently demonstrating ethical strategies and business behavior by addressing unmet noneconomic needs of society. Corporate sustainability involves strategic efforts to meet the needs of current customers, suppliers, shareholders, employees, and other stakeholders, while protecting, and perhaps enhancing, the resources needed by future generations.

ASSURANCE OF LEARNING EXERCISES

1. Consider the following portrayal of strategies employed by the major recording studios:

   Some recording artists and the Recording Artists' Coalition claim that the world's five major music recording studios—Universal, Sony, Time Warner, EMI/Virgin, and Bertelsmann—deliberately employ strategies calculated to take advantage of musicians who record for them. One practice to which they strenuously object is that the major-label record companies frequently require artists to sign contracts committing them to do six to eight albums, an obligation that some artists say can entail an indefinite term of indentured servitude. Further, it is claimed that audits routinely detect unpaid royalties to musicians under contract; according to one music industry attorney, record companies misreport and underpay artist royalties by 10 to 40 percent and are "intentionally fraudulent." One music writer was recently quoted as saying the process was "an entrenched system whose prowess and conniving makes Enron look like amateur hour." Royalty calculations are based on complex formulas that are paid only after artists pay for recording costs and other expenses and after any advances are covered by royalty earnings.

   A *Baffler* magazine article outlined a hypothetical but typical record deal in which a promising young band is given a $250,000 royalty advance on a new album. The album subsequently sells 250,000 copies, earning $710,000 for the record company; but the band, after repaying the record company for $264,000 in expenses ranging from recording fees and video budgets to catering, wardrobe, and bus tour costs for promotional events related to the album, ends up $14,000 in the hole, owes the record company money, and is thus paid no royalties on any of the $710,000 in revenues the recording company receives from the sale of the band's music. It is also standard practice in the music industry for recording studios to sidestep payola laws by hiring independent promoters to lobby and compensate radio stations for playing certain records. Record companies are often entitled to damages for undelivered albums if an artist leaves a recording studio for another label after seven years. Record companies also retain the copyrights in perpetuity on all music recorded under contract, a practice that artists claim is unfair. The Dixie Chicks, after a year-long feud with Sony over contract terms, ended up refusing to do another album; Sony sued for breach of contract, prompting a countersuit by the Dixie Chicks charging "systematic thievery" to cheat them out of royalties. The suits were settled out of court. One artist said, "The record companies are like cartels." Recording studios defend their strategic practices by pointing out that fewer than 5 percent of the signed artists ever deliver a hit and that they lose money on albums that sell poorly.[56]

    a. If you were a recording artist, would you be happy with some of the strategic practices of the recording studios? Would you feel comfortable signing a recording contract with studios engaging in any of the practices?

    b. Which, if any, of the practices of the recording studios do you view as unethical?

2. Suppose you found yourself in the following situation: In preparing a bid for a multimillion-dollar contract in a foreign country, you are introduced to a "consultant" who offers to help you in submitting the bid and negotiating with the customer company. You learn in conversing with the consultant that she is well connected in local government and business circles and knows key personnel in the customer company extremely well. The consultant quotes you a six-figure fee. Later, your local coworkers tell you that the use of such consultants is normal in this country—and that a large fraction of the fee will go directly to people working for the customer company. They further inform you that bidders who reject the help of such consultants have lost contracts to competitors who employed them. What would you do, assuming your company's code of ethics expressly forbids the payments of bribes or kickbacks in any form?

3. Assume that you are the sales manager at a European company that makes sleepwear products for children. Company personnel discover that the chemicals used to flameproof the company's line of children's pajamas might cause cancer if absorbed through the skin. Following this discovery, the pajamas are then banned from sale in the European Union and the United States, but senior executives of your company learn that the children's pajamas in inventory and the remaining flameproof material can be sold to sleepwear distributors in certain countries where there are no restrictions against the material's use. Your superiors instruct you to make the necessary arrangements to sell the inventories of banned pajamas and flameproof materials to distributors in those countries. Would you comply if you felt that your job would be in jeopardy if you didn't?

4. Review Microsoft's statements about its corporate citizenship programs at www.microsoft.com/about/corporatecitizenship. How does the company's commitment to global citizenship provide positive benefits for its stakeholders? How does Microsoft plan to improve social and economic empowerment in developing countries through its Unlimited Potential program? Why is this important to Microsoft shareholders?

5. Go to www.nestle.com and read the company's latest sustainability report. What are Nestlé's key sustainable environmental policies? How is the company addressing sustainable social development? How do these initiatives relate to the company's principles, values, and culture and its approach to competing in the food industry?

EXERCISES FOR SIMULATION PARTICIPANTS

1. Is your company's strategy ethical? Why or why not? Is there anything that your company is doing that could be considered shady by your competitors?

2. In what ways, if any, is your company exercising social responsibility and good corporate citizenship? Could (should) the list of things your company is doing be longer? If so, indicate what additional actions you think your company could take (assuming it had the option to do so).

3. Is your company conducting its business in an environmentally sustainable manner? What specific actions could your company take that would make an even greater contribution to environmental sustainability?

10 Building an Organization Capable of Good Strategy Execution

LEARNING OBJECTIVES

1. Gain command of what managers must do to promote successful strategy execution.

2. Understand why good strategy execution requires astute managerial actions to build core competencies and competitive capabilities.

3. Learn what issues to consider in organizing the work effort and why strategy-critical activities should be the main building blocks of the organizational structure.

4. Become aware of the pros and cons of centralized and decentralized decision making in implementing and executing the chosen strategy.

Once managers have decided on a strategy, the emphasis turns to converting it into actions and good results. Putting the strategy into place and getting the organization to execute it well call for different sets of managerial skills. Whereas crafting strategy is largely a market-driven activity, implementing and executing strategy is primarily an operations-driven activity revolving around the management of people and business processes. Whereas successful strategy making depends on business vision, solid industry and competitive analysis, and shrewd market positioning, successful strategy execution depends on doing a good job of working with and through others, building and strengthening competitive capabilities, motivating and rewarding people in a strategy-supportive manner, and instilling a discipline of getting things done. Executing strategy is an action-oriented, make-things-happen task that tests a manager's ability to direct organizational change, achieve continuous improvement in operations and business processes, create and nurture a strategy-supportive culture, and consistently meet or beat performance targets.

Experienced managers are emphatic in declaring that it is a whole lot easier to develop a sound strategic plan than it is to execute the plan and achieve the desired outcomes. According to one executive, "It's been rather easy for us to decide where we wanted to go. The hard part is to get the organization to act on the new priorities."[1] In a recent study of 1,000 companies, government agencies, and not-for-profit organizations in over 50 countries, 60 percent of employees rated their organizations poor in terms of strategy implementation.[2] *Just because senior managers announce a new strategy doesn't mean that organizational members will agree with it or enthusiastically move forward in implementing it.* Senior executives cannot simply direct immediate subordinates to abandon old ways and take up new ways, and they certainly cannot expect the needed actions and changes to occur in rapid-fire fashion and lead to the desired outcomes. Some managers and employees may be skeptical about the merits of the strategy, seeing it as contrary to the organization's best interests, unlikely to succeed, or threatening to their departments or careers. Moreover, different employees may have misconceptions about the new strategy or have different ideas about what internal changes are needed to execute it. Long-standing attitudes, vested interests, inertia, and ingrained organizational practices don't melt away when managers decide on a new strategy and begin efforts to implement it—especially when only a few people have been involved in crafting the strategy and when the rationale for strategic change requires quite a bit of salesmanship. It takes adept managerial leadership to convincingly communicate the new strategy and the reasons for it, overcome pockets of doubt and disagreement, secure the commitment and enthusiasm of key personnel, build consensus on all the hows of implementation and execution, and move forward to get all the pieces into place. Company personnel have to understand—in their heads and in their hearts—why a new strategic direction is necessary and where the new strategy is taking them.[3] Instituting change is, of course, easier when the problems with the old strategy have become obvious and/or the company has spiraled into a financial crisis.

But the challenge of successfully implementing new strategic initiatives goes well beyond managerial adeptness in overcoming resistance to change. What really makes executing strategy a tougher, more time-consuming management challenge than crafting strategy are the wide array of managerial activities that have to be attended to and the number of bedeviling issues that must be worked out. It takes first-rate "managerial smarts" to zero in on what exactly needs to be done to put new strategic initiatives in place and, further, how best to get these things done in a timely manner that yields good results. Highly demanding people-management skills are required. Plus, it takes follow-through and perseverance to get a variety of initiatives launched and moving, and to integrate the efforts of many different work groups into a smoothly functioning whole. Depending on how much consensus building and organizational change is involved, the process of implementing strategy changes can take several months to several years. And it takes still longer to achieve *real proficiency* in executing the strategy.

Like crafting strategy, *executing strategy is a job for the whole management team, not just a few senior managers.* While an organization's chief executive officer and the heads of major units (business divisions, functional departments, and key operating units) are ultimately responsible for seeing that strategy is executed successfully, the process typically affects every part of the firm, from the biggest operating unit to the smallest frontline work group. Top-level managers have to rely on the active support and cooperation of middle and lower managers in launching new strategic initiatives, in putting all of the pieces of the strategy into place, and in getting rank-and-file employees to execute the strategy with real proficiency and dedication. It is middle and lower-level managers who ultimately must ensure that work groups and frontline employees do a good job of performing strategy-critical value chain activities and produce the operating results that allow companywide performance targets to be met. Hence, the role of middle and lower-level managers on the company's strategy execution team is by no means minimal.

CORE CONCEPT

Good strategy execution requires a *team effort.* All managers have strategy-executing responsibility in their areas of authority, and all employees are participants in the strategy execution process.

Strategy execution thus requires every manager to think through the answer to "What does my area have to do to implement its part of the strategic plan, and what should I do to get these things accomplished effectively and efficiently?" The bigger the organization or the more geographically scattered its operating units, the more that successful strategy execution depends on the cooperation and implementing skills of operating managers who can push the needed changes at the lowest organizational levels and, in the process, deliver good results. Only in small organizations can top-level managers get around the need for a team effort on the part of management and personally orchestrate the action steps required for good strategy execution and operating excellence.

A FRAMEWORK FOR EXECUTING STRATEGY

Executing strategy entails figuring out all the hows—the specific techniques, actions, and behaviors that are needed for a smooth strategy-supportive operation—and then following through to get things done and deliver results. The idea is to make things happen and make them happen right. The first step in implementing strategic changes is for management to communicate the case for organizational change so clearly and persuasively to organizational members that a determined commitment takes hold throughout the ranks to find ways to put the strategy into place, make it work, and meet performance targets. The ideal condition is for managers to arouse enough enthusiasm for the strategy to turn the implementation process into a companywide crusade. *Management's handling of the strategy implementation process can be considered successful if and when the company achieves the targeted strategic and financial performance and shows good progress in making its strategic vision a reality.*

The specific hows of executing a strategy—the exact items that need to be placed on management's action agenda—always have to be customized to fit the particulars of a company's situation. Making minor changes in an existing strategy differs from implementing radical strategy changes. The hot buttons for successfully executing a low-cost provider strategy are different from those in executing a high-end differentiation strategy. Implementing and executing a new strategy for a struggling company in the midst of a financial crisis is a different job from that of improving strategy execution in a company where the execution is already pretty good. Moreover, some managers are more adept than others at using this or that approach to achieving the desired kinds of organizational changes. Hence, there's no definitive managerial recipe for successful strategy execution that cuts across all company situations and all types of strategies or that works for all types of managers. Rather, the specific hows of implementing and executing a strategy—the "to-do list" that constitutes management's agenda for action—always represents management's judgment about how best to proceed in light of the prevailing circumstances.

The Principal Managerial Components of the Strategy Execution Process

Despite the need to tailor a company's strategy-executing approaches to the particulars of its situation, certain managerial bases have to be covered no matter what the circumstances. Eight managerial tasks crop up repeatedly in company efforts to execute strategy (see Figure 10.1):

1. Building an organization with the competencies, capabilities, and resource strengths to execute strategy successfully.
2. Marshaling sufficient money and people behind the drive for strategy execution.
3. Instituting policies and procedures that facilitate rather than impede strategy execution.

Figure 10.1   The Eight Components of Strategy Execution

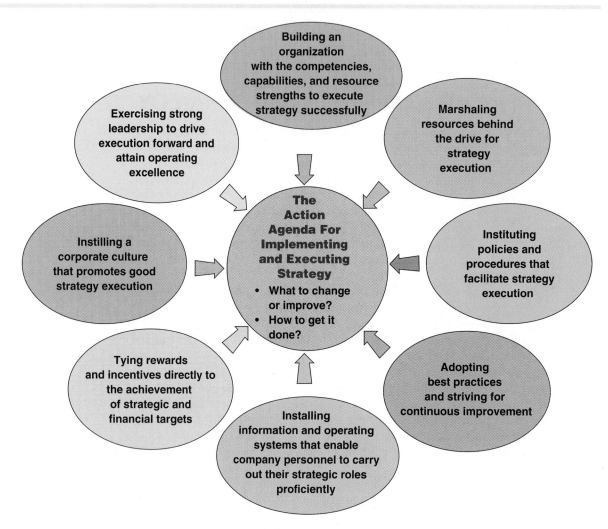

4. Adopting best practices and pushing for continuous improvement in how value chain activities are performed.
5. Installing information and operating systems that enable company personnel to carry out their strategic roles proficiently.
6. Tying rewards directly to the achievement of strategic and financial targets and to good strategy execution.
7. Instilling a corporate culture that promotes good strategy execution.
8. Exercising strong leadership to drive execution forward, keep improving on the details of execution, and achieve operating excellence as rapidly as feasible.

How well managers perform these eight tasks has a decisive impact on whether the outcome is a spectacular success, a colossal failure, or something in between.

In devising an action agenda for implementing and executing strategy, the place for managers to start is with *a probing assessment of what the organization must do differently and better to carry out the strategy successfully.* They should then consider *precisely how to make the necessary internal changes* as rapidly as possible. Successful strategy implementers have a knack for diagnosing what their organizations need to do to execute the chosen strategy well and figuring out how to get things done—they are masters in promoting results-oriented behaviors on the part of company personnel and following through on making the right things happen in a timely fashion.[4]

> When strategies fail, it is often because of poor execution—things that were supposed to get done slip through the cracks.

In big organizations with geographically scattered operating units, the action agenda of senior executives mostly involves communicating the case for change to others, building consensus for how to proceed, installing strong allies to push implementation along in key organizational units, urging and empowering subordinates to keep the process moving, establishing deadlines and measures of progress, recognizing and rewarding those who achieve implementation milestones, directing resources to the right places, and personally leading the strategic change process. Thus, the bigger the organization, the more successful strategy execution depends on the cooperation and implementing skills of operating managers who can push needed changes at the lowest organizational levels and deliver results. In small organizations, top managers can deal directly with frontline managers and employees, personally orchestrating the action steps and implementation sequence, observing firsthand how implementation is progressing, and deciding how hard and how fast to push the process along. Regardless of the organization's size and whether implementation involves sweeping or minor changes, the most important leadership traits are a strong, confident sense of what to do and how to do it. Having a strong grip on these two things comes from understanding the circumstances of the organization and the requirements for effective strategy execution. Then it remains for those managers and company personnel in strategy-critical areas to step up to the plate and produce the desired results.

What's Covered in Chapters 10, 11, and 12   In the remainder of this chapter and the next two chapters, we will discuss what is involved in performing the eight key managerial tasks (shown in Figure 10.1) that shape the process of implementing and executing strategy. This chapter explores building resource strengths and organizational capabilities. Chapter 11 looks at marshaling resources, instituting strategy-facilitating policies and procedures, adopting best practices, installing operating systems, and tying rewards to the achievement of good results. Chapter 12 deals with creating a strategy-supportive corporate culture and exercising appropriate strategic leadership.

BUILDING AN ORGANIZATION CAPABLE OF GOOD STRATEGY EXECUTION

Proficient strategy execution depends heavily on competent personnel, better-than-adequate competitive capabilities, and effective internal organization. Building a capable organization is thus always a top priority in strategy execution. As shown in Figure 10.2, three types of organization-building actions are paramount:

1. *Staffing the organization*—putting together a strong management team, and recruiting and retaining employees with the needed experience, technical skills, and intellectual capital.

Figure 10.2   The Three Components of Building an Organization Capable of Proficient Strategy Execution

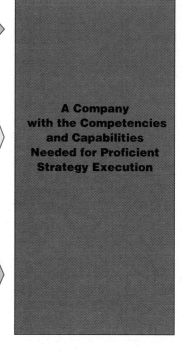

Staffing the Organization
- ■ Putting together a strong management team
- ■ Recruiting and retaining talented employees

Building Core Competencies and Competitive Capabilities
- ■ Developing a set of competencies and capabilities suited to the current strategy
- ■ Updating and revising this set as external conditions and strategy change
- ■ Training and retraining Company personnel as needed to maintain skills-based competencies

Structuring the Organization and Work Effort
- ■ Instituting organizational arrangements that facilitate good strategy execution
- ■ Deciding how much decision-making authority to push down to lower-level managers and frontline employees

A Company with the Competencies and Capabilities Needed for Proficient Strategy Execution

2. *Building core competencies and competitive capabilities*—developing proficiencies in performing strategy-critical value chain activities and updating them to match changing market conditions and customer expectations.

3. *Structuring the organization and work effort*—organizing value chain activities and business processes and deciding how much decision-making authority to push down to lower-level managers and frontline employees.

STAFFING THE ORGANIZATION

No company can hope to perform the activities required for successful strategy execution without attracting and retaining talented managers and employees with suitable skills and *intellectual capital.*

Putting Together a Strong Management Team

Assembling a capable management team is a cornerstone of the organization-building task.[5] While different strategies and company circumstances sometimes call for different mixes of backgrounds, experiences, management styles, and know-how, *the most important consideration is to fill key managerial slots with smart people who are clear thinkers, good at figuring out what needs to be done, skilled in "making it happen" and delivering good results.*[6] The task of implementing and executing challenging strategic initiatives must be assigned to executives who can be counted on to turn their decisions and actions into results that meet or beat the established performance targets. It helps enormously when a company's top management team has several people who are particularly good change agents—true believers who champion change, know how to make it happen, and love every second of the process.[7] Without a smart, capable, results-oriented management team, the implementation-execution process ends up being hampered by missed deadlines, misdirected or wasteful efforts, and/or managerial ineptness.[8] Weak executives are serious impediments to getting optimal results because they are unable to differentiate between ideas and approaches that have merit and those that are misguided—the caliber of work done under their supervision suffers.[9] In contrast, managers with strong strategy-implementing capabilities have a talent for asking tough, incisive questions. They know enough about the details of the business to ensure the soundness of the approaches and decisions of the people around them, and they can discern whether the resources people are asking for to put the strategy in place make sense. They are good at getting things done through others, typically by making sure they have the right people under them and that these people are put in the right jobs.[10] They consistently follow through on issues, monitor progress carefully, make adjustments when needed, and keep important details from slipping through the cracks. In short, they know how to drive organizational change, and they have the managerial skills to promote first-rate strategy execution.

> **CORE CONCEPT**
> Putting together a talented management team with the right mix of experiences, skills, and abilities to get things done is one of the first strategy-implementing steps.

Sometimes a company's existing management team is up to the task; at other times it may need to be strengthened or expanded by promoting qualified people from within or by bringing in outsiders whose experiences, talents, and leadership styles better suit the situation. In turnaround and rapid-growth situations, and in instances when a company doesn't have insiders with the requisite know-how, filling key management slots from the outside is a fairly standard organization-building approach. In addition, it is important to ferret out and replace managers who, for whatever reasons, either do not buy into the case for making organizational changes or do not see ways to make things better.[11] For a top management team to be truly effective, it has got to consist of true believers who recognize that organizational changes are needed and are ready to get on with the process. Weak executives and diehard resisters have to be replaced or sidelined, perhaps by shifting them to positions of lesser influence where they cannot hamper new strategy execution initiatives.

The overriding aim in building a management team should be to assemble a *critical mass* of talented managers who can function as agents of change and further the cause of first-rate strategy execution—every manager's success is enhanced (or limited) by the quality of his or her managerial colleagues and the degree to which they freely exchange ideas, debate how to improve approaches that have merit, and join forces to tackle issues and solve problems.[12] When a first-rate manager enjoys the help and support of other first-rate managers, it's possible to create a managerial whole that is greater than the sum of individual efforts—talented managers who work well together as a team can produce organizational results that are dramatically better than what one or two star managers acting individually can achieve. The chief lesson here is that *a company needs to get the right executives on the bus—and the wrong executives off the bus—before trying to drive the bus in the desired direction.*[13]

Illustration Capsule 10.1 describes General Electric's widely acclaimed approach to developing a top-caliber management team.

Recruiting and Retaining Capable Employees

Assembling a capable management team is not enough. Staffing the organization with the right kinds of people must go much deeper than managerial jobs in order for value chain activities to be performed competently. *The quality of an organization's*

ILLUSTRATION CAPSULE 10.1
How General Electric Develops a Talented and Deep Management Team

General Electric (GE) is widely considered to be one of the best-managed companies in the world, partly because of its concerted effort to develop outstanding managers. For starters, GE strives to hire talented people with high potential for executive leadership; it then goes to great lengths to expand the leadership, business, and decision-making capabilities of all its managers. The company spends about $1 billion annually on training and education programs. In 2008, all of its 189 most-senior executives had spent at least 12 months in training and professional development.

Four key elements undergird GE's efforts to build a talent-rich stable of managers:

1. GE makes a practice of transferring managers across divisional, business, or functional lines for sustained periods. Such transfers allow managers to develop relationships with colleagues in other parts of the company, help break down insular thinking in business "silos," and promote the sharing of cross-business ideas and best practices. There is an enormous emphasis at GE on transferring ideas and best practices from business to business and making GE a "boundaryless" company.

2. In selecting executives for key positions, GE is strongly disposed to candidates who exhibit what are called the four Es—enormous personal *energy*, the ability to *energize* others, *edge* (a GE code word for instinctive competitiveness and the ability to make tough decisions in a timely fashion, saying yes or no, and not maybe), and *execution* (the ability to carry things through to fruition). Considerable attention is also paid to problem-solving ability, experience in multiple functions or businesses, and experience in driving business growth (as indicated by good market instincts, in-depth knowledge of particular markets, customer touch, and technical understanding).

3. All managers are expected to be proficient at what GE calls *workout*—a process in which managers and employees come together to confront issues as soon as they come up, pinpoint the root cause of the issues, and bring about quick resolutions so the business can

move forward. Workout is GE's way of training its managers to diagnose what to do and how to do it.

4. Each year GE sends about 10,000 newly hired and longtime managers to its John F. Welch Leadership Development Center (generally regarded as one of the best corporate training centers in the world) for a three-week course on the company's Six Sigma quality initiative. Close to 10,000 "Master Black Belt" and "Black Belt" Six Sigma experts have graduated from the program to drive forward thousands of quality initiatives throughout GE. Six Sigma training is an iron-clad requirement for promotion to any professional or managerial position and any stock option award. GE's Leadership Development Center also offers advanced courses for senior managers that may focus on a single management topic for a month. All classes involve managers from different GE businesses and different parts of the world. Some of the most valuable learning comes in between formal class sessions when GE managers from different businesses trade ideas about how to improve processes and better serve the customer. This knowledge sharing not only spreads best practices throughout the organization but also improves each GE manager's knowledge.

Each of GE's 85,000 managers and professionals is graded in an annual process that divides them into five tiers: the top 10 percent, the next 15 percent, the middle 50 percent, the next 15 percent, and the bottom 10 percent. Everyone in the top tier gets stock awards, nobody in the fourth tier gets shares of stock, and most of those in the fifth tier become candidates for being weeded out. Business heads are pressured to wean out "C" players. GE's CEO personally reviews the performance of the top 3,000 managers. Senior executive compensation is heavily weighted toward Six Sigma commitment and producing successful business results. In 2007, over 70 percent of total compensation for GE's five most-senior executives was contingent on the company's performance.

According to Jack Welch, GE's CEO from 1980 to 2001, "The reality is, we simply cannot afford to field anything but teams of 'A' players."

Sources: GE's 1998, 2003, and 2007 annual reports; www.ge.com; John A. Byrne, "How Jack Welch Runs GE," *BusinessWeek,* June 8, 1998, p. 90; Miriam Leuchter, "Management Farm Teams," *Journal of Business Strategy,* May 1998, pp. 29–32; and "The House That Jack Built, *The Economist,* September 18, 1999.

people is always an essential ingredient of successful strategy execution—knowledgeable, engaged employees are a company's best source of creative ideas for the nuts-and-bolts operating improvements that lead to operating excellence. Companies like Google, Microsoft, McKinsey & Company, Southwest Airlines, Cisco Systems, Amazon.com, Procter & Gamble, PepsiCo, Nike, Electronic Data Systems (EDS), Goldman Sachs, and Intel make a concerted effort to recruit the best and brightest people they can find and then retain them with excellent compensation packages, opportunities for rapid advancement and professional growth, and challenging and interesting assignments. Having a pool of "A" players with strong skill sets and lots of brainpower is essential to their business. Microsoft makes a point of hiring the very brightest and most talented programmers it can find and motivating them with both good monetary incentives and the challenge of working on cutting-edge software design projects. McKinsey & Company, one of the world's premier management consulting companies, recruits only cream-of-the-crop MBAs at the nation's top 10 business schools; such talent is essential to McKinsey's strategy of performing high-level consulting for the world's top corporations. The leading global accounting firms screen candidates not only on the basis of their accounting expertise but also on whether they possess the people skills needed to relate well with clients and colleagues. Southwest Airlines goes to considerable lengths to hire people who can have fun and be fun on the job; it uses special interviewing and screening methods to gauge whether applicants for customer-contact jobs have outgoing personality traits that match its strategy of creating a high-spirited, fun-loving, in-flight atmosphere for passengers; it is so selective that only about 3 percent of the people who apply are offered jobs.

> **CORE CONCEPT**
> In many industries, adding to a company's talent base and building intellectual capital is more important to good strategy execution than additional investments in plants, equipment, and capital projects.

In high-tech companies, the challenge is to staff work groups with gifted, imaginative, and energetic people who can bring life to new ideas quickly and inject into the organization what one Dell executive calls "hum."[14] The saying "People are our most important asset" may seem hollow, but it fits high-technology companies dead-on. Besides checking closely for functional and technical skills, Dell tests applicants for their tolerance of ambiguity and change, their capacity to work in teams, and their ability to learn on the fly. Companies like Amazon.com, Google, and Cisco Systems have broken new ground in recruiting, hiring, cultivating, developing, and retaining talented employees—most of whom are in their 20s and 30s. Cisco goes after the top 10 percent, raiding other companies and endeavoring to retain key people at the companies it acquires. Cisco executives believe that a cadre of star engineers, programmers, managers, salespeople, and support personnel is the backbone of the company's efforts to execute its strategy and remain the world's leading provider of Internet infrastructure products and technology.

In instances where intellectual capital greatly aids good strategy execution, companies have instituted a number of practices aimed at staffing jobs with the best people they can find:

1. Spending considerable effort in screening and evaluating job applicants, selecting only those with suitable skill sets, energy, initiative, judgment, aptitudes for learning, and personality traits that mesh well with the company's work environment and culture.

2. Putting employees through training programs that continue throughout their careers.

3. Providing promising employees with challenging, interesting, and skill-stretching assignments.

4. Rotating people through jobs that not only have great content but also span functional and geographic boundaries. Providing people with opportunities to gain experience in a variety of international settings is increasingly considered an essential part of career development in multinational or global companies.

5. Encouraging employees to challenge existing ways of doing things, to be creative and innovative in proposing better ways of operating, and to push their ideas for new products or businesses. Progressive companies work hard at creating an environment in which ideas and suggestions bubble up from below and employees are made to feel that their views and suggestions count.

6. Making the work environment stimulating and engaging such that employees will consider the company a great place to work.

7. Striving to retain talented, high-performing employees via promotions, salary increases, performance bonuses, stock options and equity ownership, fringe benefit packages, and other perks.

8. Coaching average performers to improve their skills and capabilities, while weeding out underperformers and benchwarmers.

> The best companies make a point of recruiting and retaining talented employees—the objective is to make the company's entire workforce (managers and rank-and-file employees) a genuine resource strength.

It is very difficult for a company to competently execute its strategy and achieve operating excellence without a large band of capable employees who are actively engaged in the process of making ongoing operating improvements.

BUILDING CORE COMPETENCIES AND COMPETITIVE CAPABILITIES

High among the organization-building priorities in the strategy implementing/executing process is the need to build and strengthen competitively valuable core competencies and organizational capabilities. Whereas managers identify the desired competencies and capabilities in the course of crafting strategy, good strategy execution requires putting the desired competencies and capabilities in place, upgrading them as needed, and then modifying them as market conditions evolve. Sometimes a company already has some semblance of the needed competencies and capabilities, in which case managers can concentrate on strengthening and nurturing them to promote better strategy execution. More often, however, company managers have to significantly broaden or deepen certain capabilities or even add entirely new competencies in order to put strategic initiatives in place and execute them proficiently.

A number of prominent companies have succeeded in establishing core competencies and capabilities that have been instrumental in making them winners in the marketplace. Intel's core competence is in the design and mass production of complex chips for personal computers, servers, and other electronic products. Procter & Gamble's core competencies reside in its superb marketing/distribution skills and its R&D capabilities in five core technologies—fats, oils, skin chemistry, surfactants, and emulsifiers. Ciba Specialty Chemicals has technology-based competencies that allow it to quickly manufacture products for customers wanting customized products relating to coloration, brightening and whitening, water treatment and paper processing, freshness, and cleaning. Disney has core competencies in theme park operation and family entertainment.

The Three-Stage Process of Developing and Strengthening Competencies and Capabilities

Building core competencies and competitive capabilities is a time-consuming, managerially challenging exercise. While some organization-building assist can be gotten from discovering how best-in-industry or best-in-world companies perform a particular activity, trying to replicate and then improve on the competencies and capabilities of others is much easier said than done, for the same reasons that one is unlikely to ever become a good golfer just by studying what Tiger Woods does. Putting a new capability in place is more complicated than charging a group of people to become highly competent in performing the desired activity, using whatever information can be gleaned from other companies having similar competencies or capabilities. Rather, it takes a series of deliberate and well-orchestrated organizational steps to achieve mounting proficiency in performing an activity. The capability-building process has three stages:

> *Stage 1*—First, the organization must develop the *ability* to do something, however imperfectly or inefficiently. This entails selecting people with the requisite skills and experience, upgrading or expanding individual abilities as needed, and then molding the efforts and work products of individuals into a collaborative effort to create organizational ability.
>
> *Stage 2*—As experience grows and company personnel learn how to perform the activity *consistently well and at an acceptable cost,* the ability evolves into a tried-and-true *competence* or *capability.*
>
> *Stage 3*—Should company personnel continue to polish and refine their know-how and otherwise sharpen their performance of an activity such that the company eventually becomes *better than rivals* at performing the activity, the core competence rises to the rank of a *distinctive competence* (or the capability becomes a competitively superior capability), thus providing a path to competitive advantage.

Many companies are able to get through stages 1 and 2 in performing a strategy-critical activity, but comparatively few achieve sufficient proficiency in performing strategy-critical activities to qualify for the third stage.

Managing the Process   Four traits concerning core competencies and competitive capabilities are important in successfully managing the organization-building process:[15]

1. *Core competencies and competitive capabilities are bundles of skills and know-how that most often grow out of the combined efforts of cross-functional work groups and departments performing complementary activities at different locations in the firm's value chain.* Rarely does a core competence or capability consist of narrow skills attached to the work efforts of a single department. For instance, a core competence in speeding new products to market involves the collaborative efforts of personnel in R&D, engineering and design, purchasing, production, marketing, and distribution. Similarly, the capability to provide superior customer service is a team effort among people in customer call centers (where orders are taken and inquiries are answered), shipping and delivery, billing and accounts receivable, and after-sale support. Complex activities (like designing and manufacturing an ultra-fuel-efficient SUV using innovative engine technology or creating software security systems that can foil the efforts of hackers) usually involve a number

of component skills, technological disciplines, competencies, and capabilities—some performed in-house and some provided by suppliers/allies. An important part of the organization-building function is to think about which activities of which groups need to be linked and made mutually reinforcing and then to forge the necessary collaboration both internally and with outside resource providers.

> **CORE CONCEPT**
> Building competencies and capabilities is a multistage process that occurs over months and years, not something that is accomplished overnight.

2. *Normally, a core competence or capability emerges incrementally* out of company efforts either to bolster skills that contributed to earlier successes or to respond to customer problems, new technological and market opportunities, and the competitive maneuverings of rivals. Migrating from the one-time ability to do something up the ladder to a core competence or competitively valuable capability is usually an organization-building process that takes months and often years to accomplish—it is definitely not an overnight event.

3. The key to leveraging a core competence into a distinctive competence (or a capability into a competitively superior capability) is *concentrating more effort and more talent than rivals on deepening and strengthening the competence or capability, so as to achieve the dominance needed for competitive advantage.* This does not necessarily mean spending more money on such activities than competitors, but it does mean consciously focusing more talent on them and striving for best-in-industry, if not best-in-world, status. To achieve dominance on lean financial resources, companies like Cray in large computers and Honda in gasoline engines have leveraged the expertise of their talent pool by frequently re-forming high-intensity teams and reusing key people on special projects. The experiences of these and other companies indicate that the usual keys to successfully building core competencies and valuable capabilities are superior employee selection, thorough training and retraining, powerful cultural influences, effective cross-functional collaboration, empowerment, motivating incentives, short deadlines, and good databases—not big operating budgets.

4. Evolving changes in customers' needs and competitive conditions often require *tweaking and adjusting a company's portfolio of competencies and intellectual capital to keep its capabilities freshly honed and on the cutting edge.* This is particularly important in high-tech industries and fast-paced markets where important developments occur weekly. As a consequence, wise company managers work at anticipating changes in customer-market requirements and staying ahead of the curve in proactively building a package of competencies and capabilities that can win out over rivals.

Managerial actions to develop core competencies and competitive capabilities generally take one of two forms: either strengthening the company's base of skills, knowledge, and intellect, or coordinating and networking the efforts of the various work groups and departments. Actions of the first sort can be undertaken at all managerial levels, but actions of the second sort are best orchestrated by senior managers who not only appreciate the strategy-executing significance of strong competencies/capabilities but also have the clout to enforce the necessary networking and cooperation among individuals, groups, departments, and external allies.

One organization-building question is whether to develop the desired competencies and capabilities internally or to outsource them by partnering with key suppliers or forming strategic alliances. The answer depends on what can be safely delegated to outside suppliers or allies versus what internal capabilities are key to the company's long-term success. Either way, though, calls for action. Outsourcing means launching initiatives to identify the most attractive providers and to establish collaborative relationships. Developing the capabilities in-house means marshaling personnel with relevant skills and experience, collaboratively networking the individual skills and related cross-functional activities to form organizational capability, and building the desired levels of proficiency through repetition (practice makes perfect).[16]

Sometimes the tediousness of internal organization building can be shortcut by buying a company that has the requisite capability and integrating its competencies into the firm's value chain. Indeed, a pressing need to acquire certain capabilities quickly is one reason to acquire another company—an acquisition aimed at building greater capability can be every bit as competitively valuable as an acquisition aimed at adding new products or services to the company's business lineup. Capabilities-motivated acquisitions are essential (1) when a market opportunity can slip by faster than a needed capability can be created internally, and (2) when industry conditions, technology, or competitors are moving at such a rapid clip that time is of the essence. But usually there's no good substitute for ongoing internal efforts to build and strengthen the company's competencies and capabilities in performing strategy-critical value chain activities.

Updating and Remodeling Competencies and Capabilities as External Conditions and Company Strategy Change Even after core competencies and competitive capabilities are in place and functioning, company managers can't relax. Competencies and capabilities that grow stale can impair competitiveness unless they are refreshed, modified, or even phased out in response to ongoing market changes and shifts in company strategy. Indeed, the buildup of knowledge and experience over time, coupled with the imperatives of keeping capabilities in step with ongoing strategy and market changes, makes it appropriate to view a company as *a bundle of evolving competencies and capabilities.* Management's organization-building challenge is one of deciding when and how to recalibrate existing competencies and capabilities, and when and how to develop new ones. Although the task is formidable, ideally it produces a dynamic organization with "hum" and momentum as well as a distinctive competence.

Toyota, en route to overtaking General Motors as the global leader in motor vehicles, has aggressively upgraded its capabilities in fuel-efficient hybrid engine technology and constantly fine-tuned its famed Toyota Production System to enhance its already proficient capabilities in manufacturing top-quality vehicles at relatively low costs—see Illustration Capsule 10.2. Likewise, Honda, which has long had a core competence in gasoline engine technology and small engine design, has recently accelerated its efforts to broaden its expertise and capabilities in hybrid engines so as to stay close behind Toyota. Microsoft totally retooled the manner in which its programmers attacked the task of writing code for its Vista operating systems for PCs and servers. TV broadcasters have upgraded their capabilities in digital broadcasting technology in readiness for the 2009 switchover from analog to digital signal transmission.

The Strategic Role of Employee Training

Training and retraining are important when a company shifts to a strategy requiring different skills, competitive capabilities, managerial approaches, and operating methods. Training is also strategically important in organizational efforts to build skills-based competencies. And it is a key activity in businesses where technical know-how

ILLUSTRATION CAPSULE 10.2
Toyota's Legendary Production System: A Capability That Translates into Competitive Advantage

The heart of Toyota's strategy in motor vehicles is to outcompete rivals by manufacturing world-class, quality vehicles at low costs and selling them at competitive price levels. Executing this strategy requires top-notch manufacturing capability and superefficient management of people, equipment, and materials. Toyota began conscious efforts to improve its manufacturing competence over 50 years ago. Through tireless trial and error, the company gradually took what started as a loose collection of techniques and practices and integrated them into a full-fledged process that has come to be known as the Toyota Production System (TPS). The TPS drives all plant operations and the company's supply chain management practices. TPS is grounded in the following principles, practices, and techniques:

- *Use just-in-time delivery of parts and components to the point of vehicle assembly.* The idea here is to cut out all the bits and pieces of transferring materials from place to place and to discontinue all activities on the part of workers that don't add value (particularly activities where nothing ends up being made or assembled).

- *Develop people who can come up with unique ideas for production improvements.* Toyota encourages employees at all levels to question existing ways of doing things—even if it means challenging a boss on the soundness of a directive. Toyota president Katsuaki Watanabe encourages the company's employees to "pick a friendly fight." Also, Toyota doesn't fire its employees who, at first, have little judgment for improving work flows; instead, the company gives them extensive training to become better problem solvers.

- *Emphasize continuous improvement.* Workers are expected to use their heads and develop better ways of doing things, rather than mechanically follow instructions. Toyota managers tout messages such as "Never be satisfied" and "There's got to be a better way." Another mantra at Toyota is that the *T* in TPS also stands for "Thinking." The thesis is that a work environment where people have to think generates the wisdom to spot opportunities for making tasks simpler and easier to perform, increasing the speed and efficiency with which activities are performed, and constantly improving product quality.

- *Empower workers to stop the assembly line when there's a problem or a defect is spotted.* Toyota views worker efforts to purge defects and sort out the problem immediately as critical to the whole concept of building quality into the production process. According to TPS, "If the line doesn't stop, useless defective items will move on to the next stage. If you don't know where the problem occurred, you can't do anything to fix it."

- *Deal with defects only when they occur.* TPS philosophy holds that when things are running smoothly, they should not be subject to control; if attention is directed to fixing problems that are found, quality control along the assembly line can be handled with fewer personnel.

- *Ask yourself "Why?" five times.* While errors need to be fixed whenever they occur, the value of asking "Why?" five times enables identifying the root cause of the error and correcting it so that the error won't recur.

- *Organize all jobs around human motion to create a production/assembly system with no wasted effort.* Work organized in this fashion is called "standardized work," and people are trained to observe standardized work procedures (which include supplying parts to each process on the assembly line at the proper time, sequencing the work in an optimal manner, and allowing workers to do their jobs continuously in a set sequence of subprocesses).

- *Find where a part is made cheaply and use that price as a benchmark.*

The TPS utilizes a unique vocabulary of terms (such as *kanban, takt-time, jikoda, kaizen, heijunka, monozukuri, poka yoke,* and *muda*) that facilitates precise discussion of specific TPS elements. In 2003, Toyota established a Global Production Center to efficiently train large numbers of shop-floor experts in the latest TPS methods and better operate an increasing number of production sites worldwide.

There's widespread agreement that Toyota's ongoing effort to refine and improve on its renowned TPS gives it important manufacturing capabilities that are the envy of other motor vehicle manufacturers. Not only have such auto manufacturers as Ford, Daimler, Volkswagen, and General Motors attempted to emulate key elements of TPS, but elements of Toyota's production philosophy has been adopted by hospitals and postal services.

Sources: Information posted at www.toyotageorgetown.com; Hirotaka Takeuchi, Emi Osono, and Norihiko Shimizu, "The Contradictions That Drive Toyota's Success," *Harvard Business Review* 86, no. 6 (June 2008), pp. 96–104; and Taiichi Ohno, *Toyota Production System: Beyond Large-Scale Production* (New York: Sheridan, 1988).

is changing so rapidly that a company loses its ability to compete unless its skilled people have cutting-edge knowledge and expertise. Successful strategy implementers see to it that the training function is both adequately funded and effective. If the chosen strategy calls for new skills, deeper technological capability, or building and using new capabilities, training should be placed near the top of the action agenda.

The strategic importance of training has not gone unnoticed. Over 600 companies have established internal "universities" to lead the training effort, facilitate continuous organizational learning, and help upgrade company competencies and capabilities. Many companies conduct orientation sessions for new employees, fund an assortment of competence-building training programs, and reimburse employees for tuition and other expenses associated with obtaining additional college education, attending professional development courses, and earning professional certification of one kind or another. A number of companies offer online, just-in-time training courses to employees around the clock. Increasingly, employees at all levels are expected to take an active role in their own professional development, assuming responsibility for keeping their skills and expertise up-to-date and in sync with the company's needs.

From Competencies and Capabilities to Competitive Advantage

While strong core competencies and competitive capabilities are a major assist in executing strategy, they are an equally important avenue for securing a competitive edge over rivals in situations where it is relatively easy for rivals to copy smart strategies. Anytime rivals can readily duplicate successful strategy features, making it difficult or impossible to outstrategize rivals and beat them in the marketplace with a superior strategy, the chief way to achieve lasting competitive advantage is to outexecute them (beat them by performing certain value chain activities in superior fashion). *Building core competencies and competitive capabilities that are difficult or costly for rivals to emulate and that push a company closer to true operating excellence promotes proficient strategy execution.* Moreover, because cutting-edge core competencies and competitive capabilities represent resource strengths that are often time-consuming and expensive for rivals to match or trump, any competitive edge they produce tends to be sustainable and pave the way for above-average company performance.

> **CORE CONCEPT**
>
> Building competencies and capabilities that are very difficult or costly for rivals to emulate has a huge payoff—improved strategy execution and a potential for competitive advantage.

It is easy to cite instances where companies have gained a competitive edge based on superior competencies and capabilities. Dell's competitors have spent years and millions of dollars in what so far is a futile effort to match Dell's cost-efficient supply chain management capabilities. FedEx has unmatched capabilities in reliable overnight delivery of documents and small parcels. Various business news media have been unable to match the competence of *The Wall Street Journal* to report business news with such breadth and depth.

EXECUTION-RELATED ASPECTS OF ORGANIZING THE WORK EFFORT

There are few hard-and-fast rules for organizing the work effort to support good strategy execution. Every firm's organization chart is partly a product of its particular situation, reflecting prior organizational patterns, varying internal circumstances, executive judgments about reporting relationships, and the politics of who gets which assignments.

Moreover, every strategy is grounded in its own set of key success factors and value chain activities. But some organizational considerations are common to all companies. These are summarized in Figure 10.3 and discussed in turn in the following sections.

Deciding Which Value Chain Activities to Perform Internally and Which to Outsource

The advantages of a company having an outsourcing component in its strategy were discussed in Chapter 6 (pp. 164–205), but there is also a need to consider the role of outsourcing in executing the strategy. Aside from the fact than an outsider, because of its expertise and specialized know-how, may be able to perform certain value chain activities better or cheaper than a company can perform them internally, outsourcing can also have several organization-related benefits. Managers too often spend inordinate amounts of time, mental energy, and resources haggling with functional support groups and other internal bureaucracies over needed services, leaving less time for them to devote to performing strategy-critical activities in the most proficient manner. One way to reduce such distractions is to outsource the performance of assorted administrative support functions and perhaps even selected core or primary value chain activities to outside vendors, thereby enabling the company to *concentrate its full energies and resources on even more competently performing those value chain activities that are at the core of its strategy and for which it can create unique value.*

Figure 10.3   Structuring the Work Effort to Promote Successful Strategy Execution

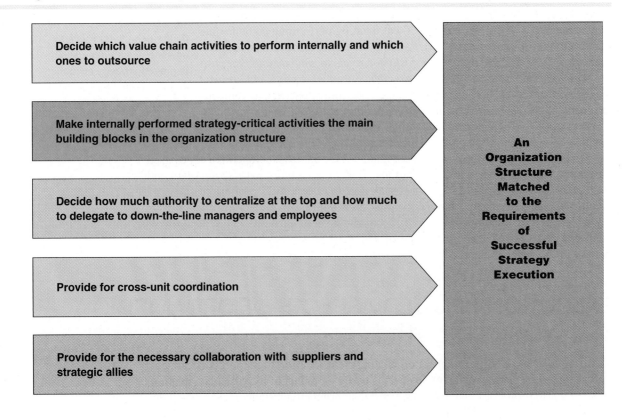

For example, E. & J. Gallo Winery outsources 95 percent of its grape production, letting farmers take on the weather and other grape-growing risks while it concentrates its full energies on wine production and sales.[17] A number of PC makers outsource the mundane and highly specialized task of PC assembly, concentrating their energies instead on product design, sales and marketing, and distribution.

When a company uses outsourcing to zero in on ever better performance of those truly strategy-critical activities where its expertise is most needed, then it may be able to realize three very positive benefits:

1. *The company improves its chances for outclassing rivals in the performance of these activities and turning a core competence into a distinctive competence.* At the very least, the heightened focus on a performing a select few value chain activities should meaningfully strengthen the company's existing core competencies and promote more innovative performance of those activities—either of which could lower costs or materially improve competitive capabilities. ING Insurance, Circuit City, Hugo Boss, Japan Airlines, Whirlpool, and Chevron have outsourced their data processing activities to computer service firms, believing that outside specialists can perform the needed services at lower costs and equal or better quality. A relatively large number of companies outsource the operation of their Web sites to Web design and hosting enterprises. Many business that get a lot of inquiries from customers or that have to provide 24/7 technical support to users of their products across the world have found that it is considerably less expensive to outsource these functions to specialists (often located in foreign countries where skilled personnel are readily available and worker compensation costs are much lower) than to operate their own call centers.

2. *The streamlining of internal operations that flows from outsourcing often acts to decrease internal bureaucracies, flatten the organization structure, speed internal decision making and shorten the time it takes to respond to changing market conditions.*[18] In consumer electronics, where advancing technology drives new product innovation, organizing the work effort in a manner that expedites getting next-generation products to market ahead of rivals is a critical competitive capability. The world's motor vehicle manufacturers have found that they can shorten the cycle time for new models, improve the quality and performance of those models, and lower overall production costs by outsourcing the big majority of their parts and components from independent suppliers and then working closely with their vendors to advance the design and functioning of the items being supplied, to swiftly incorporate new technology, and to better integrate individual parts and components to form engine cooling systems, transmission systems, and electrical systems.

3. *Partnerships can add to a company's arsenal of capabilities and contribute to better strategy execution.* By building, continually improving, and then leveraging partnerships, a company enhances its overall organizational capabilities and builds resource strengths—strengths that deliver value to customers and consequently pave the way for competitive success. Soft-drink and beer manufacturers all cultivate their relationships with their bottlers and distributors to strengthen access to local markets and build the loyalty, support, and commitment for corporate marketing programs, without which their own sales and growth are weakened. Similarly, fast-food enterprises like McDonald's and Taco Bell find it essential to work hand-in-hand with franchisees on outlet cleanliness, consistency

> **CORE CONCEPT**
> Wisely choosing which activities to perform internally and which to outsource can lead to several strategy-executing advantages—lower costs, heightened strategic focus, less internal bureaucracy, speedier decision making, and a better arsenal of competencies and capabilities.

of product quality, in-store ambience, courtesy and friendliness of store personnel, and other aspects of store operations. Unless franchisees continuously deliver sufficient customer satisfaction to attract repeat business, a fast-food chain's sales and competitive standing will suffer quickly. Companies like Boeing, Aerospatiale, Verizon Communications, and Dell have learned that their central R&D groups cannot begin to match the innovative capabilities of a well-managed network of supply chain partners having the ability to advance the technology, lead the development of next-generation parts and components, and supply them at a relatively low price.[19]

As a general rule, companies refrain from outsourcing those value chain activities over which they need direct strategic and operating control in order to build core competencies, achieve competitive advantage, and effectively manage key customer–supplier–distributor relationships. It is the strategically less important activities—like handling customer inquiries and providing technical support, doing the payroll, administering employee benefit programs, providing corporate security, managing stockholder relations, maintaining fleet vehicles, operating the company's Web site, conducting employee training, and managing an assortment of information and data processing functions—where outsourcing is most used.

Even so, a number of companies have found ways to successfully rely on outside vendors to perform strategically significant value chain activities.[20] Broadcom, a global leader in chips for broadband communications systems, outsources the manufacture of its chips to Taiwan Semiconductor, thus freeing company personnel to focus their full energies on R&D, new chip design, and marketing. Nike concentrates on design, marketing, and distribution to retailers, while outsourcing virtually all production of its shoes and sporting apparel. Cisco Systems outsources virtually all of its manufacturing of its routers, switches, and other Internet gear; yet, it protects its market position by retaining tight internal control over product design and it closely monitors the daily operations of its manufacturing vendors. Large numbers of electronics companies outsource the design, engineering, manufacturing, and shipping of their products to such companies as Flextronics and Solectron, both of which have built huge businesses as providers of such services to companies worldwide. So while performing *core* value chain activities in-house normally makes good sense, there can be times when outsourcing some of them works to good advantage.

The Dangers of Excessive Outsourcing   Critics contend that a company can go overboard on outsourcing and so hollow out its knowledge base and capabilities as to leave itself at the mercy of outside suppliers and short of the resource strengths to be a master of its own destiny.[21] The point is well taken, but most companies appear alert to the danger of taking outsourcing to an extreme or failing to maintain control of the work performed by specialist vendors or offshore suppliers. Many companies refuse to source key components from a single supplier, opting to use two or three suppliers as a way of avoiding single supplier dependence or giving one supplier too much bargaining power. Moreover, they regularly evaluate their suppliers, looking not only at the supplier's overall performance but also at whether they should switch to another supplier or even bring the activity back in-house. To avoid loss of control, companies typically work closely with key suppliers, meeting often and setting up online systems to share data and information, collaborate on work in progress, monitor performance, and otherwise document that suppliers' activities are closely integrated with their own requirements and expectations. Indeed, the advent of sophisticated online systems makes it feasible for companies to work in "real time" with suppliers 10,000 miles away, making rapid response possible whenever concerns or problems arise. Hence, *the real debate surrounding outsourcing is not about whether too much outsourcing risks loss of control but about how to use outsourcing in a manner that produces greater competitiveness.*

Making Strategy-Critical Activities the Main Building Blocks of the Organization Structure

In any business, some activities in the value chain are always more critical to strategic success and competitive advantage than others. For instance, hotel/motel enterprises have to be good at fast check-in/check-out, housekeeping and facilities maintenance, food service, and creating a pleasant ambience. In discount stock brokerage, the strategy-critical activities are fast access to information, accurate order execution, efficient record keeping and transactions processing, and good customer service. In specialty chemicals, the critical activities are R&D, product innovation, getting new products onto the market quickly, effective marketing, and expertise in assisting customers. Where such is the case, it is important for management to build its organization structure around proficient performance of these activities, making them the centerpieces or main building blocks on the organization chart.

The rationale for making strategy-critical activities the main building blocks in structuring a business is compelling: If activities crucial to strategic success are to have the resources, decision-making influence, and organizational impact they need, they have to be centerpieces in the organizational scheme. Plainly, implementing a new or changed strategy is likely to entail new or different key activities, competencies, or capabilities and therefore to require new or different organizational arrangements. If workable organizational adjustments are not forthcoming, the resulting mismatch between strategy and structure can open the door to execution and performance problems.[22] Attempting to carry out a new strategy with an old organizational structure is usually unwise.

What Types of Organization Structures Fit Which Strategies?   It is generally agreed that some type of *functional or specialized-activity structure* is the best organizational arrangement when a company is in just one particular business (irrespective of which of the five competitive strategies it opts to pursue). The primary organizational building blocks within a business are usually traditional *functional departments* (R&D, engineering and design, production and operations, sales and marketing, information technology, finance and accounting, and human resources) and *process departments* (where people in a single work unit have responsibility for all the aspects of a certain process like supply chain management, new product development, customer service, quality control, or Web sales). For instance, a technical instruments manufacturer may be organized around research and development, engineering, supply chain management, assembly, quality control, marketing, technical services, and corporate administration. A hotel may have a functional organization based on front-desk operations, housekeeping, building maintenance, food service, convention services and special events, guest services, personnel and training, and accounting. A discount retailer may organize around such functional units as purchasing, warehousing and distribution, store operations, advertising, merchandising and promotion, customer service, and corporate administrative services.

In enterprises with operations in various countries around the world (or with geographically scattered organizational units within a country), the basic building blocks may also include *geographic organizational units,* each of which has profit/loss responsibility for its assigned geographic area. In vertically integrated firms, the major building blocks are *divisional units performing one or more of the major processing steps along the value chain* (raw materials production, components manufacture, assembly, wholesale distribution, retail store operations); each division in the value chain may operate as a profit center for performance measurement purposes.

The typical building blocks of a diversified company are its *individual businesses,* with each business unit usually operating as an independent profit center and with corporate headquarters performing assorted support functions for all of its business units. But a divisional business-unit structure can present problems to a company pursuing related diversification because independent business units—each running its own business in its own ways—inhibit cross-business collaboration and the capture of cross-business strategic fits.

Determining the Degree of Authority and Independence to Give Each Unit and Each Employee

In executing the strategy and conducting daily operations, companies must decide how much authority to delegate to the managers of each organization unit—especially the heads of business subsidiaries, functional and process departments, and plants, sales offices, distribution centers and other operating units—and how much decision-making latitude to give individual employees in performing their jobs. The two extremes are to *centralize decision making* at the top (the CEO and a few close lieutenants) or to *decentralize decision making* by giving managers and employees considerable decision-making latitude in their areas of responsibility. As shown in Table 10.1, the two approaches are based on sharply different underlying principles and beliefs, with each having its pros and cons.

Centralized Decision Making: Pros and Cons   *In a highly centralized organization structure, top executives retain authority for most strategic and operating decisions and keep a tight rein on business-unit heads, department heads, and the managers of key operating units; comparatively little discretionary authority is granted to frontline supervisors and rank-and-file employees.* The command-and-control paradigm of centralized structures is based on the underlying assumption that frontline personnel have neither the time nor the inclination to direct and properly control the work they are performing, and that they lack the knowledge and judgment to make wise decisions about how best to do it—hence the need for managerially prescribed policies and procedures, close supervision, and tight control. The thesis underlying authoritarian structures is that strict enforcement of detailed procedures backed by rigorous managerial oversight is the most reliable way to keep the daily execution of strategy on track.

> There are disadvantages to having a small number of top-level managers micromanage the business either by personally making decisions or by requiring lower-level subordinates to gain approval before taking action.

The big advantage of an authoritarian structure is tight control by the manager in charge—it is easy to know who is accountable when things do not go well. But there are some serious disadvantages. Hierarchical command-and-control structures make an organization sluggish in responding to changing conditions because of the time it takes for the review/approval process to run up all the layers of the management bureaucracy. Furthermore, to work well, centralized decision making requires top-level managers to gather and process whatever information is relevant to the decision. When the relevant knowledge resides at lower organizational levels (or is technical, detailed, or hard to express in words), it is difficult and time-consuming to get all of

TABLE 10.1 Advantages and Disadvantages of Centralized versus Decentralized Decision Making

Centralized Organizational Structures	Decentralized Organizational Structures
Basic Tenets • Decisions on most matters of importance should be pushed to managers up the line who have the experience, expertise, and judgment to decide what is the wisest or best course of action. • Front-line supervisors and rank-and-file employees can't be relied upon to make the right decisions—because they seldom know what is best for the organization and because they do not have the time or the inclination to properly manage the tasks they are performing (letting them decide what to do is thus risky). **Chief Advantage** • Tight control from the top fixes accountability. **Primary Disadvantages** • Lengthens response times because management bureaucracy must decide on a course of action. • Does not encourage responsibility among lower level managers and rank-and-file employees. • Discourages lower level managers and rank-and-file employees from exercising any initiative—they are expected to wait to be told what to do.	**Basic Tenets** • Decision-making authority should be put in the hands of the people closest to and most familiar with the situation and these people should be trained to exercise good judgment. • A company that draws on the combined intellectual capital of all its employees can outperform a command-and-control company. **Chief Advantages** • Encourages lower level managers and rank-and-file employees to exercise initiative and act responsibly. • Promotes greater motivation and involvement in the business on the part of more company personnel. • Spurs new ideas and creative thinking. • Allows fast response times. • Entails fewer layers of management. **Primary Disadvantages** • Puts the organization at risk if many bad decisions are made at lower levels—top management lacks full control. • Impedes cross-business coordination and capture of strategic fits in diversified companies.

the facts and nuances in front of a high-level executive located far from the scene of the action—full understanding of the situation cannot be readily copied from one mind to another.[23] Hence, centralized decision making is often impractical—the larger the company and the more scattered its operations, the more that decision-making authority has to be delegated to managers closer to the scene of the action.

Decentralized Decision-Making: Pros and Cons *In a highly decentralized organization, decision-making authority is pushed down to the lowest organizational level capable of making timely, informed, competent decisions.* The objective is to put adequate decision-making authority in the hands of the people closest to and most familiar with the situation and train them to weigh all the factors and exercise good judgment. Decentralized decision making means that the managers of each organizational unit are delegated lead responsibility for deciding how best to execute strategy (as well as some role in shaping the strategy for the units they head). Decentralization thus requires selecting strong managers to head each organizational unit and holding them accountable for crafting and executing appropriate strategies for their units. Managers who consistently produce unsatisfactory results have to be weeded out.

> The ultimate goal of decentralized decision making is to put decision-making authority in the hands of those persons or teams closest to and most knowledgeable about the situation.

The case for empowering down-the-line managers and employees to make decisions related to daily operations and executing the strategy is based on the belief that a company that draws on the combined intellectual capital of all its employees can outperform a command-and-control company.[24] Decentralized decision making means, for example, that in a diversified company the various business-unit heads have broad authority to execute the agreed-on business strategy with comparatively little interference from corporate headquarters; moreover, the business-unit heads delegate considerable decision-making latitude to functional and process department heads and the heads of the various operating units (plants, distribution centers, sales offices) in implementing and executing their pieces of the strategy. In turn, work teams may be empowered to manage and improve their assigned value chain activity, and employees with customer contact may be empowered to do what it takes to please customers. At Starbucks, for example, employees are encouraged to exercise initiative in promoting customer satisfaction—there's the story of a store employee who, when the computerized cash register system went offline, enthusiastically offered free coffee to waiting customers.[25] *With decentralized decision making, top management maintains control by limiting empowered managers' and employees' discretionary authority and holding people accountable for the decisions they make.*

The benefits of decentralized organization structures are considerable. Delegating greater authority to subordinate managers and employees creates a more horizontal organization structure with fewer management layers. Whereas in a centralized vertical structure managers and workers have to go up the ladder of authority for an answer, in a decentralized horizontal structure they develop their own answers and action plans—making decisions in their areas of responsibility and being accountable for results is an integral part of their job. Pushing decision-making authority down to middle and lower-level managers and then further on to work teams and individual employees shortens organizational response times and spurs new ideas, creative thinking, innovation, and greater involvement on the part of subordinate managers and employees. In worker-empowered structures, jobs can be defined more broadly, several tasks can be integrated into a single job, and people can direct their own work. Fewer managers are needed because deciding how to do things becomes part of each person's or team's job. Further, today's online communication systems make it easy and relatively inexpensive for people at all organizational levels to have direct access to data, other employees, managers, suppliers, and customers. They can access information quickly (via the Internet or company intranet), readily check with superiors or whomever else as needed, and take responsible action. Typically, there are genuine gains in morale and productivity when people are provided with the tools and information they need to operate in a self-directed way. Decentralized decision making can not only shorten organizational response times but also spur new ideas, creative thinking, innovation, and greater involvement on the part of subordinate managers and employees.

In the past 15 years, there has been a pronounced shift from authoritarian, multilayered hierarchical structures to flatter, more decentralized structures that stress employee empowerment. There's strong and growing consensus that authoritarian, hierarchical organization structures are not well suited to implementing and executing strategies in an era when extensive information and instant communication are the norm and when a big fraction of the organization's most valuable assets consists of intellectual capital and resides in the knowledge and capabilities of its employees. Many companies have therefore begun empowering lower-level managers and employees throughout their organizations, giving them greater discretionary authority to make strategic adjustments in their areas of responsibility and to decide what needs to be done to put new strategic initiatives into place and execute them proficiently.

Maintaining Control in a Decentralized Organization Structure   Pushing decision-making authority deep down into the organization structure and empowering employees presents its own organizing challenge: *how to exercise adequate control* *over the actions of empowered employees so that the business is not put at risk at the same time that the benefits of empowerment are realized.*[26] Maintaining adequate organizational control over empowered employees is generally accomplished by placing limits on the authority that empowered personnel can exercise, holding people accountable for their decisions, instituting compensation incentives that reward people for doing their jobs in a manner to contributes to good company performance, and creating a corporate culture where there's strong peer pressure on individuals to act responsibly.

Capturing Strategic Fits in a Decentralized Structure   Diversified companies striving to capture cross-business strategic fits have to beware of allowing business heads to operate independently when cross-business collaboration is essential in order to gain strategic fit benefits. Cross-business strategic fits typically have to be captured either by enforcing close cross-business collaboration or by centralizing performance of functions having strategic fits at the corporate level.[27] For example, if businesses with overlapping process and product technologies have their own independent R&D departments—each pursuing their own priorities, projects, and strategic agendas—it's hard for the corporate parent to prevent duplication of effort, capture either economies of scale or economies of scope, or broaden the company's R&D efforts to embrace new technological paths, product families, end-use applications, and customer groups. Where cross-business R&D fits exist, the best solution is usually to centralize the R&D function and have a coordinated corporate R&D effort that serves both the interests of individual business and the company as a whole. Likewise, centralizing the related activities of separate businesses makes sense when there are opportunities to share a common sales force, use common distribution channels, rely on a common field service organization to handle customer requests or provide maintenance and repair services, use common e-commerce systems and approaches, and so on.

The point here is that efforts to decentralize decision making and give organizational units leeway in conducting operations have to be tempered with the need to maintain adequate control and cross-unit coordination—decentralization doesn't mean delegating authority in ways that allow organization units and individuals to do their own thing. There are numerous instances when decision-making authority must be retained at high levels in the organization and ample cross-unit coordination strictly enforced.

Providing for Internal Cross-Unit Coordination

The classic way to coordinate the activities of organizational units is to position them in the hierarchy so that the most closely related ones report to a single person (a functional department head, a process manager, a geographic area head, a senior executive). Managers higher up in the ranks generally have the clout to coordinate, integrate, and arrange for the cooperation of units under their supervision. In such structures, the chief executive officer, chief operating officer, and business-level managers end up as central points of coordination because of their positions of authority over the whole unit. When a firm is pursuing a related diversification strategy, coordinating the related activities of independent business units often requires the centralizing authority of a single corporate-level officer. Also, diversified companies commonly centralize such staff support functions as public relations, finance and accounting, employee benefits, and information technology at the corporate level both to contain the costs of support activities and to facilitate uniform and coordinated performance of such functions within each business unit.

However, close cross-unit collaboration is usually needed to build core competencies and competitive capabilities in such strategically important activities as speeding new products to market and providing superior customer service which involve employees scattered across several internal organization units (and perhaps the employees of outside strategic partners or specialty vendors). A big weakness of traditional functionally organized structures is that pieces of strategically relevant activities and capabilities often end up scattered across many departments, with the result that no one group or manager is accountable. Consider, for example, how the following strategy-critical activities cut across different functions:

- *Filling customer orders accurately and promptly*—a process that involves personnel from sales (which wins the order); finance (which may have to check credit terms or approve special financing); production (which must produce the goods and replenish warehouse inventories as needed); warehousing (which has to verify whether the items are in stock, pick the order from the warehouse, and package it for shipping); and shipping (which has to choose a carrier to deliver the goods and release the goods to the carrier).[28]

- *Fast, ongoing introduction of new products*—a cross-functional process involving personnel in R&D, design and engineering, purchasing, manufacturing, and sales and marketing.

- *Improving product quality*—a process that entails the collaboration of personnel in R&D, design and engineering, purchasing, in-house components production, manufacturing, and assembly.

- *Supply chain management*—a collaborative process that cuts across such functional areas as purchasing, inventory management, manufacturing and assembly, and warehousing and shipping.

- *Building the capability to conduct business via the Internet*—a process that involves personnel in information technology, supply chain management, production, sales and marketing, warehousing and shipping, customer service, finance, and accounting.

- *Obtaining feedback from customers and making product modifications to meet their needs*—a process that involves personnel in customer service and after-sale support, R&D, design and engineering, purchasing, manufacturing and assembly, and marketing research.

Handoffs from one department to another lengthen completion time and frequently drive up administrative costs, since coordinating the fragmented pieces can soak up hours of effort on the parts of many people.[29] This is not a fatal flaw of functional organization—organizing around specific functions normally works to good advantage in support activities like finance and accounting, human resource management, and engineering, and in such primary activities as R&D, manufacturing, and marketing. But the tendency for pieces of a strategy-critical activity to be scattered across several functional departments is an important weakness of functional organization and accounts for why a company's competencies and capabilities are typically cross-functional and don't reside in the activities of a single functional department.

Many companies have found that rather than continuing to scatter related pieces of a strategy-critical business process across several functional departments and scrambling to integrate their efforts, it is better to reengineer the work effort and pull the people who performed the pieces in functional departments into a group that works together to perform the whole process, thus creating *process departments* (like customer service or new product development or supply chain management). And sometimes the coordinating mechanisms involve the use of cross-functional task forces, dual reporting relationships, informal organizational networking, voluntary cooperation, incentive compensation tied to measures of group performance, and strong executive-level insistence on teamwork and cross-department cooperation (including removal of recalcitrant managers who stonewall collaborative efforts). At one European-based company, a top executive promptly replaced the managers of several plants who were not fully committed to collaborating closely on eliminating duplication in product development and production efforts among plants in several different countries. Earlier, the executive, noting that negotiations among the managers had stalled on which labs and plants to close, had met with all the managers, asked them to cooperate to find a solution, discussed with them which options were unacceptable, and given them a deadline to find a solution. When the asked-for teamwork wasn't forthcoming, several managers were replaced.

Providing for Collaboration with Outside Suppliers and Strategic Allies

Someone or some group must be authorized to collaborate as needed with each major outside constituency involved in strategy execution. Forming alliances and cooperative relationships presents immediate opportunities and opens the door to future possibilities, but nothing valuable is realized until the relationship grows, develops, and blossoms. Unless top management sees that constructive organizational bridge-building with strategic partners occurs and that productive working relationships emerge, the value of alliances is lost and the company's power to execute its strategy is weakened. If close working relationships with suppliers are crucial, then supply chain management must be given formal status on the company's organization chart and a significant position in the pecking order. If distributor/dealer/franchisee relationships are important, someone must be assigned the task of nurturing the relationships with forward channel allies. If working in parallel with providers of complementary products and services contributes to enhanced organizational capability, then cooperative organizational arrangements have to be put in place and managed to good effect.

Building organizational bridges with external allies can be accomplished by appointing "relationship managers" with responsibility for making particular strategic partnerships or alliances generate the intended benefits. Relationship managers have many roles and functions: getting the right people together, promoting good rapport, seeing that plans for specific activities are developed and carried out, helping adjust internal organizational procedures and communication systems, ironing out operating dissimilarities, and nurturing interpersonal cooperation. Multiple cross-organization ties have to be established and kept open to ensure proper communication and coordination.[30] There has to be enough information sharing to make the relationship work and periodic frank discussions of conflicts, trouble spots, and changing situations.[31]

Current Organizational Trends

Many of today's companies are winding up the task of remodeling their traditional hierarchical structures once built around functional specialization and centralized authority. Much of the corporate downsizing movement in the late 1980s and early 1990s was aimed at recasting authoritarian, pyramidal organizational structures into flatter, decentralized structures. The change was driven by growing realization that command-and-control hierarchies were proving a liability in businesses where customer preferences were shifting from standardized products to custom orders and special features, product life cycles were growing shorter, custom mass production methods were replacing standardized mass production techniques, customers wanted to be treated as individuals, technological change was ongoing, and market conditions were fluid. Layered management hierarchies with lots of checks and controls that required people to look upward in the organizational structure for answers and approval were failing to deliver responsive customer service and timely adaptations to changing conditions.

The organizational adjustments and downsizing of companies in 2001–2003 brought further refinements and changes to streamline organizational activities and shake out inefficiencies. The goals have been to make companies leaner, flatter, and more responsive to change. Many companies are drawing on five tools of organizational design: (1) managers and workers empowered to act on their own judgments, (2) work process redesign (to achieve greater streamlining and tighter cohesion), (3) self-directed work teams, (4) rapid incorporation of Internet technology applications, and (5) networking with outsiders to improve existing organization capabilities and create new ones. Considerable management attention is being devoted to building a company capable of outcompeting rivals on the basis of superior resource strengths and competitive capabilities—capabilities that are increasingly based on intellectual capital and cross-unit collaboration.

Several other organizational characteristics are emerging:

- Extensive use of Internet technology and e-commerce business practices—real-time data and information systems, greater reliance on online systems for transacting business with suppliers and customers, and Internet-based communication and collaboration with suppliers, customers, and strategic partners.

- Fewer barriers between different vertical ranks, between functions and disciplines, between units in different geographic locations, and between the company and its suppliers, distributors/dealers, strategic allies, and customers—an outcome partly due to pervasive use of online systems.

- Rapid dissemination of information, rapid learning, and rapid response times—also an outcome partly due to pervasive use of online systems.

- Collaborative efforts among people in different functional specialties and geographic locations—essential to create organization competencies and capabilities.

- Assembling work teams that include more members and have a greater geographic dispersion of team members. During the 1990s, most formal team arrangements contained 20 or fewer members. Today, teams at many multinational corporations include 100 or more members that might be scattered across 10 or more countries.

KEY POINTS

Implementing and executing strategy is an operation-driven activity revolving around the management of people and business processes. The managerial emphasis is on converting strategic plans into actions and good results. *Management's handling of the process of implementing and executing the chosen strategy can be considered success-ful if and when the company achieves the targeted strategic and financial performance and shows good progress in making its strategic vision a reality.* Shortfalls in perfor-mance signal weak strategy, weak execution, or both.

The place for managers to start in implementing and executing a new or different strategy is with *a probing assessment of what the organization must do differently and better to carry out the strategy successfully.* They should then consider *precisely how to make the necessary internal changes* as rapidly as possible.

Like crafting strategy, executing strategy is a job for a company's whole manage-ment team, not just a few senior managers. Top-level managers have to rely on the active support and cooperation of middle and lower managers to push strategy changes into functional areas and operating units and to see that the organization actually oper-ates in accordance with the strategy on a daily basis.

Eight managerial tasks crop up repeatedly in company efforts to execute strategy:

1. Building an organization with the competencies, capabilities, and resource strengths to execute strategy successfully.
2. Marshaling sufficient money and people behind the drive for strategy execution.
3. Instituting policies and procedures that facilitate rather than impede strategy execution.
4. Adopting best practices and pushing for continuous improvement in how value chain activities are performed.
5. Installing information and operating systems that enable company personnel to carry out their strategic roles proficiently.
6. Tying rewards directly to the achievement of strategic and financial targets and to good strategy execution.
7. Shaping the work environment and corporate culture to fit the strategy.
8. Exercising strong leadership to drive execution forward, keep improving on the details of execution, and achieve operating excellence as rapidly as feasible.

Building an organization capable of good strategy execution entails three types of organization-building actions: (1) *staffing the organization*—assembling a talented, can-do management team, and recruiting and retaining employees with the needed experience, technical skills, and intellectual capital, (2) *building core competencies and competitive capabilities* that will enable good strategy execution and updating them as strategy and external conditions change, and (3) *structuring the organization and work effort*—organizing value chain activities and business processes and decid-ing how much decision-making authority to push down to lower-level managers and frontline employees.

Building core competencies and competitive capabilities is a time-consuming, managerially challenging exercise that involves three stages: (1) developing the *ability* to do something, however imperfectly or inefficiently, by selecting people with the req-uisite skills and experience, upgrading or expanding individual abilities as needed, and then molding the efforts and work products of individuals into a collaborative group effort; (2) coordinating group efforts to learn how to perform the activity *consistently well and at an acceptable cost,* thereby transforming the ability into a tried-and-true *competence* or *capability;* and (3) continuing to polish and refine the organization's know-how and otherwise sharpen performance such that it becomes *better than rivals* at performing the activity, thus raising the core competence (or capability) to the rank of a *distinctive competence* (or competitively superior capability) and opening an avenue to competitive advantage. Many companies manage to get through stages 1 and 2 in performing a strategy-critical activity but comparatively few achieve sufficient proficiency in performing strategy-critical activities to qualify for the third stage.

Strong core competencies and competitive capabilities are an important avenue for securing a competitive edge over rivals in situations where it is relatively easy for rivals to copy smart strategies. Anytime rivals can readily duplicate successful strategy features, making it difficult or impossible to *outstrategize* rivals and beat them in the marketplace with a superior strategy, the chief way to achieve lasting competitive advantage is to *outexecute* them (beat them by performing certain value chain activities in superior fashion). *Building core competencies and competitive capabilities that are difficult or costly for rivals to emulate and that push a company closer to true operating excellence is one of the best and most reliable ways to achieve a durable competitive edge.*

Structuring the organization and organizing the work effort in a strategy-supportive fashion has five aspects: (1) deciding which value chain activities to perform internally and which ones to outsource; (2) making internally performed strategy-critical activities the main building blocks in the organization structure; (3) deciding how much authority to centralize at the top and how much to delegate to down-the-line managers and employees; (4) providing for internal cross-unit coordination and collaboration to build and strengthen internal competencies/capabilities; and (5) providing for the necessary collaboration and coordination with suppliers and strategic allies.

ASSURANCE OF LEARNING EXERCISES

1. Review the Careers link on L'Oréal's worldwide corporate Web site (go to www. loreal.com and click on the company's worldwide corporate Web site option). The section provides extensive information about personal development, international learning opportunities, integration of new hires into existing teams, and other areas of management development. How do the programs discussed help build core competencies and competitive capabilities at L'Oréal? Please use the chapter's discussion of building core competencies and competitive capabilities as a guide for preparing your answer.

2. Examine the overall corporate organizational structure chart for Exelon Corporation. The chart can be found by going to www.exeloncorp.com and using the Web site search feature to locate "organizational charts." Does it appear that strategy-critical activities are the building blocks of Exelon's organizational arrangement? Is its organizational structure best characterized as a departmental structure tied to functional, process, or geographic departments? Is the company's organizational structure better categorized as a divisional structure? Would you categorize Exelon's organizational structure as a matrix arrangement? Explain your answer.

3. Using Google Scholar or your university library's access to EBSCO, InfoTrac, or other online databases, do a search for recent writings on decentralized decision making and employee empowerment. According to the articles you found in the various management journals, what are the conditions for effectively pushing decision making down to lower levels of management?

EXERCISES FOR SIMULATION PARTICIPANTS

1. How would you describe the organization of your company's top management team? Is some decision making decentralized and delegated to individual managers? If so, explain how the decentralization works. Or are decisions made more by consensus, with all co-managers having input? What do you see as the advantages and disadvantages of the decision-making approach your company is employing?

2. Have you and your co-managers made a special effort to develop any core competencies or competitive capabilities that can contribute to achieving a competitive advantage? Why or why not? Explain.

3. Does your company have the ability to outsource any value chain activities? If so, have you and your co-managers opted to engage in outsourcing? Why or why not?

11

Managing Internal Operations: Actions That Promote Good Strategy Execution

LEARNING OBJECTIVES

1. Learn why resource allocation should always be based on strategic priorities.

2. Understand why policies and procedures should be designed to facilitate good strategy execution.

3. Understand why and how benchmarking, best-practices adoption, and tools for continuously improving the performance of value chain activities help an organization achieve operating excellence and superior strategy execution.

4. Understand the role of information and operating systems in enabling company personnel to carry out their strategic roles proficiently.

5. Learn how and why the use of well-designed incentives and rewards can be management's single most powerful tool for promoting proficient strategy execution and operating excellence.

Winning companies know how to do their work better.

—Michael Hammer and James Champy

If you want people motivated to do a good job, give them a good job to do.

—Frederick Herzberg

Companies that make best practices a priority are thriving, thirsty, learning organizations. They believe that everyone should always be searching for a better way. Those kinds of companies are filled with energy and curiosity and a spirit of can-do.

—Jack Welch
Former CEO, General Electric

You ought to pay big bonuses for premier performance . . . Be a top payer, not in the middle or low end of the pack.

—Lawrence Bossidy
Former CEO, Honeywell International

In Chapter 10 we emphasized the importance of building organization capabilities and structuring the work effort so as to perform strategy-critical activities in a coordinated and highly competent manner. In this chapter we discuss five additional managerial actions that promote successful strategy execution:

1. Marshaling resources behind the drive for good strategy execution.
2. Instituting policies and procedures that facilitate strategy execution.
3. Adopting best practices and striving for continuous improvement in how value chain activities are performed.
4. Installing information and operating systems that enable company personnel to carry out their strategic roles proficiently.
5. Tying rewards and incentives directly to the achievement of strategic and financial targets and to good strategy execution.

MARSHALLING RESOURCES BEHIND THE DRIVE FOR GOOD STRATEGY EXECUTION

Early in the process of implementing and executing a new or different strategy, managers need to determine what resources will be needed and then consider whether the current budgets of organizational units are suitable. Plainly, organizational units must have the budgets and resources for executing their parts of the strategic plan effectively and efficiently. Developing a strategy-driven budget requires top management to determine what funding is needed to execute new strategic initiatives and to strengthen or modify the company's competencies and capabilities. This includes careful screening of requests for more people and new facilities and equipment, approving those that hold promise for making a contribution to strategy execution, and turning down those that don't. Should internal cash flows prove insufficient to fund the planned strategic initiatives, then management must raise additional funds through borrowing or selling additional shares of stock to willing investors.

A company's ability to marshal the resources needed to support new strategic initiatives and steer them to the appropriate organizational units has a major impact on the strategy execution process. Too little funding (stemming either from constrained financial resources or from sluggish management action to adequately increase the budgets of strategy-critical organizational units) slows progress and impedes the efforts of organizational units to execute their pieces of the strategic plan proficiently. Too much funding wastes organizational resources and reduces financial performance. Both outcomes argue for managers to be deeply involved in reviewing budget proposals and directing the proper kinds and amounts of resources to strategy-critical organization units.

A change in strategy nearly always calls for budget reallocations and resource shifting. Previously important organizational units having a lesser role in the new strategy may need downsizing. Units that now have a bigger and more critical strategic role may need more people, new equipment, additional facilities, and above-average increases in their operating budgets. More resources may have to be devoted to quality control or to adding new product features or to building a better brand image or to cutting costs or to employee retraining. Strategy implementers need to be active and forceful in downsizing some functions and upsizing others, not only to amply fund activities with a critical role in the new strategy but also to avoid inefficiency and achieve profit projections. They have to put enough resources behind new strategic initiatives to make things happen, and they have to make the tough decisions to kill projects and activities that are no longer justified. Honda's strong support of R&D activities allowed it to develop the first motorcycle airbag, the first low-polluting four-stroke outboard marine engine, a wide range of ultralow-emission cars, the first hybrid car (Honda Insight) in the U.S. market, and the first hydrogen fuel cell car (Honda Clarity). However, Honda managers had no trouble stopping production of the Insight in 2006 when its sales failed to take off and then shifting resources to the development and manufacture of other promising new models.

Visible actions to reallocate operating funds and move people into new organizational units signal a determined commitment to strategic change and frequently are needed to catalyze the implementation process and give it credibility. Microsoft has made a practice of regularly shifting hundreds of programmers to new high-priority programming initiatives within a matter of weeks or even days. At Harris Corporation, where the strategy was to diffuse research ideas into areas that were commercially viable, top management

CORE CONCEPT

The funding requirements of a new strategy must drive how capital allocations are made and the size of each unit's operating budgets. Underfunding organizational units and activities pivotal to strategic success impedes execution and the drive for operating excellence.

regularly moved groups of engineers out of low-opportunity activities into its most promising new commercial venture divisions. Fast-moving developments in many markets are prompting companies to abandon traditional annual or semiannual budgeting and resource allocation cycles in favor of speedily adapting the strategy to newly developing events.

Merely fine-tuning the execution of a company's existing strategy seldom requires big movements of people and money from one area to another. But the bigger the change in strategy (or the more obstacles that lie in the path of good strategy execution), the bigger the resource shifts that tend to be required. The desired improvements can usually be accomplished through above-average budget increases to organizational units launching new initiatives and below-average increases (or even small budget cuts) for the remaining organizational units. However, there are times when strategy changes or new execution initiatives need to be made without boosting budget requirements. In such circumstances, managers have to work their way through the existing budget line by line and activity by activity, looking for ways to shift resources from low-value-adding activities to high-priority activities where new execution initiatives are needed.

INSTITUTING POLICIES AND PROCEDURES THAT FACILITATE STRATEGY EXECUTION

A company's policies and procedures can either assist or block good strategy execution. Anytime a company moves to put new strategy elements in place or improve its strategy-execution capabilities, managers are well advised to undertake a careful review of existing policies and procedures, proactively revising or discarding those that are out of sync. A change in strategy or a push for better strategy execution generally requires some changes in work practices and the behavior of company personnel. One way of promoting such changes is to institute a select set of new policies and procedures deliberately aimed at steering the actions and behavior of company personnel in a direction more conducive to good strategy execution and operating excellence.

> **CORE CONCEPT**
> Well-conceived policies and procedures aid strategy execution; out-of-sync ones are barriers.

As shown in Figure 11.1, prescribing new policies and operating procedures acts to facilitate strategy execution in three ways:

1. *Instituting new policies and procedures provides top-down guidance regarding how certain things now need to be done.* Asking people to alter established habits and procedures, of course, always upsets the internal order of things. It is normal for pockets of resistance to develop and for people to exhibit some degree of stress and anxiety about how the changes will affect them, especially when the changes may eliminate jobs. But when existing ways of doing things pose a barrier to improving strategy execution, actions and behaviors have to be changed. The managerial role of establishing and enforcing new policies and operating practices is to paint a different set of white lines, place limits on independent behavior, and channel individual and group efforts along a path more conducive to executing the strategy. Instituting new policies and procedures to steer the actions and behavior of company personnel in strategy-supportive directions becomes especially important when there are doubts among rank-and-file employees about the soundness of a new strategy or the necessity of change. Most employees will refrain from violating company policy or going against recommended practices and procedures without first gaining clearance or having strong justification.[1]

Figure 11.1   How Prescribed Policies and Procedures Facilitate Strategy Execution

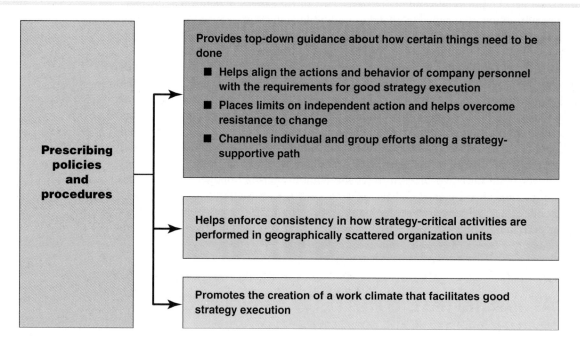

2. *Policies and procedures help enforce needed consistency in how particular strategy-critical activities are performed in geographically scattered operating units.* Standardization and strict conformity are sometimes desirable components of good strategy execution. Eliminating significant differences in the operating practices of different plants, sales regions, customer service centers, or the individual outlets in a chain operation helps a company deliver consistent product quality and service to customers. Good strategy execution nearly always entails an ability to replicate product quality and the caliber of customer service at every location where the company does business—anything less blurs the company's image and fails to meet customer expectations.

3. *Well-conceived policies and procedures promote the creation of a work climate that facilitates good strategy execution.* Because discarding old policies and procedures in favor of new ones invariably alters the internal work climate, managers can use the policy-changing process as a powerful lever for changing the corporate culture in ways that produce a stronger fit with the new strategy. The trick here, obviously, is to hit on a new policy that will catch the immediate attention of the whole organization, quickly shift actions and behavior, and then become embedded in how things are done.

In an attempt to steer "crew members" into stronger quality and service behavior patterns, McDonald's policy manual spells out detailed procedures that personnel in each McDonald's unit are expected to observe; for example, "Cooks must turn, never flip, hamburgers. If they haven't been purchased, Big Macs must be discarded in 10 minutes after being cooked and French fries in 7 minutes. Cashiers must make eye contact with and smile at every customer."

Nordstrom's strategic objective is to make sure that each customer has a pleasing shopping experience in its department stores and returns time and again; to get store personnel to dedicate themselves to outstanding customer service, Nordstrom has a policy of promoting only those people whose personnel records contain evidence of "heroic acts" to please customers—especially customers who may have made "unreasonable requests" that require special efforts. To keep its R&D activities responsive to customer needs and expectations, Hewlett-Packard requires R&D people to make regular visits to customers to learn about their problems and learn their reactions to HP's latest new products.

One of the big policymaking issues concerns what activities need to be rigidly prescribed and what activities ought to allow room for independent action on the part of empowered personnel. Few companies need thick policy manuals to direct the strategy-execution process or prescribe exactly how daily operations are to be conducted. Too much policy promotes excessive and stifling bureaucracy, erecting as many obstacles as wrong policy and being as confusing as no policy. There is wisdom in a middle approach: *Prescribe enough policies to give organization members clear direction in implementing strategy and to place desirable boundaries on employees' actions; then empower them to act within these boundaries however they think makes sense.* Allowing company personnel to act anywhere between the "white lines" is especially appropriate when individual creativity and initiative are more essential to good strategy execution than standardization and strict conformity. Instituting strategy-facilitating policies can therefore mean more policies, fewer policies, or different policies. It can mean policies that require things to be done a certain way or policies that give employees leeway to do activities the way they think best.

ADOPTING BEST PRACTICES AND STRIVING FOR CONTINUOUS IMPROVEMENT

Company managers can significantly advance the cause of competent strategy execution by pushing organization units and company personnel to identify and adopt the best practices for performing value chain activities and, further, insisting on continuous improvement in how internal operations are conducted. One of the most widely used and effective tools for gauging how well a company is executing pieces of its strategy entails benchmarking the company's performance of particular activities and business processes against "best-in-industry" and "best-in-world" performers.[2] It can also be useful to look at "best-in-company" performers of an activity if a company has a number of different organizational units performing much the same function at different locations. Identifying, analyzing, and understanding how top companies or individuals perform particular value chain activities and business processes provides useful yardsticks for judging the effectiveness and efficiency of internal operations and setting performance standards for organization units to meet or beat.

> **CORE CONCEPT**
> Managerial efforts to identify and adopt best practices are a powerful tool for promoting operating excellence and better strategy execution.

Identifying and Incorporating Best Practices to Improve Operating Effectiveness and Efficiency

A **best practice** is a technique for performing an activity or business process that at least one company has demonstrated works particularly well. To qualify as a legitimate best practice, the technique must have a proven record in significantly lowering costs, improving quality or performance,

> **CORE CONCEPT**
> A *best practice* is any practice that at least one company has proved works particularly well.

shortening time requirements, enhancing safety, or delivering some other highly positive operating outcome. Best practices thus identify a path to operating excellence. For a best practice to be valuable and transferable, it must demonstrate success over time, deliver quantifiable and highly positive results, and be repeatable.

Benchmarking is the backbone of the process of identifying, studying, and implementing outstanding practices. A company's benchmarking effort looks outward to find best practices and then proceeds to develop the data for measuring how well a company's own performance of an activity stacks up against the best-practice standard. A strong commitment to and belief in benchmarking involves being humble enough to admit that others have come up with world-class ways to perform particular activities yet wise enough to try to learn how to match, and even surpass, them. But, as shown in Figure 11.2, the payoff of benchmarking comes from adapting the top-notch approaches pioneered by other companies in the company's own operation and thereby boosting, perhaps dramatically, the proficiency with which value chain tasks are performed.

However, benchmarking is more complicated than simply identifying which companies are the best performers of an activity and then trying to imitate their approaches—especially if these companies are in other industries. Normally, the outstanding practices of other organizations have to be *adapted* to fit the specific circumstances of a company's own business and operating requirements. Since most companies believe "our work is different" or "we are unique," the telling part of any best-practice initiative is how well the company puts its own version of the best practice into place and makes it work.

Indeed, a best practice remains little more than another company's interesting success story unless company personnel buy into the task of translating what can be learned from other companies into real action and results. The agents of change must be frontline employees who are convinced of the need to abandon the old ways of doing things and switch to a best-practice mind-set. *The more that organizational units use best practices in performing their work, the closer a company moves toward performing its value chain activities as effectively and efficiently as possible.* This is what operational excellence is all about.

Legions of companies across the world now engage in benchmarking to improve their strategy execution efforts and, ideally, gain a strategic, operational, and financial advantage over rivals. Scores of trade associations and special interest organizations have undertaken efforts to collect best-practice data relevant to a particular industry or business function and make their databases available online to members—good examples include The Benchmarking Exchange (www.benchnet.com); Best Practices, LLC

Figure 11.2 From Benchmarking and Best-Practice Implementation to Operating Excellence

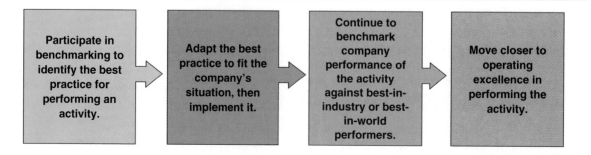

(www.best-in-class.com); and the American Productivity and Quality Center (www.apqc.org). Benchmarking and best-practice implementation have clearly emerged as legitimate and valuable managerial tools for promoting operational excellence.

Business Process Reengineering, Six Sigma Quality Programs, and TQM: Tools for Promoting Operating Excellence

In striving for operating excellence, many companies have also come to rely on three other potent management tools: business process reengineering, Six Sigma quality control techniques, and total quality management (TQM) programs. Indeed, these three tools have become globally pervasive techniques for implementing strategies keyed to cost reduction, defect-free manufacture, superior product quality, superior customer service, and total customer satisfaction. The following sections describe how business process reengineering, Six Sigma, and TQM can contribute to operating excellence and better strategy execution.

Business Process Reengineering Companies scouring for ways to improve their operations have sometimes discovered that the execution of strategy-critical activities is hindered by an organizational arrangement where pieces of the activity are performed in several different functional departments, with no one manager or group being accountable for optimum performance of the entire activity. This can easily occur in such inherently cross-functional activities as customer service (which can involve personnel in order filling, warehousing and shipping, invoicing, accounts receivable, after-sale repair, and technical support); new product development (which can typically involve personnel in R&D, design and engineering, purchasing, manufacturing, and sales and marketing); and supply chain management (which cuts across such areas as purchasing, inventory management, manufacturing and assembly, warehousing, and shipping). Even if personnel in all the different departments and functional areas are inclined to collaborate closely, the activity may not end up being performed optimally or cost-efficiently.

To address such shortcomings in strategy execution, many companies during the past decade have opted to *reengineer the work effort* by pulling the pieces of strategy-critical activities out of different departments and unifying their performance in a single department or cross-functional work group. Reorganizing the people who performed the pieces in functional departments into a close-knit group that has charge over the whole process and that can be held accountable for performing the activity in a cheaper, better, and/or more strategy-supportive fashion is called business process reengineering.[3]

When done properly, business process reengineering can produce dramatic operating benefits. In the order-processing section of General Electric's circuit breaker division, elapsed time from order receipt to delivery was cut from three weeks to three days by consolidating six production units into one, reducing a variety of former inventory and handling steps, automating the design system to replace a human custom-design process, and cutting the organizational layers between managers and workers from three to one. Productivity rose by 20 percent in one year, and unit manufacturing costs dropped by 30 percent. Northwest Water, a British utility, used business process reengineering to eliminate 45 work depots that served as home bases to crews who installed and repaired water and sewage lines and equipment. Now crews work directly from their vehicles, receiving assignments and reporting work completion from computer terminals in their trucks. Crew members are no longer employees but contractors to Northwest Water. These reengineering efforts not only eliminated the need for the work depots but also allowed Northwest Water to eliminate a big percentage of the bureaucratic personnel and supervisory organization that managed the crews.[4]

Since the early 1990s, reengineering of value chain activities has been undertaken at many companies in many industries all over the world, with some companies achieving excellent results.[5] While reengineering has produced only modest results in some instances, usually because of ineptness and/or lack of wholehearted commitment, it has nonetheless proved itself as a useful tool for streamlining a company's work effort and moving closer to operational excellence.

Total Quality Management Programs   *Total quality management (TQM) is a philosophy of managing a set of business practices that emphasizes continuous improvement in all phases of operations, 100 percent accuracy in performing tasks, involvement and empowerment of employees at all levels, team-based work design, benchmarking, and total customer satisfaction.*[6] While TQM concentrates on the production of quality goods and fully satisfying customer expectations, it achieves its biggest successes when it is also extended to employee efforts in *all departments*—human resources, billing, R&D, engineering, accounting and records, and information systems—that may lack pressing, customer-driven incentives to improve. It involves reforming the corporate culture and shifting to a total quality/continuous improvement business philosophy that permeates every facet of the organization.[7] TQM aims at instilling enthusiasm and commitment to doing things right from the top to the bottom of the organization. Management's job is to kindle an organizationwide search for ways to improve, a search that involves all company personnel exercising initiative and using their ingenuity. TQM doctrine preaches that there's no such thing as "good enough" and that everyone has a responsibility to participate in continuous improvement. TQM is thus a race without a finish. Success comes from making little steps forward each day, a process that the Japanese call *kaizen*.

TQM takes a fairly long time to show significant results—very little benefit emerges within the first six months. The long-term payoff of TQM, if it comes, depends heavily on management's success in implanting a culture within which TQM philosophies and practices can thrive. TQM is a managerial tool that has attracted numerous users and advocates over several decades, and it can deliver good results when used properly.

Six Sigma Quality Control   *Six Sigma quality control consists of a disciplined, statistics-based system aimed at producing not more than 3.4 defects per million iterations for any business process—from manufacturing to customer transactions.*[8] The Six Sigma process of define, measure, analyze, improve, and control (DMAIC, pronounced *Dee-may-ic*) is an improvement system for existing processes falling below specification and needing incremental improvement. The Six Sigma process of define, measure, analyze, design, and verify (DMADV) is used to develop *new* processes or products at Six Sigma quality levels. DMADV is sometimes referred to as a Design for Six Sigma (DFSS). Six Sigma programs for both improving existing processes or developing new processes are executed by personnel who have earned Six Sigma "green belts" and Six Sigma "black belts," and are overseen by personnel who have completed Six Sigma "master black belt" training. According to the Six Sigma Academy, personnel with black belts can save companies approximately $230,000 per project and can complete four to six projects a year.[9]

The statistical thinking underlying Six Sigma is based on the following three principles: All work is a process, all processes have variability, and all processes create data that explains variability.[10] To illustrate how these three principles drive the metrics of DMAIC, consider the case of a janitorial company that wants to improve the caliber of work done by its cleaning crews and thereby boost customer satisfaction. The janitorial company's Six Sigma team can pursue quality enhancement and continuous improvement via the DMAIC process as follows:

- *Define.* Because Six Sigma is aimed at reducing defects, the first step is to define what constitutes a defect. Six Sigma team members might decide that leaving streaks on windows is a defect because it is a source of customer dissatisfaction.

- *Measure.* The next step is to collect data to find out why, how, and how often this defect occurs. This might include a process flow map of the specific ways that cleaning crews go about the task of cleaning a commercial customer's windows. Other metrics may include recording what tools and cleaning products the crews use to clean windows.

- *Analyze.* After the data are gathered and the statistics analyzed, the company's Six Sigma team discovers that the tools and window cleaning techniques of certain employees are better than those of other employees because their tools and procedures leave no streaked windows—a "best practice" for avoiding window streaking is thus identified and documented.

- *Improve.* The Six Sigma team implements the documented best practice as a standard way of cleaning windows.

- *Control.* The company teaches new and existing employees the best practice technique for window cleaning. Over time, there's significant improvement in customer satisfaction and increased business.

Six Sigma's DMAIC process is a particularly good vehicle for improving performance when there are *wide variations* in how well an activity is performed.[11] For instance, airlines striving to improve the on-time performance of their flights have more to gain from actions to curtail the number of flights that are late by more than 30 minutes than from actions to reduce the number of flights that are late by less than 5 minutes. Likewise, FedEx might have a 16-hour average delivery time for its overnight package service operation, but if the actual delivery time varies around the 16-hour average from a low of 12 hours to a high of 26 hours, such that 10 percent of its packages are delivered over 6 hours late, then it has a huge *reliability* problem.

Since the mid-1990s, thousands of companies and nonprofit organizations around the world have begun using Six Sigma programs to promote operating excellence. Such manufacturers as Motorola, Allied Signal, Caterpillar, DuPont, Xerox, Alcan Aluminum, BMW, Volkswagen, Nokia, Owens Corning, and Emerson Electric have employed Six Sigma techniques to good advantage in improving production quality. General Electric (GE), one of the most successful companies implementing Six Sigma training and pursuing Six Sigma perfection, estimated benefits on the order of $10 billion during the first five years of implementation. GE first began Six Sigma in 1995 after Motorola and Allied Signal blazed the Six Sigma trail. One of GE's successes was in its Lighting division where Six Sigma was used to cut invoice defects and disputes by 98 percent, a particular benefit to Wal-Mart, the division's largest customer. GE Capital Mortgage improved the chances of a caller reaching a "live" GE person from 76 to 99 percent.[12] Illustration Capsule 11.1 describes Whirlpool's use of Six Sigma in its appliance business.

ILLUSTRATION CAPSULE 11.1
Whirlpool's Use of Six Sigma to Promote Operating Excellence

Top management at Whirlpool Corporation, the leading global manufacturer and marketer of home appliances in 2007, with 72 manufacturing and technology centers around the globe and sales in some 170 countries, has a vision of Whirlpool appliances in "Every Home . . . Everywhere with Pride, Passion, and Performance." One of management's chief objectives in pursuing this vision is to build unmatched customer loyalty to the Whirlpool brand. Whirlpool's strategy to win the hearts and minds of appliance buyers the world over has been to produce and market appliances with top-notch quality and innovative features that users will find appealing. In addition, Whirlpool's strategy has been to offer a wide selection of models (recognizing that buyer tastes and needs differ) and to strive for low-cost production efficiency, thereby enabling Whirlpool to price its products very competitively. Executing this strategy at Whirlpool's operations in North America (where it is the market leader), Latin America (where it is also the market leader), Europe (where it is ranks third), and Asia (where it is number one in India and has a foothold with huge growth opportunities elsewhere) has involved a strong focus on continuous improvement, lean manufacturing capabilities, and a drive for operating excellence. To marshal the efforts of its 73,000 employees in executing the strategy successfully, management developed a comprehensive Operational Excellence program with Six Sigma as one of the centerpieces.

The Operational Excellence initiative, which began in the 1990s, incorporated Six Sigma techniques to improve the quality of Whirlpool products, while at the same time lowering costs and trimming the time it took to get product innovations into the marketplace. The Six Sigma program helped Whirlpool save $175 million in manufacturing costs in its first three years.

To sustain the productivity gains and cost savings, Whirlpool embedded Six Sigma practices within each of its manufacturing facilities worldwide and instilled a culture based on Six Sigma and lean manufacturing skills and capabilities. Beginning in 2002, each of Whirlpool's operating units began taking the Six Sigma initiative to a higher level by first placing the needs of the customer at the center of every function—R&D, technology, manufacturing, marketing, and administrative support—and then striving to consistently improve quality levels while eliminating all unnecessary costs. The company systematically went through every aspect of its business with the view that company personnel should perform every activity at every level in a manner that delivers value to the customer and that leads to continuous improvement on how things are done.

Whirlpool management believes that the company's Operational Excellence process has been a major contributor in sustaining the company's global leadership in appliances.

Source: www.whirlpool.com (accessed September 25, 2003; November 15, 2005; and August 16, 2008).

Six Sigma is, however, not just a quality-enhancing tool for manufacturers. At one company, product sales personnel typically wined and dined customers to close their deals.[13] But the costs of such entertaining were viewed as excessively high in many instances. A Six Sigma project that examined sales data found that although face time with customers was important, wining, dining, and other types of entertainment were not. The data showed that regular face time helped close sales, but that time could be spent over a cup of coffee instead of golfing at a resort or taking clients to expensive restaurants. In addition, analysis showed that too much face time with customers was counterproductive. A regularly scheduled customer picnic was found to be detrimental to closing sales because it was held at a busy time of year, when customers preferred not to be away from their offices. Changing the manner in which prospective customers were wooed resulted in a 10 percent increase in sales. Six Sigma has also been used to improve processes in health care. A Milwaukee hospital used Six Sigma to map the process of filling prescriptions—the prescriptions originated with a doctor's write-up, were filled by the hospital pharmacy, and then administered by nurses. DMAIC analysis revealed that most mistakes came from misreading the doctor's handwriting.[14] The hospital implemented a program requiring doctors to type the prescription into a computer, which slashed the number of errors dramatically.

A problem tailor-made for Six Sigma occurs in the insurance industry, where it is common for top agents to outsell poor agents by a factor of 10 to 1 or more. If insurance executives offer a trip to Hawaii in a monthly contest to motivate low-performing agents, the typical result is to motivate top agents to be even more productive and make the performance gap even wider. A DMAIC Six Sigma project to reduce the variation in the performance of agents and correct the problem of so many low-performing agents would begin by measuring the performance of all agents, perhaps discovering that the top 20 percent sell seven times more policies than the bottom 40 percent. Six Sigma analysis would then consider such steps as mapping how top agents spend their day, investigating the factors that distinguish top performers from low performers, learning what techniques training specialists have employed in converting low-performing agents into high performers, and examining how the hiring process could be improved to avoid hiring underperformers in the first place. The next step would be to *test* proposed solutions—better training methods or psychological profiling to identify and weed out candidates likely to be poor performers—to identify and measure which alternative solutions really work, which don't, and why. Only those actions that prove statistically beneficial are then introduced on a wide scale. The DMAIC method thus entails empirical analysis to diagnose the problem (*design, measure, analyze*), test alternative solutions (*improve*) and then *control* the variability in how well the activity is performed by implementing actions shown to truly fix the problem.

However, while Six Sigma programs often improve the efficiency of many operating activities and processes, there is evidence that innovation can be stifled by Six Sigma programs. The essence of Six Sigma is to reduce variability in processes, but creative processes include quite a bit of variability. In many instances, breakthrough innovations occur only after thousands of ideas have been abandoned and promising ideas have gone through multiple iterations and extensive prototyping. James McNerney, a GE executive schooled in constructive use of Six Sigma, became CEO at 3M Corporation and proceeded to institute a series of Six Sigma-based principles. McNerney's dedication to Six Sigma and his elimination of 8 percent of the company's workforce did cause 3M's profits to jump shortly after his December 2000 arrival, but the application of Six Sigma in 3M's R&D and new product development activities soon proved to stifle innovation and new product introductions, undermining 3M's long-standing reputation for innovation. 3M's researchers complained that the innovation process did not lend itself well to the extensive data collection and analysis required under Six Sigma and that too much time was spent completing reports that outlined the market potential and possible manufacturing concerns for projects in all stages of the R&D pipeline. Six Sigma rigidity and a freeze on 3M's R&D budget from McNerney's first year as CEO through 2005 was blamed for the company's drop from first to seventh place on the Boston Consulting Group's Most Innovative Companies list.[15]

Moreover, there are several other prominent instances when Six Sigma proponents who used Six Sigma to great advantage at one company fell flat when trying to utilize Six Sigma principles in managing another company. Robert Nardelli, another executive whose management skills were honed at GE and based on the Six Sigma philosophy, struggled during short tenure as CEO at The Home Depot because a number of the changes he introduced ended up damaging worker morale and customer satisfaction. Under Nardelli, The Home Depot's ranking on the American Customer Satisfaction Index for major U.S. retailers dropped from first to last among major U.S.

retailers. Ann Fudge, a GE board member who was also well versed in GE's management approaches, failed as CEO of Young & Rubicam after attempting to implement Six Sigma processes at the advertising agency. So while Six Sigma principles have certainly been used to good advantage in numerous companies and have a track record of promoting operating excellence, Six Sigma is not a panacea for improving operations at all organizations—there are occasions where it has been used unwisely and inadvertently produced counterproductive outcomes.

A blended approach to Six Sigma implementation that is gaining in popularity pursues incremental improvements in operating efficiency, while R&D and other processes that allow the company to develop new ways of offering value to customers are given freer rein. Managers of these *ambidextrous organizations* are adept at employing continuous improvement in operating processes but allowing R&D to operate under a set of rules that allows for the development of breakthrough innovations. However, the two distinctly different approaches to managing employees must be carried out by tightly integrated senior managers to ensure that the separate and diversely oriented units operate with a common purpose. Ciba Vision, a global leader in contact lenses, has dramatically reduced operating expenses through the use of continuous improvement programs, while simultaneously and harmoniously developing new series of contact lens products that have allowed its revenues to grow by 300 percent over a 10-year period.[16]

In summary, a company that systematically and wisely applies Six Sigma methods to its value chain, activity by activity, can make major strides in improving the proficiency with which its strategy is executed. As is the case with TQM, obtaining managerial commitment, establishing a quality culture, and fully involving employees are the three most intractable challenges encountered in the implementation of Six Sigma quality programs.[17]

The Difference between Business Process Reengineering and Continuous Improvement Programs like Six Sigma and TQM   Business process reengineering and continuous improvement efforts like TQM and Six Sigma both aim at improved efficiency and reduced costs, better product quality, and greater customer satisfaction. The essential difference between business process reengineering and continuous improvement programs is that reengineering aims at *quantum gains* on the order of 30 to 50 percent or more, whereas total quality programs stress *incremental progress,* striving for inch-by-inch gains again and again in a never-ending stream.

> Business process reengineering aims at one-time quantum improvement; continuous improvement programs like TQM and Six Sigma aim at ongoing incremental improvements.

The two approaches to improved performance of value chain activities and operating excellence are not mutually exclusive; it makes sense to use them in tandem. Reengineering can be used first to produce a good basic design that yields quick, dramatic improvements in performing a business process. Total quality programs can then be used as a follow-on to reengineering and/or best-practice implementation, delivering gradual improvements. Such a two-pronged approach to implementing operational excellence is like a marathon in which you run the first four miles as fast as you can, then gradually pick up speed the remainder of the way.

Capturing the Benefits of Initiatives to Improve Operations

Usually, the biggest beneficiaries of benchmarking and best-practice initiatives, reengineering, TQM, and Six Sigma are companies that view such programs not as ends in themselves but as tools for implementing and executing company strategy more effectively. The skimpiest payoffs occur when company managers seize them as something worth trying—novel ideas that could improve things. In most such instances, they result in strategy-blind efforts to simply manage better. There's an important lesson here. Best practices, TQM, Six Sigma quality, and business process reengineering all need to be seen and used as part of a bigger-picture effort to execute strategy proficiently. Only strategy can point to which value chain activities matter and what performance targets make the most sense. Absent a strategic framework, managers lack the context in which to fix things that really matter to business-unit performance and competitive success.

To get the most from initiatives to better execute strategy, managers must have a clear idea of what specific outcomes really matter. Is it a Six Sigma defect rate, high on-time delivery percentages, low overall costs relative to rivals, fewer customer complaints, shorter cycle times, a higher percentage of revenues coming from recently introduced products, or what? Benchmarking best-in-industry and best-in-world performance of most or all value chain activities provides a realistic basis for setting internal performance milestones and longer-range targets.

Once initiatives to improve operations are linked to the company's strategic priorities, then comes the managerial task of building a total quality culture that is genuinely committed to achieving the performance outcomes that strategic success requires.[18] Managers can take the following action steps to realize full value from TQM or Six Sigma initiatives and promote a culture of operating excellence:[19]

> **CORE CONCEPT**
> The purpose of using benchmarking, best practices, business process reengineering, TQM, Six Sigma, or other operational improvement programs is to improve the performance of strategy-critical

1. Visible, unequivocal, and unyielding commitment to total quality and continuous improvement, including a quality vision and specific, measurable objectives for boosting quality and making continuous improvement.

2. Nudging people toward quality-supportive behaviors by:
   a. Screening job applicants rigorously and hiring only those with attitudes and aptitudes right for quality-based performance.
   b. Providing quality training for most employees.
   c. Using teams and team-building exercises to reinforce and nurture individual effort. (The creation of a quality culture is facilitated when teams become more cross-functional, multitask-oriented, and increasingly self-managed.)
   d. Recognizing and rewarding individual and team efforts regularly and systematically.
   e. Stressing prevention (doing it right the first time), not inspection (instituting ways to correct mistakes).

3. Empowering employees so that authority for delivering great service or improving products is in the hands of the doers rather than the overseers—*improving quality has to be seen as part of everyone's job.*

4. Using online systems to provide all relevant parties with the latest best practices and actual experiences with them, thereby speeding the diffusion and adoption of best practices throughout the organization and also allowing them to exchange data and opinions about how to upgrade the prevailing best practices.

5. Preaching that performance can, and must, be improved because competitors are not resting on their laurels and customers are always looking for something better.

If the targeted performance measures are appropriate to the strategy and if all organizational members (top executives, middle managers, professional staff, and line employees) buy into a culture of operating excellence, then a company's work climate becomes decidedly more conducive to proficient strategy execution. Benchmarking, best practices implementation, reengineering, TQM, and Six Sigma initiatives can greatly enhance a company's product design, cycle time, production costs, product quality, service, customer satisfaction, and other operating capabilities—and they can even deliver competitive advantage.[20] Not only do improvements from such initiatives add up over time and strengthen organizational capabilities, but the benefits they produce have hard-to-imitate aspects. While it is relatively easy for rivals to undertake benchmarking, process improvement, and quality training, it is much more difficult and time-consuming for them to instill a deeply ingrained culture of operating excellence (as occurs when such techniques are religiously employed) and top management exhibits lasting commitment to operational excellence throughout the organization.

INSTALLING INFORMATION
AND OPERATING SYSTEMS

Company strategies can't be executed well without a number of internal systems for business operations. Southwest Airlines, Singapore Airlines, Lufthansa, British Airways, and other successful airlines cannot hope to provide passenger-pleasing service without a user-friendly online reservation system, an accurate and speedy baggage handling system, and a strict aircraft maintenance program that minimizes equipment failures requiring at-the-gate service and delaying plane departures. FedEx has internal communication systems that allow it to coordinate its 70,000-plus vehicles in handling an average of 5.5 million packages a day. Its leading-edge flight operations systems allow a single controller to direct as many as 200 of FedEx's 650 aircraft simultaneously, overriding their flight plans should weather or other special emergencies arise. In addition, FedEx has created a series of e-business tools for customers that allow them to ship and track packages online (either at FedEx's Web site or on their own company intranets or Web sites), create address books, review shipping history, generate custom reports, simplify customer billing, reduce internal warehousing and inventory management costs, purchase goods and services from suppliers, and respond quickly to changing customer demands. All of FedEx's systems support the company's strategy of providing businesses and individuals with a broad array of package delivery services (from premium next-day to economical five-day deliveries) and boosting its competitiveness against United Parcel Service, Airborne Express, and the U.S. Postal Service.

Otis Elevator, the world's largest manufacturer of elevators, has a 24-hour communications service center called OtisLine to coordinate its maintenance efforts for the 1.5 million-plus elevators and escalators it has installed worldwide.[21] Electronic monitors installed on each user's site can detect when an elevator or escalator has any of 325 problems and will automatically place a service call to the nearest service center. Trained operators take all trouble calls, input critical information into a computer, and dispatch trained mechanics from one of 325 locations across the world to the local trouble spot. All customers have online access to performance data on each of their Otis elevators. More than 80 percent of mechanics in North America carry Web-enabled phones connected to Otis's e*Service that transport needed information quickly and allow mechanics to update data in Otis computers for future reference. The OtisLine system helps keep outage times to less than two and a half hours. All the trouble-call data is relayed to design and manufacturing personnel, allowing them to quickly alter design specifications or manufacturing procedures when needed to correct recurring problems.

Amazon.com ships customer orders from fully computerized, 1,300-by-600-foot warehouses containing about 3 million books, CDs, toys, and houseware items.[22] The warehouses are so technologically sophisticated that they require about as many lines of code to run as Amazon's Web site does. Using complex picking algorithms, computers initiate the order-picking process by sending signals to workers' wireless receivers, telling them which items to pick off the shelves in which order. Computers also generate data on misboxed items, chute backup times, line speed, worker productivity, and shipping weights on orders. Systems are upgraded regularly, and productivity improvements are aggressively pursued. In 2003, Amazon's six warehouses were able to handle three times the volume handled in 1999 at costs averaging 10 percent of revenues (versus 20 percent in 1999); in addition, they turned their inventory over 20 times annually in an industry whose average was 15 turns. Amazon's warehouse efficiency and cost per order filled was so low that one of the fastest-growing and most profitable parts of Amazon's business was using its warehouses to run the e-commerce operations of Toys "R" Us and Target.

Most telephone companies, electric utilities, and TV broadcasting systems have online monitoring systems to spot transmission problems within seconds and increase the reliability of their services. At eBay, there are systems for real-time monitoring of new listings, bidding activity, Web site traffic, and page views. Kaiser Permanente spent $3 billion to digitize the medical records of its 8.2 million members so that it could manage patient care more efficiently.[23] IBM has created a database of 36,000 employee profiles that enable it to better assign the most qualified IBM consultant to the projects it is doing for clients. In businesses such as public accounting and management consulting, where large numbers of professional staff need cutting-edge technical know-how, companies have developed systems that identify when it is time for certain employees to attend training programs to update their skills and know-how. Many companies have cataloged best-practice information on their intranets to promote faster transfer and implementation organizationwide.[24]

Well-conceived state-of-the-art operating systems not only enable better strategy execution but also strengthen organizational capabilities—perhaps enough to provide a competitive edge over rivals. For example, a company with a differentiation strategy based on superior quality has added capability if it has systems for training personnel in quality techniques, tracking product quality at each production step, and ensuring that all goods shipped meet quality standards. A company striving to be a low-cost provider is competitively stronger if it has a benchmarking system that identifies opportunities to implement best practices and drive costs out of the business. Fast-growing companies get an important assist from having capabilities in place to recruit and train new employees in large numbers and from investing in infrastructure that gives them the capability to handle rapid growth as it occurs. It is nearly always better to put infrastructure and support systems in place before they are actually needed than to have to scramble to catch up to customer demand.

> **CORE CONCEPT**
> State-of-the-art support systems can be a basis for competitive advantage if they give a firm capabilities that rivals can't match.

Instituting Adequate Information Systems, Performance Tracking, and Controls

Accurate and timely information about daily operations is essential if managers are to gauge how well the strategy execution process is proceeding. Information systems need to cover five broad areas: (1) customer data, (2) operations data, (3) employee data, (4) supplier/partner/collaborative ally data, and (5) financial performance data. All key strategic performance indicators have to be tracked and reported as often as practical. Monthly profit-and-loss statements and monthly statistical summaries, long the norm, are fast being replaced by daily statistical updates and even up-to-the-minute performance monitoring that online technology makes possible. Many retail companies have automated online systems that generate daily sales reports for each store and maintain up-to-the-minute inventory and sales records on each item. Manufacturing plants typically generate daily production reports and track labor productivity on every shift. Many retailers and manufacturers have online data systems connecting them with their suppliers that monitor the status of inventories, track shipments and deliveries, and measure defect rates.

Real-time information systems permit company managers to stay on top of implementation initiatives and daily operations, and to intervene if things seem to be drifting off course. Tracking key performance indicators, gathering information from operating personnel, quickly identifying and diagnosing problems, and taking corrective actions are all integral pieces of the process of managing strategy implementation and execution and exercising adequate organization control. A number of companies have recently begun creating "electronic scorecards" for senior managers that gather daily or weekly statistics from different databases about inventory, sales, costs, and sales trends; such information enables these managers to easily stay abreast of what's happening and make better decisions in real time.[25] Telephone companies have elaborate information systems to measure signal quality, connection times, interrupts, wrong connections, billing errors, and other measures of reliability that affect customer service and satisfaction. British Petroleum (BP) has outfitted rail cars carrying hazardous materials with sensors and global-positioning systems (GPS) so that it can track the status, location, and other information about these shipments via satellite and relay the data to its corporate intranet. Companies that rely on empowered customer-contact personnel to act promptly and creatively in pleasing customers have installed online information systems that put essential customer data on their computer monitors with a few keystrokes so that they can respond effectively to customer inquiries and deliver personalized customer service.

CORE CONCEPT

Having good information systems and operating data is integral to competent strategy execution and operating excellence.

Statistical information gives managers a feel for the numbers, briefings and meetings provide a feel for the latest developments and emerging issues, and personal contacts add a feel for the people dimension. All are good barometers. Managers have to identify problem areas and deviations from plan before they can take actions to get the organization back on course, by either improving the approaches to strategy execution or fine-tuning the strategy. Jeff Bezos, Amazon's CEO, an ardent proponent of managing by the numbers, says, "Math-based decisions always trump opinion and judgment. The trouble with most corporations is that they make judgment-based decisions when data-based decisions could be made."[26]

Exercising Adequate Controls over Empowered Employees

Another important aspect of effectively managing and controlling the strategy execution process is monitoring the performance of empowered workers to see that they are acting within the specified limits.[27] Leaving empowered employees to their own devices in meeting performance standards without appropriate checks and balances can expose an organization to excessive risk.[28] Instances abound of employees' decisions or behavior having gone awry, sometimes costing a company huge sums or producing lawsuits, aside from just generating embarrassing publicity.

Managers shouldn't have to devote big chunks of their time to making sure that the decisions and behavior of empowered employees stay between the white lines—this would defeat the major purpose of empowerment and, in effect, lead to the reinstatement of a managerial bureaucracy engaged in constant over-the-shoulder supervision. Yet managers have a clear responsibility to exercise sufficient control over empowered employees to protect the company against out-of-bounds behavior and unwelcome surprises. Scrutinizing daily and weekly operating statistics is one of the important ways in which managers can monitor the results that flow from the actions of empowered subordinates—if the operating results flowing from the actions of empowered employees look good, then it is reasonable to assume that empowerment is working.

But close monitoring of real-time or daily operating performance is only one of the control tools at management's disposal. Another valuable lever of control in companies that rely on empowered employees, especially in those that use self-managed work groups or other such teams, is peer-based control. Most team members feel responsible for the success of the whole team and tend to be relatively intolerant of any team member's behavior that weakens team performance or puts team accomplishments at risk (especially when team performance has a big impact on each team member's compensation). Because peer evaluation is such a powerful control device, companies organized into teams can remove some layers of the management hierarchy and rely on strong peer pressure to keep team members operating between the white lines. This is especially true when a company has the information systems capability to monitor team performance daily or in real time.

TYING REWARDS AND INCENTIVES TO STRATEGY EXECUTION

It is important for both organization units and individuals to be enthusiastically committed to executing strategy and achieving performance targets. Company managers typically use an assortment of motivational techniques and rewards to enlist organizationwide commitment to executing the strategic plan. A manager has to do more than just talk to everyone about how important new strategic practices and performance targets are to the organization's well-being. No matter how inspiring, talk seldom commands people's best efforts for long. *To get employees' sustained, energetic commitment, management has to be resourceful in designing and using motivational incentives—both monetary and nonmonetary.* The more a manager understands what motivates subordinates and the more he or she relies on motivational incentives as a tool for achieving the targeted strategic and financial results, the greater will be employees' commitment to good day-in, day-out strategy execution and achievement of performance targets.[29]

> **CORE CONCEPT**
> A properly designed reward structure is management's most powerful tool for mobilizing organizational commitment to successful strategy execution.

Strategy-Facilitating Motivational Practices

Financial incentives generally head the list of motivating tools for trying to gain wholehearted employee commitment to good strategy execution and operating excellence. Monetary rewards generally include some combination of base pay increases, performance bonuses, profit-sharing plans, stock awards, company contributions to employee 401(k) or retirement plans, and piecework incentives (in the case of production workers). But successful companies and managers normally make extensive use of such nonmonetary carrot-and-stick incentives as frequent words of praise (or constructive criticism), special recognition at company gatherings or in the company newsletter, more (or less) job security, stimulating assignments, opportunities to transfer to attractive locations, increased (or decreased) autonomy, and rapid promotion (or the risk of being sidelined in a routine or dead-end job). In addition, companies use a host of other motivational approaches to make their workplaces more appealing and spur stronger employee commitment to the strategy execution process; the following are some of the most important:[30]

- *Providing attractive perks and fringe benefits*—The various options here include full coverage of health insurance premiums; full tuition reimbursement for work on college degrees; paid vacation time of three or four weeks; on-site child care at major facilities; on-site gym facilities and massage therapists; getaway opportunities at company-owned recreational facilities (beach houses, ranches, resort condos); personal concierge services; subsidized cafeterias and free lunches; casual dress every day; personal travel services; paid sabbaticals; maternity leaves; paid leaves to care for ill family members; telecommuting; compressed workweeks (four 10-hour days instead of five 8-hour days); reduced summer hours; college scholarships for children; on-the-spot bonuses for exceptional performance; and relocation services.

- *Relying on promotion from within whenever possible*—This practice helps bind workers to their employer and employers to their workers; plus, it is an incentive for good performance. Promotion from within also helps ensure that people in positions of responsibility actually know something about the business, technology, and operations they are managing.

- *Making sure that the ideas and suggestions of employees are valued and that those with merit are promptly acted on*—Many companies find that their best ideas for nuts-and-bolts operating improvements come from the suggestions of employees. Moreover, research indicates that the moves of many companies to push decision making down the line and empower employees increases employee motivation and satisfaction, as well as boosting their productivity. The use of self-managed teams has much the same effect.

- *Creating a work atmosphere in which there is genuine sincerity, caring, and mutual respect among workers and between management and employees*—A "family" work environment where people are on a first-name basis and there is strong camaraderie promotes teamwork and cross-unit collaboration.

- *Stating the strategic vision in inspirational terms that make employees feel they are a part of doing something very worthwhile in a larger social sense*—There's strong motivating power associated with giving people a chance to be part of something exciting and personally satisfying. Jobs with noble purpose tend to turn employees on. At Pfizer, Merck, and most other pharmaceutical companies, it is the notion of helping sick people get well and restoring patients to full life. At Whole Foods Market (a natural foods grocery chain), it is helping customers discover good eating habits and thus improving human health and nutrition.

- *Sharing information with employees about financial performance, strategy, operational measures, market conditions, and competitors' actions*—Broad disclosure and prompt communication send the message that managers trust their workers. Keeping employees in the dark denies them information useful to performing their job, prevents them from being "students of the business," and usually turns them off.

- *Having knockout facilities*—An appealing work environment with appealing features and amenities usually has decidedly positive effects on employee morale and productivity.

- *Being flexible in how the company approaches people management (motivation, compensation, recognition, recruitment) in multinational, multicultural environments*—There is usually some merit in giving local managers in foreign operations leeway to adapt their motivation, compensation, recognition, and recruitment practices to fit local customs, habits, values, and business practices rather than insisting on consistent people-management practices worldwide. But the one area where consistency is essential is conveying the message that the organization values people of all races and cultural backgrounds and that discrimination of any sort will not be tolerated.

For specific examples of the motivational tactics employed by several prominent companies (many of which appear on *Fortune*'s annual list of the 100 best companies to work for in America), see Illustration Capsule 11.2.

Striking the Right Balance between Rewards and Punishment

While most approaches to motivation, compensation, and people management accentuate the positive, companies also embellish positive rewards with the risk of punishment. At General Electric, McKinsey & Company, several global public accounting firms, and other companies that look for and expect top-notch individual performance, there's an "up-or-out" policy—managers and professionals whose performance is not good enough to warrant promotion are first denied bonuses and stock awards and eventually weeded out. A number of companies deliberately give employees heavy workloads and tight deadlines—personnel are pushed hard to achieve "stretch" objectives and expected to put in long hours (nights and weekends if need be). At most companies, senior executives and key personnel in underperforming units are pressured to boost performance to acceptable levels and keep it there or risk being replaced.

As a general rule, it is unwise to take off the pressure for good individual and group performance or play down the stress, anxiety, and adverse consequences of shortfalls in performance. There is no evidence that a no-pressure/no-adverse-consequences work environment leads to superior strategy execution or operating excellence. As the CEO of a major bank put it, "There's a deliberate policy here to create a level of anxiety. Winners usually play like they're one touchdown behind."[31] *High-performing organizations nearly always have a cadre of ambitious people who relish the opportunity to climb the ladder of success, love a challenge, thrive in a performance-oriented environment, and find some competition and pressure useful to satisfy their own drives for personal recognition, accomplishment, and self-satisfaction.*

However, if an organization's motivational approaches and reward structure induce too much stress, internal competitiveness, job insecurity, and unpleasant consequences, the impact on workforce morale and strategy execution can be counterproductive. Evidence shows that managerial initiatives to improve strategy execution should incorporate more positive than negative motivational elements because when cooperation

ILLUSTRATION CAPSULE 11.2
What Companies Do to Motivate and Reward Employees

Companies have come up with an impressive variety of motivational and reward practices to help create a work environment that energizes employees and promotes better strategy execution. Here's a sampling of what companies are doing:

- Google has a sprawling four-building complex known as the Googleplex where the roughly 1,000 employees are provided with free food, unlimited ice cream, pool and Ping-Pong tables, and complimentary massages—management built the Googleplex to be "a dream environment." Moreover, the company gives its employees the ability to spend 20 percent of their work time on any outside activity. Google has helped extend its social mission to employees' lives away from work by giving employees $1,000 toward the purchase of a hybrid car and covering a portion of the cost of having solar panels installed at their homes.

- Lincoln Electric, widely known for its piecework pay scheme and incentive bonus plan, rewards individual productivity by paying workers for each nondefective piece produced. Workers have to correct quality problems on their own time—defects in products used by customers can be traced back to the worker who caused them. Lincoln's piecework plan motivates workers to pay attention to both quality and volume produced. In addition, the company sets aside a substantial portion of its profits above a specified base for worker bonuses. To determine bonus size, Lincoln Electric rates each worker on four equally important performance measures: dependability, quality, output, and ideas and cooperation. The higher a worker's merit rating, the higher the incentive bonus earned; the highest rated workers in good profit years receive bonuses of as much as 110 percent of their piecework compensation.

- At JM Family Enterprises, a Toyota distributor in Florida, employees get a great lease on new Toyotas and are flown to the Bahamas for cruises on the 172-foot company yacht, plus the company's office facility has such amenities as a heated lap pool, a fitness center, on-site child care, and a free nail salon. Employees get free prescriptions delivered by a "pharmacy concierge" and professionally made take-home dinners.

- Wegmans, a family owned grocer with 71 stores on the East Coast of the United States, provides employees with flexible schedules and benefits that include on-site fitness centers. The company's approach to managing people allows it to provide a very high level of customer service not found in other grocery chains. Employees ranging from cashiers to butchers to store managers are all treated equally and viewed as experts in their jobs. Employees receive 50 hours of formal training per year and are allowed to make decisions that they believe are appropriate for their jobs. The company's annual turnover rate is only 6 percent, which is less than one-half the 14 percent average turnover rate in the U.S. supermarket industry.

- Nordstrom, widely regarded for its superior in-house customer service experience, typically pays its retail salespeople an hourly wage higher than the prevailing rates paid by other department store chains plus a commission on each sale. Spurred by a culture that encourages salespeople to go all out to satisfy customers and to seek for and promote new fashion ideas, Nordstrom salespeople often earn twice the average incomes of sales employees at competing stores. The typical Nordstrom salesperson earns nearly $38,000 a year, and sales department managers earn, on average, $48,500 a year. Nordstrom's rules for employees are simple: "Rule #1: Use your good judgment in all situations. There will be no additional rules."

- Employees at W. L. Gore (the maker of Gore-Tex) get to choose what project/team they work on, and each team member's compensation is based on other team members' rankings of his or her contribution to the enterprise.

- At Ukrop's Super Markets, a family-owned chain, stores stay closed on Sunday; the company pays out 20 percent of pretax profits to employees in the form of quarterly bonuses; and the company picks up the membership tab for employees if they visit their health club 30 times a quarter.

- At biotech leader Amgen, employees get 16 paid holidays, generous vacation time, tuition reimbursements up to $10,000, on-site massages, a discounted car wash, and the convenience of shopping at on-site farmers' markets.

Sources: Fortune's lists of the 100 best companies to work for in America, 2002, 2004, 2005, and 2008; Jefferson Graham, "The Search Engine That Could," *USA Today,* August 26, 2003, p. B3; and Fred Vogelstein, "Winning the Amazon Way," *Fortune,* May 26, 2003, p. 73.

is positively enlisted and rewarded, rather than strong-armed by orders and threats (implicit or explicit), people tend to respond with more enthusiasm, dedication, creativity, and initiative.[32] Something of a middle ground is generally optimal—not only handing out decidedly positive rewards for meeting or beating performance targets but also imposing sufficiently negative consequences (if only withholding rewards) when actual performance falls short of the target. But the negative consequences of underachievement should never be so severe or demoralizing as to impede a renewed and determined effort to overcome existing obstacles and hit the targets in upcoming periods.

Linking the Reward System to Strategically Relevant Performance Outcomes

The most dependable way to keep people focused on strategy execution and the achievement of performance targets is to *generously* reward and recognize individuals and groups who meet or beat performance targets and deny rewards and recognition to those who don't. *The use of incentives and rewards is the single most powerful tool management has to win strong employee commitment to diligent, competent strategy execution and operating excellence.* Decisions on salary increases, incentive compensation, promotions, key assignments, and the ways and means of awarding praise and recognition are potent attention-getting, commitment-generating devices.[33] Such decisions seldom escape the closest employee scrutiny, saying more about what is expected and who is considered to be doing a good job than about any other factor. Hence, when meeting or beating strategic and financial targets becomes *the dominating basis* for designing incentives, evaluating individual and group efforts, and handing out rewards, company personnel quickly grasp that it is in their own self-interest to do their best in executing the strategy competently and achieving key performance targets.[34] Indeed, it is usually through the company's system of incentives and rewards that workforce members emotionally ratify their commitment to the company's strategy execution effort.

Ideally, performance targets should be set for every organization unit, every manager, every team or work group, and perhaps every employee—targets that measure whether strategy execution is progressing satisfactorily. If the company's strategy is to be a low-cost provider, the incentive system must reward actions and achievements that result in lower costs. If the company has a differentiation strategy predicated on superior quality and service, the incentive system must reward such outcomes as Six Sigma defect rates, infrequent need for product repair, low numbers of customer complaints, speedy order processing and delivery, and high levels of customer satisfaction. If a company's growth is predicated on a strategy of new product innovation, incentives should be tied to factors such as the percentages of revenues and profits coming from newly introduced products.

Illustration Capsule 11.3 provides two vivid examples of how companies have designed incentives linked directly to outcomes reflecting good strategy execution.

CORE CONCEPT
A properly designed reward system aligns the well-being of organization members with their contributions to competent strategy execution and the achievement of performance targets.

The Importance of Basing Incentives on Achieving Results, Not on Performing Assigned Duties   To create a strategy-supportive system of rewards and incentives, a company must emphasize rewarding people for accomplishing results,

ILLUSTRATION 11.3
Nucor and Bank One: Two Companies That Tie Incentives Directly to Strategy Execution

The strategy at Nucor Corporation, one of the two largest steel producers in the United States, is to be *the* low-cost producer of steel products. Because labor costs are a significant fraction of total cost in the steel business, successful implementation of Nucor's low-cost leadership strategy entails achieving lower labor costs per ton of steel than competitors' costs. Nucor management uses an incentive system to promote high worker productivity and drive labor costs per ton below rivals'. Each plant's workforce is organized into production teams (each assigned to perform particular functions), and weekly production targets are established for each team. Base pay scales are set at levels comparable to wages for similar manufacturing jobs in the local areas where Nucor has plants, but workers can earn a 1 percent bonus for each 1 percent that their output exceeds target levels. If a production team exceeds its weekly production target by 10 percent, team members receive a 10 percent bonus in their next paycheck; if a team exceeds its quota by 20 percent, team members earn a 20 percent bonus. Bonuses, paid every two weeks, are based on the prior two weeks' actual production levels measured against the targets.

Nucor's piece-rate incentive plan has produced impressive results. The production teams put forth exceptional effort; it is not uncommon for most teams to beat their weekly production targets anywhere from 20 to 50 percent. When added to their base pay, the bonuses earned by Nucor workers make Nucor's work force among the highest-paid in the U.S. steel industry. From a management perspective, the incentive system has resulted in Nucor having labor productivity levels 10 to 20 percent above the average of the unionized workforces at several of its largest rivals, which in turn has given Nucor a significant labor cost advantage over most rivals.

At Bank One (recently acquired by JPMorgan Chase), management believed it was strategically important to boost its customer satisfaction ratings in order to enhance its competitiveness vis-à-vis rivals. Targets were set for customer satisfaction and monitoring systems for measuring customer satisfaction at each branch office were put in place. Then, to motivate branch office personnel to be more attentive in trying to please customers and also to signal that top management was truly committed to achieving higher levels of overall customer satisfaction, top management opted to tie pay scales in each branch office to that branch's customer satisfaction rating—the higher the branch's ratings, the higher that branch's pay scales. Management believed its shift from a theme of equal pay for equal work to one of equal pay for equal performance contributed significantly to its customer satisfaction priority.

It is folly to reward one outcome in hopes of getting another outcome.

not for just dutifully performing assigned tasks. Focusing jobholders' attention and energy on what to *achieve* as opposed to what to *do* makes the work environment results-oriented. It is flawed management to tie incentives and rewards to satisfactory performance of duties and activities in hopes that the by-products will be the desired business outcomes and company achievements.[35] In any job, performing assigned tasks is not equivalent to achieving intended outcomes. Diligently showing up for work and attending to job assignments does not, by itself, guarantee results. As any student knows, the fact that an instructor teaches and students go to class doesn't necessarily mean that the students are learning. The enterprise of education would no doubt take on a different character if teacher compensation dropped when student learning was unacceptably low and rose when student learning increased. Employee productivity among employees at Best Buy's corporate headquarters rose by 35 percent after the company began to focus on the results of each employee's work rather than on whether employees came to work early and stayed late.

Incentive compensation for top executives is typically tied to such financial measures as revenue and earnings growth, stock price performance, return on investment, and creditworthiness and perhaps such strategic measures as market share, product quality, or customer satisfaction. However, incentives for department heads, teams, and individual workers may be tied to performance outcomes more closely related to their strategic area of responsibility. In manufacturing, incentive compensation may be tied to unit manufacturing costs, on-time production and shipping, defect rates, the number and extent of work stoppages due to labor disagreements and equipment breakdowns, and so on. In sales and marketing, there may be incentives for achieving dollar sales or unit volume targets, market share, sales penetration of each target customer group, the fate of newly introduced products, the frequency of customer complaints, the number of new accounts acquired, and customer satisfaction. Which performance measures to base incentive compensation on depends on the situation—the priority placed on various financial and strategic objectives, the requirements for strategic and competitive success, and what specific results are needed in different facets of the business to keep strategy execution on track.

Guidelines for Designing Incentive Compensation Systems   The concepts and company experiences discussed above yield the following prescriptive guidelines for creating an incentive compensation system to help drive successful strategy execution:

1. *Make the performance payoff a major, not minor, piece of the total compensation package.* Payoffs must be at least 10 to 12 percent of base salary to have much impact. Incentives that amount to 20 percent or more of total compensation are big attention-getters, likely to really drive individual or team effort; incentives amounting to less than 5 percent of total compensation have comparatively weak motivational impact. Moreover, the payoff for high-performing individuals and teams must be meaningfully greater than the payoff for average performers, and the payoff for average performers meaningfully bigger than for below-average performers.

2. *Have incentives that extend to all managers and all workers, not just top management.* It is a gross miscalculation to expect that lower-level managers and employees will work their hardest to hit performance targets just so a few senior executives can get lucrative rewards.

3. *Administer the reward system with scrupulous objectivity and fairness.* If performance standards are set unrealistically high or if individual/group performance evaluations are not accurate and well documented, dissatisfaction with the system will overcome any positive benefits.

4. *Tie incentives to performance outcomes directly linked to good strategy execution and financial performance.* Incentives should never be paid just because people are thought to be "doing a good job" or because they "work hard." Performance evaluation based on factors not tightly related to good strategy execution signal that either the strategic plan is incomplete (because important performance targets were left out) or management's real agenda is something other than the stated strategic and financial objectives.

5. *Make sure that the performance targets each individual or team is expected to achieve involve outcomes that the individual or team can personally affect.* The role of incentives is to enhance individual commitment and channel behavior in beneficial directions. This role is not well served when the performance measures by which company personnel are judged are outside their arena of influence.

6. *Keep the time between achieving the target performance outcome and the payment of the reward as short as possible.* Companies like Nucor and Continental

> **CORE CONCEPT**
> The role of the reward system is to align the well-being of organization members with realizing the company's vision, so that organization members benefit by helping the company execute its strategy competently and fully satisfy customers.

Airlines have discovered that weekly or monthly payments for good performance work much better than annual payments. Nucor pays weekly bonuses based on prior-week production levels; Continental awards employees a monthly bonus for each month that on-time flight performance meets or beats a specified percentage companywide. Annual bonus payouts work best for higher-level managers and for situations where target outcome relates to overall company profitability or stock price performance.

7. *Make liberal use of nonmonetary rewards; don't rely solely on monetary rewards.* When used properly, money is a great motivator, but there are also potent advantages to be gained from praise, special recognition, handing out plum assignments, and so on.

8. *Absolutely avoid skirting the system to find ways to reward effort rather than results.* Whenever actual performance falls short of targeted performance, there's merit in determining whether the causes are attributable to subpar individual/group performance or to circumstances beyond the control of those responsible. An argument can be made that exceptions should be made in giving rewards to people who've tried hard, gone the extra mile, yet still come up short because of circumstances beyond their control. The problem with making exceptions for unknowable, uncontrollable, or unforeseeable circumstances is that once good excuses start to creep into justifying rewards for subpar results, the door is open for all kinds of reasons why actual performance failed to match targeted performance. A "no excuses" standard is more evenhanded and certainly easier to administer.

CORE CONCEPT

The unwavering standard for judging whether individuals, teams, and organizational units have done a good job must be whether they meet or beat performance targets that reflect good strategy execution.

Once the incentives are designed, they have to be communicated and explained. Everybody needs to understand how their incentive compensation is calculated and how individual/group performance targets contribute to organizational performance targets. The pressure to achieve the targeted strategic and financial performance and continuously improve on strategy execution should be unrelenting, with few (if any) loopholes for rewarding shortfalls in performance. People at all levels have to be held accountable for carrying out their assigned parts of the strategic plan, and they have to understand their rewards are based on the caliber of results that are achieved. But with the pressure to perform should come meaningful rewards. Without an ample payoff, the system breaks down, and managers are left with the less workable options of barking orders, trying to enforce compliance, and depending on the goodwill of employees.

Performance-Based Incentives and Rewards in Multinational Enterprises

In some foreign countries, incentive pay runs counter to local customs and cultural norms. Professor Steven Kerr cites the time he lectured an executive education class on the need for more performance-based pay and a Japanese manager protested, "You shouldn't bribe your children to do their homework, you shouldn't bribe your wife to prepare dinner, and you shouldn't bribe your employees to work for the company."[36] Singling out individuals and commending them for unusually good effort can also be a problem; Japanese culture considers public praise of an individual an affront to the harmony of the group. In some countries, employees have a preference for nonmonetary rewards—more leisure time, important titles, access to vacation villages, and nontaxable perks. Thus, multinational companies have to build some degree of flexibility into the design of incentives and rewards in order to accommodate cross-cultural traditions and preferences.

KEY POINTS

Managers implementing and executing a new or different strategy must identify the resource requirements of each new strategic initiative and then consider whether the current pattern of resource allocation and the budgets of the various subunits are suitable.

Anytime a company alters its strategy, managers should review existing policies and operating procedures, proactively revise or discard those that are out of sync, and formulate new ones to facilitate execution of new strategic initiatives. Prescribing new or freshly revised policies and operating procedures aids the task of strategy execution (1) by providing top-down guidance to operating managers, supervisory personnel, and employees regarding how certain things need to be done and what the boundaries are on independent actions and decisions; (2) by enforcing consistency in how particular strategy-critical activities are performed in geographically scattered operating units; and (3) by promoting the creation of a work climate and corporate culture that promotes good strategy execution.

Competent strategy execution entails visible, unyielding managerial commitment to best practices and continuous improvement. Benchmarking, the discovery and adoption of best practices, business process reengineering, and continuous improvement initiatives like total quality management (TQM) or Six Sigma programs all aim at improved efficiency, lower costs, better product quality, and greater customer satisfaction. *These initiatives are important tools for learning how to execute a strategy more proficiently.*

Company strategies can't be implemented or executed well without a number of support systems to carry on business operations. Well-conceived state-of-the-art support systems not only facilitate better strategy execution but also strengthen organizational capabilities enough to provide a competitive edge over rivals. Real-time information and control systems further aid the cause of good strategy execution.

Strategy-supportive motivational practices and reward systems are powerful management tools for gaining employee commitment. The key to creating a reward system that promotes good strategy execution is to make strategically relevant measures of performance *the dominating basis* for designing incentives, evaluating individual and group efforts, and handing out rewards. Positive motivational practices generally work better than negative ones, but there is a place for both. There's also a place for both monetary and nonmonetary incentives.

For an incentive compensation system to work well (1) the monetary payoff should be a major percentage of the compensation package, (2) the use of incentives should extend to all managers and workers, (3) the system should be administered with care and fairness, (4) the incentives should be linked to performance targets spelled out in the strategic plan, (5) each individual's performance targets should involve outcomes the person can personally affect, (6) rewards should promptly follow the determination of good performance, (7) monetary rewards should be supplemented with liberal use of nonmonetary rewards, and (8) skirting the system to reward nonperformers or subpar results should be scrupulously avoided. Companies with operations in multiple countries often have to build some degree of flexibility into the design of incentives and rewards in order to accommodate cross-cultural traditions and preferences.

ASSURANCE OF LEARNING EXERCISES

1.   Using your favorite search engine, do a search on the term *best practices*. Browse through the search results to identify at least five organizations that have gathered a set of best practices and are making the best-practices library they have assembled available to members.

2. Do an Internet search on Six Sigma quality programs. Browse through the search results and (*a*) identify at least three companies that offer Six Sigma training and (*b*) find lists of companies that have implemented Six Sigma programs in their pursuit of operational excellence—be prepared to cite at least 10 companies that are Six Sigma users.

3. Read some of the recent Six Sigma articles posted at www.isixsigma.com. Prepare a one-page report to your instructor detailing how Six Sigma is being used in various companies and what benefits these companies are reaping from Six Sigma implementation.

4. Review the profiles and applications of the latest Malcolm Baldrige National Quality Award recipients at www.quality.nist.gov. What are the standout features of the companies' approaches to managing operations? What do you find impressive about the companies' policies and procedures, use of best practices, emphasis on continuous improvement, and use of rewards and incentives?

5. Go to www.dell.com/casestudies and read how Dell's clients have used information and operating systems to facilitate good strategy execution. Choosing one of the case studies provided in PDF format, describe how the information systems solution improved the effectiveness of the client's value creating business processes.

6. Consult the latest issue of *Fortune* containing the annual "100 Best Companies to Work For" (usually a late-January or early-February issue), or go to www.fortune.com to access the list, and identify at least five compensation incentives and work practices that these companies use to enhance employee motivation and reward them for good strategic and financial performance. You should identify compensation methods and work practices that are different from those cited in Illustration Capsule 11.2.

7. Using Google Scholar or your university library's access to online business periodicals, search for the term *incentive compensation* and prepare a one- to two-page report to your instructor discussing the successful (or unsuccessful) use of incentive compensation plans by various instructors. Given the results of your research, what factors seem to determine whether incentive compensation plans succeed or fail?

EXERCISES FOR SIMULATION PARTICIPANTS

1. Do you and your co-managers deliberately shift resources from one area to another to better support strategy execution efforts? If so, cite at least three such instances.

2. Is benchmarking data available in the simulation exercise in which you are participating? If so, do you and your co-managers regularly study the benchmarking data to see how well your company is doing? Do you consider the benchmarking information provided to be valuable? Why or why not? Cite three recent instances in which your examination of the benchmarking statistics has caused you and your co-managers to take corrective actions to boost company performance.

3. Do you and your co-managers have an opportunity to (*a*) adopt best practices or (*b*) use TQM or Six Sigma tools? If so, explain how your company has used these tools to try to improve strategy execution and boost company performance.

4. Does your company have opportunities to use incentive compensation techniques? If so, explain your company's approach to incentive compensation. Is there any hard evidence you can cite that indicates your company's use of incentive compensation techniques has worked? For example, have your company's compensation incentives actually boosted productivity? Can you cite evidence indicating that the productivity gains have resulted in lower labor costs? If the productivity gains have *not* translated into lower labor costs, then is it fair to say that your company's use of incentive compensation is a failure?

5. Are you and your co-managers consciously trying to achieve operating excellence? What are the indicators of operating excellence at your company? Given these indicators, how well does your company measure up? Is there any evidence indicating that your company's management team is doing a better job of achieving operating excellence than are the management teams at rival companies?

12 Corporate Culture and Leadership

Keys to Good Strategy Execution

LEARNING OBJECTIVES

1. Be able to identify the key features of a company's corporate culture.
2. Understand how and why a company's culture can aid the drive for proficient strategy execution and operating excellence.
3. Learn the kinds of actions management can take to change a problem corporate culture.
4. Learn why corporate cultures tend to be grounded in core values and ethical principles and help establish a corporate conscience.
5. Understand what constitutes effective managerial leadership in achieving superior strategy execution and operating excellence.

In the previous two chapters we examined six of the managerial tasks that are important to good strategy execution and operating excellence—building a capable organization, marshaling the needed resources and steering them to strategy-critical operating units, establishing policies and procedures that facilitate good strategy execution, adopting best practices and pushing for continuous improvement in how value chain activities are performed, creating internal operating systems that enable better execution, and employing motivational practices and compensation incentives that gain wholehearted employee commitment to the strategy execution process. In this chapter we explore the two remaining managerial tasks that shape the outcome of efforts to execute a company's strategy: creating a strategy-supportive corporate culture and exerting the internal leadership needed to drive the implementation of strategic initiatives forward and achieve higher plateaus of operating excellence.

INSTILLING A CORPORATE CULTURE THAT PROMOTES GOOD STRATEGY EXECUTION

Every company has its own unique culture. The character of a company's culture or work climate is a product of the core values and business principles that executives espouse, the standards of what is ethically acceptable and what is not, the work practices and behaviors that define "how we do things around here," its approach to people management and style of operating, the "chemistry" and the "personality" that permeates its work environment, and the stories that get told over and over to illustrate and reinforce the company's values, business practices, and traditions. The meshing together of stated beliefs, business principles, style of operating, ingrained behaviors and attitudes, and work climate define a company's **corporate culture.** A company's culture is important because it influences the organization's actions and approaches to conducting business—in a very real sense, the culture is the company's "operating system" or organizational DNA.[1]

Corporate cultures vary widely. For instance, the bedrock of Wal-Mart's culture is dedication to customer satisfaction, zealous pursuit of low costs and frugal operating practices, a strong work ethic, ritualistic Saturday-morning headquarters meetings to exchange ideas and review problems, and company executives' commitment to visiting stores, listening to customers, and soliciting suggestions from employees. General Electric's culture is founded on a hard-driving, results-oriented atmosphere (where all of the company's business divisions are held to a standard of being number one or two in their industries as well as achieving good business results); extensive cross-business sharing of ideas, best practices, and learning; the reliance on "workout sessions" to identify, debate, and resolve burning issues; a commitment to Six Sigma quality; and globalization of the company. At Nordstrom, the corporate culture is centered on delivering exceptional service to customers; the company's motto is "Respond to unreasonable customer requests"—each out-of-the-ordinary request is seen as an opportunity for a "heroic" act by an employee that can further the company's reputation for a customer-pleasing shopping environment. Illustration Capsule 12.1 relates how Google and Alberto-Culver describe their corporate cultures.

Identifying the Key Features of a Company's Corporate Culture

A company's corporate culture is mirrored in the character or "personality" of its work environment—the factors that underlie how the company tries to conduct its business and the behaviors that are held in high esteem. The chief things to look for include the following:

- The values, business principles, and ethical standards that management preaches and *practices*—actions speak much louder than words here.
- The company's approach to people management and the official policies, procedures, and operating practices that paint the white lines for the behavior of company personnel.
- The spirit and character that pervades the work climate. Is the workplace vibrant and fun? Methodical and all-business? Tense and harried? Highly competitive and

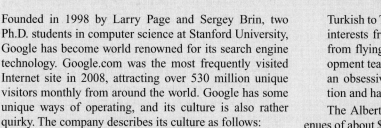

ILLUSTRATION CAPSULE 12.1
The Corporate Cultures at Google and Alberto-Culver

Founded in 1998 by Larry Page and Sergey Brin, two Ph.D. students in computer science at Stanford University, Google has become world renowned for its search engine technology. Google.com was the most frequently visited Internet site in 2008, attracting over 530 million unique visitors monthly from around the world. Google has some unique ways of operating, and its culture is also rather quirky. The company describes its culture as follows:

> Though growing rapidly, Google still maintains a small company feel. At the Googleplex headquarters almost everyone eats in the Google café (known as "Charlie's Place"), sitting at whatever table has an opening and enjoying conversations with Googlers from all different departments. Topics range from the trivial to the technical, and whether the discussion is about computer games or encryption or ad serving software, it's not surprising to hear someone say, "That's a product I helped develop before I came to Google."
>
> Google's emphasis on innovation and commitment to cost containment means each employee is a hands-on contributor. There's little in the way of corporate hierarchy and everyone wears several hats. The international webmaster who creates Google's holiday logos spent a week translating the entire site into Korean. The chief operations engineer is also a licensed neurosurgeon. Because everyone realizes they are an equally important part of Google's success, no one hesitates to skate over a corporate officer during roller hockey.
>
> Google's hiring policy is aggressively non-discriminatory and favors ability over experience. The result is a staff that reflects the global audience the search engine serves. Google has offices around the globe and Google engineering centers are recruiting local talent in locations from Zurich to Bangalore. Dozens of languages are spoken by Google staffers, from

Turkish to Telugu. When not at work, Googlers pursue interests from cross-country cycling to wine tasting, from flying to Frisbee. As Google expands its development team, it continues to look for those who share an obsessive commitment to creating search perfection and having a great time doing it.

The Alberto-Culver Company, with fiscal 2007 revenues of about $1.5 billion, is the producer and marketer of Alberto VO5, TRESemmé, Motions, Soft & Beautiful, Just for Me, and Nexxus hair care products; St. Ives skin care products; and such brands as Molly McButter, Mrs. Dash, Sugar Twin, and Static Guard. Alberto-Culver brands are sold in more than 100 countries.

At the careers section of its Web site, the company described its culture in the following words:

> Building careers is as important to us as building brands. We believe that passionate people create powerful growth. We believe in a workplace built on values and believe our best people display those same values in their families and their communities. We believe in recognizing and rewarding accomplishment and celebrating our victories.
>
> We believe the best ideas work their way—quickly—up an organization, not down. We believe that we should take advantage of every ounce of your talent on teams and cross-functional activities, not just assign you to a box.
>
> We believe in open communication. We believe that you can improve what you measure, so we survey and spot check all the time. For that same reason, everyone has specific goals so that their expectations are in line with their managers' and the company's.
>
> We believe that victory is a team accomplishment. We believe in personal development. We believe if you talk with us you will catch our enthusiasm and want to be a part of the Alberto-Culver team.

Sources: Information posted at www.google.com and www.alberto.com (accessed August 18, 2008).

politicized? Are people excited about their work and emotionally connected to the company's business, or are they just there to draw a paycheck? Is there an emphasis on empowered worker creativity, or do people have little discretion in how jobs are done?

- How managers and employees interact and relate to each other—the reliance on teamwork and open communication, the extent to which there is good camaraderie, whether people are called by their first names, whether coworkers spend little or lots of time together outside the workplace, and what the dress codes are (the accepted styles of attire and whether there are casual days).

- The strength of peer pressures to do things in particular ways and conform to expected norms—what actions and behaviors are approved (and rewarded by management in the form of compensation and promotion) and which ones are frowned on.

- The company's revered traditions and oft-repeated stories about "heroic acts" and "how we do things around here."

- The manner in which the company deals with external stakeholders (particularly vendors and local communities where it has operations)—whether it treats suppliers as business partners or prefers hardnosed, arm's-length business arrangements and the strength and genuineness of the commitment to corporate citizenship and environmental sustainability.

Some of these sociological forces are readily apparent, and others operate quite subtly.

The values, beliefs, and practices that undergird a company's culture can come from anywhere in the organization hierarchy, most often representing the business philosophy and managerial style of influential executives but also resulting from exemplary actions on the part of company personnel and consensus agreement about "how we ought to do things around here."[2] Typically, key elements of the culture originate with a founder or certain strong leaders who articulated them as a set of business principles; company policies; operating approaches; and ways of dealing with employees, customers, vendors, shareholders, and local communities where the company has operations. Over time, these cultural underpinnings take root, become embedded in how the company conducts its business, come to be accepted by company managers and employees alike, and then persist as new employees are encouraged to adopt and follow the professed values, behaviors, and work practices.

The Role of Stories   Frequently, a significant part of a company's culture is captured in the stories that get told over and over again to illustrate to newcomers the importance of certain values and the depth of commitment that various company personnel have displayed. One of the folktales at FedEx, world renowned for the reliability of its next-day package delivery guarantee, is about a deliveryman who had been given the wrong key to a FedEx drop box. Rather than leave the packages in the drop box until the next day when the right key was available, the deliveryman unbolted the drop box from its base, loaded it into the truck, and took it back to the station. There, the box was pried open and the contents removed and sped on their way to their destination the next day. Nordstrom keeps a scrapbook commemorating the heroic acts of its employees and uses it as a regular reminder of the above-and-beyond-the-call-of-duty behaviors that employees are encouraged to display. At Frito-Lay, there are dozens of stories about truck drivers who went to extraordinary lengths in overcoming adverse weather conditions in order to make scheduled deliveries to retail customers and keep store shelves stocked with Frito-Lay products. At Microsoft, there are stories of the long hours programmers put in, the emotional peaks and valleys in encountering and overcoming coding problems, the exhilaration of completing a complex program on schedule, the satisfaction of working on cutting-edge projects, the rewards of being part of a team responsible for a popular new software program, and the tradition of competing aggressively. Such stories serve the valuable purpose of illustrating the kinds of behavior the company encourages and reveres. Moreover, each retelling of a legendary story puts a bit more peer pressure on company personnel to display core values and do their part in keeping the company's traditions alive.

Perpetuating the Culture   Once established, company cultures are perpetuated in six important ways: (1) by screening and selecting new employees that will mesh well with the culture, (2) by systematic indoctrination of new members in the culture's fundamentals, (3) by the efforts of senior group members to reiterate core values in daily conversations and pronouncements, (4) by the telling and retelling of company legends, (5) by regular ceremonies honoring members who display desired cultural behaviors, and (6) by visibly rewarding those who display cultural norms and penalizing those who don't.[3] *The more new employees a company is hiring, the more important it becomes to screen job applicants every bit as much for how well their values, beliefs, and personalities match up with the culture as for their technical skills and experience.* For example, a company that stresses operating with integrity and fairness has to hire people who themselves have integrity and place a high value on fair play. A company whose culture revolves around creativity, product innovation, and leading change has to screen new hires for their ability to think outside the box, generate new ideas, and thrive in a climate of rapid change and ambiguity. Southwest Airlines—whose two core values, "LUV" and fun, permeate the work environment and whose objective is to ensure that passengers have a positive and enjoyable flying experience—goes to considerable lengths to hire flight attendants and gate personnel who are witty, cheery, and outgoing and who display "whistle while you work" attitudes. Fast-growing companies risk creating a culture by chance rather than by design if they rush to hire employees mainly for their talents and credentials and neglect to screen out candidates whose values, philosophies, and personalities aren't a good fit with the organizational character, vision, and strategy being articulated by the company's senior executives.

As a rule, companies are careful to hire people who they believe will fit in and embrace the prevailing culture. And, usually, job seekers lean toward accepting jobs at companies where they feel comfortable with the atmosphere and the people they will be working with. Employees who don't hit it off at a company tend to leave quickly, while employees who thrive and are pleased with the work environment stay on, eventually moving up the ranks to positions of greater responsibility. The longer people stay at an organization, the more that they come to embrace and mirror the corporate culture—their values and beliefs tend to be molded by mentors, fellow workers, company training programs, and the reward structure. Normally, employees who have worked at a company for a long time play a major role in indoctrinating new employees into the culture.

Forces That Cause a Company's Culture to Evolve   However, even stable cultures aren't static—just like strategy and organization structure, they evolve. New challenges in the marketplace, revolutionary technologies, and shifting internal conditions—especially eroding business prospects, an internal crisis, or top executive turnover—tend to breed new ways of doing things and, in turn, cultural evolution. An incoming CEO who decides to shake up the existing business and take it in new directions often triggers a cultural shift, perhaps one of major proportions. Likewise, diversification into new businesses, expansion into foreign countries, rapid growth, an influx of new employees, and merger with or acquisition of another company can all precipitate cultural changes of one kind or another.

Company Subcultures: The Problems Posed by New Acquisitions and Multinational Operations   Although it is common to speak about corporate culture in the singular, it is not uncommon for companies to have multiple cultures (or subcultures).[4] Values, beliefs, and practices within a company sometimes vary significantly by department, geographic location, division, or business unit. A company's subcultures can clash, or at least not mesh well, if they embrace conflicting business philosophies or operating approaches, if key executives employ different approaches to people management, or if important differences between a company's culture and those of recently acquired companies have not yet been ironed out. *Global and multinational companies tend to be at least partly multicultural* because cross-country organization units have different operating histories and work climates, as well as members who have grown up under different social customs and traditions and who have different sets of values and beliefs. The human resources manager of a global pharmaceutical company who took on an assignment in the Far East discovered, to his surprise, that one of his biggest challenges was to persuade his company's managers in China, Korea, Malaysia, and Taiwan to accept promotions—their cultural values were such that they did not believe in competing with their peers for career rewards or personal gain, nor did they relish breaking ties to their local communities to assume cross-national responsibilities.[5] Many companies that have merged with or acquired foreign companies have to deal with language- and custom-based cultural differences.

Nonetheless, the existence of subcultures does not preclude important areas of commonality and compatibility. For example, General Electric's cultural traits of boundarylessness, workout, and Six Sigma quality have been implanted and practiced successfully in many different countries. AES, a global power company with operations in 29 countries, has found that the core values of integrity, fun, sharing knowledge, and social responsibility underlying its culture are readily embraced by people in different countries. Moreover, AES tries to define and practice its cultural values the same way in all of its locations while still being sensitive to differences in languages, geography, lifestyles, and local customs.

In today's globalizing world, multinational companies are learning how to make strategy-critical cultural traits travel across country boundaries and create a workably uniform culture worldwide. Likewise, company managements are quite alert to the importance of cultural compatibility in making acquisitions and the need to address how to merge and integrate the cultures of newly acquired companies—cultural due diligence is often as important as financial due diligence in deciding whether to go forward on an acquisition or merger.[6] On a number of occasions, companies have decided to pass on acquiring particular companies because of culture conflicts that they believed would be hard to resolve.

Strong versus Weak Cultures

Company cultures vary widely in strength and influence. Some are strongly embedded and have a big impact on a company's practices and behavioral norms. Others are weak and have comparatively little influence on company operations.

Strong-Culture Companies   The hallmark of a strong-culture company is the dominating presence of certain deeply rooted values and operating approaches that "regulate" the conduct of a company's business and the climate of its workplace.[7] Strong cultures take years (sometimes decades) to emerge and are never an overnight phenomenon. In strong-culture companies, senior managers make a point of reiterating these principles and values to organization members and explaining how they relate to its business environment. But, more important, they make a conscious effort to display these principles in their own actions and behavior—they walk the talk, and they *insist* that *company values and business principles be reflected in the decisions and actions taken by all company personnel*. An unequivocal expectation that company personnel will act and behave in accordance with the adopted values and ways of doing business leads to two important outcomes: (1) over time the values come to be widely shared by rank-and-file employees—people who dislike the culture tend to leave; and (2) individuals encounter strong peer pressure from coworkers to observe the culturally approved norms and behaviors. Hence, a strongly implanted corporate culture ends up having a powerful influence on "how we do things around here" because so many company personnel are accepting of cultural traditions and because this acceptance is reinforced by both management expectations and coworker peer pressure. Since cultural traditions and norms have such a dominating influence in strong-culture companies, the character of the culture becomes the company's soul or psyche.

> **CORE CONCEPT**
> In a strong-culture company, culturally approved behaviors and ways of doing things are nurtured while culturally disapproved behaviors and work practices get squashed.

Three factors contribute to the development of strong cultures: (1) a founder or strong leader who establishes values, principles, and practices that are consistent and sensible in light of customer needs, competitive conditions, and strategic requirements; (2) a sincere, long-standing company commitment to operating the business according to these established traditions, thereby creating an internal environment that supports decision making and strategies based on cultural norms; and (3) a genuine concern for the well-being of the organization's three biggest constituencies—customers, employees, and shareholders. Continuity of leadership, small group size, stable group membership, geographic concentration, and considerable organizational success all contribute to the emergence and sustainability of a strong culture.[8]

In strong-culture companies, values and behavioral norms are so ingrained that they can endure leadership changes at the top—although their strength can erode over time if new CEOs cease to nurture them or move aggressively to institute cultural adjustments. And the cultural norms in a strong-culture company may not change much as strategy evolves and the organization acts to make strategy adjustments, either because the new strategies are compatible with the present culture or because the dominant traits of the culture are somewhat strategy-neutral and compatible with evolving versions of the company's strategy.

> In a strong-culture company, values and behavioral norms are like crabgrass: deeply rooted and hard to weed out.

Weak-Culture Companies In direct contrast to strong-culture companies, weak-culture companies lack values and principles that are consistently preached or widely shared (usually because the company has had a series of CEOs with differing values and differing views about how the company's business ought to be conducted). As a consequence, the company has few widely revered traditions and few culture-induced norms are evident in operating practices. Because top executives at a weak-culture company don't repeatedly espouse any particular business philosophy or exhibit long-standing commitment to particular values or extol particular operating practices and behavioral norms, individuals encounter little coworker peer pressure to do things in particular ways. Moreover, a weak company culture breeds no strong employee allegiance to what the company stands for or to operating the business in well-defined ways. While individual employees may well have some bonds of identification with and loyalty toward their department, their colleagues, their union, or their boss, there's neither passion about the company nor emotional commitment to what it is trying to accomplish—a condition that often results in many employees viewing their company as just a place to work and their job as just a way to make a living. Very often, cultural weakness stems from moderately entrenched subcultures that block the emergence of a well-defined companywide work climate.

As a consequence, *weak cultures provide little or no assistance in executing strategy* because there are no traditions, beliefs, values, common bonds, or behavioral norms that management can use as levers to mobilize commitment to executing the chosen strategy. The only plus of a weak culture is that it does not usually pose a strong barrier to strategy execution, but the negative of not providing any support means that culture-building has to be high on management's action agenda. Absent a work climate that channels organizational energy in the direction of good strategy execution, managers are left with the options of either using compensation incentives and other motivational devices to mobilize employee commitment or trying to establish cultural roots that will in time start to nurture the strategy execution process.

Unhealthy Cultures

The distinctive characteristic of an unhealthy corporate culture is the presence of counterproductive cultural traits that adversely impact the work climate and company performance.[9] The following four traits are particularly unhealthy:

1. A highly politicized internal environment in which many issues get resolved and decisions made on the basis of which individuals or groups have the most political clout to carry the day.
2. Hostility to change and a general wariness of people who champion new ways of doing things.
3. An insular "not-invented-here" mind-set that makes company personnel averse to looking outside the company for best practices, new managerial approaches, and innovative ideas.
4. A disregard for high ethical standards and overzealous pursuit of wealth and status on the part of key executives.

Politicized Cultures   What makes a politicized internal environment so unhealthy is that political infighting consumes a great deal of organizational energy, often with the result that what's best for the company takes a backseat to political maneuvering. In companies where internal politics pervades the work climate, empire-building managers jealously guard their decision-making prerogatives. They have their own agendas and operate the work units under their supervision as autonomous "fiefdoms," and the positions they take on issues are usually aimed at protecting or expanding their turf. Collaboration with other organizational units is viewed with suspicion (What are "they" up to? How can "we" protect "our" flanks?), and cross-unit cooperation occurs grudgingly. When an important proposal moves to the front burner, advocates try to ram it through and opponents try to alter it in significant ways or even kill it. The support or opposition of politically influential executives and/or coalitions among departments with vested interests in a particular outcome typically weigh heavily in deciding what actions the company takes. All this maneuvering takes away from efforts to execute strategy with real proficiency and frustrates company personnel who are less political and more inclined to do what is in the company's best interests.

Change-Resistant Cultures   In less-adaptive cultures where skepticism about the importance of new developments and resistance to change are the norm, managers prefer waiting until the fog of uncertainty clears before steering a new course, making fundamental adjustments to their product line, or embracing a major new technology. They believe in moving cautiously and conservatively, preferring to follow others rather than take decisive action to be in the forefront of change. Change-resistant cultures place a premium on not making mistakes, prompting managers to lean toward safe, don't-rock-the-boat options that will have only a ripple effect on the status quo, protect or advance their own careers, and guard the interests of their immediate work groups.

Change-resistant cultures encourage a number of undesirable or unhealthy behaviors—avoiding risks, not making bold proposals to pursue emerging opportunities, a lax approach to both product innovation and continuous improvement in performing value chain activities, and following rather than leading market change. In change-resistant cultures, word quickly gets around that proposals to do things differently face an uphill battle and that people who champion them may be seen as something of a nuisance. Executives who don't value managers or employees with initiative and new ideas quickly put a damper on product innovation, experimentation, and efforts to improve. At the same time, change-resistant companies have little appetite for being first-movers or fast-followers, believing that being in the forefront of change is too risky and that acting too quickly increases vulnerability to costly mistakes. They are more inclined to adopt a wait-and-see posture, carefully analyze several alternative responses, learn from the missteps of early movers, and then move forward cautiously and conservatively with initiatives that are deemed safe. Hostility to change is most often found in companies with multilayered management bureaucracies that have enjoyed considerable market success in years past and that are wedded to the "We have done it this way for years" syndrome.

When such companies encounter business environments with accelerating change, going slow on altering traditional ways of doing things can be become a liability rather than an asset. General Motors, IBM, Sears, and Eastman Kodak are classic examples of companies whose change-resistant bureaucracies were slow to respond to fundamental changes in their markets; clinging to the cultures and traditions that made them successful, they were reluctant to alter operating practices and modify their business approaches. As strategies of gradual change won out over bold innovation and being an early mover, all four lost market share to rivals that quickly moved to institute changes more in tune with evolving market conditions and buyer preferences. These companies are now struggling to recoup lost ground with cultures and behaviors more suited to market success—the kinds of fit that caused them to succeed in the first place.

Insular, Inwardly Focused Cultures   Sometimes a company reigns as an industry leader or enjoys great market success for so long that its personnel start to believe they have all the answers or can develop them on their own. There is a strong tendency to neglect what customers are saying and how their needs and expectations are changing. Such confidence in the correctness of how it does things and in the company's skills and capabilities breeds arrogance—company personnel discount the merits of what outsiders are doing and what can be learned by studying best-in-class performers. Benchmarking and a search for the best practices of outsiders are seen as offering little payoff. Any market share gains on the part of up-and-coming rivals are regarded as temporary setbacks, soon to be reversed by the company's own forthcoming initiatives (which, it is confidently predicted, will be an instant market hit with customers).

Insular thinking, internally driven solutions, and a must-be-invented-here mindset come to permeate the corporate culture. An inwardly focused corporate culture gives rise to managerial inbreeding and a failure to recruit people who can offer fresh thinking and outside perspectives. The big risk of insular cultural thinking is that the company can underestimate the competencies and accomplishments of rival companies and overestimate its own progress—with a resulting loss of competitive advantage over time.

Unethical and Greed-Driven Cultures   Companies that have little regard for ethical standards or that are run by executives driven by greed and ego gratification are scandals waiting to happen. Enron's collapse in 2001 was largely the product of an ethically dysfunctional corporate culture—while the culture embraced the positives of product innovation, aggressive risk-taking, and a driving ambition to lead global change in the energy business, its executives exuded the negatives of arrogance, ego, greed, and an "ends-justify-the-means" mentality in pursuing stretch revenue and profitability targets.[10] A number of Enron's senior managers were all too willing to wink at unethical behavior, to cross over the line to unethical (and sometimes criminal) behavior themselves, and to deliberately stretch generally accepted accounting principles to make Enron's financial performance look far better than it really was. In the end, Enron came unglued because a few top executives chose unethical and illegal paths to pursue corporate revenue and profitability targets—in a company that publicly preached integrity and other notable corporate values but was lax in making sure that key executives walked the talk. Unethical cultures and executive greed have produced scandals at WorldCom, Quest, HealthSouth, Adelphia, Tyco, McWane, Parmalat, Rite Aid, Hollinger International, Refco, and Marsh & McLennan, with executives being indicted and/or convicted of criminal behavior. The U.S. Attorney's office elected not to prosecute KPMG with "systematic" criminal acts to market illegal tax shelters to wealthy clients (which KPMG tried mightily to cover up) because a criminal indictment would have resulted in the immediate collapse of KPMG and cut the number of global public accounting firms from four to just three; instead, criminal charges were filed against the company officials deemed most responsible. In 2005, U.S. prosecutors elected not to press criminal charges against Royal Dutch Petroleum (Shell Oil) for repeatedly and knowingly reporting inflated oil reserves to the Securities and Exchange Commission and not to indict Tommy Hilfiger USA for multiple tax law violations—but both companies agreed to sign nonprosecution agreements, the terms of which were not made public but almost certainly involved fines and a long-term company commitment to cease and desist.

High-Performance Cultures

Some companies have so-called high-performance cultures where the standout cultural traits are a can-do spirit, pride in doing things right, no-excuses accountability, and a pervasive results-oriented work climate where people go the extra mile to meet or beat stretch objectives. In high-performance cultures, there's a strong sense of involvement on the part of company personnel and emphasis on individual initiative and creativity. Performance expectations are clearly delineated for the company as a whole, for each organizational unit, and for each individual. Issues and problems are promptly addressed—a strong bias for being proactive instead of reactive exists. There's a razor-sharp focus on what needs to be done. Results-oriented cultures are permeated with a spirit of achievement and have a good track record in meeting or beating performance targets.

The challenge in creating a high-performance culture is to inspire high loyalty and dedication of the part of employees, such that they are both energized and preoccupied with putting forth their very best efforts to do things right and be unusually productive. Managers have to take pains to reinforce constructive behavior, reward top performers, and purge habits and behaviors that stand in the way of high productivity and good results. They must work at knowing the strengths and weaknesses of their subordinates, so as to better match talent with task and enable people to make meaningful contributions by doing what they do best.[11] They have to stress learning from mistakes and building on strengths, and put an unrelenting emphasis on moving forward and making good progress—in effect, there has to be a disciplined, performance-focused approach to managing the organization.

Adaptive Cultures

The hallmark of adaptive corporate cultures is willingness on the part of organizational members to accept change and take on the challenge of introducing and executing new strategies.[12] Company personnel share a feeling of confidence that the organization can deal with whatever threats and opportunities come down the pike; they are receptive to risk taking, experimentation, innovation, and changing strategies and practices. In direct contrast to change-resistant cultures, adaptive cultures are very supportive of managers and employees at all ranks who propose or help initiate useful change. Internal entrepreneurship on the part of individuals and groups is encouraged and rewarded. Senior executives seek out, support, and promote individuals who exercise initiative, spot opportunities for improvement, and display the skills to implement them. Managers openly evaluate ideas and suggestions, fund initiatives to develop new or better products, and take prudent risks to pursue emerging market opportunities. As in high-performance cultures, the company exhibits a proactive approach to identifying issues, evaluating the implications and options, and quickly moving ahead with workable solutions. Strategies and traditional operating practices are modified as needed to adjust to or take advantage of changes in the business environment.

> **CORE CONCEPT**
> In adaptive cultures, there's a spirit of doing what's necessary to ensure long-term organizational success provided the new behaviors and operating practices that management is calling for are seen as legitimate and consistent with the core values and business principles underpinning the culture.

But why is change so willingly embraced in an adaptive culture? Why are organization members not fearful of how change will affect them? Why does an adaptive culture not become unglued with ongoing changes in strategy, operating practices, and behavioral norms? The answers lie in two distinctive and dominant traits of an adaptive culture: (1) Any changes in operating practices and behaviors must *not* compromise core values and long-standing business principles, and (2) the changes that are instituted must satisfy the legitimate interests of stakeholders—customers, employees, shareowners, suppliers, and the communities where the company operates.[13] In other words, what sustains an adaptive culture is that organization members perceive the changes that management is trying to institute as legitimate and in keeping with the core values and business principles that form the heart and soul of the culture.

Thus, for an adaptive culture to remain intact over time, top management must orchestrate organizational changes in a manner that (1) demonstrates genuine care for the well-being of all key constituencies and (2) tries to satisfy all their legitimate interests simultaneously. Unless fairness to all constituencies is a decision-making principle and a commitment to doing the right thing is evident to organization members, the changes are not likely to be seen as legitimate and thus be readily accepted and implemented wholeheartedly.[14] Making changes that will please customers and/or that protect, if not enhance, the company's long-term well-being are generally seen as legitimate and are often seen as the best way of looking out for the interests of employees, stockholders, suppliers, and communities where the company operates.

At companies with adaptive cultures, management concern for the well-being of employees is nearly always a big factor in gaining employee support for change—company personnel are usually receptive to change as long as employees understand that changes in their job assignments are part of the process of adapting to new conditions and that their employment security will not be threatened unless the company's business unexpectedly reverses direction. In cases where workforce downsizing becomes necessary, management concern for employees dictates that separation be handled humanely, making employee departure as painless as possible. Management efforts to make the process of adapting to change fair and equitable for customers, employees, stockholders, suppliers, and communities where the company operates breeds acceptance of and support for change among all organization stakeholders.

> Adaptive cultures are exceptionally well suited to companies with fast-changing strategies and market environments.

Technology companies, software companies, and Internet-based companies are good illustrations of organizations with adaptive cultures. Such companies thrive on change—driving it, leading it, and capitalizing on it (but sometimes also succumbing to change when they make the wrong move or are swamped by better technologies or the superior business models of rivals). Companies like Google, Intel, Cisco Systems, eBay, Nokia, Amazon.com, and Dell cultivate the capability to act and react rapidly. They are avid practitioners of entrepreneurship and innovation, with a demonstrated willingness to take bold risks to create altogether new products, new businesses, and new industries. To create and nurture a culture that can adapt rapidly to changing to shifting business conditions, they make a point of staffing their organizations with people who are proactive, rise to the challenge of change, and have an aptitude for adapting.

In fast-changing business environments, a corporate culture that is receptive to altering organizational practices and behaviors is a virtual necessity. However, adaptive cultures work to the advantage of all companies, not just those in rapid-change environments. Every company operates in a market and business climate that is changing to one degree or another and that, in turn, requires internal operating responses and new behaviors on the part of organization members. *As a company's strategy evolves, an adaptive culture is a definite ally in the strategy-implementing, strategy-executing process as compared to cultures that have to be coaxed and cajoled to change.*

Culture: Ally or Obstacle to Strategy Execution?

A company's present culture and work climate may or may not be compatible with what is needed for effective implementation and execution of the chosen strategy. *When a company's present work climate promotes attitudes and behaviors that are well suited to first-rate strategy execution, its culture functions as a valuable ally in the strategy execution process.* When the culture is in conflict with some aspect of the company's direction, performance targets, or strategy, the culture becomes a stumbling block.[15]

How a Company's Culture Can Promote Better Strategy Execution   A culture grounded in strategy-supportive values, practices, and behavioral norms adds significantly to the power and effectiveness of a company's strategy execution effort. For example, a culture characterized by frugality and thrift nurtures employee actions to identify cost-saving opportunities—the very behavior needed for successful execution of a low-cost leadership strategy. A culture built around such business principles as pleasing customers, operating excellence, and employee empowerment promotes employee behaviors that facilitate execution of strategies keyed to high product quality and superior customer service. A culture that includes taking initiative, challenging the status quo, exhibiting creativity, embracing change, and working collaboratively is conducive to successful execution of product innovation and technological leadership strategies.[16] Good alignment between ingrained cultural norms and the behaviors needed for good strategy execution makes the culture a valuable ally in the strategy execution process. In a company where strategy and culture are misaligned, some of the very behaviors needed to execute strategy successfully run contrary to the behaviors and values imbedded in the prevailing culture. Such a clash nearly always poses a formidable hurdle that has to be cleared for strategy execution to get very far.

> **CORE CONCEPT**
> The tighter the culture–strategy fit, the more that the culture steers company personnel into displaying behaviors and adopting operating practices that promote good strategy execution.

A tight culture–strategy matchup furthers a company's strategy execution effort in three ways:[17]

1. *A culture that encourages actions, behaviors, and work practices supportive of good strategy execution not only provides company personnel with clear guidance regarding "how we do things around here" but also produces significant peer pressure from coworkers to conform to culturally acceptable norms.* The stronger the admonishments from top executives about "how we need to do things around here" and the stronger the peer pressures from coworkers, the more the culture influences people to display behaviors and observe operating practices that support good strategy execution.

2. *A deeply embedded culture tightly matched to the strategy aids the cause of competent strategy execution by steering company personnel to culturally approved behaviors and work practices, thus making it far simpler for management to root out operating practices that are a misfit.* This is why it is very much in management's best interests to build and nurture a deeply rooted culture where ingrained behaviors and operating practices marshal organizational energy behind the drive for good strategy execution.

3. *A culture imbedded with values and behaviors that facilitate strategy execution promotes strong employee identification with and commitment to the company's vision, performance targets, and strategy.* When a company's culture is grounded in many of the needed strategy-executing behaviors, employees feel genuinely better about their jobs, the company they work for, and the merits of what the company is trying to accomplish. As a consequence, greater numbers of company personnel exhibit some passion about their work and exert their best efforts to execute the strategy and achieve performance targets. All this helps move the company closer to realizing its strategic vision and, from employees' standpoint, makes the company a more engaging place to work.

These benefits of close culture–strategy alignment say something important about the task of managing the strategy executing process: *Closely aligning corporate culture with the requirements for proficient strategy execution merits the full attention of senior executives.* The culture-building objective is to create a work climate and style of operating that mobilize the energy and behavior of company personnel squarely behind efforts to execute strategy competently. The more deeply that management can embed strategy-supportive ways of doing things, the more that management can rely on the culture to automatically steer company personnel toward behaviors and work practices that aid good strategy execution.[18]

Furthermore, culturally astute managers understand that nourishing the right cultural environment not only adds power to their push for proficient strategy execution but also promotes strong employee identification with and commitment to the company's vision, performance targets, and strategy. A culture–strategy fit prompts employees with emotional allegiance to the culture to feel genuinely better about their jobs, the company they work for, and the merits of what the company is trying to accomplish. As a consequence, their morale is higher and their productivity is higher. In addition, greater numbers of company personnel exhibit passion for their work and exert their best efforts to make the strategy succeed and achieve performance targets. All this helps move the company closer to realizing its strategic vision and, from employees' standpoint, makes the company a more engaging place to work.

The Perils of Strategy–Culture Conflict   Conflicts between behaviors approved by the culture and behaviors needed for good strategy execution pose a real dilemma for company personnel. Should they be loyal to the culture and company traditions (to which they are likely to be emotionally attached) and thus resist or be indifferent to actions and behaviors that will promote better strategy execution? Or should they go along with the strategy execution effort and engage in actions and behaviors that run counter to the culture—a choice that will likely impair morale and lead to less-than-wholehearted commitment to management's strategy execution efforts? Neither choice leads to desirable outcomes, and the solution is obvious: Eliminate the conflict.

When a company's culture is out of sync with the actions and behaviors needed to execute the strategy successfully, the culture has to be changed as rapidly as can be managed—this, of course, presumes that it is one or more aspects of the culture that are out of whack rather than the strategy execution approaches management wishes to institute. While correcting a strategy–culture conflict can occasionally mean revamping a company's approach to executing the strategy to produce good cultural fit, more usually it means altering aspects of the mismatched culture to ingrain new behaviors and work practices that will enable first-rate strategy execution. The more entrenched the mismatched aspects of the culture, the greater the difficulty of implementing and executing new or different strategies until better strategy–culture alignment emerges. A sizable and prolonged strategy–culture conflict weakens and may even defeat managerial efforts to make the strategy work.

Changing a Problem Culture

Changing a problem culture is among the toughest management tasks because of the heavy anchor of ingrained behaviors and ways of doing things. It is natural for company personnel to cling to familiar practices and to be wary, if not hostile, to new approaches of how things are to be done. Consequently, it takes concerted management action over a period of time to root out certain unwanted behaviors and replace an out-of-sync culture with behaviors and ways of doing things that are more conducive to executing the strategy. *The single most visible factor that distinguishes successful culture-change efforts from failed attempts is competent leadership at the top.* Great power is needed to force major cultural change and overcome the springback resistance of entrenched cultures—and great power is possessed only by the most senior executives, especially the CEO. However, while top management must be out front leading the effort, instilling new cultural behaviors is a job for the whole management team. Middle managers and frontline supervisors play a key role in implementing the new work practices and operating approaches, helping win rank-and-file acceptance of and support for the desired behavioral norms.

As shown in Figure 12.1, the first step in fixing a problem culture is for top management to identify those facets of the present culture that are dysfunctional and pose obstacles to executing new strategic initiatives and meeting or beating company performance targets. Second, managers have to clearly define the desired new behaviors and features of the culture they want to create. Third, managers have to convince company personnel why the present culture poses problems and why and how new behaviors and operating approaches will improve company performance—the case for cultural reform has to be persuasive. Finally, and most important, all the talk about remodeling the present culture has to be followed swiftly by visible, forceful actions to promote the desired new behaviors and work practices—actions that company personnel will interpret as a determined top management commitment to bring about a different work climate and new ways of operating.

Making a Compelling Case for Culture Change   The place for management to begin a major remodeling of the corporate culture is by selling company personnel on the need for new-style behaviors and work practices. This means making a compelling

Figure 12.1   Changing a Problem Culture

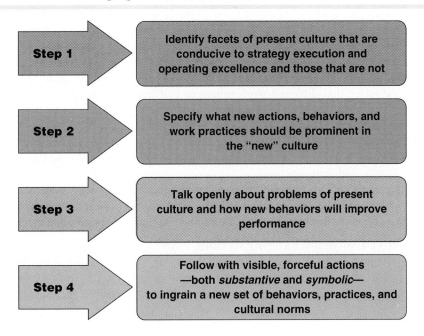

Step 1 — Identify facets of present culture that are conducive to strategy execution and operating excellence and those that are not

Step 2 — Specify what new actions, behaviors, and work practices should be prominent in the "new" culture

Step 3 — Talk openly about problems of present culture and how new behaviors will improve performance

Step 4 — Follow with visible, forceful actions —both *substantive* and *symbolic*— to ingrain a new set of behaviors, practices, and cultural norms

case for why the company's new strategic direction and culture-remodeling efforts are in the organization's best interests and why company personnel should wholeheartedly join the effort to doing things somewhat differently. Skeptics and opinion leaders have to be convinced that all is not well with the status quo. This can be done by:

- Citing reasons why the current strategy has to be modified and why new strategic initiatives that are being undertaken will bolster the company's competitiveness and performance. The case for altering the old strategy usually needs to be predicated on its shortcomings—why sales are growing slowly, why rivals are doing so much better, why too many customers are opting to go with the products of rivals, why costs are too high, why the company's price has to be lowered, and so on. In some instances, management must sell the case for culture change when signs of problems are just emerging. It is far easier to change elements of a problem culture before they become deeply ingrained work behaviors.[19] Building the case for culture change is easier if managers and other key personnel are forced to listen to dissatisfied customers, the complaints of strategic allies, alienated employees, or disenchanted stockholders.

- Explaining why and how certain behavioral norms and work practices in the current culture pose obstacles to good execution of new strategic initiatives.

- Explaining how new behaviors and work practices that are to have important roles in the new culture will be more advantageous and produce better results. Effective culture-change leaders are good at telling stories to describe the new values and desired behaviors and connect them to everyday practices.

It is essential for the CEO and other top executives to personally talk to company personnel all across the company about the reasons for modifying work practices and culture-related behaviors. Senior officers and department heads have to play the lead role in explaining the behaviors, practices, and operating approaches that are to be introduced and why they are beneficial—and the explanations will likely have to be repeated many times. For the culture-change effort to be successful, front-line supervisors and employee opinion leaders must be won over to the cause, which means convincing them of the merits of *practicing* and *enforcing* cultural norms at the lowest levels in the organization. Arguments for new ways of doing things and new work practices tend to be embraced more readily if employees understand how they will benefit company stakeholders (particularly customers, employees, and shareholders). Until a big majority of employees accept the need for a new culture and agree that different work practices and behaviors are called for, there's more work to be done in selling company personnel on the whys and wherefores of culture change. Building widespread organizational support requires taking every opportunity to repeat the messages of why the new work practices, operating approaches, and behaviors are good for company stakeholders (particularly customers, employees, and shareholders).

Management's efforts to make a persuasive case for changing what is deemed to be a problem culture must be *quickly followed* by forceful, high-profile actions across several fronts. The actions to implant the new culture must be both substantive and symbolic.

Substantive Culture-Changing Actions No culture change effort can get very far with just talk about the need for different actions, behaviors, and work practices. Company executives have to give the culture-change effort some teeth by initiating *a series of actions* that company personnel will see as credible and unmistakably indicative of the seriousness of management's commitment to new strategic initiatives and the associated cultural changes. The strongest signs that management is truly committed to instilling a new culture include:

1. Replacing key executives who are strongly associated with the old culture and are stonewalling needed organizational and cultural changes.

2. Promoting individuals who are known to possess the desired cultural traits, who have stepped forward to advocate the shift to a different culture, and who can serve as role models for the desired cultural behavior.

3. Appointing outsiders with the desired cultural attributes to high-profile positions—bringing in new-breed managers to serve as role models and help drive the culture-change movement sends an unmistakable message that a new era is dawning and acts to reinforce company personnel who have already gotten on board the culture-change effort.

4. Screening all candidates for new positions carefully, hiring only those who appear to fit in with the new culture—this helps build a critical mass of people to help turn the tide in favor of the new culture.

5. Mandating that all company personnel attend culture-training programs to learn more about the new work practices and operating approaches and to better understand the cultured-related actions and behaviors that are expected.

6. Pushing hard to implement new-style work practices and operating procedures.

7. Designing compensation incentives that boost the pay of teams and individuals who display the desired cultural behaviors and hit change-resisters in the pocketbook—company personnel are much more inclined to exhibit the desired kinds of actions and behaviors when it is in their financial best interest to do so.

8. Granting generous pay raises to individuals who step out front, lead the adoption of the desired work practices, display the new-style behaviors, and achieve pace-setting results.

9. Revising policies and procedures in ways that will help drive cultural change.

Executives must take care to launch enough companywide culture-change actions at the outset to leave no room for doubt that management is dead serious about changing the present culture and that a cultural transformation is inevitable. To convince doubters and skeptics that they cannot just wait things out in hopes the culture-change initiative will soon die out, the series of actions initiated by top management must create lots of hallway talk across the whole company, get the change process off to a fast start, and be followed by unrelenting efforts to firmly establish the new work practices and style of operating as standard.

Symbolic Culture-Changing Actions   There's also an important place for symbolic managerial actions to alter a problem culture and tighten the strategy–culture fit. The most important symbolic actions are those that top executives take to *lead by example*. For instance, if the organization's strategy involves a drive to become the industry's low-cost producer, senior managers must display frugality in their own actions and decisions: inexpensive decorations in the executive suite, conservative expense accounts and entertainment allowances, a lean staff in the corporate office, scrutiny of budget requests, few executive perks, and so on. At Wal-Mart, all the executive offices are simply decorated; executives are habitually frugal in their own actions, and they are zealous in their own efforts to control costs and promote greater efficiency. At Nucor, one of the world's low-cost producers of steel products, executives fly coach class and use taxis at airports rather than limousines. If the culture change imperative is to be more responsive to customers' needs and to pleasing customers, the CEO can instill greater customer awareness by requiring all officers and executives to spend a significant portion of each week talking with customers about their needs. Top executives must be alert to the fact that company personnel will be watching their actions and decisions to see if they are walking the talk. Hence they need to make sure that their current decisions will be construed as consistent with new-culture values and behaviors.[20]

Another category of symbolic actions includes holding ceremonial events to single out and honor people whose actions and performance exemplify what is called for in the new culture. A point is made of holding events to celebrate each culture-change success (and any other outcome that management would like to see happen again). Executives sensitive to their role in promoting strategy–culture fits make a habit of appearing at ceremonial functions to praise individuals and groups that get with the program. They show up at employee training programs to stress strategic priorities, values, ethical principles, and cultural norms. Every group gathering is seen as an opportunity to repeat and ingrain values, praise good deeds, expound on the merits of the new culture, and cite instances of how the new work practices and operating approaches have worked to good advantage.

The use of symbols in culture-building is widespread. Many universities give outstanding teacher awards each year to symbolize their commitment to good teaching and their esteem for instructors who display exceptional classroom talents. Numerous businesses have employee-of-the-month awards. The military has a long-standing custom of awarding ribbons and medals for exemplary actions. Mary Kay Cosmetics awards an array of prizes—from ribbons to pink automobiles—to its beauty consultants for reaching various sales plateaus.

How Long Does It Take to Change a Problem Culture?   Planting and growing the seeds of a new culture require a determined effort by the chief executive and other senior managers. Neither charisma nor personal magnetism is essential. But a sustained and persistent effort to reinforce the culture at every opportunity through both word and deed is very definitely required. Changing a problem culture is never a short-term exercise. It takes time for a new culture to emerge and prevail. Overnight transformations simply don't occur. And it takes even longer for a new culture to become deeply embedded. The bigger the organization and the greater the cultural shift needed to produce a strategy–culture fit, the longer it takes. In large companies, fixing a problem culture and instilling a new set of attitudes and behaviors can take two to five years. In fact, it is usually tougher to reform an entrenched problematic culture than it is to instill a strategy-supportive culture from scratch in a brand-new organization. Sometimes executives succeed in changing the values and behaviors of small groups of managers and even whole departments or divisions, only to find the changes eroded over time by the actions of the rest of the organization—what is communicated, praised, supported, and penalized by an entrenched majority undermines the new emergent culture and halts its progress. Executives, despite a series of well-intended actions to reform a problem culture, are likely to fail at weeding out embedded cultural traits when widespread employee skepticism about the company's new directions and culture-change effort spawns covert resistance to the cultural behaviors and operating practices advocated by top management. This is why management must take every opportunity to convince employees of the need for culture change and communicate to them how new attitudes, behaviors, and operating practices will benefit the interests of organizational stakeholders.

ILLUSTRATION CAPSULE 12.2
Changing the "Old Detroit" Culture at Chrysler

Shortly after Robert Nardelli became CEO of Chrysler in August 2007, he announced that the company, which had just been spun off from DaimlerChrysler AG in May, would record an annual loss of $1.6 billion. Nardelli believed that Chrysler's problems in the marketplace and its inability to control costs were rooted in a corporate culture formed during an era when U.S. automobile manufacturers had no serious competition from abroad, gasoline was inexpensive, and high profit margins from the sale of trucks, SUVs, and minivans helped disguise weaknesses in the company's passenger car lineup. In early 2008, Nardelli placed himself in charge of a wide-ranging culture change program that included the following elements:

- Chrysler's top 300 executives were required to participate in multiday in-house management seminars aimed at creating the mind-set that decisions should be based on what is best for the customer. Chrysler executives participating in the seminars are not allowed to accept phone calls or e-mails via PDAs and wireless phones during the sessions.

- Nardelli has replaced Chrysler managers unwilling to break from past work behaviors and attitudes. A well-regarded engineer who was put in charge of a key vehicle project was ousted after resisting key principles of the new culture Nardelli hoped to install at Chrysler.

- Chrysler's compensation plan and promotion policies were changed to reward performance rather than seniority.

- Chrysler's purchasing managers were required to abandon the procurement policies that gave preference to the cheapest parts even if the parts were of inferior quality. Purchasing managers were retrained to consider the ownership experience of the customers who purchase Chrysler vehicles when making decisions about the quality and price of parts used in the company's vehicles.

- Nardelli selected a former Toyota executive to become vice chairman of the company to help with the culture change effort and push the drive for improved product quality forward. When given an opportunity to test-drive the new Dodge Challenger as it was headed to production, the former Toyota executive sent the new vehicle back to engineering because its push-button starter needed be held down too long before the engine turned over. Chrysler's vice chairman sent other new vehicles back to engineering after his test drives—including the Chrysler Sebring, which received new bushings and more sound-deadening materials.

Chrysler's culture-change program was expected to take years of effort on the part of management at all levels to break the ingrained behaviors that damaged the company's reputation for quality and had been in place for decades. In mid-2008, Chrysler, Dodge, and Jeep all ranked below the industry average on J. D. Power and Associates' initial quality survey, with Jeep placing last among all automobile manufacturers.

Source: Based on information in Neal E. Boudette, "Nardelli Tries to Shift Chrysler's Culture," *The Wall Street Journal,* June 18, 2008, p. B1.

Illustration Capsule 12.2 discusses the approaches being used at Chrysler in 2007–2008 to change a culture that was grounded in a 1970s view of the automobile industry.

Grounding the Culture in Core Values and Ethics

The foundation of a company's corporate culture nearly always resides in its dedication to certain core values and the bar it sets for ethical behavior. The culture-shaping significance of core values and ethical behaviors accounts for why so many companies have developed a formal values statement and a code of ethics—see Table 12.1 for representative core values and the ground usually covered in codes of ethics. Many companies today convey their values and codes of ethics to stakeholders and interested parties in their annual reports and on their Web sites The trend of making stakeholders aware of a company's commitment

> **CORE CONCEPT**
> **A company's culture is grounded in and shaped by its core values and the bar it sets for ethical behavior.**

Table 12.1   Representative Content of Company Values Statements and Codes of Ethics

Typical Core Values	Areas Covered by Codes of Ethics
• Satisfying and delighting customers • Dedication to superior customer service, top-notch quality, product innovation, and/or technological leadership • A commitment to excellence and results • Exhibiting such qualities as integrity, fairness, trustworthiness, pride of workmanship, Golden Rule behavior, respect for coworkers, and ethical behavior • Creativity, exercising initiative, and accepting responsibility • Teamwork and cooperative attitudes • Fair treatment of suppliers • Making the company a great place to work • A commitment to having fun and creating a fun work environment • Being stewards of shareholders' investments and remaining committed to profits and growth • Exercising social responsibility and being a good community citizen • Caring about protecting the environment • Having a diverse workforce	• Expecting all company personnel to display honesty and integrity in their actions and avoid conflicts of interest • Mandating full compliance with all laws and regulations, specifically: 　—Antitrust laws prohibiting anticompetitive practices, conspiracies to fix prices, or attempts to monopolize 　—Foreign Corrupt Practices Act 　—Securities laws and prohibitions against insider trading 　—Environmental and workplace safety regulations 　—Discrimination and sexual harassment regulations 　—Political contributions and lobbying activities • Prohibiting giving or accepting bribes, kickbacks, or gifts • Engaging in fair selling and marketing practices • Not dealing with suppliers that employ child labor or engage in other unsavory practices • Being above-board in acquiring and using competitively sensitive information about rivals and others • Avoiding use of company assets, resources, and property for personal or other inappropriate purposes • Responsibility to protect proprietary information and not divulge trade secrets

to core values and ethical business conduct is attributable to three factors: (1) greater management understanding of the role these statements play in culture-building, (2) a renewed focus on ethical standards stemming from the numerous corporate scandals that hit the headlines during 2001–2005, and (3) the sizable fraction of consumers and suppliers who prefer doing business with ethical companies.

At Darden Restaurants—the world's largest casual dining company that employs more than 180,000 people and serves 350 million meals annually at 1,700 Red Lobster, Olive Garden, LongHorn Steakhouse, Capital Grille, Bahama Breeze, and Seasons 52 restaurants in North America—the core values are operating with integrity and fairness, caring and respect, being of service, teamwork, excellence, always learning and teaching, and welcoming and celebrating workforce diversity. Top executives at Darden believe the company's practice of these values has been instrumental in creating a culture characterized by trust, exciting jobs and career opportunities for employees, and a passion to provide "a terrific dining experience to every guest, every time, in every one of our restaurants."[21]

Of course, sometimes a company's stated core values and codes of ethics are cosmetic, existing mainly to impress outsiders and help create a positive company image. But more usually they have been developed to shape the culture. Many executives want the work climate at their companies to mirror certain values and ethical standards, partly because they are personally committed to these values and ethical standards but mainly because they are convinced that adherence to such values and ethical principles will make the company a much better performer and improve its image with both insiders and external constituents alike. As discussed earlier, values-related cultural norms promote better strategy execution and mobilize company personnel behind the drive to achieve stretch objectives and the company's strategic vision. Hence, a corporate culture grounded in well-chosen core values and high ethical standards contributes mightily to a company's long-term strategic success.[22] And, not incidentally, strongly ingrained values and ethical standards reduce the likelihood of lapses in ethical and socially approved behavior that mar a company's reputation and put its financial performance and market standing at risk.

> A company's values statement and code of ethics communicate expectations of how employees should conduct themselves in the workplace.

The Culture-Building Role of Values and Codes of Ethics At companies where executives believe in the merits of practicing the values and ethical standards that have been espoused, *the stated core values and ethical principles are the cornerstones of the corporate culture.* As depicted in Figure 12.2, a company's stated core values and ethical principles have two roles in the culture-building process. One, a company that works hard at putting its stated core values and ethical principles into practice fosters a work climate where company personnel share strongly held convictions about how the company's business is to be conducted. Second, the stated values and ethical principles provide company personnel with guidance about the manner in which they are to do their jobs—which behaviors and ways of doing things are approved (and expected) and which are out of bounds.

Transforming Core Values and Ethical Standards into Cultural Norms Once values and ethical standards have been formally adopted, they must be institutionalized in the company's policies and practices and embedded in the conduct of company personnel. This can be done in a number of different ways.[23] Tradition-steeped companies with a rich folklore rely heavily on word-of-mouth indoctrination

Figure 12.2 The Two Culture-Building Roles of a Company's Core Values and Ethical Standards

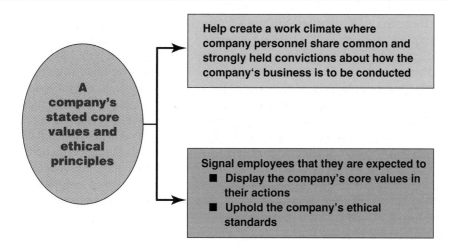

A company's stated core values and ethical principles

Help create a work climate where company personnel share common and strongly held convictions about how the company's business is to be conducted

Signal employees that they are expected to
■ Display the company's core values in their actions
■ Uphold the company's ethical standards

and the power of tradition to instill values and enforce ethical conduct. But most companies employ a variety of techniques to hammer in core values and ethical standards, using some or all of the following:

1. Giving explicit attention to values and ethics in recruiting and hiring to screen out applicants who do not exhibit compatible character traits.

2. Incorporating the statement of values and the code of ethics into orientation programs for new employees and training courses for managers and employees.

3. Having senior executives frequently reiterate the importance and role of company values and ethical principles at company events and internal communications to employees.

4. Using values statements and codes of ethical conduct as benchmarks for judging the appropriateness of company policies and operating practices.

5. Making the display of core values and ethical principles a big factor in evaluating each person's job performance—there's no better way to win the attention and commitment of company personnel than by using the degree to which individuals observe core values and ethical standards as a basis for compensation increases and promotion.

6. Making sure that managers, from the CEO down to frontline supervisors, are diligent in stressing the importance of ethical conduct and observance of core values. Line managers at all levels must give serious and continuous attention to the task of explaining how the values and ethical code apply in their areas.

7. Encouraging everyone to use their influence in helping enforce observance of core values and ethical standards—strong peer pressures to exhibit core values and ethical standards are a deterrent to outside-the-lines behavior.

8. Periodically having ceremonial occasions to recognize individuals and groups who display the values and ethical principles.

9. Instituting ethics enforcement procedures.

To deeply ingrain the stated core values and high ethical standards, companies must turn them into *strictly enforced cultural norms*. They must put a stake in the ground, making it unequivocally clear that living up to the company's values and ethical standards has to be a way of life at the company and that there will be little toleration of outside-the-lines behavior

The Benefits of Cultural Norms Grounded in Core Values and Ethical Principles   The more that managers succeed in making the espoused values and ethical principles the main drivers of "how we do things around here," the more that the values and ethical principles function as cultural norms. Over time, a strong culture grounded in the display of core values and ethics may emerge. As shown in Figure 12.3, *cultural norms* rooted in core values and ethical behavior are highly beneficial in three respects.[24] One, the advocated core values and ethical standards accurately communicate the company's good intentions and validate the integrity and above-board character of its business principles and operating methods. There's nothing cosmetic or fake about the company's values statement and code of ethics—company personnel actually strive to practice what is being preached. Second, the values-based and ethics-based cultural norms steer company personnel toward both doing things right and doing the right thing. Third, they establish a "corporate conscience" and provide yardsticks for gauging the appropriateness of particular actions, decisions, and policies.

Figure 12.3   The Benefits of Cultural Norms Strongly Grounded in Core Values and Ethical Principles

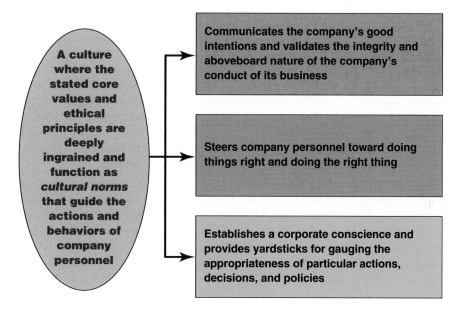

Establishing a Strategy–Culture Fit in Multinational and Global Companies

In multinational and global companies, establishing a tight strategy–culture fit is complicated by the diverse societal circumstances surrounding the company's operations in different countries. The nature of the local economies, living conditions, per capita incomes, and lifestyles can give rise to considerable cross-border diversity in a company's workforce and to subcultures within the corporate culture. Leading cross-border culture-change initiatives requires sensitivity to prevailing differences in local circumstances; company managers must discern when local subcultures have to be accommodated and when cross-border differences in the company's corporate culture can and should be narrowed.[25] Cross-country diversity in a multinational enterprise's corporate culture are more tolerable if the company is pursuing a multicountry strategy and if the company's culture in each country is well aligned with its strategy in that country. But significant cross-country differences in a company's culture are likely to impede execution of a global strategy and have to be addressed.

As discussed earlier in this chapter, *the trick to establishing a workable strategy–culture fit in multinational companies is to ground the culture in strategy-supportive values and operating practices that travel well across country borders* and strike a chord with managers and workers in many different areas of the world, despite varying local customs and traditions. A multinational enterprise with a misfit between its strategy and culture in certain countries where it operates can attack the problem by rewording its values statement so as to express core values in ways that have universal appeal. The alternative is to allow *some leeway* for certain core values to be reinterpreted

> **CORE CONCEPT**
>
> A multinational company needs to build its corporate culture around values and operating practices that travel well across borders.

or de-emphasized or applied somewhat differently from country to country whenever local customs and traditions in a country really need to be accommodated. But such accommodation needs to be done in ways that do not impede good strategy execution.

Aside from trying to build the corporate culture around a set of core values that have universal appeal, management can seek to minimize the existence of subcultures and promote greater cross-country cultural uniformity by:

- *Instituting culture training in each country to (1) communicate the meaning of core values in language that resonates with company personnel in that country and (2) explain the case for common operating approaches and work practices.* The use of uniform work practices becomes particularly important when the company's work practices are more efficient and aid good strategy execution as compared to others—in such instances, local managers have to find ways to skirt local preferences and win support for "how we do things around here."

- *Creating a cultural climate where it is the norm to adopt best practices, use common work procedures, and pursue operating excellence.* Companies may find that a values-based corporate culture is less conducive to good strategy execution than a cultural climate of operating excellence where company personnel are energized to do things in the best possible manner, achieve continuous improvement, and meet or beat performance targets. A results-oriented culture keyed to operating excellence and meeting stretch objectives sidesteps many of the problems with trying to get people from different societies and traditions to embrace common values.

- *Giving local managers the flexibility to modify people management approaches or operating styles in those situations where adherence to companywide cultural traditions simply doesn't work well.* But local modifications have to be infrequent and done in a manner that doesn't undermine the establishment of a mostly uniform corporate culture.

- *Giving local managers discretionary authority to use somewhat different motivational and compensation incentives to induce local personnel to adopt and practice the desired cultural behaviors.* Personnel in different countries may respond better to some compensation structures and reward systems than others.

Generally, a high degree of cross-country homogeneity in a multinational company's corporate culture is desirable and has to be pursued, particularly when it comes to ingraining universal core values and companywide enforcement of such ethical standards as the payment of bribes and kickbacks, the use of underage labor, and environmental stewardship. Having too much variation in the culture from country to country not only makes it difficult to use the culture to drive the strategy execution process but also works against the establishment of a one-company mind-set and a consistent corporate identity.

LEADING THE STRATEGY-EXECUTION PROCESS

For an enterprise to execute its strategy in truly proficient fashion and approach operating excellence, top executives have to be out front personally leading the implementation/execution process and driving the pace of progress. Top executives—and, to some degree, the enterprise's entire management team—must seek to engage the full organization. A fully engaged workforce, one where individuals bring their best every day, is a necessary element to producing great results.[26] So is having a group of high-impact people looking to make a big difference at work. Top-level executives can usually best create a fully engaged organization by delegating authority to middle and lower-level managers to get the implementation/execution process moving and by creating a sense of empowerment among employees as well. It is unwise for company personnel to feel powerless to change anything significant and just wait to follow orders from top executives.

But delegating and empowering does not mean that senior managers can stay in their offices, content to receive reports from subordinates and monitor the latest metrics. Rather, they have to be out in the field, seeing for themselves how well operations are going, gathering information firsthand, and gauging the progress being made. Proficient strategy execution requires company managers to be diligent and adept in spotting gridlock, ferreting out problems and issues, learning what obstacles lie in the path of good execution, and then clearing the way for progress—the goal must be to produce better results speedily and productively. And there has to be constructive, but unrelenting, pressure on organizational units to (1) demonstrate growing consistency in strategy execution and (2) achieve performance targets—ultimately, it's all about producing excellent strategy execution and financial results.

Making Corrective Adjustments in Timely Fashion

The leadership challenge in achieving consistently good strategy execution ultimately boils down to two things: deciding when corrective adjustments are needed and deciding what adjustments to make. Both decisions are a normal and necessary part of managing the strategy execution process, since no scheme for implementing and executing strategy can foresee all the events and problems that will arise. There comes a time at every company when managers have to fine-tune or overhaul the approaches to strategy execution and push for better results. Clearly, when a company's strategy execution effort is not delivering good results and making measurable progress toward operating excellence, it is the leader's responsibility to step forward and push corrective actions—*there is no substitute for decisive and effective action to resolve problems and improve outcomes.*

The *process* of making corrective adjustments varies according to the situation. In a crisis, taking remedial action fairly quickly is of the essence. But it still takes time to review the situation, examine the available data, identify and evaluate options (crunching whatever numbers may be appropriate to determine which options may generate the best outcomes), and decide what to do. The organizational leader then usually meets with key subordinates and personally presides over extended discussions of the proposed responses, trying to build a quick consensus among members of the executive inner circle. If no consensus emerges and/or if action is required so swiftly that consultation with others is infeasible, the burden falls on the manager in charge to make the decision and get the chosen actions under way.

When the situation allows managers to proceed more deliberately in deciding when to make changes and what changes to make, most managers seem to prefer a process of incrementally solidifying commitment to a particular course of action.[27] The process that managers go through in deciding on corrective adjustments is essentially the same for both proactive and reactive changes: They sense needs, gather information, broaden and deepen their understanding of the situation, develop options and explore their pros and cons, put forth action proposals, generate partial (comfort-level) solutions, strive for a consensus, and finally formally adopt an agreed-on course of action.[28] The time frame for deciding what corrective changes to initiate can take a few hours, a few days, a few weeks, or even a few months if the situation is particularly complicated.

Success in initiating corrective actions usually hinges on thorough analysis of the situation, the exercise of good business judgment in deciding what actions to take, and good implementation of the corrective actions that are initiated. Successful managers are skilled in getting an organization back on track rather quickly; they (and their staffs) are good at discerning what actions to take and in ramrodding them through to a successful conclusion. Managers that struggle to show measurable progress in generating good results and improving the performance of strategy-critical value chain activities are candidates for being replaced.

The challenges of leading a successful strategy execution effort are, without question, substantial.[29] But the job is definitely doable. Because each instance of executing strategy occurs under different organizational circumstances, the managerial agenda for executing strategy always needs to be situation-specific—there's no neat generic procedure to follow. And, as we said at the beginning of Chapter 10, executing strategy is an action-oriented, make-the-right-things-happen task that challenges a manager's ability to lead and direct organizational change, create or reinvent business processes, manage and motivate people, and achieve performance targets. If you now better understand what the challenges are, what approaches are available, which issues need to be considered, and why the action agenda for implementing and executing strategy sweeps across so many aspects of administrative and managerial work, then we will look on our discussion in Chapters 10, 11, and 12 as a success.

A FINAL WORD ON MANAGING THE PROCESS OF CRAFTING AND EXECUTING STRATEGY

In practice, it is hard to separate the leadership requirements of executing strategy from the other pieces of the strategy process. As we emphasized in Chapter 2, the job of crafting, implementing, and executing strategy is a five-task process with much looping and recycling to fine-tune and adjust strategic visions, objectives, strategies, capabilities, implementation approaches, and cultures to fit one another and to fit changing circumstances. The process is continuous, and the conceptually separate acts of crafting and executing strategy blur together in real-world situations. The best tests of good strategic leadership are whether the company has a good strategy and whether the strategy execution effort is delivering the hoped-for results. If these two conditions exist, the chances are excellent that the company has good strategic leadership.

KEY POINTS

The character of a company's culture is a product of the core values and business principles that executives espouse, the standards of what is ethically acceptable and what is not, the work practices and behaviors that define "how we do things around here," the company's approach to people management and style of operating, the chemistry and the personality that permeates its work environment, and the stories that get told over and over to illustrate and reinforce the company's values, business practices, and traditions. A company's culture is important because it influences the organization's actions and approaches to conducting business—in a very real sense, the culture is the company's "operating system" or organizational DNA.[30]

The psyche of corporate cultures varies widely. Moreover, company cultures vary widely in strength and influence. Some are strongly embedded and have a big impact on a company's practices and behavioral norms. Others are weak and have comparatively little influence on company operations. There are four types of unhealthy cultures: (1) those that are highly political and characterized by empire building, (2) those that are change resistant, (3) those that are insular and inwardly focused, and (4) those that are ethically unprincipled and are driven by greed. High-performance cultures and adaptive cultures both have positive features that are conducive to good strategy execution.

A culture grounded in values, practices, and behavioral norms that match what is needed for good strategy execution helps energize people throughout the company to do their jobs in a strategy-supportive manner, adding significantly to the power of a company's strategy execution effort and the chances of achieving the targeted results. But when the culture is in conflict with some aspect of the company's direction, performance targets, or strategy, the culture becomes a stumbling block. Thus, an important part of managing the strategy execution process is establishing and nurturing a good fit between culture and strategy.

A company's present culture and work climate may or may not be compatible with what is needed for effective implementation and execution of the chosen strategy. *When a company's present work climate promotes attitudes and behaviors that are well suited to first-rate strategy execution, its culture functions as a valuable ally in the strategy execution process.* When the culture is in conflict with some aspect of the company's direction, performance targets, or strategy, the culture becomes a stumbling block.

Changing a company's culture, especially a strong one with traits that don't fit a new strategy's requirements, is a tough and often time-consuming challenge. Changing a culture requires competent leadership at the top. It requires symbolic actions and substantive actions that unmistakably indicate serious commitment on the part of top management. The more that culture-driven actions and behaviors fit what's needed for good strategy execution, the less managers have to depend on policies, rules, procedures, and supervision to enforce what people should and should not do.

The taproot of a company's corporate culture nearly always is its dedication to certain core values and the bar it sets for ethical behavior. Of course, sometimes a company's stated core values and codes of ethics are cosmetic, existing mainly to impress outsiders and help create a positive company image. But more usually they have been developed to shape the culture. If management practices what it preaches, a company's core values and ethical standards nurture the corporate culture in three highly positive ways: (1) they communicate the company's good intentions and validate the integrity and above-board character of its business principles and operating methods; (2) they steer company personnel toward both doing the right thing and doing things right; and (3) they establish a corporate conscience that gauges the appropriateness of particular actions, decisions, and policies. Companies that really care about how they conduct their business put a stake in the ground, making it unequivocally clear that company personnel are expected to live up to the company's values and ethical standards—how well individuals display core values and adhere to ethical standards is often part of the job performance evaluations. Peer pressure to conform to cultural norms is quite strong, acting as an important deterrent to outside-the-lines behavior.

Leading the drive for good strategy execution and operating excellence calls for five actions on the part of the manager in charge:

1. Staying on top of what is happening, closely monitoring progress, ferreting out issues, and learning what obstacles lie in the path of good execution.
2. Putting constructive pressure on the organization to achieve good results and operating excellence.
3. Leading the development of stronger core competencies and competitive capabilities.
4. Displaying ethical integrity and leading social responsibility initiatives.
5. Pushing corrective actions to improve strategy execution and achieve the targeted results.

ASSURANCE OF LEARNING EXERCISES

1. Go to www.google.com. Click on the "About Google" link and then on the "Corporate Info" link. Read what Google has to say about its culture under the "Culture" link. Also, read the "Ten Things Google Has Found to Be True" in the "Our Philosophy" section. How do the "Ten Things" and Google's culture aid in management's attempts to execute the company's strategy?

2. Go to the Jobs section at www.intel.com and see what Intel has to say about its culture under the links for Careers, Diversity, and The Workplace. Does what's on this Web site appear to be just recruiting propaganda, or does it convey the type of work climate that management is actually trying to create? Explain your answer.

3. Using Google Scholar or your university library's access to EBSCO, Lexis-Nexis, or other databases, search for recent articles in business publications on culture change. Give examples of three companies that have recently undergone culture-change initiatives. What are the key features of each company's culture-change program? What results did management achieve at each company?

4. Go to www.jnj.com, the Web site of Johnson & Johnson, and read the "J&J Credo," which sets forth the company's responsibilities to customers, employees, the community, and shareholders. Then read the "Our Company" section. Why do you think the credo has resulted in numerous awards and accolades that recognize the company as a good corporate citizen?

5. Go to www.avoncompany.com/investor and read the "Management Discussion and Analysis of Financial Condition and Results of Operations" section of Avon's 2007 annual report. The company provides a great deal of information about its turnaround plan launched in 2005 and its ongoing corrective actions to achieve operating excellence. Describe in one to two pages how management at Avon demonstrates the internal leadership needed for superior strategy execution.

EXERCISES FOR SIMULATION PARTICIPANTS

1. If you were making a speech to company personnel, what would you tell them about the kind of corporate culture you would like to have at your company? What specific cultural traits would you like your company to exhibit? Explain.

2.   What core values would you want to ingrain in your company's culture? Why?

3.   Following each decision round, how important is it for you and your co-managers to make corrective adjustments in either your company's strategy or how well the strategy is being executed? Explain. What will happen to your company's performance if you and your co-managers stick with the status quo and fail to make corrective adjustments?

part two 2

Readings in Crafting and Executing Strategy

READING

1

Can You Say What Your Strategy Is?

David J. Collis
Harvard Business School

Michael G. Rukstad
Harvard Business School

Can you summarize your company's strategy in 35 words or less? If so, would your colleagues put it the same way?

It is our experience that very few executives can honestly answer these simple questions in the affirmative. And the companies that those executives work for are often the most successful in their industry. One is Edward Jones, a St. Louis–based brokerage firm with which one of us has been involved for more than 10 years. The fourth-largest brokerage in the United States, Jones has quadrupled its market share during the past two decades, has consistently outperformed its rivals in terms of ROI through bull and bear markets, and has been a fixture on *Fortune*'s list of the top companies to work for. It's a safe bet that just about every one of its 37,000 employees could express the company's succinct strategy statement: Jones aims to "grow to 17,000 financial advisers by 2012 [from about 10,000 today] by offering trusted and convenient face-to-face financial advice to conservative individual investors who delegate their financial decisions, through a national network of one-financial-adviser offices."

Conversely, companies that don't have a simple and clear statement of strategy are likely to fall into the sorry category of those that have failed to execute their strategy or, worse, those that never even had one. In an astonishing number of organizations, executives, frontline employees, and all those in between are frustrated because no clear strategy exists for the company or its lines of business. The kinds of complaints that abound in such firms include:

Reprinted from *Harvard Business Review* 86, no. 4 (April 2008), pp. 82–90.

- "I try for months to get an initiative off the ground, and then it is shut down because 'it doesn't fit the strategy.' Why didn't anyone tell me that at the beginning?"

- "I don't know whether I should be pursuing this market opportunity. I get mixed signals from the powers that be."

- "Why are we bidding on this customer's business again? We lost it last year, and I thought we agreed then not to waste our time chasing the contract!"

- "Should I cut the price for this customer? I don't know if we would be better off winning the deal at a lower price or just losing the business."

Leaders of firms are mystified when what they thought was a beautifully crafted strategy is never implemented. They assume that the initiatives described in the voluminous documentation that emerges from an annual budget or a strategic-planning process will ensure competitive success. They fail to appreciate the necessity of having a simple, clear, succinct strategy statement that everyone can internalize and use as a guiding light for making difficult choices.

Think of a major business as a mound of 10,000 iron filings, each one representing an employee. If you scoop up that many filings and drop them onto a piece of paper, they'll be pointing in every direction. It will be a big mess: 10,000 smart people working hard and making what they think are the right decisions for the company—but with the net result of confusion. Engineers in the R&D department are creating a product with "must have" features for which (as the marketing group could have told them) customers will not pay; the sales force is selling customers on quick turnaround times and customized offerings even though the manufacturing group has just invested in equipment designed for long production runs; and so on.

If you pass a magnet over those filings, what happens? They line up. Similarly, a well-understood statement of strategy aligns behavior within the business. It allows everyone in the organization to make individual choices that reinforce one another, rendering those 10,000 employees exponentially more effective.

What goes into a good statement of strategy? Michael Porter's seminal article "What Is Strategy?" (HBR November–December 1996) lays out the characteristics of strategy in a conceptual fashion, conveying the essence of strategic choices and distinguishing them from the relentless but competitively fruitless search for operational efficiency. However, we have found in our work both with executives and with students that Porter's article does not answer the more basic question of how to describe a particular firm's strategy.

It is a dirty little secret that most executives don't actually know what all the elements of a strategy statement are, which makes it impossible for them to develop one. With a clear definition, though, two things happen: First, formulation becomes infinitely easier because executives know what they are trying to create. Second, implementation becomes much simpler because the strategy's essence can be readily communicated and easily internalized by everyone in the organization.

ELEMENTS OF A STRATEGY STATEMENT

The late Mike Rukstad, who contributed enormously to this article, identified three critical components of a good strategy statement—objective, scope, and advantage—and rightly believed that executives should be forced to be crystal clear about them. These elements are a simple yet sufficient list for any strategy (whether business or military) that addresses competitive interaction over unbounded terrain.

Any strategy statement must begin with a definition of the ends that the strategy is designed to achieve. "If you don't know where you are going, any road will get you there" is the appropriate maxim here. If a nation has an unclear sense of what it seeks to achieve from a military campaign, how can it have a hope of attaining its goal? The definition of the objective should include not only an end point but also a time frame for reaching it. A strategy to get U.S. troops out of Iraq at some distant point in the future would be very different from a strategy to bring them home within two years.

Since most firms compete in a more or less unbounded landscape, it is also crucial to define the scope, or domain, of the business: the part of the landscape in which the firm will operate. What are the boundaries beyond which it will not venture? If you are planning to enter the restaurant business, will you provide sit-down or quick service? A casual or an upscale atmosphere? What type of food will you offer—French or Mexican? What geographic area will you serve—the Midwest or the East Coast?

Alone, these two aspects of strategy are insufficient. You could go into business tomorrow with the goal of becoming the world's largest hamburger chain within 10 years. But will anyone invest in your company if you have not explained how you are going to reach your objective? Your competitive advantage is the essence of your strategy: What your business will do differently from or better than others defines the all-important means by which you will achieve your stated objective. That advantage has complementary external and internal components: a value proposition that explains why the targeted customer should buy your product above all the alternatives, and a description of how internal activities must be aligned so that only your firm can deliver that value proposition.

Defining the objective, scope, and advantage requires trade-offs, which Porter identified as fundamental to strategy. If a firm chooses to pursue growth or size, it must accept that profitability will take a back seat. If it chooses to serve institutional clients, it may ignore retail customers. If the value proposition is lower prices, the company will not be able to compete on, for example, fashion or fit. Finally, if the advantage comes from scale economies, the firm will not be able to accommodate idiosyncratic customer needs. Such trade-offs are what distinguish individual companies strategically.

DEFINING THE OBJECTIVE

The first element of a strategy statement is the one that most companies have in some form or other. Unfortunately, the form is usually wrong. Companies tend to confuse their statement of values or their mission with their strategic objective. A strategic objective is *not*, for example, the platitude of "maximizing shareholder wealth by exceeding customer expectations for _____ [insert product or service here] and providing opportunities for our employees to lead fulfilling lives while respecting the environment and the communities in which we operate." Rather, it is the single precise objective that will drive the business over the next five years or so. (See Figure 1, "A Hierarchy of Company Statements.") Many companies do have—and all firms should have—statements of their ultimate purpose and the

Figure 1   A Hierarchy of Company Statements

Organizational direction comes in several forms. The mission state-ment is your loftiest guiding light— and your least specific. As you work your way down the hierarchy, the statements become more concrete, practical, and ultimately unique. No other company will have the same strategy statement,which defines your competitive advantage, or balanced scorecard, which tracks how you implement your particular strategy.

MISSION
Why we exist

VALUES
What we believe in
and how we will behave

VISION
What we want to be

STRATEGY – – – – – – –
What our competitive
game plan will be

BALANCED
SCORECARD
How we will monitor
and implement that plan

The BASIC
ELEMENTS
of a Strategy
Statement

OBJECTIVE = Ends

SCOPE = Domain

ADVANTAGE = Means

ethical values under which they will operate, but neither of these is the strategic objective.

The mission statement spells out the underlying motivation for being in business in the first place—the contribution to society that the firm aspires to make. (An insurance company, for example, might define its mission as providing financial security to consumers.) Such statements, however, are not useful as strategic goals to drive today's business decisions. Similarly, it is good and proper that firms be clear with employees about ethical values. But principles such as respecting individual differences and sustaining the environment are not strategic. They govern how employees should behave ("doing things right"); they do not guide what the firm should do ("the right thing to do").

Firms in the same business often have the same mission. (Don't all insurance companies aspire to provide financial security to their customers?) They may also have the same values. They might even share a vision: an indeterminate future goal such as being the "recognized leader in the insurance field." However, it is unlikely that even two companies in the same business will have the same strategic objective. Indeed, if your firm's strategy can be applied to any other firm, you don't have a very good one.

It is always easy to claim that maximizing shareholder value is the company's objective. In some sense all strategies are designed to do this. However, the question to ask when creating an actionable strategic statement is, Which objective is most likely to maximize shareholder value over the next several years? (Growth? Achieving a certain market share? Becoming the market leader?) The strategic objective should be specific, measurable, and time bound. It should also be a single goal. It is not sufficient to say, "We seek to grow profitably." Which matters more—growth or profitability? A salesperson needs to know the answer when she's deciding how aggressive to be on price. There could well be a host of subordinate goals that follow from the strategic objective, and these might serve as metrics on a balanced scorecard that monitors progress for which individuals will be held accountable. Yet the ultimate objective that will drive the operation of the business over the next several years should always be clear.

The choice of objective has a profound impact on a firm. When Boeing shifted its primary goal from being the largest player in the aircraft industry to being the most profitable, it had to restructure the entire organization, from sales to manufacturing. For example, the company dropped its policy of competing with Airbus to the last cent on every deal and abandoned its commitment to maintain a manufacturing capacity that could deliver more than half a peak year's demand for planes.

Another company, after years of seeking to maximize profits at the expense of growth, issued a corporate mandate to generate at least 10 percent organic growth per year. The change in strategy forced the firm to switch its focus from shrinking to serve only its profitable core customers and competing on the basis of cost or efficiency to differentiating its products, which led to a host of new product features and services that appealed to a wider set of customers.

At Edward Jones, discussion among the partners about the firm's objective ignited a passionate exchange. One said, "Our ultimate objective has to be maximizing profit per partner." Another responded, "Not all financial advisers are partners—so if we maximize revenue per partner, we are ignoring the other 30,000-plus people who make the business work!" Another added, "Our ultimate customer is the client. We cannot just worry about partner profits. In fact, we should start by maximizing value for the customer and let the profits flow to us from there!" And so on. This intense debate not only drove alignment with the objective of healthy growth in the number of financial advisers but also ensured that every implication of that choice was fully explored. Setting an ambitious growth target at each point in its 85-year history, Edward Jones has continually increased its scale and market presence. Striving to achieve such growth has increased long-term profit per adviser and led the firm to its unique configuration: Its only profit center is the individual financial adviser. Other activities, even investment banking, serve as support functions and are not held accountable for generating profit.

DEFINING THE SCOPE

A firm's scope encompasses three dimensions: customer or offering, geographic location, and vertical integration. Clearly defined boundaries in those areas should make it obvious to managers which activities they should concentrate on and, more important, which they should not do.

The three dimensions may vary in relevance. For Edward Jones, the most important is the customer. The firm is configured to meet the needs of one very specific type of client. Unlike just about every other brokerage in the business, Jones does not define its archetypal customer by net worth or income. Nor does it use demographics, profession, or spending habits. Rather, the definition is psychographic: The company's customers are long-term investors who have a conservative investment philosophy and are uncomfortable making serious financial decisions without the support of a trusted adviser. In the terminology of the business, Jones targets the "delegator," not the "validator" or the "do-it-yourselfer."

The scope of an enterprise does not prescribe exactly what should be done within the specified bounds. In fact, it encourages experimentation and initiative. But to ensure that the borders are clear to all employees, the scope should specify where the firm or business will not go. That will prevent managers from spending long hours on projects that get turned down by higher-ups because they do not fit the strategy.

For example, clarity about who the customer is and who it is not has kept Edward Jones from pursuing day traders. Even at the height of the Internet bubble, the company chose not to introduce online trading (it is still not available to Jones customers). Unlike the many brokerages that committed hundreds of millions of dollars and endless executive hours to debates over whether to introduce online trading (and if so, how to price and position it in a way that did not cannibalize or conflict with traditional offerings), Jones wasted no money or time on that decision because it had set clear boundaries.

Similarly, Jones is not vertically integrated into proprietary mutual funds, so as not to violate the independence of its financial advisers and undermine clients' trust. Nor will the company offer penny stocks, shares from IPOs, commodities, or options—investment products that it believes are too risky for the conservative clients it chooses to serve. And it does not have metropolitan offices in business districts, because they would not allow for the convenient, face-to-face interactions in casual settings that the firm seeks to provide. Knowing not to extend its scope in these directions has allowed the firm to focus on doing what it does well and reap the benefits of simplicity, standardization, and deep experience.

DEFINING THE ADVANTAGE

Given that a sustainable competitive advantage is the essence of strategy, it should be no surprise that advantage is the most critical aspect of a strategy statement. Clarity about what makes the firm distinctive is what most helps employees understand how they can contribute to successful execution of its strategy.

As mentioned above, the complete definition of a firm's competitive advantage consists of two parts. The first is a statement of the customer value proposition. Any strategy statement that cannot explain why customers should buy your product or service is doomed to failure. A simple graphic that maps your value proposition against those of rivals can be an extremely easy and useful way of identifying what makes yours distinctive. (See Figure 2, "Wal-Mart's Value Proposition.")

The second part of the statement of advantage captures the unique activities or the complex combination of activities allowing that firm alone to deliver the customer value proposition. This is where the strategy statement draws from Porter's definition of strategy as making consistent choices about the configuration of the firm's activities. It is also where the activity-system map that Porter describes in "What Is Strategy?" comes into play.

As Figure 3, "Edward Jones's Activity-System Map," shows, the brokerage's value proposition is to provide convenient, trusted, personal service and advice. What is most distinctive about Jones is that it has only one financial adviser in an office, which allows it to have more offices (10,000 nationally) than competitors do. Merrill Lynch has about 15,000 brokers but only 1,000 offices. To make it easy for its targeted customers to visit at their convenience—and to provide a relaxed, personable, nonthreatening environment—Jones puts its offices in strip malls and the retail districts of rural areas and suburbs rather than high-rise buildings in the central business districts of big cities. These choices alone require Jones to differ radically from other brokerages in the configuration of its activities. With no branch-office management providing direction or support, each financial adviser must be an entrepreneur who delights in running his or her own operation. Since

Figure 2   Wal-Mart's Value Proposition

Wal-Mart's value proposition can be summed up as "everyday low prices for a broad range of goods that are always in stock in convenient geographic locations." It is those aspects of the customer expeience that the company overdelivers relative to competitors. Under-performance on other dimensions, such as ambience and sales help, is a strategic choice that generates cost savings, which fuel the company's price advantage.

If the local mom-and-pop hardware store has survived, it also has a value proposition: convenience, proprietors who have known you for years, free coffee and doughnuts on Saturday mornings, and so on.

Sears falls in the middle on many criteria. As a result, customers lack a lot of compelling reasons to shop there, which goes a long way toward explaining why the company is struggling to remain profitable.

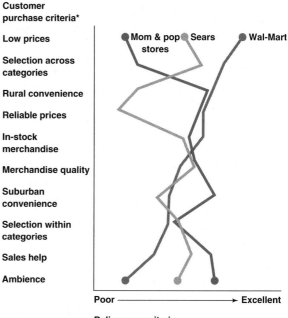

*in approximate order of importance to Wal-Mart's target customer group.
Source: Jan Rivkin, Harvard Business School.

such people are an exception in the industry, Jones has to bring all its own financial advisers in from other industries or backgrounds and train them, at great expense. Until 2007, when it switched to an Internet-based service, the firm had to have its own satellite network to provide its widely dispersed offices with real-time quotes and allow them to

Figure 3 Edward Jones's Activity-System Map

This map illustrates how acitivities at the brokerage Edward Jones connect to deliver competitive advantage. The firm's customer value proposition appears near the center of the map—in the "customer relationship" bubble—and the supporting activities hang off it. Only the major connections are shown.

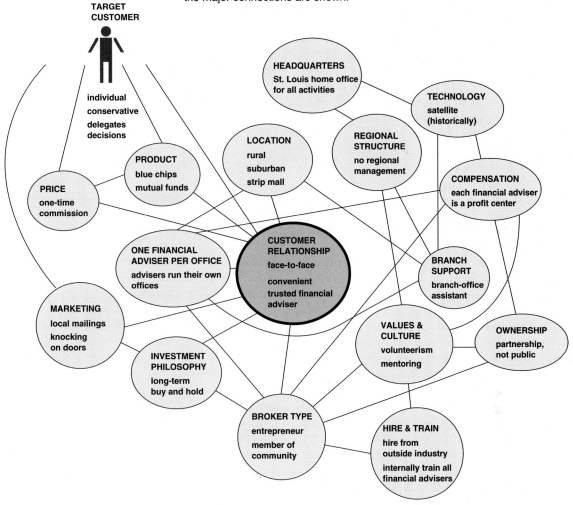

execute trades. Because the company has 10,000 separate offices, its real estate and communication costs are about 50 percent higher than the industry average. However, all those offices allow the financial advisers who run them to deliver convenient, trusted, personal service and advice.

Other successful players in this industry also have distinctive value propositions and unique configurations of activities to support them.

Merrill Lynch

During the five-year tenure of former CEO Stan O'Neal, who retired in October 2007, Merrill Lynch developed an effective strategy that it called "Total Merrill." The company's value proposition: to provide for all the financial needs of its high-net-worth customers—those with liquid financial assets of more than $250,000—*through retirement*. While a lot of brokerages cater to people with a high net worth, they focus on asset accumulation *before retirement.* Merrill's view is that as baby boomers age and move from the relatively simple phase of accumulating assets to the much more complex, higher-risk phase of drawing cash from their retirement accounts, their needs change. During this stage, they will want to consolidate their financial assets with a single trusted partner that can help them figure out how to optimize income over their remaining years by making the best decisions on everything from annuities to payout ratios to long-term-care insurance. Merrill offers coherent financial plans for such customers and provides access to a very wide range of sophisticated products based on a Monte Carlo simulation of the probabilities of running out of money according to different annual rates of return on different categories of assets.

How does Merrill intend to deliver this value to its chosen customers in a way that's unique among large firms? First, it is pushing brokers—especially new ones—to become certified financial planners and has raised internal training requirements to put them on that road. The certified financial planner license is more difficult for brokers to obtain than the standard Series 7 license, because it requires candidates to have a college degree and to master nearly 100 integrated financial-planning topics. Second, Merrill offers all forms of insurance, annuities, covered calls, hedge funds, banking services, and so on (unlike Edward Jones, which offers a much more limited menu of investment products). Since several of these products are technically complex, Merrill needs product specialists to support the client-facing broker. This "Team Merrill" organization poses very different HR and compensation issues from those posed by Edward Jones's single-adviser offices. Merrill's compensation system has to share income among the team members and reward referrals.

Wells Fargo

This San Francisco bank competes in the brokerage business as part of its tactic to cross-sell services to its retail banking customers in order to boost profit per customer. (It aims to sell each customer at least eight different products.) Wells Fargo's objective for its brokerage arm, clearly stated in a recent annual report, is to triple its share of customers' financial assets. The brokerage's means for achieving this goal is the parent company's database of 23 million

customers, many of them brought into the firm through one particular aspect of the banking relationship: the mortgage. Wells Fargo differs from Edward Jones and Merrill Lynch in its aim to offer *personalized*, rather than *personal*, service. For example, the firm's IT system allows a bank clerk to know a limited amount of information about a customer (name, birthday, and so on) and appear to be familiar with him or her, which is quite different from the ongoing individual relationships that Jones and Merrill brokers have with their clients.

LPL Financial

Different again is LPL Financial, with offices in Boston, San Diego, and Charlotte, North Carolina. LPL sees its brokers (all of whom are independent financial advisers affiliated with the firm) rather than consumers as its clients and has configured all of its activities to provide individualized solutions and the highest payouts to its brokers. This means that the vast majority of the activities performed by the corporate headquarters staff are services, such as training, that brokers choose and pay for on an à la carte basis. As a result, LPL's headquarters staff is very small (0.20 people per broker) compared with that of Edward Jones (1.45 people per broker). Low overhead allows LPL to offer a higher payout to brokers than Jones and Merrill do, which is its distinctive value proposition to its chosen customer: the broker.

By now it should be apparent how a careful description of the unique activities a firm performs to generate a distinctive customer value proposition effectively captures its strategy. A relatively simple description in a strategy statement provides an incisive characterization that could not belong to any other firm. This is the goal. When that statement has been internalized by all employees, they can easily understand how their daily activities contribute to the overall success of the firm and how to correctly make the difficult choices they confront in their jobs.

DEVELOPING A STRATEGY STATEMENT

How, then, should a firm go about crafting its strategy statement? Obviously, the first step is to create a great strategy, which requires careful evaluation of the industry landscape. This includes developing a detailed understanding of customer needs, segmenting customers, and then identifying unique ways of creating value for the ones the firm chooses to serve. It also calls for an analysis of competitors' current strategies and a prediction of how they might change in the future. The process must involve a rigorous, objective assessment of the firm's capabilities and resources and those of competitors, as described in "Competing on Resources: Strategy in the 1990s," by David J. Collis and Cynthia A. Montgomery (HBR July–August 1995)—not just a feel-good exercise of identifying core competencies. The creative part of developing strategy is finding the sweet spot that aligns the firm's capabilities with customer needs in a way that competitors cannot match given the changing external context—factors such as technology, industry demographics, and regulation. (See Figure 4, "The Strategic Sweet Spot.") We have found that one of the best ways to do this is to develop two or three plausible but very different strategic options.

For example, fleshing out two dramatically different alternatives—becoming a cheap Red Lobster or a fish McDonald's—helped executives at the Long John Silver's chain of restaurants understand the strategic choices that they had to make. They had been trying to do a bit of everything, and this exercise showed them that their initiatives—such as offering early-evening table service and expanding drive-through service—were strategically inconsistent. (Competing on the basis of table service requires bigger restaurants and more employees, while drive-through service requires high-traffic locations and smaller footprints.) As a result, they chose to be a fish McDonald's, building smaller restaurants with drive-through service in high-traffic locations.

The process of developing the strategy and then crafting the statement that captures its essence in a readily communicable manner should involve employees in all parts of the company and at all levels of the hierarchy. The wording of the strategy statement should be worked through in pains-taking detail. In fact, that can be the most powerful part of the strategy development process. It is usually in heated discussions over the choice of a single word that a strategy is crystallized and executives truly understand what it will involve.

The end result should be a brief statement that reflects the three elements of an effective strategy.

Figure 4 The Strategic Sweet Spot

The strategic sweet spot of a company is where it meets customers' needs in a way that rivals can't, given the context in which it competes.

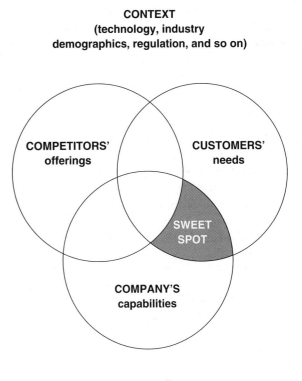

CONTEXT
(technology, industry demographics, regulation, and so on)

COMPETITORS' offerings

CUSTOMERS' needs

SWEET SPOT

COMPANY'S capabilities

It should be accompanied by detailed annotations that elucidate the strategy's nuances (to preempt any possible misreading) and spell out its implications. (See Figure 5, "Leaving No Room for Misinterpretation.")

When the strategy statement is circulated throughout the company, the value proposition chart and activity-system map should be attached. They serve as simple reminders of the twin aspects of competitive advantage that underpin the strategy. Cascading the statement throughout the organization, so that each level of management will be the teacher for the level below, becomes the starting point for incorporating strategy into everyone's behavior. The strategy will really have traction only when executives can be confident that the actions of empowered frontline employees will be guided by the same principles that they themselves follow.

Figure 5 Leaving No Room for Misinterpretation

Executives at Edward Jones have developed a detailed understanding of every element of the firm's strategy. Here is an example.

Edward Jones's Strategy Statement

To grow to 17,000 financial advisers by 2012 by offering trusted and convenient face-to-face financial advice to conservative individual investors who delegate their financial decisions, through a national network of one-financial-adviser offices.

"Conservative"

Our investment philosophy is long-term buy and hold. We do not sell penny stocks, commodities, or other high-risk instruments. As a result we do not serve day traders and see no need to offer online trading.

We charge commissions on trades because this is the cheapest way to buy stocks (compared with a wrap fee, which charges annually as a percentage of assets) when the average length of time the investor holds the stock or mutual fund is over 10 years.

"Individual"

We do not advise institutions or companies.

We do not segment according to wealth, age, or other demographics. The company will serve all customers that fit its conservative investment philosophy. Brokers will call on any and every potential customer. Stories abound within Jones of millionaires who live in trailers—people all the other brokerages would never think of approaching.

"Investors"

Our basic service is investment. We do not seek to offer services such as checking accounts for their own sake, but only as part of the management of a client's assets.

"who delegate their financial decisions"

We do not target self-directed do-it-yourselfers, who are comfortable making their own investment decisions. We are also unlikely to serve validators, who are merely looking for reassurance that their decisions are correct.

The value of rhetoric should not be underestimated. A 35-word statement can have a substantial impact on a company's success. Words do lead to action. Spending the time to develop the few words that truly capture your strategy and that will energize and empower your people will raise the long-term financial performance of your organization.

Enabling Bold Visions

Douglas A. Ready
London Business School

Jay A. Conger
London Business School

I t was a beautiful, sunny day in Miami. Inside a darkened auditorium, however, 3,500 senior executives of one of the world's largest financial companies, flown in for just this purpose, sat awaiting their new CEO. The scene resembled the beginning of a pro basketball game: Loud rock music set the beat, and laser images peppered the crowd and the stage. As the audience members stomped their feet and swayed with the music, the CEO appeared on stage. His task? To pitch his newly minted enterprise vision to the already energized crowd.

His speech, as well choreographed as the buildup, was brief and upbeat. The message was simple: "We will become 'the breakout firm.' And to achieve breakout status, we will rely on the three I's of innovation, integration, and inspiration." Given the tight schedule of events for this one-day meeting, the CEO took no questions. But the speech had caught the executives' attention, and the new vision created a buzz of excitement.

Months later, the buzz had worn off. Reality had intruded, as it always does. The company, successful for more than a hundred years, had always proceeded conservatively. Its organizational culture was anything but "breakout." It wasn't innovative; its businesses, products and customers were not integrated; and its leaders were not known for being inspirational.

In short, following their initial enthusiasm, the company's senior executives were having a hard time reconciling the new vision with day-to-day realities as they met in planning sessions with the next levels of management and front-line employees. Within the top executive team, there were few role models for the three I's, and there were no signs of rewards for behaving as breakout leaders.

Within a year, the term "breakout" had slipped quietly into the background. Few senior executives could even remember the three I's. About two years after the speech in Miami, the CEO declared victory and went on to lead another company. But the confusion sowed by the unrealized vision cost the company both market share and the harder to quantify elements of trust and momentum with employees and customers.

This gap between inspiration and implementation is a common one. We set out to find out why, and what CEOs and their top teams could do to translate bold visions into operational realities. (See the box, "About the Research.") In this article, we'll first explain several common reasons behind the derailment of bold visions. We will then offer a framework that executives can use to ensure that their visions become more than just pipe dreams. Examples of companies that have successfully followed this path will both illustrate the challenges and provide guidance to those who want to actively address them.

WHY MANY BOLD VISIONS DERAIL

New visions can fade away for many apparently unique reasons. However, as a result of a search of the literature on organizational change and our discussions with executives from 40 companies, we were able to categorize the reasons for failure into a set of themes.[1]

Reprinted from *MIT Sloan Management Review* 49, no. 2 (Winter 2008), pp. 69–76. Reproduced with permission of the copyright owner. Further reproduction prohibited without permission.

About the Research

To gain a better understanding of the challenges companies face in enabling bold visions, we conducted research on approximately 40 global companies. We conducted surveys within the companies and then came up with an initial research protocol for the dialogue component of the project. We then met with representatives from those companies to engage in discussions—mostly in groups, but sometimes individually—about how to move bold visions from the initial phase of inspiration to a sustainable aspect of company operations. Our goal: to determine a best-practice model. Finally, we gathered in-depth detail from people in several companies that had successfully turned visions into reality.

Failing to Focus

How many initiatives can any company handle at once? In our experience, an organization can be confronted with a dozen or more major initiatives at a time. If the top team attempts to wrestle with all of them at once, middle managers and front-line employees will likely be confused. The bold vision will get mired in a haze of other priorities, with various initiative champions roaming through the company like prophets crying in the wilderness.

Sitting Out This Dance

It's awkward dancing without a partner. But that's essentially what too many leaders of the companies we researched tried to do: They started the dance by explaining the vision but didn't engage a partner to make it work. They didn't communicate how others in the company could learn the steps to the new dance. Moreover, employees could walk away from the dance floor without fear, since there was no short-term price to pay for not engaging to make the new vision an operating reality.

Skipping the Skill Building

By its nature, a bold vision can't simply be retrofitted onto a company. (If it could, it would be a tame or gentle new vision.) But many of the companies we examined did not invest to develop the new skills their people would need to realize the vision. Some leaders didn't even want to hear that their organizations lacked the capability to execute it. For example, the CEO of the "breakout" financial services company didn't want to talk about the need to develop collaborative managers and leaders—an obvious prerequisite for the integration plank of his vision.

Mismatching Messages and Metrics

Much is made of people's tendency to talk the talk without walking the walk—and that general problem applies in this instance, too. Many executives told us that a bold new vision often bumped up against subtle reinforcements of business as usual. For example, it would become clear through the stories floating through the organization that yesterday's leadership behaviors were still seen to be of paramount importance in spite of the need for changes to fit the vision. Further, we learned that performance management processes and organizational performance measures often remain unchanged, even though newly articulated visions require new behaviors and mindsets.

Clashing Powers

In many cases, an organization's political dynamics and culture can become a major barrier to the success of the new vision. Powerful groups are often tied to existing core activities that made the company thrive in the past. If the new vision threatens the supremacy of the old guard, political infighting may stall it out and defeat the change agents.

Figure 1   The Five-Phase Model for Enabling Visions

Companies that successfully put new visions of the enterprise into practice follow a process that takes the organization through five phases. In today's competitive landscape, this is an iterative process. While companies may be able to stick with a single vision for a few years, most will need to return to the process regularly.

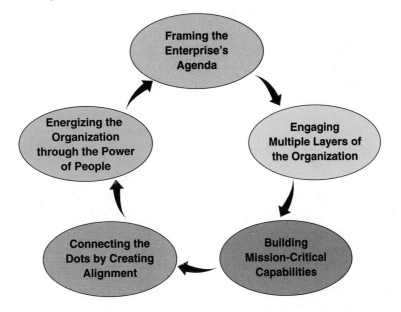

Neglecting the Talent Pipeline

According to the managers in our study, the challenge of bringing about a new vision is, in essence, a change management challenge. What's needed to make it work? Layers of change agents, from top to bottom—a critical mass of people who embody the behaviors and values of the new call to action. But many companies lack such pipelines of talent, filled with people who are capable of this critical task.

These six problem areas explain why many bold visions fail to produce measurable change, far less ignite their companies to reach new heights. But a model of change can help companies avoid this trap.

THE CHANGE MODEL

While our research uncovered reasons for the failure of bold visions, it also led us to discern a pattern followed by companies that successfully translated a vision into action. We observed five critical activities, performed in sequence, that together form a systems approach to enabling visions. This approach can be described as a framework for leading large-scale, enterprisewide change initiatives. (See Figure 1, "The Five-Phase Model for Enabling Visions.")

Phase I: Framing the Agenda

If an organization's top executives are spending much of their time attending to competing "top priorities," they'll gradually put the CEO's vision on the back burner, where it will slowly simmer down to nothing. The leaders in our study who successfully brought about change framed their organizations' challenges as compelling stories that created an urgent agenda for action.

They used the stories to set priorities among the many challenges facing their organizations, with a laser focus on the need to drive performance and to develop the right organizational climate. They often cast the need to drive performance in present and future terms—as a matter of finding pathways to future growth while maintaining the edge that enabled the company to deliver value to customers in the short

Figure 2 The Enterprise Agenda

An enterprise agenda must take into account, on one axis, both present and future performance — both the company's future growth strategy and its current customer value proposition. This reflects the company's focus on "doing." On the other axis, the agenda must reflect an organization's state of "being" — the way employees and other insiders are affected by the climate of change, as well as the way customers and other external stakeholders perceive the company's new vision.

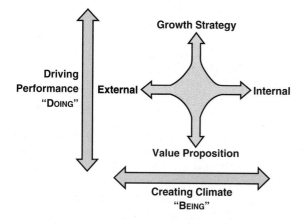

term. In addressing the need to create an organizational climate that was consistent with the company's performance objectives, these change leaders took into consideration both external (brand, corporate social responsibility) and internal (culture, values, behaviors) concerns. (See Figure 2, "The Enterprise Agenda.")

Consider the approach to change taken by the British Broadcasting Corporation (BBC). Like many established media companies, the BBC has been under assault by the proliferation of media options, a problem that has intensified with the advent of inexpensive and easy-to-use digital technology. Customer choice has fragmented, and the network's market share has steadily eroded. Gone are the days when a popular sitcom could attract more than 28 million viewers, as one did in the 1960s.

The company needed to change to meet these challenges, but it had to navigate risks. It had to chart a course that would not destroy its proud heritage or instigate a flight of the talent that had always been the bedrock of its core competence.

When Mark Thompson was hired as the BBC's new director general a few years ago, he inherited an organization deeply entrenched in the analog world. Innovators elsewhere in the industry were already

moving with dispatch into the digital world. But Thompson didn't move immediately to bring about big changes. He took some time to make sure he understood the core competencies of the organization and how they matched up against the future direction of the industry. He got to know the cutting-edge elements of the future of the business as well as the best way to frame the BBC's new vision for success.

After a great deal of listening to industry experts, customers, and employees, Thompson framed the BBC's new enterprise agenda: Creative Future. His message was simple. In order to drive performance, the BBC would invest heavily in digital technology and become leaner and smaller (by becoming better at aligning programming with an improved customer segmentation capability). And in order to create the climate suitable to achieve these performance objectives, the BBC's leaders and managers would need to become more agile and collaborative. This framing of the agenda was clear: As the competitive landscape shifted, the BBC would not sacrifice quality, but it would make tough decisions about programming and head count.

Another storied company facing the imperative to change recently was Deutsche Bank AG, based in Frankfurt, Germany. In this case, globalization, not technology, was the primary force at work. By the early 1990s, the 150-year-old retail and commercial bank still had its roots firmly planted in Germany. Its top executives and managers were virtually all German, and nearly 70 percent of its core business was conducted in Germany. But a strategic analysis of the company's future prospects revealed the likelihood of trouble in the near future: The bank's growth potential in both retail and commercial banking in Germany amounted to roughly 2 percent per year.

In contrast, growth prospects in other areas were much more robust: 10 percent per year in capital markets and investment banking, 5 percent in asset and wealth management, and unquantifiably huge growth prospects in the Asia Pacific region and throughout the rest of Europe. But to exploit these opportunities, the bank would have to undergo two major transformations—from domestic to global player and from a narrow focus to a broad one, as a fully integrated financial services institution with new core competencies in capital markets and investment banking.

Facing possible extinction if it continued on its present path, Deutsche Bank, led by Josef Ackermann, responded with a bold new vision: the One Bank initiative. Ackermann, chairman of the Deutsche Bank Group's executive committee, knew that One Bank wouldn't work if it was just a slogan. "We had to make sure that we were moving from a one-culture bank to a one-bank culture." And today the bank's executives are quick to point out that One Bank is only a part of the story of the company's impressive transformation.

In framing the bank's enterprise agenda, Ackermann launched the Business Realignment Program in conjunction with the One Bank initiative. This program ensured that the Group's executives and managers would know precisely what the company's priorities were and where the Group was heading over the next decade. The program also placed the capital markets and investment banking divisions at the core of the bank's growth strategy while stressing the importance of integration. Again, driving performance and creating climate—within a construct of ruthless prioritization—were the twin goals.

As Ackermann put it, "We must view ourselves as one bank and one team with one shared goal. We intend to implement the idea of 'One Bank–One Team' as swiftly as possible. Utmost priority will be given to removing the silo mentality."[2] To reinforce this dual emphasis, Ackermann approved new leadership standards and cultural values that were directly linked to the One Bank initiative. With these changes, Ackermann made it clear that performance and climate would go hand in hand at Deutsche Bank.

Sometimes companies find themselves in dire situations but still need a leader to spell out, in detail, just how serious the problems are. This bad-news-first approach can be critical to the framing of a bold vision that will get a company moving away from the status quo as quickly as possible. In 1999, when Carlos Ghosn took the helm at Nissan Motor Co. Ltd., he stressed several dismal facts. Nissan had just lost its position as Japan's second-largest carmaker. Market share had, in fact, been declining for two and a half decades. Fewer than 1 Nissan model in 10 was profitable. Against this background, Ghosn told the company that the Nissan Revival plan was the company's "last chance." Employees got the message.

Phase II: Engaging the Organization

Once change leaders have framed their agendas, they must do whatever they can to distribute "ownership" of that vision as broadly as possible. But this has to be done the right way. We found that while managers and even executives yearn for more leadership in their organizations, they don't want to be cast simply as followers. Instead, they want a different style of leadership, one characterized by authentic collaboration and broad-based engagement.

This finding gets to the heart of why we emphasize that bold visions must be enabled rather than merely executed. Visions that are truly bold will create tension and anxiety within an organization's business-as-usual stakeholders. Great change leaders understand this, and they don't make those who have succeeded under yesterday's business model enemies of the new vision. They invite differing views and perspectives and listen carefully to those who contribute legitimate arguments concerning the tensions created by the newly framed enterprise agenda.

Carlos Ghosn was particularly keen to solicit new ideas and to get new voices to speak up. At the beginning of his tenure at Nissan, he created nine cross-functional teams and staffed them with middle managers in their 30s and 40s from different functions, divisions and countries. Each team had only 10 members. To keep discussions fluid, a facilitator was assigned to each; to ensure that the teams had authority and were not influenced by a single function, each had two board-level sponsors.

Only three guidelines were set out for the teams' work. They had one goal: to make proposals to reduce costs and develop the business. They had one rule: no sacred cows, no constraints. And they had one deadline: three months for final recommendations. In the end, the cross-functional teams were a powerful vehicle for returning Nissan to profitability. Critically, Ghosn had not simply issued orders from the top about how to realize the new vision. Instead, he had engaged the company's managers to find their own routes to success.

Mark Thompson's strategy to engage the BBC's stakeholder communities with his Creative Future vision started at the top. The director general engaged the BBC's board of directors in a series of dialogues that eventually produced a set of recommendations for restructuring the BBC along four criteria: creative, digital, simple, and open. The board owned the overarching direction of the restructuring. It left to Thompson the task of engaging his managers and executives so that the restructuring would come to life in day-to-day operations.

Thompson followed through by bringing teams together from different BBC groups—Vision, Journalism, Audio & Music, and Future Media and Technology. The task was to work through the details of how the BBC would transform itself from a collection of separate units to a unified organization that relied heavily on cross-unit collaboration. Eventually this engagement process also paved the way for Thompson to restructure the company into three multimedia output groups and to merge the Future Media and Technology team with the new Operations team. Collaboration moved from being an articulated but unrealized value to an ingrained way of working at the BBC.

Similarly, Deutsche Bank's Ackermann launched a variety of engagement initiatives to enable his vision. For senior-level leaders, he led a series of dialogues called the Spokesman's Challenge. These were open discussions led by Ackermann and his top executive team that focused on listening to the concerns of his enterprise leadership team. The outcome? A better understanding of the tensions that might get in the way of making the One Bank initiative come to life.

Ackermann also created the One Bank Task Force, a group focused on engaging successive layers of management so that they would also own the vision and become part of the solution. In addition, he skillfully used Deutsche Bank's Learning and Leadership Development Operation to initiate programs that were directly linked to implementing the One Bank vision.

While Deutsche Bank and the BBC faced compelling reasons to change, their situations were not as dire as that of Mattel Inc. in 2000. In May of that year, Bob Eckert became CEO of an organization that was in deep trouble. The company had fired its previous CEO over the disastrous acquisition of an electronic games company. Morale was low and finger-pointing was high. Eckert set out to engage the organization with a vision of greater collaboration—a vision that would eventually be called One Mattel. In that spirit, a team of line managers approached Eckert and asked if they could craft a set of new values for the company conveying collaboration. The team came back with four values that all built on the word "play"—Play Fair, Play Together, Play with Passion, and Play to Grow. Since these values accurately captured the aspirations of many employees, they were quickly and enthusiastically adopted by

the organization. Just as important to the success of One Mattel: the engagement of the company's line managers.

Phase III: Building Mission-Critical Capabilities

While engagement with the new vision is critical, it's not enough. The development of new capabilities is also necessary, as companies usually have gaps in what they want to do and what they can do.

The process of building mission-critical capabilities is no small challenge, however. We identified two significant problems in the course of our research. First, there are the practical concerns: How do you go about identifying which capabilities will provide differentiated competitive advantage? Second, there are political concerns: How do you identify and address capability gaps without turning the process into an enterprisewide blame game? Either or both of these concerns can become cancerous if matched with a CEO with a short attention span who "just wants to get on with it." This underscores the importance of following the phases sequentially. After all, it is difficult for a CEO to have a serious conversation about building new capabilities without first framing the enterprise agenda and engaging the organization in an active dialogue.

Without proper leadership, the BBC's Creative Future initiative could have foundered during this phase. In order to realize the full benefits of Thompson's bold vision, the BBC required new skills and capabilities and cross-unit collaboration. But the organization was constructed of durable silos with a "craftsmanship culture" in each silo that guided career development decisions of its managers and employees.

Addressing these challenges was not the work of a moment—or of a single program. Thompson attacked the problems in a variety of ways. He brought the BBC's technologists together from across the organization to create what he referred to as a "powerhouse resource." He brought in or developed the expertise required to launch new multiplatform initiatives—that is, initiatives that transcended a single medium or product. He oversaw the introduction of Stepping Stones, a program to create a better understanding of different parts of the Vision Studios and to enable BBC producers to work more flexibly. He launched Hot Shoes, a developmental program that encouraged hundreds of staff to try out their expertise in other disciplines throughout the BBC, allowing them to see what new skills they might need to span boundaries or develop capabilities for new growth areas in the industry. Finally, he initiated the Journalism College Web site, enabling more than 8,500 journalists to sharpen their skills in editorial policy and in emerging fields of the craft. The sum of these programs was a newly skilled base of employees who could work across platforms and had a deep understanding of digital media.

Despite the differences in industry, Deutsche Bank's capability-building challenges were strikingly similar to those of the BBC. Its organizational structure was also formed by silos, and its future depended upon how well Ackermann could break them down.

But in Deutsche Bank's case, more than just skill building was needed. The bank also had to cut costs deeply in order to become more operationally efficient. Ackermann shed some of the bank's portfolio of businesses and acquired and reorganized new businesses that would serve as growth platforms. He targeted markets in other parts of Europe, the Americas and particularly Asia. He made English the official language of Deutsche Bank and carefully moved executives and managers across business and geographic boundaries to build a global mind-set and a collaborative culture. And he used the leadership and learning programs not only as phase II engagement mechanisms but also as critical capability-building tools for his managers.

Phase IV: Connecting the Dots by Creating Alignment

Bold visions rarely succumb to frontal attacks. The companies that collaborated with us in our study mentioned repeatedly that bold visions get derailed by more subtle means: by mind-sets, systems, and processes that are out of sync or, ironically, by the unintentional messages sent out by the very executives who are trying to enable the visions to take root.

For example, one of us was engaged by one of Korea's leading "chaebols" (conglomerates) to facilitate a leadership initiative. The goal was to build a global mind-set among the group's senior executive team. In the audience were 55 Korean business-unit presidents, all men. The discussion was proceeding well until the topic of reconstructing the top team came up. The suggestion was made to establish a guideline metric that would call for one or two of the group's presidents to be either female or non-Korean.

The suggestion was greeted with amused disbelief. But that response illuminates a broad problem that afflicts people in any country: Companies and their employees are hard-wired to resist change. We have observed similar roadblocks when companies attempt to align processes—such as those for performance management and rewards—with new visions.

For example, many companies today are trying to break down silos to deliver integrated solutions to their customers. They are trying to enact "one company" visions. And yet they frequently continue to measure and reward their managers solely on their ability to meet unit objectives. Such outdated processes do nothing to encourage cross-unit collaboration in the service of enhanced customer-value propositions.

What can be done to align processes with a new vision? When Josef Ackermann first launched Deutsche Bank's One Bank initiative, there was a good deal of discussion but little actual business transacted as a result of cross-unit collaboration. That began to change when two of the bank's executives, Anshu Jain, head of Global Markets, and Pierre de Weck, head of Private Wealth Management, signed a Global Partnership Agreement. The agreement set the stage for a robust collaboration between the two divisions. The two business heads figured out how to work together to satisfy clients' needs, as well as how to share revenues and profits from those clients.

This wasn't the only example of parts of the bank learning to collaborate. Other approaches to aligning the company's systems, processes and mind-sets with the One Bank vision include:

• executive development activities undertaken as a team, with leaders from different divisions taking part;

• the establishment of a unit-by-unit performance measurement process that tracked business generated by boundary spanning;

- changes to the executive succession process that took into consideration the extent to which emerging leaders exhibited cross-boundary behaviors;
- and the institution of the One Bank award, a formal recognition by the Group Executive Committee of exceptional behavior in service of the new vision.

The alignment of vision and process can also be reinforced by changing organizational structure and its support mechanisms. For example, following the restructuring of the BBC's departments, Mark Thompson created a new Operations Group. The group was set up to bring leadership, direction, and consistency to the BBC's big infrastructure projects, a critical element of the Creative Future vision. Thompson also linked cost-cutting measures in functional departments to the enablement of the vision, since cost savings could be funneled directly into new investments. Thus, members of the finance department could see how their efforts to develop new accounting and finance systems were contributing $100 million toward the Creative Future initiative. By such simple yet creative means are the hearts and minds of large organizations won.

Phase V: Energizing the Organization through the Power of People

No vision of the enterprise can come to life without the enthusiastic support and follow-through of literally thousands of managers and employees. Individuals in every business, function, and region play a critical role in enabling a bold vision to move from inspiration to implementation.

But do companies have the talent they need to see a vision through to completion? The respondents in our study expressed deep concern about this issue. Specifically, they worried that their leaders were placing too little emphasis on identifying and nurturing the talent pools that would be needed. The problem was not a lack of talent management and succession systems—97 percent of those participating in the research indicated that their companies had such systems in place. However, an almost equally large percentage indicated that their companies lacked a free and flowing pipeline of talent sufficient to execute their organizations' competitive strategies. Pressed further, the respondents indicated that most companies' talent management systems were not in sync with their future capability requirements.

This finding leads us to conclude that leadership failures are not so much a matter of struggling individuals, the focus of most leadership studies. Instead, such failures stem from executive inattention to the connections between talent requirements and competitive capability requirements. All too often, the problem is not that leaders are failing their companies, but rather that a company's talent policies are failing its leaders.

Great change leaders are deeply committed to, engaged in, and accountable for building robust talent processes. They do not delegate this job to the human resources department. The BBC's Mark Thompson brought in a new head of BBC People, as it is called, with the express purpose and mandate to create a human capital strategy that is directly linked to the corporation's Creative Future vision. All division heads engaged in and signed off on the strategy and committed to implement it with the same rigor they would apply to their marketing or operations strategies.

Deutsche Bank's Ackermann demanded that the company's entire leadership curriculum be re-engineered in accordance with the Business Realignment Program and the One Bank vision. The bank's programs now are focused directly on global leadership, managing networks and organizational complexity, and leading across business and geographic boundaries—all essential ingredients in making the One Bank vision a sustainable success.

Even companies that do not face immediate threats need to consider how to keep their people energized. Starbucks Corp., for example, has yet to face major barriers to its growth. In 2006, however, the company launched the Grow and Stay Small initiative. Its focus has been to determine how Starbucks ensures that its partners (employees) and customers have the same positive experiences that they had when the company was much smaller as well as identify the forces affecting the culture. Through the engagement of partners and customers, the company is identifying the common ground needed to "stay small" culturally while building support for enterprisewide initiatives that build on this common ground.

CONTINUOUS REVISION

Just a few decades ago, organizations could stay the course with a strategy for a period of years. The idea that a new vision would be needed, perhaps with some frequency, would have been treated with mild amusement, if not outright derision. But competitive realities have forced executives to rethink what their companies are doing, and how they are doing it, over and over again. Auto manufacturers like Nissan see profitability and market share evaporating. Media companies like the BBC face the hostile world of disruptive technology. Financial institutions like Deutsche Bank discover that a one-country focus is a path to extinction. In such conditions, bold visions are called for—and will be called for again, probably sooner than any executive would like.

Let's stipulate: A bold vision that fundamentally misreads the competitive landscape has no chance of success, regardless of the process used to make it reality. The vision has to be on target, sophisticated, inspiring, and far-seeing. Once those difficult criteria have been met, however, a process is needed to take the vision from its birth—as words thundered from a podium by the CEO as rock star, for example—to a new way of doing business. By following the model outlined here, executives can sustain the momentum, and see through the changes, of enabling bold new visions.

References

1. See, for example, J. P. Kotter, "Leading Change: Why Transformation Efforts Fail," *Harvard Business Review* (March–April 1995): 59–67; L. Bossidy, R. Charan and C. Burck, *Execution: The Discipline of Getting Things Done* (New York: Crown Business, 2002); D. A. Ready, "Leading at the Enterprise Level," *MIT Sloan Management Review* 45, no. 3 (Spring 2004): 87–91; D. A. Ready, "How Storytelling Builds Next-Generation Leaders," *MIT Sloan Management Review* 43, no. 4 (Summer 2002): 63–69; J. C. Collins and J. I. Porras, "Building Your Company's Vision," *Harvard Business Review* (September 1996): 65–77; M. A. Roberto and L. C. Levesque, "The Art of Making Change Initiatives Stick," *MIT Sloan Management Review* 46, no. 4 (Summer 2005): 53–60; C. K. Prahalad and G. Hamel, "The Core Competence of the Corporation," *Harvard Business Review* 68, no. 3 (May–June 1990): 79–91; M. Beer and N. Nohria, "Cracking the Code of Change," *Harvard Business Review* (May–June 2000): 133–41; D. A. Ready and J. Conger, "Make Your Company a Talent Factory," *Harvard Business Review* (June 2007): 68–77; E. G. Chambers, M. Foulon, H. Handfield-Jones, S. M. Hankin, and E. G. Michaels III, "The War for Talent," *McKinsey Quarterly* 3 (August 1998): 44–57; D. C. Hambrick, "The Top Management Team: Key to Strategic Success," *California Management Review* 30, no. 1 (Fall 1987): 88–108; and G. Probst and K. Marmenout, "Deutsche Bank: Becoming a Global Leader with European Tradition," European Case Clearing House no. 306-529-1 (Geneva: University of Geneva, 2007).

2. Probst and Marmenout, "Deutsche Bank."

Location, Location: The Geography of Industry Clusters

Holger Schiele
Leibniz University

lusters are a fashionable topic. The theory has been refined and hundreds of such regional-sectoral agglomerations have been "discovered" during the last decade and their functionality studied. It seems to be a characteristic of modern economies that successful industrial activities cluster in a few regions:

- Every third brush sold in the world is manufactured in Bechhofen in Franconia; the Italian region of Friaul holds about one-third of the world's chair manufacturers, half of the world's tiles are produced in two regions in Italy and Spain, and the region of Yiwu in China controls about half of the market for Christmas decorations (Schiele, 2003). These are only a few striking examples. A meta-study counted more than 800 documented clusters around the world (van der Linde, 2003).

- Most of China's export success is driven by firms located in "one-product towns" where hundreds of firms agglomerate along a single value chain (Sim, 2006).

- In Germany, every second manufacturing sector hosts clusters (Brenner, 2004), including paper manufacturing, watches, the optical industry and foundries. Clusters also exist in some service sectors, such as media and finance.

The clustering of entire value chains in single locations has considerable consequences for firms. For instance, Nokia officials explained that they closed the last mobile phone factory in Germany because they had failed to attract a cluster of suppliers near the factory. Most suppliers are located in Asia and even though transport costs are negligible, the distance to

Reprinted from *Journal of Business Strategy* 29, no. 3 (2008), pp. 29–36.

the industry center and the resulting long lead times prevented Nokia from achieving the necessary flexibility to react quickly to market changes.

Of course, clusters do not form in every industry (Steinle and Schiele, 2002), but "in industries characterized by dominant regional clusters, membership in a cluster is essential for sustained strategic equality" (Tallman et al., 2004, p. 268)

Recently, a new school in strategic thinking has started to consider clusters. The "ecosystem theory" not only attributes the success of firms to their presence in attractive markets or to the availability of superior resources for production, but also offers a new perspective, arguing that the entire value-creating system of a firm contributes to its success. This explicitly includes its network of business partners and the relationship toward them (Jarzabkowski and Wilson, 2006). One of the ecosystem theories is the cluster approach, which attaches a geographic dimension to a value-creating system.

The cluster approach has been extensively applied in the marketing of regions and regional development, but not in corporate management. While theoretically compelling, what have largely been missing are answers to the questions of what the clustering phenomenon really means for firms and how management can actively seize the opportunities arising from this trend.

Addressing these two issues, we will briefly explain the concept of clusters. Then, two pairs of case studies illustrate clusters' vital relevance for management. Each pair contrasts a successful with an unsuccessful firm. The first two cases cover firms located within a cluster, and the second two cases firms outside the strongest cluster of their industry.

PRODUCTIVITY BENEFITS, INNOVATION, AND HIGHER PROFITABILITY: COMPETITIVE ADVANTAGES OF COMPANIES LOCATED WITHIN CLUSTERS

In the 1990s, the century-old cluster concept was revitalized by the seminal work of Porter. He defines a cluster as a group of firms and institutions of one industrial sector that are complementing each other along a value chain and also overlapping in a limited geographical area (Porter, 1998). Several producers of a particular product, their specialized suppliers, customers who anticipate international trends and supporting organizations, such as educational institutions or associations, agglomerate on a national or even a regional basis within a country (see Figure 1).

To fully describe a cluster, though, it is not sufficient to merely list the organizations present in a region. It is also necessary to consider how these firms and institutions behave toward each other. Is their behavior toward cluster members different from their behavior toward other firms? Are they aware of being located in a cluster? Take the example of a region that called itself "medical valley" yet almost half of firms surveyed indicated that they had never been aware of forming a cluster. Workshops have subsequently been conducted in the region to create awareness. In one workshop, for instance, a firm that was sending its samples to be tested overseas discovered that another firm, located almost next door, also had a testing facility. Firms in agglomerations can miss opportunities through not communicating with each other sufficiently.

However, some agglomerations have developed an "innovative milieu" with intensive interaction that fosters collaboration while simultaneously maintaining competition (Crevoisier, 2004; Steinle et al., 2007). Firms located within such clusters have often been found to enjoy productivity, innovation and profitability advantages compared to their isolated competitors. British and American studies showed that almost double the density of employees in a specific sector within a region correlated with 7 percent and 6 percent higher productivity, respectively (Ciccone and Hall, 1996; Baptista, 2003). There are even more dramatic examples, such as that of the Flemish tufted carpet industry, where the average productivity of the same machines—expressed in terms of the number of meters produced by the plant—was 40 percent higher in the cluster than in isolated companies (Vanhaverbeke, 1992).

An explanation: in clusters, numerous specialized suppliers can emerge through spin-offs, which then start to compete intensively with one another. Owing to the presence of this supply base, producers located within clusters can more easily concentrate on their core competencies and increase productivity.

Another form of specialization found in agglomerations is a "labor-pool" of employees trained in specialties (Marshall, 1961). In clusters, it is easier for companies to recruit suitable employees and for employees to specialize in terms of their education. However, a wage-spiral may arise in a very dynamic cluster if employees frequently switch from one firm to another.

The significance of employees moving from company to company becomes clearer still when viewed as a mechanism for knowledge exchange. People take their knowledge with them to their new jobs, combining it with the knowledge acquired at

Figure 1   Elements of a Cluster (The Amplified Porterian Diamond)

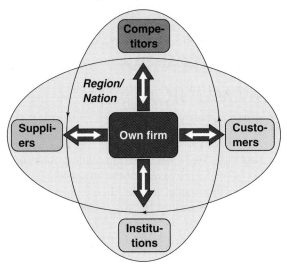

How to Recognize a Cluster

Firms can use Porter's "diamond of competitive advantage" to determine if they are members of any cluster (or if their competitors are). Managers may ask the following questions:

- Are our internationally successful competitors headquartered in the same region (as us)?
- Does our home country host innovation-oriented customers who tend to anticipate global trends?

- Can we rely on a complete set of leading suppliers being present locally?
- Is our sector characterized by an abundance of institutions in our region, such as associations, specialized educational institutions, research institutes, and the like?
- Are there close ties among these organizations—"everyone knows each other"? Does our cluster resemble a club?

their new firms and thus developing the common knowledge base further. This provides an explanation for research findings showing that a few selected centres are host to most of the innovations in an industry (Feldman, 1999; Breschi and Lissoni, 2001).

Higher productivity and innovative power result in companies within clusters tending to be, on average, more profitable than their isolated competitors:

- The Banca d'Italia analyzed 64,000 balance sheets, which revealed that companies within clusters showed a return on investment of 10 percent, whereas comparable but isolated companies achieved only 6 percent (Fabiani and Pellegrini, 1998).
- In another study with data from Mediobanca, there was a difference of at least 2 percent between companies within clusters and isolated companies (Hermes Lab, 2000).

Conclusion

Individual sectors within an economy form national or regional focal points. Companies anchored in such clusters can yield, on average, higher productivity than isolated companies and also benefit from greater innovative strength. Consequently, they are more profitable. The competitive success of a firm is thus influenced by location as well as such factors as wages paid or the quality of management.

Although the cluster approach argues that the success of firms depends more strongly on their

environment than commonly assumed, it does not imply the irrelevance of management action. Management decides how to address the opportunities and challenges clusters present. This point will be illustrated by the following case studies. The cases were developed over the past five years in several companies through research and participant observation and data analysis, which were supplemented by semi-structured interviews (Punch, 2005).

The cases do not aim to "prove" the theory, an objective for which larger-scale empirical studies may be more suitable, but rather to fill the application gap for management and provide evidence that may suggest a new focus in strategic management thinking.

CASE STUDY 1: ANATOMY OF A VEHICLE CLUSTER WITH INTENSIVE COMMUNICATION AMONG PLAYERS

The first case study deals with a leading manufacturer of rail vehicles in one of the strongest German clusters. In this sector, the German export share of the world market was 25 percent in 2003, larger than the average German world market share of this product (10.6 percent) by a factor of 2.4.

In terms of the four dimensions of Porter's diamond—competitors of a company, customers, suppliers, and institutions—until a short while ago, two global players and half a dozen smaller manufacturers located in Germany were producing the final product. On average, the German market alone has constituted about 20 percent of overall global sales volume over the last few years. The industry is supported by at least 30 associations, institutes, and technical training establishments. According to the cluster concept, it is not surprising that the supplier side is also very strongly represented.

In this case, we studied the supply structure of the leading manufacturer in the cluster. We studied the 30 largest suppliers, who also supplied the three most important competitors of the firm. Twenty of these core suppliers were from Germany, five were from Austria or Switzerland, and only five were not located in the German-speaking area.

These suppliers, who sold their components to all the major players in this industry, were invited to participate in a "reverse rating." They were asked to evaluate their four most important customers with respect to ten dimensions. In six dimensions the suppliers rated their customers similarly. In four dimensions, though, significant deviations among them appeared. The German company located within the same cluster as most of the suppliers was evaluated more positively for the "communication with suppliers," "supplier development," and "knowledge about the supplier" dimensions than its international competitors located outside the cluster. The various suppliers' evaluations of their international customers revealed only minimal deviation between these non-cluster firms.

Conclusion

A typical feature of a leading cluster is that the leading suppliers are also anchored in the cluster, such as in this case. There was good mutual knowledge and intensive communication within the cluster. However, in this case study, it is noteworthy that for the "cooperation/partnership" dimension no deviation was evident among the four companies assessed by their common suppliers. This shows that the company located within the cluster did not consistently exploit its advantage of having a better relationship with suppliers.

Establishing personal contact through informal events is one technique used to make teams work well together, for instance in new product development projects. Typically, in a cluster, such "intimacy" already exists due to the employees sharing the same educational background, for instance. Thus, clusters create opportunities but these opportunities must be actively seized, which the firm in the case study above did not do. The case study below illustrates how a firm actively used its cluster location successfully.

CASE STUDY 2: COOPERATION WITH SUPPLIERS IN A CLUSTER LEADS TO PRODUCTIVITY GAINS

The company in this second case, which has won many prizes for innovation, is located within a sectoral agglomeration. It is a manufacturer of milled metal products, a sector where Germany has a world market share of 12 percent, hence holding third position according to the export statistics. This firm's home region is in one of the clusters identified in the study by Brenner (2004).

Case company 2 is the world market leader for a particular alloy and one of its largest competitors is located only 30 kilometers away in the same cluster. The second largest manufacturer, an American company, had to apply for creditor protection under Chapter 11. The world market share of the company in the case was relatively stable at 11 percent by the end of the 1990s, but rose sharply to 17 percent between 1997 and 2002. Although global demand decreased by 15 percent during the same period, this company was able to increase its production by a further 6 percent against this market trend.

If one observes the procurement structure of the company, it is striking that 85 percent of its purchasing volume is sourced within a radius of 50 kilometers. Almost all of its machine equipment is manufactured in this region as well. The exceptions were two Italian machines, which had been purchased from the assets of a bankrupt French competitor.

In the present case, the case study firm wanted to analyze how the costs for a specific production step could be reduced. In the context of global sourcing, the first consideration was to find economically viable suppliers for an important consumable, because it accounted for 70 percent of costs. Six of the eight potential suppliers for this consumable were within the cluster. Testing the material of one of the non-local suppliers resulted in serious damage to the company's equipment, and its engineers were reluctant to try out any more new suppliers. The firm decided on a specific, partner-oriented strategy of cooperation with its traditional supplier. Such a strategy can best be implemented in a cluster.

A joint project was initiated among:

- the buyer, as the user of the consumable (the case company);
- the manufacturer of the consumable whose costs should be reduced;
- the manufacturer of the machine on which the material was used; and
- a research institute, which would support the necessary tests.

The team formulated a target for reducing consumption and costs linked to the following agreement: if the productivity target was not reached, the supplier would have to lower its price. In the end, this constellation resulted in a win–win situation for the participants. The buyer reduced its costs while the manufacturer of the consumable gained, for the first time, an opportunity to use its own testing plant thanks to its cooperation with the machine manufacturer.

The results underline the importance of several organizations, all of which are well integrated with one another, comprising one localized value chain. The cost-efficiency of the newly developed consumable is linked to the entire context, including the type of machine used. It is unlikely to perform in a similar way in a completely different (application) context, such as with a foreign competitor that uses different equipment. The literature refers to the "technology transfer paradox" (Gertler, 1993). Added to this is the need to conduct the tests on the same physical machine with all the parties working at the same geographical location, namely, where the test unit is installed.

Conclusion

Within a cluster, forms of cooperation are possible which are not available to partners scattered far and wide without unduly taxing effort. Partner-oriented projects are a good example. Systematically searching for partnering opportunities within the cluster and implementing such cooperation agreements is at the core of a cluster strategy.

The cases below consider two companies, which, unlike those in the first two case studies, do not belong to strong sector clusters.

CASE STUDY 3: RISKS TO THE COMPETITIVE POSITION OF COMPANIES OUTSIDE CLUSTERS

Case 3 deals with a German oil-field equipment supplier and illustrates the problems that can arise due to remoteness from clusters. The strongest cluster, comprising well over 5,000 companies, is located in Houston, Texas. Aberdeen, Scotland, with over 1,000 companies, is second in importance and can be termed "the oil capital of Europe." The German agglomeration in Celle registers about 60 firms.

The company in Case 3 has seven major competitors, among which the American firms are clearly dominant and include the world market leader. In terms of institutions, the American Petroleum Institute is the main standardization body. On the demand side, the firm in Case 3 has a very close relationship with one customer, from whose repair department the firm originated in the first place. Meanwhile, both companies have been taken over by a foreign group.

Remoteness from the main clusters and the consequences of this can be clearly demonstrated by analysis of the sourcing structure: 55 percent of goods purchased by the Case 3 company were classified as highly specialized, including, for instance, pumps that are made just for the oil industry. Only a single home supplier, which accounted for about 3 percent of purchasing volume, was supplying this strategic category of goods. The remaining 97 percent of the externally sourced specially made parts came from abroad, primarily from the strongest cluster in the United States. An "inverse supply structure" is present, which is exactly the opposite of Cases 1 and 2, where almost all specialized suppliers were located in the home cluster.

In the present case there were supply problems, including delays and non-adherence to the specifications established at the time of ordering. Repeated trips to the cluster in the United States did not improve the situation. Even delegating a permanent agent to the cluster in Houston failed to solve the problem.

Conclusion

Companies anchored outside strong sector clusters must be regarded as marginal firms. It may be possible for such marginal firms to exist in niches. However, it may be difficult for peripheral companies to obtain a leading position in terms of technology or a significant world market share when their most important competitors are the "preferred customers" of the core suppliers located in a foreign cluster.

CASE STUDY 4: SALES GROWTH AFTER JOINING A CLUSTER

The company in Case 4 may be described as a mixture of trading house and technical services provider, providing end customers with sophisticated products as well as on-site installation. The steel parts are used in industrial buildings.

After changing over to sourcing its main product from a cluster-based firm rather than from an isolated manufacturer, the company was able to increase sales by 30 percent. This increase was not due only to the cluster effect—an increase in sales staff also played a role. However, successfully tapping the cluster provided the basic prerequisites for this improvement.

When the Case Study 4 company signed a new contract, the new partner was a company which focuses on its core competencies and was anchored in a cluster. Importantly, instead of the end product, only an intermediate product is made by the large core firm. The intermediate product is then further

refined by small suppliers. Six companies, all of which are located in the immediate vicinity of the main factory, qualified for this processing work. Owing to the high transportation costs of this steel product, it is only possible to allocate this work among companies located in a small area.

Sourcing the products from a regional network of suppliers rather than from an integrated company created many advantages for the buyer. First, the processing companies are largely interchangeable and hence have to compete for orders. Cost and efficiency advantages are thus transferred quickly. Secondly, the competitive situation led to differentiation efforts on the part of the small processing companies, even in the first year of the new model being put into practice. Thus, for instance, one company offered a surface treatment that made it possible to use the product under unfavorable environmental conditions with high humidity. This is a typical example of innovative force created through competition in a cluster, which in turn leads to an expansion of the market and therefore to a win–win situation for all participants.

Conclusion

Within the cluster, the value chain is more strongly differentiated and is characterized by companies that compete with one another. Such a competitive structure can contribute to lower costs and higher innovative force. From this perspective, it is advisable to procure products from a cluster-based supplier instead of from an isolated company, all other things being equal.

IMPLICATIONS OF CLUSTERS FOR MANAGEMENT

The four case studies illustrate various aspects of the practical relevance of a cluster perspective for companies. The spatial concentration of competitive suppliers has repeatedly become evident. This finding may also alert strategists to the necessity of closely monitoring supply markets as a factor in strategic decisions. Further, it has been possible to observe that cooperation as well as productivity and innovation advantages have emerged in clusters. Clearly, the cluster phenomenon deserves a space in managers' decision making.

Managers need to ascertain whether their firms are located in a cluster or not. Firms located outside a strong industry cluster may need to link up with the cluster. Avoiding the home market of the company's strongest competitors would be the wrong approach. Another option would be to find a niche.

From a portfolio perspective, firms outside a cluster may be candidates for divestiture.

Firms anchored in strong industry clusters must take advantage of their location. Rather than ignoring their cluster through undifferentiated global sourcing, for instance, firms should actively search for partnering opportunities with local firms (Steinle and Schiele, 2008). Finally, the cluster approach has substantial implications for decisions regarding firm relocations. If a new location is needed, moving into a regional cluster in the host market may be the preferable option.

Above all it is clear that, contrary to the prematurely proclaimed "death of distance," proximity matters and is a factor that deserves attention in strategic management. The cluster approach is one way to operationalize proximity.

References

Baptista, R. (2003). "Productivity and the density of regional clusters," in Bröcker, J., Dohse, D. and Soltwedel, R. (Eds), *Innovation Clusters and Interregional Competition,* Springer, Berlin, pp. 163–81.

Brenner, T. (2004), *Local Industrial Clusters: Existence, Emergence, and Evolution,* Routledge, London.

Breschi, S. and Lissoni, F. (2001), "Knowledge spillovers and local innovation systems: a critical survey," *Industrial and Corporate Change,* Vol. 10 No. 4, pp. 975–1005.

Ciccone, A. and Hall, R. E. (1996), "Productivity and the density of economic activity," *American Economic Review,* Vol. 86 No. 1, pp. 54–70.

Crevoisier, O. (2004), "The innovative milieu approach: towards a territorialized understanding of the economy?" *Economic Geography,* Vol. 80 No. 4, pp. 367–79.

Fabiani, S. and Pellegrini, G. (1998), "Uanalisi quantitativa delle imprese nei distretti industriali italiani: redditività, produttività e costo del lavoro" ("A quantitative analysis of the firms in industrial districts: profitability, productivity and labour costs"), *L'Industria. Rivista di economia e politica industriale,* Vol. 19 No. 4, pp. 811–31.

Feldman, M. P. (1999), "The new economics of innovation, spillovers and agglomeration: a review of empirical studies," *Economy Innovation New Technology,* Vol. 8, pp. 5–25.

Gertler, M. S. (1993), "Implementing advanced manufacturing technologies in mature industrial regions: towards a social model of technology production," *Regional Studies,* Vol. 27 No. 7, pp. 665–80.

Hermes Lab (2000), *Check-Up economico finanziario dei distretti industriali. Rapporto esplorativo sui risultati economici dei distretti industriali italiani 1997–1998 (Economic and Financial Check-up of the Industrial Districts),* Club dei Distretti Industriali, Montebelluna.

Jarzabkowski, P. and Wilson, D. C. (2006), "Actionable strategy knowledge: a practical perspective," *European Management Journal,* Vol. 24 No. 5, pp. 348–67.

Marshall, A. (1961), *Principles of Economics. An Introductory Volume,* 9th (variorum) ed., Macmillan, London.

Porter, M. E. (1998), *On Competition,* Harvard Business School Press, Boston, MA.

Punch, K. (2005), *Introduction to Social Research. Quantitative and Qualitative Approaches,* 2nd ed., Sage, Thousand Oaks, CA.

Schiele, H. (2003), *Der Standort-Faktor. Wie Unternehmen durch regionale Cluster Produktivität und Innovationskraft steigern (The Location Factor[[check]]. How Firms Increase their Productivity and Power of Innovation through Regional Clusters),* Wiley-VCH, Weinheim.

Sim, T. (2006), "Supply clusters: a key to China's cost advantage," *Supply Chain Management Review,* Vol. 10 No. 2, pp. 46–51.

Steinle, C. and Schiele, H. (2002), "When do industries cluster? A proposal on how to assess an industry's propensity to concentrate at a single region or nation," *Research Policy,* Vol. 31, pp. 849–58.

Steinle, C. and Schiele, H. (2008), "Limits to global sourcing? Strategic consequences of dependency on international suppliers: cluster theory, resource-based view and case studies," *Journal of Purchasing and Supply Management,* Vol. 14 (forthcoming).

Steinle, C., Schiele, H. and Mietzner, K. (2007), "Merging a firm-centred and a regional policy perspective for the assessment of regional clusters: concept and application of a 'dual' approach to a medical technology cluster," *European Planning Studies,* Vol. 15 No. 2, pp. 235–51.

Tallman, S., Jenkins, M., Henry, N. and Pinch, S. (2004), "Knowledge, clusters, and competitive advantage," *Academy of Management Review,* Vol. 29 No. 2, pp. 258–71.

van der Linde, C. (2003), "The demography of clusters—findings from the cluster meta-study," in Bröcker, J., Dohse, D. and Soltwedel, R. (Eds), *Innovation Clusters and Interregional Competition,* Springer, Berlin, pp. 130–49.

Vanhaverbeke, W. (1992), *The Tufted Carpets Industry in Belgium,* IESE, Barcelona.

Identifying Valuable Resources

Cliff Bowman
Cranfield School of Management

Veronique Ambrosini
Cranfield School of Management

INTRODUCTION

The resource-based view of the firm argues that an organization can be regarded as a bundle of resources (Barney, 1991; Amit and Shoemaker, 1993), and that resources that are valuable, rare, imperfectly imitable and imperfectly substitutable (the VRIN criteria; Barney, 1991) are an organization's main source of sustainable competitive advantage from which sustained performance results. The resource-based view (RBV) has received considerable attention; however, empirical work, as well as the dissemination of the view to a managerial audience, has been limited. This has been hampered partly by the difficulties in operationalizing the view. In particular it is difficult to identify resources within a firm if there is no agreed definition of what "valuable" means (Barney, 2001; Priem and Butler, 2001). Hence the RBV does little to inform managers about how they might identify these key assets. Hoopes, Madsen, and Walker (2003) suggest that "concentrating on value and inimitability gets to the heart of the RBV" (2003, 890). Valuable resources give advantage to the firm today, and inimitability addresses how sustainable this advantage might be over time.[1]

The aim of this paper is to survey the RBV literature and try to clarify what is meant by "valuable" resources, and to set out how such resources could be identified within the firm.

We begin by reviewing the range of definitions of "valuable resources" proposed in the RBV literature. To summarize this literature, a valuable

resource is a resource that permits premium pricing, or enables costs to be lowered relative to competitors. Thus the key aspect of a resource is its use value, i.e., how it impacts on customers' perception of utility and on unit cost (Bowman and Ambrosini, 2000). In the next section we distinguish between the *identification* of a valuable resource, and the *valuation* of that resource. We then set out some of the major difficulties encountered in assessing the value of a resource in monetary terms. We follow this investigation by arguing that despite all of these problems it is still worth trying to attempt to identify resources in order to develop insights into the sustainability of a firm's resource base and, as a corollary, into the firm's sustainable competitive advantage. Our approach focuses on the use value of resources, their utility in the processes of firm value creation, and their consequent impact on profit flows. Our intention is to develop an approach to the identification of resources that recognizes the theoretical difficulties involved. Hence, as a result this may facilitate empirical work and enhance theoretical development and the development of normative prescriptions that may enhance the wider adoption by managers of some of the insights generated by the RBV.

WHAT IS A VALUABLE RESOURCE?

We know that resources must be simultaneously valuable, rare, inimitable, and non-substitutable to be a source of sustainable competitive advantage

Reprinted from *European Management Journal* 25, no. 4 (2007), pp. 320–29.

(Barney, 1991). While this is well acknowledged by RBV advocates, there is, however, not a clear understanding of what "valuable" means within the view. In what follows we have reviewed the definitions of "valuable" in the RBV literature.

Barney states that a valuable resource "must enable a firm to do things and behave in ways that lead to high sales, low costs, high margins, or in other ways add financial value to the firm" (1986, 658). He later adds that "resources are valuable when they enable a firm to conceive of or implement strategies that improve its efficiency and effectiveness" (1991, 105). In the same paper he suggests that a valuable resource "exploits opportunities and/or neutralizes threats in a firm's environment" (1991, 105). Priem and Butler (2001) acknowledge the importance of Barney's (1991) original definitions, but they add that "most researchers have defined any new terms of interest without formally specifying the original, underlying RBV terms. Indeed, in much of the conceptual and empirical RBV work, researchers have either paraphrased Barney's (1991) RBV statements or simply cited his article without augmented definition" (2001, 23–24).

Amit and Schoemaker (1993) and Collis and Montgomery (1995) take a market orientation, an approach supported by Bogner and Thomas (1994) and Verdin and Williamson (1994). Amit and Shoemaker (1993) suggest that resources are valuable in relation to a specific market, and Collis and Montgomery (1995) suggest that "a valuable resource must contribute to the production of something customers want at a price they are willing to pay" (1995, 120). This position was also recently adopted by Peteraf and Bergen (2003) when they linked value to specific product markets: a resource's value is ". . . derive[d] from its application in product markets. It traces back from the ultimate satisfaction of customer needs" (2003, 1028).

Other contributors have emphasized the notion of the "economic value" of the resource: a valuable resource "enabl[es] the firm to do things that lead to economic value" (Fiol, 1991, 195) or a valuable resource is a resource that has ". . . some capacity to generate profits and prevent losses" (Miller and Shamsie, 1996, 520). Combs and Ketchen (1999) have a similar view when they specifically link the source of profits to premium pricing: ". . . valuable, meaning buyers are willing to purchase the resources' outputs at prices significantly above

their costs" (1999, 869). Finally, Hoopes, Madsen, and Walker (2003) return to the notion of rents and economic profits: "a valuable resource enables a firm to improve its market position relative to competitors. For example, resources acquired at a price below their discounted net present value can generate rents" (2003, 890), and Bowman and Ambrosini (2003) stress the importance of rent capture: "a resource is valuable to the firm if it generates rents that can be captured by the firm" (2003, 291) and "a resource must not only generate rents but ex-ante limits to competition also need to be present in order to prevent costs from offsetting the rents" (2003, 291).

Synthesizing from these definitions, most of which are complementary, we can conclude that a valuable resource must generate in some way a rent stream from a product market, and it therefore must contribute or be involved in some way in the creation of a product or service that has use value to customers. In most of these definitions resources have a *current* value based on an existing rent stream, and, reflecting upon the notions of *economic* value in some of these definitions, the resource must contribute to firm profits in excess of the cost of capital. This suggests that valuable resources are likely to permit premium pricing, or enable costs to be lowered, or drive additional profitable growth and this in turn implies that some notion of *relative* firm performance is being invoked. However, resources generate rents that may not in fact lead through to improve firm profitability. Following Coff (1999), rents may be appropriated by other stakeholders through the exercise of their bargaining power. So a resource-endowed firm may actually display indifferent profit performance in comparison to rival firms. Note that these stakeholders need not be involved in supplying or providing resources; their ability to capture rent may be unrelated to their contribution to the firm's performance.

This being said, these definitions, while helping our understanding of what "valuable" means still leave many questions and dilemmas that have yet to be resolved. We need to be able to distinguish between the need to *identify* resources that are valuable, and the related problem of resource *valuation*. Before we consider some of the problems of resource valuation we would like to note that we use the term "resource" in its broad sense (Barney, 1991) and hence it includes activities, capabilities, etc.

VALUING RESOURCES: THE KEY PROBLEMS

We explore below the problems associated with resource valuation. Then we suggest that attempting to value resources may not be at this stage a fruitful avenue to pursue due to some of the complexities we explore and that we should concentrate on attempting to *identify* resources.

Rent Attribution

In the resource-based view valuable resources generate rents, and rents from valuable resources derive from asymmetry in resource endowment, rarity, limited transferability, and appropriability (Amit and Schoemaker, 1993). In this sense, the rent value of a resource is an absolute amount, and does not require us to compare the resource, or the firm that possesses it, with other firms. However, this does not mean that the rent stream of resources is easy to identify as firm performance is based on a complex pattern of inter-linked, context-specific factors, and a single specific resource is unlikely to be isolatable as the sole source of firm performance (Dierickx and Cool, 1989). Furthermore, as we will develop later, a firm may be endowed with rent-generating resources but its profits may be unremarkable. This could be because (*a*) the rents are captured by resource suppliers (Coff, 1999), or (*b*) the positive impacts of the resources are counteracted by the presence of competitive disadvantages (Powell, 2001). Another dilemma ensues: Are we valuing a specific resource or a bundle of resources?

Valuing a Resource or Resources?

As argued by many authors (Dierickx and Cool, 1989; Lippman and Rumelt, 2003; Verdin and Williamson, 1994), the value of a resource is often contingent upon the presence of other resources. Moreover, not only is there co-specialization among resources (Lippman and Rumelt, 2003), many resources have value only in a particular context (Castanias and Helfat, 1991), and what works in one context may not be as effective in another. All this compounds the problem of resource valuation as it means that the effect of the resource, its impact, is moderated by the presence of complementary resources.

Past, Present, or Future Value?

Beyond the questions of rent attribution and resource complementarity, when trying to tackle the problem of resource valuation we also need to address whether we are interested in past, present, or future value. One can argue that the most reliable valuation of a resource would be its *past* contribution. Assessing the *present* value of a resource could be undertaken, first, from the perspective of its current impact on cost and revenue flows, or, second, its current value as an investment, which would require tracking its impact on future revenue and cost streams, which will be at best informed guesses. Valuing future cash streams, like "strategy" itself, is "an adventure into the unknown" (McGee, 2003, 415). Resources may change over time, their value can be altered by management decisions, for instance, or even if they do not change, their positive impact may decline or indeed increase due to exogenous or endogenous changes.

Objective or Subjective Valuations?

This leads us to a further issue: Are we seeking for an objective valuation, or a subjective assessment of a resource's value? For example, we may value a resource in its current context as $x, which could at least in principle be established against some explicit criteria, but an entrepreneur may be able to spot a far more effective context for the resource, and would be prepared to pay a sum greater than $x for it. This suggests that value is in the eye of the beholder, or should we assume this entrepreneur could employ the same assessment criteria as us, the difference being her tacit knowledge about other opportunities?

We could suppose that most executives would derive a valuation in fairly intuitive ways. For example, an executive may have a well-formed insight into the "business model" of the firm. This executive may intuitively understand the significance and importance of certain activities, individuals, relationships, etc. This insight may have been formed through several years of experience of working in the firm, or it may be the result of some diagnostic heuristics this executive has developed over time that enable him to distill the essential processes in a firm. These are perhaps necessarily imprecise, and impressionistic valuations of resources or potential resources. Differences in subjective valuation would form the basis of resource "picking" activity where resources were separable from the firm.

Investors are usually attracted to a firm in the expectation of future profits, but their expectations are based on their perceived risk (Chatterjee, Wiseman, Fiegenbaum, and Devers, 2003) or on judgments about the firm's future, the future state of the firm's product markets, likely competitor behavior, etc. Moreover, typically they can only invest in the firm as a gestalt; they cannot invest in specific current resources or hoped-for future resources. So the firm as a whole is appraised as an investment, which factors in not only the perceived current stock of resources but also prospects for future resource enhancements and current and future competitive disadvantages, "factors and processes that impede the development of or offset the effects of such advantages" (West and DeCastro, 2001, 418). As one of the typical features of resources that are inimitable over a significant time period is that they are embedded within the firm, there is thus no market for the resource that we can readily turn to in order to establish a market-based valuation.

The Costs of Resources

If we were to attempt a monetary valuation of a resource, from a shareholder perspective we would need to balance the positive impact of the resource with its procurement, development, and operating costs. If resources are "bought rather than built" the acquisition cost of the resource may well be clearly measurable, and for some "built" resources, such as patents, it may also be possible to attribute development costs. However, for many valuable resources like tacit knowledge or organizing routines (Kogut and Zander, 1992), tracing their development costs may be complicated. When examining the cost of a resource we must also think not only of acquisition and development costs but also of the ongoing costs associated with owning and deploying the resource. As we noted earlier, rents may be captured by, for example, employees in the form of high relative wages or in managerial salaries and benefits (Coff, 1999).

Shareholder Value and the Cost of Capital

In accordance with the RBV we assume that within a capitalist economy production is undertaken in the pursuit of profit. In other words, resources are a form of investment, and what is key is their contribution to shareholder value. We have explained that it is immensely difficult to isolate the profit contribution of a resource from the complex agglomeration of resources and other assets that typify the firm. A further complexity is introduced when we focus on shareholder value, which is the "cost of capital," the opportunity cost or the rate of return that a firm would have been able to earn had it invested in some other avenue at the same risk level. Indeed some strategists argue that it is not sufficient for firms to make profits; they also have to create "economic value," which can be defined as a level of profitability above the cost of capital (after tax-earnings minus the opportunity cost of capital). Hence the question: Should "costs" include the cost of capital and, if so, what variant of this cost is appropriate?

Why Be Concerned about Valuing Resources?

Given the extent of the difficulties that resource valuation poses it is worth asking the question: Why should we endeavor to value resources? In view of the numerous difficulties listed above, one can only suggest that resources will resist any attempt at precise valuation. However, in practice, managers need to, at the very least, understand the approximate value of the resources in their care. If one subscribes to the RBV explanation of the sources of sustained advantage, it would seem essential for managers to be able to identify the extant resources available to the firm. This knowledge should allow researchers and practitioners to better understand how to sustain and develop competitive advantage, and it may help managers exploit their firm's resources more extensively. At least armed with these insights, executives would be able to avoid inadvertently destroying resources through inappropriate action. It is very difficult to manage for shareholder value unless one knows which resources or resource systems are currently delivering performance. One could argue that many executives establish approximate resource valuations based on insights and tacit knowledge they may have acquired through experience (Castaniat and Helfat, 2001). However, we could also suggest that managers' perceptions are often inaccurate (Mezias and Starbuck, 2003) and hence that it may be useful to make some suggestions that would facilitate the identification and valuation of resources.

The difficulties involved in attempting to attach a monetary valuation to a resource or resources suggest that this is not a fruitful endeavor. However, it should be more feasible to be able to *identify* valuable resources, or at least candidates for VRIN resource status, based on their role in delivering firm profits. With this aim in mind we propose a workable approach to resource *identification* that may help us progress both the academic developments of the RBV, and its wider adoption within the practitioner community. The resource valuation approach we propose is based on the current performance of the firm in specific product markets. Identification of valuable resources would be a first step in enabling these resources to be deliberately managed. The resources identified are valuable in a specific sense: they help produce a margin advantage for the firm in a specific product market.

Toward a Workable Approach to Resource Identification

The RBV is essentially a theory to explain performance differences between firms, and it is assumed that these firms are competing in similar or the same product market. Valuable and rare resources generate competitive advantage, with competitive advantage being the means through which the firm can achieve superior profits. As Figure 1 shows, competitive advantage leads to above-average profit performance in the industry (Arend, 2004). This means that the RBV is concerned with competing, and hence with *relative* performance (the search for "superior" performance in comparison to competitors) and therefore any definition of "valuable" must address *relative* performance. This suggests that if we assume a set of competing firms, there will be an average level of performance that could act as the benchmark.

In Figure 1, building on the literature and the argument we have developed so far, we set out a model showing how resources can generate competitive advantage and positively impact profit flow. It represents the firm's operations in relation to a specific

Figure 1   The Impact of Resources on Profit Flow

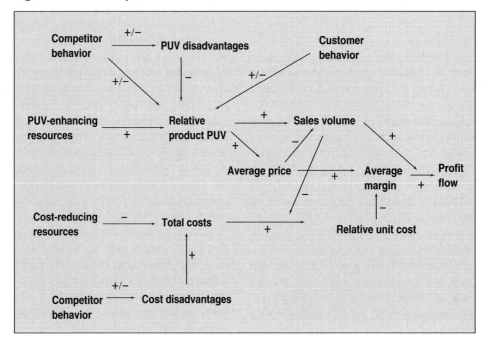

market, and not the firm in its entirety. We take as given that the firm is managed in the interests of its owners, the shareholders, and that owners invest for returns above the "average," however that may be estimated. All the main components of the figure are relative to the "average" firm in the industry.

Valuable resource impacts are mediated through the realm of use values, which are properties of products and services that provide utility (Bowman and Ambrosini, 2000). Valuable resources may increase revenues, but they operate indirectly through, say, improvements in product design that are valued by customers. Similarly, they may have the effect of reducing input costs but this is achieved via, for example, better negotiating skills with suppliers. In other words valuable resources impact indirectly on both the supply side, by reducing input costs (Lippman and Rumelt's [2003] "cost"), and demand side of the firm, by increasing perceived use value (PUV) (Lippman and Rumelt's [2003] "simple rents"). Hence if we are to understand a resource's value, we need to engage with the domain of use values.

We assume an extant stock of valuable resources that has resulted from resource creation processes that may have been deliberate or emergent. Valuable resources, singly or in combination, confer use value or utility benefits on the operations of the firm. These benefits can impact to reduce relative unit costs or they can cause improvements in the relative use value perceived by the customers of the firm's products or services (Bowman and Ambrosini, 2000). These are broadly in line with Peteraf and Barney's (2003) "efficiency" benefits.

The improvements in relative PUV can impact either on sales volumes achieved or on prices that can be charged. This reflects the benefits of product differentiation that can either increase sales volumes, assuming competitive prices, or can increase margins where premium prices can be charged (Porter, 1980). Premium prices, assuming unit costs are equivalent to the average firm, can lead to enhanced margins and, assuming average sales volumes, this should lead to above-average profit flow. The revenues captured by the firm from customers (Sales volumes × Unit price) are Lippman and Rumelt's (2003) "simple rents."

The potential benefits to investors of having valuable resources, in terms of returns on their investments, depend *inter alia* on the costs incurred in developing or acquiring these resources. For instance, an acquired resource, like a brand, may well confer PUV benefits that could permit premium prices, but the costs of acquiring the brand may well result in no net increase in returns on shareholder's capital. In this case the rents that the brand can generate have been capitalized and captured by the firm that sold the brand.

The profit flow benefits of PUV-enhancing resources are not straightforward if the benefits are manifested in improved sales volumes. In order for enhanced sales volumes to impact profits, the firm needs to have valuable resources enabling it to reduce its capital costs, or develop experience advantage that would impact on variable costs. So the benefits of resources that enhance sales volumes may need to have a resultant impact in the creation of cost-reducing resources in the form of scale or experience advantage. Alternatively, taking a dynamic view, if the rate at which sales revenues increase outstrips the rate the associated costs of sales are increasing, profit flows will expand.

This suggests that there may be precursor or antecedent factors that do not directly impact to improve margins; their impact is consequent on the development or exploitation of other valuable resources, like large-scale production units. Similarly, although firm reputation is often cited as a valuable resource, it is more likely to be the *outcome* of other factors that helped to create it, e.g., groundbreaking product designs, excellent quality assurance processes. Thus, valuable resources can be the results of a series of factors configured together *simultaneously* to deliver advantage. They may also be connected sequentially over time where, for instance, excellent quality systems may result in more reliable products and lower scrap and rework costs. Here the resources impact positively on both PUV and unit costs.

Before embarking on the discussion of the "disadvantages" in Figure 1, we can suggest that there are essentially three ways in which valuable resources can create competitive advantage and ultimately enhanced profit flows. In Figure 2 we adapt the Value, Price, and Cost framework of Hoopes et al. (2003) to illustrate these alternative competitive strategies. We have on the left of the figure the average firm, with products delivering average perceived use value (PUV), average prices (P), and average levels of cost (C). In order to relate perceived use value,

Figure 2   Three Resource-Based Competitive Strategies

CS: average consumer surplus, CS+: above average consumer surplus, CS++: well above average consumer surplus
M: average margin, M+: above average margin
C: average cost, C–: below average cost
$PUV: average perceived use value, $PUV+: above average PUV
P: average price, P–: below average price, P+: above average price

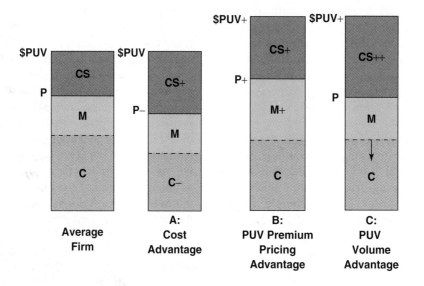

which is a subjective evaluation, with the objective monetary variables of price and cost, we have "monetized" perceived use value: the height of the column ($PUV) represents the price the customer would be *prepared to pay* for this product (see Collis and Montgomery [1995] or and Bowman and Ambrosini [2000] for an explanation of this approach). The columns refer to a single product/customer relationship, thus the costs are unit costs. In the case of the average firm, consumer surplus would be the difference between $PUV and P (labeled CS), and the average margin would be P − C, labeled M in the figure. CS+ represents above-average consumer surplus, and C++ would be well-above-average consumer surplus.

Exploiting Cost Advantage

This would be equivalent to Porter's (1980) cost leadership strategy. The firm delivers average or equivalent product perceived use value compared to rival firms, but the firm's unit costs are lower than the industry average. Prices are average for the industry, leading to above-average margins, and superior

profit flows. An example of a company achieving competitive advantage this way would be Ryan Air. They have cost-efficient systems allowing them to maximize plane utilization, they use secondary airports, and have stripped down non-essential services that have little if any impact on customers' PUV on short-haul flights. The Ryan Air recipe was a variation on the Southwest Airlines strategy, adapted and extended for a European context. Initially, the combination of systems, aircraft utilization, and other configurational advantages gave Ryan Air a cost advantage that did not rely on any resources derived from economies of scale. This is Case A in the figure, where this cost advantage enabled Ryan Air to price below competitors, so customers experienced superior consumer surplus. Over time Ryan Air has grown to the point where it has immense bargaining power over suppliers, particularly Boeing. So the initial resource advantage delivered the margin advantage in A, which over time has been augmented by a scale advantage. As a result they probably now have not only lower prices but better margins than the average European short-haul carrier (i.e., M moves to M+).

Exploiting Perceived Use Value Advantage through Premium Pricing

In Case B the firm's product PUV is higher than the average industry's PUV (PUV+), enabling the firm to charge premium prices (P+). This would be Porter's differentiation strategy. The unit costs are average for the industry, leading to superior margins (M+) and enhanced profit flows. Here in Case B the resource-based advantage enables the firm to offer superior products, but these resources do not result in any increase over average unit costs, hence the margin enhancement.

If the suppliers of these valuable resources were able to bid up their prices, the ongoing costs to the firm would rise, possibly offsetting the margin benefits of premium prices. So here the configuration of resources must be such that there is no net cost penalty involved in delivering superior PUV.

If in providing superior PUV the unit costs were above the industry average, then in order to sustain a margin advantage the firm would need to raise prices accordingly. However, in most markets the higher the price, the lower the resulting sales volume, so if there are scale and experience-based resource advantages to be had in this industry, high premium prices would prevent this firm from achieving these particular resource benefits.

An example of such a company might be Innocent, the purveyor of fruit smoothies. By using only fresh products and clever targeted advertising, their products are perceived to have unique benefits and hence they are able to sell their products at a premium prices.

Exploiting Perceived Use Value Advantage through Superior Sales Volumes

In Case C the firm has a product PUV advantage (PUV+) but elects not to premium-price. If, initially, the firm has average unit costs, there would be no margin advantage. However, the superior PUV would attract more customers and, even if costs remained at the average, the superior sales volumes could lead to superior profit flows (Higher sales × Average margin). A more likely outcome is that the enhanced relative sales volumes would enable the firm to develop scale and experience based resources, e.g., more efficient plant, which would lower unit costs over time and the firm might get a higher margin (the arrow in the figure). An example might be pop music. If we assume the production costs of an unknown performer are more or less the same, the band that has the knack of producing a hit song will earn the label a volume-based PUV advantage. This example also highlights the importance of the timing of contracts for productive inputs. The unknown band is unlikely to be in a position to bargain for an advantageous deal, so the costs to the production company would not be prohibitive. Of course, should the band be subsequently able to re-negotiate their deal with the record company, they may be able to capture a larger share of future rents, assuming naturally they are capable of repeating their recording success.

By focusing on the domain of *use* values inside the firm, this approach can not only help us in identifying resources where the firm is enjoying an enhanced profit flow relative to competitors, it can also help us identify the less straightforward case highlighted by Coff (1999) where generated rents are appropriated by other stakeholders. If we are able to understand what dimensions of the firm's products are particularly valued by clients, and if we are also able to identify areas of relative firm efficiency, even where the rents generated by these valuable resources are appropriated by stakeholders like employees, managers, or suppliers, we can still gain insights into the resource base of the firm.

Competitive Disadvantages

The model in Figure 1 incorporates competitive *disadvantages* that may counteract the positive benefits of resources. They are weaknesses and inadequacies within the firm that have a negative effect on competitive advantage (Arend, 2004). Competitive disadvantages are hence moderating factors in the generation of profits. As explained by Powell (2001) "competitive disadvantage is not merely the non-existence of such [VRIN] resources (which would create economic parity) but rather the failure even to satisfy the minimum success requirements [. . .] required of any firm" (2001, 877). Moreover "if all competitors shared the same weakness and inadequacy it would not be a source of disadvantage. Under such circumstances all firms would suffer on an equal footing" (West and Castro, 2001, 425). A firm can find itself with both valuable resources that can lead to competitive advantage, e.g., they deliver product with high relative PUV (e.g., Caterpillar in large earth-moving equipment in the 1980s) and competitive disadvantages simultaneously (e.g., Caterpillar's high labor costs), and competitive disadvantages may outweigh the positive effects of the valuable resources: "firms may do many things well, but if they do one thing wrong it may negate all the other good" (West and Castro, 2001, 424). For example, the product may be perceived to be superior, but availability may be a problem, or after-sales service could be inferior, below the industry average. For example, local speciality shops such as delicatessens are often seen to offer quality products, but their limited range often pushes time-poor customers to shop in large out-of-town retailers. A further example of disadvantages outweighing competitive advantage could be that of Boo.com. PUV for Boo was high, its range of high-fashion-oriented designer items was sought after, and it benefited from positive word of mouth and editorial comment, but many of its potential customers could not use the Web site because it was too rich in graphics and hence too slow to access, so Boo.com never reached the sales volumes required.

Similarly the resources may enable lower variable costs, e.g., through superior work scheduling systems, which may be counteracted by inefficiencies in some other part of the production process. Moreover, valuable resources may deliver PUV-based competitive advantage that does not lead to profit improvements because of cost disadvantages. Sainsbury's, the British retailer, is recognized for having quality products, a broad choice, and similar prices to its main rival Tesco, but has historically been plagued by high supply chain costs and lower sales volumes compared to Tesco and it cannot achieve the same margins (2.43 percent versus 6 percent in 2005). Firms may also well have valuable resources that allow them to have below-average costs that are unable to deliver margin improvements because of, e.g., sales or marketing weaknesses, leading to inferior relative PUV, that result in the firm having to discount relative prices. Where the provider of a valuable resource is able to appropriate the rents their resource generates, this will be reflected in cost disadvantages for the firm (Lippman and Rumelt, 2003). For example, a "star" consultant

with a wide portfolio of clients may be able to bargain for a large salary and bonus. The question for the firm's management would be whether the *net* impact of this consultant was positive for the firm, i.e., if the overall impact was a net positive for profit flows. We would add that current valuable resources may potentially be sources of competitive disadvantage: if the environment changes and the resources are not modified, they may lead to disadvantage. In other words as Leonard-Barton (1992) explains, today's valuable resources can become tomorrow's core rigidities.

The clear managerial implication is that if the valuable resources that generate advantage can be identified and if the sources of competitive *dis*advantages can also be identified, then even if there were no obvious actions that could be undertaken to enhance the resource stock, then at least if actions were taken to diminish some of the impact of the disadvantages, profits would improve. For instance Marks and Spencer always had strong links with their suppliers and above-average supply chain and retailer systems; however, in the 1990s their women's clothing range was perceived as being outdated and boring. In short, their cost-competitive advantage was outweighed by their lack of sales volume due to their inferior design capability. They have now recognized that design was critical to enhancing their products' PUV and to achieving competitive advantage, and hence they have hired talented designers and they are on the way to recovery.

Thus while many firms (if not all "going concerns") are likely to have at least some valuable resources, the problem is that some of the competitive advantage generated from these resources is moderated by the presence of *dis*advantages.

Exogenous Changes

The model in Figure 1 also incorporates competitor and customer behavior as exogenous variables that can cause the resource stock to become more or less valuable. For instance, changes in competitor behavior can cause relative PUV to increase or decrease, regardless of any actions by the firm, and changes in customer preferences can have a similar relative impact. Car producers are currently facing such a situation with increasing customer interest in the causes and effects of global warming, which are likely to advantage some firms perceived to be addressing a "green" agenda, e.g., Toyota, Honda, while disadvantaging other firms, e.g., GM. Competitors and customers together can also cause the prices charged by the firm to rise or fall relatively, again regardless of the firm's actions, and by definition, if a competitor achieves a lower cost position, this impacts negatively on the *relative* cost position of the focal firm.

Thus the model explains the different ways through which valuable resources can impact on the firm's profit flow, and it incorporates circumstances where firms have resources, but the profit benefits of them are counteracted by competitive disadvantages. It shows how PUV-enhancing resources can impact margins directly by enabling the firm to premium price, or these resources can lead to sales volume increases that can lead to the development of scale and/or experience advantage. It also recognizes that the RBV is a theory of *relative* advantage, which is consistent with the resource-based view, and that exogenous actions by competitors and customers can cause resources to be created or destroyed, again regardless of firm behavior.

In the next section we discuss how, given the definitions of "valuable" set out earlier, we could embark on the empirical identification of valuable resources.

Empirically Identifying Valuable Resources

From Figure 1 resources have value if they impact to either produce superior product/service perceived use value, or if they help reduce relative unit costs. To be precise, valuable resources must be involved in the generation of current revenue streams, and, if their impact is to lower costs, they must be lowering the costs involved in producing that revenue stream. This helps us to be very clear then about activities of the firm that are *not* resources generating competitive advantage. For example, in a manufacturing firm R&D cannot be a resource, nor can training. These activities may be capable of *creating* valuable resources that will impact on PUV or unit cost in the *future,* but currently they are merely a cost to the firm. So, using this approach we can also clearly distinguish between firm resources and "dynamic capabilities" (Teece et al., 1997). Dynamic capabilities create resources; they are not resources themselves

because they are not connected to an identifiable *current* product creation process and a consequent revenue stream.

As we have explained, resources operate in the domain of use values, and therefore we need to interrogate the use value creation processes inside the firm to find valuable resources. A starting point would be an understanding of current customers, and what their perceptions of product use value are. If they are satisfied clients, then assuming we are not competing on price, there must be some dimensions of customer perceived use value that the firm excels in. For instance, it could be after-sales service, or product reliability, or design. If this relative PUV advantage can be reliably and precisely identified (and focus groups may provide this data), then the next step would be to track back inside the firm's processes to uncover the origins of product advantage.

With regard to cost-reducing resources, these could be identified through benchmarking against close rival firms. Where the firm has a competitive cost advantage in a part of the value creation process, this can be the starting point for an investigation into the sources of this advantage. In this way we would uncover a source of relative advantage, which would be a candidate for an RBV resource. To then be assured that the resource was not only valuable but also passed the other VRIN criteria as well is a more difficult exercise, involving rather more judgment than analysis. For example, in assessing "imitability" we would need insights into how the particular resource was created, and we would need to make judgments about the extent of rival firm's capabilities to replicate the resource. As far as assessing substitutability, this may be more straightforward. Taking our use value perspective, if we can understand the use value role or impact of the resource on the creation of PUV, or on the costs of use value creation, it should be possible to determine how else these effects could be achieved.

While it is important to assess resource imitability and substitutability, here we have concentrated on current resources and current advantage rather than deal with building other sources of advantage and envisaging how firms can grow. We have focused on identifying what is currently giving the firm some advantage rather than hypothesizing on the *duration* of this advantage. Insights into the extant resource stock help managers manage today's organization.

They can use these insights to protect these often subtle and vulnerable resources, and they may be able to find new ways to deploy or leverage these resources. The starting point is a deep insight into what actually is delivering advantage and hence the empirical identification by managers of their own firm's resource stock must, in our view, form the basis for a more confident stewardship of the assets in an executive's charge. We would go further and suggest that insights into the extant resource stock, whether they are generated through experience, structured reflection, or appropriate analysis should be the starting point for any strategic interventions. By understanding what is currently giving the firm competitive advantage, and by also being apprised of the nature of the firm's competitive *dis*advantages, executives can implement strategies with a great deal more confidence. In essence, what we are advocating here is a more structured and theoretically grounded approach to the well-known but often badly applied SWOT analysis.

CONCLUSION

Although the value creation is critical to organizational success, there is still some confusion surrounding various aspects of what is meant by "value" and the process of value creation. In this paper we have attempted to bring some clarity into the debate, and in particular we have examined what is a valuable resource and how can it become a coherent concept for both the academic and practitioner communities. We have also explored some problems in operationalizing the RBV, particularly the problem of identifying resources, and we concluded with some suggestions about how this may be done. We have elaborated on the notion of valuable resources, specifying that value is relative and that we should be concerned with current value. We have explained that valuable resources can generate three types of competitive advantage: cost advantage, the ability to premium price, and volume-based advantage. And finally we have explained how unit margin can be used as measure of resource impact. We have also argued that probably all firms have some valuable resources, but the problem is that these often co-exist with competitive *dis*advantages, negating the positive effects of these valuable resources. We have acknowledged that the firm's ability to iden-

tify valuable resources and "to mitigate or eliminate resources weaknesses" (West and DeCastro, 2001, 420) is crucial in the pursuit of superior profit flows. In short we have shown how the concept of "valuable" resource can be operationalized and hence become a meaningful construct for managers to deploy in their quest to outperform their competitors. Throughout, though, we have assumed the perspective of the executive trying to manage the firm in the shareholders' interests. Although investors are not only interested in current profit flows but also interested in profit growth, we have not tackled the problem of identifying and valuing potential resources. This would require a different approach, and would involve *inter alia* the identification and valuation of the firm's dynamic capabilities.

Note

1. Valuable and rare resources, on their own, lead to (temporary) competitive advantage; when inimitability and non-substitutability are also present, we have sustained competitive advantage. A valuable but not rare resource leads to competitive parity. This means that the "V" element is central to the VRIN framework.

References

Amit, R. and Shoemaker, P. (1993) Strategic assets and organizational rents. *Strategic Management Journal* **14,** 33–46.

Arend, R.J. (2004) The definition of strategic liabilities, and their impact on firm performance. *Journal of Management Studies* **41,** 1003–1027.

Barney, J.B. (1991) Firm resources and sustained competitive advantage. *Journal of Management* **17,** 99–120.

Barney, J.B. (2001) Is the resource-based "view" a useful perspective for strategic management research? Yes. *Academy of Management Review* **26,** 41–56.

Bogner, W.C. and Thomas, H. (1994) Core competence and competitive advantage: A model and illustrative evidence from the pharmaceutical industry. In *Competence-Based Competition,* (eds.) G. Hamel and A. Heene. John Wiley and Sons, Chichester.

Bowman, C. and Ambrosini, V. (2000) Value creation versus value capture: Towards a coherent definition of value in strategy. *British Journal of Management* **11,** 1–15.

Bowman, C. and Ambrosini, V. (2003) How the resource-based and the dynamic capability views of the firm inform corporate-level strategy. *British Journal of Management* **14,** 204–289.

Castanias, R.P. and Helfat, C.E. (1991) Managerial resources and rents. *Journal of Management* **17,** 155–171.

Chatterjee, S.R., Wiseman, M., Fiegenbaum, A. and Devers, C.E. (2003) Integrating behavioural and economic concepts of risk into strategic management: The twain shall meet. *Long Range Planning* **36,** 61–79.

Coff, R.W. (1999) When competitive advantage doesn't lead to performance: The resource-based view and stakeholder bargaining power. *Organizational Science* **10,** 119–133.

Collis, D. and Montgomery, C. (1995) Competing on resources: strategy in the 1990s. *Harvard Business Review* **73,** 118–128.

Combs, G. and Ketchen, D. (1999) Explaining interfirm cooperation and performance: Toward a reconciliation of predictions from the resource-based view and organizational economics. *Strategic Management Journal* **20,** 867–888.

Dierickx, I. and Cool, K. (1989) Asset stock accumulation and sustainability of competitive advantage. *Management Science* **35,** 1504–1511.

Fiol, C.M. (1991) Managing culture as a competitive resource: An identity-based view of sustainable competitive advantage. *Journal of Management* **17,** 191–211.

Hoopes, D., Madsen, T. and Walker, G. (2003) Guest editors' introduction to the special issue: Why is there a resource-based view? Toward a theory of competitive heterogeneity. *Strategic Management Journal* **20,** 889–902.

Kogut, B. and Zander, U. (1992) Knowledge of the firm, combinative capabilities, and the replication of technology. *Organization Science* **3,** 383–396.

Leonard-Barton, D. (1992) Core capabilities and core rigidities: A paradox in managing new product development. *Strategic Management Journal* **13,** 111–125.

Lippman, S.A. and Rumelt, R.P. (2003) The payments perspective: Micro-foundations of resource analysis. *Strategic Management Journal* **24,** 903–927.

McGee, J. (2003) Commentary on 'taking strategy seriously,' the rules of evidence and bandwagon effects. *Journal of Management Inquiry* **12,** 414–417.

Mezias, J.M. and Starbuck, W.H. (2003) Studying the accuracy of managers' perceptions: A research odyssey. *British Journal of Management* **14,** 3–17.

Miller, D. and Shamsie, J. (1996) The resource-based view of the firm in two environments: The Hollywood film studios from 1936 to 1965. *Academy of Management Journal* **39,** 519–543.

Peteraf, M.A. and Barney, J.B. (2003) Unraveling the resource-based tangle. *Managerial and Decision Economics* **24,** 309–323.

Peteraf, M. and Bergen, M. (2003) Scanning dynamic competitive landscapes: A market-based and resources-based framework. *Strategic Management Journal* **24,** 1027–1041.

Porter, M.E. (1980) *Competitive Strategy: Techniques for Analysing Industries and Competitors.* Free Press, New York.

Powell, T.C. (2001) Competitive advantage: Logical and philosophical considerations. *Strategic Management Journal* **22,** 875–888.

Priem, R.L. and Butler, J.E. (2001) Is the resource-based "view" a useful perspective for strategic management research? *Academy of Management Review* **26,** 22–40.

Teece, D.J., Pisano, G. and Shuen, S. (1997) Dynamic capabilities and strategic management. *Strategic Management Journal* **18,** 509–533.

Verdin, P.J. and Williamson, P.J. (1994) Core competences, competitive advantage and market analysis: Forging the links. In *Competence-Based Competition,* (eds.) G. Hamel and A. Heene. John Wiley and Sons, Chichester.

West, G.P. and DeCastro, J. (2001) The Achilles' heel of firm strategy: Resource weaknesses and distinctive inadequacies. *Journal of Management Studies* **38,** 417–442.

The Battle of the Value Chains: New Specialized versus Old Hybrids

Gillis Jonk
A. T. Kearney

Martin Handschuh
A. T. Kearney

Sandra Niewiem
A. T. Kearney

Imagine taking a week's vacation in a tiny rural village, with only one store to supply your needs—from food and drink to clothes, hardware, and entertainment. Such temporary simplicity has its attractions—yet sooner or later most of us would happily return to civilization, where we can buy exactly what we want at our favorite niche outlets, on the Internet, or at the mall. Goodbye, simple life; hello, specialization.

This metaphor of the Village Store versus the Internet illustrates how customers have embraced this trend of commercial specialization, demanding and rewarding constantly multiplying permutations of choice. Increasingly, specialized offerings are within almost everyone's reach, and the village store, where it still survives, is an artifact of an earlier era. In fact, the shift toward specialization—driven by globalization, buying via the Internet, modular value chains, and the growth of low-wage economies—is playing out faster than some big companies can adapt. Especially at risk are companies that continue to view their customers in terms of unique buying segments, instead of realizing that today the same customer may demand different varieties of a product or service at different times.

To illustrate this trend we have identified examples of the challenges posed to established firms in various industries as new fronts of specialization emerge. To counter these threats we propose that they adopt a practical approach for discovering where

Reprinted from *Strategy & Leadership* 36, no. 2 (2008), pp. 24–29.

they are likely to be effectively attacked by emerging rivals, and for developing both preemptive first strikes and successful counterattacks. Our recommendation is that established players compete by first considering and then creating a number of specialized value chains. This suggestion contradicts the conventional wisdom that established firms are more competitive if they continued to adjust and augment a single value chain.

WHO IS AT RISK?

As the following examples show, it's not the small, fast-growing focused companies that are at risk; they're often the ones exploiting the opportunity to specialize. Those in danger are well-established leaders, in particular those that cling to old assumptions. Behaviors to watch out for include:

- Serving your customers just as you always have, not realizing these customers are changing their expectations—for example, by wanting newer, faster, and better services and products at the high end, while expecting to get better quality than once might have been expected, and for lower prices, on the low end.

- Attempting to fight back via business process improvement alone, since this is always easier than implementing radical structural changes. Such business process improvement efforts treat the symptoms, not the disease, and they offer no guarantee of success. You may find yourself making continuous process improvements with little to show for it, even as you lose more and more of your business to focused players.

- Not recognizing that things are likely to get worse. Even if today you can cope, tomorrow you may find that focused competitors have poached parts of your business so successfully you lack the resources to fight back.

Here are some typical examples of challenges in various industries that show why competition has gained a foothold and why large existing players find it so difficult to respond.

INFRASTRUCTURE MADE EASY: RETAIL COMPUTER

Once upon a time IBM happily sold laptops and PCs through a class-leading network of retailers; its strength in this channel made competition difficult for new entrants. Then Dell discovered it could bypass the reseller channel altogether by selling online, and in the process allow customers to customize the features of their computer and thus control the price. IBM found itself in a quandary as to how to respond. If it followed Dell down the direct channel route, it would instantly cannibalize its existing reseller channel. However, it couldn't compete using only its resellers because they couldn't afford to configure customized computers and sell them at competitive prices. Such dilemmas are one of several signs that specialization will soon make a competitive challenge and must be addressed.

GLOBALIZATION AND LOW-COST PLAYERS: LIGHT BULBS, AUTOS

In several industries, low-cost players have taken advantage of globalization, new ways to find customers, and specialization. An example is the lighting industry, particularly the lamps market. Until a decade ago, this market was dominated by large and sophisticated players such as General Electric, Osram, and Philips Electronics. These companies built their dominance in part on the strength of being able to supply every conceivable light source to meet every possible lighting need—from basic incandescent lamps in all shapes and wattages to specialty lamps of all kinds, including sophisticated energy-saving lamps.

But as lamps became more sophisticated, they also became more expensive. A high-end energy-saving lamp, for example, can cost 30 times more than a basic incandescent lamp, making transportation costs a smaller fraction of the price tag. New players in China seized this opening to begin exporting halogen and energy-saving lamps to Europe and North America. These entrants focused on producing only the most popular models, avoiding the costs of a more varied line. They also found consumers would accept slightly inferior products at lower prices—for example, cheaper energy-saving lamps that don't come on instantly, but flicker for a few moments before burning at full brightness.

The large do-it-yourself chains and furniture chains such as IKEA happily sell these low-cost lights, while still keeping the full range of lights made by the market leaders on their shelves to satisfy every consumer demand.

The global auto industry provides a dramatic example. In India, the Tata conglomerate is working on the Rs 1-lakh car, which is being designed to cost about $2,275. Sales are anticipated to be millions of cars per model. Clearly this offering will require a specialized value chain not only to engineer, source, produce, and assemble the cars but also to sell and service them.

Initially such a car will compete primarily in India and other emerging world markets—but other low-cost cars are already penetrating the developed world. We can see this from the success of Dacia, with its Logan and MPV car model—attractively priced basic cars sold in Western Europe, with a waiting list longer than many if not all mainstream brand cars.

Can the big automakers serve this low-cost need simply by stripping goodies from cars and selling them with as little service as possible? No, for it is impossible by mere tinkering to compete against a setup that is not only entirely specialized but has huge and appropriate scale just for the low-cost market. This is an example of why specialization is such a potential risk to leading players in industries everywhere; the big players may lead in overall market share, but that doesn't mean they're scaled right to compete in multiple specialized theaters.

MODULARIZATION: SPECIALTY MINERAL WATERS AND NON-ALCOHOLIC BEVERAGES

Modular value chains are another factor in specialization; they help smaller companies overcome their scale disadvantage by tapping into scaled-up parts of the value chains of other companies.

This frequently happens in the consumer goods market segment. Many new and highly differentiated premium products are brought to market—often by relatively small companies. The high-concept mineral waters and non-alcoholic beverages such as Fuji, POM, and VitaminWater are good examples. The companies behind these products have taken advantage of plug 'n play value chains to reduce their scale disadvantage and efficiently bring their products into today's consolidated retail market.

Innovation based on this sort of partnering isn't easy for established fast-moving consumer goods (FMCG) leaders to duplicate—an indication of this is Coca-Cola's $4.1 billion purchase of VitaminWater in the spring of 2007. Yet some are finding ways to do so just the same. Procter & Gamble, for example,

has made it a goal to adopt the entrepreneurial and modular approach toward innovation: its Connect + Develop Web sites reach out to tens of thousands of outside developers and scientists, indicating P&G's willingness to partner when such arrangements are mutually beneficial.

HYBRID VERSUS SPECIALIZED VALUE CHAINS

The difference between a hybrid value chain and a specialized value chain is that a hybrid focuses on the full breadth of the needs of specific customer segments, whereas the specialized value chain focuses on segments of specific customer needs (see Figures 1–3).

How do you know when your hybrid value chain can't compete effectively against specialized competitors? How do you know when there is sufficient potential to warrant the effort of creating multiple specialized chains? Here are some telltale signs:

- Your business segment is having a hard time finding growth, yet focused competitors are gaining ground.
- Internal complexity is rising; customer satisfaction isn't.

Figure 1 Hybrid versus Specialized Value Chains

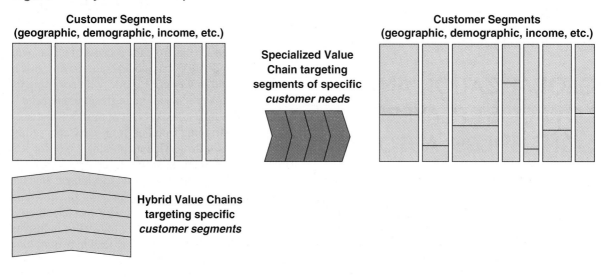

Figure 2 Moving from Hybrid to Specialized Value Chains

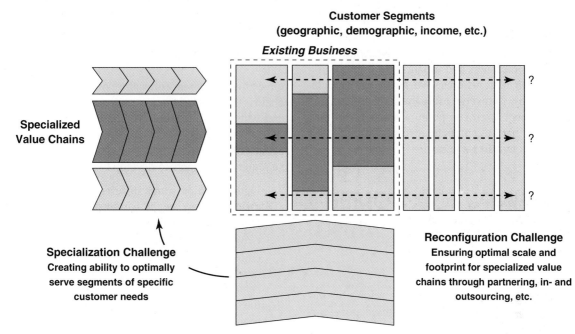

Figure 3 Hybrid versus Specialized Value Chains

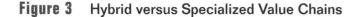

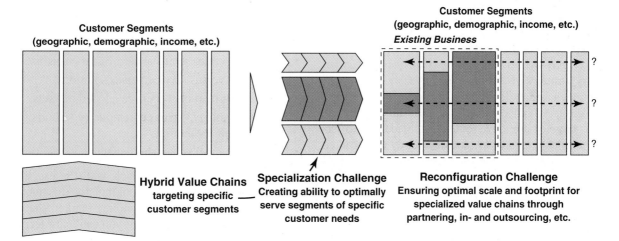

- The potential for horizontal synergies between units can no longer be ignored.
- You need to find external partners, but find more obstacles than opportunities.
- Channel conflicts and price cannibalizations are increasing.

- Customers are being cherry-picked, their loyalty is eroding, and competitive requests for proposals (RFPs) and tender situations are on the rise.

If you're experiencing such symptoms, you may nonetheless be tempted to stay with your hybrid chain, rather than take on the seemingly high-effort exercise of developing specialized chains. Such a shift would require new, often non-traditional organization and governance structures, a thorough analysis of scale versus scope strategies, the pursuit of new customers for the newly specialized chains, and many more interfaces and alliances to manage. Yet it's important to remember that customer expectations are likely to diverge more, rather than less, and that once specialized competitors reach scale, they will be very hard to compete against if your firm is still using its hybrid value chain.

REDEFINING CUSTOMER FOCUS; ORCHESTRATING CANNIBALIZATION

For well-established companies with a long history of success, two aspects of specialization pose particular challenges.

First, customer focus has to be redefined. Instead of trying to figure out how to better serve existing customer segments, the focus shifts. Now it becomes a hunt to uncover segments of specific customer needs that benefit from being served by a more specialized value chain, especially those segments of customer needs that are underserved by the current hybrid value chains. Consider the market entry strategy of the low-cost air carriers. Companies such as EasyJet, Ryan Air, and Southwest didn't look for customers around specific hubs—instead, they targeted attractive routes, and made their offering available to anybody and everybody who wanted no-frills transportation on these routes. For a network carrier, such a switch would represent a radical departure from the decades of building customer bases around hubs and improving connections and services.

This brings us to the second challenge: if a network airline carrier does decide to set up a low-cost operation, it must inevitably cannibalize its existing network operations to make the new unit a success. Mergers and acquisitions can help provide the scale needed for specialization, an example of this being the merger that created Air France–KLM a few years ago.

THE VALUE CHAIN SPECIALIZATION ASSESSMENT

Given the highly strategic nature of specializing value chains, there's obviously a need for assessing where and when parts of the value chain might have to be specialized. This will help evaluate opportunities against other strategic opportunities and threats. To do so requires managers to develop two insights:

Understanding which different segments of specific customer needs would potentially benefit from increased value chain specialization.

Creating strategic business plans for such specialization opportunities that address customer needs, market offerings, competition, and resources. The plans should assess both the impact on the current business and the reconfiguration requirements.

In our experience, evaluating which segments of specific customer needs would gain from value chain specialization requires comprehensive analysis. Typical dimensions to consider are:

- High-end versus midrange versus low-end products and pricing.
- Standard versus semi-standard versus customized.
- Products versus service versus solutions.
- Emerging markets versus developed markets.
- Old technology versus contemporary technology versus new technology.
- Single channel versus multichannel distribution.

Another important approach is to assess the competitive playing field, looking for instances where focused players are gaining market share; they are likely doing something you can learn from. It's also important to search for emerging needs; it may be that a specialized value chain to cater to them effectively doesn't yet exist.

Once opportunities for value chain specialization have been identified, they will have to be strategically evaluated during the regular strategic decision-making processes—for example, by developing business plans.

Understanding the Limitations of Customer Segmentation

One reason companies stick with traditional business optimization in the face of focused competition is that one of key tools for understanding the market—customer segmentation—is no longer as helpful as it used to be.

Most air travelers, for example, don't limit themselves to charter flights, or network flights, or low-cost flights; they treat air travel as a smorgasbord and choose based on their present needs. Likewise, people buying books and CDs from Amazon are also likely to frequent Waterstone's or Barnes & Noble, where they can actually handle books and CDs and also get together with friends for a Starbucks coffee and muffin—that is, a complete shopping and leisure experience.

In such cases, to continue thinking in terms of customer segments can only cloud our thinking about real customer needs. We will mistakenly continue to believe that our value chains should be responsive, agile, and lean and mean, all at the same time—rather than realizing that value chain specialization and scale reconsideration would be far more effective.

The answer is simple: give up the old assumptions, and start segmenting in terms of customer needs, not individual customers. Then the dialog on value chain specialization can begin in earnest.

THE END OF THE VILLAGE STORE

Aligning the segments of present or future customer needs, on the one hand, and the company's degree of value chain specialization, on the other, can represent an important source of growth and value for established firms and new entrants alike.

Customers, who have learned how to rapidly value new offerings, are the main drivers of the trend toward specialized value chains. To return to the metaphor we began with, if our customers have said goodbye to the village store, then so must we.

Playing Hardball: Why Strategy Still Matters

George Stalk

The Boston Consulting Group

For a time, it seemed that strategy didn't matter anymore, particularly during the e-commerce boom. The brilliant promise of Web-based business temporarily blinded many managers, academics, and investors to the fundamentals of strategy. Strategy has always been about allocating resources to stimulate customer demand and create competitive advantage. The greater the advantage, the faster a company can grow, the more profitable it can be, and the greater value it can create. But in the first rush of e-commerce, a lot of investment dollars and management talent went into ventures that did not have competitive advantage from the get-go—like Boo.com, BBQ.com, Lifejacketstore.com—and were doomed.

The bust of e-commerce reminded everyone, all too painfully, that strategy always matters. Today, it matters more than ever. Competitive intensity is at an all-time high as a result of globalization, technology, fragmented consumer groups, and shifting power along the supply/demand chain. But while gaining a competitive advantage is harder than ever, strategy is again being pushed off the management agenda—not by e-commerce, but by "managerially correct" demands. Even when managers want to focus on creating and reinforcing competitive advantage, they are being distracted by a plethora of "soft" issues. Not only must managers cope with the intense scrutiny and burdensome demands of corporate governance, they must deal with the recriminations for outsourcing and offshoring, demands to motivate employees in times of increased uncertainty, and unceasing pressure to produce quick results or face replacement. The time has come to put strategy back on the agenda again. That is why we wrote *Hardball*.

THE FIVE PRINCIPLES OF HARDBALL

Today there are two extremes in business competition. Companies can play softball, relying on weak tactics that look like strategies but do little more than keep the company in the game for the short term. Or they can play hardball, employing tough strategies designed to rout, not simply beat, competitors. Which of today's companies are playing hardball? What strategies are they using to win? And what will it take for firms to adopt and execute these strategies successfully?

1. *Hardball players focus relentlessly on competitive advantage.* Competitive advantage is something I have that you don't. Too bad for you. But too bad for me, too. When I have the advantage, you are forced to accept defeat or find a way around my advantage to build your own. So hardball competitors are never satisfied with today's competitive advantage—they want tomorrow's.

Richard Ivey School of Business
The University of Western Ontario

Reprinted from *Ivey Business Journal* 69, no. 2 (November/December 2004), pp. 1–8. Ivey Management Services prohibits any form of reproduction, storage or transmittal of this material without its written permission. This material is not covered under authorization from any reproduction rights organization. To order copies or request permission to reproduce materials, contact Ivey Publishing, Ivey Management Services, c/o Richard Ivey School of Business, The University of Western Ontario, London, Ontario, Canada, N6A 3K7: phone (519) 661-3208, fax (519) 661-3882, e-mail cases@ivey.uwo.ca. Copyright © 2004, Ivey Management Services. One time permission to reproduce granted by Ivey Management Services on December 1, 2008.

2. *Hardball competitors strive to convert competitive advantage into decisive advantage.* Competitive advantage, as essential as it is, can be fleeting. That's why hardball players seek to put themselves out of reach of their competitors by building their competitive advantage into decisive, or unassailable, advantage. Decisive advantage is systemically reinforcing. The better you get at it, the harder it is for competitors to compete against it or take it away. And the more likely it is that your competitors will "pick up their marbles" and leave that particular playing field.

3. *Hardball players employ the indirect attack.* When a company makes a direct attack, it does exactly what its opponent expects and is prepared for. The attacker hopes that superior resources and persistence will carry the day. An indirect attack means that you surprise a competitor with your actions and apply resources where the opponent is least able to defend himself.

4. *Hardball players exploit their employees' will to win.* To achieve competitive advantage, people must be action-oriented, and always impatient with the status quo. The will to win can be fostered; softball players can be transformed into hardball players. But as your competitive advantage grows, it gets harder to exploit your employees' will to win.

5. *Hardball players draw a bright line at the edge of the caution zone.* To play hardball means to be aware of when you are entering the "caution zone," that area so rich in possibility that lies between the place where society clearly says you can play the game of business and the place where society clearly says you can't.

Generally, hardball strategies do not require entry into the caution zone. Company leaders are responsible for drawing a bright line that defines the boundary, and for letting everybody know when they're getting close to it.

In rare instances, however, a hardball player will deliberately enter the caution zone. When he does, he must take extra care. Every move must be evaluated in the light of the following questions:

- Will the proposed action break any laws?
- Will the proposed action be bad for the customer?
- Will competitors be directly hurt by an action?
- Will an action hit a nerve with a special interest group in a way that might damage the company?
- Will the action harm the industry or society?

If the answer to any of the questions is "yes," it means the company has ventured too far into the caution zone. The leader must immediately take corrective action.

SIX CLASSIC HARDBALL STRATEGIES

Any strategy that provides a decisive competitive advantage is a hardball strategy. In our book, we describe six classic hardball strategies that have proved, over the decades, to be particularly effective in generating competitive advantage.

1. *Unleash massive and overwhelming force.* Although hardball players prefer the indirect attack, they sometimes surprise and overcome their competitors with a full frontal assault. Massive and overwhelming force must be deployed like the blow of a hammer—accurate, direct, and swift. It must not be used until the company is ready to put all its energy behind it. The company must also be certain that the competitive advantage it believes it has is ready to be deployed.

When a company chooses the direct attack strategy, it may be necessary for it to completely overhaul its business in order to unleash the force. The process can feel like the turnaround of a successful company, a paradoxical situation that is uncomfortable for entrenched leaders. Only those with vision and courage should engage in this bold, and often very public, hardball strategy. And companies must be careful not to put their competitors out of business and into bankruptcy protection, from which they may emerge stronger than ever.

When the president of Frito-Lay, Roger Enrico, had had enough of Eagle Snack's incursion into its market for salty snacks, his first response was to slim down and focus the organization, to reduce costs and concentrate investments. He then launched an all-out attack on Eagle's stronghold, the supermarkets, by increasing promotions and advertising, upping in-store service, and, where necessary, reducing prices.

> Hardball executives relish anomalies because they may conceal opportunities that can be exploited.

He wrote a check that was larger than Eagle could afford to match. Eagle crumpled under the assault and withdrew.

2. *Exploit anomalies.* Sometimes a growth opportunity lies hidden in a phenomenon that, at first glance, seems irrelevant to the business or contradictory to current practice. But anomalies—such as idiosyncratic customer preferences, unexpected employee behaviors, or odd insights from another industry—can show the way to competitive advantage, even decisive advantage.

When Rose Marie Bravo took over Burberry, the English manufacturer of raincoats that was dead in the water, she noticed that Burberry's sales in Spain were inexplicably strong. Her interest was piqued because, as she pointed out, "It doesn't rain in Spain." She learned that the country manager had extended the Burberry brand into many other categories. She took this insight to the United States, to Asia, and throughout Europe. Burberry's sales have more than tripled, and its EBITDA has increased sevenfold.

Softball players want to ignore anomalies or to suppress them because they don't conform to standard practice. Hardball executives relish anomalies because they may conceal opportunities that can be exploited.

3. *Threaten your competitor's profit sanctuaries.* Profit sanctuaries are the parts of a business where a company makes the most money and steadily accumulates wealth. In certain circumstances, the hardball player can influence a competitor's behavior and gain competitive advantage by attacking the competitor's profit sanctuaries.

This strategy is risky. It can take you deep into the caution zone, so each use must be considered on its own legal merits. Also, your competitor is likely to retaliate by attacking *your* profit sanctuaries. And he may have greater financial resources than you thought, or a "sugar daddy" waiting in the wings to save his hide.

Toyota has overrun its opponents' sanctuaries. The profit sanctuaries of GM, Ford, and Chrysler are light trucks and SUVs, where they earn between $10,000 and $15,000 per vehicle. Toyota now offers equivalent vehicles and has enough cash that it could give them away. Instead, it is plowing its earnings back into hybrid vehicles and capacity expansions. Toyota effectively controls the strategies of the Big 3 by occupying their profit sanctuaries.

4. *Take it and make it your own.* Softball competitors like to think their bright ideas are sacred. Hardball players know better. They're willing to take any good idea they see (any one that isn't nailed down by a patent or other legal protection), and use it to create competitive advantage for themselves.

This needn't be restricted to borrowing from competitors. You can pick up ideas from one geographic market and transplant them to another. Ideas can also be transplanted between industries. But the "making it your own" part is just as important as the "taking it." Every hardball company finds a way to build on, improve, and customize the borrowed idea so that it's not just a me-too copy.

Batesville Casket is the world-leading manufacturer of welded steel caskets. In the 1970s, Batesville endeavored to reduce its manufacturing costs by transplanting automotive manufacturing techniques to its industry. The impact on Batesville's less sophisticated competitors was stunning. In the 1990s, Batesville set its sights on those competitors with positions in major metropolitan markets. To get at them, Batesville had to offer greater variety and faster response times at affordable prices. Batesville Casket accomplished this with remarkable success by transplanting Toyota's production system.

5. *Entice your competitors into retreat.* Sometimes, through a superior understanding of your business and your industry, you can take actions that confuse your competitors and entice them to behave in ways that they believe will be beneficial to them, but that actually will weaken them. This opportunity hinges on the existence of certain customers that are not worth having because they cost too much to serve. These are the customers you want your competitors to have.

Federal Mogul discovered that smaller engine manufacturers were not as profitable as large OEMs despite having higher gross margins. The cost impact of smaller production runs and higher service needs were hidden from management by the company's standard costing system. Federal Mogul repriced its small OEM business high enough to make money if it won the bid, but low enough to ensure that any competitor who won the bid would not recover its true costs. Over time, the cost position of Federal Mogul's competitors worsened as they continued to win more business with the smaller OEMs.

Enticing your competitors to focus on a business that drives up their costs is one of the most complex strategies of hardball competition. You must have a superb understanding of your own costs and how customers make purchase decisions. For example, you can set prices so your competitors respond by seeking business that they think will be profitable for them, but that will, in fact, drive up their costs and depress their profits. This is a risky, bet-the-company strategy. It works best in complex businesses where costs may be misallocated. There is lots of potential for error. Your analysis of the actual-versus-apparent costs associated with a product, service, or customer—and the strategy that grows out of that analysis—has to be right.

6. *Break compromises.* When a hardball player wants to achieve explosive growth, he looks for a compromise to break. A compromise is a concession that an industry forces on its customers, who often accept it because they have come to believe it is endemic—"just the way things work"?—like the never-changing 3 p.m. check-in time at hotels.

Wausau Paper bet that the standard industry practice of requiring its paper merchants to accept long and unreliable deliveries and large minimum-order quantities was a huge compromise, resulting in higher inventories and greater costs for the merchants. Wausau "retooled" its business to provide merchants with 10 times faster delivery times, three times the variety, and 1/20th the minimum-order quantities. Wausau merchants loved the new model, and Wausau grew like a weed; in the past 15 years, it has created more shareholder value than any other paper company.

If compromises can be identified and businesses altered to create a new model, the result is often fast and profitable growth. Getting rid of a compromise usually confuses your competitors, because they are still locked in the mind-set that generated the compromises.

HARDBALL M&A

Despite their high failure rate, mergers and acquisitions can be a powerful means of pursuing a hardball strategy more quickly, or on a much larger scale, than could be done organically. Mergers made without a strategic rationale, and acquisitions pursued on the whim of the CEO, are softball moves. A good M&A deal creates competitive advantage; a great deal can help a company achieve decisive advantage, enabling it to lock up critical assets or build superior economics.

Companies often pursue M&A to rapidly expand, nationally or globally, or annex a rival and reduce competition. There can be so much strategic benefit in merging or acquiring companies that some hardball players become serial acquirers. Hardball serial acquirers have a clear idea of how to build competitive advantage, and have the capabilities to consummate deals and digest acquisitions for maximum strategic benefit. Companies often begin their M&A activity as a way of pursuing a modest strategic goal, but end up achieving decisive advantage.

The lessons from serial acquirers that use M&A to carry out their hardball strategies are straightforward in concept, but difficult to execute:

- Acquire only if the opportunity fits with the strategy.
- Do not be tempted to step outside your proven process.
- Build an internal M&A capability.
- Seek outside advice and assistance.
- Take a rigorous approach to valuation.
- Invest in post-merger integration capabilities.

CHANGES IN THE FIELD OF PLAY

The strategies in *Hardball* are classics, but "classic" should not be interpreted to mean "static." The game of hardball is dynamic and always evolving. New barriers to achieving competitive advantage emerge, and new roadblocks to building decisive advantage are erected. Several issues will affect the way hardball must be played in the future. They will change the rules for players who wish to be winners, especially on the global field.

Playing the China card. Over the next decade, China will be the biggest and most contentious issue for hardball players, even if they are not global companies themselves. The most important China issue is not that it is a source of low-cost production or even that it is a huge market for companies. The critical China issue today is that this country will be the source of tomorrow's toughest new competitors, who will become a thorn in the side for all Western companies as the Japanese were in the 1980s. Nokia and Motorola know this, and have dramatically intensified their handset investments in China to retain leadership positions there.

Getting stuck in the middle. During the past decade, the U.S. economy has shifted from being producer-driven to consumer-driven. This has become an important issue for companies in virtually every industry and business segment, but many of them have yet to recognize it, or they have leaders that refuse to believe it.

As a result of changes in consumer demographics and behavior, in combination with changes in retailing, the market for consumer goods has become polarized. At the very high end, some luxury brands continue to succeed by selling super-expensive goods at very high margins and in very small quantities.

At the low end, a wide variety of brands of commodities and utilitarian items—including house-hold and office products, food staples, home electronics, toys, and hardware—compete with each other on price and minor product differentiations. These brands, including private-label or generic brands, may grow in volume but must fight ferociously to retain or grow profits.

And then there is the middle, where no consumer or manufacturer wants to be—the territory where hundreds of companies and brands have gotten stuck. Companies like Kmart, Mitsubishi Motors, General Electric appliances, and Samsonite are frozen in the headlights of competitors who are stealing customers at the low and high price points.

The fastest-growing segment in the market is in premium goods that are still affordable for middle-market consumers. These are goods and services, priced from 20 to 200 percent above mid-priced offerings, which offer enough technical differences and performance improvements, along with emotional engagement, that consumers are willing to pay extra for them. These new luxury brands include small, low-priced items such as Aveda personal care, Grey Goose and Belvedere vodka,

and Starbucks coffee. They also include more expensive items such as a Viking stove or a set of Callaway golf clubs, and go all the way up to big-ticket purchases, such as a premium sea cruise or a Mercedes C-class sedan.

Dealing with stranded assets. A nasty side effect of gaining competitive advantage and creating a virtuous cycle that builds into decisive advantage is the stranding of assets. This happens when an asset that was once a contributor to competitive advantage becomes irrelevant or, worse, a drag on competitiveness. Forces such as globalization, technological change and corporate self-interest continuously intensify competition and strand many kinds of assets—including plants and facilities, as well as customers and suppliers.

> The fastest-growing segment in the market is in premium goods that are still affordable for middle-market consumers. These are goods and services, priced from 20 to 200 percent above mid-priced offerings, which offer enough technical differences and performance improvements, along with emotional engagement, that consumers are willing to pay extra for them.

Softball competitors rally around stranded assets, attempting to delay the day of reckoning when the assets will have to be written off. They seek government aid; they try to push the problem onto the public, as the auto industry is attempting to do with health care costs. The longer the delay, the greater the pain will be in the long run.

As early as the 1970s, both Cadillac and Lincoln faced the problems of an aging and shrinking customer base. Ford flip-flopped: Lincoln was a marketing brand, then it was a company, and then it was part of Ford Division.

In contrast, GM invested in bold, risky new product designs and higher quality, in an attempt to woo new customers and revive the Cadillac customer base. Cadillac's new models have gotten a lot of media attention and are selling well enough that the company has been emboldened to market its vehicles in Europe. Hardball competitors like GM strive to eliminate and, when possible, re-purpose their stranded assets.

Being "Wal-Marted." Wal-Mart is the largest retailer on the planet. Its sales exceed those of the second-largest retailer, Carrefour, by more than three times. Wal-Mart is the largest retailer—or among the top three largest—of goods in many consumer categories. Wal-Mart continues to push into new categories with catastrophic consequences for traditional competitors. Its cost position is so strong that its competitors' attempts to match it on "everyday low prices" end in failure.

For its suppliers, Wal-Mart is a dilemma. It is the most profitable customer for many suppliers, on an absolute basis and often on the basis of percentage. These suppliers are naturally wary of upsetting Wal-Mart.

But there are chinks in the monolith's armor. While customers find great value at Wal-Mart, they are also forced into a compromise when they shop there. They usually have to travel a long distance to get to a store; they have to park in a large, crowded lot; they must roam through acres of retail space, through aisles designed to take them ever deeper into the store. Sales help is scarce, and not always knowledgeable. The prices are dramatically low, but the shopping experience is mediocre at best, and unpleasant at worst.

Internet retailers such as Tesco and Grocerygateway.com are tapping into the willingness of some customers to pay higher prices for a better experience. Internet-savvy consumers who value their time and want competitive prices, but don't need the very lowest prices, find shopping online to be a perfectly acceptable substitute for shopping at Wal-Mart and other big-box retailers. At Grocerygateway.com, shoppers can get groceries at competitive prices, hardware from The Home Depot, liquor, and more at the click of a mouse. The goods are delivered within an agreed-upon time and unloaded into the house. No driving. No parking. No crowds. No wandering the endless aisles. No lugging packages. No Wal-Mart.

THE HARDBALL MIND-SET

To play the game of hardball to its fullest requires a hardball state of mind. Hardball players possess a number of admirable characteristics. They have an intellectual toughness that enables them to face facts and see reality. They are emotionally aware, which means they know themselves well, and also their people. They are always dissatisfied with the status quo, no matter how fine things may seem. They have the will to catalyze change. They're tough, but not bullies. They're serious about their business. They

have such an intense passion for winning that it rubs off on others.

The hardball player needs all of these qualities, and more, in order to accomplish his most important task: to get to the heart of the matter and stay there. The heart of the matter is that set of fundamental, often systemic, issues that is limiting the growth and success of the business. These issues are often so challenging in so many ways that no one in the organization has the guts to take them on, or the ability to actually solve them.

Getting to the heart of the matter is not easy. Organizations do not like addressing heart-of-the-matter issues. These issues are hard, time-consuming, fraught with risks, and prone to defeat individual efforts.

An organization that is unwilling, or not ready, to face the heart of the matter is one doomed to inaction. It will be like a sitting duck in comparison to competitors that are able to face the heart of the matter. It is the job of the hardball leader to compel his organization to face those fundamental issues and then plunge into addressing them.

Hardball leaders succeed in staying at the heart of the matter by keeping their organizations in "perpetual turnaround" mode, no matter how successful they are. They make themselves, and their people, believe that they are in constant danger of losing their advantage because, in fact, they are. A management team in turnaround mode cannot allow itself to be distracted from the central objectives of the turnaround.

Hardball players are often deceptive in appearance and demeanor. They are brave, but not necessarily boastful. They are bold, but never bullying. They may not be flashy; sometimes they may even seem rather bland. But the ones that achieve strong competitive advantage, and especially those that go on to create decisive advantage, tend to have much longer successful runs than their competitors. There is no limit to the duration of advantage, nor are we aware of any average lifespan for advantaged companies. It is the leader that usually causes a company to lose decisive advantage, sometimes as the result of a serious mistake, but most often through complacency and failure to adapt. If a company is aggressive at renewing its competitive advantage, it may enjoy a very long run indeed, and watch as the softball players limp away from the playing field, never to return.

Hitting Back: Strategic Responses to Low-Cost Rivals

Jim Morehouse
A. T. Kearney

Bob O'Meara
A. T. Kearney

Christian Hagen
A. T. Kearney

Todd Huseby
A. T. Kearney

By the late 1990s, global network manufacturer Cisco Systems was sitting pretty in China. Offering hardware, software, and services for Internet solutions, the firm had a 60 percent market share for high-end equipment there. But as Cisco was being lauded in cover stories in the world's leading business publications, Huawei Technologies, a little-known Chinese start-up, quietly entered the networking industry. Beginning in 1998 by importing and developing PBX telephone products, Huawei was unencumbered by inherited costs, was able to hire newly minted Chinese engineers at starting salaries of $8,500 a year, and enjoyed a multibillion-dollar credit line from the Chinese government.

Huawei took full advantage of its competitive strengths, reducing networking equipment costs 70 percent compared with Cisco, its much larger rival. Through partnerships with 3Com and Siemens, Huawei entered new markets, and in the United Kingdom, it won British Telecom's business, ultimately forcing the domestic incumbent Marconi Corporation onto the selling block. From 2001 to 2005, Huawei's revenue rose from $2.3 billion to nearly $6 billion, and it cut Cisco's market share in China to less than 40 percent.[1]

Huawei's brashly competitive move was built around low costs. But successful low-cost competitors don't just sap margins incrementally. What makes them so dangerous is their ability to redefine the entire competitive landscape. The low-cost competitor transforms its value chain to reduce prices drastically. With low costs as a pivot, it shifts the ground beneath larger, less flexible opponents and turns their mass and momentum against them. Responses often come too late to be effective, and are hampered by strategic assumptions that no longer apply. Larger rivals soon find they are fighting a war on the new competitor's terms. Wanting to move quickly, they often cut back on prices to retain customers. If they do so before performing a thoughtful analysis, this action may punish them further. Meanwhile, the Huaweis of the world thrive and continue to gain market share.

The way to beat low-cost competitors that have the potential to become serious competitors is to identify and deal with them early, before they get a foothold in a market.

STING LIKE A BEE

As Cisco learned, even high-tech firms with strong brand identities are not safe from low-cost rivals. Nimble competitors exploit their offshore advantage, partnerships, and inexpensive technologies to break down barriers and rewrite the rules of competition, almost overnight. Following widely different strategies, these firms succeed for one reason: they redesign their value chain to cut costs substantially in an established market.

Reprinted from *Strategy & Leadership* 36, no.1 (2008), pp. 4–13. Reproduced with permission of the copyright owner. Further reproduction prohibited without permission.

Figure 1 highlights some of the attributes of low-cost competitors, which can be seen in a variety of different companies. Consider Nike's face-off with Steve & Barry's, a discount clothing chain that captured a niche market in athletic shoes. At under $15 a pair, its Starbury One basketball shoe is leading a full-court press on the youth market for budget-priced athletic shoes. Three million pairs of Starbury sneakers have sold since their August 2006 debut. Meanwhile, Nike's footwear inventory is 15 percent larger than a year ago.[2]

Then there is Southwest Airlines. Although known for its no-frills service, the most overlooked aspect of Southwest's profit-winning strategy is its superior asset utilization. By structuring flight schedules to return planes from the gate to the air in as little as 20 minutes, Southwest flies its planes 20 to 30 percent more hours than the other major airlines. By deploying a point-to-point route network, instead of the hub-and-spoke approach used by most major carriers, Southwest minimizes the domino effect of flight delays and gains maximum use of its assets.

Even Wal-Mart and IKEA, low-cost competitors in their own right, must constantly be on alert for their next threat. While these firms compete on price rather than product differentiation, their retail model is now being challenged by Japanese retailer, Muji. Its stores combine low prices with a high-concept minimalism so that customers don't have to sacrifice status for cost. The retailer, well established in Europe and Asia, is now moving into the U.S. market.

Low-cost competitors can be right under your nose. A current partner, a supplier or even a contract manufacturer can walk away with key elements of your value chain, establishing its own operations on a modest scale and positioning itself to take more value later by moving upstream or increasing its leverage. That same contract manufacturer may cross boundaries to apply what it learned in one industry to break into another. Case in point is Huawei's challenge to Cisco.

Figure 1   Attributes of a Low-Cost Competitor

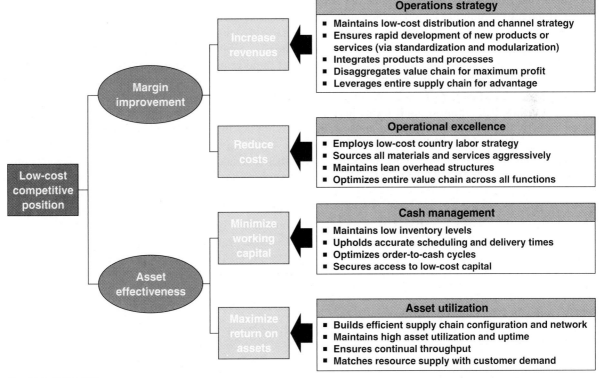

Source: A. T. Kearney.

Figure 2   A Low-Cost Competitor Optimizes Its Value Chain across Multiple Dimensions

Design engineering	Procurement and supplier management	Assembly	Quality	Order and distribute	Market	Support
• Focuses on process design rather than product design • "Copycats" on design ideas • Maintains low number of SKUs • Has low R&D budget • Develops products jointly with suppliers • Standardizes and modularizes to reduce complexity	• Co-locates with suppliers in low-cost country • Offers procurement insight in design • Gains transparency into supplier costs • Standardizes products to consolidate purchases • Focuses on long-term, win–win contracting • Designs strategies around supplier base structure	• Establishes low-cost location • Leverages excess capacity at plants for own-brand production • Employs just-in-time delivery • Utilizes data exchange for notification shipments • Keeps supplier representatives on plant floor • Utilizes flexible manufacturing resources and plants	• Conducts quality testing in LCC • Integrates suppliers into quality process • Increases standardization to improve quality testing • Optimizes warranty pricing • Connects suppliers to manufacturing via effective IT and data integration	• Outsources logistics • Pursues unique channel sources such as Internet • Increases order efficiency with standardized products • Uses vendor-managed replenishment • Plans manufacturing with order information • Key customers have multiple points of contact along supply chain	• Co-brands with partners to reduce marketing spend • Sells directly through e-channels to minimize sales force overhead • Lets order influence marketing • Minimizes marketing spend through use of e-channels • Focuses on emerging economies (China, India, Africa)	• Establishes automated bug tracking system • Sets up Web-based and self-service customer support systems • Leverages innovative customer-support models

Source: A. T. Kearney.

As Figure 2 illustrates, a low-cost competitor can pursue several strategies along various points of the value chain, and rarely focuses on just one area. These competitors minimize complex and expensive activities such as R&D, product design, and marketing, and focus instead on ruthless efficiency. At each step, the new rival chooses the strategies that best deliver lower costs. It keeps the number of SKUs low, standardizes its design and products, outsources assembly to low-cost countries, and forms partnerships for activities too costly to build in-house. Cutting costs across the value chain not only enhances its ability but makes it all the more difficult for larger, less flexible companies to respond.

YOUR HANDS CAN'T HIT WHAT YOUR EYES CAN'T SEE

Many companies fail to recognize the significance of a low-cost competitor until it's too late. For one reason, because they are too wedded to the status quo, they develop their strategies in functional silos and according to internal objectives without considering the entire spectrum of competitor strategies or changes to the external environment. In other words, firms make a serious mistake by benchmarking their position against competitors' existing value chain. In a world of the extended enterprise, analyzing competitors' capabilities is like trying to hit a target capable of rapid transformation. With more diffuse industry barriers, low-cost rivals are outsourcing some parts of their value chain and building partnerships in others. This obscures the true competitive picture and multiplies the number of benchmarking variables.

The best way to identify and thwart a low-cost rival is to adopt its mind-set, anticipate its next competitive move, and measure your costs against its costs. This requires digging deeper than the qualitative, theoretical approach of war-gaming or the internally focused tools of business-process redesign and lean manufacturing. The goal is to defeat the low-cost rival by compelling actions that allow you to become more competitive and grow or maintain a profitable position in your market segment.

This best practice analysis requires four steps:

1. *Identify likely low-cost rivals.* Identifying low-cost competitors early in the game is crucial. The sooner they can be detected, the less likely it is you'll be competing on their terms, and the

more time you'll have to plan a response. What to look for? Focus on strategies that offer a cost advantage against your own, for each area of the value chain. Emerging rivals are firms that:

- Concentrate on a cost-effective design process rather than a unique product design. Reducing complexity in design has a ripple effect on other areas of the value chain, from cost management to procurement and quality. In the 1980s, while U.S. automakers were rolling out large, customized vehicles, Japanese competitors focused on streamlining their processes to cut down on costs and offer affordable models.

- Involve suppliers early in the process, during initial product design and development.

- Assemble products in low-cost countries. Companies that develop this mind-set and capability give themselves a significant head start and source of advantage.

- Standardize products to reduce testing. Effective firms also engage their suppliers in the quality process.

- Engage consumer-to-consumer online communities (eBay and grassfire.com are good examples) and develop low-cost shipping and distribution models via third-party logistics providers.

- Sell in large volume to developing economies. Low-cost rivals often cover their fixed costs and build up their brands and capabilities by serving emerging markets before moving into established ones. If incumbents are not scanning competitors outside their national markets, they might not spot the new rivals until late in the game.

- Offer unique online and self-service customer support systems—or find creative solutions in call-center strategies. For example, JetBlue Airways routes customer service calls to call-center representatives who work from home, thus saving millions of dollars in real estate overhead

Internally, consider whether your company is still as profitable as it was six months or a year ago. Because shrinking margins often indicate that a new competitor is undercutting you on price, have a process in place for an ongoing analysis.

2. *Perform a total-cost analysis.* A total-cost analysis is used to translate a likely competitor's advantages into a hypothetical total product or service-cost analysis. This compares your opponent's "should cost" to actual costs. Questions that should guide the analysis at this point include: How significant is the advantage? How does the cost advantage translate into pricing options? Is it sustainable over time? Most importantly, can we replicate it, and if so, how? Figure 3 shows what happened when a global electronics component supplier used a total-cost analysis to identify potential threats from companies with more efficient supply chains. The analysis was based on detailed plant-by-plant assumptions, which were validated against known cost structures both inside and outside the company. By employing operational best practices, regardless of location, this company could cut costs by 20 percent or more.

3. *Develop all potential scenarios.* Developing "what-if" scenarios allows you to ascertain likely next steps. Will the low-cost rival reposition itself? Enter new markets? Launch new products? Move into new services? Of course, effective forecasting depends on understanding where the market is going and which low-cost companies have sustainable capabilities. For example, a supplier that is not a low-cost rival today could become one tomorrow if it develops the right capabilities or if a number of suppliers consolidate. A private-equity firm could even step in and provide funding to enable such a transformation.

These scenarios will probably cause some internal angst as the company weighs whether or not it can make the necessary changes, and if it is likely to lose its most valuable customers as a result. This leads to a crucial fourth step in our analysis.

4. *Determine your best strategic moves.* At this point you want to make sure the goal is to compete against a low-cost rival by using the information from the what-if scenarios to

Figure 3 Total-Cost Analysis Reveals Competitor's Advantage

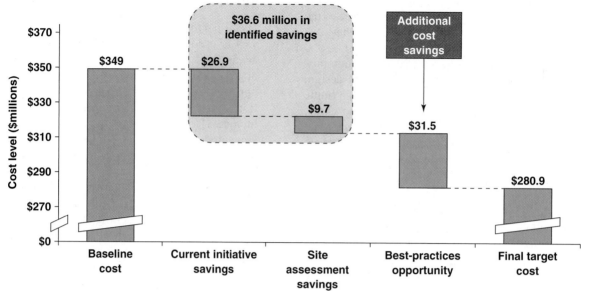

Source: A. T. Kearney.

improve operations and become more competitive overall. The analysis should prompt new questions:

- Are we focusing on the right things to remain competitive?
- What can we do immediately to protect our position?
- What should we do to compete over the medium to long term given our current strategy?
- What should we concentrate on first to remain competitive and create value?

Defeating low-cost competitors involves two separate but related tasks: First, "stop the bleeding," and second, reposition the company for success in the new market. Leaders should break down potential moves into short-term tactics and long-term strategies (see Figure 4).

SHORT-TERM TACTICS

Short-term tactics should reinforce a firm's existing strengths and gain time for the internal and external analysis needed to develop the long-term strategy. These tactics keep low-cost rivals at bay while the company repositions its business. For example, when first confronted by a low-cost rival, companies often respond by lowering prices or providing sales incentives to maintain their market share. Although there are obvious disadvantages and risks to this tactic, it sometimes works, especially if the competitor is relatively weak and doesn't have the product mix or capabilities to sustain its cash flow. Before attempting this, an incumbent needs to assess the true likelihood that it will outlast its competition and go on to reclaim lost market share. Sometimes another way to protect market share in the short term is through legal action. As a case in point. Cisco hit Huawei with a patent infringement lawsuit to slow its entry into American and European markets, but eventually dropped its suit when Huawei agreed to modify its products.[3]

Often the better tactic is to shift the competition away from price alone. The newer rival may be less competitive in other areas. Use product differentiation to appeal to customers' needs for features or benefits they can't get from the low-cost competitor. In the short term, differentiation may be enhanced by crafty marketing. Shell Oil did this back in the 1950s when oil companies were all essentially on par. Shell decided to promote the merits of "platformate," a little-known mileage-boosting additive that was, in fact,

Figure 4 Low-Cost Competitor Alternatives

Focus	Possible Strategies	Advantages	Disadvantages	Market Examples
Short-term tactics	• Lower price or provide incentives to maintain share and validate low-cost competitors' sustainability	• Works if low-cost competitor does not have product mix or capabilities to sustain cash flow • Maintains capacity to cover fixed costs	• Reduces profit margins unambiguously • Sets stage for price war • Removes value in industry for all players • Allows competitors to gain capabilities and customers	• GM • American Airlines • Akamai
	• Emphasize product or service differentiation through advertising and sales channels	• Increases marketing focus • Enhances brand • Can help shift focus on solutions and messages	• Might backfire if customers do want or understand differentiated features or benefits • Increases advertising and marketing budgets	• Apple • CopyCo. (see case study in reading) • Shell Oil
	• Narrow target to attractive customers and allow low-cost rivals to capture unprofitable customers	• Increases margins in short-term • Allows company to trim unprofitable customers • Promises further benefits if competitors continue to try to attract customers that are unprofitable to serve	• Constrains future flexibility as focus narrows • Risks ability to acquire currently low-profit customers that may become more profitable • Shrinks customer base to grow and cross-sell	• Ecolab • Sprint • TXU • Fidelity
Long-term strategies	• Focus organization on differentiation or premium segments	• Allows organization to focus on narrower set of core strengths and profitable customers	• Risks losing a potential future higher-profit segment • Requires company to adjust manufacturing and supply chain to more targeted demand	• British Airways • Wegmans • Starbucks • Dell • Ferrellgas
	• Expand product or services into related, profitable offerings or geographies	• Focuses company on expanding presence and not just riding one product for full life cycle • Diversifies portfolio of products	• Forces company to have solid discipline on evaluation of markets and products—bad bets can be costly	• Cisco • Whole Foods • Tesco
	• Learn from competitors—become a low-cost player or develop low-cost offshoot or product	• Forces efficiencies through the organization • Increases long-term competitive position • Can keep premium pieces of brand	• Requires difficult change management • Demands that company truly become low-cost player—not just market it • Forces company to truly eliminate legacy costs from low-cost offshoot	• Ted Airlines • Delta Airlines • Siebel • Marriott
	• Bundle products with solutions, services, or other products	• Allows company to move upstream and develop new capabilities • More toward higher margin products or services • Based on innovation—not volume	• Forces skill-set and company transformation • Customer may want to decouple products and services • Requires new skills set: sales is trained to push products—not develop solutions • Change management cannot be overlooked	• IBM • Xerox • Motorola

Source: A. T. Kearney.

What Not to Do When Battling Low-Cost Competition

A key part of your battle plan is establishing what not to do when fighting low-cost competition:

- Don't wait for the new rivals to hit you. For example, Sears, Kmart, and other department stores were slow to respond to Wal-Mart.

- Don't respond without first developing a plan. Otherwise, you waste resources on all potential rivals rather than focusing on those that pose an actual threat.

- Don't focus solely on current competitors and current products. Companies that may not be direct competitors today could move in with similar products or services tomorrow.

- Don't drop your guard against traditional competitors. Old fights don't end when new ones begin.

- Don't try to defeat low-cost rivals by cutting prices alone. Given your competitors' margins, a price war will almost never work in your favor, unless the competitor can't sustain its advantage over time.

- Don't understimate the extent of the change management involved. Competing against low-cost rivals is a companywide effort. Engineering, distribution, and marketing, for example, must be realigned to a new strategy, which requires managing change across all aspects of the organization.

---

used by other firms as well. The sales effort began with a television ad campaign where a car fueled by Shell gas without platformate raced against a car powered by gas with the additive. The non-platformate car ran out of gas and stopped while the platformate car was shown passing the stopped car and bursting through a huge paper banner with a Shell logo on it. The ad was a visible illustration of product differentiation, and the marketing campaign is credited with launching Shell as a major player in the industry.

Finally, focus on your more attractive customers and leave the less profitable ones to your new rivals. Not all customers are equally valuable. Some are prohibitively expensive to serve and draw resources that could be directed elsewhere for bigger gains. Let new rivals take these customers off your hands, so you can concentrate on the more profitable ones. Just don't make a public announcement of this tactic with a letter, as Sprint did recently.[4]

LONG-TERM STRATEGIES

While long-term strategies involve more risk, the rewards are often worth it. Firms build these strategies to adapt to changed conditions and seize new opportunities—which can sometimes result in a very different company. IBM was the premier manufacturer of personal computers until the 1990s, when Dell and Gateway began selling lower-priced models directly to customers. In the early 1990s it posted a nearly $5 billion loss, the largest of its kind for any American company in a single year. Undaunted, the company set about reinventing its business. By 1995, with the acquisition of Lotus, IBM had a new strategy. Instead of selling components and hardware, it began selling software and service "solutions," bundling products together for a higher-value offer.

Another example comes from the retail propane gas industry where the focus is traditionally on price. One company beat its rivals by ramping up customer service and expanding its delivery options. The gas company decided to invest in technology (global positioning systems, scheduling software, etc.) to transform its field-service operations. These efforts improved deliveries, reduced fixed costs, enhanced asset allocation, increased its ability to match supply with demand, and strengthened customer service—leading to nearly 300 new customers within nine months. The company's investment had a short payback period and, perhaps more important, the move fundamentally altered the industry's landscape and performance expectations by creating significant barriers to entry.

Lastly, if you can't beat your low-cost rivals, steal a page from their playbook and form a low-cost offshoot. United Airlines, tired of competing with the likes of Southwest and other low-cost flyers, came up with its own low-cost rival, Ted.

LOW-COST RIVAL IN THE RING

To see how companies can use analysis of a potential low-cost rivalry situation to guide strategy, let's look at the example of a copy manufacturer. Any company in this industry is either in a margin squeeze between high costs and declining prices, or its products are being commoditized by companies in low-cost markets such as China. Well aware of the challenges within its industry, this manufacturer, we'll call it CopyCo, was looking beyond known competitors to identify potential outside threats. It found two: Huawei Technologies and its current contract manufacturer.

A company such as Huawei, well-known for moving into new industries, could readily become a competitor if it wanted—or form the low-cost backbone for yet another company. As evidence of its capability, it was already becoming a factor in the mobile phone business; in 2006, Vodafone introduced its latest branded consumer mobile phone, and announced that Huawei was its first choice to manufacture the handset. Typical of the emerging Asian white-label manufacturers, Huawei could produce the new handset at a cost 30 percent lower than Vodafone could hope to receive from a larger equipment maker.[5] From networking components to cell phones, Huawei was proving to be a flexible and formidable force.

Another threat was CopyCo's existing contract manufacturer. It could use the knowledge gained in the current partnership—product designs, engineering and manufacturing specifications—to become a ruthless competitor as well.

Alert to these threats, the analysis identified a handful of other potential foes in the market—expanding on CopyCo's list to include several white-label manufacturers. CopyCo could see how potential competitors might optimally design their products, set up their value chains and manage total costs. This is where companies see the break-even point at which they can manufacture a product and where a competitor could make it for much less (see Figure 5). CopyCo was already selling its smaller copiers at a loss to drive sales and encourage repeat purchases of link cartridges—it didn't realize a profit until several replacement cartridges were sold. In contrast, its known competitors were closer to making money on the initial sale and realizing additional profits on repeat cartridge sales. A company such as Huawei would no doubt improve these prospects even further. CopyCo put pencil to paper, finding that a low-cost competitor could harm them in the following ways:

- Enter and dominate the low-cost market segment. The company could then partner with another competitor to move up the value chain and compete in the high-price/high-quality market segment. This would squeeze CopyCo out of both markets, just as Huawei did to Cisco.

- Develop white-label products to sell to CopyCo's top customers. CopyCo would lose retail channels due to white-label competition. Huawei's partnership with Vodafone is an example of such a strategy.

- Enter developing countries early, exploiting cost advantages and capturing market share. Meanwhile, CopyCo would be slow to enter, fail to gain market share, and miss planned growth projections.

- Leverage low-cost country research and development or exploit lax intellectual property rights protection to leapfrog CopyCo technologically, win on price, and capture key market segments.

- Be acquired by a separate cash-rich or debt-averse computer-hardware company.

Realizing that several firms had the potential to become rivals, CopyCo was motivated to adopt a proactive plan. While a company like Huawei was certainly a potential threat, the scenarios demonstrated that other, still unknown competitors could be just as competitive. After prioritizing its plans, CopyCo chose the strategy it was most capable of implementing quickly. In the short term, it increased its advertising and stepped up sales efforts to maintain its share.

Long term, it is tailoring its strategies around two different markets. For the low-end brand, it is shifting to pursue profitable customer segments that account for the largest volume of replacement ink cartridge sales. In the high-end market, it is focusing on industry-specific solutions to raise its margins and produce an offering rivals can't emulate. Also, CopyCo executives are reevaluating their current contract-manufacturer relationships.

Figure 5   Average Unit Cost for Copier Low-Cost Competitor versus CopyCo

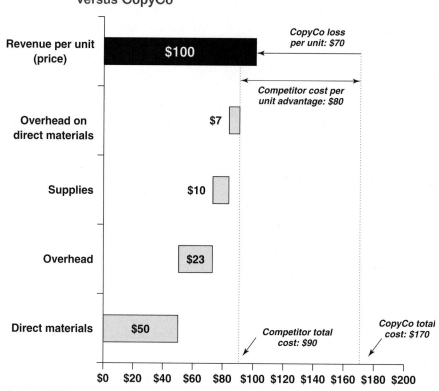

Source: A. T. Kearney.

THRIVING AGAINST AGGRESSIVE LOW-COST COMPETITORS

It is unlikely and unrealistic that any company will start with a clean sheet in response to low-cost competition, but all companies can develop action plans by considering their situation along with a competitor analysis. The following are three things to keep in mind:

1. *Don't get caught off guard.* Scour your market and others for current and future threats. Recognize that competitors can come from anywhere and attack at any time. They could be a real and urgent threat. They could come from a different industry or segment. Or they could be holding back, waiting to enter the market given favorable conditions. This competitor could also be

a "best of" amalgamation of current and hypothetical competitors. Engage your top managers to identify the most likely competitors.

2. *Be action-oriented.* American automakers lost ground to Toyota because they failed not only to see the threat soon enough but also to deploy their relevant sources of competitive advantage. They could have met the challenge when it was a potential threat rather than an actual one. Hyundai, for example, took a clean-sheet approach and came up with the car company of the future—one that avoids high fixed costs, captures the full lifetime value of a car through leasing rather than selling, outsources operations, and offers low-cost modular designs. All of these principles could have been adopted by U.S. and EU car companies. Eventually, Hyundai's strong quality performance allowed it to move upstream from producing low-cost to high-end cars.

3. *Develop a robust plan of action.* No company should ever underestimate its ability to outsmart the competition. Companies can turn even the toughest challenge into an opportunity to reexamine and intensify their efforts. The recent turnaround at Cisco Systems proves that it is possible to come back strong against low-cost rivals. After taking a hit in the networking business from the likes of Huawei, Cisco realized it needed a new strategic direction. While it remained committed to its traditional business, it also began expanding into new product areas, including business equipment and consumer technologies. The key was recognizing market transitions and entering at the appropriate time: Bad bets can be costly, so the company put resources into understanding markets, developing the right capabilities, and perfecting its timing. As a result, Cisco recently posted an 18 percent revenue increase from the previous year. The company expects years of steady growth from a second Internet boom (Web 2.0) as consumers upgrade to the next generation of Web-based technologies such as video conferencing and Internet telephony. "Web 2.0 is an opportunity to be an instant replay of what happened to Cisco in the early 1990s." CEO John Chambers said in an interview.[6]

For Cisco and others, the Huaweis of the world are everywhere. You may beat some and ignore some, but others will be lurking in the shadows. While no industry is impervious to such rivals, the winner every time will be the company that identifies the genuine threats, takes on the serious competition, adapts to its tactics quickly, and hits back with a well-placed blow.

Notes

1. Huawei 2005 annual report; Bruce Einhorn, "Cisco's Middle Kingdom alliance," *BusinessWeek Online,* 23 November 2005; Craig Simons, "The Huawei way," *Newsweek International Edition,* 16 January 2006.
2. Stanley Holmes, "Changing the game on Nike," *BusinessWeek,* 22 January 2007.
3. Laurie J. Flynn, "Cisco drops patent infringement lawsuit," *New York Times,* 29 July 2004.
4. Samar Srivastava, "Sprint drops clients over excessive inquiries," *Wall Street Journal,* 7 July 2007.
5. Cassell Brian-Low, "Vodafone to unveil self-branded mobile phone," *Wall Street Journal,* 27 September 2006.
6. Michelle Kessler, "Cisco is entering a new boom period, CEO says," *USA Today,* 8 August 2007; see also Bobby White, "No longer just plumbers," *Wall Street Journal,* 7 August 2007.

Limited-Potential Niche or Prospective Market Foothold? Five Tests

Ken Hutt
Deloitte Consulting

Ruben Gavieres
Deloitte Consulting

Betosini Chakraborty
Deloitte Consulting

Successful companies eventually discover that the larger and more mature they get, the more difficult it is to maintain their growth rate. Even continuously innovative companies—such as Johnson & Johnson, Microsoft, IBM, and Cisco—must struggle to sustain their growth rates because of the difficulty of identifying and developing early footholds in nascent markets.

Writing about the challenges of managing large, mature businesses, Professor Clayton Christensen[1] and consultant Michael Raynor[2] described the innovation and growth life cycle and the specter of diminishing returns. A key and counterintuitive observation made by Christensen and Raynor is that much of the management commitment that makes for an effective sustaining strategy is likely to prevent participation in the next wave of growth opportunities.

For large companies, the majority of product development and R&D resources are focused on sustaining, incremental innovation. As a result, stage-gate processes and portfolio tools are refined and improved to become ever better at finding and supporting just the sort of products that will appeal to traditional customers, ideally in a low-risk, predictable way.[3] It is very difficult to push a genuinely new idea through specialized processes and metrics designed to enable low-risk, well-understood, and incremental product improvements.

The reality, however, is that most budding business opportunities won't grow into billion-dollar business units, and therefore few have true potential to drive big-company growth. So how can managers distinguish between limited-potential niche and crucial market foothold opportunities? The distinction is crucial in order to make the case for funding and supporting for the small, but potentially important, foothold business areas. Over the past few years we have worked with a number of large companies that are applying the Christensen/Raynor disruption theory. Because of the counterintuitive nature of much of the theory, its adoption by all levels of management can be a struggle. This is because most of the existing processes and policies that have made a company successful run counter to incubating new opportunities. To this end, we have found several straightforward tests to be very useful when incorporated within a development process. Our findings so far are not intended to be the last word on identifying footholds, but instead a starting point for managers who want to apply disruption theory in a fact-based manner and move beyond experience and intuition.

DISTINGUISHING BETWEEN A NICHE AND A FOOTHOLD OPPORTUNITY

Niches tend to be near-term opportunities with well-defined requirements and fixed market or customer boundaries. The product or capabilities developed

Reprinted from *Strategy & Leadership* 35, no. 4 (2007), pp. 18–22.

Working Definitions

Foothold market, a position usable as a base for further advancement. Innovations in foothold markets appeal to a variety of market segments and can lead to significant and surprising growth.

Niche market, a customer segment for which a product or service is best fitted. These are opportunities with well-defined requirements and fixed market or customer boundaries.

do not provide a springboard for expansion of the market. In many ways, personal digital assistants (PDAs) have represented a series of niches. The BlackBerry, the Palm V, and the Sidekick have each in their day had passionate customers, but so far none has evolved much beyond the initial distinctive application. Indeed, the core functionality of PDAs has been subsumed into the mobile phone and, because of the intense competition for continuous innovation by mobile-phone designers, to date there has been little significant differentiation. Even the long-anticipated iPhone has critics wondering whether it can distinguish itself from the competitive pack and offer a truly unique and valuable proposition.

LIMITED-POTENTIAL NICHE OR PROSPECTIVE MARKET FOOTHOLD? FIVE TESTS

Initially, footholds look a lot like niches. The crucial difference is that foothold markets evolve and grow in valuable ways, and it is this difference that managers can identify using a series of five tests. We should point out that these tests are intended to trigger data-gathering to substantiate or highlight the major issues. They are not intended to be only qualitative, but rather also to produce a quantitative product and market strategy. These tests should also be codified into an appropriate evaluation process.[4]

As a starting point, we propose that a strong foothold opportunity exists if managers answer "yes" to five tests:

1. Does the product provide clear value to new customers?
2. Can an initial, viable product be brought to the market sooner rather than later?
3. Will the first customers pay for the improvements needed to enter larger markets?
4. Will initial applications diffuse the product across traditional market segments?
5. Is there limited reliance on third parties for major product improvements?

Here's how each of these tests work in practice:

1. *Does the product provide clear value to new customers?* The intended customers should be passionate about the product; this should be clear from user studies, observations, or field trials. While this test, and the associated data, may give some indication of how many customers might be inclined to buy a product or service, its real value is that it rates the degree of excitement and feeling shown by first-adopter customers.

   To generate value for new customers, it is imperative to understand the customers' needs. This can be accomplished through a Jobs–Outcome–Constraints (JOC) analysis that provides a better understanding of the "jobs" that the intended users are trying to accomplish. A "job" is something that users have to do (i.e., a task, an assigned piece of work to be finished within a certain time, a specific duty or function). An "outcome" is a metric that the customer uses to define success in accomplishing a job, while a "constraint" is an imposed limitation that keeps the customer from using a given solution. The JOC analysis differs from other market research tools—such as conjoint analysis, voice-of-the-customer—in that it segments based on different usage situations rather than buying behaviors. JOC analysis captures—via observation, in-depth interviews, and surveys—the priorities and the trade-offs that early users are prepared to make in particular aspects of a product.

Based on research by consultant Anthony Ulwick,[5] we have overlaid an Importance/Satisfaction measure on the JOC framework that has allowed early markets to be segmented and products redesigned. We recommend that a JOC or similar analysis be conducted to allow trade-offs to be quantified against a backdrop of real user preferences.

2. *Can an initial, viable product be brought to the market sooner rather than later?* The output of the first test was an understanding of the needs of those less demanding customers that are prepared to make trade-offs well suited to an early product. This second question and the associated follow-up analysis must determine (1) that the early product will be profitable at initial volumes, and (2) that no daunting challenges will prevent a relatively quick market launch. Of course, notions of timing and profitability will vary by industry and application, but the crucial guideline at this stage is, "Managers should be impatient for profit and patient for growth."[6] It would likely be much more valuable for a company to introduce a viable "good enough" product into the market sooner, which would allow the market to respond quickly and enable the innovators to learn from market inputs.

3. *Will initial customers pay for the improvements needed to enter larger markets?* At this stage, managers have identified a segment, made trade-offs, and developed a profitable route to get to market. But the opportunity may still be a niche, not a foothold, if the natural product-improvement route doesn't lead to larger, more mainstream markets. The support of initial customers is crucial at this point because they are, in effect, funding product improvements (see Figure 1).

Figure 1   Applying Niche-Foothold Tests to Established Products

Litmus Tests	Blackberry	iPod	Toyota
Did the product provide clear value to new customers?	◐	●	◐
Was an initial, viable product brought to the market sooner rather than later?	●	●	●
Did the customers pay for the improvements needed to enter larger markets?	○	◐	●
Did initial applications diffuse the product across traditional market segments?	○	●	●
Limited reliance on third parties for major product improvements?	◐	◐	●
RESULT	**Niche**	**Foothold**	**Foothold**

● Yes   ◐ Maybe   ○ No

Note: For illustration we applied the tests, qualitatively, to well-known products, RIM's BlackBerry, Apple's iPod, and Toyota's hybrid. Clearly, this is after the fact and so we've changed the tense of the questions a little. One conclusion is that Black-Berry is constrained by a narrow customer base, whereas Toyota's customers are eager for a more mainstream product.

Are the initial customers impatient for special attributes? For example, an early market for digital imaging during the 1990s was in corporate ID badges, where Polaroid technology was dominant. Digital allowed image storage and fast clean printing, and could support the high early costs per digital print. However, this market was impatient to see improvements in such areas as printing onto badge PVC substrates, image rub-resistance, and overall durability under continuous use. These attributes were all very important for that customer group, but not very important for mainstream photo-replacement applications. Printing badges was very profitable for most of the early players, but it turned out to be a niche, not a foothold.

In the high-tech world, Cisco's acquisition of Linksys is often cited as an example of how a large company can grow by incorporating a potentially disruptive business. Linksys does indeed give Cisco an option to move its low-cost-routing technology upmarket to ever more complex segments, including disrupting Cisco's core router business. But is that likely to happen? Based upon this opportunity test, Linksys looks more niche than foothold and the answer appears to be "no." The most important customers for Linksys are fairly undemanding technically, but very discriminating in areas such as standardization, cost, and simplicity. For example, satisfying the home and small-business segment is unlikely to directly open more demanding technical segments. Linksys will need to make the case for investing in these more technically challenging segments despite, and not because of, the needs of the current business.

In contrast, the hybrid engine pioneered by Toyota has passionate customers who are impatient to see just the sort of improvements that will help prepare the engine for a larger, more mainstream market. These potential improvements include lower upfront cost, even more efficient fuel consumption, improved performance, and lifetime reliability. Thus the hybrid engine market passes this test and has all the hallmarks of a foothold.

4. *Will initial applications enable the product to appeal to a number of traditional market segments?* Is the first product aimed at a specific customer? Without that specificity it would be very difficult to satisfy test 1 or 2. But can you imagine other users who may wish to experiment with your product having both access and interest? Through such strategies as channel choice, initial price point, and peripheral or product bundling, can you envision other groups having an opportunity to find surprising applications? That's the key for this test. Footholds require learning from early applications and responding to the resulting market feedback by improving the product in ways that not only satisfy current customers but also open larger and, ideally, more diverse markets. The more diverse the applications, the more likely it is that the initial product will become a platform for serving a number of markets and won't be overly reliant on one segment for continued growth.

Two examples with very different diffusion properties: iPod and BlackBerry. There is no typical iPod user; it seems that almost everyone has one and has a favorite way to use it. The level of experimentation is very high, and Apple is in the enviable position of being able to absorb or participate in the most valuable results, such as Podcasting. In contrast, RIM's BlackBerry has passionate users, too, but they tend to be corporate e-mail junkies. The product has not been widely adopted by other segments so far, and product improvements have consistently been driven by inputs from a homogenous user base. As a result, the BlackBerry has become increasingly easy to use for the same customer segment. This unambiguous specialization on the corporate segment has made BlackBerry hard to dislodge in this core market but effectively precluded penetration across other market segments. One can conclude that the BlackBerry has created an extremely satisfied, profitable, homogenous user base, effectively carving out a niche position. To move beyond this niche and establish a new growth platform probably doesn't involve adding mainstream features, like a camera phone, to a Blackberry. Instead the company may need to launch a new distinct platform; RIM appears to be exploring this with its new wireless phone, the Pearl.

5. *Is there little or no reliance on third parties for major product improvements?* Based on the four previous questions, a foothold is defined as a segment that is willing to buy the initial product

and is impatient for you to improve it in ways that make the product increasingly useful to a larger, more diverse customer population. The next step is to evaluate the ease or difficulty of capturing profits as the product improves. To reap profits, a company must be free to solve the most significant problem with the design or the business model.

Consider a case of extreme reliance, wireless telecom networks, where the performance of the network is often decided by the performance of the underlying network elements—such as base station antennas, spectrally efficient coding regimes, and radio performance of the handset. Improving network performance means improving each of these elements in a coordinated manner. Such a set of sustaining innovations is difficult to achieve and is also extremely dependent on third parties. The ability to capture above-average profits from distinctive innovation is not easy for any player in the wireless industry because of the dependent nature of the network. Footholds have been difficult to find.

On the other hand, consider Toyota's hybrid engine. Toyota has a leading technical position and, so far, is not beholden to any third party for major enabling components, so the chances are good that Toyota can capture much of the hybrid's value.

After asking all five questions, if your analysis of a potential business opportunity indicates that it is a strong foothold, then it's likely it has a significant long-term potential for your business.

Working with company management, we have successfully incorporated these tests into early product- and market-development activities through process steps and metrics. Foothold tests begin the formal process of exploring potential markets effectively—enabling even a large company to act more like an entrepreneurial start-up.

Notes

1. Christensen, Clayton, *The Innovator's Dilemma: When New Technologies Cause Great Firms to Fail,* HBS Press, 1997.
2. Christensen, Clayton and Raynor, Michael, *The Innovator's Solution: Creating and Sustaining Successful Growth,* HBS Press, 2003.
3. Cooper, Robert, Egettt, Scott, and Kleinschmidt, Elko. *Portfolio Management for New Products,* 2nd ed., Basic Books, 2001.
4. Hutt, Ken and Shah, Pragnesh, *Managing the Front End of Innovation,* Conference, Boston, Management Roundtable, 2006.
5. Ulwick, Anthony, *What Customers Want: Using Outcome-Driven Innovation to Create Breakthrough Products and Services,* McGraw-Hill, 2005.
6. Christensen, Clayton and Raynor, Michael, *The Innovator's Solution: Creating and Sustaining Successful Growth,* HBS Press, 2003.

Further Reading

Hutt, Ken and Davidson, Alistair (2005), "Strategies for Managing Mature Products," *Strategy & Leadership,* April 2005.

Johansson, Frans (2004), *The Medici Effect: Breakthrough Insights at the Intersection of Ideas, Concepts and Cultures,* HBS Press, 2004.

Raynor, Michael (2007), *The Strategy Paradox,* Doubleday, 2007.

Value Innovation: A Leap into the Blue Ocean

W. Chan Kim
INSEAD

Renée Mauborgne
INSEAD

Corporate strategy is heavily influenced by its military roots. The very language of strategy is imbued with military references—chief executive "officers" in "headquarters," "troops" on the "front lines." Described this way, strategy is about confronting an opponent and fighting over a given piece of land that is both limited and constant. Traditionally, strategy focused on beating the competition, and strategic plans are still couched in warlike terminology. They exhort companies to seize competitive advantage, battle for market share, and fight over price. Competition is a bloody battlefield.

The trouble is that if the opposing army is doing exactly same thing, such strategies often cancel each other out, or trigger immediate tit-for-tat retaliation. Strategy quickly reverts to tactical opportunism. So where should companies turn for a more innovative approach to strategy?

The answer lies with something we call blue ocean strategy. We argue that head-to-head competition results in nothing but a bloody red ocean as rivals fight over shrinking profits. Success comes not from battling competitors, but from making the competition irrelevant by creating "blue oceans" of uncontested market space. The creators of blue oceans don't use the competition as their benchmark. Instead, they follow a different strategic logic that we call value innovation. Value innovation is the cornerstone of blue ocean strategy. We call it value innovation because instead of focusing on beating the competition in existing market space, you focus on getting out of existing market boundaries by creating a leap in value for buyers and your company which leaves the competition behind.

These ideas challenge conventional strategic thinking and are supported by extensive research. Over the past decade, we have created a database that covers more than 30 industries going back over 100 years. So what does all this data show?

We believe that the business world has been overlooking one of the key lessons of wealth creation in history. Our research indicates that the major source of wealth creation over time is not the industry that a company plays in per se. Nor did we find permanently great companies that consistently created and captured wealth.

History reveals that there are neither perpetually excellent companies nor perpetually excellent industries. Companies and industries rise and fall based on the strategic moves that are made. Consider *In Search of Excellence*, the bestselling business book published in 1982. Within just five years, two-thirds of the identified model firms in the book had declined. Likewise for those sample companies in *Built to Last*, another bestselling business book. It was later found that if industry performance was removed from the equation, some of the companies in *Built to Last* were no longer excellent. As Foster and Kaplan point out in their book *Creative Destruction*, while the companies listed certainly outperformed the market, some did not outperform the competition within their entire industries.

Reprinted from *Journal of Business Strategy* 26, no. 4 (2005), pp. 22–26. Adapted by permission of Harvard Business School Press. "Blue Ocean Strategy: How to Create Uncontested Market Space and Make the Competition Irrelevant," by W. Chan Kim and Renée Mauborgne. Copyright © 2005 by the Harvard Business School Publishing Corporation; all rights reserved.

The Performance Consequences of Blue Oceans

We set out to quantify the impact of creating blue oceans on a company's growth in both revenues and profits in a study of the business launches of 108 companies (see Figure 1).

We found that 86 percent of the launches were line extensions, that is, incremental improvement within the red ocean of existing market space. Yet they accounted for only 62 percent of total revenues and a mere 39 percent of total profits. The remaining 14 percent of the launches were aimed at creating new blue oceans. They generated 38 percent of total revenues and 61 percent of total profits.

Given that business launches included the total investments made for creating red and blue oceans (regardless of their subsequent revenue and profit consequences, including failures), the performance benefits of creating blue waters are evident.

So if there is no perpetually high-performing company and if the same company can be brilliant at one moment and wrongheaded another, it appears that the company is not the appropriate unit of analysis in exploring the roots of high performance. There are no perpetually excellent industries, either. Five years ago, for example, people envied companies in the IT industry, yet today the reverse is largely true.

Our analysis of industry history shows that the strategic move, and not the company or the industry, is the right unit of analysis for explaining the root of profitable growth. And the strategic move that we found matters centrally is the creation and capturing of blue oceans.

Figure 1   The Profit and Growth Consequences of Blue Ocean Strategy

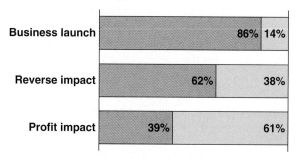

- Launches within red oceans
- Launches for creating blue oceans

STRATEGIC MOVES

By strategic move, we mean the set of managerial actions and decisions involved in making a major market-creating business offering. The strategic moves we discuss—moves that have delivered products and services that opened and captured new market space, with a significant leap in demand—contain great stories of profitable growth. We built our study around these strategic moves (over 150 from more than 30 industries spanning from 1880 to 2000) to understand the pattern by which blue oceans are created and captured and high performance is achieved.

A snapshot of the auto industry from 1900 to 1940 is instructive. In 1908 Henry Ford created the auto industry as we know it with the Ford Model T. Prior to Ford, consumers had two choices: horse-drawn buggies or expensive custom-made automobiles. Ford created a blue ocean by making the automobile easy to use, reliable, and priced so that the majority of Americans could afford it. Ford's market share went from 9 to 61 percent. The Model T, then, was the strategic move that ignited the automotive industry. But in 1924, it was overtaken by another strategic move, this time by General Motors. Contrary to Ford's functional one-color, one-car, single-model strategy, GM created the new market space of emotional, stylized cars with "a car for every purpose and purse." Not only was the auto industry's growth and profitability again catapulted

Head-to-head competition results in nothing but a bloody red ocean as rivals fight over shrinking profits. Success comes not from battling competitors, but from making the competition irrelevant by creating "blue oceans" of uncontested market space.

to new heights, but GM's market share jumped from 20 to 50 percent while Ford's fell from 50 to 20 percent.

Move forward to the 1970s when Japanese car companies created the blue ocean of small, gas-efficient autos. And then to the 1980s when Chrysler created the blue ocean of minivans. All these companies were incumbents. Moreover, the blue oceans made by incumbents were usually within their core businesses. In fact, most blue oceans are created from within, not beyond, red oceans of existing industries. This challenges the view that new markets are in distant waters. Blue oceans are right next to you in every industry. Issues of perceived cannibalization or creative destruction for established companies also proved to be exaggerated. Blue oceans created profitable growth for every company launching them, start-ups and incumbents alike.

Over our study period of more than 100 years, we found a similar pattern in other sectors. In short, the strategic move that matters most to both an industry's long-run profitable growth and that of individual companies is the repeated creation over time of new market space that captured a mass of buyers. Blue ocean strategy is about creating and executing such strategic moves that unlock uncontested market space which render competitors irrelevant. In contrast, red ocean strategy is about how to outcompete in the existing market space.

SAILING INTO A BLUE OCEAN

To understand the power of strategic moves that create blue oceans consider the U.S. wine market. Conventional wisdom caused wineries to compete on the prestige and the quality of wine at a price point—traditional competitive strategy. Prestige and quality were viewed as a function of adding complexity to the wine based on taste profiles shared by winemakers and reinforced by the wine show judging system. The wine experts concur that complexity—layered personality and characteristics that reflect the

uniqueness of the soil, season, and winemaker's skill in tannins, oak, and aging processes—equates with quality.

Then along came Casella Wines, an Australian winery. Casella redefined the problem of the wine industry as how to make a fun and nontraditional wine that's easy to drink. Why? In looking at the demand side of alternatives of beer, spirits, and ready-to-drink cocktails, which captured three times as many consumer alcohol sales as wine, Casella Wines found that the mass of American adults saw wine as a turnoff. It was intimidating and pretentious, and the complexity of taste—even though it was where the industry sought to excel—created a challenge to the inexperienced palate. With this insight, Casella was ready to challenge the industry's strategic logic and business model. To do so it considered four key questions outlined in an analytical tool we call the four actions framework.

First, which of the factors that the industry takes for granted should be eliminated? Second, which factors should be reduced well below the industry's standard? Third, which factors should be raised well above the industry's standard? Fourth, which factors should be created that the industry has never offered?

The upshot of this analysis was that Casella Wines created [yellow tail], a wine whose strategic profile broke from the competition and created a blue ocean. Instead of offering wine as wine, Casella created a social drink accessible to everyone. By looking at the alternatives of beer and ready-to-drink cocktails, Casella Wines created three new factors in the U.S. wine industry—easy drinking, easy to select, and fun and adventure. It eliminated or reduced everything else. [Yellow tail] was a completely new combination of characteristics that produced an uncomplicated wine structure that was instantly appealing to the mass of alcohol drinkers. The result was an easy drinking wine that did not require years to develop an appreciation for.

This allowed the company to dramatically reduce or eliminate all the factors the wine industry had long competed on—tannins, complexity and aging. With the need for aging reduced, the working capital required was also reduced. The wine industry criticized the sweet fruitiness of [yellow tail] but consumers loved the wine.

Casella also made selection easy by offering only two choices of [yellow tail]—Chardonnay, the most popular white wine in the United States; and a red Shiraz. It removed all technical jargon from the bottle and created instead a striking and instantly recognizable label featuring a kangaroo in vibrant colors. It also scored a home run by making wine shop employees ambassadors of [yellow tail], introducing fun and adventure into the sales process by giving them Australian outback clothing, including bushman hats and oilskin jackets to wear at work. Recommendations to consumers to buy [yellow tail] flew out of their mouths.

From the moment [yellow tail] hit the retail shelves in July 2001, sales took off. In the space of three years, [yellow tail] emerged as the fastest-growing brand in the histories of both the Australian and U.S. wine industries and the number one imported wine into the United States, surpassing the wines of France and Italy. By August 2003, it was the number one red wine in a 750 ml bottle sold in America, outstripping California labels. By the end of 2004, [yellow tail's] moving average annual sales were tracking at 11.2 million cases. What's more, whereas large wine companies developed strong brands over decades of marketing investment, [yellow tail] leap-frogged tall competitors with no promotional campaign or mass media or consumer advertising. It didn't just steal sales from competitors; it grew the overall market. [Yellow tail] brought over 6 million non-wine drinkers—beer and ready-to-drink cocktail drinkers—into the market. Novice table wine drinkers started to drink wine more frequently, jug wine drinkers moved up, and drinkers of more expensive wines moved down to become consumers of [yellow tail].

A MARKET UNIVERSE OF TWO OCEANS

To understand what Casella achieved, imagine a market universe composed of two sorts of oceans—red oceans and blue oceans. Red oceans represent all the industries in existence today. This is the known market space. Blue oceans denote all the industries not in existence today. This is the unknown market space.

In the red oceans, industry boundaries are defined and accepted, and the competitive rules of the game are known. Here, companies try to outperform their rivals to grab a greater share of existing demand. As the market space gets more crowded, prospects for profits and growth are reduced. Products become commodities, and cut-throat competition turns the red ocean bloody.

Blue oceans, in contrast, are defined by untapped market space, demand creation, and the opportunity for highly profitable growth. Although some blue oceans are created well beyond existing industry boundaries, most are created from within red oceans by expanding existing industry boundaries, as [yellow tail] did. In blue oceans, competition is irrelevant because the rules of the game are waiting to be set.

It will always be important to swim successfully in the red ocean by outcompeting rivals. Red oceans will always matter and will always be a fact of business life. But with supply exceeding demand in more industries, competing for a share of contracting markets, while necessary, is not sufficient to sustain high performance. Companies need to go beyond competing. To seize new profit and growth opportunities, they also need to create blue oceans.

Unfortunately, blue oceans are largely uncharted. The dominant focus of strategy work over the past 25 years has been on competition-based red ocean strategies. Some discussions around blue oceans exist. But until now there has been little practical guidance on how to create them. That's why in our book *Blue Ocean Strategy,* we provide practical frameworks and analytics for the systematic pursuit and capture of blue oceans.

> Our analysis of industry history shows that the strategic move, and not the company or the industry, is the right unit of analysis for explaining the root of profitable growth.

THE EXPANSION OF BLUE OCEANS

Although the term *blue oceans* is new, their existence is not. They are a feature of business life, past and present. Look back one hundred years and ask, how many of today's industries were then unknown? The answer: Many industries as basic as automobiles, music recording, aviation, petrochemicals, health care, and management consulting were unheard of or had just begun to emerge at that time. Now turn the clock back only 30 years. Again, a plethora of multibillion-dollar industries jumps out—mutual funds, mobile phones, gas-fired electricity plants, biotechnology, discount retail, express package delivery, snowboards, coffee bars, and home videos, to name a few. Just three decades ago, none of these industries existed.

Now put the clock forward 20 years—or perhaps 50 years—and ask yourself: How many now unknown industries will likely exist then? If history is any predictor of the future, again the answer is many of them.

The reality is that industries never stand still. They continuously evolve. Operations improve, markets expand, and players come and go. History teaches us that we have a hugely underestimated capacity to create new industries and re-create existing ones.

In fact, the half-century-old Standard Industrial Classification (SIC) system published by the U.S. Census Bureau was replaced in 1997 by the North American Industry Classification Standard (NAICS) system. The new system expanded the 10 SIC industry sectors into 20 sectors to reflect the emerging realities of new industry territories. The service sector under the old system, for example, is now expanded into seven business sectors ranging from information to health care and social assistance. Given that these systems are designed for standardization and continuity, such a replacement shows how significant the expansion of blue oceans has been.

THE IMPORTANCE OF CREATING BLUE OCEANS

There are several driving forces behind a rising imperative to create blue oceans. Accelerated technological advances have substantially improved industrial productivity and have allowed suppliers to produce an unprecedented array of products and services. The result is that in increasing numbers of industries, supply exceeds demand. The trend toward globalization compounds the situation. As trade barriers between nations and regions are dismantled

and as information on products and prices becomes instantly and globally available, niche markets and havens for monopoly continue to disappear.

The result has been accelerated commoditization of products and services—something the financial services industry knows all about. The effect is to increase price wars and shrink profit margins. In overcrowded industries, differentiating brands becomes harder in both economic upturns and downturns.

All this suggests that the business environment in which most strategy and management approaches of the 20th century evolved is increasingly disappearing. As red oceans become more and more bloody, management will need to be more concerned with blue oceans than ever before. That is why the future belongs to companies that can create and execute on blue ocean strategy.

The war or competitive battle analogy we have used for strategy so far has its limits. It is based on an assumption that there's only so much territory that exists. So it's been about dividing up that territory by competing against one another. There's been a winner and a loser. But our research shows it's not a zero-sum game. You can create new land. Business history shows us that contrary to perceived wisdom, the number of market spaces that can be created is infinite.

There is, however, a hugely underestimated capacity to create new territory—new industries and markets. The number of industries is ever expanding—and the pace is accelerating. The implications for chief executives and their advisers are profound. Some industries die, some persist. But new industries are constantly being created. It is like a galaxy of stars—infinite. Transpose that onto the future, and the obvious conclusion is that the biggest industries today are unlikely to be the biggest industries 30 years hence.

MINIMIZING RISK AND MAXIMIZING OPPORTUNITY

Some would think that blue ocean strategy may be inherently more risky. Far from it, blue ocean strategy is about risk minimization and not about risk taking. Of course, there is no such thing as a riskless strategy. Any strategy, whether red or blue, will always involve risk. Nonetheless, when it comes to venturing beyond the red ocean to create and capture blue oceans there are six key risks companies face: search risk, planning risk, scope risk, business model risk, organizational risk, and management risk. The first four risks revolve around strategy formulation, and the latter two around strategy execution.

Each of the six principles in *Blue Ocean Strategy* expressly addresses how to mitigate each of these risks. The first blue ocean principle—reconstruct market boundaries—addresses the search risk of how to successfully identify, out of the haystack of possibilities that exist, commercially compelling blue ocean opportunities. The second principle—focus on the big picture, not the numbers—tackles how to mitigate the planning risk of investing lots of effort and lots of time but delivering only tactical red ocean moves. The third principle—reach beyond existing demand—addresses the scope risk of aggregating the greatest demand for a new offering.

The fourth principle—get the strategic sequence right—addresses how to build a robust business model to ensure that you make a healthy profit on your blue ocean idea, thereby mitigating business model risk. The fifth principle—overcome key organizational hurdles—tackles how to knock over organizational hurdles in executing a blue ocean strategy addressing organizational risk. The sixth principle—build execution into strategy—tackles how to motivate people to execute blue ocean strategy to the best of their abilities, overcoming management risk.

These six principles aim to make the formulation and execution of blue ocean strategy as systematic and actionable as competing in the red oceans of existing market space. In creating blue oceans, they guide companies in a way that is both opportunity maximizing and risk minimizing.

BLUE OCEAN STRATEGY IS A DYNAMIC PROCESS

Blue ocean strategy should not be a static process. It must be a dynamic one. Consider The Body Shop. In the 1980s. The Body Shop was highly successful, and rather than compete head-on with large cosmetics companies, it invented a whole new market space for natural beauty products. More recently The Body Shop has struggled. But that does not diminish the brilliance of its original strategic move. The problem was that The Body Shop didn't realize what made it a brilliant strategic move. Its genius lay in creating a new market space in an intensely competitive industry that historically competed on glamour. Once it had created a blue ocean, the company focused on mining that new market space. That was OK while few players imitated it, but as more and more competitors jumped into its blue ocean and it became red, the company became involved in a bruising battle for market share. This was the wrong strategy.

Once a company has created a blue ocean, it should prolong its profit and growth sanctuary by swimming as far as possible in the blue ocean, making itself a moving target, distancing itself from potential imitators, and discouraging them in the process. The aim here is to dominate the blue ocean over imitators for as long as possible. But, as other companies' strategies converge on your market and the blue ocean turns red with intense competition, companies need to reach out to create a new blue ocean to break away from the competition again. This is where The Body Shop stumbled.

Blue ocean strategy shows companies not only how to create and capture blue oceans but also how to monitor when it is time to reach out for a new blue ocean. In this way, blue ocean strategy presents a dynamic iterative process to create uncontested market space across time.

Racing to Be 2nd: Conquering the Industries of the Future

Costas Markides
London Business School

Paul A. Geroski
London Business School

Many ideas have been developed in the last fifty years on how big, established companies could create entirely new markets. This advice has been hungrily consumed by large, established corporations as well as smaller firms. After all, which company does not want to become more innovative and which CEO does not dream about leading their organization into virgin territories, discovering in the process exciting new markets?

Yet despite all this advice and good intentions, it is very rare to find a big, established company among the innovators that create radical new markets. Why not?

The simple answer is that the advice given is either inadequate or plainly wrong. What people often forget is that "innovation" is not one entity. There are different kinds of innovations, with different competitive effects. For example, what a firm needs to do to achieve product innovation may be entirely different from what it needs to do to achieve process innovation. Lumping the two kinds of innovation together is like mixing oil with water.

What this implies is that the generic question "How can the modern corporation be more innovative and create new markets?" only gets us generic answers—and these answers may or may not help the company achieve the kind of innovation that creates radical new markets. In other words, prescriptions to help a firm become more "innovative" may or may not be the ones that lead to radical new market creation.

It's virtually impossible to offer proper advice on how to create or colonize radical new markets without first understanding where these kinds of markets come from, what they look like, and what it takes to succeed in them. A better opening question is, "Where do radical new markets come from, what are their structural characteristics, and what skills are needed to create and compete effectively in them?" This helps us identify the skills and competences needed—and the strategies that must be adopted—if a firm is to be a successful colonizer of radical new markets.

In fact, as we show in our book *Fast Second: How Smart Companies Bypass Radical Innovation to Enter and Dominate New Markets,* the full extent of what established companies need to change to be successful pioneers is such a formidable challenge that many of them are better off not even trying.

WHERE DO RADICAL NEW MARKETS COME FROM?

Radical new markets get created through radical innovation. It's important to appreciate this point because it is only by promoting this specific type of innovation inside a firm that the company can hope to create radical new markets.

Innovations are considered radical if they meet two conditions: first, they introduce major new value propositions that disrupt existing consumer habits and behaviors—what on earth did our ancestors do in the evenings without television?—and second, the markets they create undermine the competences and complementary assets on which existing competitors have built their success.

Reprinted from *Business Strategy Review* 15, no. 4 (Winter 2004), pp. 25–31. Reprinted with permission of Blackwell Publishing Ltd.

Figure 1   Different Types of Innovation

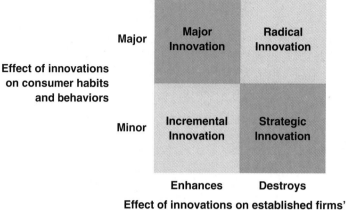

Effect of innovations on consumer habits and behaviors

	Enhances	**Destroys**
Major	Major Innovation	Radical Innovation
Minor	Incremental Innovation	Strategic Innovation

Effect of innovations on established firms' competences and complementary assests

Not all innovations are radical. When we classify innovations along the two dimensions mentioned above—disrupting customers' activities and undermining competitors—we get four types of innovation, as shown in Figure 1. The dividing points in the matrix are subjective, and our intention is not to defend the boundaries of a particular definition. Rather, our goal is to simply suggest that innovation can mean different things to different people, that different types of innovation exist, and that one particular innovation may be more or less radical than another.

We focus on radical innovations here because these are the kind of innovations that give rise to brand-new markets. They are innovations that disrupt both customers and producers. They are based on a different set of scientific principles from the prevailing set, create radical new markets, demand new consumer behaviors, and present major challenges to the existing competitors. The introduction of the car at the end of the 19th century is an example of radical innovation.

Academic researchers have been studying radical innovation for the past fifty years. As a result, we know many things about this kind of innovation. Specifically, we have learned the following about radical innovation over the years:

- Radical innovations that create new-to-the-world markets are disruptive for both customers and producers.

- As a result, these kinds of innovations are rarely driven by demand or immediate customer needs. Instead, they result from a supply-push process that originates from those responsible for developing the new technology.

- Such innovations typically lack champions, either in the form of lead consumers or existing market leaders.

- Supply-push innovations share certain characteristics: they are developed in a haphazard manner without a clear customer need driving them; they emerge from the efforts of a large number of scientists working independently on totally unrelated research projects who devise the technology for their own uses; and they go through a long gestation process when seemingly nothing happens until they suddenly explode onto the market.

- These kinds of innovation create small niches on the periphery of well-established markets. This makes them unattractive to established firms.

The fact that radical innovations result from a haphazard supply-push process has a serious implication for the modern corporation. Specifically, since this process cannot be easily replicated in the R&D facility of a single firm, it is highly unlikely that brand-new markets will be created by a single firm.

Consider the development of the Internet over the last forty years. The associated technology, both hardware and software, was developed in a haphazard way without a clear customer need driving it. No one involved with the technology in the early days had any idea that things would end up where they are today; there was no master plan linking the development of new client-server relations between users and mainframe computers to the possibility of booking a hotel room by computer from a mobile phone.

This unplanned, unsystematic development of the underlying technology seems to have largely been a consequence of how the work was done, and by whom—scientists and engineers in research institutes and universities in this case. Even the major early user, the U.S. Department of Defense, took a remarkably hands-off attitude toward the research work sponsored by DARPA, rarely insisting that it be linked explicitly to defense needs but instead giving it a blue skies mandate. Furthermore, the research efforts that "suddenly" culminated in the Internet were undertaken by a host of scientists from a number of institutions and government agencies over a very long period of time. Such a process can hardly be planned or coordinated.

SUPPLY PUSH AND THE EMERGENCE OF NEW MARKETS

Different innovations produce different kinds of markets. Figure 2 lists a number of markets that have been created through innovation. Those on the left came about through radical innovation, while those on the right came about through strategic innovation. Our interest here is with the markets that are created through the supply-push process of radical innovation—how and when they emerge and how firms ought to compete in these markets.

So what kind of markets do supply-push innovation processes produce? What are their structural characteristics, and what skills and competences are needed to compete effectively?

Supply-push innovation processes have one very important property, and this property has a profound impact on how new markets develop. Since the ultimate consumers of the new products or services which embody a new radical technology typically

Figure 2 New Markets Created through Innovation

New Markets Created through Radical Innovation	New Markets Created through Strategic Innovation
• Television	• Internet banking
• Personal computers	• Low-cost flights
• Personal digital assistants (PDAs)	• Private-label consumer goods
• Cars	• Screen-based electronic trading systems
• Supercomputers	• Generic drugs
• Semiconductors	• Online distribution of groceries
• Mobile phones	• Catalog retailing
• Videocassette recorders (VCRs)	• Department stores
• Medical diagnostic imaging	• Steel minimills
• Computer operating systems	• Online universities

have very little knowledge of what the products have to offer them and how they would feel about them, the race to bring the fruits of the new technology to market is wide open.

No one knows what consumers really want and no one knows just what new technology can do, nor how to produce economically whatever it is that results from the innovation. Your guess is, therefore, as good as ours. Since there are no real barriers to entry into the (as yet) underdeveloped new market, there will not in principle be any shortage of entrepreneurs who are willing to try out their own particular vision of what the new technology has to offer. Anyone who understands the new technology is a potential entrant; anyone sufficiently enthused by what the new technology might ultimately offer will try to become an actual entrant.

This is what happens in all new markets created by radical innovation. Consider the television market. Thirty firms were producing television sets in the United States in 1947, 40 more entered the following year, and another 71 entered between 1949 and 1953. The peak population of television producers in the United States was 71 in 1951, a number larger than the entire number of TV manufacturers that exist today. This massive wave of entry is a phenomenon that always happens in the early days of new markets. Since all of these entrants bring their own product variants to the market, the massive swelling in the population of producers is usually matched by a widening in the range of product variety which is wholly unmatched by anything that happens later on.

Eventually the wave of entry subsides and is in turn followed by what is sometimes a sharp, sudden, and very sizable shakeout that leads to the death of most of the early pioneers. The shakeout is associated with the emergence of a dominant design in the market; this is an event that signals the beginning of growth in the industry.

The dominant design is a basic template or core product that defines what the product is and what it does. It is a consensus good that commands the support of a wide range of early consumers (even if it is not their first preference). It is a product standard that sends signals to suppliers upstream, retailers downstream and producers of complementary goods everywhere. Finally, it is a platform good that allows different manufacturers to offer differentiated versions of the product without destroying the consensus or requiring new complementary goods.

The emergence of a dominant design is the decisive step in establishing a new market. It signals the emergence of a standard product that is capable of forming the basis of a mass market. For the many potential consumers who have yet to enter and make a choice, it signals the end of choice and therefore reduces their risk. A successful dominant design almost always triggers massive entry by consumers into the market, and ushers in the early heavy growth phase that most markets undergo.

The emergence of a dominant design is important for a second reason. The hundreds of early pioneers who entered the new market on the basis of different product designs die soon after the dominant design emerges. On the other hand, the champion whose product forms the basis of the dominant design often develops substantial and very long lived first-mover advantages from being the product champion. Notice that most of these so-called "first movers" were not, in fact, the first into the market. All of them were preceded by many, now forgotten, entrepreneurial start-ups whose work formed the foundation upon which these slightly later entrants built. These "first

movers" were first only in the sense that they were the first to champion the particular product variant that became the dominant design. They were first when the market, not the product, emerged—and this is why they ended up with most of the profits.

It is important to emphasize three points that emerge from this.

- Very few of the original entrants (the pioneers) survive the consolidation of the market. Most disappear, never to be heard of again.

- The consolidators who ultimately win are rarely the first in the new market. Their success is based precisely on not moving fast—but by choosing the right time to move.

- Consolidators' activities—entering at the right time, standardizing the product, cutting prices, scaling up production, creating distribution networks, segmenting the market, investing in advertising and marketing—are the activities that create what we somewhat inaccurately call "first-mover advantages." Consolidators' shrewd movements create buyer loyalty, obtain preemptive control of scarce assets, go down the learning curve, create brands and reputation, and enjoy economies of scale benefits—all of which give them advantages that potential new entrants don't have. Thus, even though pioneers are chronologically first to market, consolidators are the "real" first movers. They are the first to the market that counts—the mass market!

The upshot of all this is that the *companies that end up capturing and dominating the new-to-the-world markets are almost never the ones that created these markets.* Henry Ford did not create the car market, but his company ended up capturing most of the value in that market in its first century of existence. Procter & Gamble did not create the market for disposable nappies, but it harvested most of the value from the mass market. And General Electric did not create the CAT scanner market, yet it was GE that made most of the money.

It turns out that when it comes to radical new markets, this is more the norm than the exception. So—given this fact—why would any company want to create a new market? Surely, the advice we should be giving companies is how to scale up and consolidate new markets, not how to create them.

HOW TO "CREATE" THE INDUSTRIES OF THE FUTURE

All this has serious implications for big, established companies. Specifically:

- The innovation process that creates radical new markets cannot be replicated inside the modern corporation.
- The companies that create brand-new markets are almost never the ones that end up consolidating and dominating these markets.

These two facts suggest to us that big, established firms should leave the task of creation to "the market"—the thousands of small, start-up firms around the world that have the requisite skills and attitudes to succeed at this game. Established firms should, instead, concentrate on what they are good at— which is to consolidate young markets into big mass markets.

They could do this by creating a network of feeder firms—young, entrepreneurial companies that are busy colonizing new niches. Through its business development function, the established company could serve as a venture capitalist to these feeder firms. It may also help them with their own R&D, more to keep close to technological developments than for any other reason. Then, when it is time to consolidate the market, it could build a new mass-market business on the platform that these feeder firms have provided. Since the younger firms do not have the resources, power, marketing, and distribution to scale up their creations, they should—in principle— be happy to subcontract this activity to the bigger firms, subject to a fair division of the spoils.

What we are proposing here is for the modern corporation to subcontract the creation of radical new products to the market and for start-up firms to subcontract the consolidation of these products to big, established firms. This will strike some people as too radical an idea, but it is in fact a business model that is widely accepted in industries where companies live and die on their ability to bring creative new products continuously to the market. We are talking about creative industries such as movies, plays, art galleries, book publishing, and music publishing.

Think about it. A major book publisher does not try to create any of its "new products" (the books) internally. It could, of course, attempt to do so. It would involve hiring thousands of employees, giving them an office and a computer and asking them to produce new books in return for a fixed salary. But how silly does that sound? An organizational structure like that would be the fastest way to destroy the very creativity and innovation it seeks to generate!

Instead of attempting to do everything internally, a major book publisher goes out in the market, identifies potential product creators (authors) and signs them up to deliver their product. Once the product is created (outside the bureaucracy of the big firm), the author subcontracts the marketing, promotion, and distribution of their creation to the book publisher. Just as it would be silly for the big publisher to attempt to create the new products internally, it would be a similar act of folly for individual authors to attempt to sell and promote their books on their own. The division of labor builds upon the strengths of each participant and is a solution that maximizes the welfare of everyone involved. There may be disagreements and problems between publisher and author, but that's what management is there for.

Professor Richard Caves is to be thanked for this insight. Caves alerted us to the striking similarity between what we are proposing (division of labor between young and established firms) and what he was observing in his study of creative industries. This is an arrangement which appears to be the norm in several creative industries. How many art galleries do you know that create their own "products" (paintings) every year? Equally, how many famous painters do you know who used to be full-time employees of major art houses? The image of Picasso or van Gogh laboring away in the R&D lab of a major gallery, straining to create his next masterpiece, is so laughable that no one would take it seriously. Yet this is exactly how we have organized the modern corporation to deliver new radical products.

As a final example, consider the record industry. It would be hard to imagine any famous singers actually working as full-time employees of the big record companies. Professor Caves' research on the subject has shown that there is a very clear division of labor in this market: "Large and small firms play different roles in the recruitment of performers and promotion of their albums. The large companies' distinctive competence lies in promotion and record distribution on a large—increasingly international—scale. The small or independent company performs the gatekeeping function of recruiting new artists and, particularly, identifies and promotes new styles of music and types of performers. The distinction closely parallels that between contemporary art galleries that focus on identifying and developing artists with promise and those devoted to promoting successful artists."

A similar proposition to ours was developed by Reid McRae Watts. In *The Slingshot Syndrome,* he makes the same link between creative industries and the creation of new radical products, showing how the modern corporation could structure itself along the lines that one sees in creative industries. The interested reader is directed to both books.

Some people might object that the division of labor between creators and promoters that we see in creative industries is easy to achieve because the creators of the product are mostly individuals (authors, singers, painters). Therefore, the argument goes, it is easy to allow them to operate as free agents and simply sign them up whenever they have something to offer. By contrast, the creation of a new radical product often requires many scientists to work together, usually in the same laboratory, building upon the knowledge and expertise of the organization. This requires some coordination and supervision of the work.

Although this is a valid concern, we only have to look at the film industry to understand how the division of labor that we are advocating here could be achieved even when there are many people involved in the creation of the product and coordination is necessary. In the film business, a new product (a movie) starts with a screenplay, often written by an independent agent (the writer). The writer approaches several producers to seek financing. The producers may be independent or employed by distribution companies such as Disney, Sony, or Time-Warner. Once a producer acquires the rights to the screenplay, it is their job to provide the financing as well as the director and the actors to make the movie.

Once again, these are all independent agents, willing to offer their services to a specific project for a specific fee. It is only when the product is finally created that the big established firm—the studio—moves into action. The studio acquires the rights to distribute the new product and uses its massive marketing power and existing distribution infrastructure to sell, promote, and distribute the film.

Therefore, in several creative industries we see a clear separation between those who create the product and those who promote, distribute, and sell it. Needless to say, the "promoters" must be knowledgeable about the latest technology and products so that they can make an intelligent assessment of whether a painting, book, or record is good enough for them to promote. But they do not have to be actively involved in its creation. If this organization of work functions well in creative industries, shouldn't we at least attempt to import it into other industries that aspire to become more creative?

In fact, when we compare the basic economic properties of creative industries with the features that characterize new radical markets, the two types of market are amazingly similar. Given this fact, we would be surprised if the organizational structure that characterizes creative industries cannot be readily imported into any industry that aspires to create radical new markets.

Resources

Markides, Costas, and Geroski, Paul A. (2004), *Fast Second: How Smart Companies Bypass Radical Innovation to Enter and Dominate New Markets,* Jossey Bass.

Caves, Richard (2000), *Creative Industries: Contracts between Art and Commerce,* Harvard University Press.

Watts, Reid McRae (2000), *The Slingshot Syndrome: Why America's Leading Technology Firms Fail at Innovation,* Writers Club Press.

Globalization Is an Option, Not an Imperative. Or, Why The World Is Not Flat

Pankaj Ghemawat
Harvard Business School

Most managers—88 percent in a recent online survey I conducted—think of global expansion as an imperative rather than an option to be evaluated. At one level, this can be seen as yet another outlet for expansionary energies once one starts to think of multiple markets rather than just a single one. But at another level, one can argue that expansionary excesses distinguish how most people think about global strategy—as strategy for a company operating in multiple countries—from how they think about corporate strategy for a company operating in multiple lines of business. Cross-border expansion commands wider support and is conceived as optimally proceeding farther than cross-business expansion. For example, 64 percent of the respondents in my survey agreed that "The truly global company should aim to compete in all major markets," whereas there is no comparable presumption in terms of competing in all major lines of business (not within most advanced, open economies, at least).[1]

The intent of this article is to counteract such biases, not only by pointing out the problems with them (the principal focus of the next section) but also but by providing an actionable alternative, namely a framework for valuing cross-border moves (the topic of the section on the ADDING Value Scorecard).

GLOBAL EXPANSION: AN IMPERATIVE OR AN OPTION?

Writers on the globalization of business rarely examine the question of why, if at all, so many follow the urge to globalize. Although there are several reasons for this, perhaps the most important is the widespread tendency to believe in an apocalyptic scenario in which globalization erases borders or, in popular parlance, flattens the world. If true, this would obviate the question of "Why": Think of a blue ocean submerging a flat world and encouraging expansion into all major markets simply because they are there. But talk of a borderless world turns

Richard Ivey School of Business
The University of Western Ontario

Reprinted from *Ivey Business Journal* 72, no. 6 (January–February 2008), pp. 1–11. Ivey Management Services prohibits any form of reproduction, storage or transmittal of this material without its written permission. This material is not covered under authorization from any reproduction rights organization. To order copies or request permission to reproduce materials, contact Ivey Publishing, Ivey Management Services, c/o Richard Ivey School of Business, The University of Western Ontario, London, Ontario, Canada, N6A 3K7: phone (519) 661-3208, fax (519) 661-3882, e-mail cases@ivey.uwo.ca. Copyright © 2008, Ivey Management Services. One time permission to reproduce granted by Ivey Management Services on December 1, 2008.

out, upon examination of the data, to be so much *globaloney*.[2]

A second reason for believing that the world is flat is that, since the late 1980s, much of the literature on globalization written from a business perspective has focused on concerns related to *how*, and not why: how to link far-flung units, build global networks, find and train global managers, create truly global corporate cultures.[3] Furthermore, to the extent that the literature *does* deal with global strategy as opposed to global organization, it mostly focuses on achieving global presence: entering the right markets, making the right acquisitions, or choosing the right alliance partners.[4] I should add that this bias appears to apply to MBA strategy curricula as well as to research and writings for practitioners.[5]

The two broad biases above are probably reinforced by a third—a sense that cross-border moves are so complex and uncertain that they need to become acts of faith. This can be seen as an extension of the tendency to do detailed cost-benefit analyses of small decisions in single-country strategy but to simply throw up one's hands and surrender to animal spirits in making large decisions. Or as Parkinson put it in his Law of Triviality, "The time spent on any item of the agenda will be in inverse proportion to the sum involved."

Whatever the precise reasons, executives in global companies or wannabes often spout slogans rather than substance when asked for their reasons for globalizing operations. Verdin and Van Heck have compiled a confection of these that would be funny if they weren't so familiar:[6] "Our home market is too small." "We need to be where the market is." "Eat or be eaten." And so on. Such *dinosaurism* largely died out in single-country or local strategy more than two decades ago. It is time to put them to rest by articulating criteria for evaluating global expansion rather than treating it as an imperative.

VALUE ANALYSIS AS A MODE OF EVALUATION

There are two broad approaches to evaluating strategies: in terms of principles (e.g., fit with the strategy in place, with corporate financial balances, and with the reputations of managerial sponsors) or in terms of analyzing their implications for value. I have explained at some length elsewhere why principles may be fine for guiding routine decisions, but need to be seen, in the context of important strategic decisions (with large components of irreversibility), as ways of triangulating or complementing the analysis of value rather than acting as substitutes for it.[7]

While this article focuses mostly on the value analysis of specific strategic decisions, even general-purpose value analysis can shed interesting light on action implications—and non-implications. Consider, for example, one of the most widely taught case studies on global business strategy, Cemex, the Mexican cement multinational that has managed to outperform its global competitors, mostly headquartered in Europe, in a capital-intensive industry where it probably suffers a capital-cost disadvantage. Cemex is often celebrated in textbooks and elsewhere for its tight integration/standardization, which it describes as "the Cemex Way" and which an academic who has studied the company terms "[CEO] Zambrano's bear hug." My own value analysis of the situation shifted my attention to Cemex's apparent ability to pick more attractive markets (or to make them more attractive) in ways that let it raise prices. And it helped prevent overgeneralization about the Cemex Way from the relative homogeneity of cement to industries exhibiting more cross-country variation. In other words, a focus on value can help with implementation as well as with analysis.

Yet another reason value analysis is important is that many companies lose money in many geographies over long periods of time. Thus, according to multiyear data on 16 companies that Marakon Associates generated at my request,

> We found that half of the companies we have looked at have significant geographic units that earn negative economic returns. . . . [We] know from our clients that their profitability by geography has stayed fairly stable over time unless they have specifically targeted action at specific countries.

HOW THE ADDING VALUE SCORECARD CAN HELP

To figure out how to analyze value ahead of time, it is useful to start out with the observation that value is the product of margins and volume (with growth rates warranting independent attention in more dynamic terms).[8] In the context of expansionary biases, it was argued above that volume/growth-related considerations are already allotted too much weight in global strategy. So what merits more attention in value analysis are the implications of cross-border moves for margins.

The rigorous focus on value analysis of single-country strategy—in companies, by consultants, and in the classroom—is helpful in this regard because it unbundles margins into the average attractiveness of the environment in which a business operates and its competitive advantage or disadvantage relative to its average competitor within that environment.[9] These quantities are linked by what might be called the fundamental equation of business strategy:

$$\text{Your margin} = \text{Industry} + \text{Your competitive} \atop \text{margin} \quad \text{advantage}$$

Michael Porter's famous five forces framework for the structural analysis of industries has explored the strategic determinants of industry margin or profitability.[10] And Porter and other strategists have probed the determinants of competitive advantage with more recent, rigorously value-theoretic work suggesting the usefulness of separating it into willingness-to-pay and (opportunity) costs:[11]

$$\begin{aligned} \text{Your competitive} &= [\text{Willingness-to-pay} - \text{Cost}] \\ \text{advantage} &\quad \text{for your company} \\ &- [\text{Willingness-to-pay} - \text{Cost}] \\ &\quad \text{for your competitor} \\ &= \text{Your relative willingness-to-} \\ &\quad \text{pay} - \text{Your relative cost} \end{aligned}$$

In other words, in single-country strategy, the notion of a competitive edge has evolved into an understanding of the economics of what might be called "the competitive wedge." A firm is said to have created a competitive advantage over its rivals if it has driven a wider wedge between willingness-to-pay and costs than its competitors. The ADDING Value Scorecard adapts and extends this logic to multiple countries. (ADDING is an acronym that is explained below.)

The Scorecard's first component is Adding volume, and it is followed by the three levers for improving margins discussed above: Decreasing costs, Differentiating, and Improving industry attractiveness. Its last two components, Normalizing risks and Generating knowledge (and other resources), are add-ons that reflect the large discontinuities that can arise at national borders. It is worth adding that this structure, involving commensurability and adding up, distinguishes ADDING Value from other scorecards widely used in business that simply summarize an assortment of more-or-less arbitrary items.

Applications of the scorecard will be aided by a detailed application to a cross-border move that clearly failed the ADDING Value test (as I wrote about roughly at the time),[12] namely the merger, recently dissolved, of Daimler-Benz and Chrysler. Figure 1 summarizes the ADDING Value analysis and the rest of this section elaborates.

Adding Volume

Through its merger with Chrysler, Daimler-Benz hoped to turn itself into one of the Big 5 automakers in terms of total scale of production. But the limitation of this logic is that profitability in cars, particularly luxury cars, doesn't really seem related to volume. GM, with the biggest scale at the time and scale/brand as well, scrapes along at the bottom of the profitability rankings, while Daimler's arch-rival, BMW, which barely makes the Top 10, ranks just behind Toyota in profitability. And even if one believes, despite these data, that size does matter, note that DC's total volume actually dipped after the merger!

Decreasing Costs

What about decreasing costs? As Figure 1 indicates, the proposed one-year savings of $1.4 billion in operating costs were focused on SG&A, excluding advertising, which amounted to only 7 percent of revenues. This is small change. In addition, automakers generally count on substantial annual productivity gains anyway, so the target looks even punier in that light. And on the other side of the coin, there were increased expenses: investment bankers' fees that exceeded $100 million, more than $400 million a year in recurring expenditures to bring the pay of the merged company's German managers up to their American counterparts', not to mention the much larger premiums (28 percent) paid for Chrysler's stock, and the costs of increased coordination complexity.

And then there was the issue of saving an additional $3 billion through shared engineering and manufacturing know-how. Daimler and Chrysler had almost zero product-line overlap, which spelled trouble for attempts at such sharing. To aggravate

Figure 1   The Adding Value Scorecard and the DaimlerChrysler (DC) Merger

Levers of Value Addition	DC's Attempts/Achievements	Limitations
Adding volume	Became one of the Big 5 in terms of total scale of production	• Performance not really driven by scale • Scale requirements lower in luxury: BMW overtook DC despite lower scale and scale/brand • DC share slippage after merger

Decreasing costs	1-year operating cost savings of $1.4b, mostly procurement and back-end activities (finance, control, IT, and logistics)	• $1.4b only 1% of revenues (SG&A focus—only 7% of revenues, excluding advertising)
		• Some improvement even without merger: Chrysler previously saved $1.5b over 5 years with an internal ideas program
		• Some higher costs as well:
		  • $00s of millions in inv. bankers' fees etc.
		  • $00s of millions (ongoing) pay increases to German top managers for parity with U.S.
		  • 28% premium for Chrysler stock
		  • No allowance for complexity/coordination costs of
		• Source of additional $3.0b unclear given limited segment overlap, zero cross-brand platforms, "Purity Laws"
		• Share backflow to Europe, triggering rapid ejection from S&P500; possible increase in volatility: cf. row on risk

Differentiating/increasing willingness-to-pay	Transfer of superior quality, technology, image (particularly from DB to Chrysler)	• Brand Bible mandate of strict separation • Perception that Mercedes' recent quality and profitability problems reflect management focus on fixing Chrysler
Improving industry attractiveness/bargaining power	Increased Big 5 share from 52% to 54% → another step in industry restructuring	• Restructuring excess capacity weaker basis for consolidation by mid-sized players, than need for scale economies: public vs. private benefits • Unfavorable dynamics: intensifying competition in light commercial vehicles (Chrysler focus) in U.S.
Normalizing risk	Risk pooling across different segments or geographies	• Limited value to pooling for public firms with access to efficient capital markets • Possible increase in share volatility/shareholder pressure (new investors, weakened Deutsche Bank ties)
Generating and upgrading resources	Some joint development efforts; some attempts at cultural integration	• Joint work in strictly demarcated (and limited) areas • Institutionalized "Marrying Up/Marrying Down" barriers with "Purity Laws" • Poor communication (Schrempf did not visit U.S. HQ)

matters, a so-called "Brand Bible" issued after the merger decreed that the two divisions' marques would be kept *completely separate,* including their European dealerships.

Finally, in the decreasing-costs category, Daimler apparently hoped that a broader global shareholder base would lead to reduced capital costs for the merged company. In fact, the large "backflow" of shares from the United States to Europe in the wake of the merger triggered the company's removal from the S&P 500, which may have led to more volatility, which may in turn have *increased* capital costs.

Differentiating/Increasing Willingness-to-Pay

The notion here, glanced at above, was that Mercedes' cachet would somehow rub off on Chrysler and make the latter's products more attractive: "Mass with class," as one periodical put it. Two things went wrong. First, the Brand Bible (and similar barriers) prevented this kind of cross-pollination. Second, Chrysler turned out to be a far shakier company than Daimler-Benz's due diligence had suggested. Its aging product line and significant overcapacity contributed to losses of $4.7 billion in 2001 alone. This necessitated an intensive focus on rehabbing Chrysler—distracting management's attention—as well as compromises at Daimler to keep reported profits up. BMW ended up overtaking Mercedes as the number one luxury car brand in the world in 2004.

Improving Industry Attractiveness/ Bargaining Power

What about improving industry attractiveness? Did the DaimlerChrysler merger fix the auto industry in some way that was useful to DaimlerChrysler? Unfortunately, no. The merger *did* increase the Big 5's share of production from 52 to 54 percent, but that change pales against the backdrop of prior decreases in auto industry concentration, which had fallen substantially and more or less continuously since Ford's Model T accounted for about one-half of the world's total stock of cars in the 1920s. The global auto industry's problem today is not one of fewer and fewer players surmounting escalating scale thresholds but, instead, of more and more

fragmentation and, related to that, chronic excess capacity.

Normalizing Risk

The problem with applying this piece of the ADDING template to the DaimlerChrysler merger is that risk-pooling across different segments or georgraphies—one of the stated aims of the merger—doesn't make much sense in the context of a public firm with access to efficient capital markets. On the flip side, the market-value plunge of the overall company soured the traditionally cozy relationship between Daimler and Deutsche Bank, and there was operational risk as well: DC's management proved unable to attend to more than one crisis at a time.

Generating Knowledge/Resources

While the DaimlerChrysler merger created opportunities for information exchange, it appears that few were pursued. This is not too surprising given the very limited attempts at integration. For example, CEO Jurgen Schrempf didn't speak at Chrysler's headquarters in Auburn Hills until *seven months* after the merger had officially been finalized.

CONCLUSION

The detailed discussion of the DaimlerChrysler merger was meant to help you apply the ADDING Value Scorecard to your own business situation. Other help is provided by the even more detailed discussion of the Cemex case in particular and conceptual material in Chapter 3 of my recent book, *Redefining Global Strategy* and by the ADDING Value electronic tool available from *Harvard Business Online.*

Another way of wrapping up this article is with the reminder that in analyzing the implications of cross-border moves for value, strategists need to ask—and address—deeper questions about the different components of the ADDING Value Scorecard. Figure 2 provides a 30-odd list of generic questions of this sort. Addressing some or even all of these questions will not eliminate the possibility of error. But the alternative—expansion across borders driven by *dinosaurism*—is likely to yield results that are substantially worse.

Figure 2   Generic Questions about Components of Value

Components of Value	Questions
Adding volume/growth	• What is the true economic profitability of incremental volume? • At what level does additional volume really boost profitability or margins: total scale, other (disaggregated) geographic scale, plant scale, share of customer wallet. . . .? • Are the effects on the cost side or differentiation side? • How significant are the scale effects (slope, percentage of costs/revenues affected)? • What's the sustainable growth rate? • Where will economics start to deteriorate (or capacity to pinch) first if expanding volume: procurement, production, logistics, pricing?
Decreasing costs	• To what extent can you use actual costs as a proxy for opportunity costs? • Have you unbundled price effects and cost effects by looking at costs/unit? • Have you looked at cost increases (e.g., due to cross-border adaptation, complexity, or size) as well as decreases, and to net them out? • Have you considered cost drivers other than scale? • Have you distinguished between ongoing costs (e.g., operating costs) and one-time costs—ultimately stacking them up against each other? • Are there any implications for rivals' costs? (Raising rivals' costs can help added value as much as one's own, although legal/antitrust risks.)
Differentiating/increasing willingness-to-pay	• Have you thought about the full range of benefits to buyers? • Have you segmented the market appropriately? • To what extent can price be used as a proxy for willingness-to-pay (otherwise, have to devise willingness-to-pay calculator)? • How are any benefits of volume affected by downward sloping demand? • How does cross-country heterogeneity reduce willingness-to-pay for the products on offer? • What are the R&D/sales and advertising/sales intensities for the industry? • Are there any implications for rivals' willingness-to-pay?
Improving industry attractiveness/ bargaining power	• Do you understand international differences in industry profitability? • Are moves significant enough to substantially affect the structural correlates of industry attractiveness (particularly concentration)? • Do you have to account for changes in bargaining power associated with shifts to multinational customers/suppliers? • Can you overcome free-rider problems: is your stake in the industry large enough to pay to improve its general attractiveness? • Are there regulatory/non-market restraints that are important?
Normalizing (or optimizing) risk	• How significant is risk (capital-intensity and specialization of assets, volatility of demand. . . .)? • How reducible is risk by pooling across geographies, products, etc. (inversely related to their integration/correlation)? • Are there other ways of diversifying or managing risk (e.g., can shareholders do it)? • In which ways does cross-border expansion increase risk (e.g., foreign exchange volatility)? • Are there any benefits to increasing risk (e.g., option value of emerging markets to multinationals in mature developed markets)? • How reversible is the move being considered?
Generating and upgrading resources	• Is knowledge geographically specific or portable? • What are the other modes of acquiring the requisite knowledge? (Similar questions can be applied to resources other than knowledge/learning)

References

1. Highly diversified groups, particularly in small, closed markets, provide an important exception to this rule.

2. For more extended discussions of the empirical underpinnings, or rather, lack thereof, of flat-earth beliefs, see my article "Why the World Isn't Flat" in the March–April 2007 issue of *Foreign Policy* or, for a full-length academic treatment, Edward Leamer's review of Thomas Friedman's book, *The World Is Flat,* in the *Journal of Economic Literature* in March 2007. My "What in the World" blog for HBS Online at http://discussionleader.hbsp.com/ghemawat/ supplies additional data, on exaggerated conceptions of flatness and evoked biases.

3. Cf. the most prominent writers in this vein, Christopher A. Bartlett and Sumantra Ghoshal, 1989, *Managing Across Borders: The Transnational Solution,* Boston: Harvard Business School Press. As they put it, "For all the companies we studied, the key challenge in responding to the demands of the 1980s was not to define a strategy, but to overcome the one-dimensional organizational capabilities and management biases that stood in the way of building a new, more complex, and dynamic transnational posture." Just in case you didn't get it, the objectives and content of cross-border strategy—the why and the what—are supposed to be obvious, but organization—the how— is not. To me, this is placing the cart squarely before the horse given the general acknowledgment, even by organizational scholars, that organizational structure, broadly defined, has to be contingent on strategy. For more detail, see my "Reconceptualizing Research in International Strategy and Organization," *Strategic Organization,* May 2008.

4. For some survey work that makes these points, see Steven Werner, "Recent Developments in International Management Research: A Review of 20 Top Management Journals," *Journal of Management,* No. 3, 2002, and Niccolò Pisani, "International Management Research: An Updated Review," unpublished draft, IESE Business School, June 2007.

5. Pankaj Ghemawat and Jordan Siegel, "Study of Core Strategy Curricula," and Pankaj Ghemawat, "Study of the Core Curriculum of a Leading Business School."

6. Paul Verdin and Nick Van Heck, *From Local Champions to Global Masters,* London: Palgrave, 2001.

7. See Pankaj Ghemawat, "Choice: Making Commitments," Chapter 3 in *Commitment: The Dynamic of Strategy,* New York: Free Press, 1991, especially pp. 46–51.

8. The implied margin-volume trade-off was first discussed systematically in Chapter 3 of my book, *Commitment* (op cit.).

9. For more discussion of this logic, see Pankaj Ghemawat, *Strategy and the Business Landscape,* Englewood Cliffs (NJ): Prentice-Hall, 2006.

10. Michael E. Porter, *Competitive Strategy,* New York: Free Press, 1980.

11. See, in particular, see Adam. M. Brandenburger and Harborne W. Stuart, Jr., "Value-Based Business Strategy," *Journal of Economics and Management Strategy* 5, No. 1 (1996).

12. Pankaj Ghemawat and Fariborz Ghadar, "The Dubious Logic of Global Megamergers," *Harvard Business Review,* July–August 2000.

The Challenge for Multinational Corporations in China: Think Local, Act Global

Seung Ho Park
Samsung Economic Research Institute

Wilfried R. Vanhonacker
HKUST Business School

The view of multinational corporations in China has changed dramatically since the late 1970s, when the nation opened its economy and welcomed foreign direct investment, and global players such as Volkswagen, Coca-Cola, and 3M began exploring the market. During the 1980s, other MNCs such as Motorola, Philips, and NEC were received with open arms. They enjoyed corporate tax rates half those imposed on local companies, and they paid no duties on their capital goods imports. In general, they were revered by government and consumers alike. Even into the 1990s, as China and its people developed a better understanding of MNCs, the foreign companies were the objects of awe and admiration. At that time, Chinese consumers exhibited an almost unconditional preference for MNCs' products and services.

However, beginning in 2000, when per capita GDP climbed above U.S.$1,000,[1] and especially since 2001, when China joined the World Trade Organization, both the Chinese government and consumers have changed their perceptions of MNCs drastically. MNC projects now are scrutinized much more for their fit with national interests. Furthermore, MNCs increasingly are getting local treatment. The coming equalization of the corporate tax rates (to be phased in as of January 1, 2008) between local and foreign companies attests to this. MNCs are now held to the same, if not stricter, standards than local competitors

Reprinted from *MIT Sloan Management Review* 48, no. 4 (Summer 2007), pp. W8–W15.

in terms of areas such as employment standards and environmental standards. And they are finding that those standards are enforced much more rigorously.

Chinese consumers also have become more demanding. As a rule, shoppers no longer see much difference between products made by Chinese companies and those made by MNCs. Indeed, their expressed purchase choices often are cast as negative reflections of how much more they had expected of MNCs. In some ways, China's consumers feel let down. The cachet of the MNC is no longer there; savvy shoppers now emphasize objective details and product quality.

MNCs clearly have made significant contributions to China's development. In 2004, 28 percent of China's industrial output and 19 percent of its tax revenue was accounted for by MNCs.[2] Furthermore, MNCs produced 57 percent of all exports from China in that year.[3] By the end of 2004, 400 of the Fortune 500 companies had offices in China. Technology transfer and managerial knowledge are less tangible, but they represent other areas in which MNCs have had an impact, even though a recent government report declared that roughly 85 percent of intellectual property rights used in China are owned by MNCs.[4]

When China opened up, the initial expectation was that MNCs would bring cash, know-how, and skills. But the nation's economy has shifted very rapidly—more rapidly than many outsiders have appreciated. As such, much of what the MNCs first contributed is prized less. At its current stage of

Figure 1   Adapting the MNCs' Behavior to China's Expectations

Given China's current stage of economic development, MNCs are now valued as teachers and role models rather than sources of cash, know-how and skills. But they are falling short in those roles and therefore can expect more government scrutiny.

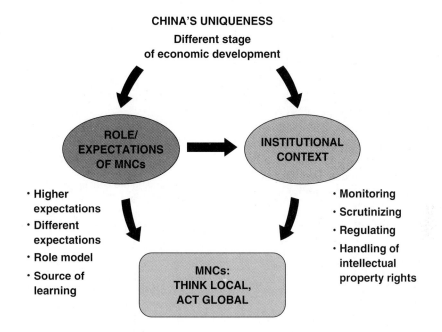

economic development, China has plenty of cash and has benefited from technology and management transfer (although the government remains concerned about the lack of intellectual property in Chinese hands). The current expectations of MNCs are much more qualitative and behavioral: They are supposed to be teachers and role models. (See Figure 1, "Adapting the MNCs' Behavior to China's Expectatons.") And it is in those roles that they often fall short.

Less than two years ago, for example, fast-food giant McDonald's Corp. was forced to cancel a television ad in China after viewers there found it offensive. The commercial depicted a Chinese man kneeling before an electronics salesman and begging for a discount. Viewers said that the commercial depicted the Chinese as poor and lacking in dignity. Explaining that it had been vetted by government authorities, McDonald's China said the ad was trying to convey a message in an exaggerated, humorous way. Chinese viewers

obviously thought otherwise: 80 percent considered the ad insulting.[5]

Toyota Motor Corp. ran into a similar situation in 2003 with two different print ads. One advertisement depicted a popular cultural symbol, a Chinese-style stone-carved lion, saluting a moving Prado GX, whose Mandarin translation means "despotic manner." The slogan read: "You have to pay respect to it." Many Chinese connected the lion with those carved on the Lugou Bridge in Beijing, the site of the first battle of the Second Sino-Japanese War in 1937. The second ad showed a Toyota Land Cruiser pulling a Chinese-made truck on a bumpy road. The truck's trademark was too small to be identified, but the vehicle looked very similar to the Jiefang trucks built by First Automotive Works Corp., a Toyota joint-venture partner in China. A flood of comments on online auto forums claimed the ads were offensive; some citizens used the Web to call for boycotts against Japanese cars. Public resentment against

Japanese companies is aroused easily in China due to Japan's wartime occupation of the country. Toyota withdrew the ads from 30 Chinese publications and published apologies in response to the widespread indignation that the ads provoked.[6]

Such missteps and misunderstandings are not trivial matters. Although localized operations are congruent with the MNCs' efficiency and effectiveness rationales and are essential to their bottom lines, localized behavior can prove disastrous. Toshiba found that out especially quickly in 2000. After an alleged defect in Toshiba's laptops came to light worldwide that year, Toshiba paid about U.S.$1.5 billion (or U.S.$445 per person) in compensation to its American customers. But it did not offer the same settlement to Chinese customers, providing only corrective software. After widespread condemnation in the Chinese media, Toshiba fell from its position as China's top laptop supplier to number three. Its market share dropped from 19 percent to 15 percent in a matter of months.[7]

INDIGNATION AND LOSING FACE

Making mistakes can be particularly costly in China. News travels quickly, and consumers can get surprisingly involved in the discussion. Their general admiration for foreign MNCs translates into high expectations, which quickly can turn into disappointment and disapproval. There are already more than 100 million "netizens" in China,[8] many of them busily filling online billboards and chat rooms with comments, opinions, and their own misconceptions and exaggerations.

MNCs must become more closely attuned to the role they are expected to play at this stage of the development of China's economy. They are under increasing scrutiny by the Chinese government, so it is all the more important for them to understand their "face," or status, in China—how they are perceived and thus how they should act.

In China, few things are worse than losing face. The concept has two bases: social prestige and moral integrity. The two factors are interdependent in that social status implies certain expectations about one's behavior and that the face one is accorded by

others will depend on how well one lives up to those expectations. This applies as much to organizations as to individuals. Although MNCs still are very well placed, their lofty status brings with it high expectations about their integrity. The higher they are in the hierarchy of corporations, the higher the expectations. China expects to benefit from the MNCs' positive influence on the nation's business environment and practices. (See Figure 2, "The Factors Determining an MNC's 'Face.'") A loss of face casts a long shadow over the MNCs' competitiveness and hence their future in China. To gain respect and face, global behavioral standards must be pursued.

Figure 2   The Factors Determining An MNC's "Face"

Understanding the concept of face is fundamental to success in China. The concept has two bases: social prestige and moral integrity. For now, MNCs have prestige, but with prestige come expectations of integrity.

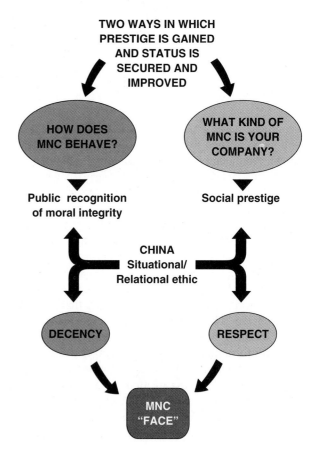

THINK LOCAL—ACT GLOBAL

Put simply, MNCs in China must turn the familiar mantra "think global, act local" on its head. They must "think local," which means fitting business models and approaches to the local reality with respect for the local culture and norms, with a sensitivity to the local political context and with appreciation for the roles that the Chinese government expects MNCs to play. Local managerial talent and input clearly are important factors. Local managers instinctively know the subtleties of the Chinese market and how to navigate the often murky environment. MNCs not only need to have their hands and feet in China—they must have their heads there too, in all senses of the word.

However, MNCs in China must also "act global"—that is, they must ensure that their behavior in China is in line with their behavior around the world. Localized behavior can come in many forms and can be disastrous. The following examples illustrate the kind of ill-advised localized behavior in which some MNCs have engaged. (See Figure 3, "The Behavioral Mistakes of MNCs in China.") For any company wishing to succeed in China, they provide some lessons in what to avoid.

Don't Apply Double Standards

MNCs can get into trouble in China when allowing local standards and practices to trump global standards and concerns. Both Colgate-Palmolive Co. and the Procter & Gamble Co. came under fire in the Chinese media in April 2005 for selling toothpaste containing triclosan, an antibacterial compound that a U.S. study, which did not involve toothpaste, found might cause cancer under certain conditions.[9] When the study findings were reported by the British *Evening Standard* newspaper, British retailer Marks & Spencer Group PLC decided to take the triclosan-enhanced toothpastes off its shelves. China's national toothpaste standard does not stipulate how much triclosan is allowed; both Colgate and P&G claimed that the British response was an over-reaction and kept their Chinese products on the shelf. Their response was backed by a subsequent report in the *People's Daily,* China's main newspaper.[10] (Some retailers in China, including Carrefour SA in Shanghai, did refund consumers for the toothpaste brands that contained triclosan.) At that time, Colgate and P&G's Crest brands accounted for 30 percent and 15 percent, respectively, of China's toothpaste market. Colgate and Crest remain on the Chinese market today but are reportedly seeing declines in sales volumes.

Figure 3   The Behavioral Mistakes of MNCs in China

Multinational corporations often make a mess of their attempts to localize their brand outreach in China. Here are eight types of gaffes that many MNCs have been making.

Mistakes	Consequences
• Double standards	• Associated with discrimination
• Ignorance of the law	• Embarrassment; loss of face
• Bending the rules	• Losing licenses; losing first-mover advantage
• Making "symbolic" acquisitions	• Perceived monopolistic behavior
• Overly aggressive tactics over intellectual property rights	• Viewed as eager to suppress Chinese companies
• Management insensitivity	• Negative public relations
• "Strip-mining" profits	• Tax audits and investigation; difficulties with profit repatriation
• Using China as a lab	• Perceived as taking without giving

Sina.com reported that Colgate's brand trust ratings dropped from 88 percent to 9 percent in one week.[11]

It is worth noting that MNCs must not interpret food safety concerns in the sole context of China's regulatory framework. They must listen to the sensibilities and views of Chinese consumers as well. A case in point: Kraft Foods Inc. and Campbell Soup Co. have been criticized for applying double standards, since they use genetically modified soybeans in China but not in Europe. Legally, both companies are in the right: China does not forbid the use of GM soybeans as long as the product labels disclose the information. (Indeed, China has been an early adopter of the technology and has granted six licenses for GM crops.) The core issue, however, is that global worries about genetically modified crops—circulated by organizations such as Greenpeace International—find their way into China, and into the eyes and ears of Chinese consumers.[12]

Know the Law and Follow It

Many MNCs undermine their local credibility with their ignorance of regulations. Samsung Corp. ran afoul of Chinese regulators in just this way. When the South Korea–based consumer electronics giant was ranked as 2004's top consumer electronics brand in terms of brand equity,[13] a local distributor promptly included this information in its in-store promotional materials. Government authorities were not amused, however: Strict laws prohibit the use of "No. 1," "best," and similar status-oriented references in any advertising in China.

Don't Bend the Rules

Some MNC executives characterize Chinese business practices as immature or corrupt. Yet most Chinese believe that corruption was not part of local business practices until MNCs appeared on the scene. This argument is based on the MNCs not understanding China's business environment and the cultural fabric that characterizes behavior and social interaction in China. Many Chinese feel that MNCs do not understand guanxi, or social networks, and therefore, to get ahead, the companies often buy their way into the market.

One company that paid dearly for such behavior is insurance and financial services giant American International Group Inc. After the China Insurance Regulatory Commission opened a regulatory investigation on illegal selling practices, AIG admitted in January 2005 that its Hong Kong and Macau agents were illegally selling insurance policies in China. As a consequence, CIRC asked AIG to withdraw its application for a group license. The result was that Trieste, Italy–based Assicurazioni Generali SpA was able to jump into the top spot, even though AIG had been the "first mover" in China's insurance industry. Indeed AIG had enjoyed a unique legal arrangement as the only wholly foreign-owned insurance operation in China, so one can imagine how the Chinese government felt about the insurer's behavior.[14]

Lucent Technologies, the U.S. communications equipment company, was at the center of a similar outcry. In a case that was well publicized in the United States, Lucent dismissed its China operations president and three senior executives in April 2004 for offering "commissions" to suppliers in China.[15] Reports show that of the 500,000 bribery cases investigated in China over the last 10 years, 64 percent involved foreign companies.[16] MNCs should note that Chinese law attributes commercial bribery by local employees to the employer, even if management is unaware of the practices.

Avoid Making "Symbolic" Acquisitions

These involve the purchase of local brands, sometimes with the promise of strengthening them, but instead diminishing their presence or killing them off. Chinese observers often view such acquisitions as deliberate attempts to keep local companies at bay or to liquidate them altogether. For example, in 1994, Unilever acquired a five-year lease for Maxam, at that time China's leading toothpaste brand, through a joint venture with a local company. Three years later, it stopped advertising the brand. A Shanghai business acquired Maxam from Unilever in 2001 and spent more than RMB500 million to revive it. But its move came too late; the damage had been done.[17]

Avoid Employing Aggressive Tactics Over Intellectual Property Rights

Another contentious issue has been the aggressive, litigious handling of intellectual property rights disputes by some MNCs in China. Approaches such as those undertaken in recent years by Cisco Systems Inc.,[18] Royal Philips Electronics NV,[19] Sigma Tel Inc.[20] and

Microsoft Corp.,[21] while certainly based on legal grounds within and outside China, are locally perceived as attempts to deter the emergence of local businesses and are in line with the historical Chinese view of imperialistic behavior in China. Apart from damaging the company's corporate image, such aggressive behavior can play into the hands of competitors that have opted for more of a partnership approach.

Guard Against Management Insensitivity

With restructuring going on in many MNCs in China, some companies have been labeled as having particularly insensitive management styles. In the restructuring process that followed the June 2005 sale of Siemens AG's mobile phone unit to Taiwanese electronics company BenQ Corp., laid-off employees accused Siemens of following improper legal processes and of discrimination and unfair salary differences between German and Chinese managers. They took their grievances to the streets, garnering ample media attention.

Don't "Strip-Mine" Profits

MNCs in China also come under scrutiny for their profit-recognition practices. According to Chinese tax authorities, two-thirds of the MNCs that claim to be losing money on their China operations use transfer pricing mechanisms to take profits out of the country. A recent estimate by the tax authorities puts the profits taken out by transfer pricing (on which no taxes are paid) at RMB30 billion (about U.S.$3.85 billion at press time). At the same time, other reports question the credibility of MNCs' reported operating losses in China. For example, manufacturers in China reported average profit increases of 15.6 percent from January 2005 to April 2005, but MNCs reported an average 3.5 percent drop in earnings for the same period.[22]

Don't Use China as a Lab

Sohu.com Inc., a popular Internet service provider in China, ran an online survey of its users in June 2005.[23] Half of the participants felt that MNCs had been changing in a negative way. No specific companies were named, but two views were common. One was that MNCs had been undermining their credibility and public image with their practices and behavior.

The other view was that many MNCs treated the Chinese marketplace as a lab. This is supported by arguments that new technologies are tested in China because it is cheap to do so, but very little of that technology is transferred to China or integrated into the nation's developing industrial base.

WHAT MANAGERS MUST DO

Whether, as has been argued by some, the Chinese media are irresponsible and consumers are overreacting and oversensitive, the fact is that MNCs can find themselves rapidly cast in a negative light if they are not aware of, and do not avoid, behavioral pitfalls.

The question is whether local managers understand the need for behavioral standards and, indeed, whether they know what those standards are. Localization naturally implies that managers and management should move away from a global posture and perspective. Although local managers have an intuitive feel for the local market and know how to get things done in China, they might be less familiar with what a global company really is and, more important, what is expected of those companies at this stage of China's development. Local managers might not be the best at understanding and appreciating how important it is for MNCs to act global rather than trying to appear Chinese. Furthermore, "acting global" might conflict with what they feel needs to be done to get results on the ground. Local ad agencies and other service providers also might not be familiar with what is required. In essence, MNCs are being held to a behavioral standard that changes as China evolves.

The "think local, act global" strategy implies a need for seemingly contradictory management skills. Managers do need to be local in their understanding, but they also must be global in their behavior. They must have real global experience and a mature understanding of (and appreciation for) MNCs' global business conduct. Such managerial talent is in very short supply in China, and unfortunately it is not nurtured by the MNCs' current localization drive.

For its part, the Chinese government is concerned most about the gap it sees between MNCs' expected behavior and how they behave in practice. Beijing has been looking to MNCs to set global standards in China—a particularly important contribution at this stage in the development of the country's economy. Interestingly, guanxi with high government officials—viewed by many MNCs as the best way to protect their interests—is an unreliable tool. Although guanxi does play a role, it is a very poor protector against some MNCs' localization practices. Since so many MNCs have fallen short of expectations so frequently, the government has felt it necessary to crack down, monitoring the behavior of foreign companies more actively.

Multinational corporations in China can succeed over the long term only if they show they have acute awareness of and sensitivity to local laws and cultural imperatives and demonstrate that they deeply understand the concept of face. They must demonstrate they understand their exemplar roles and can police their own behavior effectively. If they do not, they can surely expect Beijing and the provincial governments to do it for them. In China, one gets prestige from who one is, but one easily can lose it from what one does.

References

1. *China Statistical Yearbook* (Beijing: China Statistics Press, 2006).

2. Ibid.; and *Tax Year Book of China* (Beijing: China Tax Press, 2006).

3. In 2004, China's total exports reached U.S.$593.3 billion, and MNCs contributed U.S.$338.6 billion to that figure. See *China Statistical Yearbook.*

4. "The Proposal to Raise China's Capacity in Innovating Independent Intellectual Property Rights" (in Chinese), Mar. 14, 06, www.china.org.cn; and "Each China-Made PC Is Liable to Pay Foreign Companies 30% Royalty, 20% For Each Mobile Telephone" (in Chinese), April 28, 2006, *Western China Metropolis Daily.*

5. T. X. Li, "McDonald's New Ad Depicting Customers Begging on Their Knees for Discounts Offends Customers" (in Chinese), *Chengdu Commercial Daily,* Jun. 17, 2005; and "Chinese Kneeling for Discount in McDonald's Ad," *China Daily,* Jun. 22, 2005.

6. J. Li, "The Beginning and End of Tantrums Caused By Toyota's Ad Depicting Stone Lions Saluting a Prado" (in Chinese), *Star Daily,* Dec. 3, 2003; and "Toyota Car Ads Belittle Dignity of the Chinese Nation," Dec. 6, 2003, http://english.peopledaily.com.cn.

7. B. B. Shou, "Outbursts Created By the Toshiba Incident Not to End Easily" (in Chinese), *Nanfang Weekend,* Jun. 3, 2000; "Toshiba Notebook Sales Decline Due to Compensation Refusal," Dec. 20, 2000, http://english.peopledaily.com.cn; and "Toshiba's 'Favoring One While Slighting the Other' Helps Little to Reverse Declining Sales" (in Chinese), Dec. 20, 2000, http://news.zol.com.cn.

8. "CNNIC Released the 16th Internet Report: China Has 103 Million Net Users" (in Chinese), *Sohu IT,* July 21, 2005, http://it.sohu.com.

9. "Doubts Hanging Over Colgate and Crest: Former Competitors Now Become Fellow Sufferers" (in Chinese), *Beijing News,* April 19, 2005.

10. M. Prigg, "Cancer Alert Over Toothpaste," *Evening Standard,* April 15, 2005; X. H. Shi, "The Colgate Incident: Conducting Studies Is Not Equivalent to Giving Warning Signs" (in Chinese), *People's Daily,* April 20, 2005; W. Shao, "Toothpaste Will Not Be Recalled," April 21, 2005, www.newsgd.com; and L. X. Gao, "Cancer-Causing Toothpaste: People Become Frightened Under the Butterfly Effect" (in Chinese), *China Youth Daily,* April 22, 2005.

11. "Internet Survey Indicated That 90% of Net Users Trusted Crest in the Past" (in Chinese), April 18, 2005, http://finance.sina.com.cn; H. F. Xu, "A Market Cold Front Encountered By Colgate Toothpaste Caused Its Sales Turnover to Dive" (in Chinese), *Shanghai Daily,* April 20, 2005; and Y. F. Zou, "Colgate and Crest in Credibility Crisis: Long- Standing Brand Names Become New Choice" (in Chinese), *Sanxia Commercial Daily,* April 22, 2005.

12. C. Qin, "Greenpeace Alleges Double Standards Over GM Food Practices," *China Daily,* Mar. 15, 2005; K. Xu, "Kraft and Campbell Soup Products Suspected of Involvement in Genetic Modification" (in Chinese), *International Finance News,* Mar. 16, 2005; and F. Lei, "Kraft and Campbell Soup's Genetically Modified Food Strategy For China Faces Challenge" (in Chinese), *First Chinese Business Daily,* Mar. 18, 2005.

13. Y. Liu, "100 Most-Valued Consumer Brand Names Announced: Samsung Tops the List" (in Chinese), *Huaxia Times,* Dec. 20, 2004; H. T. Fan, "Samsung Chosen As Most-Valued Consumer Brand Name, Haier and Nokia Rank 2nd and 3rd Respectively" (in Chinese), *Beijing Youth Daily,* Dec. 21, 2004; Q. W. Lu, "Most-Valued Consumer Brand Names Announced" (in Chinese), *Jiefang Daily,* Dec. 22, 2004; and L. M. Zhang, "Samsung Tops the List Followed by Haier" (in Chinese), *Beijing Morning Post,* Dec. 22, 2004.

14. Y. Wan, "Invalid Insurance Policy Schemes Again Become Rampant Towards Year End: China Insurance Regulatory Commission Again Vows to Crush the Scam" (in Chinese), *China Business News,* Nov. 20, 2004; G. Z. Chen, "Overflow of Invalid

Insurance Policy Schemes, When Will This End?" (in Chinese), *International Finance News,* Nov. 26, 2004; P. Zhao, "AIA Hong Kong Forbids Its Agents From Selling Insurance Policies to Mainland Customers: Payment to 'Invalid Insurance Policies' Solely Determined by Mr. Edmund Tse" (in Chinese), *21st Century Business Herald,* Jan. 30, 2005; and M. Yuan, "AIA China Errs For the First Time: Group Insurance Application Withdrawn as a Result of Long Delay" (in Chinese), *Economic Observer,* Jun. 5, 2005.

15. "Alcatel-Lucent China Fired Four High-Level Managers Suspected of Involvement in Bribery" (in Chinese), *Shanghai Securities Daily,* April 8, 2004; W. Wu, "Four Discharged High-Level Managers of Alcatel-Lucent May Throw Light On the Mainland Company's Corruption Cases" (in Chinese), *Nanfang Daily,* April 8, 2004; Y. C. Wang and F. Zhang, "Alcatel-Lucent China's 'Door to Bribery" (in Chinese), *Caijing Magazine,* April 20, 2004; and N. Lu, "FCPA: The Case of Alcatel-Lucent's Overseas Company in Accepting Bribe Becomes a Known Law in the Realm of Commerce" (in Chinese), *Global Entrepreneur,* Sept. 5, 2005.

16. C. Chang, N.F. Xiao and Y.L. Wu, "Investigating a Foreign Telecom Enterprise for Bribery" (in Chinese), *Asia Pacific Economic Times,* July 23, 2004; J. Zeng, "Revealing Secrets of the Telecom Industry On How to Perfect Cases of Bribery" (in Chinese), *China Business News,* Aug. 16, 2004; and "Investigating Cases of Bribery Involving Foreign Enterprises in China: Has China Become a Tax-Evasion Haven for Multinational Companies?" (in Chinese), *International Herald Leader,* May 30, 2005.

17. Z. S. Zheng, "MaXan Faces the Pain of Losing Control over Its Brand Name After 7 Years in a Joint Venture" (in Chinese), *Market Daily,* Jun. 14, 2001; L. Yu, "MaXan: The Illusion of Staging a Comeback" (in Chinese), *Chinese Business Daily,* Jan. 30, 2005; and F. Yao, "MaXan: From Being Ignored to Achieving Breakthrough" (in Chinese), *21st Century Business Herald,* Mar. 30, 2005.

18. "CISCO Accuses China of Infringement on Its Intellectual Property Rights" (in Chinese), Reuters, Jan. 24, 2003; "CISCO Files Legal Action Against Chinese Companies for Infringement on Its Patent Rights" (in Chinese), *Wall Street Journal,* Jan. 24, 2003; H. H. Qiu and M. G. Li, "CISCO Sues China as Backing" (in Chinese), *21st Century Business Herald,* Jan. 25, 03; L. Yang and S. K. Yu, "CISCO Sues China" (in Chinese), *Beijing Youth Daily,* Jan. 25, 2003; and C. Q. Zhang, "CISCO's Legal Action Against China on Intellectual Property Rights Infringement Ends" (in Chinese), *Guangming Daily,* July 30, 2004.

19. L. Zhou, "Philips Files Action in Hong Kong Against Orient Power Electronics Alleging the Latter's Refusal to Pay DVD Royalties" (in Chinese), *Oriental Morning Post,* May 26, 2005; J. Huang, "Philips Invoking Its Patent Rights to Crush China's DVD Companies: Orient Power Is Sued" (in Chinese), *National Business Daily,* May 27, 2005; and Z. Wang, "Philips Counterclaims Orient Power: Chinese Party to Submit New Pleadings Against 3C Alliance" (in Chinese), *First Chinese Business Daily,* May 27, 2005.

20. Z. P. Liang, "China MP3 Export Troubled By Royalty: No Optimism For the Future" (in Chinese), *First Chinese Business Daily,* Feb. 4, 2005; Y. B. Sun, "Actions Semiconductor, Involved in a MP3 Royalty Dispute, Counterattacks by Launching a Section 337 Investigation" (in Chinese), *First Chinese Business Daily,* Mar. 29, 2005; and R. Huang, "First Legal Action Raised in China on MP3 Core Chip Patent Rights" (in Chinese), *Oriental Morning Post,* April 22, 2005.

21. X. D. Fang, "Project Venus: Good Fortune or Misfortune?" (in Chinese), *Nanfang Weekend,* Mar. 12, 1999; X. D. Fang and J. X. Wang, "Analysis: The Shadow of Intellectual Imperialism" (in Chinese), *Guangming Daily,* Jun. 2, 1999; "See Through Microsoft's China Strategy" (in Chinese), *Zhangjiang Daily,* Jun. 3, 1999; J. J. Lang and G. Z. Jin, "Microsoft Throws Its Net, Yadu Gnaws Through It to Launch Counterattacks" (in Chinese), *Economic Information Daily,* Jun. 10, 99; J. Pi, L. Hou, and L. Gu, "Microsoft Not Considered by Government Purchase?" (in Chinese), *Beijing Times,* Jan. 5, 02; H. L. Wang, "Beijing Takes the Lead to Say NO, Microsoft Fails to Bid for Government Projects" (in Chinese), *Economic Observer,* Jan. 7, 2002; and Y. Zhou, "After 10-Year Struggle of Kingsoft and Microsoft, Will the Situation Be Changed by the Government Purchase?" (in Chinese), *China Entrepreneur,* Sept. 29, 2002.

22. R. W. Zhang, "60% of the Losses Incurred by Foreign Enterprises Are Abnormal: State Administration of Taxation Kick-Starts Anti-Tax Evasion Activities" (in Chinese), *China Business News,* May 29, 2005; "China Becomes a Tax-Evasion Haven for Multinational Companies" (in Chinese), *Economic Herald,* May 30, 2005; "Multinational Companies Seriously Suspected of Tax Evasion: How Much That Ought to Have Been Paid Has Remained Unpaid?" (in Chinese), *China Business Times,* July 6, 2005; and "China Must Not Serve as a Tax-Evasion Haven for Multinational Companies" (in Chinese), July 11, 2005, www.peopledaily.com.cn.

23. H. W. Chen, "Multinational Companies Fall Into 'Localization Trap'" (in Chinese), *China Economic Times,* Jun. 22, 2005.

13 How to Win in Emerging Markets

Satish Shankar
Bain & Co.

Charles Ormiston
Bain & Co.

Nicolas Bloch
Bain & Co.

Robert Schaus
Bain & Co.

Vijay Vishwanath
Bain & Co.

Village roads can be impassable, home cooking is still a way of life, product prices can be below the cost of production in developed markets, and local products often have generations of loyal customers. Nevertheless, emerging markets in Asia, Latin America, and Eastern Europe are delivering some of the strongest revenue and profit growth for global makers of fast-moving consumer goods—everything from snacks to toothpaste—despite concerns that lower prices translate into lower profits.

Emerging-market leaders like Coca-Cola, Unilever, Colgate-Palmolive, Groupe Danone, and PepsiCo earn 5 percent to 15 percent of their total revenues from the three largest emerging markets in Asia: China, India, and Indonesia. The story is similar in Russia and Eastern Europe, where these companies often dominate their target categories and routinely exceed internal corporate benchmarks for profitability. And the trend is likely to continue: The gross domestic product of emerging markets equaled the gross domestic product of advanced nations for the first time in 2006, with much of the growth coming from the "BRICET" nations—Brazil, Russia, India, China, Eastern Europe, and Turkey.

Until the past few years, emerging markets were a relatively low priority for the leading consumer

Reprinted from *MIT Sloan Management Review* 49, no. 3 (Spring 2008), pp. 19–23.

products companies with a few exceptions, even though these markets are home to about 85 percent of the world's population. The obstacles are still real—in emerging markets, multinationals compete on unfamiliar terrain dominated by local players, sell at price points below those in their home countries, and wrestle with deep-seated social and cultural customs. But with growth slowing in the mature markets of North America, Japan, and Western Europe, some consumer goods companies have figured out how to tap into the purchasing power of a new and growing middle class—which has rising income, credit cards, and access to personal loans—in these emerging markets. The fast-moving consumer goods market leaders have proved that, when armed with the right strategies, they can beat domestic competitors. But what separates the winners from the losers?

Flexible thinking, to begin with. Successful companies are willing to break away from business as usual. They reconfigure global products to compete with consumers' preferences for popular local brands, both in price and taste. Or, as with Rossiya—the leading chocolate brand in Nestlé S.A.'s Russian portfolio—companies skillfully steer acquired brands with 50 years of tradition under their own umbrella. They adapt Western marketing and business management practices to local customs. And they develop the resourcefulness to overcome

Figure 1 Keys to Emerging-Market Success

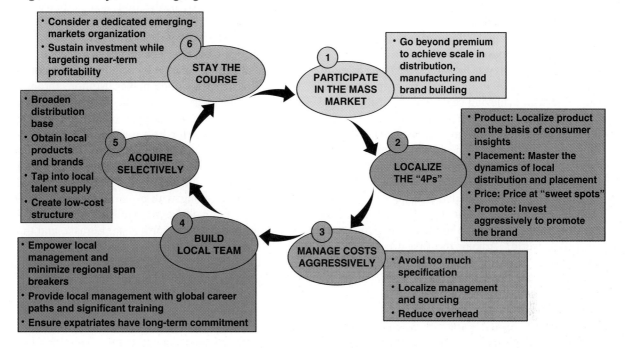

inevitable barriers. For example, where the transportation infrastructure is poor, they might develop workarounds to distribute their products, as Unilever Group did with its fleet of motorcycles to reach customers in remote villages in Indonesia.

For those that surmount the obstacles, the rewards can be great. In some consumer product categories, growth in emerging markets is three times that of developed markets. While each market requires different adaptations, the emerging-market winners share six common practices. (See Figure 1, "Keys to Emerging-Market Success.")

THEY ENTER THE MASS MARKET TO ACHIEVE SCALE IN DISTRIBUTION, BRAND BUILDING, AND OPERATIONS

Historically, multinationals in developing nations targeted niche premium segments—those that traditionally delivered the highest profit margins.

Typically, these companies could not bring their costs low enough to sell to less affluent consumers, many of whom still lived in the countryside. The multinationals often were stuck with low growth, while local players were expanding rapidly in the low-end segments. And local players—making the most of their low costs, better distribution, and increasing sophistication—also began launching brands in the premium segment as the middle class started to grow.

A good example is the cigarette business in Indonesia, where foreign players were limited to less than 10 percent of the market with brands like Marlboro, Dunhill, and Lucky Strike. In 2003, one local player, PT Hanjaya Mandala Sampoerna Tbk., launched A Mild, a kretek (clove-and-tobacco) cigarette for the premium segment. The success of that brand propelled local players like PT Djarum to attack the premium and near-premium segments with brands like L.A. Lights.

As local companies moved into the premium and near-premium market segments, multinationals realized that the mass-market opportunity was too big and important to ignore—they needed to enter the mass market for both the opportunity and to play defense. What's more, participating in the mass segment allows multinationals to drive down the costs of their premium products by achieving economies of scale in raw materials purchasing, manufacturing, sales, distribution, and brand building.

In 2005, for example, Philip Morris International Inc. purchased family-owned Sampoerna in a $5.2 billion transaction. It was the largest deal by a foreign investor in Indonesia. In addition to the many benefits that come with achieving scale, the acquisition will help Philip Morris and Sampoerna make the most of distribution synergies that can help them expand both companies' brands in Indonesia and in markets like Malaysia, Singapore, Brunei, and Brazil. Said Sampoerna president director Martin King, "In Indonesia, Sampoerna has an unparalleled distribution network, whereas Philip Morris has a very good distribution system and sales force in many other countries around the world." Among the first offspring from the corporate marriage: In July 2007, Philip Morris introduced Marlboro Kretek Filter, a new cigarette aimed at extending the Marlboro brand in Indonesia's market for clove-and-tobacco cigarettes.

The Philip Morris–Sampoerna acquisition has been an enormous success—the combined company's volume jumped 9.1 percent in the first year, and market share rose 1.5 percent, to more than 28 percent, enabling it to overtake Jakarta-based PT Gudang Garam Tbk. as market leader.

THEY LOCALIZE AT EVERY LEVEL

Homegrown competitors have several incumbent advantages, including consumer understanding and loyalty, lower costs and home court advantages with government regulators. But by taking the time to learn and master local market complexities, multinationals can gain a competitive edge. That often requires fundamental changes to the product offering—switching to significantly smaller pack sizes, using unconventional distribution channels, and developing products in local flavors, to name a few.

For its part, Procter & Gamble Co. knew that winning over Chinese toothpaste consumers meant catering to local preferences and health beliefs. After extensive research, P&G rolled out a reformulated version of Crest. Chinese consumers can find the Crest brand in fruit and tea flavors, with herbal elements, and there's even a salt version, catering to

the Chinese belief that salt promotes whiter teeth. P&G's approach to localization helped boost its toothpaste sales in China from nearly zero in 1997 to 25 percent of the market in 2007.

The Coca-Cola Co. accelerated its growth in the Russian soft drinks market by acquiring the second-largest Russian fruit juice maker, Multon, through its Greek subsidiary, Coca-Cola Hellenic Bottling Co. S.A., in 2005. It thus positioned itself to ride the local preference for fruit juice drinks. Russia is the largest producer and consumer of fruit juice in Eastern Europe, where fruit juice sales shot up 64 percent between 1998 and 2003. Coca-Cola credited the acquisition, along with a marketing push, with helping deliver an above-average sales increase of 7 percent in 2005 across North Asia, Eurasia, and the Middle East.

Unilever has used innovative distribution solutions to tap the consumer market in rural India. It trained more than 25,000 Indian village women to serve as distributors, extending its reach to 80,000 villages. The program generates about $250 million yearly from villages that otherwise would be too costly to serve.

Localizing also means taking an aggressive approach to brand building. That was the foundation for Coca-Cola's dramatic success in China, where it leads all carbonated soft-drink sales, with a 51 percent market share led by its Coke and Sprite brands against PepsiCo's 30 percent share. Coca-Cola's sales maintained a 16 to 17 percent annual growth rate in the latest five years, and it even hit 18 percent in the second quarter of 2007. By spending twice as much as PepsiCo on advertising and promotion—including sponsoring sports events in China, Chinese Olympic teams and Beijing's 2008 Olympic bid—Coca-Cola eclipsed domestic and multinational competitors alike to attain the number one position. Now, China is Coca-Cola's fourth-largest market, approximately 5 percent of its worldwide sales.

At the crux of all localization strategies is pricing. Global marketers cannot beat out local brands unless they find the local pricing sweet spot—a price that is competitive in the local marketplace and that also delivers a profit. (See Figure 2, "Can Mass Yield Profits?") Finding that affordable price point usually requires reconfiguring existing products or creating new ones specific to a market. For example, Singapore-based Petra Foods Ltd., the world's fourth-largest chocolate maker, prices its popular chocolate

Figure 2 Can Mass Yield Profits?

Price points in India are low, but players still make reasonable profits.

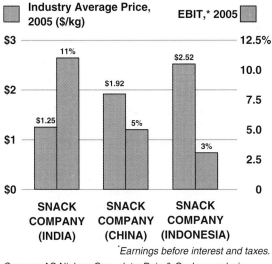

*Earnings before interest and taxes.

Sources: AC Nielsen Corp. data: Bain & Co. Inc. analysis.

Figure 3 Subsidiaries Growing

Equity markets are rewarding the Indian subsidiaries of multinationals with high market caps.

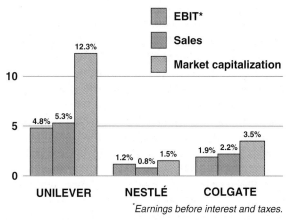

*Earnings before interest and taxes.

Sources: Annual reports; Bloomberg; Reuters; market cap numbers for India from last fiscal year end to match EBIT and sales data.

treat for Indonesian consumers at two pricing sweet spots—500 and 1,000 rupiahs (approximately five and 10 U.S. cents). Those prices coincide with the pocket money typically given to children for treats.

THEY DEVELOP A "GOOD-ENOUGH" COST MENTALITY

Between the traditional premium and low-end market segments is the large and flourishing market for what we call "good-enough" products, with higher quality than low-end goods but affordable prices that still generate profits. Feeding the good-enough market requires aggressive management of costs. Among the techniques: taking advantage of used capital equipment or more labor-intensive production processes, using local suppliers, and outsourcing. For example, a major multinational food company discovered that it could source capital equipment from India at a third of the price it paid to European suppliers without compromising its stringent quality

standards. Cost discipline also means reducing overhead and localizing management.

Winners look at everything they can control to shift the competitive dynamics in their favor—from changing the specifications for packaging material to imposing greater operating efficiency to lowering overhead and using local equipment.

For multinationals catering to the premium end of the market, a strategic acquisition can help slash costs enough to make them competitive. (See Figure 3, "Subsidiaries Growing.") For example, in 2000, Colgate-Palmolive Co. invested $21 million for a 40 percent stake in Sanxiao, a low-cost toothpaste brand in China. The domestic company had a 30 percent cost advantage over Colgate. By localizing manufacturing at a Sanxiao facility, Colgate was able to reduce its costs by 60 percent, which allowed the company to lower the price of its goods by an equal percentage and thus expand into the good-enough segment. Colgate's benefits multiplied when it started using the factory as a worldwide distribution center.

THEY THINK GLOBALLY, HIRE LOCALLY

Too often, multinationals count on expatriates to guide their entry into emerging markets, an approach that can backfire. Expatriates can drive up costs and frequently fail to deliver the deep market understanding offered by local managers. Instead of parachuting in expert expatriates on short assignments, winning multinationals cultivate world-class local management teams that provide a competitive edge in product design, promotion and distribution. The primary role of expatriates shifts from managing to developing local talent and transferring knowledge.

Market leaders foster loyalty by empowering local teams and providing them with global opportunities. It's a talent pool they can tap when entering other emerging markets. Procter & Gamble, the most successful consumer products company in China, has staked its future on its Chinese recruits, who represent nearly all of its employees in China—with one-quarter of them holding Chinese university degrees. When companies do hire expatriates, they make sure there's a long-term commitment.

But the tight local management pools also require creativity, flexibility and commitment. Fast-moving consumer goods players risk becoming the training ground for their local competitors, which are sometimes ready to promote faster and pay better than traditional pay scales allow. A sales force turnover exceeding 50 percent per year can result.

THEY MAKE SURE LOCAL ACQUISITIONS HAVE A STRONG BUSINESS FIT

A strategic acquisition can accelerate a multinational's entry into an emerging market by adding popular local brands to its product lineup, broadening its reach with a stronger distribution network, providing a local talent pool and lowering operating costs. In July 2007, Coca-Cola acquired the Russian beverage group Aquavision, giving itself state-of-the-art, expanded production capabilities. The move builds on Coca-Cola's previous purchase of Multon, the leading Russian fruit juice maker, strengthening the multinational's position in Eastern Europe's hotly contested soft drinks market.

In India, Frito-Lay Inc. increased its market share—and profits—when it bought the local brand Uncle Chipps in 2000. The Indian chips complemented Frito-Lay's brand portfolio, both in price and flavors. After the acquisition, Frito-Lay relaunched the Uncle Chipps brand at a lower price, positioning it as cheaper than Lay's, its flagship potato chip brand. Instead of competing against each other, Frito-Lay has two products targeted at different consumer segments. It also trimmed the number of Uncle Chipps flavors, dropping one that was similar to its saucy ketchup offering. Again, the goal was to have complementary, not competing, flavors. To reduce manufacturing costs, Lay's moved production to a local plant.

Gillette, which was acquired by P&G in 2005 and is the world's largest battery maker, scored a major coup in 2003 by acquiring the Fujian Nanping Nanfu Battery Co. Ltd., the major Chinese rival to its Duracell batteries. The acquisition gave Gillette much more than just a hot-selling Chinese battery brand. The deal had hidden assets: a state-of-the-art manufacturing plant and a distribution network with over three million retailers throughout China. With Nanfu's low-cost factory, Gillette was able to reduce production costs and use the retailing network to extend the reach of its Duracell product line. Gillette protected both Duracell's and Nanfu's brands in their respective segments. The dual branding, cost synergies, sales growth, broadened product portfolio, economies of scale and superior distribution access to more than three million retail outlets in China enabled Gillette to increase its operating margins in the country significantly.

THEY ORGANIZE FOR EMERGING MARKETS

The leaders maximize their investments by building dedicated emerging-market capabilities. This enables them to approach each emerging market with strategies crafted to distinguish the characteristics they find there from the established practices they pursue in developed economies. For example, British American Tobacco PLC, one of the most successful consumer goods companies in emerging markets, has long had a stable of international management talent that it deploys across Asia, Africa, and Latin America.

A U.K. multinational has taken this a step further by creating a formal emerging-markets organization separate from its other international operations. By putting the emerging-markets operations under one tent, it expects to sharpen management's focus and improve managers' ability to evaluate the relative risk-return trade-offs across its emerging-markets portfolio. This will also promote cross-market learning about what works and what doesn't—crucial lessons that otherwise might be lost if emerging-market insights were blurred in a vast global operation.

Groupe Danone, the French food conglomerate, has substantial presence in major emerging markets in Asia such as India, Indonesia, and China, which share several common characteristics—huge geographic area; a high proportion of mom-and-pop outlets, especially in rural areas; and low price points. The company has learned a lot from operating in these markets, such as positioning brands to appeal to local consumers, using low-cost Asian production equipment, keeping a tight lid on overhead, and changing the specifications for packaging and raw materials to produce "good-enough" products. These lessons have been effectively cross-pollinated across the various emerging markets in which Danone operates.

With consumer markets in Asia and Eastern Europe growing at double-digit rates, multinationals are moving fast to build their brands—and the expertise to manage them in emerging markets. Indeed, succeeding in emerging markets is essential if multinationals are to defend—and increase—their share of the global market. How they fare in emerging markets is a critical indicator of how they will fare in the world.

Why Is Synergy So Difficult in Mergers of Related Businesses?

Sayan Chatterjee
Case Western Reserve University

The belief in potential synergy by merger adherents has not diminished very much over the last twenty years despite a record of extravagant promises, mixed successes, and many outright disasters. Often the proponents of new mergers justify them by describing how the value chains of the merging firms "fit" together and how there is potential for rapid growth via cross-selling. As a famous example, in the early 1980s United Airlines acquired Hertz car rental, Westin Hotels, and a few other service businesses with the idea that they could cross-sell travel customers. These mergers were considered "related" because these firms shared some customers. But growth and profits from the expected cross-selling never materialized and eventually the acquired companies were spun out. In a more recent example, AOL and Time Warner merged to benefit from cross-selling synergies created by combining complementary functions. After the merger, AOL's subscribers were bombarded with pitches for Time Warner products, such as broadband access and music by Time artist Brandy, which did not have the expected success. So instead of creating valuable synergy, the merger led to the loss of enormous shareholder value for Time Warner.

Even with such striking failures in the news, until relatively recently not many managers questioned the likelihood of merger synergy between related companies.[1] Likewise there exists voluminous but inconclusive academic research that seeks to justify synergy as a valid reason for undertaking mergers. However, one of the earliest empirical studies of this genre questioned the validity of synergy in related

Reprinted from *Strategy & Leadership* 35, no. 2 (2007), pp. 46–52.

mergers[2] (as contrasted with horizontal-business or same-business mergers). So how do the drivers of merger success—from due diligence, to valuation, to integration—promote synergy between related business? And what evidence is there that supports or contradicts what the adherents of synergy believe? And what types of related mergers are more likely to fail?

Synergy, the golden prize of related mergers, flourishes when the combination of disparate parts within the new organization can lead to more revenues, more efficiency, or more of both than what the individual parts could muster as stand-alone units. Such synergy is difficult to achieve merely by adding new technology or talented employees, especially when the process by which the interconnected activities increase efficiency, or value to customers, is complex—such as the supply chains of Dell or Wal-Mart.[3] In almost all cases, such complex business operations were developed internally and often over a long period of time. There have been many mergers, such as AOL/Time-Warner, that have tried to create these complex interactions following the merger. Among these, the ones that get the most attention are synergistic mergers of equals. Another reason such unions grab headlines is because these are often a bet-the-company gamble. In contrast, the acquisition of a small company is unlikely to change the business model of the acquiring firm significantly and so is less newsworthy.[4] While mergers of equals can sometimes lead to spectacular successes, such as Kraft-General Foods and Novartis, we argue the odds are heavily stacked against them. Perhaps the most significant obstacle to a merger of equals, or large complex mergers in general, is that these are difficult to integrate.[5]

SYNERGY AND INTEGRATION

Synergistic mergers may, at least in theory, create competitive advantage when their complexity makes imitation difficult by would-be competitors. But this same complexity can also lead to integration problems. The acquiring firm in a synergistic merger is typically looking at an idiosyncratic situation and, therefore, its inability to draw upon previous experience often leads to an underestimation of the integration issues and difficulties. Consider a synergistic merger that is studied as a classic of this genre: AOL/Time Warner. This deal was sold to the shareholders on a promise of cross-selling and other synergies. If AOL had thoroughly explored the organizational constraints and cultural differences during due diligence, then they would have been a little less optimistic about achieving some of the synergies. Consider these events:

> On Valentine's Day (2001), AOL Time Warner Inc.'s America Online service hosted an online chat with movie star Keanu Reeves. . . . As part of the chat, AOL set up links to other online sources on Mr. Reeves, including an article created by People. com, the online version of *People* magazine, which is published by the company's Time Inc. unit. According to people familiar with the details, AOL asked People.com to edit out the phrase "He may not be Oscar material (so far, at least)," because it wasn't Keanu friendly. People.com editors refused, and AOL didn't link to the story during the chat.[6]

Soon after this, much to the reluctance of AOL management, they were forced to add "editorial independence" as prominently in their list of company values as "teamwork"—a prerequisite for synergy.[7]

There are numerous other such instances of planned synergy that failed to materialize. Consider the cross-promotion that was supposed to bring in more revenues. One market that Time Warner had targeted was the Internet radio stations accessible to AOL subscribers. The basic idea was to increase the royalties for Time Warner's recording artists played over the Internet radio stations. Time expected these radio stations to go along with the royalty increase because of AOL's subscriber base. Instead the Internet radio stations severed their links with AOL. AOL's subscribers ended up with only AOL radio

stations. It seems the issue of royalty conflicts was not carefully reviewed during the negotiation stage before this source of revenue was booked as synergy. The clearest admission that the merger synergy was abandoned came from the 2002 directive by the new CEO Richard Parsons: each individual unit would focus on what they are good at individually. Overemphasizing the potential for collective good is a common mistake in synergistic mergers, and AOL is not alone in misjudging the opportunities.

SYNERGISTIC MERGERS AND VALUATIONS

There is research evidence that the premiums paid in mergers perceived to be synergistic by managers (termed "related mergers" in the strategy literature) are higher[8] than purely financial (unrelated) mergers as well as horizontal (same-industry) mergers. However, there is also evidence the acquiring firms in "related" mergers do not benefit or are actually worse off compared to unrelated as well as horizontal mergers.[9] Our interviews with practicing managers confirm this research evidence. In a related merger, the seller knows much more of the true value than the buyer, even though the buyer may think that it knows what it is buying.

Consider the case of Kellogg's acquisition of Lender's Bagels. In late 1990s, Kellogg bought Lender's Bagels (a maker of frozen bagels) from Kraft in a desperate effort to get into a high-growth market—bagels. However, the true growth market was in fresh bagels and not the frozen bagels that Lender's sold. To compound this mistake, Kellogg saw Lender's as a related business because Kellogg was selling Eggo waffles in the grocery freezer. In sum, Kellogg did not know the entire bagel business. To paraphrase a former Kellogg executive: "Kraft got a good deal out of the sale."

It should be common sense that mergers that are dependent on coordination of partially familiar activities (complex or otherwise) by two former independent entities will be more difficult to value. Our advice to managers who are contemplating so-called related mergers: it is absolutely imperative to have much more clarity with these mergers than you think you have. The fact that parts of the acquired business are related to yours can lull you into complacency, which can be disastrous. On top of that, if the coordination of the integration is complex, this unwarranted confidence increases the risk even more. In three well-documented mergers—AT&T/NCR, Quaker Oats/Snapple, and AOL/Time Warner—the acquirers all assumed that they could precisely predict the revenue increases that would only arise from such complex coordination of activities of the merging firms. Moreover, they thought that they could achieve these increases very quickly. It turns out they were very wrong.

HOW TO REDUCE THE VALUATION RISKS OF A SYNERGISTIC MERGER

Managers should expect synergistic mergers to be difficult and success elusive. For one reason, they tend to be one-off initiatives, and thus unique. Because of this, it is very difficult to develop a repeatable acquisition process. Thus, synergistic mergers or acquisitions are likely to be excessively costly and to experience integration problems.

The following checklist—based on our assessment of problematic mergers and on conversations with successful acquirers—may enable potential purchasers to avoid some of the major pitfalls:

- *Avoid high-pressure deals.* If the combination is truly unique, then it avoids a major pitfall for all acquisitions—a high-pressure competitive bidding process. Further, negotiations of such deals are more likely to be friendly and transparent. Leadership's goal should be to manage one-off synergistic mergers much the same way that serial acquirers such as Danaher or RPM do deals. These firms often pursue a target for years and even decades. Not only does their long-term perspective give these acquirers much better insight into what they are buying, but they often receive favorable treatment from the seller because of the long-standing relationship.

- *Same industry mergers are less risky.* Travelers/ Citicorp and Hewlett-Packard/Compaq mergers were secretly negotiated over a long period of time, which allowed all the participants to develop realistic expectations. In both cases, all the parties were in the same industry, so everyone

understood the business and the industry dynamics. Surprisingly, both mergers exceeded their basic goals.

- *Synergies in cost reductions are easier than revenue increase.* Based on a survey of academic research, interviews and anecdotal evidence, it is my conclusion that it is much easier to achieve success when the stated goal of a merger is its potential for cost reduction rather than its potential to increase revenue. For example, following its disastrous acquisition of Lender's, Kellogg's next purchase was the frozen vegetarian burgers unit of Worthington Foods. However, with this acquisition Kellogg fared much better because they focused on the cost side of the synergy and did not assume that the market would grow by itself.[10] Likewise, the Hewlett-Packard/ Compaq merger was largely predicated on a consolidation of capacity that could be accurately measured. Despite Carly Fiorina's sudden departure before integration was complete, all the cost targets of the merger were met earlier than predicted. HP had established an objective of achieving $1.3 billion in cost savings by November 2003. Yet within a year, according to Forrester Research, HP had posted savings of $3.7 billion, and acquired new strength in servers and IT services.[11]

The previous observation also solidifies our belief about mergers in the same industry faring better than related mergers. In a merger or acquisition driven solely by consolidation of capacity in a market or industry, the revenue increase would come from simple supply–demand dynamics that are much easier to understand. In contrast, the typical related merger expects revenue increases from complicated cross-selling and other interfunctional coordination. In general, there is strong and uniform academic evidence that horizontal industry consolidations, motivated by capacity reduction, are one of the few merger categories that seem to succeed.[12]

- *Clarify the source of revenue increase.* On the other hand, the evidence regarding related (as opposed to horizontal) mergers that can lead to new revenue opportunities is extremely mixed. Consider, for example, AT&T's effort to develop a broadband strategy by acquiring the leading cable companies TCI and MediaOne in the early 1990s. This was an entry strategy that required paying an excessive premium to overcome the entry barriers. As time has shown, AT&T's rival, Comcast, became the beneficiary when this strategy failed and it acquired all of AT&T's cable assets at fire-sale prices.

In sum, it is very difficult to come to a definitive conclusion in advance about the potential for revenue increase, especially for related (as opposed to financial or unrelated) mergers. This makes it highly risky to establish revenue increase as the primary justification for such mergers. As one former Kellogg executive commented on the failed Lender's Bagel merger, "Very often you do not know what you do not know."

So how can managers mitigate this risk? An alternative approach is to seek a merger as a last resort and instead try to determine if the synergies can be obtained through contractual mechanisms. For example, in the case of United's merger with Hertz car rentals and the Westin hotel chains, United could have reaped the significant benefits of cross-selling between its car-rental and hotel partners by simply referring customers to each other without getting into a merger[13]—as most airlines do at present.

- *Do not make a bad situation worse.* In 1999, Prudential acquired the boutique Silicon Valley investment bank Volpe Brown Whelan in order to get into the booming Internet firm's underwriting business. This is a classic "fit"-driven merger where the acquiring firm buys a complementary resource. During its negotiations with Volpe, Prudential's dealmakers drew up a list of 12 bankers and analysts considered critical to the firm's value. Yet many of these vital personnel left when Prudential closed Volpe's trading desk and integrated the trading operations with Prudential's own. Prudential was trying to extract cost synergy. Yes, Prudential paid a premium to buy the underwriting business. However, trying to recover the premium by consolidating the trading desk was the wrong integration priority. Instead, Prudential may have been able to generate the cost savings it sought through the merger by integrating the trading desk, if they did not hurry the process and antagonize the key traders. These traders were the first line of contact with the customers. The cost reduction was not worth losing these key personnel.

The case of the Volpe acquisition by Prudential illustrates an important lesson. Let's suppose that your firm has acquired a profitable business. You have paid a premium for it. Now you realize that it is difficult to achieve the synergy and you probably will not recover the premium. Our advice is not to try to squeeze the acquisition to produce a quick profit. Trying to force the issue may well lead to the target firm losing ground to its competitors. This is exactly what happened when Rubbermaid acquired Little Tikes in 1984 and wanted to integrate it with its other product lines. The end result was that the founder of Little Tikes quit Rubbermaid, and started step 2, a company that effectively competed with Little Tikes. As a result, the Little Tikes division suffered a string of annual losses and was divested in November 2006. As these cases show, in certain situations the mishandled acquisition of a relatively small target can lead to painful consequences for the acquiring firm.

TWO TYPES OF SPECIAL CASES

Opportunistic Acquisitions

The problem with opportunistic acquisitions, whether they are synergistic or not, is that they are likely to be ad hoc ventures that cannot draw upon previous experience. Research suggests that, as a defense, decision makers must try to develop an in-depth understanding of the acquisition's market. A case in point, in 1993 Merck wanted to use the disease management database of the leading pharmaceutical benefit management company, Medco, to get into the formularies of the managed care companies. Merck's investment paid off in the 1990s mainly because Merck had invested in in-house disease management programs before making the $6 billion hostile bid for Medco. Thus, it had a slight information/knowledge advantage over pharmaceutical companies that acquired pharmaceutical benefit management companies in the wake of the Merck/Medco acquisition. Any kind of information advantage will be a buffer against paying too much. As another method of defense against overpaying, Cisco routinely tries to develop products in-house first before making an acquisition.

Hostile Bids

What about hostile bids? The Medco acquisition ultimately ended up as a friendly merger, but there are acquisitions that remain hostile to the end. Many hostile bids are not built around synergy but rather a short-term opportunity to create value by restructuring or breaking up the acquired company, a common ploy in the 1980s. These acquirers motivated by restructuring did not really suffer from an information disadvantage because they could not care less about the internal goings-on of the acquired company. They simply applied their skill at restructuring and breaking up companies over and over again—so in some sense they benefited from repetition. For this reason, restructuring acquisitions also have a good track record.[14]

A hostile bid can also be justifiable if the value proposition and the value extraction processes are understood by the purchaser. Consider Oracle's hostile bid to acquire PeopleSoft. Oracle was willing to pay $6 billion (an initial offer that was subsequently raised) simply to buy PeopleSoft's 3,000 customers. There was no information disadvantage because Oracle made the calculation that the market power that it would generate by removing PeopleSoft as a competitor (or of avoiding the formation of a stronger competitor through the merger of PeopleSoft and J. D. Edwards) was worth $6 billion.[15] Note that, there was no complicated plan to integrate PeopleSoft with Oracle. In sum, hostile bids that have a purely financial goal are likely to work, provided the acquiring firm has done its homework and has complete clarity about the viability of the value proposition.

However, hostile bids that expect to create value by a complex melding of the acquiring and acquired firm are much less likely to succeed. Commenting on AT&T's hostile bid for NCR in 1990, NCR chairman Chuck Exley said that AT&T was "like an electricity company that wants to get into the Mixmaster business!"[16] In fact, the NCR acquisition was an unmitigated disaster. Our advice: never attempt a synergistic hostile takeover.

SOME FINAL ADVICE TO LEADERS

Research shows that acquiring firms that rely on a repeatable acquisition process have the highest probability of success. The reverse is also true: occasional acquirers that seek synergy or a unique opportunity have to contend with all the impediments to acquisition success and are less likely to succeed. Even experienced acquirers should approach synergistic mergers with great care and not put too much faith in their prior success record. Phillip Morris found out that its success with the Miller acquisition did not help it when it undertook the *ad hoc* acquisition of 7UP. Similarly, Quaker Oats' experience acquiring Gatorade did not ensure success when it attempted the opportunistic acquirement of Snapple. Our conclusion: managers should be extremely circumspect when contemplating one-off mergers or acquisitions.

Notes

1. Mark L. Sirower (1997). *The Synergy Trap: How Companies Lose the Acquisition Game,* The Free Press, New York, NY. This book summarizes a stream of research starting with Sayan Chatterjee's article "Types of synergy and economic value: the impact of acquisitions on merging and rival firms," *Strategic Management Journal,* Vol. 7, pp. 119–139 (1986).

2. Chatterjee (1986) op. cit.

3. This is in effect a "merger" of the procurement activity of Dell/Wal-Mart with the manufacturing activity of their vendors. The reason that competitors have not been able to imitate these supply chains is because of their complexity.

4. This complexity can be a problem even for smaller acquisitions—the types that we have previously argued are more likely to pay off. However, the previous sections deal with an increase in the productivity of the small target's assets and not synergy from a comprehensive combination of the acquirer and acquired companies' activities. In fact, sometimes these smaller firms targeted as synergistic acquisitions can become a money pit if the acquired firm is not careful (Joseph L. Bower "Not all M&As are alike—and that matters," *Harvard Business Review,* March 2001, Vol. 79 No. 3, pp. 92–101). Recall AT&T's acquisition of NCR and Quaker Oats' acquisition of Snapple.

5. Chatterjee (1986) op. cit. hinted at this possibility but did not provide any evidence.

6. Julia Angwin and Matthew Rose, "Creating a 'new media' concept," *Wall Street Journal,* Eastern Edition, 03/09/2001, Vol. 237 No. 48, p. B1, p. 1

7. Julia Angwin and Matthew Rose op. cit

8. Singh, H. and Montgomery. C. (1987), "Corporate acquisition strategies and economic performance," *Strategic Management Journal.*

9. Anand and Singh. 1997 op. cit. Lubatkin (1987), "Merger strategies and stockholder value," *Strategic Management Journal,* pp. 25–37. D. J. Flanagan (1996). "Announcements of purely related and purely unrelated mergers and shareholder returns: Reconciling the relatedness paradox," *Journal of Management,* pp. 823–835. Chatterjee (1986) op. cit., E.B. Eckbo (1983), "Horizontal mergers, collusion, and stockholder wealth," *Journal of Financial Economics,* pp. 241–273.

10. According to the Kellogg executive who integrated the Worthington merger, the revenue estimates were not borne out.

11. Charles Rutstein, with Galen Schreck (2003). "A year later: HP can claim integration success," Forrester Research, May 9.

12. Chatterjee (1986); Anand and Singh (1997) op. cit.

13. The principles for deciding between a contractual arrangement versus and organizational arrangement were well developed in the mid-1960s by Oliver Williamson.

14. Michael E. Porter (1987), "From competitive advantage to corporate strategy," *Harvard Business Review,* May/Jun, Vol. 65 No. 3, pp. 43-59.

15. Porter (1987) op. cit. calls it the better-off test.

16. Paul Carroll, "Is it synergy or just sin?" *Context,* Winter 2002/2003

Corporate Social Responsibility: Why Good People Behave Badly in Organizations

Pratima Bansal
University of Western Ontario

Sonia Kandola
University of Western Ontario

WHAT IS CORPORATE SOCIAL IRRESPONSIBILITY?

It is not difficult to identify socially irresponsible companies. Examples that come to mind easily include Enron, Arthur Andersen, Philip Morris, and Union Carbide. In fact, it is much easier to identify firms that are irresponsible than those that are responsible. Most people agree that firms should operate within legal parameters and not knowingly harm stakeholders. Yet despite the risks and consequences, some firms still operate outside of these parameters. Take the cases of Enron and Arthur Andersen.

On Nov. 8, 2001, following the Securities and Exchange Commission's investigations into its accounting irregularities, Enron was forced to write down its earnings dating back to 1997 by 20 percent and reduce its retained earnings by $2.2 billion (all currency in U.S. dollars). Enron had excluded its partnerships with Chewco and Joint Energy

Development Investments from its consolidated financial statements. By keeping the $600 million debt associated with these partnerships off the balance sheet, Enron had been able to maintain its strong credit rating and share price. It was clear, however, that this practice was improper; Enron had a large stake in these partnerships, and several senior Enron officials were part of their management.

This accounting practice clearly misled shareholders, analysts, and creditors. Andrew Fastow, the ex-CFO of Enron, was accused of knitting together this complex web of transactions and earning about $30 million in management fees in addition to his Enron salary. He has been indicted by a federal grand jury on 78 counts of fraud, money laundering, and conspiracy. Because of the erosion of investor and public confidence, Enron filed for bankruptcy on Dec. 2, 2001.

Arthur Andersen, Enron's auditors for over 16 years, should have caught this malpractice. Sherry Watkins, the Enron employee who brought the accounting irregularities to the attention of Kenneth Lay, Enron's then-CEO and a former Andersen employee, stated that "[Andersen] should have known what they were signing off." Outsiders have stated that the audit team, led by Andersen's Houston partner, David Duncan, should have questioned the exclusion of the partnerships from the beginning. Why it didn't is open to speculation, but the matter of conflict of interest is inevitably raised; Andersen earned $25 million in revenues for auditing Enron and $27 million in revenues for consulting. Its actions have led to a criminal charge for obstructing justice and to the sale of its foreign branches and non-tax divisions.

Enron's and Arthur Andersen's actions were unquestionably irresponsible. It is important to ask, then, what caused such behavior and disregard for ethical principles. We discuss those causes in this article.

WHY FIRMS ACT IRRESPONSIBLY: THE ROLE OF INDIVIDUALS

For organizations to act irresponsibly, individuals must act irresponsibly. When individual irresponsible actions become systemic and significant, the problem then becomes an organizational one. The fact that some people in organizations act irresponsibly is not surprising. While most people resist the temptation to become involved in illegitimate activities, some inevitably succumb.

While it is possible to understand why some individuals act badly, it is more difficult to explain why other individuals, especially senior management, condone or even become involved in such actions, especially given that the consequences are often serious and can lead to the company's failure. After all, everything that we know about good leadership suggests that leaders must demonstrate integrity.

In the case of Arthur Andersen, the behavior of senior management, David Duncan, and his audit team all contributed to organizational failure. It was clear that Duncan benefited financially from managing the lucrative and prestigious Enron account, though he did seem to have some misgivings about Enron's accounting irregularities. In 1997, Andersen appointed Duncan to be its lead partner for Enron's global engagement; in addition, as the firm's lead partner on the Enron audit, he was responsible for all of the accounting team's decisions.

Managing the account proved challenging for Duncan. He continued to uncover accounting irregularities and brought these to the attention of Andersen's professional standards board. However, Enron management and Andersen's senior managers pressured him to accept the accounting practices, likely because of the revenues generated from the audit

and non-audit work. Once the SEC had uncovered Enron's misdemeanors and the spotlight had moved to Arthur Andersen, Duncan sent an e-mail message to his staff that he knew would result in the destruction of documents that the SEC would soon request. On May 13, 2002, although he knew that his confession could lead to a sentence of 10 years in prison, and that Arthur Andersen would be held criminally liable, Duncan admitted to obstructing justice. During these proceedings, several people indicated that they were aware of the accounting irregularities but could nevertheless not curb the malpractice.

WHY GOOD PEOPLE BEHAVE BADLY IN ORGANIZATIONS: THE PERSPECTIVE OF SOCIAL PSYCHOLOGY

Psychologists often argue that our personality traits or dispositions govern our behavior. In other words, people act in similar ways in different situations. While our dispositions are formed by socialization, some may be genetically coded. It could be argued, then, that if people are honest and trustworthy in their personal life, they will be so in their professional life. However, considerable research shows that situational factors are more relevant than personal dispositions in explaining individuals' actions. People who act responsibly in one situation may act irresponsibly in another because of the context in which their actions occur. Just what is it about the organizational context that can lead good people to behave badly? Social psychologists have looked for answers.

Consider the situation of Kitty Genovese, a 28-year-old woman who was murdered in Queens, N.Y., in 1964. Thirty-eight witnesses watched the assault. The assailant returned to the scene of the crime three times over a period of 30 minutes, but it was not until the final stabbing that an observer finally called the police; they arrived within two minutes. The community was shocked that not one of the 38 witnesses had attempted to stop the killing. This behavior, commonly called the "bystander effect," was explained by researchers John Darley and Bibb Latané, who found that people have a tendency to not intervene in emergency situations. In fact, the more bystanders there are, the longer it takes for someone to intervene. Extending the research of Darley and Latané, we suggest three ways in which the bystander effect can explain how individual actions contribute to corporate social irresponsibility.

Watching Other Bystanders

Individuals are guided in their behavior by observing other bystanders. They may be aware that the individuals they are observing are acting irresponsibly, yet they may do nothing to intervene because they assume that keeping silent is the norm. The more people, especially senior management, who are aware of the situation, the longer the irresponsible practices will continue. In the case of Arthur Andersen, most of the audit team was likely aware of the accounting irregularities, and the anomalies were reported to the firm's professional standards board. Yet ironically, as more people became aware of the situation, it became less likely that something would be done, because the actions were seemingly deemed acceptable by the organization.

The Ambiguity of Irresponsible Actions

Second, the ambiguity contributes to bystander apathy. If it is not absolutely clear that the action is unacceptable, or it is not clear who is responsible for resolving the problem, the issue is less likely to be addressed. It is ultimately the responsibility of the CEO to ensure that the firm operates within legal parameters, but if an infraction is not addressed, there will inevitably arise much uncertainty about when it occurred, how serious it is, and whether it is illegal or just bad practice. If ambiguity exists, employees will often continue to engage in the irresponsible practice, not admitting that there really is a problem.

In the case of Arthur Andersen, David Duncan and the audit team may have initially been uncertain about the seriousness of the problem. As evidence mounted about the accounting irregularity, Duncan attempted to reduce the ambiguity by taking it to

Andersen's professional standards board. Given that the board did not rule that the practices should be discontinued, the acceptability of the situation continued to remain an unanswered question.

Diffused Responsibility

Responsibility for addressing ethical issues is diffused among the people involved in the situation. In larger organizations, responsibility for bad organizational behavior lies with all employees, so it is assumed that everyone in the organization will share the consequences of irresponsible actions—despite the fact that only a few individuals may be rewarded. David Duncan earned $700,000 in the year prior to his indictment, and Andersen's senior management profited even more from the lucrative audit and non-audit contracts with Enron. These individuals had little incentive to expose the scandal. Those that did not profit likely did not believe it was their responsibility to report the problem or did not know to whom they should go.

CONSEQUENCES OF IRRESPONSIBLE ACTIONS

Most of us would like to believe that we would not behave irresponsibly in organizations. Yet there is considerable evidence to suggest that many people just like us do behave irresponsibly. At some time or other, every general manager will likely be placed in a situation requiring them to decide whether to engage in a practice that compromises what they deem to be acceptable. If they make the wrong choice, there are consequences for the individual and the organization.

Employee Commitment and Turnover

First, and maybe most importantly, employees who engage in irresponsible actions, or merely stand by watching, often experience guilt and anxiety. These feelings could influence their relationships with their staff, colleagues, and family members. Ultimately, the commitment of these employees to the organization will wane, leading to poor personal performance and, potentially, their departure.

Enron's Values

COMMUNICATION

We have an obligation to communicate. Here, we take the time to talk with one another . . . and to listen. We believe that information is meant to move and that information moves people.

RESPECT

We treat others as we would like to be treated ourselves. We do not tolerate abusive or disrespectful treatment.

INTEGRITY

We work with customers and prospects openly, honestly and sincerely. When we say we will do something, we will

do it; when we say we cannot or will not do something, then we won't do it.

EXCELLENCE

We are satisfied with nothing less than the very best in everything we do. We will continue to raise the bar for everyone. The great fun here will be for all of us to discover just how good we can really be.

Corporate Norms

Second, employees who act irresponsibly will likely influence those around them. Those who observe the behavior start to treat it as the norm. Irresponsible actions often beget further irresponsible actions, which can cause a contagion of irresponsibility.

While individuals initiate irresponsible actions, it is the organization that will ultimately be labeled as socially irresponsible, especially as the number of actions and degree of harm mount. While a few isolated incidents may be blamed on individuals, the legitimacy of the organization will be challenged as the number of bystanders increases or the actions become systemic. The share price of such firms experiences greater volatility, and ultimately, the organization may fail, as was the case with Enron and Arthur Andersen.

PREVENTING CORPORATE SOCIAL IRRESPONSIBILITY

Two conditions are necessary to prevent corporate social irresponsibility: a set of strong and consistent organizational values that espouse corporate social

responsibility, and employee empowerment that permits and encourages individuals to express their concerns to senior management.

Organizational Values

Organizations need to adhere to a set of values that dictate appropriate individual actions. These values establish a framework for what is considered to be acceptable within the organization. Employees will often turn to these values to determine how they should act. As a result, the values must be clear and consistent. If the firm espouses shareholder wealth as an important value, it must be framed in the context of the firm's commitment to social responsibility. Further, it is important that the firm actually practices its values, rather than merely list them in the annual reports and elsewhere. The organization's actions must be framed in the context of the value statements, and all of the values must be exercised throughout the year. Activities that do not support those values must be stopped.

Ironically, Enron espoused a set of values that clearly articulated integrity (see box). It is clear that Enron articulated appropriate values, but did not exercise them. The company also did not provide a mechanism for employees to express their concerns, which is the second necessary condition to prevent corporate social irresponsibility.

Individual Concerns

Employee empowerment is necessary so that employees can express their concerns to senior management. Employees need to be able to voice ideas that support the organization's values or warn of violations. Individuals will naturally be concerned about issues that interest them personally, such as the impact of the firm's operations on the environment, or about an issue that has arisen on the job, such as the way in which a client's account is being handled. By enabling employees to express their concerns, the organization can prevent corporate social irresponsibility and instill responsibility.

Employees may perceive issues that others miss and issues that may have compromised the health and reputation of the organization. They will make those issues part of their own agenda and attempt to initiate corporate action. If the organization acts on those concerns, bystander apathy can be at least partially curbed. Such individual actions can take place at all levels of the organization, and will reflect well on the company as a whole.

Take, for example, Johnson & Johnson and its reaction to the Tylenol incident. Seven people died in the Chicago area in 1982 after reportedly taking Extra Strength Tylenol capsules. Because Johnson & Johnson suspected product tampering on store shelves, it could have chosen to deny responsibility, which was the financially prudent decision at that time. But Johnson & Johnson's credo states:

> We believe our first responsibility is to the doctors, nurses and patients, to mothers and fathers and all others who use our products and services. In meeting their needs we must do everything of high quality.

The CEO, James Burke, used the credo to govern the company's response to the crisis. To reflect its concern for consumers of the Tylenol brand, Johnson & Johnson recalled more than 31 million bottles of the drug at a cost of more than $100 million. The speed with which Johnson & Johnson addressed the issue serves as an example of a company standing firmly by the values it espouses. Although the crisis could have destroyed the Tylenol brand, sales of the product rebounded after an initial loss to capture more than its original 32 percent market share of over-the-counter pain medication. These actions are typical of decision making at Johnson & Johnson, which first enunciated its credo in 1943. The firm has a strong tradition of developing products and policies that positively influence its consumers, employees, communities and, ultimately, its shareholders.

FROM IRRESPONSIBILITY TO RESPONSIBILITY

The practice of developing a strong organizational value system while giving employees and management the opportunity to express their concerns not only prevents corporate social irresponsibility; it promotes corporate social responsibility. Corporate social responsibility is defined as meeting the needs or expectations of all stakeholders. Employees provide a window into what stakeholders desire. Employee relationships with customers, investors, suppliers, the local community, and other employees give them insights into significant issues that should be addressed. Senior management needs to respond to the most significant issues that threaten the organization's values.

By implementing easy actions that fit with organizational values and address the concerns of a large number of employees, the organization will build commitment. For example, Xerox encourages all employees to participate in Earth Day activities. Such activities fuel personal initiatives because people attach environmental concerns to their daily activities. The organization also has a mechanism that enables employees to suggest ways in which environmental initiatives can extend to organizational-level actions. Through these initiatives, Xerox has shown leadership in its response to environmental issues.

The corporate accounting scandals in recent years are notable for the bystander apathy that permitted widespread and significant accounting irregularities. The resulting corporate failures have underlined the importance of keeping corporate social irresponsibility in check. By subscribing to a set of consistent organizational values that attempt to safeguard both financial and social performance, and by empowering and enabling employees to articulate their concerns, organizations can prevent corporate social irresponsibility, and promote responsibility.

Competing Responsibly

Bert van de Ven
University of Tilburg

Ronald Jeurissen
Nyenrode Business University

Abstract: In this paper we examine the effects of different competitive conditions on the determination and evaluation of strategies of corporate social responsibility (CSR). Although the mainstream of current thinking in business ethics recognizes that a firm should invest in social responsibility, the normative theory on how specific competitive conditions affect a firm's social responsibility remains underdeveloped. Intensity of competition, risks to reputation, and the regulatory environment determine the competitive conditions of a firm. Our central thesis is that differential strength of competition produces differential moral legitimacy of firm behavior. When competition is fierce or weak, different acts or strategies become morally acceptable, as well as economically rational. A firm has to develop its own strategy of social responsibility, in light of its competitive position, as well as ethical considerations.

1. INTRODUCTION

It is widely accepted in business ethics that a moral evaluation of firm behavior should focus on the impact of the firm on the rights and legitimate interests of its stakeholders.[1] CSR is often defined in stakeholder terms as well. The European Commission, for example, defines CSR as "a concept whereby companies integrate social and environmental concerns in their business operations and in their interaction with their stakeholders on a voluntary basis, as they are increasingly aware that responsible behavior leads to sustainable business success."[2]

When we define the responsibilities of a firm in stakeholder terms, we should realize that the firm itself is a nexus of stakeholders. A firm is a cooperative venture for mutual benefit, a coalition of participants[3] (clients, employees, share owners, suppliers), who are all economic stakeholders of each other, and who all depend on the continuity of the firm for their wealth and well-being. Hence, the ability of a firm to survive is an important *instrumental* moral goal, in view of the legitimate interests and rights of many stakeholders. This means that policies and strategies of companies directed at the continuity of the firm (operationalized in terms of profitability, market share, growth, future cash flows, etc.) must be considered as morally justified activities, prima facie. The continuity of the firm is an important moral value, albeit of an instrumental nature.

This has a bearing on CSR. Contrary to what the European Commission suggests, in the above quotation, there is not always a positive relationship between responsible behavior and sustainable business success. The relationship depends on many factors, important ones of which are the competitive conditions of a firm. Depending on the competitive conditions, some CSR initiatives can be beneficial to a firm, others not. Therefore, not all forms of CSR are feasible for a firm given the actual market in which the firm has to be successful. Competitive conditions are an intervening variable, influencing the relationship between CSR and business success, and even deciding over whether this relationship is positive or negative.

In our view, competitive conditions affect a firm's social responsibility with respect to specific

Reprinted from *Business Ethics Quarterly* 15, no. 2 (April 2005), pp. 299–317. Used by permission of the Philosophy Documentation Center.

dilemmas, as well as with respect to the CSR strategy a firm can or should adopt. This is so, because competitive conditions are determinants of a firm's survivability, which is an instrumental moral value. In light of the moral value of survivability, managers have a duty to take the competitive conditions of their firm into account in all the strategic decisions that they make, including decisions about CSR. From this, it does not follow, however, that the survivability of the firm should always override other considerations. Sometimes the stakeholders would be better off if a certain business activity were terminated immediately. Take, for instance, the production of CFCs that erode the ozone layer. All living creatures on planet Earth have a high stake in stopping the production of CFCs. So a law that forbids the production of CFCs, as it was actually adopted in, among others, the United States, is morally desirable, even if it means that certain CFC-producing firms would not survive as a result. Furthermore, sometimes the timely liquidation of a firm is legitimate in order to secure the financial interests of stakeholders. Finally, if a certain business violates human rights to stay in business, this could not be legitimized by referring to the instrumental moral value of the firm's survivability. In other words, if the evil of putting the continuance of a firm in jeopardy is the lesser evil, survival of the firm will be overruled by other moral considerations.

Following John Kay, we define business strategy as a firm's scheme for handling the relationships with its environment. Such a scheme includes market entry decisions, product positioning decisions, and an approach to relationship building with stakeholders. A scheme may be articulated or implicit, preprogrammed or emergent. The level of conscious design by management of a scheme may vary, since all strategies are based on a mixture of calculation and opportunism, of vision and experiment.[4] CSR as a strategy aims particularly at social and environmental aspects of doing business. Assessing CSR from a strategic perspective may seem to imply that ethical responsibilities are subordinated to economic imperatives. It may seem as if CSR is not intrinsically valued, but only instrumentally. The suspicion arises that the motivation of firms behind CSR is not truly ethical, since it is in their self-interest. We cannot treat this problem fully within the scope of this paper, because we would then have to deal with the philosophical question what exactly constitutes the moral worth of an action. Is it the respect for the moral law, as Kant suggested? Or are moral sentiments like empathy and sympathy necessary conditions for a truly ethical motivation? For the purpose of this paper, it suffices to assume that for a strategy of CSR to be qualified as ethical or moral it is not required that self-interested reasons be completely absent. Beyond this, we stress the instrumental moral value of the continuation of a firm with respect to the fulfillment of the legitimate expectations of stakeholders.[5] From the perspective of the social responsibility of a firm, it can only be considered a good thing when ethics contribute to the continuation of the firm, since this way a firm will be able to contribute more to the well-being of stakeholders and of non-stakeholders such as the environment. Furthermore, the fact that CSR can serve strategic purposes does not say anything about the motivations behind it. Maybe the members of the board of directors are truly motivated by a sense of moral duty; maybe they are only backing the CSR efforts because it is good for business or for themselves. They will probably have mixed motives to integrate CSR in their corporate strategy. We suggest that the qualification of a strategy as a strategy of CSR should not depend on the motivation of managers, but only on goals and outcomes, just like this is the case for any other business strategy.

CSR should make sense from the perspective of the overall competitive strategy of a firm (and the other way around), and should be treated as an integral part of it, not only because this furthers the long-term survival of a firm but also because this way the moral claims of stakeholders have the best chance of becoming an accepted part of the firm's decision-making structure and its organizational culture. This way, the relationship between ethics and economics becomes in large measure a matter of strategic choice rather than discovery, as Lynn Sharp Paine has argued.[6]

Many business ethicists agree that, regardless of what a firm does to improve its social performance and to take on its moral responsibilities, it should also be profitable in the long run. Mostly, however, this relationship is discussed only in general terms. Little attention is paid to the relationship between *specific* competitive conditions and the possibilities of a firm to adopt a specific CSR strategy. Sethi and Sama developed a descriptive model of the effect of marketplace competition, industry structure, and firm resources on ethical business conduct.[7] It is important to describe how competitive conditions influence ethical business behavior, but this does not tell us to what extent and in what sense it is morally acceptable that market conditions influence the outcomes of the decision-making process. To answer this question, we will have to look more specifically into the relationship between competitive conditions and CSR. This brings us to the following research question:

> How can firms compete in a morally acceptable way, given the fact that they have to survive in an environment where competition is (*a*) more or less intense, (*b*) more or less regulated, and (*c*) more or less susceptible to the scrutiny of influential stakeholders?

By specifying the relationships between specific competitive conditions and CSR strategies, greater justice can be done to the special circumstances that confront a firm that tries to balance its social responsibility with the need to be profitable.

To develop a specifying model of the relationship between CSR and competition, we will first discuss the assumption of perfect competition in economic theory. This assumption totally paralyzes the debate on CSR from an economic perspective, so we will first have to show why, from an ethical perspective, this assumption must be rejected. Next, in section three, we will introduce a conceptualization of competitive forces and competitive strategies, based on the work of Porter. In sections four to six, we will examine what CSR strategies are feasible for firms, under different competitive conditions. In section seven we will draw a number of conclusions.

2. INTENSITY OF COMPETITION AND CSR STRATEGIES

Why should firms pursue profitability? Profits are not the purpose of a business activity, but a means of building the business and rewarding employees, executives, and investors, says Solomon.[8] According to Peter Drucker, profits are not the explanation, cause, or rationale of a firm's behavior and management decisions, but the test of their validity.[9] Steinmann and Löhr express a similar view when they call profitability the formal criterion of success of business activities. This criterion does not say anything as to *how* a firm can or should become profitable.[10] Although the market system functions in such a way that only profitable firms will eventually survive, this does not tell management which roads will lead to corporate success. As part of the social world, the world of business is socially constructed, rather than economically determined.[11] Corporate strategies are formed in sense-making processes, which involve a degree of freedom. This implies that a firm can choose to integrate social responsibility into its corporate strategy. If a firm does so, management will probably be convinced that it is good for business. Whether a certain CSR strategy is indeed good for business depends on how the market and other stakeholders will respond.

Ex ante, no one can point to competitive pressures as a condition that completely eliminates the firm's social responsibility. Only the hypothetical case of *perfect competition* would possibly qualify as an excuse for not engaging in CSR. Standard economic theory says that, under the condition of perfect competition, firms do not have the financial means to bear costs that are unilateral, or that cannot be recovered by means of setting a premium price. Therefore, CSR efforts leading to marginal cost increases are simply not a viable option under the condition of perfect competition.[12] When CSR efforts lead to cost savings, or to profitable new business opportunities as they often do, perfect competition not only allows for these kinds of efforts, but they are necessary, since they will lead to the maximization of profits. The tension between profits and morality is therefore limited to those CSR efforts that do not lead to a win–win situation.

But even when CSR efforts do not result in a win–win situation under perfect competition, we would argue that corporate responsibility is not completely eliminated. A firm has the moral duty to prevent posing a serious threat to health, safety, or the environment, even when this means that the firm will go bankrupt. Harsh market conditions are no excuse here. Short of unilateral measures, a firm could in this case encourage government regulations or self-regulation of the industry to ensure that every competitor in the business faces the same costs. Firms always have a moral responsibility to (help) counteract a market situation in which immorality leads to a competitive advantage by seeking a solution on a higher institutional level. This is an instance of what De George has called "the principle of ethical displacement."[13] We suggest that this is one of the key ethical principles of CSR, since in this way a firm helps to counter the negative side effects (or the external costs, as economists would say) of the free market system. As one of the players in the market, each firm bears a part of the collective responsibility of all players to promote the ethical functioning of their market.

In a situation of perfect competition, a firm has no room to take on moral responsibilities that involve more costs than benefits relative to the costs and benefits of the competitors. However, since perfect competition is a theoretical ideal type which does not have much in common with most real markets, it is not justified to simply assume that firms have to deal with the extreme conditions of perfect markets.[14] That is why we reject the view of Milton Friedman, who bases part of his criticism of CSR on this ideal description of the market, as is shown by the next quotation: "The participant in a competitive market has no appreciable power to alter terms of exchange; he is hardly visible as a separate entity; hence it is hard to argue that he has any 'social responsibility' except that which is shared by all citizens to obey the law of this land and to live according to his rights."[15] This view of the firm as an entity that is barely visible and has no power to change things for the better or for the worse is clearly flawed as a general theory of the firm. It does not acknowledge that multinational firms in particular are becoming more and more visible to a global public and that in many markets firms have the power to influence the terms of the exchange. Friedman's assumption that most markets could be treated as if they were perfectly competitive is therefore not a methodologically proper one to make for present purposes. Nor is his conclusion acceptable which is based on this assumption, that a firm cannot have any responsibilities other than increasing its profits within the limits of the law and moral custom. Since competition in most real markets is less than perfect, we can conclude that firms in general do have at least some market power and therefore some financial room to enhance CSR.

Although we do not agree with Friedman that in general there is no room for individual firms to engage in CSR efforts that involve more costs than benefits relative to the competitors, we do want to acknowledge that the functioning of markets does put limitations on what a firm can afford with respect to CSR. This leads to a number of ethical questions. Is it morally relevant that some firms have to deal with fierce competition whereas other firms enjoy the comfort of less intense competition, when it comes to determining the moral responsibilities of a firm? Does it make a difference from a moral perspective when a firm bears considerable costs in order to comply with the law, while most of its competitors do not, because the law is not enforced consistently? Finally, what is the relevance of corporate reputation for CSR? Does reputation as a coordination mechanism always stimulate socially responsible behavior? In the next sections, we set out to answer these questions.

3. COMPETITIVE FORCES AND COMPETITIVE STRATEGIES

We will base our analysis of the relationship between competition and CSR on Porter's seminal research into the competitive strategies of firms. Porter has introduced a distinction between *competitive forces* and *competitive strategies*.[16] Competitive forces determine the degree of competitiveness within an industry. They are: the entry of new competitors, the threat of substitutes, the bargaining power of buyers, the bargaining power of suppliers, and the rivalry among the existing competitors.[17] These five forces influence a firm's prices, costs, and required investments, which are the constituents of return on investment. The entry of new competitors depends on economies of scale, brand identity, and capital requirements. The threat of substitutes is dependent on the relative price performance of substitutes and the buyer's propensity to substitute. The bargaining power of buyers is dependent on buyer concentration versus firm concentration, buyer volume, and the buyer's ability to integrate backward, as well as on the price sensitivity of buyers, among other things. The bargaining power of the supplier is dependent, among other things, on supplier concentration versus firm concentration, the importance of volume to the supplier, and the presence of substitute inputs. Finally, the rivalry among the existing competitors is dependent on things like the growth of the industry, intermittent overcapacity, product differences, brand identity, and switching costs.

For our purpose, it is important to note that, according to Porter, a firm is usually not a prisoner of its industry's structure. "Firms, through their strategies, can influence the five forces. If a firm can shape structure, it can fundamentally change an industry's attractiveness for better or worse. Many successful strategies have shifted the rules of competition in this way."[18] Competitive strategies are ways for a firm to increase its competitiveness within an industry. Porter distinguishes three such strategies, namely cost leadership, differentiation, and focus.[19]

In cost leadership, a firm sets out to become *the* low-cost producer in its industry. To achieve the status of low-cost producer, a firm must find and exploit all sources of cost advantage. Typically, low-cost producers sell a standard product and place emphasis on reaping scale or absolute cost advantages. Having a low-cost position yields a firm above average returns in its industry, despite the presence of strong competitive forces. Its cost position gives the firm a defense against rivalry from competitors, because its lower costs mean that it can still earn returns after its competitors have lost their profits through rivalry.

A firm differentiates itself from its competitors if it is unique in something that is widely valued by buyers. It selects one or more attributes that many buyers in an industry perceive as important, and uniquely positions itself to meet these. If a firm pursues forms of uniqueness that buyers do not value, it may be different from its competitors but not differentiated. The best way to learn whether a product is truly differentiated is to see if it is rewarded for its uniqueness with a premium price.

The focus strategy rests on the choice of a narrow competitive scope within an industry. The focuser selects a segment or group of segments in the industry and tailors its strategy to serving them to the exclusion of others. This can be a particular buyer group, a segment of the product line, or a specific market region. The strategy rests on the premise that the firm is thus able to serve its narrow strategic target more effectively or efficiently than competitors who are competing more broadly.

If strategies of CSR do qualify as (part of) a competitive strategy, then we have a sound argument to back up the claim that CSR can contribute to a sustainable competitive advantage and hence to profitability. To investigate this, we will examine a number of markets with varying degrees of competition and briefly explore some ways in which strategies of CSR can lead to a competitive advantage, or are affected by the competitive characteristics of these types of markets. To determine which CSR strategies could succeed, we will also take into account some features of the legal environment and the effect of the strategy on reputation. The combination of these three competitive conditions—intensity of competition, legal environment, and the effect on reputation—determines which strategy of CSR is commercially appropriate.

We will assume that a certain industry structure will result in more or less intense competition, depending on the five competitive forces. It takes an extensive and laborious analysis to present a complete picture of the competitive forces for an industry. For the theoretical purpose of this study, we do not need such a level of detail. For practical reasons, therefore, we will distinguish between three ideal types, or "frozen moments," of markets, that capture the intensity of the competition for an imaginary firm, at a certain point in time. We will refer to the three levels of competitiveness as "fierce," "strong," and "weak." This distinction is based on stipulations, which are, of course, artificial. Empirically, the intensity of competition varies gradually along the five competitive forces.

For each level of competitiveness, we will investigate the strategic opportunities and limitations for firms to engage in CSR efforts and to deal with moral problems and dilemmas. In general, we can say that a strategy of low costs is the dominant competitive strategy under fierce competition. Only forms of CSR that are reconcilable with a low-cost strategy are competitively feasible under fierce competition. Differentiation is the dominant strategy under strong competition. CSR strategies that help a firm to differentiate itself from its competitors are appropriate under strong competition. Under weak competition, there is no dominant strategy. This market lacks competitive pressure altogether, so that very different strategies can lead to business success. Table 1 outlines the specific CSR strategies that are available to firms under different levels of competitiveness. In sections four to six, we will explain these strategies in greater detail.

Table 1   Specific CSR Strategies under Different Levels of Industry Competitiveness

Intensity of Competition	Fierce	Strong	Weak
Dominant generic competitive strategy	Low-cost strategy	Product-differentiation strategy	Low-cost or product-differentiation
Specific CSR strategy	Ethical displacement strategy: Self-regulation	Compliance with the spirit of the law	All CSR strategies are possible
	Legal compliance	Stakeholder management	
	Reputation protection	Brand reputation management and ethical reporting	
		Ethical product differentiation	

4. CSR STRATEGIES UNDER CONDITIONS OF FIERCE COMPETITION

We define fierce competition as a market in which a firm has little or no power to influence prices, because several or all of the following features of the industry structure make the five forces of competition very strong: (i) the entry barriers are low, for instance, because of low capital requirements and because brand identity is not important; (ii) the product can easily be substituted, because there is a high buyer propensity to substitute; (iii) the buyers have a strong bargaining power, because their concentration is relatively high; (iv) the bargaining power of suppliers is relatively high, due to a lack of substitute inputs; and (v) the concentration within the industry is low whereas the product is (almost) homogeneous (no product differentiation), causing the rivalry between competitors to be high. In general, one can say that fierce competition leads to low profitability and forces companies to follow a low cost strategy.

Under fierce competition, firms cannot afford to invest in CSR, if this will lead to higher costs than the competitors have to bear, because the buyers will almost immediately switch to a cheaper competitor. Under conditions of fierce competition, a firm has no financial room to bear costs that are structurally higher than those of competitors. Even under these conditions, there are some CSR strategies that

are recommendable for firms. These are strategies which, although costly in the short term, are sufficiently beneficial to make them the rational option under fierce competition. We will consider three of them, namely ethical displacement, legal compliance, and reputation protection.

Ethical Displacement

Ethical displacement means that if an ethical conflict cannot be solved at a certain level of social aggregation (the individual, the organization, the industry, or the national/international political level), then one should look for a solution at a level other than that at which the dilemma occurs. Ethical displacement is relevant not only for a market with perfect competition but also for a market with fierce competition, since individual firms cannot afford high unilateral investments in CSR. Firms in this situation have a duty to look for competitively neutral means to promote CSR at the industry level. A system of self-regulation of the industry should impose the same costs on all the competitors. This way no individual firm runs the risk of a competitive disadvantage. In a market with fierce competition it is, therefore, a viable form of CSR to take the initiative for industry self-regulation.

Legal Compliance

Under conditions of fierce competition, a firm usually has to set modest goals with respect to its strategy of CSR. It can start by trying to comply with the law. Carroll identifies legal responsibilities as one of the dimensions of CSR.[20] Lynn Sharp Paine considers legal compliance to be an important strategy for ethics management. Both authors agree that obedience to the law is not the highest possible achievement in business ethics, but that it is an important beginning. We would like to stress here that even this beginning can be difficult for firms, and sometimes presents a serious ethical and competitive challenge.

From an ethical perspective (assuming the instrumental moral value of the firm), a firm has to ensure itself that even the legalistic minimum level of CSR will not lead to a competitive disadvantage. To be sure, not all cost disadvantages are a competitive disadvantage. To become a competitive disadvantage the additional costs would have to be so high, or so persistent, that the firm risks losing its business to its competitors. Whether legal compliance will lead to a competitive disadvantage depends for an important part on certain features of the legal environment. Compliance with the law will probably lead to a competitive disadvantage when competitors structurally bear less costs by using loopholes in the law, or when the law is not enforced effectively. In a situation of fierce competition, an acceptable degree of enforcement would have to be determined by the probabilities of detection and conviction, and the size of the fine, compared to the cost advantage resulting from transgression.

Under fierce competition, a firm can be pressured strongly to take advantage of loopholes in the law, when not doing so would lead to a considerable relative cost disadvantage. Likewise, a firm is pressured to break the law when the law is not enforced effectively enough to create a satisfactorily level playing field among the competition.[21] In both cases, compliance with the law could lead to bankruptcy. Hence, if a firm wants to secure its own survival, the competitive condition of fierce competition could force it to choose between its own survival and the duty to comply with the law. Under such extreme circumstances, a firm faces a moral dilemma. As we argued in section one, the continuation of the firm presents an instrumental moral value to all the stakeholders. Securing the survival of the firm is therefore morally desirable, provided that the business itself is not of an immoral nature.[22] On the other hand, securing the continuation of the firm would imply that one breaches the moral and legal

duty to comply with the law. How should a firm deal with this dilemma? The *fairness of competitive conditions* provides an important clue to answering this question.

Legal institutions can create circumstances that entail unfair competitive disadvantages for some firms. An example would be legislation which forbids companies to pay bribes to government officials in other countries. The United States has such legislation, under the Foreign Corrupt Practices Act of 1977. Similar legislation has recently been introduced in the Netherlands as well. Until now, the Prosecution Council has only started a few bribery cases. This is not because Dutch managers are so law abiding when it comes to bribery. On the contrary, paying money or giving gifts to government officials in order to get them to do their work (which would be a form of extortion) is widely understood as being an unfortunate but unavoidable part of doing business in some parts of the world. The rather weak enforcement of antibribery laws in the Netherlands creates a cost disadvantage for the compliant firms. The obedient firms are worse off as a result of their legally correct behavior, whereas the firms that violate the law benefit. A lack of law enforcement that creates a competitive disadvantage for compliant firms is an example of unfair competition. If this occurs in a fiercely competitive environment, then we believe the responsibility of firms not to pay bribes might be mitigated to some extent. Here we take recourse to the rule, introduced by Velasquez, that the moral responsibility for an act is mitigated (but not annihilated) by the difficulty to avoid the act, among other things.[23] It is primarily the responsibility of the government to ensure that the legal environment does not create unfair competition. According to the principle of ethical displacement, however, employer organizations and industrial organizations have a responsibility to lobby for legal improvements in this context.

A situation of unfair and fierce competition does not generally justify bribery. Paying bribes, whether one takes the initiative or not, poses a serious moral problem, because it contributes to corruption and makes markets less efficient. Therefore, it is morally better if a firm tries to stay in business without paying bribes. The only point we want to make here is that following the moral duty to comply with the law can take its toll for a firm, when competition is fierce. Managers can be confronted with tough moral choices, when compliance with the law has to be pitted against company survival. Since legal compliance in a fiercely competitive market involves a moral commitment and moral choices from a firm's management, we believe that this strategy can rightly be called a form of CSR.

Reputation Protection

Another possible strategy of CSR in a market with fierce competition is the protection of a good reputation among customers. We call this a form of CSR because reputation protection involves taking care of social aspects of the relationship that cannot be completely captured in a contractual form. Although a firm's reputation is not restricted to the assessment of past performance by customers (both individual and/or industrial), but comprises the assessment by all stakeholders,[24] we will limit ourselves to the reputation of the firm among its customers. This focus on the customer is motivated by the fact that in a fiercely competitive market the relation between corporate reputation and actual buying behavior is very important for the continuation of the firm. We define effect on reputation as the cumulative effect of a certain issue on the customers' beliefs with respect to those features of an organization and its product that influence their buying behavior. The opportunities of firms to use reputation protection as a CSR strategy depend on the interests of the customers. These interests can involve characteristics of the core product, but they can also involve company policies.

The condition of fierce competition involves that brand identity is not so important and the product is almost homogeneous. The customers' interests, as far as the product itself is concerned, are closely related to features of the core product, such as product quality, price, and availability. The product has to be reliable and the price has to be on a level comparable to the prices competitors ask; otherwise, the customers will buy a competitor's product next time. In general, we can say that under the condition of fierce competition, reputation will be negatively affected if a certain breach of morality has repercussions for the features of the core product, such as its reliability and safety, and if the customers know about these repercussions. The magnitude of the negative effect will, of course, depend on the perceived importance of the impacts on health or safety. If, for instance,

beef is suspected to contain growth hormones, some consumers will look for alternative meat products. Even under fierce competition, such reputational risks can be well worth avoiding.

Company policies, even when they do not affect the quality of products, can cause negative reputational effects among customers, when they perceive the policy as immoral or indecent. This might be a reason for customers to boycott a product or a firm, even if no customer's interest is being hurt directly. Companies like Heineken, Ikea, Nike, and Shell have, each in their own way, experienced what risks a public perception of social irresponsibility can mean to the business, especially when nongovernmental organizations (NGOs) target a firm with their campaign.

Public perceptions of a company's social and environmental performance sometimes strongly influence the buying behavior of consumers, but the pressure of public perception is felt less strongly on the business-to-business market. Here, other consumers come into play, who are often less concerned about social and environmental issues. Business-to-business markets can also be fiercely competitive. Under such conditions, a firm cannot always afford to worry much about a declining reputation in the eyes of the wider public, when their business clients are insensitive to moral issues, or even benefit from them. In business-to-business markets, this parting of public anxiety and consumer interests can be observed frequently. An example of this is the case of the Dutch-based firm IHC Caland in Burma (Myanmar). IHC Caland had agreed to produce an offshore storage and offloading system for oil and gas for Premier Oil, off the coast of Burma. The deal was not illegal under European Union legislation at the time. Like so many other firms, IHC Caland was criticized by pressure groups for its presence in Burma. According to these groups, IHC Caland was supporting the military regime in Burma, by contributing to the economy and hence to the means of existence of the regime. IHC Caland, however, could expect only a few orders of this size each year. Failing one of them could seriously harm their results. Moreover, IHC Caland had already signed a contract with Premier Oil. Leaving Burma would imply a breach of contract which would be detrimental to IHC Caland's reputation within the industry. This would be a threat to the continued existence of IHC Caland, in a market where buyers have great bargaining power. IHC Caland's conclusion on the Burma deal was that they would only pull out if it was forbidden by the government. By taking the matter to a higher (political) level of social organization, IHC Caland in fact invoked the principle of ethical displacement.

We conclude that even under fierce competition, several strategies of CSR are available to firms. Legal compliance is required also under fierce competition, although there should be greater understanding for the costs that legal compliance sometimes poses to companies under fierce competition. Ethical displacement is a CSR strategy that involves relatively low costs, as it aims at equalizing costs between competitors. Inquiring about the problem-solving potential of ethical displacement should always be considered morally imperative for firms, when fierce competition makes unilateral CSR initiatives unattractive. Reputation protection, finally, is a means to prevent great costs for companies, which is not only economically feasible but even economically imperative under fierce competition. On the business-to-business market, however, the reputation mechanism may not always make a firm align with the CSR expectations of the larger public. Inevitably, firms under fierce competition will sometimes disappoint the public at large from a CSR perspective. We believe that a competitive analysis helps to understand why these disappointments are not always justified.

5. CSR STRATEGIES UNDER CONDITIONS OF STRONG COMPETITION

The term "strong competition" refers to markets in which competitors have more financial room to bear costs due to choices made as a result of their moral and social responsibilities. Competition is strong, rather than fierce, if one or two of the five forces of competition are weak, while the other forces remain strong. For instance, the entry barriers are high because of the importance of brand identity and the high costs involved in developing it. Competition is still strong because of the other forces of competition. In these kinds of markets, profit margins need not be as razor-thin as they are in markets with

fierce competition. When it comes to exploring the possibilities of the strategies of CSR, strongly competitive markets will be less restrictive.

The dominant generic strategy in a market with strong competition is product differentiation. Firms will try to differentiate their products or services in the eyes of the customers to justify a premium price. The distinctive capabilities of architecture of relational contract, reputation, innovation, as well as the strategic assets of a firm (such as exclusive dealing contracts) are the basis for product differentiation.[25] John Kay defines architecture as a network of relational contracts within, or around, the firm. Architectures depend on the ability of the firm to build and sustain long-term relationships and to establish an environment that penalizes opportunistic behavior.[26]

If a strategy of product differentiation succeeds, the competition in the market becomes less intense than in a market with fierce competition, because product differentiation results in a higher entry barrier. This way a firm can avoid the low-cost strategy which is dominant in a market with fierce competition. CSR initiatives can contribute to a strategy of product differentiation and are therefore appropriate for a market with strong competition. Sometimes, they even lie at the core of the differentiation strategy itself. The chosen strategy of CSR may build on an already developed distinctive capability of the firm, such as reputation or the high quality of the architecture of relational contracts. A good reputation and high-quality architecture can, however, also be the result of a long-term engagement with moral issues and stakeholders' interests in business. Below, we will discuss four ways in which CSR can become an integral part of business strategy, under conditions of strong competition: compliance with the spirit of the law, stakeholder management, brand reputation management and ethical reporting, and ethical product differentiation.

Compliance with the Spirit of the Law

Under conditions of strong competition, a firm has financial room to comply not only with the letter but also with the spirit of the law. This requires paying attention to the rationale of the law, in order to interpret it correctly and arrive at a proper understanding of how the law should be interpreted in new situations.[27] An example of this is how firms respond to loopholes in tax legislation. If the intention of the legislator is known, but imperfectly expressed in the letter of the law, a firm can consider it its social responsibility to comply with the spirit of the law. Also, a firm has more to gain from this strategy, since distinctive capabilities like a sustainable network of long-term relationships (architecture) and reputation presuppose at least that a firm is able and willing to comply with its contracts in a non-opportunistic way, aimed at establishing long term relationships. Furthermore, the adaptations of the decision-making structure and the organizational culture necessary to enable compliance with the spirit of the law are first steps in the direction of a full-fledged approach to integrating moral considerations in the decision making of the firm.[28] Stakeholder management is such an approach, and this will be discussed next.

Stakeholder Management

The management and guarding of the interests of stakeholders is essential if a firm wants to strengthen its architecture. According to Kay, architecture is one of the distinctive capabilities on which a competitive advantage can be built. One of the ways in which architecture adds value to individual contributions is through the establishment of a cooperative ethic. In our view, stakeholder management can contribute to building an environment that penalizes opportunistic behavior by monitoring the relationship of the firm with each stakeholder, so that appropriate action can be taken if anything goes wrong. Measures that could be taken to achieve this goal are social and ethical auditing, introducing an ethical committee or ethics officer, and a procedure for dealing with complaints, among other things.

It may seem that presently powerless stakeholders are irrelevant from a strategic perspective. Mitchell, Agle, and Wood have argued, however, that powerless stakeholders who are affected in their interests, will aspire for power vis-à-vis the company, in order to promote their interests.[29] One can never tell in advance whether a stakeholder who has no power at all to act against a certain firm will not one day find the means to do so. Often, such powerless stakeholders are helped by NGOs to promote their cases. This possibility will always be of some importance to the sustainability of a firm in the long run. Take for example the victims of the Nazi regime's robbery of gold and other possessions during the Second World War. Banks that cooperated with the Nazis during the war had to deal with the claims of Holocaust survivors at a much later date. More recently one can think of the protest of the Ogoni against Shell's activities in Nigeria. The environmentalist movement of the Ogoni did not seem powerful enough to influence Shell's policy. It was only after the killing of Ken Saro-Wiwa by the Nigerian regime that Shell was forced to address the problem of the Ogoni in a new way.

Brand Reputation Management and Ethical Reporting

Another important distinctive capability that can be used widely in strongly competitive markets is brand reputation management. The importance of brand reputation as a distinctive capability can be seen in markets where product quality is important, but it can only be identified through long-term experience.[30] The market for accountancy services provides a good example. A certified public accountant adds value only if he represents a firm that has an established reputation of independence and trustworthiness. When a public accountancy firm loses its reputation among the users of financial reports, the added value of the audit for the client disappears. Only accountancy firms that succeed in upholding a reputation of independence and trustworthiness will stay in business in the long run. This example shows how the social responsibility of a firm can be addressed at the strategic level of decision making.

Brands can serve several strategic functions. They are a means by which a producer can establish the reputation of a product. They can provide continuity. And the consumption of branded products may be a means by which consumers can express their identity.[31] CSR becomes important from a branding perspective, when many consumers appreciate a corporate image of CSR. Global brands like Motorola, Nike, and Heineken run great financial risks if their brand names become associated with child labor, human rights violations, or discrimination. Consumers seem to be extra critical of the CSR performance of a company when it represents a famous brand.[32] Nevertheless, one should not overestimate the impact of consumer sovereignty on the assessment of the qualities of a product or of ethical issues. Consumers face cognitive and motivational limitations, and limited opportunities to gather information about products or firms.[33]

Some global brands have responded to the greater public scrutiny by setting up a system of ethical and social reporting. For instance, Shell and British Telecom publish independently audited reports, covering issues like environmental impact, health, child labor, and corruption. Reporting can be an important tool of brand management and stakeholder management alike, by gathering information about the needs of stakeholders and about the firm's own performance. By reporting about its ethical and social performance, a firm can at least appear to be making an effort to inform its stakeholders. No matter how imperfect the quality of ethical auditing and reporting may be, the firm will be perceived as being more open and trustworthy. The assurance that the firm is trustworthy already comes from the mere fact that it publishes ethical and social reports. The signal to the stakeholders is clear: a firm that invests in ethical and social reporting not only commits itself to the market, but acknowledges that it has to earn the approval of the public at large by showing that it tries to take on its responsibilities. Whether a firm actually does take its responsibilities seriously is of course not guaranteed by ethical and social reporting as such. To answer this question, independent monitoring of a firm's behavior remains necessary. Social and ethical reporting however, does give stakeholders information about the policies and measures of a firm with respect to CSR. This is at least a good starting point for further dialogue between stakeholders and the firm.

From a strategic point of view, an investment in ethical and social reporting makes sense for global brands in particular. Firstly, they are most likely to become the target of public scrutiny. Secondly, these brands build on their reputation and, therefore, not only have a lot to lose, but also a lot to gain from a reputation of good corporate citizenship.

Ethical Product Differentiation

It is possible to differentiate a product based on some ethical quality or aspect, if the consumer is ready to pay a premium price because he or she values the particular strategy of CSR that a firm intends to follow. There are many examples of such strategies.

Take, for instance, the firms that use fair-trade labels to sell coffee or bananas at a premium price, claiming that part of the premium will benefit small farmers who are dependent on such a premium for a "reasonable and fair income." By convincing customers of the social value offered at the premium price, the firms succeed in differentiating their "fair" product form normal, "unfair" trade.

Although the strategy of ethical product differentiation might be appropriate in the case of strong competition, it is also risky. If the customer fails to attach value to the ethical product claim, the firm loses business to competitors. The premium price will be perceived as unjustified. Furthermore, it is risky to claim that a product has some ethical quality to it that is lacking in the products of competitors. As The Body Shop has experienced, a firm that claims to safeguard ethical values in the production process will receive extra critical attention from journalists[34] and consumers. The company was accused of misleading the public, since among other things only a fraction of the product ingredients were actually bought from fair-trade supply channels, while the bulk of the ingredients were bought from normal (purportedly unfair) supply channels. To counter this kind of criticism, The Body Shop has invested in social and ethical auditing and reporting.

6. CSR STRATEGIES UNDER CONDITIONS OF WEAK COMPETITION

A market with weak competition has several characteristics that change the strategic importance of CSR. Competition in a market is weak when all five forces of competition are weak or tend to be weak: (i) the threat of entry of new competitors is low, because of economies of scale and well-established brand identity; (ii) the product cannot easily be substituted, because of high switching costs; (iii) the buyers have little bargaining power, because their concentration is relatively low; (iv) the bargaining power of suppliers is relatively low due to the threat of backward integration; and (v) the concentration within the industry is high, causing the rivalry between competitors to be low. Taken together, these five forces of competition lead to weak competition.

Markets with weak competition can be either oligopolistic or monopolistic. Because of the lack of competition in such markets, firms have market power, which means that they can ask higher prices or reduce their quality, without losing too much business. Because of the lack of efficiency and quality in many markets with weak competition, intervention of the government through antitrust legislation and supervisory organs is often undertaken to safeguard the interests of consumers and the public. Market power, however, can have some positive effects as well. It enables a firm to invest in CSR. A firm in a weakly competitive market has the financial and managerial room to choose any of the CSR strategies described in the previous chapters. It is another issue whether all these strategies would be equally wise choices.

Compliance with the spirit of the law makes sense in a market with weak competition, because in this way a firm can prevent or reduce the chance of (further) government intervention. Most firms will consider it in their interests to prevent government intervention, because this way they have more control of the situation. If a firm in a market with weak competition refrains from misusing its market power, it indeed takes away the necessity of government intervention. However, when important interests of consumers or the public at large are at stake, for instance in public transport or energy supply, compliance with the law may not suffice. If important interests are at stake, dissatisfaction of consumers or the public can easily become a political issue. That is why, in these kinds of markets, it is in the interests of a firm to at least keep their key stakeholders satisfied, by using the strategy of stakeholder management or some form of ethical reporting. After all, these tools of ethical management not only benefit the stakeholders but also improve the overall quality of management, by keeping in touch with changing social expectations.

7. CONCLUSIONS

In this paper, we addressed the question of how specific competitive conditions affect CSR, and which CSR strategies are feasible for a firm under different competitive conditions. The competitive condition can be defined by three characteristics: the intensity of competition, the legal environment, and the risks to reputation.

The central moral argument underlying our analysis is that, in general, the continuation of a firm has an instrumental moral value because normally all stakeholders have a legitimate stake in this continuation. If, however, a person or group is better off if a business activity is terminated, management has to balance rights and obligations in such a way that the lesser evil is chosen. If this means that a firm will not be able to survive then this is the lesser evil in such a case. If, however, most stakeholders with legitimate claims on a firm have an interest in the continuance of the firm in order to secure their stakes and if this continuation means that the interests of a certain stakeholder or nonstakeholder cannot be secured fully, this could be the lesser evil that should be chosen. It all depends on the nature of what is at stake. From a deontological perspective, for example, the stakes of all stakeholders do not override fundamental rights to liberty, life, and property. Starting from these premises, we conclude that fierce competition can be a morally mitigating factor for making use of loopholes in the law or to violate the law. The latter, of course, depends on the moral issues surrounding a certain law. We conclude that legal compliance can already be an ambitious strategy of CSR, for firms that have to deal with fierce competition.

In the case of strong competition, there is more room for other strategies of CSR that can contribute to product differentiation. We briefly explored the strategies of compliance with the spirit of the law, stakeholder management, brand reputation management and ethical reporting, and ethical product differentiation. To a great extent, these strategies are a necessary response to the demands of different stakeholders who have the option of taking their business to a competitor.

It is a defining characteristic of a market with weak competition that it lacks this kind of competitive pressure altogether. The legal environment, however, does provide a reason for firms in such a market to adopt some form of CSR, because of the risk of government intervention. Other reasons for firms in a market with weak competition to adopt a more ambitious strategy of CSR are of a more intrinsic nature, like the desire of management to be part of a "good" or "well-managed" company.

We analyzed the correspondences between the chosen strategy of CSR and the competitive conditions that confront a firm. From a strategic perspective, this may seem self-evident. From a moral perspective, however, it is anything but self-evident to stress the moral value of a firm's survival. Are we not prioritizing the self-interest of the firm above all other stakeholder interests, and hence, above moral duties that override self-interest? In a way we are, but only in so far as we want to acknowledge that every functioning system has to reproduce itself in order to be able to comply with whatever duty is imposed on it ("ought implies be"). Only if morality is best served by the immediate termination of business activities does this prioritization lose its validity. After all, the reasons for prioritizing a firm's survival are moral reasons.

We have outlined the main features of a normative framework that specifies how firms can compete in a morally acceptable way, given the characteristics of their competitive environment. Further empirical research could provide more detailed insight into the mechanisms through which competitive conditions actually influence the CSR strategies that firms implement. A hypothesis derived from our framework is that the more firms integrate CSR into their corporate strategy, the better they will be able to cater for the legitimate demands of their stakeholders. Also, more in-depth research is needed, from both a moral and strategic perspective, into the strategic potentials of different CSR strategies under different competitive conditions. In this way business ethics could develop a contingency approach to CSR, instead of looking for the one best ethics for all firms.

Notes

1. R. E. Freeman, *Strategic Management: A Stakeholder Approach* (Boston: Pitman, 1984); R. E. Freeman and W. M. Evan, "Corporate Governance: A Stakeholder Approach," *Journal of Behavioral Economics* 19 (1990): 337–59; A. Wicks, D. Gilbert, and E. Freeman, "A Feminist Reinterpretation of the Stakeholder Concept," *Business Ethics Quarterly* 4(4) (October 1994); Th. Donaldson and L. E. Preston, "The Stakeholder Theory of the Corporation: Concepts, Evidence and Implications," *Academy of Management Review* 20(1) (1995): 65–91; N. E. Bowie, *Business Ethics: A Kantian Perspective* (Malden, Mass.: Blackwell, 1999); R. K. Mitchell, B. R. Agle, and D. J. Wood, "Toward a Theory of Stakeholder Identification and Salience: The Principle of Who and What Really Counts," *Academy of Management Review* 22(4) (1997): 853–86.

2. Commission of the European Communities, *Communication from the Commission Concerning Corporate Social Responsibility: A Business Contribution to Sustainable Development* (Brussels: COM [2002]): 347 final, p. 3 (http://europa.eu.int/comm/employment_social/soc-dial/csr/csr_index.htm).

3. S. Douma, H. Schreuder, *Economic Approaches to Organizations* (New York: Prentice Hall, 1991): 66.

4. J. Kay, *Foundations of Corporate Success* (Oxford: Oxford University Press, 1993): 8–9.

5. Compare C. W. Hill and T. M. Jones, "Stakeholder-Agency Theory," *Journal of Management Studies* 29 (1992): 145: "[O]bviously, the claims of different groups may conflict.... However, on a more general level, each group can be seen as having a stake in the continued existence of the firm." This passage is also quoted with approval in a recent article by R. Phillips, R. E. Freeman, and A. C. Wicks, "What Stakeholder Theory Is Not," *Business Ethics Quarterly* 13(4) (2003): 484.

6. L. Sharp Paine, Does Ethics Pay? *Business Ethics Quarterly* 10(1) (2000): 319–30.

7. S. P. Sethi and L. M. Sama, "Ethical Behavior as a Strategic Choice by Large Corporations: The Interactive Effect of Marketplace Competition, Industry Structure, and Firm Resources," *Business Ethics Quarterly* 8(1) (1998): 85–104.

8. R. Solomon, *Ethics and Excellence. Cooperation and Integrity in Business* (Oxford: Oxford University Press, 1992), 44.

9. P. Drucker, *Management: Tasks, Responsibilities, Practices* (New York: Harper & Row, 1974), 60.

10. H. Steinmann and A. Löhr, "Unternehmensethik: Ein republikanisches Programm in der Kritik," in *Markt und Moral: Die Diskussion um die Unternehmensethik*, ed. S. Blasche, W. Köhler, and P. Rohs (Bern: Haupt, 1994), 156.

11. Steinmann and Löhr, "Unternehmensethik," 147.

12. W. Baumol, "(Almost) Perfect Competition (Contestability) and Business Ethics," in W. Baumol and S. Batey Blackman, *Perfect Markets and Easy Virtues: Business Ethics and the Invisible Hand* (Cambridge, Mass.: Blackwell, 1991), 1–23; K. Homann and F. Blome-Drees, *Wirtschafts- und Unternehmensethik* (Göttingen: Vandenhoeck and Ruprecht, 1992), 42; Sethi and Sama, "Ethical Behavior as a Strategic Choice by Large Corporations," 90.

13. R. De George, *Competing with Integrity in International Business* (Oxford: Oxford University Press, 1993), 97.

14. Steinmann and Löhr, "Unternehmensethik," 170.

15. M. Friedman, *Capitalism and Freedom* (Chicago: University of Chicago Press, 1962), 120.

16. M. E. Porter, *Competitive Strategy: Techniques for Analyzing Industries and Competitors* (New York: Free Press, 1980); M. E. Porter, *Competitive Advantage: Creating and Sustaining Superior Performance* (New York: Free Press, 1985).

17. Porter, *Competitive Advantage,* 4.

18. Ibid., 7.

19. Porter, *Competitive Strategy,* 35.

20. A. Carroll, *Business and Society* (Boston: Little Brown, 1981); L. Sharp Paine, "Managing for Organizational Integrity," *Harvard Business Review* (March–April 1994): 106–17.

21. Sethi and Sama, "Ethical Behavior as a Strategic Choice by Large Corporations," 90.

22. One could object that bankruptcy might also mean that the interests of some stakeholders are protected. Although bankruptcy can be the best solution in the case of insolvency, it also means that the interests of the stakeholders are terminated. One could argue that this is not a moral problem, since after the bankruptcy, the assets will be put to more efficient use. Hence, total utility would benefit from bankruptcy. This argument, however, is built on the assumption that the market is efficient. This means, among other things, that the rules governing the marketplace affect all the competitors in the same way. However, as we argued above, a lack of law enforcement punishes legal compliance and rewards noncompliance. In these circumstances, it may happen that an efficient and obedient firm goes bankrupt, while an inefficient disobedient firm survives. As a result, the social optimum will not be achieved.

23. M. Velasquez, *Business Ethics: Concepts and Cases,* 3rd ed. (Englewood Cliffs, N.J.: Prentice Hall, 1992), 40.

24. Fombrun and Rindova define corporate reputation as follows: "A corporate reputation is a collective representation of a firm's past actions and results that describes the firm's ability to deliver valued outcomes to multiple stakeholders. It gauges a firm's relative standing both internally with employees and externally with its stakeholders, in both its competitive and institutional environments." C. Fombrun and C. van Riel, "The Reputational Landscape," in *Revealing the Corporation. Perspectives on Identity, Image, Reputation, Corporate Branding, and Corporate-Level Marketing,* ed. J. Balmer and S. Greyser (London/New York: Routledge, 2003), 230.

25. Key, *Foundations of Corporate Success.*

26. Ibid., 66–86.

27. H. Steinmann and T. Olbrich, "Business Ethics in U.S. Corporations: Results from an Interview Series," in P. Ulrich and J. Wieland, *Unternehmensethik in der Praxis. Impulse aus den USA, Deutchland und der Schweiz,* (Bern: Haupt, 1998), 72.

28. Steinmann and Olbrich, "Business Ethics in U.S. Corporations," 75.

29. "We suggest that a theory of stakeholder identification and salience must somehow account for latent stakeholders if it is to be both comprehensive and useful, because such identification can, at a minimum, help organizations avoid problems and perhaps even enhance effectiveness." Mitchell, Agle, and Wood, "Toward a Theory of Stakeholder Identification and Salience," 859.

30. Kay, *Foundations of Corporate Success,* 87.

31. Ibid., 263.

32. N. Klein, *No Logo: No Space, No Choice, No Jobs: Taking Aim at the Brand Bullies* (London: Flamingo, 2000).

33. M. J. Sirgy and C. Su, "The Ethics of Consumer Sovereignty in an Age of High Tech," *Journal of Business Ethics* 28 (2000): 1–14, 2–9.

34. See, for example, the writings of John Entine, who has followed The Body Shop critically for a decade now: J. Entine, "The Body Shop: Truth and Consequences," *Drugs and Cosmetics Industry* (January 1995), 57–60; J. Entine, "Body Flop: Anita Roddick Proclaimed That Business Could Be Caring as Well as Capitalist. Today The Body Shop Is Struggling on Both Counts," *R.O.B.: Toronto Globe and Mail's Report on Business Magazine* (May 31, 2002).

The Secrets to Successful Strategy Execution

Gary L. Neilson
Booz & Company

Karla L. Martin
Booz & Company

Elizabeth Powers
Booz & Company

A brilliant strategy, blockbuster product, or break-through technology can put you on the competitive map, but only solid execution can keep you there. You have to be able to deliver on your intent. Unfortunately, the majority of companies aren't very good at it, by their own admission. Over the past five years, we have invited many thousands of employees (about 25 percent of whom came from executive ranks) to complete an online assessment of their organizations' capabilities, a process that's generated a database of 125,000 profiles representing more than 1,000 companies, government agencies, and not-for-profits in over 50 countries. Employees at three out of every five companies rated their organization weak at execution—that is, when asked if they agreed with the statement "Important strategic and operational decisions are quickly translated into action," the majority answered no.

Execution is the result of thousands of decisions made every day by employees acting according to the information they have and their own self-interest. In our work helping more than 250 companies learn to execute more effectively, we've identified four fundamental building blocks executives can use to influence those actions—clarifying decision rights, designing information flows, aligning motivators, and making changes to structure. (For simplicity's sake we refer to them as decision rights, information, motivators, and structure.)

In efforts to improve performance, most organizations go right to structural measures because moving lines around the org chart seems the most obvious solution and the changes are visible and concrete. Such steps generally reap some short-term efficiencies quickly, but in so doing address only the symptoms of dysfunction, not its root causes. Several years later, companies usually end up in the same place they started. Structural change can and should be part of the path to improved execution, but it's best to think of it as the capstone, not the cornerstone, of any organizational transformation. In fact, our research shows that actions having to do with decision rights and information are far more important—about twice as effective—as improvements made to the other two building blocks. (See Figure 1, "What Matters Most to Strategy Execution.")

Take, for example, the case of a global consumer packaged-goods company that lurched down the reorganization path in the early 1990s. (We have altered identifying details in this and other cases that follow.) Disappointed with company performance, senior management did what most companies were doing at that time: They restructured. They eliminated some layers of management and broadened spans of control. Management-staffing costs quickly fell by 18 percent. Eight years later, however, it was déjà vu. The layers had crept back in, and spans of control had once again narrowed. In addressing only structure, management had attacked the visible symptoms of poor performance but not the underlying cause—how people made decisions and how they were held accountable.

Reprinted from *Harvard Business Review* 86, no. 6 (June 2008), pp. 61–70.

Figure 1   What Matters Most to Strategy Execution

When a company fails to execute its strategy, the first thing managers often think to do is restructure. But our research shows that the fundamentals of good execution start with clarifying decision rights and making sure information flows where it needs to go. If you get those right, the correct structure and motivators often become obvious.

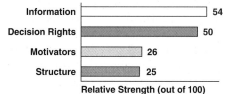

Relative Strength (out of 100)

Information	54
Decision Rights	50
Motivators	26
Structure	25

This time, management looked beyond lines and boxes to the mechanics of how work got done. Instead of searching for ways to strip out costs, they focused on improving execution—and in the process discovered the true reasons for the performance shortfall. Managers didn't have a clear sense of their respective roles and responsibilities. They did not intuitively understand which decisions were theirs to make. Moreover, the link between performance and rewards was weak. This was a company long on micromanaging and second-guessing, and short on accountability. Middle managers spent 40 percent of their time justifying and reporting upward or questioning the tactical decisions of their direct reports.

Armed with this understanding, the company designed a new management model that established who was accountable for what and made the connection between performance and reward. For instance, the norm at this company, not unusual in the industry, had been to promote people quickly, within 18 months to two years, before they had a chance to see their initiatives through. As a result, managers at every level kept doing their old jobs even after they had been promoted, peering over the shoulders of the direct reports who were now in charge of their projects and, all too frequently, taking over. Today, people stay in their positions longer so they can follow through on their own initiatives, and they're still around when the fruits of their labors start to kick in. What's more, results from those initiatives continue to count in their performance reviews for some time after they've been promoted, forcing managers to live with the expectations they'd set in their previous jobs. As a consequence, forecasting has become more accurate and reliable. These actions did yield a structure with fewer layers and greater spans of control, but that was a side effect, not the primary focus, of the changes.

THE ELEMENTS OF STRONG EXECUTION

Our conclusions arise out of decades of practical application and intensive research. Nearly five years ago, we and our colleagues set out to gather empirical data to identify the actions that were most effective in enabling an organization to implement strategy. What particular ways of restructuring, motivating, improving information flows, and clarifying decision rights mattered the most? We started by drawing up a list of 17 traits, each corresponding to one or more of the four building blocks we knew could enable effective execution—traits like the free flow of information across organizational boundaries or the degree to which senior leaders refrain from getting involved in operating decisions. With these factors in mind, we developed an online profiler that allows individuals to assess the execution capabilities of their organizations. Over the next four years or so, we collected data from many thousands of profiles, which in turn allowed us to more precisely calibrate the impact of each trait on an organization's ability to execute. That allowed us to rank all 17 traits in order of their relative influence. (See Figure 2, "The 17 Fundamental Traits of Organizational Effectiveness.")

Ranking the traits makes clear how important decision rights and information are to effective strategy execution. The first eight traits map directly to decision rights and information. Only 3 of the 17 traits relate to structure, and none of those ranks higher than 13th. We'll walk through the top five traits here.

1. *Everyone has a good idea of the decisions and actions for which he or she is responsible.* In companies strong on execution, 71 percent of individuals agree with this statement; that figure drops to 32 percent in organizations weak on execution.

Blurring of decision rights tends to occur as a company matures. Young organizations are generally too busy getting things done to define roles and responsibilities clearly at the outset. And why should they? In a small company, it's not so difficult to know what other people are up to. So for a time, things work out well enough. As the company grows, however, executives come and go, bringing in with them and taking away different expectations,

Figure 2   The 17 Fundamental Traits of Organizational Effectiveness

From our survey research drawn from more than 26,000 people in 31 companies, we have distilled the traits that make organizations effective at implementing strategy. Here they are, in order of importance.

RANK	ORGANIZATION TRAIT	STRENGTH INDEX (OUT OF 100)
1	Everyone has a good idea of the decisions and actions for which he or she is responsible.	81
2	Important information about the competitive environment gets to headquarters quickly.	68
3	Once made, decisions are rarely second-guessed.	58
4	Information flows freely across organizational boundaries.	58
5	Field and line employees usually have the information they need to understand the bottom-line impact of their day-to-day choices.	55
6	Line managers have access to the metrics they need to measure the key drivers of their business.	48
7	Managers up the line get involved in operating decisions.	32
8	Conflicting messages are rarely sent to the market.	32
9	The individual performance-appraisal process differentiates among high, adequate, and low performers.	32
10	The ability to deliver on performance commitments strongly influences career advancement and compensation.	32
11	It is more accurate to describe the culture of this organization as "persuade and cajole" then "command and control."	29
12	The primary role of corporate staff here is to support the business units rather than to audit them.	29
13	Promotions can be lateral moves (from one position to another on the same level in the hierarchy).	29
14	Fast-track employees here can expect promotions more frequently than every three years.	23
15	On average, middle managers here have five or more direct reports.	19
16	If the firm has a bad year, but a particular division has a good year, the division head would still get a bonus.	13
17	Besides pay, many other things motivate individuals to do a good job.	10

BUILDING BLOCKS
☐ Decision rights ☐ Information ■ Motivators ▨ Structure

and over time the approval process gets ever more convoluted and murky. It becomes increasingly unclear where one person's accountability begins and another's ends.

One global consumer-durables company found this out the hard way. It was so rife with people making competing and conflicting decisions that it was hard to find anyone below the CEO who felt truly accountable for profitability. The company was organized into 16 product divisions aggregated into three geographic groups—North America, Europe, and International. Each of the divisions was charged with reaching explicit performance targets, but functional staff at corporate headquarters controlled spending targets—how R&D dollars were allocated, for instance. Decisions made by divisional and geographic leaders were routinely overridden by functional leaders. Overhead costs began to mount as the divisions added staff to help them create bulletproof cases to challenge corporate decisions.

Decisions stalled while divisions negotiated with functions, each layer weighing in with questions. Functional staffers in the divisions (financial analysts, for example) often deferred to their higher-ups in corporate rather than their division vice president, since functional leaders were responsible for rewards and promotions. Only the CEO and his executive team had the discretion to resolve disputes. All of these symptoms fed on one another and collectively hampered execution—until a new CEO came in.

The new chief executive chose to focus less on cost control and more on profitable growth by redefining the divisions to focus on consumers. As part of the new organizational model, the CEO designated accountability for profits unambiguously to the divisions and also gave them the authority to draw on functional activities to support their goals (as well as more control of the budget). Corporate functional roles and decision rights were recast to better support the divisions' needs and also to build the cross-divisional links necessary for developing the global capabilities of the business as a whole. For the most part, the functional leaders understood the market realities—and that change entailed some adjustments to the operating model of the business. It helped that the CEO brought them into the organizational redesign process, so that the new model wasn't something imposed on them as much as it was something they engaged in and built together.

About the Data

We tested organizational effectiveness by having people fill out an online diagnostic, a tool comprising 19 questions (17 that describe organizational traits and two that describe outcomes).

To determine which of the 17 traits in our profiler are most strongly associated with excellence in execution, we looked at 31 companies in our database for which we had responses from at least 150 individual (anonymously completed) profiles, for a total of 26,743 responses. Applying regression analysis to each of the 31 data sets, we correlated the 17 traits with our measure of organizational effectiveness, which we defined as an affirmative response to the outcome statement, "Important strategic and operational decisions are quickly translated into action." Then we ranked the traits in order, according to the number of data sets in which the trait exhibited a significant correlation with our measure of success within a 90 percent confidence interval. Finally, we indexed the result to a 100-point scale. The top trait—"Everyone has a good idea of the decisions and actions for which he or she is responsible"—exhibited a significant positive correlation with our success indicator in 25 of the 31 data sets, for an index score of 81.

2. *Important information about the competitive environment gets to headquarters quickly.* On average, 77 percent of individuals in strong-execution organizations agree with this statement, whereas only 45 percent of those in weak-execution organizations do.

Headquarters can serve a powerful function in identifying patterns and promulgating best practices throughout business segments and geographic regions. But it can play this coordinating role only if it has accurate and up-to-date market intelligence. Otherwise, it will tend to impose its own agenda and policies rather than defer to operations that are much closer to the customer.

Consider the case of heavy-equipment manufacturer Caterpillar.[1] Today it is a highly successful $45 billion global company, but a generation ago, Caterpillar's organization was so badly misaligned that its very existence was threatened. Decision rights were hoarded at the top by functional general offices located at headquarters in Peoria, Illinois, while much of the information needed to make those decisions resided in the field with sales managers. "It just took a long time to get decisions going up and down the functional silos, and they really weren't good business decisions; they were more functional decisions," noted one field executive. Current CEO Jim Owens, then a managing director in Indonesia, told us that such information that did make it to the top had been "whitewashed and varnished several times over along the way." Cut off from information about the external market, senior executives focused on the organization's internal workings, overanalyzing issues and second-guessing decisions made at lower levels, costing the company opportunities in fast-moving markets.

Pricing, for example, was based on cost and determined not by market realities but by the pricing general office in Peoria. Sales representatives across the world lost sale after sale to Komatsu, whose competitive pricing consistently beat Caterpillar's. In 1982, the company posted the first annual loss in its almost-60-year history. In 1983 and 1984, it lost $1 million a day, seven days a week. By the end of 1984, Caterpillar had lost a billion dollars. By 1988, then-CEO George Schaefer stood atop an entrenched bureaucracy that was, in his words, "telling me what I wanted to hear, not what I needed to know." So he convened a task force of "renegade" middle managers and tasked them with charting Caterpillar's future.

Ironically, the way to ensure that the right information flowed to headquarters was to make sure the right decisions were made much further down the organization. By delegating operational responsibility to the people closer to the action, top executives were free to focus on more global strategic issues. Accordingly, the company reorganized into business units, making each accountable for its own P&L statement. The functional general offices that had been all-powerful ceased to exist, literally overnight. Their talent and expertise, including engineering, pricing, and manufacturing, were parceled out to the new business units, which could now design their own products, develop their own manufacturing processes and schedules, and set their own prices. The move dramatically decentralized decision rights, giving the units control over market decisions. The business unit P&Ls were now measured consistently across the enterprise, as return on assets became the universal measure of success. With this accurate, up-to-date, and directly comparable information, senior decision makers at headquarters could make smart strategic choices and trade-offs rather than use outdated sales data to make ineffective, tactical marketing decisions.

Within 18 months, the company was working in the new model. "This was a revolution that became a renaissance," Owens recalls, "a spectacular transformation of a kind of sluggish company into one that actually has entrepreneurial zeal. And that transition was very quick because it was decisive and it was complete; it was thorough; it was universal, worldwide, all at one time."

3. *Once made, decisions are rarely second-guessed.* Whether someone is second-guessing depends on your vantage point. A more senior and broader enterprise perspective can add value to a decision, but managers up the line may not be adding incremental value; instead, they may be stalling progress by redoing their subordinates' jobs while, in effect, shirking their own. In our research, 71 percent of respondents in weak-execution companies thought that decisions were being second-guessed, whereas only 45 percent of those from strong-execution organizations felt that way.

Recently, we worked with a global charitable organization dedicated to alleviating poverty. It had a problem others might envy: It was suffering from the strain brought on by a rapid growth in donations and a corresponding increase in the depth and breadth of its program offerings. As you might expect, this nonprofit was populated with people on a mission who took intense personal ownership of projects. It did not reward the delegation of even the most mundane administrative tasks. Country-level managers, for example, would personally oversee copier repairs. Managers' inability to delegate led to decision paralysis and a lack of accountability as the organization grew. Second-guessing was an art form. When there was doubt over who was empowered to make a decision, the default was often to have a series of meetings in which no decision was reached. When decisions were finally made, they had generally been vetted by so many parties that no

one person could be held accountable. An effort to expedite decision making through restructuring—by collocating key leaders with subject-matter experts in newly established central and regional centers of excellence—became instead another logjam. Key managers still weren't sure of their right to take advantage of these centers, so they didn't.

The nonprofit's management and directors went back to the drawing board. We worked with them to design a decision-making map, a tool to help identify where different types of decisions should be taken, and with it they clarified and enhanced decision rights at all levels of management. All managers were then actively encouraged to delegate standard operational tasks. Once people had a clear idea of what decisions they should and should not be making, holding them accountable for decisions felt fair. What's more, now they could focus their energies on the organization's mission. Clarifying decision rights and responsibilities also improved the organization's ability to track individual achievement, which helped it chart new and appealing career-advancement paths.

4. *Information flows freely across organizational boundaries.* When information does not flow horizontally across different parts of the company, units behave like silos, forfeiting economies of scale and the transfer of best practices. Moreover, the organization as a whole loses the opportunity to develop a cadre of up-and-coming managers well versed in all aspects of the company's operations. Our research indicates that only 21 percent of respondents from weak-execution companies thought information flowed freely across organizational boundaries whereas 55 percent of those from strong-execution firms did. Since scores for even the strong companies are pretty low, though, this is an issue that most companies can work on.

A cautionary tale comes from a business-to-business company whose customer and product teams failed to collaborate in serving a key segment: large, cross-product customers. To manage relationships with important clients, the company had established a customer-focused marketing group, which developed customer outreach programs, innovative pricing models, and tailored promotions and discounts. But this group issued no clear and consistent reports of its initiatives and progress to the product units and had difficulty securing time with the regular cross-unit management to discuss key performance issues.

Each product unit communicated and planned in its own way, and it took tremendous energy for the customer group to understand the units' various priorities and tailor communications to each one. So the units were not aware, and had little faith, that this new division was making constructive inroads into a key customer segment. Conversely (and predictably), the customer team felt the units paid only perfunctory attention to its plans and couldn't get their cooperation on issues critical to multiproduct customers, such as potential trade-offs and volume discounts.

Historically, this lack of collaboration hadn't been a problem because the company had been the dominant player in a high-margin market. But as the market became more competitive, customers began to view the firm as unreliable and, generally, as a difficult supplier, and they became increasingly reluctant to enter into favorable relationships.

Once the issues became clear, though, the solution wasn't terribly complicated, involving little more than getting the groups to talk to one another. The customer division became responsible for issuing regular reports to the product units showing performance against targets, by product and geographic region, and for supplying a supporting root-cause analysis. A standing performance-management meeting was placed on the schedule every quarter, creating a forum for exchanging information face-to-face and discussing outstanding issues. These moves bred the broader organizational trust required for collaboration.

5. *Field and line employees usually have the information they need to understand the bottom-line impact of their day-to-day choices.* Rational decisions are necessarily bounded by the information available to employees. If managers don't understand what it will cost to capture an incremental dollar in revenue, they will always pursue the incremental revenue. They can hardly be faulted, even if their decision is—in the light of full information—wrong. Our research shows that 61 percent of individuals in strong-execution organizations agree that field and line employees have the information they need to understand the bottom-line impact of their decisions. This figure plummets to 28 percent in weak-execution organizations.

We saw this unhealthy dynamic play out at a large, diversified financial-services client, which had been built through a series of successful mergers of small regional banks. In combining operations, managers had chosen to separate front-office bankers who sold loans from back-office support groups who did risk assessments, placing each in a different reporting relationship and, in many cases, in different locations. Unfortunately, they failed to institute the necessary information and motivation links to ensure smooth operations. As a result, each pursued different, and often competing, goals.

For example, salespeople would routinely enter into highly customized one-off deals with clients that cost the company more than they made in revenues. Sales did not have a clear understanding of the cost and complexity implications of these transactions. Without sufficient information, sales staff believed that the back-end people were sabotaging their deals, while the support groups considered the front-end people to be cowboys. At year's end, when the data were finally reconciled, management would bemoan the sharp increase in operational costs, which often erased the profit from these transactions.

Executives addressed this information misalignment by adopting a "smart customization" approach to sales. They standardized the end-to-end processes used in the majority of deals and allowed for customization only in select circumstances. For these customized deals, they established clear back-office processes and analytical support tools to arm salespeople with accurate information on the cost implications of the proposed transactions. At the same time, they rolled out common reporting standards and tools for both the front- and back-office operations to ensure that each group had access to the same data and metrics when making decisions. Once each side understood the business realities confronted by the other, they cooperated more effectively, acting in the whole company's best interests—and there were no more year-end surprises.

CREATING A TRANSFORMATION PROGRAM

The four building blocks that managers can use to improve strategy execution—decision rights, information, structure, and motivators—are inextricably linked. Unclear decision rights not only paralyze decision making but also impede information flow, divorce performance from rewards, and prompt work-arounds that subvert formal reporting lines.

Blocking information results in poor decisions, limited career development, and a reinforcement of structural silos. So what to do about it?

Since each organization is different and faces a unique set of internal and external variables, there is no universal answer to that question. The first step is to identify the sources of the problem. In our work, we often begin by having a company's employees take our profiling survey and consolidating the results. The more people in the organization who take the survey, the better.

Once executives understand their company's areas of weakness, they can take any number of actions. Figure 3, "Mapping Improvement Tactics to the Building Blocks," shows 15 possible steps that can have an impact on performance. (The options listed represent only a sampling of the dozens of choices managers might make.) All of these actions are geared toward strengthening one or more of the 17 traits. For example, if you were to take steps to "clarify and streamline decision making" you could potentially strengthen two traits: "Everyone has a good idea of the decisions and actions for which he or she is responsible," and "Once made, decisions are rarely second-guessed."

You certainly wouldn't want to put 15 initiatives in a single transformation program. Most organizations don't have the managerial capacity or organizational appetite to take on more than five or six at a time. And as we've stressed, you should first take steps to address decision rights and information, and then design the necessary changes to motivators and structure to support the new design.

To help companies understand their shortcomings and construct the improvement program that will have the greatest impact, we have developed an organizational-change simulator. This interactive tool accompanies the profiler, allowing you to try out different elements of a change program virtually, to see which ones will best target your company's particular area of weakness. (For an overview of the simulation process, see the box "Test Drive Your Organization's Transformation.")

To get a sense of the process from beginning to end—from taking the diagnostic profiler, to formulating your strategy, to launching your organizational transformation—consider the experience of a leading insurance company we'll call Goodward Insurance. Goodward was a successful company with strong capital reserves and steady revenue and customer growth. Still, its leadership wanted to further enhance execution to deliver on an ambitious five-year strategic agenda

Figure 3 Mapping Improvements to the Building Blocks: Some Sample Tactics

Companies can take a host of steps to improve their ability to execute strategy. The 15 here are only some of the possible examples. Every one strengthens one or more of the building blocks executives can use to improve their strategy-execution capability: clarifying decision rights, improving information, establishing the right motivators, and restructuring the organization.

- **Focus corporate staff on supporting business-unit decision making.**
- **Clarify and streamline decision making at each operating level.**
- **Focus headquarters on important strategic questions.**
- **Create centers of excellence by consolidating similar functions into a single organizational unit.**
- **Assign process owners to coordinate activities that span organizational functions.**
- **Establish individual performance measures.**
- **Improve field-to-headquarters information flow.**
- **Define and distribute daily operating metrics to the field or line.**
- **Create cross-functional teams.**
- **Introduce differentiating performance awards.**
- **Expand nonmonetary rewards to recognize exceptional performers.**
- **Increase position tenure.**
- **Institute lateral moves and rotations.**
- **Broaden spans of control.**
- **Decrease layers of management.**

BUILDING BLOCKS ■ Decision rights □ Information ■ Motivators ■ Structure

that included aggressive targets in customer growth, revenue increases, and cost reduction, which would require a new level of teamwork. While there were pockets of cross-unit collaboration within the company, it was far more common for each unit to focus on its own goals, making it difficult to spare resources to support another unit's goals. In many cases there was little incentive to do so anyway: Unit A's goals might require the involvement of Unit B to succeed, but Unit B's goals might not include supporting Unit A's effort.

The company had initiated a number of enterprisewide projects over the years, which had been completed on time and on budget, but these often had to be reworked because stakeholder needs hadn't been sufficiently taken into account. After launching a shared-services center, for example, the company had to revisit its operating model and processes when units began hiring shadow staff to focus on priority work that the center wouldn't expedite. The center might decide what technology applications, for instance, to develop on its own rather than set priorities according to what was most important to the organization.

In a similar way, major product launches were hindered by insufficient coordination among departments. The marketing department would develop new coverage options without asking the claims-processing group whether it had the ability to process the claims. Since it didn't, processors had to create expensive manual work-arounds when the new kinds of claims started pouring in. Nor did marketing ask the actuarial department how these products would affect the risk profile and reimbursement expenses of the company, and for some of the new products, costs did indeed increase.

To identify the greatest barriers to building a stronger execution culture, Goodward Insurance gave the diagnostic survey to all of its 7,000-plus employees and compared the organization's scores on the 17 traits with those from strong-execution companies. Numerous previous surveys (employee-satisfaction, among others) had elicited qualitative comments identifying the barriers to execution excellence. But the diagnostic survey gave the company quantifiable data that it could analyze by group and by management level to determine which barriers were most hindering the people actually charged with execution. As it turned out, middle management was far more pessimistic than the top executives in their assessment of the organization's execution ability. Their input became especially critical to the change agenda ultimately adopted.

Through the survey, Goodward Insurance uncovered impediments to execution in three of the most influential organizational traits:

- *Information did not flow freely across organizational boundaries.* Sharing information was never one of Goodward's hallmarks, but managers had always dismissed the mounting anecdotal evidence of poor cross-divisional information flow as "some other group's problem." The organizational diagnostic data, however, exposed such plausible deniability as an inadequate excuse. In fact, when the CEO reviewed the profiler results with his direct reports, he held up the chart on cross-group information flows and declared, "We've been discussing this problem for several years, and yet you always say that it's so-and-so's problem, not mine. Sixty-seven percent of [our] respondents said that they do not think information flows freely across divisions. This is not so-and-so's problem—it's our problem. You just don't get results that low [unless it comes] from everywhere. We are all on the hook for fixing this."

  Contributing to this lack of horizontal information flow was a dearth of lateral promotions. Because Goodward had always promoted up rather than over and up, most middle and senior managers remained within a single group. They were not adequately apprised of the activities of the other groups, nor did they have a network of contacts across the organization.

- *Important information about the competitive environment did not get to headquarters quickly.* The diagnostic data and subsequent surveys and interviews with middle management revealed that the wrong information was moving up the org chart. Mundane day-to-day decisions were escalated to the executive level—the top team had to approve midlevel hiring decisions, for instance, and bonuses of $1,000—limiting Goodward's agility in responding to competitors' moves, customers' needs, and changes in the broader marketplace. Meanwhile, more important information was so heavily filtered as it moved up the hierarchy that it was all but worthless for rendering key verdicts. Even if lower-level managers knew that a certain project could never work for highly valid reasons, they would not communicate that dim view to the top team. Nonstarters not only started, they kept going. For instance, the company had a project under way to create new incentives for its brokers. Even though this approach had been previously tried without success, no one spoke up in meetings or stopped the project because it was a priority for one of the top-team members.

Test-Drive Your Organization's Transformation

You know your organization could perform better. You are faced with dozens of levers you could conceivably pull if you had unlimited time and resources. But you don't. You operate in the real world.

How, then, do you make the most educated and cost-efficient decisions about which change initiatives to implement? We've developed a way to test the efficacy of specific actions (such as clarifying decision rights, forming cross-functional teams, or expanding nonmonetary rewards) without risking significant amounts of time and money. You can go to www.simulator-orgeffectiveness.com to assemble and try out various five-step organizational-change programs and assess which would be the most effective and efficient in improving execution at your company.

You begin the simulation by selecting one of seven organizational profiles that most resembles the current state of your organization. If you're not sure, you can take a five-minute diagnostic survey. This online survey automatically generates an organizational profile and baseline execution-effectiveness score. (Although 100 is a perfect score, nobody is perfect; even the most effective companies often score in the 60s and 70s.)

Having established your baseline, you use the simulator to chart a possible course you'd like to take to improve your execution capabilities by selecting five out of a possible 28 actions. Ideally, these moves should directly address the weakest links in your organizational profile. To help you make the right choices, the simulator offers insights that shed further light on how a proposed action influences particular organizational elements.

Once you have made your selections, the simulator executes the steps you've elected and processes them through a Web-based engine that evaluates them using empirical-relationships identified from 31 companies representing more than 26,000 data observations. It then generates a

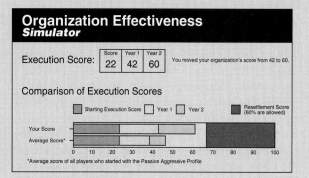

bar chart indicating how much your organization's execution score has improved and where it now stands in relation to the highest-performing companies from our research and the scores of other people like you who have used the simulator starting from the same original profile you did. If you wish, you may then advance to the next round and pick another five actions. What you will see is illustrated above.

The beauty of the simulator is its ability to consider—consequence-free—the impact on execution of endless combinations of possible actions. Each simulation includes only two rounds, but you can run the simulation as many times as you like. The simulator has also been used for team competition within organizations, and we've found that it engenders very engaging and productive dialogue among senior executives.

While the simulator cannot capture all of the unique situations an organization might face, it is a useful tool for assessing and building a targeted and effective organization-transformation program. It serves as a vehicle to stimulate thinking about the impact of various changes, saving untold amounts of time and resources in the process.

- *No one had a good idea of the decisions and actions for which he or she was responsible.* The general lack of information flow extended to decision rights, as few managers understood where their authority ended and another's began. Accountability even for day-to-day decisions was unclear, and managers did not know whom to ask for clarification. Naturally, confusion over decision rights led to second-guessing. Fifty-five

percent of respondents felt that decisions were regularly second-guessed at Goodward.

To Goodward's credit, its top executives immediately responded to the results of the diagnostic by launching a change program targeted at all three problem areas. The program integrated early, often symbolic, changes with longer-term initiatives, in an effort to build momentum and galvanize participation and ownership. Recognizing that a passive-aggressive attitude toward people perceived to be in power solely as a result of their position in the hierarchy was hindering information flow, they took immediate steps to signal their intention to create a more informal and open culture. One symbolic change: the seating at management meetings was rearranged. The top executives used to sit in a separate section, the physical space between them and the rest of the room fraught with symbolism. Now they intermingled, making themselves more accessible and encouraging people to share information informally. Regular brown-bag lunches were established with members of the C-suite, where people had a chance to discuss the overall culture-change initiative, decision rights, new mechanisms for communicating across the units, and so forth. Seating at these events was highly choreographed to ensure that a mix of units was represented at each table. Icebreaker activities were designed to encourage individuals to learn about other units' work.

Meanwhile, senior managers commenced the real work of remedying issues relating to information flows and decision rights. They assessed their own informal networks to understand how people making key decisions got their information, and they identified critical gaps. The outcome was a new framework for making important decisions that clearly specifies who owns each decision, who must provide input, who is ultimately accountable for the results, and how results are defined. Other longer-term initiatives include:

- Pushing certain decisions down into the organization to better align decision rights with the best available information. Most hiring and bonus decisions, for instance, have been delegated to immediate managers, so long as they are within preestablished boundaries relating to numbers hired and salary levels. Being clear about who needs what information is encouraging cross-group dialogue.
- Identifying and eliminating duplicative committees.
- Pushing metrics and scorecards down to the group level, so that rather than focus on solving the mystery of *who* caused a problem, management can get right to the root cause of *why* the problem occurred. A well-designed scorecard captures not only outcomes (like sales volume or revenue) but also leading indicators of those

outcomes (such as the number of customer calls or completed customer plans). As a result, the focus of management conversations has shifted from trying to explain the past to charting the future—anticipating and preventing problems.

- Making the planning process more inclusive. Groups are explicitly mapping out the ways their initiatives depend on and affect one another; shared group goals are assigned accordingly.
- Enhancing the middle management career path to emphasize the importance of lateral moves to career advancement.

Goodward Insurance has just embarked on this journey. The insurer has distributed ownership of these initiatives among various groups and management levels so that these efforts don't become silos in themselves. Already, solid improvement in the company's execution is beginning to emerge. The early evidence of success has come from employee-satisfaction surveys: Middle management responses to the questions about levels of cross-unit collaboration and clarity of decision making have improved as much as 20 to 25 percentage points. And high performers are already reaching across boundaries to gain a broader understanding of the full business, even if it doesn't mean a better title right away.

Execution is a notorious and perennial challenge. Even at the companies that are best at it—what we call "resilient organizations"—just two-thirds of employees agree that important strategic and operational decisions are quickly translated into action. As long as companies continue to attack their execution problems primarily or solely with structural or motivational initiatives, they will continue to fail. As we've seen, they may enjoy short-term results, but they will inevitably slip back into old habits because they won't have addressed the root causes of failure. Such failures can almost always be fixed by ensuring that people truly understand what they are responsible for and who makes which decisions—and then giving them the information they need to fulfill their responsibilities. With these two building blocks in place, structural and motivational elements will follow.

Note

1. The details for this example have been taken from Gary L. Neilson and Bruce A. Pasternack, *Results: Keep What's Good, Fix What's Wrong, and Unlock Great Performance* (Random House, 2005).

Some Pros and Cons of Six Sigma: An Academic Perspective

Jiju Antony
Caledonian Business School

INTRODUCTION

Six Sigma is a business strategy that seeks to identify and eliminate causes of errors or defects or failures in business processes by focusing on outputs that are critical to customers (Snee, 1999). It is also a measure of quality that strives for near elimination of defects using the application of statistical methods. A defect is defined as anything which could lead to customer dissatisfaction. The fundamental objective of the Six Sigma methodology is the implementation of a measurement-based strategy that focuses on process improvement and variation reduction. A number of papers and books have been published showing the fundamentals of Six Sigma, such as, what is Six Sigma (Hoerl, 1998; Breyfogle III, 1999; Harry and Schroeder, 1999), why do we need Six Sigma (Snee, 2000; Pande et al., 2001), what makes Six Sigma different from other quality initiatives (Pyzdek, 2001; Snee and Hoerl, 2003), Six Sigma deployment (Keller, 2001; Adams et al., 2003), critical success factors of Six Sigma implementation (Antony and Banuelas, 2002), Six Sigma project selection process (Snee, 2002), and organizational infrastructure required for implementing Six Sigma (Adams et al., 2003; Snee and Hoerl, 2003).

I personally have experienced that senior management in many organizations view Six Sigma as another quality improvement initiative or flavor of the month in their list. I am often told by many engineers and managers, in small and big companies, that there is nothing really new in Six Sigma compared to other quality initiatives we have witnessed in the past. In response, I often ask a simple question to people in organizations who practice TQM: "What do you understand by the term TQM?" I often get many varying answers to this question. However if I ask a bunch of Six Sigma practitioners, "What do you know of the term Six Sigma?" I often get an answer which means more or less the same thing and concurs with what I would have expected. The following aspects of the Six Sigma strategy are not accentuated in previous quality improvement initiatives:

- Six Sigma strategy places a clear focus on achieving measurable and quantifiable financial returns to the bottom line of an organization. No Six Sigma project is approved unless the bottom-line impact has been clearly identified and defined.

- Six Sigma strategy places an unprecedented importance on strong and passionate leadership and the support required for its successful deployment.

- Six Sigma methodology of problem solving integrates the human elements (culture change, customer focus, belt system infrastructure, etc.) and process elements (process management, statistical analysis of process data, measurement system analysis, etc.) of improvement.

- Six Sigma methodology utilizes the tools and techniques for fixing problems in business processes in a sequential and disciplined fashion. Each tool and technique within the Six Sigma methodology has a role to play and when, where, why, and how these tools or techniques should

Reprinted from *The TQM Magazine* 16, no. 4 (2004). © Emerald Group Publishing Limited. Reprinted with permission of Emerald Group Publishing Limited.

be applied is the difference between success and failure of a Six Sigma project.

- Six Sigma creates an infrastructure of champions, master black belts (MBBs), black belts (BBs), and green belts (GBs) that lead, deploy, and implement the approach.

- Six Sigma emphasizes the importance of data and decision making based on facts and data rather than assumptions and hunches! Six Sigma forces people to put measurements in place. Measurement must be considered as a part of the culture change.

- Six Sigma utilizes the concept of statistical thinking and encourages the application of well-proven statistical tools and techniques for defect reduction through process variability reduction methods (e.g., statistical process control and design of experiments).

Just like any other quality improvement initiatives we have seen in the past, Six Sigma has its own limitations. The following are some of the limitations of Six Sigma which create opportunities for future research:

- The challenge of having quality data available, especially in processes where no data is available to begin with (sometimes this task could take the largest proportion of the project time).

- In some cases, there is frustration as the solutions driven by the data are expensive and only a small part of the solution is implemented at the end.

- The right selection and prioritization of projects is one of the critical success factors of a Six Sigma program. The prioritization of projects in many organizations is still based on pure subjective judgment. Very few powerful tools are available for prioritizing projects and this should be a major thrust for research in the future.

- The statistical definition of Six Sigma is 3.4 defects or failures per million opportunities. In service processes, a defect may be defined as anything which does not meet customer needs or expectations. It would be illogical to assume that all defects are equally good when we calculate the sigma capability level of a process. For instance, a defect in a hospital could be a wrong admission procedure, lack of training required by a staff member, misbehavior of staff members,

unwillingness to help patients when they have specific queries, etc.

- The calculation of defect rates or error rates is based on the assumption of normality. The calculation of defect rates for non-normal situations is not yet properly addressed in the current literature of Six Sigma.

- Due to dynamic market demands, the critical-to-quality characteristics (CTQs) of today would not necessarily be meaningful tomorrow. All CTQs should be critically examined at all times and refined as necessary (Goh, 2002).

- Very little research has been done on the optimization of multiple CTQs in Six Sigma projects.

- Assumption of a 1.5 sigma shift for all service processes does not make much sense. This particular issue should be the major thrust for future research, as a small shift in sigma could lead to erroneous defect calculations.

- Non-standardization procedures in the certification process of black belts and green belts is another limitation. This means not all black belts or green belts are equally capable. Research has shown that the skills and expertise developed by black belts are inconsistent across companies and are dependent to a great extent on the certifying body. For more information on this aspect, readers are advised to refer to Hoerl (2001). Black belts believe they know all the practical aspects of advanced quality improvement methods such as design of experiments, robust design, response surface methodology, statistical process control, and reliability, when in fact they have barely scratched the surface.

- The start-up cost for institutionalizing Six Sigma into a corporate culture can be a significant investment. This particular feature would discourage many small and medium-size enterprises from the introduction, development, and implementation of Six Sigma strategy.

- Six Sigma can easily digress into a bureaucratic exercise if the focus is on such things as the number of trained black belts and green belts, number of projects completed, etc., instead of bottom-line savings.

- There is an overselling of Six Sigma by too many consulting firms. Many of them claim expertise in Six Sigma when they barely understand the tools and techniques and the Six Sigma roadmap.

- The relationship between cost of poor quality (COPQ) and process sigma quality level requires more justification.
- The linkage between Six Sigma and organizational culture and learning is not addressed properly in the existing literature.
- The "five sigma" wall proposed in Mikel Harry's book, *Six Sigma: The Breakthrough Management Strategy Revolutionizing the World's Top Corporations,* is questionable. Companies might redesign their processes well before even four sigma quality level. Moreover, it is illogical to assume that the "five sigma" wall approach is valid for all processes (manufacturing, service, or transactional). Moreover, the decision of re-design efforts over continuous improvement depends on a number of other variables such as risk, technology, cost, customer demands, time, complexity, etc.

WHAT DOES THE FUTURE HOLD FOR SIX SIGMA?

In my opinion, Six Sigma will be around as long as the projects yield measurable or quantifiable bottom-line results in monetary or financial terms. When Six Sigma projects stop yielding bottom-line results, it might disappear. I also feel that while Six Sigma will evolve in the forthcoming years, there are some core elements or principles within Six Sigma that will be maintained, irrespective of the "next big thing." One of the real dangers of Six Sigma has to do with the capability of black belts (the so-called technical experts) who tackle challenging projects in organizations. We cannot simply assume that all black belts are equally good, and their capabilities vary enormously across industries (manufacturing or service), depending a great deal on the certifying body. Another danger is the attitude of many senior managers in organizations that Six Sigma is "an instant pudding" solving all their ever-lasting problems.

I also believe that the Six Sigma toolkit will continue to add new tools, especially from other disciplines such as health care, finance, sales, and marketing. Having a core set of tools and techniques

is an advantage of Six Sigma that brings speed to fix problems and its ease of accessibility to black belts and green belts.

I would like to raise the point that Six Sigma does provide an effective means for deploying and implementing statistical thinking (Snee, 1990; 2002) which is based on the following three rudimentary principles:

1. All work occurs in a system of interconnected processes.
2. Variation exists in all processes.
3. Understanding and analyzing the variation are keys to success.

Statistical thinking can also be defined as thought processes, which recognize that variation is all around us and present in everything we do. All work is a series of interconnected processes, and identifying, characterizing, quantifying, controlling, and reducing variation provide opportunities for improvement (Snee, 1990). The above principles of statistical thinking within Six Sigma are robust and therefore it is fair to say that Six Sigma will continue to grow in the forthcoming years. In other words, statistical thinking may be used to create a culture that should be deeply embedded in every employee within any organization embarking on Six Sigma programs. However, the total package may change in the evolutionary process. It is important to remember that Six Sigma has a better record than total quality management (TQM) and business process reengineering (BPR), since its inception in the mid–late 1980s. The ever-changing need to improve will no doubt create needs to improve the existing Six Sigma methodology and hence develop better products and provide better services in the future. As a final note, the author believes that companies implementing or contemplating embarking on Six Sigma programs should not view it as an advertising banner for promotional purposes.

CONCLUSION

Six Sigma as a powerful business strategy has been well recognized as an imperative for achieving and sustaining operational and service excellence. While the original focus of Six Sigma was on manufacturing, today it has been widely accepted in both service and transactional processes. This paper highlights the pros and cons of Six Sigma from the viewpoint of an academician. Although the total package may change as part of the evolutionary process, the core principles of Six Sigma will continue to grow in the future. Six Sigma has made a huge impact on industry and yet the academic community lags behind in its understanding of this powerful strategy. It will therefore be incumbent on academic fraternity to provide well-grounded theories to explain the phenomena of Six Sigma. In other words, Six Sigma lacks a theoretical underpinning and hence it is our responsibility as academicians to bridge the gap between the theory and practice of Six Sigma.

References

Adams, C., Gupta, P. and Wilson, C. (2003), *Six Sigma Deployment,* Butterworth-Heinemann, Burlington, MA.

Antony, J. and Bañuelas, R. (2002), "Key ingredients for the effective implementation of Six Sigma program," *Measuring Business Excellence,* Vol. 6 No. 4, pp. 20–27.

Breyfogle, F. W. III (1999), *Implementing Six Sigma: Smarter Solutions Using Statistical Methods,* John Wiley & Sons, New York, NY.

Goh, T. N. (2002), "A strategic assessment of Six Sigma," *Quality and Reliability Engineering International,* Vol. 18 No. 2, pp. 403–10.

Harry, M. J. and Schroeder, R. (1999), *Six Sigma: The Breakthrough Management Strategy Revolutionizing the World's Top Corporations,* Doubleday, New York. NY.

Hoerl, R. W. (1998), "Six sigma and the future of the quality profession," *Quality Progress,* Vol. 31 No. 6, pp. 35–42.

Hoerl, R. W. (2001), "Six sigma black belts: what do they need to know?" *Journal of Quality Technology,* Vol. 33 No. 4, pp. 391–406.

Keller, P. A. (2001), *Six Sigma Deployment,* Quality Publishing, Tucson, AZ.

Pande, P., Neuman, R. and Cavanagh, R. (2001), *The Six Sigma Way,* McGraw-Hill, New York, NY.

Pyzdek, T. (2001), *The Six Sigma Handbook: A Complete Guide for Greenbelts, Blackbelts and Managers at All Levels,* McGraw-Hill, New York, NY.

Snee, R. D. (1990), "Statistical thinking and its contribution to total quality," *The American Statistician,* Vol. 44 No. 2, pp. 116–21.

Snee, R. D. (1999), "Why should statisticians pay attention to Six Sigma?" *Quality Progress,* September, pp. 100–3.

Snee, R. D. (2000), "Impact of Six Sigma on quality engineering," *Quality Engineering,* Vol. 12 No. 3, pp. 9–14.

Snee, R. D. (2002), "The project selection process," *Quality Progress,* September, pp. 78–80.

Snee, R. D. and Hoerl, R. W. (2003), *Leading Six Sigma Companies,* FT Prentice-Hall, Upper Saddle River, NJ.

Further Reading

ASQ (1996), *Glossary and Tables for SQC,* Quality Press, Milwaukee, WI.

Linking Goals to Monetary Incentives

Edwin A. Locke
University of Maryland

Every experienced executive knows the importance of rewarding good performance and also how difficult it is to design an incentive system that works as it is supposed to. A recent article in *The Wall Street Journal*[1] reported that Hewitt Associates found that 83 percent of companies with a pay-for-performance system said that their incentive plan was "only somewhat successful or not working at all."

Consider just some of the ideas that must be addressed in designing an incentive system:

- What should be the form of the incentive plan? That is, how, specifically, should pay be tied to performance?
- How do you keep employees from short-cutting or cheating in order to get their bonus?
- Which actions or outcomes should you pay bonuses for?
- What will be the effect of incentives on actions or outcomes that are not included in the incentive plan?
- How many different actions or outcomes can an employee actually manage?
- If more than one action or outcome is part of the plan, how should they all be combined or weighted?
- What do you do when market conditions change radically and make the incentive system ineffective or meaningless?

It is no accident that most companies constantly tinker with, and often radically overhaul, their incentive plans. Many can never seem to get it quite right. This article will try to provide some answers to the above questions, but I will start by addressing one fundamental issue. Hewitt's research indicates that one major cause of the failure of incentive plans is the lack of clear goals.

Goal-setting theory asserts that people must have goals that are both clear and challenging in order to motivate high performance. The question then arises: How do you combine goal setting with incentives?

I will describe four different methods and the pros and cons of each.

METHOD 1: STRETCH GOALS WITH BONUSES FOR SUCCESS

This method involves assigning people difficult or stretch goals, giving them a substantial bonus if they reach them and no bonus if they do not. The respective advantages and disadvantages of this method include the following:

Pros. This method provides a strong incentive to attain the goals. There is a huge difference in reward between attaining the goals and failing, even by a small amount, to attain the goals. Further, it leaves no ambiguity about what is required of the person to receive the bonus.

Cons. A weakness of this method is ironically the result of its strength. Precisely because the motivation

Reprinted from *Academy of Management Executive* 18, no. 4 (2004), pp. 130–33. Used by permission of the Academy of Management via The Copyright Clearance Center.

for goal attainment is so high, there is considerable temptation for the person to think short range, e.g., pile up excess inventory with customers (which will come back to haunt the company in the next quarter), take short cuts (e.g., lower quality, ignore maintenance, increase risk), and cheat (e.g., exaggerate or make up totally fake results, cook the books) in order to receive the bonus.

To prevent these and other dysfunctional outcomes, the organization needs rules of conduct: ethical norms or standards that are clearly communicated and consistently enforced. The moral atmosphere or climate of an organization is set by the CEO and the senior management team, who must not only be impeccable role models but who must make certain that the company's ethical standards are strictly enforced (e.g., those who flout them must be fired). If the CEO and top managers are not personally honest, it leads to demoralization and cynicism among employees. This, in turn, can lead to a whole culture of dishonesty.

Another downside of this method is that performance which is very high but just misses the goal yields no bonus at all. This can be very demoralizing to competent, hard-working employees. It can lay the seeds for future dishonesty.

METHOD 2: MULTIPLE GOAL LEVELS WITH MULTIPLE BONUS LEVELS

This method avoids some of the problems of method 1. Instead of a single goal level with the bonus being "all or none," there are multiple goal levels (for example, five), and a different bonus level is attached to each—the higher the goal level attained, the higher the reward.

Pros. There is less temptation for employees to short-cut or cheat here, because even if they do not attain the top goal level, they can get a bonus for making the next lower level. Highly competent employees who just miss a high-level goal still get rewarded.

Cons. Because there are multiple goal and bonus levels, employees may be less motivated to try for the highest level than in the case of method 1. A problem can occur if employees are content to try for the lowest goal level that is rewarded. For this bonus system

to be effective, the CEO or senior management must set some minimum goal below which performance is considered inadequate. Then the multiple-goal level can start from a level above this minimum. However, this approach still does not push everyone to try for the highest goal. Furthermore, there is no tangible motivation to exceed the top goal because no further bonus would be forthcoming. Of course, pride and recognition are powerful motivators independent of money, but most employees want consistency between tangible and intangible rewards.

METHOD 3: A LINEAR SYSTEM

This method is recommended by Michael Jensen of the Harvard Business School.[2] It is a variation on method 2, which involves increments. Consider five levels of sales goals, e.g., +5 percent, +10 percent, +15 percent, +20 percent, +25 percent. The employee who makes 24.5 percent will get rewarded, but only for reaching the 20 percent goal, so may still feel disappointed at coming close to, but just missing, the 25 percent goal. The simplest solution here is to make this a continuous bonus system, e.g., a 2 percent bonus for every 1 percent increase in sales. (Obviously 1 percent is still an increment but a very small one.)

Pros. This method eliminates two disadvantages of methods 1 and 2. First, there is no "loss" for getting close to a higher goal level and just missing it; an employee gets paid for exactly what is achieved. This, according to Jensen, further decreases the temptation to cheat or take shortcuts. Second, there is no upper limit on the bonus. Under methods 1 and 2 if a person attained the top goal for an increase in sales (say 25 percent), the employee would get the same bonus even if that person achieved a +50 percent or +100 percent sales increase. So there would be little tangible incentive to exceed +25 percent. Under method 3, however, if the person gets a 50 percent sales increase, the bonus would be 2×50 percent or 100 percent.

Cons. There is still the problem inherent in method 2: less pressure for the employee to "stretch." Setting a minimum goal would help as with method 2, but many people might not be financially motivated to go far beyond the minimum. Also some companies could have a problem with unlimited compensation for employees; it might seem unfair to people in other parts of the company (e.g., non-sales jobs) where a meaningful linear system would be hard to design.

METHOD 4: MOTIVATE BY GOALS BUT PAY FOR PERFORMANCE

This method, suggested by Gary Latham of the Rotman Business School (University of Toronto), makes the tie between goals and performance a little looser than under the other methods. The employee is given specific, challenging goals, but the decision about bonus awards is made after the fact so as to take account of the full context in which the goal is pursued. The relevant context factors might include: e.g., how much was actually achieved regardless of what the goals were, how the company as a whole did, how difficult the goals *really* were, in the light of such factors as resources, obstacles, and market conditions, as well as the methods the employee used to attain the goals (e.g., ethical behavior). Often the bonus decisions will be made by a management team because they may have more knowledge than any one executive.

Pros. The main benefit of this method is its flexibility and comprehensiveness. For example, an employee who tries for a hard goal under very difficult circumstances but does not quite reach it can still be well rewarded, whereas an employee who attains an allegedly hard goal which turned out not to be so hard in hindsight would get less (or be penalized or fired if the goal was attained unethically). This method, of course, is similar to what is called "merit-based pay," but it would require that clear goals be set for every action or outcome that was important to the organization.

Cons. This method requires the boss to be knowledgeable about the full context and also to be objective in order to minimize favoritism or bias. Many people at the CEO and top-management levels lack these qualities. Of course, with poor quality leadership, the other incentive plans may not work either, because no method is better than the people who use it.

WHICH METHOD IS BEST?

To the author's knowledge, there have been no published field studies or laboratory experiments comparing the effectiveness of the four systems described above or even comparing any two of them. Thus there is no basis for claiming that one is necessarily better than others. Much may depend on the nature of the business and the quality of the management. This topic is ripe for further study and experimentation.

Observe that GE decided to make a distinction between goals that were absolutely essential to the organization and goals that were not. Stretch goals, which allowed credit for failure, were used mainly in the latter case. This implies that different incentive rules could be applied to each type of goal.

Cheating or short-cutting can occur under any incentive system; thus, as noted earlier, all companies need a strict (and enforced) code of ethics and well-designed control systems. (GE was known for having excellent control systems.)

WHAT ACTIVITIES SHOULD GOALS BE SET FOR?

For whatever is important. This will certainly involve performance outcomes and often goal-setting for the critical actions that lead to those outcomes. For example, sales, specifically repeat sales, depend on customer satisfaction, and there are specific actions that can be taken to satisfy customers (e.g., on-time delivery, high-quality products, changing policies as a result of customer feedback, etc.). Customer satisfaction is a "soft" measure, yet it can be measured quantitatively. Information-sharing with other managers, executives, employees, and so forth is another desirable action that often can benefit the entire company. Information-sharing could be measured by means of peer assessments. Developing subordinates is another important activity required for long-term organizational success.

It is possible to make causal maps that show the relationship between behaviors and outcomes. Consider this example: knowledge sharing within the company and with customers → improved customer service and better products → improved customer satisfaction → improved customer retention and sales → increase in profits. Note that goals can be set for any part or all parts of this sequence. Observe also that the benefit of the causal map is that it forces one to formulate the plan for improving the final outcome: profits. The causal inputs constitute a plan.

Actions and outcomes for which goals are not set and which are not rewarded monetarily will probably get minimum attention unless they are causally connected to the actions and outcomes that are measured and rewarded. A poorly devised bonus system can create "tunnel vision"—a focus only on what gets rewarded to the neglect of other important outcomes. Of course, bonus systems are *supposed* to focus attention and effort in a certain direction to the exclusion of others. Thus it is critical to do a lot of thinking about which actions and outcomes are important before creating a goal and reward system.

> **It is critical to do a lot of thinking about which actions and outcomes are important before creating a goal and reward system.**

HOW MANY GOALS SHOULD THERE BE?

It is important to avoid cognitive overload. No one manager, for example, could make good progress toward achieving 17 different goals, unless most of them could be delegated, nor would the manager even have the time to track progress. One person alone could probably handle somewhere between three and seven goals, depending on how difficult and complex they were and how much time was allowed for completion.

If employees are trying to achieve multiple goals, this presents a problem with respect to designing the reward system. *Ideal reward systems are simple,* and the simplest system has only one rewarded outcome or goal. The problem is that a one-goal system is usually too narrow in scope for a job. When a one-goal system is not adequate, there is an advantage to method 4, since it can take account of as many goals as the boss or top-management team considers relevant. If methods 1, 2, or 3 are used with multiple goals, then the goals have to be weighted in terms of importance.

GOAL INTEGRATION

In any organization virtually everything that happens affects everything else, for better or for worse. Ideally, goals should be integrated across the entire organization, but this is usually impossible due to time constraints. However, through knowledge sharing within and across organizational levels and departments, it is possible to coordinate essential activities (e.g., sales, marketing, and production all need to be involved if a new product is contemplated). Such coordination is what cross-functional teams are designed to achieve.

Goal integration, including knowledge sharing, may be facilitated if part of the bonus is paid on the basis of peer ratings of knowledge sharing and/or on how well the company as a whole does.

SHOULD GOALS BE CHANGED WHEN CONDITIONS CHANGE?

If goals are changed constantly (e.g., every three months), the danger is that no one will take them seriously. But if the strategic direction of a company changes, the goals need to reflect such changes. For example, when Jack Welch decided that GE would embrace the Six Sigma quality-control process, every executive was given goals to train employees in Six Sigma principles and to initiate Six Sigma projects. Bonuses were based, in part, on performance in relation to those goals.

What if the economy or industry turns bad? At Nucor, plant workers get paid by team productivity. If steel demand goes down, they get paid less. The

> **If goals are changed constantly (e.g., every three months), the danger is that no one will take them seriously.**

same principle holds for Nucor's plant managers and executives. In some years profits drop, and no bonuses are distributed. Nucor's philosophy is: Why should plant employees and executives get bonuses when the stockholders are losing money? At Nucor they have to tough it out until business increases. A business downturn could be a signal to develop better business strategies, to cut costs, and to set new goals.

THE EFFECTIVE INCENTIVE SYSTEM

Effective bonus plans are extraordinarily difficult to set up and to maintain. It has been said that it is better to have no bonus system at all, other than simply merit pay, than to have a bad one. Bad incentive plans encourage people to do the wrong things in the wrong way, and they lead to cynicism, anger, and indifference. The first step that should be taken when considering setting up a bonus system is to ask: What do we really want people to do or accomplish? As Steve Kerr, a former GE executive, said many years ago, there is no point in rewarding A if what you want is B.[3] This issue probably takes more thought than any other aspect of an incentive system.

The second step is to set goals for desired outcomes. Make them clear and challenging. If needed, include goals for the actions that lead to the desired outcomes and not just the outcomes themselves. Make sure the number of goals assigned is doable. And do not change the goals too readily.

The third step is to consider which goals will need to be integrated within and across levels and divisions.

The fourth step is to pick the type of bonus system that is right for your company considering what you came up with in the first three steps, with full awareness of all the pros and cons of each method.

Following these steps will not guarantee that you will devise a successful bonus system, but it will definitely increase the odds.

Endnotes

1. Chu, K. Firms report lackluster results from pay-for-performance plans. *Wall Street Journal,* 15 June 2004: D-1.

2. Jensen, M. 2002. Paying people to lie: The truth about the budgeting process. Harvard Business School Working Paper 01-072.

3. Kerr, S. 1995. On the folly of rewarding A, while hoping for B. *Academy of Management Executive,* 9(1): 7–14.Core Concept

Sydney Finkelstein
Dartmouth College

The past few years have witnessed some admirable business successes—and some exceptional failures. Among the companies that have hit hard times are a few of the most storied names in business—think Arthur Andersen, Rubbermaid, and Schwinn Bicycle—as well as a collection of former high flyers like Enron, Tyco, and WorldCom. Behind each of these failures stands a towering figure, a CEO or business leader who will long be remembered for being spectacularly unsuccessful.

The truth is, it takes some special personal qualities to be spectacularly unsuccessful. I'm talking about people who took world-renowned business operations and made them almost worthless. What's remarkable is that the individuals who possess the personal qualities that make this magnitude of destruction possible usually possess other, genuinely admirable qualities. It makes sense: Hardly anyone gets a chance to destroy so much value without demonstrating the potential for creating it. Most of the great destroyers of value are people of unusual intelligence and talent who display personal magnetism. They are the leaders who appear on the covers of *Fortune* and *Forbes*.

Still, when it comes to the crunch, these people fail—and fail monumentally. What's the secret of their destructive powers? After spending six years studying more than 50 companies and conducting some 200 interviews, I found that spectacularly unsuccessful people had seven characteristics in common. Nearly all of the leaders who preside over major business failures exhibit four or five of these habits. The truly gifted ones exhibit all seven. But here's what's really remarkable: Each of these seven habits represents a quality that is widely admired in the business world. Business not only tolerates the qualities that make these leaders spectacularly unsuccessful, it celebrates them.

Here, then, are seven habits of spectacularly unsuccessful people, along with some warning signs to look out for. These habits are most destructive when a CEO exhibits them, but any manager who has these habits can do terrible harm—including you. Study them. Learn to recognize them. And try to catch these red flags before spectacular failure finds you!

HABIT #1: THEY SEE THEMSELVES AND THEIR COMPANIES AS DOMINATING THEIR ENVIRONMENT

This first habit may be the most insidious, since it appears to be highly desirable. Shouldn't a company try to dominate its business environment, shape the future of its markets, and set the pace within them? Yes, but there's a catch. Unlike successful leaders, failed leaders who never question their dominance fail to realize they are at the mercy of changing circumstances. They vastly overestimate the extent to which they actually control events and vastly underestimate the role of chance and circumstance in their success.

CEOs who fall prey to this belief suffer from the illusion of personal pre-eminence: Like certain film directors, they see themselves as the *auteurs* of their companies. As far as they're concerned, everyone else in the company is there to execute their personal vision for the company. Samsung's CEO Kun-Hee Lee was so successful with electronics that he thought he could repeat this success with automobiles. He invested $5 billion in an already oversaturated auto market. Why? There was no business case. Lee simply loved cars and had dreamed of being in the auto business.

Warning Sign: A Lack of Respect

Leaders who suffer from the illusion of personal pre-eminence tend to believe that their companies are indispensable to their suppliers and customers. Rather than looking to satisfy customer needs, CEOs who believe they run pre-eminent companies act as if their customers were the lucky ones. When asked how Johnson & Johnson lost its seemingly insurmountable lead in the medical stent business, cardiologists and hospital administrators pointed to the company's arrogance and lack of respect for customers' ideas. Motorola exhibited the same arrogance when it continued to build fancy analogue phones, rather than the digital variety its customers were clamoring for.

HABIT #2: THEY IDENTIFY SO COMPLETELY WITH THE COMPANY THAT THERE IS NO CLEAR BOUNDARY BETWEEN THEIR PERSONAL INTERESTS AND THEIR CORPORATION'S INTERESTS

Like the first habit, this one seems innocuous, perhaps even beneficial. We want business leaders to be completely committed to their companies, with their interests tightly aligned with those of the company. But digging deeper, you find that failed executives weren't identifying too little with the company, but

rather too much. Instead of treating companies as enterprises that they needed to nurture, failed leaders treated them as extensions of themselves. And with that, a "private empire" mentality took hold.

CEOs who possess this outlook often use their companies to carry out personal ambitions. The most slippery slope of all for these executives is their tendency to use corporate funds for personal reasons. CEOs who have a long or impressive track record may come to feel that they've made so much money for the company that the expenditures they make on themselves, even if extravagant, are trivial by comparison. This twisted logic seems to have been one of the factors that shaped the behavior of Dennis Kozlowski of Tyco. His pride in his company and his pride in his own extravagance seem to have reinforced each other. This is why he could sound so sincere making speeches about ethics while using corporate funds for personal purposes. Being the CEO of a sizable corporation today is probably the closest thing to being king of your own country, and that's a dangerous title to assume.

Warning Sign: A Question of Character

When it comes right down to it, the biggest warning sign of CEO failure is a question of character. We might want to believe that leaders at companies like Adelphia, Tyco, and ImClone were trustworthy stewards of those companies, but their behavior suggests otherwise. But questions about character need not be limited to dubious or unethical acts. In fact, most leaders I studied were scrupulously honest. Rather, it is denial and defensiveness that are the critical warning signs. As Tony Galban, a D&O underwriter at Chubb, told me, "Always listen to the analysts' calls because that gives you a sense of how an individual thinks on their feet. They give you a sense of whether they're in denial or whether they're being professional." It gets down to this: Do you really trust this person?

HABIT #3: THEY THINK THEY HAVE ALL THE ANSWERS

Here's the image of executive competence that we've been taught to admire for decades: a dynamic leader making a dozen decisions a minute, dealing with many crises simultaneously, and taking only seconds to size up situations that have stumped everyone else for days. The problem with this picture is that it's a fraud. Leaders who are invariably crisp and decisive tend to settle issues so quickly they have no opportunity to grasp the ramifications. Worse, because these leaders need to feel they have all the answers, they aren't open to learning new ones.

CEO Wolfgang Schmitt of Rubbermaid was fond of demonstrating his ability to sort out difficult issues in a flash. A former colleague remembers that under Schmitt, "the joke went, 'Wolf knows everything about everything.' In one discussion, where we were talking about a particularly complex acquisition we made in Europe, Wolf, without hearing different points of view, just said, 'Well, this is what we are going to do.'" Leaders who need to have all the answers shut out other points of view. When your company or organization is run by someone like this, you'd better hope the answers he comes up with are going to be the right ones. At Rubbermaid they weren't. The company went from being *Fortune*'s most admired company in America in 1993 to being acquired by the conglomerate Newell a few years later.

Warning Sign: A Leader without Followers

John Keogh, another big-time underwriter of D&O insurance, pointed out what he looks for when CEOs are being interviewed by analysts: "[Was] the management team incredibly arrogant? [Did the CEO or CFO] have all the answers and is [he or she] pretty [much] on top of his or her game?" CEOs who believe they have all the answers don't really need other people, except to do what they want them to do. One of the critical side effects of a CEO's fixation on being right is that opposition can go underground, effectively closing down dissent. As middle management begins to realize that their personal contributions aren't important, an entire organization can grind to a halt. When a leader's perspective and the management team's perspective drastically differ, take note. The difference in perception between Schmitt and his staff at Rubbermaid was striking, and was characteristic of many executives' predicament. He was a leader without followers.

HABIT #4: THEY RUTHLESSLY ELIMINATE ANYONE WHO ISN'T COMPLETELY BEHIND THEM

CEOs who think their job is to instill belief in their vision also think that it is their job to get everyone to buy into it. Anyone who doesn't rally to the cause is undermining the vision. Hesitant managers have a choice: Get with the plan or leave.

The problem with this approach is that it's both unnecessary and destructive. CEOs don't need to have everyone unanimously endorse their vision to have it carried out successfully. In fact, by eliminating all dissenting and contrasting viewpoints, destructive CEOs cut themselves off from their best chance of seeing and correcting problems as they arise. Sometimes CEOs who seek to stifle dissent only drive it underground. Once this happens, the entire organization falters. At Mattel, Jill Barad removed her senior lieutenants if she thought they harbored serious reservations about the way that she was running things. Schmitt created such a threatening atmosphere at Rubbermaid that firings were often unnecessary. When new executives realized that they'd get no support from the CEO, many of them left almost as fast as they'd come on board. Eventually, these CEOs had everyone on their staff completely behind them. But where they were headed was toward disaster. And no one was left to warn them.

Warning Sign: Executive Departures

A revolving door at the top is one of the strongest signals that there has been executive failure at a company. Whether executives leave under "false pretenses," or are sent to some distant outpost where they'll have no further influence at headquarters, a pattern of executive departures speaks volumes for what is going on at a company. At Mattel, along with firing senior lieutenants on a moment's notice, Jill Barad drove six direct reports to resign for "personal reasons." The same thing has happened at Sun Microsystems over the last year. A mass exodus may be an indication that the CEO is out to eliminate any contrary opinions, or

Conversations with Myself: Seven Disastrous Thoughts of Unsuccessful Leaders

Habit #1: "Our products are superior, and so am I. We're untouchable. My company is successful because of my leadership and intellect—I made it happen."

Habit #2: "I am the sole proprietor. This company is my baby. Obviously, my wants and needs are in the best interest of my company and stockholders."

Habit #3: "I'm a genius. I believe in myself and you should too. Don't worry, I know all the answers. I'm not micro-managing; I'm being attentive. I don't need anyone else, certainly not a team."

Habit #4: "If you're not with me, you're against me! Get with the plan, or get out of the way. Where's your loyalty?"

Habit #5: "I'm the spokesperson. It's all about image. I'm a promotions and public relations genius. I love making public appearances; that's why I star in our commercials. It's my job to be socially visible; that's why I give frequent speeches and have regular media coverage."

Habit #6: "It's just a minor roadblock. Full steam ahead! Let's call that division a 'partner company' so we don't have to show it on our books."

Habit #7: "It has always worked this way in the past. We've done it before, and we can do it again."

---

it may reflect inside information senior executives are acting on. In either case, it's a powerful warning sign. Analysts and many investors regularly track insider sales of stock, but executive departures may provide an even clearer window on the company. After all, what stronger statement can an executive make than to leave his or her job and the company entirely?

HABIT #5: THEY ARE CONSUMMATE SPOKESPERSONS, OBSESSED WITH THE COMPANY IMAGE

You know these CEOs: high-profile executives who are constantly in the public eye. The problem is that amid all the media frenzy and accolades, these leaders' management efforts become shallow and ineffective. Instead of actually accomplishing things, they often settle for the appearance of accomplishing things.

Behind these media darlings is a simple fact of executive life: CEOs don't achieve a high level of media attention without devoting themselves assiduously to public relations. When CEOs are obsessed with their image, they have little time for operational details. Tyco's Dennis Kozlowski sometimes intervened in remarkably minor matters, but left most of the company's day-to-day operations unsupervised.

As a final negative twist, when CEOs make the company's image their top priority, they run the risk of using financial-reporting practices to promote that image. Instead of treating their financial accounts as a control tool, they treat them as a public relations tool. The creative accounting that was apparently practiced by such executives as Enron's Jeffrey Skilling or Tyco's Kozlowski is as much or more an attempt to promote the company's image as it is to deceive the public: In their eyes, everything that the company does is public relations.

Warning Sign: Blatant Attention-Seeking

The types of behavior exhibited by Napoleonic CEOs tend to be so blatant that they can't be missed. Warning signs begin with the executive lifestyle—they may start to run with a very cool crowd, buy expensive art, and hobnob with political dignitaries and celebrities. The CEO will seem to spend more time with PR personnel and making public appearances than doing something as mundane as visiting customers. Other times, a company will build a striking new headquarters, designed to serve as a corporate symbol. In more extreme cases, the CEO will try to acquire the naming rights for a new sports arena or stadium.

HABIT #6: THEY UNDERESTIMATE OBSTACLES

Part of the allure of being a CEO is the opportunity to espouse a vision. Yet, when CEOs become so enamored of their vision, they often overlook or underestimate the difficulty of actually getting there. And when it turns out that the obstacles they casually waved aside are more troublesome than they anticipated, these CEOs have a habit of plunging full-steam into the abyss. For example, when Webvan's core business was racking up huge losses, CEO George Shaheen was busy expanding those operations at an awesome rate.

Why don't CEOs in this situation reevaluate their course of action, or at least hold back for a while until it becomes clearer whether their policies will work? Some feel an enormous need to be right in every important decision they make, because if they admit to being fallible, their position as CEO might seem precarious. Once a CEO admits that he or she made the wrong call, there will always be people who say the CEO wasn't up to the job. These unrealistic expectations make it exceedingly hard for a CEO to pull back from any chosen course of action, which not surprisingly causes them to push that much harder. That's why leaders at Iridium and Motorola kept investing billions of dollars to launch satellites even after it had become apparent that land-based cell phones were a better alternative.

Warning Sign: Excessive Hype

One of the things we learned from the Internet bubble is the danger of hype, which can hide problems or mask intentions that, if known, would lead people to make different decisions. Simply stated: When something sounds too good to be true . . . it usually is. One of the best signs of a company relying on hype is the missed milestone. Whenever a company announces that its quarterly earnings are below forecast, the market reacts negatively to the news. Another important warning sign to look out for is when companies avoid looking at persuasive market data. When Barneys was planning its doomed geographic expansion, someone suggested that it do a market study to make sure that its offerings could work outside New York. CEO Bob Pressman thought the idea was ludicrous. "Market studies?" he exclaimed, incredulously. "Why do we have to do market studies? We're Barneys!"

HABIT #7: THEY STUBBORNLY RELY ON WHAT WORKED FOR THEM IN THE PAST

Many CEOs on their way to becoming spectacularly unsuccessful accelerate their company's decline by reverting to what they regard as tried-and-true methods. In their desire to make the most of what they regard as their core strengths, they cling to a static business model. They insist on providing a product to a market that no longer exists, or they fail to consider innovations in areas other than those that made the company successful in the past. Instead of considering a range of options that fit new circumstances, they use their own careers as the only point of reference and do the things that made them successful in the past. For example, when Jill Barad was trying to promote educational software at Mattel, she used the promotional techniques that had been effective for her when she was promoting Barbie dolls, despite the fact that software is not distributed or bought the way dolls are.

Frequently, CEOs who fall prey to this habit owe their careers to some "defining moment," a critical decision or policy choice that resulted in their most notable success. It's usually the one thing that they're most known for and the thing that gets them all of their subsequent jobs. The problem is that after people have had the experience of that defining moment, if they become the CEO of a large company, they allow their defining moment to define the company as well—no matter how unrealistic it has become.

Warning Sign: Constantly Referring to What Worked in the Past

When CEOs continually use the same model or repeatedly make the same decision, despite its inappropriateness, it can lead to significant failure. This type of thinking is often evident in the comments of senior executives who focus on similarities across situations while ignoring the sometimes more momentous differences. Take the case of Quaker Oats' acquisition of Snapple. Quaker paid $1.7 billion for Snapple, mistakenly assuming that the drink would be another smash hit like Gatorade. The beverage division president said things such as, "We have an excellent sales and marketing team here at Gatorade. We believe we do know how to build brands; we do know how to advance Snapple as well as Gatorade to the next level." Unfortunately, they didn't realize that Snapple was not a traditional mass-market beverage, but a "quirky, cult" drink. What's more, while Gatorade was distributed via a warehouse system, Snapple relied on family-run distributorships that had little interest in cooperating with Quaker. In 1997, Quaker sold Snapple for a paltry $300 million.

These seven habits of spectacularly unsuccessful people are powerful reminders of how organizational leaders are not only instruments of growth and success, but sometimes also architects of failure. That each of the habits has elements that are valuable for leaders only serves to point out how vigilant people who enter a leader's orbit must be, whether they are other executives, board members, lower-level managers and employees, regulators, or even suppliers, customers and competitors. In small doses, each of the habits can be part of a winning formula, but when executives overdose, the habits can quickly become toxic. That is a lesson all leaders and would-be leaders should take to heart.

Chapter 1

1. Costas Markides, "What Is Strategy and How Do You Know If You Have One?" *Business Strategy Review* 15, no. 2 (Summer 2004), pp. 5–6.
2. For a discussion of the different ways that companies can position themselves in the marketplace, see Michael E. Porter, "What Is Strategy?" *Harvard Business Review* 74, no. 6 (November–December 1996), pp. 65–67.
3. For an excellent treatment of the strategic challenges posed by rapid industry change, see Shona L. Brown and Kathleen M. Eisenhardt, *Competing on the Edge: Strategy as Structured Chaos* (Boston, MA: Harvard Business School Press, 1998), Chapter 1.
4. See Henry Mintzberg and Joseph Lampel, "Reflecting on the Strategy Process," *Sloan Management Review* 40, no. 3 (Spring 1999), pp. 21–30; Henry Mintzberg and J. A. Waters, "Of Strategies, Deliberate and Emergent," *Strategic Management Journal* 6 (1985), pp. 257–72; Costas Markides, "Strategy as Balance: From 'Either-Or' to 'And,'" *Business Strategy Review* 12, no. 3 (September 2001), pp. 1–10; Henry Mintzberg, Bruce Ahlstrand, and Joseph Lampel, *Strategy Safari: A Guided Tour through the Wilds of Strategic Management* (New York: Free Press, 1998), Chapters 2, 5, and 7; and C. K. Prahalad and Gary Hamel. "The Core Competence of the Corporation." *Harvard Business Review* 70, no. 3 (May–June 1990), pp. 79–93.
5. Joseph L. Badaracco, "The Discipline of Building Character," *Harvard Business Review* 76, no. 2 (March–April 1998), pp. 115–24.
6. Joan Magretta, "Why Business Models Matter," *Harvard Business Review* 80, no. 5 (May 2002), p. 87.

Chapter 2

1. For a more in-depth discussion of the challenges of developing a well-conceived vision, as well as some good examples, see Hugh Davidson, *The Committed Enterprise: How to Make Vision and Values Work* (Oxford: Butterworth-Heinemann, 2002), Chapter 2; W. Chan Kim and Renée Mauborgne, "Charting Your Company's Future," *Harvard Business Review* 80, no. 6 (June 2002), pp. 77–83; James C. Collins and Jerry I. Porras, "Building Your Company's Vision," *Harvard Business Review* 74, no. 5 (September–October 1996), pp. 65–77;

Jim Collins and Jerry Porras, *Built to Last: Successful Habits of Visionary Companies* (New York: HarperCollins, 1994), Chapter 11; and Michel Robert, *Strategy Pure and Simple II: How Winning Companies Dominate Their Competitors* (New York: McGraw-Hill, 1998), Chapters 2, 3 and 6.
2. Davidson, *The Committed Enterprise,* pp. 20, 54.
3. Jeffrey K. Liker, *The Toyota Way* (New York: McGraw-Hill, 2004); and Steve Hamm, "Taking a Page from Toyota's Playbook," *BusinessWe*ek, August 22–29, 2005, p. 72.
4. Davidson, *The Committed Enterprise,* pp. 36, 54.
5. As quoted in Charles H. House and Raymond L. Price, "The Return Map: Tracking Product Teams," *Harvard Business Review* 60, no. 1 (January–February 1991), p. 93.
6. Mark Gottfredson, Steve Schaubert, and Hernan Saenz, "The New Leader's Guide to Diagnosing the Business, *Harvard Business Review* 86, no. 2 (February 2008), p. 73.
7. Robert S. Kaplan and David P. Norton, *The Strategy-Focused Organization* (Boston: Harvard Business School Press, 2001), p. 3.
8. Ibid., p. 7. Also, see Robert S. Kaplan and David P. Norton, *The Balanced Scorecard: Translating Strategy into Action* (Boston: Harvard Business School Press, 1996), p. 10; Kevin B. Hendricks, Larry Menor, and Christine Wiedman, "The Balanced Scorecard: To Adopt or Not to Adopt," *Ivey Business Journal* 69, no. 2 (November–December 2004), pp. 1–7; and Sandy Richardson, "The Key Elements of Balanced Scorecard Success," *Ivey Business Journal* 69, no. 2 (November–December 2004), pp. 7–9.
9. Information posted on the Web site of Bain and Company, www.bain.com (accessed March 27, 2008).
10. Information posted on the Web site of Balanced Scorecard Institute, www.balancedscorecard. org (accessed March 27, 2008).
11. The concept of strategic intent is described in more detail in Gary Hamel and C. K. Prahalad, "Strategic Intent," *Harvard Business Review* 89, no. 3 (May–June 1989), pp. 63–76; this section draws on their pioneering discussion. See also Michael A. Hitt, Beverly B. Tyler, Camilla Hardee, and Daewoo Park, "Understanding Strategic Intent in the Global Marketplace," *Academy of Management Executive* 9, no. 2 (May 1995), pp. 12–19.
12. As reported in "We Called It: Toyota Tops GM in '07," *Automotive News,* January 28, 2008, p. 6.
13. As described in "Honda Is Expected to State Plans to Break into U.S. Jet Market," *The Wall Street Journal Online,* July 24, 2006.

14. For a fuller discussion of strategy as an entrepreneurial process, see Henry Mintzberg, Bruce Ahlstrand, and Joseph Lampel, *Strategy Safari: A Guided Tour through the Wilds of Strategic Management* (New York: Free Press, 1998), Chapter 5. Also, see Bruce Barringer and Allen C. Bluedorn, "The Relationship Between Corporate Entrepreneurship and Strategic Management," *Strategic Management Journal* 20 (1999), pp. 421–44; Jeffrey G. Covin and Morgan P. Miles, "Corporate Entrepreneurship and the Pursuit of Competitive Advantage," *Entrepreneurship: Theory and Practice* 23, no. 3 (Spring 1999), pp. 47–63; and David A. Garvin and Lynned C. Levesque, "Meeting the Challenge of Corporate Entrepreneurship," *Harvard Business Review* 84, no. 10 (October 2006), pp. 102–12.
15. For an excellent discussion of why a strategic plan needs to be more than a list of bullet points and should in fact tell an engaging, insightful, stage-setting story that lays out the industry and competitive situation as well as the vision, objectives, and strategy, see Gordon Shaw, Robert Brown, and Philip Bromiley, "Strategic Stories: How 3M Is Rewriting Business Planning," *Harvard Business Review* 76, no. 3 (May–June 1998), pp. 41–50. For a valuable discussion of the role of mission, values, vision, objectives, and strategy statements in providing organizational direction, see David J. Collins and Michael G. Rukstad, "Can You Say What Your Strategy Is?" *Harvard Business Review* 86, no. 4 (April 2008), pp. 82–90.
16. Fred Vogelstein, "Winning the Amazon Way," *Fortune,* May 26, 2003, p. 64.
17. As discussed in Garvin and Levesque, "Meeting the Challenge," pp. 110–12.
18. For a more in-depth discussion of the leader's role in creating a results-oriented culture that nurtures success, see Benjamin Schneider, Sarah K. Gunnarson, and Kathryn Niles-Jolly, "Creating the Climate and Culture of Success," *Organizational Dynamics* 23, no. 1 (Summer 1994), pp. 17–29.
19. For an excellent discussion of strategy as a dynamic process involving continuous, unending creation and recreation of strategy, see Cynthia A. Montgomery, "Putting Leadership Back into Strategy," *Harvard Business Review* 86, no. 1 (January 2008), pp. 54–60.
20. James Brian Quinn, *Strategies for Change: Logical Incrementalism* (Homewood, IL: Richard D. Irwin, 1980), pp. 20–22.
21. For discussions of what it takes for the corporate governance system to function properly, see David A. Nadler, "Building Better Boards," *Harvard Business Review* 82,

no. 5 (May 2004), pp. 102–5; Cynthia A. Montgomery and Rhonda Kaufman, "The Board's Missing Link," *Harvard Business Review* 81, no. 3 (March 2003), pp. 86–93; and John Carver, "What Continues to Be Wrong with Corporate Governance and How to Fix It," *Ivey Business Journal* 68, no. 1 (September/October 2003), pp. 1–5. See also Gordon Donaldson, "A New Tool for Boards: The Strategic Audit," *Harvard Business Review* 73, no. 4 (July–August 1995), pp. 99–107.

Chapter 3

1. There are a large number of studies of the size of the cost reductions associated with experience; the median cost reduction associated with a doubling of cumulative production volume is approximately 15 percent, but there is a wide variation from industry to industry. For a good discussion of the economies of experience and learning, see Pankaj Ghemawat, "Building Strategy on the Experience Curve," *Harvard Business Review* 64, no. 2 (March–April 1985), pp. 143–49.

2. The five-forces model of competition is the creation of Professor Michael E. Porter of the Harvard Business School. For his original presentation of the model, see Michael E. Porter, "How Competitive Forces Shape Strategy," *Harvard Business Review* 57, no. 2 (March–April 1979), pp. 137–45. A more thorough discussion can be found in Michael E. Porter, *Competitive Strategy: Techniques for Analyzing Industries and Competitors* (New York: Free Press, 1980), Chapter 1. Porter's five-forces model of competition is reaffirmed and extended in Michael E. Porter, "The Five Competitive Forces That Shape Strategy," *Harvard Business Review* 86, no. 1 (January 2008), pp. 78–93.

3. The tendency of firms to counter competitive moves of rival firms tends to cause escalating competitive pressures that affect the profitability of rivals; see Pamela J. Derfus, Patrick G. Maggitti, Curtis M. Grimm, and Ken G. Smith, "The Red Queen Effect: Competitive Actions and Firm Performance," *Academy of Management Journal* 51, no. 1, (February 2008), pp. 61–80.

4. Many of these indicators of whether rivalry produces intense competitive pressures are based on Porter, *Competitive Strategy,* pp. 17–21; and Porter, "The Five Competitive Forces That Shape Strategy," pp. 85–86.

5. The role of entry barriers in shaping the strength of competition in a particular market has long been a standard topic in the literature of microeconomics. For a discussion of how entry barriers affect competitive pressures associated with potential entry, see J. S. Bain, *Barriers to New Competition* (Cambridge, MA: Harvard University Press, 1956);

F. M. Scherer, *Industrial Market Structure and Economic Performance* (Chicago: Rand McNally & Co., 1971), pp. 216–20, 226–33; and Porter, *Competitive Strategy,* pp. 7–17; and Porter, "The Five Competitive Forces That Shape Strategy," pp. 80–82.

6. Michael E. Porter, "How Competitive Forces Shape Strategy," *Harvard Business Review* 57, no. 2 (March–April 1979), p. 140; Porter, *Competitive Strategy,* pp. 14–15; and Porter, "The Five Competitive Forces That Shape Strategy," p. 82.

7. For a good discussion of this point, see George S. Yip, "Gateways to Entry," *Harvard Business Review* 60, no. 5 (September–October 1982), pp. 85–93.

8. Porter, "How Competitive Forces Shape Strategy," p. 142; Porter, *Competitive Strategy,* pp. 23–24; and Porter, "The Five Competitive Forces That Shape Strategy," pp. 82–83.

9. Porter, *Competitive Strategy,* p. 10; and Porter, "The Five Competitive Forces That Shape Strategy," p. 85.

10. Porter, *Competitive Strategy,* pp. 27–28; and Porter, "The Five Competitive Forces That Shape Strategy," pp. 82–83.

11. Porter, *Competitive Strategy,* pp. 24–27; and Porter, "The Five Competitive Forces That Shape Strategy," pp. 83–84.

12. For a more extended discussion of the problems with the life-cycle hypothesis, see Porter, *Competitive Strategy,* pp. 157–62.

13. Ibid., p. 162.

14. Most of the candidate driving forces described here are based on the discussion in ibid., pp. 164–83.

15. Ibid., Chapter 7.

16. Ibid., pp.129–30.

17. For an excellent discussion of how to identify the factors that define strategic groups, see Mary Ellen Gordon and George R. Milne, "Selecting the Dimensions that Define Strategic Groups: A Novel Market-Driven Approach," *Journal of Managerial Issues* 11, no. 2 (Summer 1999), pp. 213–33.

18. Porter, *Competitive Strategy,* pp. 152–54.

19. Strategic groups act as good reference points for predicting the evolution of an industry's competitive structure. See Avi Fiegenbaum and Howard Thomas, "Strategic Groups as Reference Groups: Theory, Modeling and Empirical Examination of Industry and Competitive Strategy," *Strategic Management Journal* 16 (1995), pp. 461–76. For a study of how strategic group analysis helps identify the variables that lead to sustainable competitive advantage, see S. Ade Olusoga, Michael P. Mokwa, and Charles H. Noble, "Strategic Groups, Mobility Barriers, and Competitive Advantage," *Journal of Business Research* 33 (1995), pp. 153–64.

20. Porter, *Competitive Strategy,* pp.130, 132–38, and 154–55.

21. For a discussion of legal and ethical ways of gathering competitive intelligence on rival companies, see Larry Kahaner, *Competitive*

Intelligence (New York: Simon & Schuster, 1996).

22. Ibid., pp. 84–85.

23. Some experts dispute the strategy-making value of key success factors. Professor Pankaj Ghemawat has claimed that the "whole idea of identifying a success factor and then chasing it seems to have something in common with the ill-considered medieval hunt for the *philosopher's stone,* a substance which would transmute everything it touched into gold." Pankaj Ghemawat, *Commitment: The Dynamic of Strategy* (New York: Free Press, 1991), p. 11.

Chapter 4

1. Many business organizations are coming to view cutting-edge knowledge and intellectual resources of company personnel as a valuable competitive asset and have concluded that explicitly managing these assets is an essential part of their strategy. See Michael H. Zack, "Developing a Knowledge Strategy," *California Management Review* 41, no. 3 (Spring 1999), pp. 125–45; and Shaker A. Zahra, Anders P. Nielsen, and William C. Bogner, "Corporate Entrepreneurship, Knowledge, and Competence Development," *Entrepreneurship Theory and Practice,* Spring 1999, pp. 169–89.

2. In the past decade, there's been considerable research into the role a company's resources and competitive capabilities play in crafting strategy and in determining company profitability. The findings and conclusions have coalesced into what is called the resource-based view of the firm. Among the most insightful publications on the topic are Birger Wernerfelt, "A Resource-Based View of the Firm," *Strategic Management Journal,* September–October 1984, pp. 171–80; Jay Barney, "Firm Resources and Sustained Competitive Advantage," *Journal of Management* 17, no. 1 (1991), pp. 99–120; Margaret A. Peteraf, "The Cornerstones of Competitive Advantage: A Resource-Based View," *Strategic Management Journal,* March 1993, pp. 179–91; Birger Wernerfelt, "The Resource-Based View of the Firm: Ten Years After," *Strategic Management Journal* 16 (1995), pp. 171–74; Jay B. Barney, "Looking Inside for Competitive Advantage," *Academy of Management Executive* 9, no. 4 (November 1995), pp. 49–61; Christopher A. Bartlett and Sumantra Ghoshal, "Building Competitive Advantage through People," *MIT Sloan Management Review* 43, no 2 (Winter 2002), pp. 34–41; Danny Miller, Russell Eisenstat, and Nathaniel Foote, "Strategy from the Inside Out: Building Capability-Creating Organizations," *California Management Review* 44, no. 3 (Spring 2002), pp. 37–54; and Jay B. Barney and Delwyn N. Clark, *Resource-Based Theory: Creating*

and Sustaining Competitive Advantage (New York: Oxford University Press, 2007).

3. George Stalk Jr. and Rob Lachenauer, "Hardball: Five Killer Strategies for Trouncing the Competition," *Harvard Business Review* 82, no. 4 (April 2004), p. 65.

4. For a more extensive discussion of how to identify and evaluate the competitive power of a company's capabilities, see David W. Birchall and George Tovstiga, "The Strategic Potential of a Firm's Knowledge Portfolio," *Journal of General Management* 25, no. 1 (Autumn 1999), pp. 1–16; and Nick Bontis, Nicola C. Dragonetti, Kristine Jacobsen, and Goran Roos, "The Knowledge Toolbox: A Review of the Tools Available to Measure and Manage Intangible Resources," *European Management Journal* 17, no. 4 (August 1999), pp. 391–401. Also see David Teece, "Capturing Value from Knowledge Assets: The New Economy, Markets for Know-How, and Intangible Assets," *California Management Review* 40, no. 3 (Spring 1998), pp. 55–79.

5. See Barney, "Firm Resources and Sustained Competitive Advantage," *Journal of Management* 17, no. 1 (1991), pp. 105–9; and Jay B. Barney and Delwyn N. Clark, *Resource-Based Theory: Creating and Sustaining Competitive Advantage* (New York: Oxford University Press, 2007). Also, see M. A. Peteraf, "The Cornerstones of Competitive Advantage: A Resource-Based View," *Strategic Management Journal* 14, (1993), pp. 179–91; and David J. Collis and Cynthia A. Montgomery, "Competing on Resources: Strategy in the 1990s," *Harvard Business Review* 73, no. 4 (July–August 1995), pp. 120–23.

6. For a more detailed discussion, see George Stalk, Philip Evans, and Lawrence E. Schulman, "Competing on Capabilities: The New Rules of Corporate Strategy," *Harvard Business Review* 70, no. 2 (March–April 1992), pp. 57–69.

7. Donald Sull, "Strategy as Active Waiting," *Harvard Business Review* 83, no. 9 (September 2005), pp. 121–22.

8. Ibid., p. 122.

9. Ibid., pp. 124–26.

10. See Jack W. Duncan, Peter Ginter, and Linda E. Swayne, "Competitive Advantage and Internal Organizational Assessment," *Academy of Management Executive* 12, no. 3 (August 1998), pp. 6–16.

11. The value chain concept was developed and articulated by professor Michael E. Porter at the Harvard Business School and is described at greater length in Michael E. Porter, *Competitive Advantage* (New York: Free Press, 1985), Chapters 2 and 3.

12. Porter, *Competitive Advantage,* p. 36.

13. Ibid., p. 34.

14. The strategic importance of effective supply chain management is discussed in Hau L. Lee, "The Triple-A Supply Chain," *Harvard*

Business Review 82, no. 10 (October 2004), pp. 102–12.

15. M. Hegert and D. Morris, "Accounting Data for Value Chain Analysis," *Strategic Management Journal* 10 (1989), p. 180; Robin Cooper and Robert S. Kaplan, "Measure Costs Right: Make the Right Decisions," *Harvard Business Review* 66, no. 5 (September–October, 1988), pp. 96–103; and John K. Shank and Vijay Govindarajan, *Strategic Cost Management* (New York: Free Press, 1993), especially Chapters 2–6, 10.

16. For more on how and why the clustering of suppliers and other support organizations matter to a company's costs and competitiveness, see Michael E. Porter, "Clusters and the New Economics of Competition," *Harvard Business Review* 76, no. 6 (November–December 1998), pp. 77–90.

17. For discussions of the accounting challenges in calculating the costs of value chain activities, see John K. Shank and Vijay Govindarajan, *Strategic Cost Management* (New York: Free Press, 1993), especially Chapters 2–6, 10, and 11; Robin Cooper and Robert S. Kaplan, "Measure Costs Right: Make the Right Decisions," *Harvard Business Review* 66, no. 5 (September–October, 1988), pp. 96–103; and Joseph A. Ness and Thomas G. Cucuzza, "Tapping the Full Potential of ABC," *Harvard Business Review* 73, no. 4 (July–August 1995), pp. 130–38.

18. For more details, see Gregory H. Watson, *Strategic Benchmarking: How to Rate Your Company's Performance Against the World's Best* (New York: John Wiley, 1993); and Robert C. Camp, *Benchmarking: The Search for Industry Best Practices That Lead to Superior Performance* (Milwaukee: ASQC Quality Press, 1989); Christopher E. Bogan and Michael J. English, *Benchmarking for Best Practices: Winning through Innovative Adaptation* (New York: McGraw-Hill, 1994); and Dawn Iacobucci and Christie Nordhielm, "Creative Benchmarking," *Harvard Business Review* 78, no. 6 (November–December 2000), pp. 24–25.

19. Jeremy Main, "How to Steal the Best Ideas Around," *Fortune*, October 19, 1992, pp. 102–3.

20. Shank and Govindarajan, *Strategic Cost Management,* p. 50.

21. Some of these options are discussed in more detail in Porter, *Competitive Advantage,* Chapter 3.

22. An example of how Whirlpool Corporation transformed its supply chain from a competitive liability to a competitive asset is discussed in Reuben E. Stone, "Leading a Supply Chain Turnaround," *Harvard Business Review* 82, no. 10 (October 2004), pp. 114–21.

23. James Brian Quinn, *Intelligent Enterprise* (New York: Free Press, 1993), p. 54.

24. Ibid., p. 34.

Chapter 5

1. This classification scheme is an adaptation of a narrower three-strategy classification presented in Michael E. Porter, *Competitive Strategy: Techniques for Analyzing Industries and Competitors* (New York: Free Press, 1980), Chapter 2, especially pp. 35–40 and 44–46. For a discussion of the different ways that companies can position themselves in the marketplace, see Michael E. Porter, "What Is Strategy?" *Harvard Business Review* 74, no. 6 (November–December 1996), pp. 65–67.

2. Michael E. Porter, *Competitive Advantage* (New York: Free Press, 1985), p. 97.

3. For a discussion of how unique industry positioning and resource combinations are linked to consumer perspectives of value and their willingness to pay more for differentiated products or services, see Richard L. Priem, "A Consumer Perspective on Value Creation," *Academy of Management Review* 32, no. 1 (2007), pp. 219–35.

4. Ibid., pp. 135–38.

5. For a more detailed discussion, see George Stalk, Philip Evans, and Lawrence E. Schulman, "Competing on Capabilities: The New Rules of Corporate Strategy," *Harvard Business Review* 70, no. 2 (March–April 1992), pp. 57–69.

6. The relevance of perceived value and signaling is discussed in more detail in Porter, *Competitive Advantage,* pp. 138–42.

7. Ibid., pp. 160–62.

Chapter 6

1. Yves L. Doz and Gary Hamel, *Alliance Advantage: The Art of Creating Value through Partnering* (Boston: Harvard Business School Press, 1998), pp. xiii, xiv.

2. Jason Wakeam, "The Five Factors of a Strategic Alliance," *Ivey Business Journal* 68, no. 3 (May–June 2003), pp. 1–4.

3. Jeffrey H. Dyer, Prashant Kale, and Harbir Singh, "When to Ally and When to Acquire," *Harvard Business Review* 82, no. 7/8 (July–August 2004), p. 109.

4. Salvatore Parise and Lisa Sasson, "Leveraging Knowledge Management across Strategic Alliances," *Ivey Business Journal* 66, no. 4 (March–April 2002), p. 42.

5. David Ernst and James Bamford, "Your Alliances Are Too Stable," *Harvard Business Review* 83, no. 6 (June 2005), p.133.

6. An excellent discussion of the portfolio approach to managing multiple alliances and how to restructure a faltering alliance is presented in ibid., pp. 133–41.

7. Michael E. Porter, *The Competitive Advantage of Nations* (New York: Free Press, 1990), p. 66. For a discussion of how to realize the advantages of strategic partnerships, see Nancy J. Kaplan and Jonathan Hurd,

"Realizing the Promise of Partnerships," *Journal of Business Strategy* 23, no. 3 (May–June 2002), pp. 38–42; Parise and Sasson, "Leveraging Knowledge Management," pp. 41–47; and Ernst and Bamford, "Your Alliances Are Too Stable," pp. 133–41.

8. For a discussion of how to raise the chances that a strategic alliance will produce strategically important outcomes, see M. Koza and A. Lewin, "Managing Partnerships and Strategic Alliances: Raising the Odds of Success," *European Management Journal* 18, no. 2 (April 2000), pp. 146–51.

9. A. Inkpen, "Learning, Knowledge Acquisition, and Strategic Alliances," *European Management Journal* 16, no. 2 (April 1998), pp. 223–29.

10. Doz and Hamel, *Alliance Advantage,* Chapters 4–8; Patricia Anslinger and Justin Jenk, "Creating Successful Alliances," *Journal of Business Strategy* 25, no. 2 (2004), pp. 18–23; Rosabeth Moss Kanter, "Collaborative Advantage: The Art of the Alliance," *Harvard Business Review* 72, no. 4 (July–August 1994), pp. 96–108; Joel Bleeke and David Ernst, "The Way to Win in Cross-Border Alliances," *Harvard Business Review* 69, no. 6 (November–December 1991), pp. 127–35; Gary Hamel, Yves L. Doz, and C. K. Prahalad, "Collaborate with Your Competitors—and Win," *Harvard Business Review* 67, no. 1 (January–February 1989), pp. 133–39; and Jonathan Hughes and Jeff Weiss, "Simple Rules for Making Alliances Work," *Harvard Business Review* 85, no. 11 (November 2007), pp. 122–31.

11. Hughes and Weiss, "Simple Rules for Making Alliances Work," p. 122.

12. Doz and Hamel, *Alliance Advantage,* pp. 16–18.

13. Denis K. Berman, "Merger Frenzy Winds Down after 6 years," *The Wall Street Journal,* October 1, 2007, p. C5.

14. For an excellent discussion of the pros and cons of alliances versus acquisitions, see Dyer, Kale, and Singh, "When to Ally and When to Acquire," pp. 109–15.

15. For an excellent review of the strategic objectives of various types of mergers and acquisitions and the managerial challenges that different kinds of mergers and acquisition present, see Joseph L. Bower, "Not All M&As Are Alike—and That Matters," *Harvard Business Review* 79, no. 3 (March 2001), pp. 93–101.

16. For a more expansive discussion, see Dyer, Kale, and Singh, "When to Ally and When to Acquire," pp. 109–10.

17. See Kathryn R. Harrigan, "Matching Vertical Integration Strategies to Competitive Conditions," *Strategic Management Journal* 7, no. 6 (November–December 1986), pp. 535–56; for a more extensive discussion of the advantages and disadvantages of vertical integration, see John Stuckey and David White, "When and When Not to Vertically Integrate," *Sloan Management Review* (Spring 1993), pp. 71–83.

18. The resilience of vertical integration strategies despite the disadvantages is discussed in Thomas Osegowitsch and Anoop Madhok, "Vertical Integration Is Dead or Is It?" *Business Horizons* 46, no. 2 (March–April 2003), pp. 25–35.

19. This point is explored in greater detail in James Brian Quinn, "Strategic Outsourcing: Leveraging Knowledge Capabilities," *Sloan Management Review* 40, no. 4 (Summer 1999), pp. 9–21.

20. For a good discussion of the problems that can arise from outsourcing, see Jérôme Barthélemy, "The Seven Deadly Sins of Outsourcing," *Academy of Management Executive* 17, no. 2 (May 2003), pp. 87–100.

21. Michael E. Porter, *Competitive Strategy* (New York: Free Press, 1980), pp. 216–23.

22. Phillip Kotler, *Marketing Management,* 5th ed. (Englewood Cliffs, NJ: Prentice Hall, 1984), p. 366; and Porter, *Competitive Strategy,* Chapter 10.

23. Several of these were pinpointed and discussed in Charles W. Hofer and Dan Schendel, *Strategy Formulation: Analytical Concepts* (St. Paul, MN: West Publishing, 1978), pp. 164–65.

24. Ibid., pp. 164–65.

25. Porter, *Competitive Strategy,* pp. 238–40.

26. The following discussion draws on ibid., pp. 241–46.

27. An in-depth analysis of 500 companies experiencing slowing growth since 1955 indicates that about 13 percent of revenue stalls result from external factors. For a discussion of strategic factors affecting slowing revenue growth, see Matthew S. Olson, Derek van Bever, and Seth Verry, "When Growth Stalls," *Harvard Business Review* 86, no. 3 (March 2008), pp. 50–61.

28. Kathryn R. Harrigan and Michael E. Porter, "End-Game Strategies for Declining Industries" *Harvard Business Review* 61, no. 4 (July–August 1983), pp. 112–13.

29. R. G. Hamermesh and S. B. Silk, "How to Compete in Stagnant Industries," *Harvard Business Review* 57, no. 5 (September–October 1979), p. 161; and Kathryn R. Harrigan, *Strategies for Declining Businesses* (Lexington, MA: D. C. Heath, 1980).

30. Hamermesh and Silk, "How to Compete in Stagnant Industries," p. 162; Harrigan and Porter, "End-Game Strategies for Declining Industries," p. 118.

31. Hamermesh and Silk, "How to Compete in Stagnant Industries," p. 165.

32. Harrigan and Porter, "End Game Strategies for Declining Industries," pp. 111–21; Harrigan, *Strategies for Declining Businesses;* and Phillip Kotler, "Harvesting Strategies for Weak Products," *Business Horizons* 21, no. 5 (August 1978), pp. 17–18.

33. The strategic issues companies must address in fast-changing market environments are thoroughly explored in Gary Hamel and Liisa Välikangas, "The Quest for Resilence," *Harvard Business Review* 81,

no. 9 (September 2003), pp. 52–63; Shona L. Brown and Kathleen M. Eisenhardt, *Competing on the Edge: Strategy as Structured Chaos* (Boston: Harvard Business School Press, 1998); and Richard A. D'Aveni, *Hyper-Competition: Managing the Dynamics of Strategic Maneuvering* (New York: Free Press, 1994). See also Richard A. D'Aveni, "Coping with Hypercompetition: Utilizing the New 7S's Framework," *Academy of Management Executive* 9, no. 3 (August 1995), pp. 45–56; and Bala Chakravarthy, "A New Strategy Framework for Coping with Turbulence," *Sloan Management Review* (Winter 1997), pp. 69–82.

34. Brown and Eisenhardt, *Competing on the Edge,* pp. 4–5.

35. Ibid., p. 4.

36. For deeper insight into building competitive advantage through R&D and technological innovation, see Shaker A. Zahra, Sarah Nash, and Deborah J. Bickford, "Transforming Technological Pioneering into Competitive Advantage," *Academy of Management Executive* 9, no. 1 (February 1995), pp. 32–41.

37. Brown and Eisenhardt, *Competing on the Edge,* pp. 14–15. See also Kathleen M. Eisenhardt and Shona L. Brown, "Time Pacing: Competing in Markets That Won't Stand Still," *Harvard Business Review* 76, no. 2 (March–April 1998), pp. 59–69.

38. The circumstances of competing in a fragmented marketplace are discussed at length in Porter, *Competitive Strategy,* Chapter 9; this section draws on Porter's treatment.

39. Porter, *Competitive Advantage,* pp. 232–33.

40. For research evidence on the effects of pioneering versus following, see Jeffrey G. Covin, Dennis P. Slevin, and Michael B. Heeley, "Pioneers and Followers: Competitive Tactics, Environment, and Growth," *Journal of Business Venturing* 15, no. 2 (March 1999), pp. 175–210; Christopher A. Bartlett and Sumantra Ghoshal, "Going Global: Lessons from Late-Movers," *Harvard Business Review* 78, no. 2 (March–April 2000), pp. 132–45; and Fernando Suarez and Guianvito Lanzolla, "The Role of Environmental Dynamics in Building a First Mover Advantage Theory," *Academy of Management Review* 32, no. 2 (April 2007), pp. 377–92.

41. For a more extensive discussion of this point, see Fernando Suarez and Gianvito Lanzolla, "The Half-Truth of First-Mover Advantage," *Harvard Business Review* 83, no. 4 (April 2005), pp. 121–27.

42. Gary Hamel, "Smart Mover, Dumb Mover," *Fortune,* September 3, 2001, p. 195.

43. W. Chan Kim and Renée Mauborgne, "Blue Ocean Strategy," *Harvard Business Review* 82, no. 10 (October 2004), pp. 76–84.

44. Porter, *Competitive Advantage,* pp.232–33.

45. Costas Markides and Paul A. Geroski," Racing to be 2nd: Conquering the Industries of the Future," *Business Strategy Review* 15, no. 4 (Winter 2004), pp. 25–31.

Chapter 7

1. For an insightful discussion of how much significance these kinds of demographic and market differences have, see C. K. Prahalad and Kenneth Lieberthal, "The End of Corporate Imperialism," *Harvard Business Review* 76, no. 4 (July–August 1998), pp. 68–79.

2. Joseph Caron, "The Business of Doing Business with China: An Ambassador Reflects," *Ivey Business Journal* 69, no. 5 (May–June 2005), p. 2.

3. U.S. Department of Labor, "International Comparisons of Hourly Compensation Costs in Manufacturing, 2006," *Bureau of Labor Statistics Newsletter,* January 25, 2008.

4. Michael E. Porter, *The Competitive Advantage of Nations* (New York: Free Press, 1990), pp. 53–54.

5. Ibid., p. 61.

6. For two especially insightful studies of company experiences with cross-border alliances, see Joel Bleeke and David Ernst, "The Way to Win in Cross-Border Alliances," *Harvard Business Review* 69, no. 6 (November–December 1991), pp. 127–35; and Gary Hamel, Yves L. Doz, and C. K. Prahalad, "Collaborate with Your Competitors—and Win," *Harvard Business Review* 67, no. 1 (January–February 1989), pp. 133–39.

7. Jan Borgonjon and David J. Hoffmann, "The Re-emergence of the Joint Venture?" *China Business Review,* May–June 2008, p. 34.

8. See Yves L. Doz and Gary Hamel, *Alliance Advantage: The Art of Creating Value through Partnering* (Boston: Harvard Business School Press, 1998), especially Chapters 2–4; Bleeke and Ernst, "The Way to Win in Cross-Border Alliances," pp. 127–33; Hamel, Doz, and Prahalad, "Collaborate with Your Competitors," pp. 134–35; and Porter, *Competitive Advantage of Nations,* p. 66;

9. H. Kurt Christensen, "Corporate Strategy: Managing a Set of Businesses," in *The Portable MBA in Strategy,* ed. Liam Fahey and Robert M. Randall (New York: Wiley, 2001), p. 43.

10. For an excellent presentation on the pros and cons of alliances versus acquisitions, see Jeffrey H. Dyer, Prashant Kale, and Harbir Singh, "When to Ally and When to Acquire," *Harvard Business Review* 82, no. 7/8 (July–August 2004), pp. 109–15.

11. For additional discussion of company experiences with alliances and partnerships, see Doz and Hamel, *Alliance Advantage,* Chapters 2–7; and Rosabeth Moss Kanter, "Collaborative Advantage: The Art of the Alliance," *Harvard Business Review* 72, no. 4 (July–August 1994), pp. 96–108.

12. Details are reported in Shawn Tully, "The Alliance from Hell," *Fortune,* June 24, 1996, pp. 64–72.

13. Jeremy Main, "Making Global Alliances Work," *Fortune,* December 19, 1990, p. 125.

14. Pralahad and Lieberthal, "The End of Corporate Imperialism," p. 77.

15. Ibid.

16. For more details on the merits of and opportunities for cross-border transfer of successful strategy experiments, see C. A. Bartlett and S. Ghoshal, *Managing Across Borders: The Transnational Solution,* 2nd ed. (Boston: Harvard Business School Press, 1998), pp. 79–80 and Chapter 9.

17. Approaches to improving a company's local relevance through adaptation of products and services to match local preferences are discussed in Pankaj Ghemawat, "Managing Differences: The Central Challenge of Global Strategy," *Harvard Business Review* 85, no. 3 (March 2007), pp. 58–68.

18. The benefits of static and dynamic arbitrage that may accompany global strategies are discussed in ibid.

19. The ability for global companies to achieve economies of scale and/or scope through aggregation is discussed in ibid., p. 65.

20. Porter, *Competitive Advantage of Nations,* pp. 53–55.

21. Arbitrage strategies that exploit cultural, governmental policy, geographic, and economic differences between countries are discussed in Pankaj Ghemawat, "The Forgotten Strategy," *Harvard Business Review* 81, no. 11 (November 2003), pp. 76–84.

22. Porter, *Competitive Advantage of Nations,* pp. 55–58.

23. C. K. Prahalad and Yves L. Doz, *The Multinational Mission* (New York: Free Press, 1987), pp. 58–60; and Ghemawat, "Managing Differences," pp. 58–68.

24. This point is discussed at greater length in Prahalad and Lieberthal, "The End of Corporate Imperialism," pp. 68–79; also see David J. Arnold and John A. Quelch, "New Strategies in Emerging Markets," *Sloan Management Review* 40, no. 1 (Fall 1998), pp. 7–20. For a more extensive discussion of strategy in emerging markets, see C. K. Prahalad, *The Fortune at the Bottom of the Pyramid: Eradicating Poverty through Profits* (Upper Saddle River, NJ: Wharton, 2005), especially Chapters 1–3.

25. Brenda Cherry, "What China Eats (and Drinks and . . .)," *Fortune,* October 4, 2004, pp. 152–53; "A Ravenous Dragon," *Economist* 386, no. 8571 (March 15, 2008), online edition; and "China: Just the Facts," *Journal of Commerce,* June 2, 2008, p. 24.

26. Prahalad and Lieberthal, "The End of Corporate Imperialism," pp. 72–73.

27. Tarun Khanna, Krishna G. Palepu, and Jayant Sinha, "Strategies That Fit Emerging Markets," *Harvard Business Review* 83, no. 6 (June 2005), p. 63; and Arindam K. Bhattacharya and David C. Michael, "How Local Companies Keep Multinationals at Bay," *Harvard Business Review* 86, no. 3 (March 2008), pp. 94–95.

28. Prahalad and Lieberthal, "The End of Corporate Imperialism," p. 72.

29. Khanna, Palepu, and Sinha, "Strategies That Fit Emerging Markets," pp. 73–74.

30. Ibid., p. 74.

31. Ibid., p. 76.

32. The results and conclusions from a study of 134 local companies in 10 emerging markets are presented in Tarun Khanna and Krishna G. Palepu, "Emerging Giants: Building World-Class Companies in Developing Countries," *Harvard Business Review* 84, no. 10 (October 2006), pp. 60–69; also, an examination of strategies used by 50 local companies in emerging markets is discussed in Bhattacharya and Michael, "How Local Companies Keep Multinationals at Bay," pp. 85–95.

33. Steve Hamm, "Tech's Future," *BusinessWeek,* September 27, 2004, p. 88.

34. Niroj Dawar and Tony Frost, "Competing with Giants: Survival Strategies for Local Companies in Emerging Markets," *Harvard Business Review* 77, no. 1 (January–February 1999), p. 122; see also Guitz Ger, "Localizing in the Global Village: Local Firms Competing in Global Markets," *California Management Review* 41, no. 4 (Summer 1999), pp. 64–84; and Khanna and Palepu, "Emerging Giants," pp. 63–66.

35. Dawar and Frost, "Competing with Giants," p. 124.

36. Ibid., p. 126; and Khanna and Palepu, "Emerging Giants," pp. 60–69.

Chapter 8

1. For a further discussion of when diversification makes good strategic sense, see Constantinos C. Markides, "To Diversify or Not to Diversify," *Harvard Business Review* 75, no. 6 (November–December 1997), pp. 93–99. For a discussion of how hidden opportunities within a corporation's existing asset base may offer growth to corporations with declining core businesses, see Chris Zook, "Finding Your Next Core Business," *Harvard Business Review* 85, no. 4 (April 2007), pp. 66–75.

2. Michael E. Porter, "From Competitive Advantage to Corporate Strategy," *Harvard Business Review* 45, no. 3 (May–June 1987), pp. 46–49.

3. Michael E. Porter, *Competitive Strategy: Techniques for Analyzing Industries and Competitors* (New York: Free Press, 1980), pp. 354–55.

4. Ibid., pp. 344–45.

5. Yves L. Doz and Gary Hamel, *Alliance Advantage: The Art of Creating Value through Partnering* (Boston: Harvard Business School Press, 1998), Chapters 1 and 2.

6. Michael E. Porter, *Competitive Advantage* (New York: Free Press, 1985), pp. 318–19 and pp. 337–53; and Porter, "From Competitive Advantage to Corporate

Strategy," pp. 53–57. For an empirical study confirming that strategic fits are capable of enhancing performance (provided the resulting resource strengths are competitively valuable and difficult to duplicate by rivals), see Constantinos C. Markides and Peter J. Williamson, "Corporate Diversification and Organization Structure: A Resource-Based View," *Academy of Management Journal* 39, no. 2 (April 1996), pp. 340–67.

7. For a discussion of the strategic significance of cross-business coordination of value chain activities and insight into how the process works, see Jeanne M. Liedtka, "Collaboration across Lines of Business for Competitive Advantage," *Academy of Management Executive* 10, no. 2 (May 1996), pp. 20–34.

8. "Beyond Knowledge Management: How Companies Mobilize Experience," *Financial Times,* February 8, 1999, p. 5.

9. For a discussion of what is involved in actually capturing strategic fit benefits, see Kathleen M. Eisenhardt and D. Charles Galunic, "Coevolving: At Last, a Way to Make Synergies Work," *Harvard Business Review* 78, no. 1 (January–February 2000), pp. 91–101. Adeptness at capturing cross-business strategic fits positively impacts performance; see Constantinos C. Markides and Peter J. Williamson, "Related Diversification, Core Competences and Corporate Performance," *Strategic Management Journal* 15 (Summer 1994), pp. 149–65.

10. Peter Drucker, *Management: Tasks, Responsibilities, Practices* (New York: Harper & Row, 1974), pp. 692–93.

11. While arguments that unrelated diversification are a superior way to diversify financial risk have logical appeal, there is research showing that related diversification is less risky from a financial perspective than is unrelated diversification; see Michael Lubatkin and Sayan Chatterjee, "Extending Modern Portfolio Theory into the Domain of Corporate Diversification: Does It Apply?" *Academy of Management Journal* 37, no. 1 (February 1994), pp. 109–36.

12. For a review of the experiences of companies that have pursued unrelated diversification successfully, see Patricia L. Anslinger and Thomas E. Copeland, "Growth through Acquisitions: A Fresh Look," *Harvard Business Review* 74, no. 1 (January–February 1996), pp. 126–35.

13. Of course, management may be willing to assume the risk that trouble will not strike before it has had time to learn the business well enough to bail it out of almost any difficulty. But there is research that shows this is very risky from a financial perspective; see, for example, Lubatkin and Chatterjee, "Extending Modern Portfolio Theory," pp. 132–33.

14. For research evidence of the failure of broad diversification and trend of companies to focus their diversification efforts more narrowly, see Lawrence G. Franko, "The Death of Diversification? The Focusing of the World's

Industrial Firms, 1980–2000," *Business Horizons* 47, no. 4 (July–August 2004), pp. 41–50.

15. For an excellent discussion of what to look for in assessing these fits, see Andrew Campbell, Michael Gould, and Marcus Alexander, "Corporate Strategy: The Quest for Parenting Advantage," *Harvard Business Review* 73, no. 2 (March–April 1995), pp. 120–32.

16. Ibid., p. 123.

17. A good discussion of the importance of having adequate resources, and also the importance of upgrading corporate resources and capabilities, can be found in David J. Collis and Cynthia A. Montgomery, "Competing on Resources: Strategy in the 90s," *Harvard Business Review* 73, no. 4 (July–August 1995), pp. 118–28.

18. Ibid., pp. 121–22.

19. Drucker, *Management,* p. 709.

20. See, for, example, Constantinos C. Markides, "Diversification, Restructuring, and Economic Performance," *Strategic Management Journal* 16 (February 1995), pp. 101–18.

21. For a discussion of why divestiture needs to be a standard part of any company's diversification strategy, see Lee Dranikoff, Tim Koller, and Antoon Schneider, "Divestiture: Strategy's Missing Link," *Harvard Business Review* 80, no. 5 (May 2002), pp. 74–83.

22. Drucker, *Management,* p. 94.

23. See David J. Collis and Cynthia A. Montgomery, "Creating Corporate Advantage," *Harvard Business Review* 76, no. 3 (May–June 1998), pp. 72–80.

24. Drucker, *Management,* p. 719.

25. Evidence that restructuring strategies tend to result in higher levels of performance is contained in Markides, "Diversification, Restructuring and Economic Performance," pp. 101–18.

26. Company press release, October 6, 2005.

27. Dranikoff, Koller, and Schneider, "Divestiture," p.76.

28. C. K. Prahalad and Yves L. Doz, *The Multinational Mission* (New York: Free Press, 1987), p. 2.

29. Ibid., p. 15.

30. Ibid., pp. 62–63.

Chapter 9

1. James E. Post, Anne T. Lawrence, and James Weber, *Business and Society: Corporate Strategy, Public Policy, Ethics,* 10th ed. (Burr Ridge, IL: McGraw-Hill/Irwin, 2002), p.103.

2. For an overview of widely endorsed guidelines for creating codes of conduct, see Lynn Paine, Rohit Deshpandé, Joshua D. Margolis, and Kim Eric Bettcher, "Up to Code: Does Your Company's Conduct Meet World-Class Standards?" *Harvard Business Review* 83, no. 12 (December 2005), pp. 122–33.

3. For research on what the universal moral values are (six are identified—trustworthiness,

respect, responsibility, fairness, caring, and citizenship), see Mark S. Schwartz, "Universal Moral Values for Corporate Codes of Ethics," *Journal of Business Ethics* 59, no. 1 (June 2005), pp. 27–44.

4. See, for instance, Mark. S. Schwartz, "A Code of Ethics for Corporate Codes of Ethics," *Journal of Business Ethics* 41, nos.1–2 (November–December 2002), pp. 27–43.

5. For more discussion of this point, see ibid. pp. 29–30.

6 . T. L. Beauchamp and N. E. Bowie, *Ethical Theory and Business* (Upper Saddle River, NJ: Prentice-Hall, 2001), p. 8.

7. U.S. Department of Labor, "The Department of Labor's 2006 Findings on the Worst Forms of Child Labor," 2006, p. 17, www.dol.gov/ilab/programs/ocft/PDF/2006OCFTreport.pdf, accessed September 8, 2008.

8. This dilemma is presented in W. M. Greenfield, "In the Name of Corporate Social Responsibility," *Business Horizons* 47, no. 1 (January–February 2004), p. 22.

9. For a study of why low per capita income, lower disparities in income distribution, and various cultural factors are often associated with a higher incidence of bribery, see Rajib Sanyal, "Determinants of Bribery in International Business: The Cultural and Economic Factors," *Journal of Business Ethics* 59, no.1 (June 2005), pp. 139–45.

10. For a study of bribe-paying frequency by country, see Transparency International, *2003 Global Corruption Report,* p. 267, www.globalcorruptionreport.org, accessed September 9, 2008.

11. Roger Chen and Chia-Pei Chen, "Chinese Professional Managers and the Issue of Ethical Behavior," *Ivey Business Journal* 69, no, 5 (May/June 2005), p. 1.

12. Thomas Donaldson and Thomas W. Dunfee, "When Ethics Travel: The Promise and Peril of Global Business Ethics," *California Management Review* 41, no. 4 (Summer 1999), p. 53.

13. For a study of "facilitating" payments to obtain a favor (such as expediting an administrative process, obtaining a permit or license, or avoiding an abuse of authority) which are sometimes condoned as unavoidable or are excused on grounds of low wages and lack of professionalism among public officials, see Antonio Argandoña, "Corruption and Companies: The Use of Facilitating Payments," *Journal of Business Ethics* 60, no. 3 (September 2005), pp. 251–64.

14. Donaldson and Dunfee, "When Ethics Travel," p. 59.

15 . Thomas Donaldson and Thomas W. Dunfee, *Ties That Bind: A Social Contracts Approach to Business Ethics* (Boston: Harvard Business School Press, 1999), pp. 35, 83.

16. Based on a report in M. J. Satchell, "Deadly Trade in Toxics," *U.S. News and World Report,* March 7, 1994, p. 64, and cited in Donaldson and Dunfee, "When Ethics Travel," p. 46.

17. Chen and Chen, "Chinese Professional Managers," p. 1.

18. Two of the definitive treatments of integrated social contracts theory as applied to ethics are Thomas Donaldson and Thomas W. Dunfee, "Towards a Unified Conception of Business Ethics: Integrative Social Contracts Theory," *Academy of Management Review* 19, no. 2 (April 1994), pp. 252–84 and Donaldson and Dunfee, *Ties That Bind,* especially Chapters 3, 4, and 6. See also Andrew Spicer, Thomas W. Dunfee, and Wendy J. Bailey, "Does National Context Matter in Ethical Decision Making? An Empirical Test of Integrative Social Contracts Theory," *Academy of Management Journal* 47, no. 4 (August 2004), p. 610.

19. P. M. Nichols, "Outlawing Transnational Bribery through the World Trade Organization," *Law and Policy in International Business* 28, no. 2 (1997), pp. 321–22.

20. Donaldson and Dunfee, "When Ethics Travel," pp. 55–56.

21. Archie B. Carroll, "Models of Management Morality for the New Millennium," *Business Ethics Quarterly* 11, no. 2 (April 2001), pp. 367–69.

22. Ibid., pp. 369–70.

23. For survey data on what managers say about why they sometimes behave unethically, see John F. Veiga, Timothy D. Golden, and Kathleen Dechant, "Why Managers Bend Company Rules," *Academy of Management Executive* 18, no. 2 (May 2004), pp. 84–89.

24. For more details see Ronald R. Sims and Johannes Brinkmann, "Enron Ethics (Or: Culture Matters More Than Codes)," *Journal of Business Ethics* 45, no. 3 (July 2003), pp. 244–46.

25. As reported in Gardiner Harris, "At Bristol-Myers, Ex-Executives Tell of Numbers Games," *Wall Street Journal,* December 12, 2002, pp. A1, A13.

26. Ibid., p. A13.

27. Veiga, Golden, and Dechant, "Why Managers Bend the Rules," p. 36.

28. The following account is based largely on the discussion and analysis in Sims and Brinkmann, "Enron Ethics," pp. 245–52. Perhaps the definitive book-length account of the corrupt Enron culture is Kurt Eichenwald, *Conspiracy of Fools: A True Story* (New York: Broadway Books, 2005).

29. Chip Cummins and Almar Latour, "How Shell's Move to Revamp Culture Ended in Scandal," *Wall Street Journal,* November 2, 2004, p. A14.

30. Anna Wilde Mathews and Barbara Martinez, "E-Mails Suggest Merck Knew Vioxx's Dangers at Early Stage," *Wall Street Journal,* November 1, 2004, pp. A1, A10.

31. Archie B. Carroll, "The Four Faces of Corporate Citizenship," *Business and Society Review* 100/101 (September 1998), p. 6.

32. Gedeon J. Rossouw and Leon J. van Vuuren, "Modes of Managing Morality: A Descriptive Model of Strategies for Managing Ethics," *Journal of Business Ethics* 46, no. 4 (September 2003), pp. 389–400.

33. Empirical evidence that an ethical culture approach produces better results than the compliance approach is presented in Terry Thomas, John R. Schermerhorn, and John W. Dienhart, "Strategic Leadership of Ethical Behavior," *Academy of Management Executive* 18, no. 2 (May 2004), p. 64.

34. Business Roundtable, "Statement on Corporate Responsibility," New York, October 1981, p. 9.

35. Sarah Roberts, Justin Keeble, and David Brown, "The Business Case for Corporate Citizenship," a study for the World Economic Forum, p. 3, www.weforum.org/ corporatecitizenship (accessed October 14, 2003),

36. Dirk Matten and Andrew Crane, "Corporate Citizenship: Toward an Extended Theoretical Conceptualization," *Academy of Management Review* 30, no. 1 (2005), pp. 166–79.

37. Gerald I. J. M. Zetsloot and Marcel N. A. van Marrewijk, "From Quality to Sustainability," *Journal of Business Ethics* 55 (2004), pp. 79–82.

38. BP's environmental record is discussed in "Beyond the Green Corporation," *BusinessWeek,* January 29, 2007, p. 50.

39. For an excellent discussion of crafting corporate social responsibility strategies capable of contributing to a company's competitive advantage, see Michael E. Porter and Mark R. Kramer, "Strategy & Society: The Link Between Competitive Advantage and Corporate Social Responsibility," *Harvard Business Review* 84, no. 12 (December 2006), pp. 78–92.

40. N. Craig Smith, "Corporate Responsibility: Whether and How," *California Management Review* 45, no. 4 (Summer 2003), p. 63.

41. Porter and Kramer, "Strategy & Society," p. 81.

42. World Business Council for Sustainable Development, "Corporate Social Responsibility: Making Good Business Sense," January 2000, p. 7, www.wbscd.ch (accessed October 10, 2003). For a discussion of how companies are connecting social initiatives to their core values, see David Hess, Nikolai Rogovsky, and Thomas W Dunfee, "The Next Wave of Corporate Community Involvement: Corporate Social Initiatives," *California Management Review* 44, no. 2 (Winter 2002), pp. 110–25. Also see Susan Ariel Aaronson, "Corporate Responsibility in the Global Village: The British Role Model and the American Laggard," *Business and Society Review* 108, no. 3 (September 2003), p. 323.

43. www.chick-fil-a.com (accessed November 4, 2005).

44. Smith, "Corporate Responsibility," p. 63; see also World Economic Forum, "Findings of a Survey on Global Corporate Leadership," www.weforum.org/corporatecitizenship (accessed October 11, 2003).

45. Roberts, Keeble, and Brown, "The Business Case for Corporate Citizenship," p. 6.

46. Ibid., p.3.

47. Wallace N. Davidson, Abuzar El-Jelly, and Dan L. Worrell, "Influencing Managers to Change Unpopular Corporate Behavior through Boycotts and Divestitures: A Stock Market Test," *Business and Society* 34, no. 2 (1995), pp. 171–96.

48. Tom McCawley, "Racing to Improve Its Reputation: Nike Has Fought to Shed Its Image as an Exploiter of Third-World Labor Yet It Is Still a Target of Activists," *Financial Times,* December 2000, p. 14, and Smith, "Corporate Social Responsibility," p. 61.

49. Based on data in Amy Aronson, "Corporate Diversity, Integration, and Market Penetration," *BusinessWeek,* October 20, 2003, pp. 138ff.

50. Smith, "Corporate Social Responsibility," p. 62.

51. See Social Investment Forum, *2001 Report on Socially Responsible Investing trends in the United States* (Washington, D.C.: Social Investment Forum, 2001).

52. Smith, "Corporate Social Responsibility," p. 63.

53. See James C. Collins and Jerry I. Porras, *Built to Last: Successful Habits of Visionary Companies,* 3rd ed. (London: HarperBusiness, 2002); Roberts, Keeble, and Brown, "The Business Case for Corporate Citizenship," p. 4; and Smith, "Corporate Social Responsibility," p. 63.

54. Roberts, Keeble, and Brown, "The Business Case for Corporate Citizenship," p. 4.

55. Smith, "Corporate Social Responsibility," p. 65; Lee E. Preston and Douglas P. O'Bannon, "The Corporate Social-Financial Performance Relationship," *Business and Society* 36, no. 4 (December 1997), pp. 419–29; Ronald M. Roman, Sefa Hayibor, and Bradley R. Agle, "The Relationship between Social and Financial Performance: Repainting a Portrait," *Business and Society* 38, no. 1 (March 1999), pp. 109–25; and Joshua D. Margolis and James P. Walsh, *People and Profits* (Mahwah, NJ: Lawrence Erlbaum, 2001).

56. Based on information in Edna Gundersen, "Rights Issue Rocks the Music World," *USA Today,* September 16, 2002, pp. D1, D2.

Chapter 10

1. As quoted in Steven W. Floyd and Bill Wooldridge, "Managing Strategic Consensus: The Foundation of Effective Implementation," *Academy of Management Executive* 6, no. 4 (November 1992), p. 27.

2. As cited in Gary L. Neilson, Karla L. Martin, and Elizabeth Powers, "The Secrets of Successful Strategy Execution," *Harvard Business Review* 86, no. 6 (June 2008), pp. 61–62.

3. Jack Welch with Suzy Welch, *Winning* (New York: HarperBusiness, 2005), p. 135.

4. For an excellent pragmatic discussion of this point, see Larry Bossidy and Ram Charan, *Execution: The Discipline of Getting Things*

Done (New York: Crown Business, 2002), Chapter 1.

5. For an insightful discussion of how important staffing an organization with the right people is, see Christopher A. Bartlett and Sumantra Ghoshal, "Building Competitive Advantage through People," *MIT Sloan Management Review* 43, no. 2 (Winter 2002), pp. 34–41.

6. The importance of assembling an executive team with exceptional ability to see what needs to be done and an instinctive talent for figuring out how to get it done is discussed in Justin Menkes, "Hiring for Smarts," *Harvard Business Review* 83, no. 11 (November 2005), pp. 100–109; and Justin Menkes, *Executive Intelligence* (New York: HarperCollins, 2005), especially Chapters 1–4.

7. Welch with Welch, *Winning*, p. 139.

8. See Bossidy and Charan, *Execution*, Chapter 1.

9. Menkes, *Executive Intelligence*, pp. 68, 76.

10. Bossidy and Charan, *Execution*, Chapter 5.

11. Welch with Welch, *Winning*, pp. 141–42.

12. Menkes, *Executive Intelligence*, pp. 65–71.

13. Jim Collins, *Good to Great* (New York: HarperBusiness, 2001), p. 44.

14. John Byrne, "The Search for the Young and Gifted," *BusinessWeek*, October 4, 1999, p. 108.

15. James Brian Quinn, *Intelligent Enterprise* (New York: Free Press, 1992), pp. 52–53, 55, 73–74, and 76. Also, see Christine Soo, Timothy Devinney, David Midgley, and Anne Deering, "Knowledge Management: Philosophy, Processes, and Pitfalls," *California Management Review* 44, no. 4 (Summer 2002), pp. 129–51; and Julian Birkinshaw, "Why Is Knowledge Management So Difficult?" *Business Strategy Review* 12, no. 1 (March 2001), pp. 11–18.

16. Robert H. Hayes, Gary P. Pisano, and David M. Upton, *Strategic Operations: Competing through Capabilities* (New York: Free Press, 1996), pp. 503–7. Also, see Jonas Ridderstråle, "Cashing in on Corporate Competencies," *Business Strategy Review* 14, no. 1 (Spring 2003), pp. 27–38; and Danny Miller, Russell Eisenstat, and Nathaniel Foote, "Strategy from the Inside Out: Building Capability-Creating Organizations," *California Management Review* 44, no. 3 (Spring 2002), pp. 37–55.

17. Quinn, *Intelligent Enterprise*, p. 43.

18. Ibid., pp. 33, 89; James Brian Quinn and Frederick G. Hilmer, "Strategic Outsourcing," *Sloan Management Review* 35, no. 4 (Summer 1994), pp. 43–55; Jussi Heikkilä and Carlos Cordon, "Outsourcing: A Core or Non-Core Strategic Management Decision," *Strategic Change* 11, no. 3 (June–July 2002), pp. 183–93; and James Brian Quinn, "Strategic Outsourcing: Leveraging Knowledge Capabilities," *Sloan Management Review* 40, no. 4 (Summer 1999), pp. 9–22. A strong case for outsourcing is presented in C. K. Prahalad, "The Art of Outsourcing," *Wall Street Journal*, June 8, 2005, p. A13.

For a discussion of why outsourcing initiatives fall short of expectations, see Jérôme Barthélemy, "The Seven Deadly Sins of Outsourcing," *Academy of Management Executive* 17, no. 2 (May 2003), pp. 87–98.

19. Quinn, "Strategic Outsourcing," p. 17

20. For a more extensive discussion of the reasons for building cooperative, collaborative alliances and partnerships with other companies, see James F. Moore, *The Death of Competition* (New York: HarperBusiness, 1996), especially Chapter 3; Quinn and Hilmer, "Strategic Outsourcing," pp. 43–55; and Quinn, "Strategic Outsourcing," pp. 9–22.

21. Quinn, *Intelligent Enterprise*, pp. 39–40; also see Barthélemy, "The Seven Deadly Sins of Outsourcing," pp. 87–98.

22. The importance of matching organization design and structure to the particular needs of strategy was first brought to the forefront in a landmark study of 70 large corporations conducted by Professor Alfred Chandler of Harvard University. Chandler's research revealed that changes in an organization's strategy bring about new administrative problems that, in turn, require a new or refashioned structure for the new strategy to be successfully implemented. He found that structure tends to follow the growth strategy of the firm—but often not until inefficiency and internal operating problems provoke a structural adjustment. The experiences of these firms followed a consistent sequential pattern: new strategy creation, emergence of new administrative problems, a decline in profitability and performance, a shift to a more appropriate organizational structure, and then recovery to more profitable levels and improved strategy execution. See Alfred Chandler, *Strategy and Structure* (Cambridge, MA: MIT Press, 1962).

23. The importance of information flows in centralized organizational structures and the value of granting decision-making rights to those close in the field is discussed in Neilson, Martin, and Powers, "The Secrets to Successful Strategy Execution," pp. 61–70.

24. The importance of empowering workers in executing strategy and the value of creating a great working environment are discussed in Stanley E. Fawcett, Gary K. Rhoads, and Phillip Burnah, "People as the Bridge to Competitiveness: Benchmarking the 'ABCs' of an Empowered Workforce," *Benchmarking: An International Journal* 11, no. 4 (2004), pp. 346–60.

25. Iain Somerville and John Edward Mroz, "New Competencies for a New World," in *The Organization of the Future*, ed. Frances Hesselbein, Marshall Goldsmith, and Richard Beckard (San Francisco: Jossey-Bass, 1997), p. 70.

26. Exercising adequate control over empowered employees is a serious issue. For example, a prominent Wall Street securities firm lost $350 million when a trader allegedly booked fictitious profits; Sears took a $60 million

write-off after admitting that employees in its automobile service departments recommended unnecessary repairs to customers. Several makers of memory chips paid fines of over $500 million when more than a dozen of their employees conspired to fix prices and operate a global cartel—some of the guilty employees were sentenced to jail. For a discussion of the problems and possible solutions, see Robert Simons, "Control in an Age of Empowerment," *Harvard Business Review* 73 (March–April 1995), pp. 80–88.

27. For a discussion of the importance of cross-business coordination, see Jeanne M. Liedtka, "Collaboration across Lines of Business for Competitive Advantage," *Academy of Management Executive* 10, no. 2 (May 1996), pp. 20–34.

28. Michael Hammer and James Champy, *Reengineering the Corporation* (New York: HarperBusiness, 1993), pp. 26–27.

29. Although functional organization incorporates Adam Smith's division-of-labor principle (every person/department involved has specific responsibility for performing a clearly defined task) and allows for tight management control (everyone in the process is accountable to a functional department head for efficiency and adherence to procedures), *no one oversees the whole process and its result*. Hammer and Champy, *Reengineering the Corporation*, pp. 26–27.

30. Rosabeth Moss Kanter, "Collaborative Advantage: The Art of the Alliance," *Harvard Business Review* 72, no. 4 (July–August 1994), pp. 105–6.

31. For an excellent review of ways to effectively manage the relationship between alliance partners, see ibid., pp. 96–108.

Chapter 11

1. For a discussion of the four types of tools that can be used by managers to bring about organizational change, see Clayton M. Christensen, Matt Marx, and Howard Stevenson, "The Tools of Cooperation and Change," *Harvard Business Review* 84, no. 10 (October 2006), pp. 73–80.

2. For a discussion of the value of benchmarking in implementing strategy, see Christopher E. Bogan and Michael J. English, *Benchmarking for Best Practices: Winning Through Innovative Adaptation* (New York: McGraw-Hill, 1994), Chapters 2, 6; Mustafa Ungan, "Factors Affecting the Adoption of Manufacturing Best Practices," *Benchmarking: An International Journal* 11, no. 5 (2004), pp. 504–20; and Paul Hyland and Ron Beckett, "Learning to Compete: The Value of Internal Benchmarking," *Benchmarking: An International Journal* 9, no. 3 (2002), pp. 293–304; and Yoshinobu Ohinata, "Benchmarking: The Japanese

Experience," *Long-Range Planning* 27, no. 4 (August 1994), pp. 48–53.

3. Michael Hammer and James Champy, *Reengineering the Corporation* (New York: HarperBusiness, 1993), pp. 26–27.

4. Gene Hall, Jim Rosenthal, and Judy Wade, "How to Make Reengineering Really Work," *Harvard Business Review* 71, no. 6 (November–December 1993), pp. 119–31.

5. For more information on business process reengineering and how well it has worked in various companies, see James Brian Quinn, *Intelligent Enterprise* (New York: Free Press, 1992), p. 162; Ann Majchrzak and Qianwei Wang, "Breaking the Functional Mind-Set in Process Organizations," *Harvard Business Review* 74, no. 5 (September–October 1996), pp. 93–99; Stephen L. Walston, Lawton. R. Burns, and John R. Kimberly, "Does Reengineering Really Work? An Examination of the Context and Outcomes of Hospital Reengineering Initiatives," *Health Services Research* 34, no. 6 (February 2000), pp. 1363–88; and Allessio Ascari, Melinda Rock, and Soumitra Dutta, "Reengineering and Organizational Change: Lessons from a Comparative Analysis of Company Experiences," *European Management Journal* 13, no. 1 (March 1995), pp. 1–13. For a review of why some company personnel embrace process reengineering and some don't, see Ronald J. Burke, "Process Reengineering: Who Embraces It and Why?" *The TQM Magazine* 16, no. 2 (2004), pp. 114–19.

6. For some of the seminal discussions of what TQM is and how it works written by ardent enthusiasts of the technique, see M. Walton, *The Deming Management Method* (New York: Pedigree, 1986); J. Juran, *Juran on Quality by Design* (New York: Free Press, 1992); Philip Crosby, *Quality Is Free: The Act of Making Quality Certain* (New York: McGraw-Hill, 1979); and S. George, *The Baldrige Quality System* (New York: Wiley, 1992). For a critique of TQM, see Mark J. Zbaracki, "The Rhetoric and Reality of Total Quality Management," *Administrative Science Quarterly* 43, no. 3 (September 1998), pp. 602–36.

7. For a discussion of the shift in work environment and culture that TQM entails, see Robert T. Amsden, Thomas W. Ferratt, and Davida M. Amsden, "TQM: Core Paradigm Changes," *Business Horizons* 39, no. 6 (November–December 1996), pp. 6–14.

8. For easy-to-understand overviews of what Six Sigma is all about, see Peter S. Pande and Larry Holpp, *What Is Six Sigma?* (New York: McGraw-Hill, 2002); Jiju Antony, "Some Pros and Cons of Six Sigma: An Academic Perspective," *TQM Magazine* 16, no. 4 (2004), pp. 303–6; Peter S. Pande, Robert P. Neuman, and Roland R. Cavanagh, *The Six Sigma Way: How GE, Motorola and Other Top Companies Are Honing Their Performance* (New York: McGraw-Hill,

2000); and Joseph Gordon and M. Joseph Gordon, Jr., *Six Sigma Quality for Business and Manufacture* (New York: Elsevier, 2002). For how Six Sigma can be used in smaller companies, see Godecke Wessel and Peter Burcher, "Six Sigma for Small and Medium-sized Enterprises," *TQM Magazine* 16, no. 4 (2004), pp. 264–72.

9. Based on information posted at www.isixsigma.com (accessed November 4, 2002).

10. Kennedy Smith, "Six Sigma for the Service Sector," *Quality Digest Magazine,* May 2003, posted at www.qualitydigest.com (accessed September 28, 2003).

11. Del Jones, "Taking the Six Sigma Approach," *USA Today,* October 31, 2002, p. 5B.

12. Pande, Neuman, and Cavanagh, *The Six Sigma Way,* pp. 5–6.

13. Smith, "Six Sigma for the Service Sector."

14. Jones, "Taking the Six Sigma Approach," p. 5B.

15 . Brian Hindo, "At 3M, a Struggle Between Efficiency and Creativity," *BusinessWeek,* June 11, 2007, pp. 8–16.

16. For a discussion of approaches to pursuing radical or disruptive innovations while also seeking incremental gains in efficiency, see Charles A. O'Reilly and Michael L. Tushman, "The Ambidextrous Organization," *Harvard Business Review* 82, no. 4 (April 2004), pp. 74–81.

17. Terry Nels Lee, Stanley E. Fawcett, and Jason Briscoe, "Benchmarking the Challenge to Quality Program Implementation," *Benchmarking: An International Journal* 9, no. 4 (2002), pp. 374–87.

18. For a recent study documenting the imperatives of establishing a supportive culture, see Milan Ambrož, "Total Quality System as a Product of the Empowered Corporate Culture," *TQM Magazine* 16, no. 2 (2004), pp. 93–104. Research confirming the factors that are important in making TQM programs successful in both Europe and the United States is presented in Nick A. Dayton, "The Demise of Total Quality Management," *TQM Magazine* 15, no. 6 (2003), pp. 391–96.

19. Judy D. Olian and Sara L. Rynes, "Making Total Quality Work: Aligning Organizational Processes, Performance Measures, and Stakeholders," *Human Resource Management* 30, no. 3 (Fall 1991), pp. 310–11; and Paul S. Goodman and Eric D. Darr, "Exchanging Best Practices Information through Computer-Aided Systems," *Academy of Management Executive* 10, no. 2 (May 1996), p. 7.

20. Thomas C. Powell, "Total Quality Management as Competitive Advantage," *Strategic Management Journal* 16 (1995), pp. 15–37. See also Richard M. Hodgetts, "Quality Lessons from America's Baldrige Winners," *Business Horizons* 37, no. 4 (July–August 1994), pp. 74–79; and Richard Reed, David J. Lemak, and Joseph C. Montgomery, "Beyond Process: TQM Content and Firm Performance," *Academy of Management Review* 21, no. 1 (January 1996), pp. 173–202.

21. Based on information at www.utc.com and www.otiselevator.com (accessed November 14, 2005).

22. Fred Vogelstein, "Winning the Amazon Way," *Fortune,* May 26, 2003, pp. 70, 74.

23. "The Web Smart 50," *BusinessWeek,* November 21, 2005, pp. 87–88.

24. Such systems speed organizational learning by providing fast, efficient communication, creating an organizational memory for collecting and retaining best-practice information, and permitting people all across the organization to exchange information and updated solutions. See Goodman and Darr, "Exchanging Best Practices Information through Computer-Aided Systems," pp. 7–17.

25. "The Web Smart 50," *BusinessWeek,* November 21, 2005, pp. 85–90.

26. Vogelstein, "Winning the Amazon Way," p. 64.

27. For a discussion of the need for putting appropriate boundaries on the actions of empowered employees and possible control and monitoring systems that can be used, see Robert Simons, "Control in an Age of Empowerment," *Harvard Business Review* 73 (March–April 1995), pp. 80–88.

28. Ibid. Also see David C. Band and Gerald Scanlan, "Strategic Control through Core Competencies," *Long Range Planning* 28, no. 2 (April 1995), pp. 102–14.

29. The importance of motivating and empowering workers so as to create a working environment that is highly conducive to good strategy execution is discussed in Stanley E. Fawcett, Gary K. Rhoads, and Phillip Burnah, "People as the Bridge to Competitiveness: Benchmarking the 'ABCs' of an Empowered Workforce," *Benchmarking: An International Journal* 11 no. 4 (2004), pp. 346–60.

30. Pfeffer and Veiga, "Putting People First for Organizational Success," pp. 37–45; Linda K. Stroh and Paula M. Caliguiri, "Increasing Global Competitiveness through Effective People Management," *Journal of World Business* 33, no. 1 (Spring 1998), pp. 1–16; and articles in *Fortune* on the 100 best companies to work for (various issues).

31. As quoted in John P. Kotter and James L. Heskett, *Corporate Culture and Performance* (New York: Free Press, 1992), p. 91.

32. Clayton M. Christensen, Matt Marx, and Howard Stevenson, "The Tools of Cooperation and Change," pp. 74–77.

33. The effect of management decisions on employees' basic drives that underlie motiviation is discussed in Nitin Nohria, Boris Groysberg, and Linda-Eling Lee, "Employee Motivation: A Powerful New Model," *Harvard Business Review* 86, no. 7/8 (July–August 2008), pp. 78–84.

34. For a provocative discussion of why incentives and rewards are actually counterproductive, see Alfie Kohn, "Why Incentive Plans Cannot Work," *Harvard Business Review* 71, no. 6 (September–October 1993), pp. 54–63.

35. See Steven Kerr, "On the Folly of Rewarding A While Hoping for B," *Academy of Management Executive* 9, no. 1 (February 1995), pp. 7–14; Steven Kerr, "Risky Business: The New Pay Game," *Fortune,* July 22, 1996, pp. 93–96; and Doran Twer, "Linking Pay to Business Objectives," *Journal of Business Strategy* 15, no. 4 (July–August 1994), pp. 15–18.

36. Kerr, "Risky Business: The New Pay Game," p. 96.

Chapter 12

1. Joanne Reid and Victoria Hubbell, "Creating a Performance Culture," *Ivey Business Journal* 69, no. 4 (March/April 2005), p. 1.

2. John P. Kotter and James L. Heskett, *Corporate Culture and Performance* (New York: Free Press, 1992), p. 7. See also Robert Goffee and Gareth Jones. *The Character of a Corporation* (New York: HarperCollins, 1998).

3. Kotter and Heskett, *Corporate Culture and Performance,* pp. 7–8.

4. Ibid., p. 5.

5. John Alexander and Meena S. Wilson, "Leading across Cultures: Five Vital Capabilities," in *The Organization of the Future,* ed. Frances Hesselbein, Marshall Goldsmith, and Richard Beckard (San Francisco: Jossey-Bass, 1997), pp. 291–92.

6. For a discussion of the steps involved in conducting cultural diligence, see David Harding and Ted Rouse, "Human Due Diligence," *Harvard Business Review* 85, no. 4 (April 2007), pp. 124–31.

7. Terrence E. Deal and Allen A. Kennedy, *Corporate Cultures* (Reading, MA: Addison-Wesley, 1982), p. 22. See also Terrence E. Deal and Allen A. Kennedy, *The New Corporate Cultures: Revitalizing the Workplace after Downsizing, Mergers, and Reengineering* (Cambridge, MA: Perseus, 1999).

8. Vijay Sathe, *Culture and Related Corporate Realities* (Homewood, IL: Richard D. Irwin, 1985).

9. Kotter and Heskett, *Corporate Culture and Performance,* Chapter 6.

10. See Kurt Eichenwald, *Conspiracy of Fools: A True Story* (New York: Broadway Books, 2005).

11. Reid and Hubbell, "Creating a Performance Culture," pp. 2, 5.

12. This section draws heavily on the discussion of Kotter and Heskett, *Corporate Culture and Performance,* Chapter 4.

13. There's no inherent reason why new strategic initiatives should conflict with core values and business principles. While conflict is always possible, most strategy makers lean toward choosing strategic initiatives that are compatible with the company's character and culture and that don't go against ingrained values and beliefs. After all, the company's culture is usually something that strategy makers have had a hand in building and perpetuating, so they are not often anxious to undermine core values and business principles without serious soul-searching and compelling business reasons.

14. Kotter and Heskett, *Corporate Culture and Performance,* p. 52.

15. Ibid., p. 5.

16. Avan R. Jassawalla and Hemant C. Sashittal, "Cultures That Support Product-Innovation Processes," *Academy of Management Executive* 16, no. 3 (August 2002), pp. 42–54.

17. Kotter and Heskett, *Corporate Culture and Performance,* pp. 15–16. Also see Jennifer A. Chatham and Sandra E. Cha, "Leading by Leveraging Culture," *California Management Review* 45, no. 4 (Summer 2003), pp. 20–34.

18. Clayton M. Christensen, Matt Marx, and Howard H. Stevenson, "The Tools of Cooperation and Change," *Harvard Business Review* 84, no. 10 (October 2006), pp. 77–78.

19. John Humphreys and Hal Langford, "Managing a Corporate Culture Slide," *MIT Sloan Management Review* 49, Issue 3 (Spring 2008), pp. 25–27.

20. Judy D. Olian and Sara L. Rynes, "Making Total Quality Work: Aligning Organizational Processes, Performance Measures, and Stakeholders," *Human Resource Management* 30, no. 3 (Fall 1991), p. 324.

21. www.dardenrestaurants.com (accessed November 25, 2005); for more specifics, see Robert C. Ford, "Darden Restaurants' CEO Joe Lee on the Importance of Core Values: Integrity and Fairness," *Academy of Management Executive* 16, no. 1 (February 2002), pp. 31–36.

22. For several perspectives on the role and importance of core values and ethical behavior, see Joseph L. Badaracco, *Defining Moments: When Managers Must Choose between Right and Wrong* (Boston: Harvard Business School Press, 1997); Joe Badaracco and Allen P. Webb. "Business Ethics: A View from the Trenches." *California Management Review* 37, no. 2 (Winter 1995), pp. 8–28; Patrick E. Murphy, "Corporate Ethics Statements: Current Status and Future Prospects," *Journal of Business Ethics* 14 (1995), pp. 727–40; Lynn Sharp Paine, "Managing for Organizational Integrity," *Harvard Business Review* 72, no. 2 (March–April 1994), pp. 106–17; and Tom Tyler, John Dienhart, and Terry Thomas, "The Ethical Commitment to Compliance: Building Value-Based Cultures," *California Management Review* 50, no. 2 (February 2008), pp. 31–51.

23. For a study of the status of formal codes of ethics in large corporations, see Emily F. Carasco and Jang B. Singh, "The Content and Focus of the Codes of Ethics of the World's Largest Transnational Corporations," *Business and Society Review* 108, no. 1 (January 2003), pp. 71–94; and Patrick E. Murphy, "Corporate Ethics Statements: Current Status and Future Prospects," *Journal of Business Ethics* 14 (1995), pp. 727–40. For a discussion of the strategic benefits of formal statements of corporate values, see John Humble, David Jackson, and Alan Thomson, "The Strategic Power of Corporate Values," *Long Range Planning* 27, no. 6 (December 1994), pp. 28–42. An excellent discussion of whether one should assume that company codes of ethics are always ethical is presented in Mark S. Schwartz, "A Code of Ethics for Corporate Codes of Ethics," *Journal of Business Ethics* 41, nos. 1–2 (November–December 2002), pp. 27–43.

24. See Schwartz, "A Code of Ethics for Corporate Codes of Ethics," p. 27.

25. Ford, "Darden Restaurants' CEO Joe Lee on the Importance of Core Values," pp. 31–36.

26. Michael T. Kanazawa and Robert H. Miles, *Big Ideas to Big Results* (Upper Saddle River, NJ: FT Press, 2008), p. 96.

27. James Brian Quinn, *Strategies for Change: Logical Incrementalism* (Homewood, IL: Richard D. Irwin, 1980), pp. 20–22.

28. Ibid., p. 146.

29. For a good discussion of the challenges, see Daniel Goleman, "What Makes a Leader," *Harvard Business Review* 76, no. 6 (November–December 1998), pp. 92–102; Ronald A. Heifetz and Donald L. Laurie, "The Work of Leadership," *Harvard Business Review* 75, no. 1 (January–February 1997), pp. 124–34; and Charles M. Farkas and Suzy Wetlaufer, "The Ways Chief Executive Officers Lead," *Harvard Business Review* 74, no. 3 (May–June 1996), pp. 110–22. See also Michael E. Porter, Jay W. Lorsch, and Nitin Nohria, "Seven Surprises for New CEOs," *Harvard Business Review* 82, no. 10 (October 2004), pp. 62–72.

30. Joanne Reid and Victoria Hubbell, "Creating a Performance Culture," *Ivey Business Journal* 69, no.4 (March/April 2005), p. 1.

Organization Index

Name Index

A

Aaronson, Susan Ariel, EN-7
Ackermann, Josef, 428–429, 430, 431, 432
Adams, C., 549, 552
Agle, Bradley R., 534, 537, 538, EN-7
Ahlstrand, Bruce, EN-1
Al-Rifai, Hani, 122
Alexander, John, EN-10
Alexander, Marcus, 239, EN-6
Aleyne, Adrian, 121
Ambrosini, Veronique, 442, 443, 447, 452
Ambroz, Milan, EN-9
Amit, R., 442, 443, 452
Amsden, Davida M., EN-9
Amsden, Robert T., EN-9
Angwin, Julia, 518
Anslinger, Patricia L., EN-4, EN-6
Antony, Jiju, 549, 552, EN-9
Arend, R. J., 446, 449, 452
Argandoña, Antonio, EN-6
Arnold, David J., EN-5
Aronson, Amy, EN-7
Ascari, Allessio, EN-9
Awtrey, Stan, 198

B

Baansal, Pratima, 520
Badaracco, Joseph L., EN-1, EN-10
Bailey, Wendy J., EN-7
Bain, J. S., EN-2
Balmer, J., 538
Bamford, James, EN-3, EN-4
Band, David C., EN-9
Bañuelas, R., 549, 552
Baptista, R., 435, 440
Barad, Jill, 560, 562
Barney, Jay B., 442, 443, 447, 452, 453, EN-2, EN-3
Barrett, Amy, 274
Barringer, Bruce, EN-1
Barthélmy, Jérôme, EN-4, EN-8
Bartlett, Christopher A., EN-2, EN-4, EN-5, EN-8
Basu, Kunal, 289
Baumol, William, 537
Beauchamp, T. L., EN-6
Beckard, Richard, EN-8, EN-10
Beckett, Ron, EN-8
Beer, M., 433
Bergen, M., 443, 453
Bettcher, Kim Eric, EN-6

Bezos, Jeff, 44–45, 201, 372
Bhattacharya, Arindam K., 234, EN-5
Bhide, Amar, 165, 385
Bickford, Deborah J., EN-4
Birchall, David W., EN-3
Birinyi, Laszlo, 55
Birkenshaw, Julian, EN-8
Blackman, S. Batey, 537
Blasche, S., 537
Bleeke, Joel, EN-4, EN-5
Bloch, Nicolas, 508
Blome-Drees, F., 537
Bluedorn, Allen C., EN-1
Bogan, Christopher E., EN-8
Bogner, William C., 443, 452, EN-2
Bontis, Nick, EN-3
Borgonjon, Jan, EN-5
Bossidy, Lawrence, 327, 357, 433, EN-7, EN-8
Boudette, Neal E., 403
Bower, Joseph L., 518, EN-4
Bowie, N. E., 537, EN-6
Bowman, Cliff, 442, 443, 447, 452
Brandenberger, Adam M., 165, 499
Brandy, 514
Bravo, Rose Marie, 462
Brenner, T., 434, 437, 440
Breschi, S., 436, 440
Breyfogle, F. W., III, 549, 552
Brian-Low, Cassell, 475
Brin, Sergey, 387
Brinkmann, Johannes, EN-7
Briscoe, Jason, EN-9
Bröcker, J., 440, 441
Bromiley, Philip, EN-1
Brown, David, EN-7
Brown, Robert, EN-1
Brown, Shona L., 193, EN-1, EN-4
Burcher, Peter, EN-9
Burck, C., 433
Burke, James, 524
Burke, Ronald J., EN-9
Burnah, Phillip, EN-8, EN-9
Burns, Lawton R., EN-9
Butler, J. E., 442, 443, 453
Byrne, John A., 334

C

Caliguiri, Paula M., EN-9
Camp, Robert C., EN-3
Campbell, Andrew, 239, EN-6
Carasco, Emily F., EN-10
Caron, Joseph, EN-5

Carroll, A., 531, 537
Carroll, Archie B., EN-7
Carroll, Lewis, 23
Carroll, Paul, 519
Carver, John, EN-2
Castanias, R. P., 443, 446, 452
Cavanaugh, Roland R., 552, EN-9
Caves, Richard, 491, 492
Cha, Sandra E., EN-10
Chakraborty, Betosini, 476
Chakravarthy, Bala, EN-4
Chambers, E. G., 433
Chambers, John, 475
Champy, James, 357, EN-8, EN-9
Chandler, Alfred, EN-8
Chang, C., 507
Charan, Ram, 327, 433, EN-7, EN-8
Chatham, Jennifer A., EN-10
Chatterjee, Sanyan R., 445, 453, 514, 518, 519, EN-6
Chen, Chia-Pei, EN-6, EN-7
Chen, G. Z., 506
Chen, H. W., 507
Chen, Roger, EN-6, EN-7
Cherry, Brenda, EN-5
Chisholm, Shirley, 289
Christensen, Clayton M., 476, 480, EN-8, EN-9, EN-10
Christiansen, H. Curt, EN-5
Chu, C., 557
Ciccone, A., 435, 440
Clark, Delwyn N., EN-2, EN-3
Coff, R. W., 443, 449, 453
Cohen, Ben, 159
Collins, David J., EN-1
Collins, James C., 433, EN-1, EN-7, EN-8
Collins, Jim, 327
Collis, David J., 139, 416, 423, 443, 448, 453, EN-3, EN-6
Combs, G., 443, 453
Comerville, Iain, EN-8
Conger, Jay A., 425, 433
Cool, K., 443, 453
Cooper, Robert, 480
Cooper, Robin, EN-3
Copeland, Thomas E., EN-6
Cordon, Carlos, EN-8
Covin, Jeffrey G., EN-1, EN-4
Crane, Andrew, EN-7
Crevoisier, O., 435, 440
Crosby, Philip, EN-9
Cucuzza, Thomas G., EN-3
Cummins, Chip, EN-7

Subject Index